Lecture Notes in Computer Science 5007

Commenced Publication in 1973
Founding and Former Series Editors:
Gerhard Goos, Juris Hartmanis, and Jan van Leeuwen

Editorial Board

David Hutchison
  Lancaster University, UK
Takeo Kanade
  Carnegie Mellon University, Pittsburgh, PA, USA
Josef Kittler
  University of Surrey, Guildford, UK
Jon M. Kleinberg
  Cornell University, Ithaca, NY, USA
Alfred Kobsa
  University of California, Irvine, CA, USA
Friedemann Mattern
  ETH Zurich, Switzerland
John C. Mitchell
  Stanford University, CA, USA
Moni Naor
  Weizmann Institute of Science, Rehovot, Israel
Oscar Nierstrasz
  University of Bern, Switzerland
C. Pandu Rangan
  Indian Institute of Technology, Madras, India
Bernhard Steffen
  University of Dortmund, Germany
Madhu Sudan
  Massachusetts Institute of Technology, MA, USA
Demetri Terzopoulos
  University of California, Los Angeles, CA, USA
Doug Tygar
  University of California, Berkeley, CA, USA
Gerhard Weikum
  Max-Planck Institute of Computer Science, Saarbruecken, Germany

T0223112

Qing Wang
Dietmar Pfahl
David M. Raffo (Eds.)

Making Globally Distributed Software Development a Success Story

International Conference on Software Process, ICSP 2008
Leipzig, Germany, May 10-11, 2008
Proceedings

 Springer

Volume Editors

Qing Wang
Chinese Academy of Sciences
Institute of Software
No. 4 South Fourth Street, Zhong Guan Cun
Beijing 100190, China
E-mail: wq@itechs.iscas.ac.cn

Dietmar Pfahl
Simula Research Laboratory
P.O. Box 134
1325 Lysaker, Norway
E-mail: dietmarp@simula.no

David M. Raffo
Portland State University
Maseeh College of Engineering and Computer Science
P.O. Box 751
Portland, OR 97207, USA
E-mail: raffod@pdx.edu

Library of Congress Control Number: 2008926108

CR Subject Classification (1998): D.2, K.6.3, K.6, K.4.3, J.1

LNCS Sublibrary: SL 2 – Programming and Software Engineering

ISSN   0302-9743
ISBN-10   3-540-79587-1 Springer Berlin Heidelberg New York
ISBN-13   978-3-540-79587-2 Springer Berlin Heidelberg New York

This work is subject to copyright. All rights are reserved, whether the whole or part of the material is concerned, specifically the rights of translation, reprinting, re-use of illustrations, recitation, broadcasting, reproduction on microfilms or in any other way, and storage in data banks. Duplication of this publication or parts thereof is permitted only under the provisions of the German Copyright Law of September 9, 1965, in its current version, and permission for use must always be obtained from Springer. Violations are liable to prosecution under the German Copyright Law.

Springer is a part of Springer Science+Business Media

springer.com

© Springer-Verlag Berlin Heidelberg 2008

Typesetting: Camera-ready by author, data conversion by Scientific Publishing Services, Chennai, India
Printed on acid-free paper   SPIN: 12265138   06/3180   5 4 3 2 1 0

Preface

This volume contains papers presented at the International Conference on Software Process (ICSP 2008) held in Leipzig, Germany, during May 10-11, 2008. ICSP 2008 was the second conference of the ICSP series. The theme of ICSP 2008 was "Making Globally Distributed Software Development a Success Story."

Software developers work in a dynamic context of frequently changing technologies and with limited resources. Globally distributed development teams are under ever-increasing pressure to deliver their products more quickly and with higher levels of quality. At the same time, global competition is forcing software development organizations to cut costs by rationalizing processes, outsourcing part of or all development activities, reusing existing software in new or modified applications, and evolving existing systems to meet new needs, while still minimizing the risk of projects failing to deliver. To address these difficulties, new and modified processes are emerging, including agile methods and plan-based product line development. Open Source, COTS, and community-developed software are becoming more and more popular. Outsourcing coupled with 24/7 development demands well-defined processes to support the coordination of organizationally—and geographically—separated teams.

The accepted papers present completed research or advanced work-in-progress in all areas of software and systems development process including: agile software processes, CMMI, novel techniques for software process representation and analysis; process tools and metrics; and the simulation and modeling of software processes. Contributions reflecting real-world experience, or derived directly from industrial or open-source software development and evolution, were particularly welcome.

In response to the Call for Papers, 106 submissions were received from 22 different countries and regions including: Australia, Argentina, Belgium, Brazil, Canada, China, Finland, France, Germany, India, Iran, Italy, Ireland, Japan, Korea, Mexico, Sweden, Spain, Thailand, Turkey, UK, and USA. Each paper was rigorously reviewed and held to very high quality standards, and finally 33 papers from 14 countries and regions were accepted as regular papers for presentations at the conference.

The papers were clustered around topics and presented in five regular sessions organized in two parallel threads. Topics included Process Content, Process Tools and Metrics, Process Management, Process Representation, Analysis and Modeling, Experience Report, and Simulation Modeling.

Highlights of the ICSP2008 program were three keynote speeches, delivered by Christian Schmidkonz (SAP, Germany), Kesav Nori (Tata Consultancy Services, India), and Colette Roland (University of PARIS-1 Panthéon Sorbonne, France). ICSP also had a panel on Global Software Development. The panelist for this session were: Christian Schmidkonz (SAP, Germany), Kesav Nori (Tata Consultancy Services, India), and Brian Fitzgerald (University of Limerick).

A conference such as this can only succeed as a team effort. All of this work would not have been possible without the dedication and professional work of many colleagues. We wish to express our gratitude to all contributors for submitting papers.

Their work formed the basis for the success of the conference. We would also like to thank the Program Committee members and reviewers because their work is the guarantee for the high quality of the workshop. Special thanks go to the keynote speakers for giving their excellent presentations at the conference. Finally, we would also like to thank the members of the Steering Committee, Barry Boehm, Mingshu Li, Leon Osterweil, and Wilhelm Schäfer, for their advice, encouragement, and support.

We wish to express our thanks to the organizers for their hard work. The conference was sponsored by the International Software Process Association (ISPA) and the Institute of Software, the Chinese Academy of Sciences (ISCAS), and the ISCAS Laboratory for Internet Software Technologies (iTechs). We also wish to thank the 30th International Conference on Software Engineering (ICSE 2008) for sponsoring this meeting as an ICSE Co-Located Event. Finally, we acknowledge the editorial support from Springer in the publication of these proceedings.

For further information, please visit our website at http://www.icsp-conferences.org/icsp2008.

March 2008   David M. Raffo
                                                                               Qing Wang
                                                                            Dietmar Pfahl

International Conference on Software Process 2008

Leipzig, Germany
May 10–11, 2008

General Chair

David M. Raffo, Portland State University, USA

Steering Committee

Barry Boehm, University of Southern California, USA
Mingshu Li, Institute of Software, Chinese Academy of Sciences, China
Leon J. Osterweil, University of Massachusetts, USA
Wihelm Schäfer, University of Paderborn, Germany

Program Co-chairs

Dietmar Pfahl, Simula Research Laboratory, Norway
Qing Wang, Institute of Software, Chinese Academy of Sciences, China

Publicity Co-chairs

Raymond Madachy, University of Southern California, USA
Jürgen Münch, Fraunhofer Institute for Experimental Software Engineering, Germany
Liming Zhu, National ICT Australia, Australia

Program Committee

Muhammad Ali Babar	University of Limerick, Ireland
Stefan Biffl	Technische Universität Wien, Austria
Thomas Birkhölzer	University of Applied Science, Konstanz, Germany
Keith Chan	Hong Kong Polytechnic University, Hong Kong, China
Sorana Cimpan	University of Savoie at Annecy, France
Jacky Estublier	French National Research Center in Grenoble, France
Anthony Finkelstein	University College London, UK
Dennis Goldenson	Carnegie Mellon University, USA
Volker Gruhn	University of Leipzig, Germany
Paul Grünbacher	Johannes Kepler University Linz, Austria
Dan Houston	Honeywell Inc., USA

LiGuo Huang   University of Southern California, USA
Hajimu Iida   Nara Institute of Science and Technology, Japan
Katsuro Inoue   Osaka University, Japan
Ross Jeffery   University of New South Wales, Australia
Natalia Juristo   Universidad Politécnica de Madrid, Spain
Rick Kazman   University of Hawaii, USA
Jyrki Kontio   Helsinki University of Technology, Finland
Barbara Staudt Lerner   Mt. Holyoke College, USA
Jian Lv   Nanjing University, China
Ray Madachy   University of Southern California, USA
Frank Maurer   University of Calgary, Canada
Jürgen Münch   Fraunhofer Institute for Experimental Software
                            Engineering, Germany
Flavio Oquendo   University of South Brittany, France
Dewayne E. Perry   University of Texas at Austin, USA
Dietmar Pfahl   Simula Research Laboratory, Norway
Dan Port   University of Hawaii, USA
Antony Powell   YorkMetrics Ltd, UK
David M. Raffo   Portland State University, USA
Juan F. Ramil   The Open University, UK
Andreas Rausch   Technische Universität Kaiserslautern, Germany
Daniel Rodriguez   University of Alcalá , Spain
Günther Ruhe   University of Calgary, Canada
Mercedes Ruiz   University of Cádiz, Spain
Ioana Rus   University of Maryland, USA
Kevin Ryan   University of Limerick, Ireland
Walt Scacchi   University of California, Irvine, USA
Stan Sutton   IBM T. J. Watson Research Center, USA
Guilherme H. Travassos   Federal University of Rio de Janeiro/COPPE, Brazil
Colin Tully   Middlesex University, UK
Qing Wang   Institute of Software, Chinese Academy of Sciences,
                            China
Yasha Wang   Peking University, China
Yongji Wang   Institute of Software, Chinese Academy of Sciences,
                            China
Brian Warboys   University of Manchester, UK
Paul Wernick   University of Hertfordshire, UK
Laurie Williams   North Carolina State University, USA
Ye Yang   Institute of Software, Chinese Academy of Sciences,
                            China
Yun Yang   Swinburne University of Technology, Australia

External Reviewers

Silvia Acuña	Universidad Autónoma de Madrid, Spain
Dante Carrizo	Universidad Complutense de Madrid, Spain
Enrique Fernández	Instituto Tecnológico de Buenos Aires, Argentina
Ramón García	Instituto Tecnológico de Buenos Aires, Argentina
Anna Grimán	Universidad Simón Bolivar, Venezuela
Lishan Hou	Institute of Software, Chinese Academy of Sciences, China
Jingzhou Li	University of Calgary, Canada
Juan Li	Institute of Software, Chinese Academy of Sciences, China
Fengdi Shu	Institute of Software, Chinese Academy of Sciences, China
Martín Solari	ORT, Uruguay
Dietmar Winkler	Vienna University of Technology, Austria
Junchao Xiao	Institute of Software, Chinese Academy of Sciences, China
Liming Zhu	National ICT Australia, Australia

Table of Contents

Process Tools and Metrics

Process Representation, Analysis and Modeling

Simulation Modeling

Experience Report

Benefits of Global Software Development:
The Known and Unknown

Pär J. Ågerfalk[1,2], Brian Fitzgerald[1], Helena Holmström Olsson[1,3],
and Eoin Ó Conchúir[1]

[1] Lero, The Irish Software Engineering Research Centre, University of Limerick, Ireland
[2] Uppsala University, Sweden
[3] IT University, Gothenburg, Sweden
par.agerfalk@dis.uu.se, bf@ul.ie, helena.holmstrom@lero.ie,
eoin.oconchuir@lero.ie

Abstract. Organizations are increasingly moving to the global software development (GSD) model because of significant benefits that can accrue. However, GSD is fraught with difficulties arising from geographical, temporal and socio-cultural distances. The emphasis in the literature to date has typically been on how to overcome these significant challenges associated with GSD. While a number of GSD benefits have been identified in the literature, there are also a number of less obvious, what we term 'unknown,' potential benefits that can accrue from GSD. Here we synthesize and integrate an overall set of potential GSD benefits and categorize them according to the organizational, team and process level to which they are most applicable. The 'unknown' includes organization benefits, such as improved resource allocation, team benefits, such as reduced coordination cost and improved team autonomy, and process benefits, such as improved documentation and clearly defined processes.

Keywords: global software development, benefits, challenges, offshoring.

1 Introduction

Global software development (GSD) is a phenomenon of increasing importance, given the perennial pressures of the need to remain profitable and competitive in the global landscape. Companies can now leverage the emergence of large multi-skilled labor forces in lower-cost economies thanks to high-speed Internet-based communication links, through which the product (software code) can be quickly transferred between development sites. India and China, in particular, offer huge multi-skilled labor forces at greatly reduced cost compared with employment markets in the US and western Europe. Other countries are also making an impact, such as Brazil, Eastern Europe and Russia, Malaysia and Vietnam.

GSD involves the three major types of distance: geographical, temporal, and socio-cultural [1]. Single teams can be separated by these distances, essentially becoming what is often termed 'virtual teams'. In other circumstances, a single team may have all of its resources co-located, but with heavy reliance on other teams at remote

Q. Wang, D. Pfahl, and D.M. Raffo (Eds.): ICSP 2008, LNCS 5007, pp. 1–9, 2008.
© Springer-Verlag Berlin Heidelberg 2008

locations. Vast geographical distances imply the difficulty of re-locating to another of the company's sites, and not being able to stroll over to a colleague's desk to chat about an implementation issue. Temporal distance across multiple time zones reduces the number of overlapping working hours, forcing a heavier reliance on asynchronous communication technologies. Socio-cultural distance arises from the different national and organizational backgrounds of the people involved and exacerbates communication breakdown.

Major benefits have been attributed with GSD despite the challenges arising from overcoming these distances. Apart from being a potential side-effect of mergers and acquisitions, GSD is purported as enabling major benefits such as lower development costs and access to huge multi-skilled labor forces, as already mentioned. However as researchers and practitioners have focused on overcoming GSD challenges, an exhaustive inventory of potential GSD benefits has not been compiled. While some benefits have been widely acknowledged in previous research, other potential benefits are evident but, nonetheless, overlooked to a large extent. In this paper, we label these two categories of benefits 'known' and 'unknown' – and explore what each benefit might offer companies aiming to leverage GSD.

1.1 Challenges of GSD

The geographical, temporal, and socio-cultural distances affect the three major processes of software development: communication, coordination, and control [1]. In fact, communication and control problems are recognized as being the most troublesome and pervasive in software development [2].

A major challenge for GSD teams is the lack of informal communication which has been found to be an essential process in traditionally co-located development [3, 4]. Written documentation is often inadequate when resolving misunderstandings, such as misunderstandings about requirements or changes in requirement specifications. Geographical and temporal distances make it more difficult to initiate contact with colleagues at other locations. While being indispensible for enabling face-to-face contact, the cost of travel can be prohibitive. A lack of overlapping working hours can lead to delays in feedback, rendering the development process less effective. Even a time zone difference of one hour can have a major effect when combined with different typical working hours in different countries.

Socio-cultural distance can result in a fundamental difference in opinion about the nature of the software development process [5]. It can lead to misunderstandings and non-native speakers struggling to follow technical discussions, especially over the phone. A general lack of familiarity with remotely located colleagues can result in a lack of 'teamness' and a reduced sense of trust.

Moreover, the distances involved increase the complexity involved in coordinating the software development process. Software development in itself is a complex task with substantial non-routine work. The GSD environment calls for increased understanding for this complexity and the ability to focus on coordination of resources, such as distributed teams and tasks. Clearly, achieving a satisfactory result can be a challenge.

1.2 Assumptions Made About GSD

Despite well-known challenges, GSD also presents practitioners with various benefits. As pointed out above, some of these are well known, while some are not as obvious. Interestingly, the 'known' benefits, which are generally considered to be the driving forces behind GSD, all seem to apply at the organizational level. That is, they contribute to top-level organizational goals, such as cost savings and increased efficiency. Admittedly, some of the 'unknown' benefits apply at the organizational level, but in addition we see benefits that more directly affect teams and basic software development processes and tasks. We would argue that the 'unknown' benefits should also be taken into consideration and that there is a need to highlight the full spectrum of GSD benefits.

Currently there is a tendency to 'localize' GSD by attempting to reduce the geographical, temporal and socio-cultural distances involved. This approach assumes that the benefits of GSD do not fully justify truly global software development. Contrary to this, we have found teams shifting their working hours to increase the temporal overlap with remote colleagues, thereby aiming towards a 'virtual 8-hour day' [6].

However, the decision of whether or not to globalize software development activities – or indeed the inclination to either 'localize' or fully leverage GSD – should be informed by the potential benefits it offers. We argue that this decision can be better informed if both 'known' and 'unknown' benefits are taken into consideration. In what follows, we outline both 'known' and 'unknown' benefits. In the end, we provide a categorization of all benefits, using the categories (1) organizational, (2) team and (3) process/task.

2 The 'Known' Benefits of GSD

In this section we outline well-known benefits of GSD. They all seem to apply at organizational level and have been previously acknowledged in research.

2.1 Cost Savings

Perhaps the original and most sought-after benefit of GSD has been that of reduced cost of development [7]. The basis for this benefit is that companies are globalizing their software development activities to leverage cheaper employees located in lower-cost economies. This has been made possible by the deployment of cross-continental high-speed communication links enabling the instantaneous transfer of the basic product at hand: software.

The difference in wages across regions can be significant, with a US software engineer's salary being multiple times greater than that of a person with equivalent skills in (at least parts) of Asia or South America. In 2005, the annual base pay of a software engineer located in India was $10,300 [8]. However, this seems to be rising and there has been hyper-growth in local I.T. employment markets such as in Bangalore. It is our experience that companies are now looking at alternative locations which offer more acceptable attrition rates with the continued promise of cheaper labor.

2.2 Access to Large Multi-skilled Workforces

GSD provides the unprecedented possibility to leverage large pools of skilled labor by coordinating across distance [9, 10, 11, 12]. Companies have the opportunity to expand their software development activities to include the contributions of thousands of skilled workers, wherever they may be located, to form virtual global corporations [13, 11, 14].

2.3 Reduced Time to Market

A controversial benefit of GSD has been that of the 'follow-the-sun' approach, described in detail by Carmel [4]. Time zone effectiveness is the degree to which an organization manages resources in multiple time zones, maximizing productivity by increasing the number of hours during a 24-hour day that software is being developed by its teams. When time zone effectiveness is maximized to span 24 hours of the day, this is referred to as the 'follow-the-sun' development model. This is achieved by handing off work from one team at the end of their day to another team located in another time zone. The approach can aid organizations which are under severe pressure to improve time-to-market [11].

2.4 Proximity to Market and Customer

By establishing subsidiaries in countries where the company's customers are located, GSD allows it to develop software close to their customers and to increase knowledge of the local market [11]. Creating new jobs can create good will with local customers, possibly resulting in more contracts [15]. Indeed, it may be a business necessity to locate closer to customers in order to expand to other markets. For example, a company that develops software for embedded systems may focus on large manufacturing companies based in China, or a software automotive company may locate part of the development in Germany. Development activities may even be located on the same campus as the organization's large customer. Companies may also look to establishing strategic partnerships to gain access to new markets [16].

3 The 'Unknown' Benefits of GSD

Above, we have highlighted the four 'known' benefits which have been cited as driving forces towards the globalization of software development activities. However, there have been individual reports of additional benefits that may be realized through GSD. Up until now, these benefits have been mostly overlooked. Indeed, and as the label reflects, the benefits covered below are not as obvious as the 'known' benefits mentioned above. While the benefits which are well-known tend to easily affect company policy, we believe that additional and sometimes 'hidden' benefits may offer great potential and indeed contribute in strategic company decisions.

While some of the 'unknown' benefits we identify are applicable at organization level (as is the case with 'known' benefits), they also seem to affect coordination and collaboration within and between GSD software teams as well as the basic software engineering tasks at hand. For the purpose of this paper, we therefore use the categories organization, team and process/task when discussing the identified benefits. By focusing on leveraging the full range of benefits, we argue that companies may reap more rewards from their GSD activities, and that GSD may not need to be seen as only a challenge for software development companies.

3.1 Organizational Benefits

Two of the unknown benefits apply primarily at the organizational level. We refer to these as 'innovation and shared best practice' and 'improved resource allocation'.

3.1.1 Innovation and Shared Best Practices

The global business environment demands and expects innovative, high-quality software that meets its needs [17]. Organizations can take advantage of increased innovation and shared best practice that arises from the collaboration of team members who come from different national and organizational backgrounds [10, 14].

In large complex organizations, decentralized, independent individuals interact in self-organizing ways to create innovative and emergent results [17]. Such organizations base their success on innovation and their innovation capabilities come from talent – from their most brilliant, intelligent and creative engineers. Companies that expand into other countries in order to tap into talent have been termed "knowledge seekers" [18]. Such organizations tend to act somewhat differently compared to organizations that offshore purely for cost reasons [14] and we can see an acknowledgement of this benefit through the action of such companies.

3.1.2 Improved Resource Allocation

As an extension to the benefit of access to large multi-skilled labor pools, the organization can benefit from the influx of new (lower-cost) labor in other countries. It may be beneficial for the organization to reassign the newly-redundant higher-cost resources to other, often more strategic, activities while also avoiding the employee turmoil and backlash associated with workforce reductions [19]. Changes in allocation can adhere to the challenge of replacing isolated expertise and instead create skill-broadening tasks and effective teamwork [10].

3.2 Team Benefits

At the team level, we find three unknown benefits, namely 'improved task modularization', 'reduced coordination cost', and 'increased team autonomy'.

3.2.1 Improved Task Modularization

According to Conway's Law, the structure of the system mirrors the structure of the organization that designed it [20]. In fact, it is the product architecture that should determine the team structure, rather than the other way around [4]. In earlier work we have seen the importance of a separation of concerns when decomposing work into modules [21], and it appears that these principles could be extremely relevant for managing coordination complexity.

The nature of GSD leads teams to splitting their work across feature content into well-defined independent modules [10, 22, 23], without "stepping on each other's toes" [4]. This allows decisions to be made about each component in isolation [20]. Partitioning work tasks horizontally results in each site having responsibility for the whole lifecycle of particular functions/modules, it decreases interdependencies and hence, coordination costs [24]. For example, source code branching enables software development teams to work on source code in parallel, and merging the sections once they have been developed [25].

3.2.2 Reduced Coordination Cost

While we acknowledge that temporal distance can prove to be a challenge for GSD teams, it can also be seen as beneficial in terms of coordination: coordination costs are reduced when team members are not working at the same time [26]. The producer of a unit of work can complete the work during the off-hours of the person who requested that work. In essence, coordination costs are reduced since no direct coordination takes place when two people are not working at the same time.

3.2.3 Increased Team Autonomy

Gumm [27] found that organizational and geographical distribution of 'software development units' imply a certain degree of autonomy for each unit. The study reported that this autonomy allowed for the necessity to maintain the different working cultures of each team. This was viewed as necessary to maintain the quality of the work of a single team even if this in turn required careful synchronization of the single processes.

3.3 Process/Task Benefits

In addition to the organizational and team oriented unknown benefits outlined above, there are three further unknown benefits that apply primarily at the process/task level. We refer to these as 'formal record of communication', 'improved documentation', and 'clearly defined processes'.

3.3.1 Formal Record of Communication

Since asynchronous communication relies on technologies such as e-mail and fax [28, 29], a written communication history is usually left [7, 30]. This provides for increased traceability and accountability [31], and allow for input from diverse stakeholders, irrespective of geographical location [30].

3.3.2 Improved Documentation

DeLone et al. [32] state that distributed teams have an increased focus on documentation in order to aid their communication. Gumm [27] reported this as an advantage, in that documentation is better supported within distributed project settings. Information is documented and distributed electronically rather than discussed face-to-face, which allows for the passing-on of project specific knowledge in distributed settings.

3.3.3 Clearly Defined Processes

Independent of a project's process maturity, the definition and structuring of processes is a challenge [27]. While distributed project settings seem to challenge process maturity, they also seem to support it. Process definitions are compiled more carefully in distributed settings. It was noted that if team members were co-located, much of the processes would probably not be formalized.

4 Conclusions

As recognized in this paper, some benefits of GSD have been widely cited and can be considered 'known' to both researchers and practitioners. However, additional benefits are evident and they have been, to some extent, overlooked. In this paper, we have identified these 'unknown' benefits in order to provide a synthesis of GSD benefits. This will hopefully lead to a more informed debate on the topic as well as more informed decisions on whether or not to pursue GSD. As can be seen, a majority of the 'unknown' benefits that we have identified apply at team and process/task level. This is probably part of the reason for them not being widely acknowledged as driving factors towards GSD. See Table 1 for a summary of our synthesis of the benefits offered by GSD.

We have also pointed out the on-going struggle between reducing the distances of GSD and making the most of the dynamic context of the global situation. For example, we see attempts to reduce coordination costs by effective modularizing work, while at the same time wishing to leverage GSD by sharing innovation and best practice between teams. The debate on this matter up until now has not been informed by a full synthesis of the benefits. Hopefully, the synthesis of benefits of GSD should lead to an even more informed debate on this matter.

Cost-benefit tradeoffs in GSD are still not fully understood [26]. The GSD community has yet to come to a consensus on which benefits are realistic, and whether or not practitioners should aim for the realization of each of them. For example, it is not yet clear to what extent cost savings can and are being realized. Also, follow-the-sun has been dismissed by many, but is still being promoted (see e.g. [33]). Most probably, certain benefits may only be realistic in specific contexts while some benefits may be mutually exclusive. Below, we present both 'known' and 'unknown' benefits of GSD, all structured according to the categories of (1) organizational, (2) teams, and (3) process/task.

Table 1. The benefits of global software development

Organizational benefits	Team benefits	Process/Task benefits
• Cost savings • Access to large multi-skilled workforces • Reduced time to market • Proximity to market and customer • Innovation and shared best practice • Resource allocation	• Improved task modularization • Reduced coordination cost • Increased team autonomy	• Formal record of communication • Improved documentation • Clearly defined processes

References

1. Ågerfalk, P.J., Fitzgerald, B., Holmström, H., Lings, B., Lundell, B., Conchúir, E.Ó.: A framework for considering opportunities and threats in distributed software development. In: International Workshop on Distributed Software Development, Paris, France, Austrian Computer Society (2005)
2. Herbsleb, J.D., Klein, H., Olson, G.M., Brunner, H., Olson, J.S., Harding, J.: Object-Oriented Analysis and Design in Software Project Teams. Human-Computer Interaction 10, 249 (1995)
3. Curtis, B., Krasner, H., Iscoe, N.: A field study of the software design process for large systems. Communications of the ACM 31(11), 1268–1287 (1988)
4. Carmel, E.: Global Software Teams: Collaborating Across Borders and Time Zones, 1st edn. Prentice-Hall, Upper Saddle River (1999)
5. Nicholson, B., Sahay, S.: Some political and cultural issues in the globalisation of software development: case experience from Britain and India. Information and Organization 11(1), 25–43 (2001)
6. Holmström Olsson, H., Conchúir, E.Ó., Ågerfalk, P.J., Fitzgerald, B.: Two-Stage Offshoring: An Investigation of the Irish Bridge. MIS Quarterly 32(2) (2008)
7. Carmel, E., Agarwal, R.: Tactical Approaches for Alleviating Distance in Global Software Development. IEEE Software 18(2), 22–29 (2001)
8. Mercer: China and India: Comparative HR Advantages. September 9 (2005) (accessed February 27, 2006), http://www.mercer.com/china-indiareport
9. Grinter, R.E., Herbsleb, J.D., Perry, D.E.: The Geography of Coordination: Dealing with Distance in R&D Work. In: International Conference on Supporting Group Work 1999, pp. 306–315 (1999)
10. Ebert, C., De Neve, P.: Surviving Global Software Development. IEEE Software 18(2), 62–69 (2001)
11. Herbsleb, J.D., Moitra, D.: Guest Editors' Introduction: Global Software Development. IEEE Software 18(2), 16–20 (2001)
12. Damian, D., Lanubile, F., Oppenheimer, H.L.: Addressing the Challenges of Software Industry Globalization: The Workshop on Global Software Development. In: 25th International Conference on Software Engineering, Portland, Oregon, IEEE Computer Society, Los Alamitos (2003)
13. Suzuki, J., Yamamoto, Y.: Leveraging distributed software development. Computer 32(9), 59–65 (1999)
14. Carmel, E., Tija, P.: Offshoring Information Technology: Sourcing and Outsourcing to a Global Workforce. Cambridge University Press, Cambridge, United Kingdom (2005)
15. Ebert, C., Parro, C.H., Suttels, R., Kolarczyk, H.: Improving validation activities in a global software development. In: Proceedings of the 23rd International Conference on Software Engineering, Toronto, Canada (2001)
16. Karolak, D.: Global software development: managing virtual teams and environments. IEEE Computer Society Press, Los Alamitos, California (1998)
17. Highsmith, J., Cockburn, A.: Agile software development: the business of innovation. Computer 34(9), 120–127 (2001)
18. Chung, W., Alcacer, J.: Knowledge sources and foreign investment location in the US. In: Conference of the Academy of International Business, June 2003, Monterrey, California (2003)

19. Weakland, T.: 2005 Global IT Outsourcing Study. DiamondCluster International, Inc. (2005) (accessed July 5, 2006), http://diamondcluster.com/Ideas/Viewpoint/PDF/DiamondCluster2005OutsourcingStudy.pdf

20. Herbsleb, J.D., Grinter, R.E.: Splitting the Organization and Integrating the Code: Conway's Law Revisited. In: 21st International Conference on Software Engineering, IEEE Computer Society Press, Los Angeles, California, United States (1999)

21. Parnas, D.L.: On the criteria to be used in decomposing systems into modules. Communications of the ACM 15(12), 1053–1058 (1972)

22. Sahay, S.: Global software alliances: the challenge of 'standardization'. Scandinavian Journal of Information Systems 15, 3–21 (2003)

23. Bass, M., Paulish, D.: Global Software Development Process Research at Siemens. In: International Workshop on Global Software Development, May 24, 2004, Edinburgh, Scotland (2004)

24. Battin, R.D., Crocker, R., Kreidler, J., Subramanian, K.: Leveraging Resources in Global Software Development. IEEE Software 18(2), 70–77 (2001)

25. Herbsleb, J.D., Paulish, D.J., Bass, M.: Global Software Development at Siemens: Experience from Nine Projects. In: 27th International Conference on Software Engineering, St. Louis, Missouri, USA, ACM Press, New York (2005)

26. Espinosa, J.A., Carmel, E.: The Effect of Time Separation on Coordination Costs in Global Software Teams: A Dyad Model. In: 37th Hawaiian International Conference on System Sciences. Big Island, Hawaii, IEEE, Los Alamitos (2004)

27. Gumm, D.: Distribution Dimensions in Software Development Projects: A Taxonomy. IEEE Software 23(5), 45–51 (2006)

28. Kiel, L.: Experiences in Distributed Development: A Case Study. In: ICSE International Workshop on Global Software Development, Portland, Oregon, USA (2003)

29. Boland, D., Fitzgerald, B.: Transitioning from a Co-Located to a Globally-Distributed Software Development Team: A Case Study and Analog Devices Inc. In: 3rd International Workshop on Global Software Development, May 24, 2004, Edinburgh, Scotland (2004)

30. Damian, D., Zowghi, D.: The impact of stakeholders geographical distribution on managing requirements in a multi-site organization. In: IEEE Joint International Conference on Requirements Engineering, IEEE Computer Society Press, Los Alamitos (2002)

31. Ågerfalk, P.J.: Investigating actability dimensions: a language/action perspective on criteria for information systems evaluation. Interacting with Computers 16(5), 957–988 (2004)

32. Delone, W., Espinosa, J.A., Lee, G., Carmel, E.: Bridging Global Boundaries for IS Project Success. In: 38th Annual Hawaii International Conference on System Sciences (HICSS 2005) - Track 1, vol. 01, IEEE Computer Society, Los Alamitos (2005)

33. Carmel, E.: Keynote speech. In: International Conference on Global Software Engineering (ICGSE), Munich, Germany, August 27-30 (2007)

Method Engineering: Towards Methods as Services

Colette Rolland

Université Paris1 Panthéon Sorbonne, CRI,
90 Rue de Tolbiac, 75013 Paris, France
rolland@univ-paris1.fr

Abstract. In the 90's it was becoming apparent that a universal method that could be applied to 'any' information system development (ISD) project is a mirage. Project specificity, differing application engineer skills and experience lead to deviations from the prescriptions made by given methods. This was revealed by several survey based studies (e.g. [6], [1], [7], [4]). For example, a survey of method use in over 100 organizations' [4] shows that more than 2/3 of the companies have developed or adapted their methods in-house. Also 89% of respondents believed that methods should be adapted on a project to project basis. These observations raised the need for techniques to rapidly build methods adapted to engineer preferences and project situations. The area of Method Engineering (ME) attempts to provide these techniques.

Method engineering represents the effort to improve the usefulness of systems development methods by creating an adaptation framework whereby methods are created to match specific organisational situations. There are at least two objectives that can be associated to this adaptation. The first objective is the production of contingency methods, that is, situation-specific methods for certain types of organisational settings. This objective represents method engineering as the creation of a multiple choice setting [3]. The second objective is one in which method engineering is used to produce method "on-the-fly". Situational method engineering [5] is the construction of methods which are tuned to specific situations of development projects. Each system development starts then, with a method definition phase where the development method is constructed on the spot.

Rapid method construction is predicated on the reuse of existing methods. Thus, methods are modularised into components that are stored in a repository. ME used the notion of a meta-model for developing method components that could be purely product or process components, or integrated product and process components. These components are kept in a method repository from where they can be retrieved. The retrieved components can be adapted and 'put together' to form a coherent whole method through an assembly process. This composition aims to build methods that address project concerns and fit with project specificity.

From the aforementioned, it can be understood that the three key issues of method engineering are, (a) defining method components, (b) finding and retrieving components and (c) assembling components.

The talk will survey the results achieved so far along these three issues.

It can be seen that ME provides engineering capability but, we believe, that it needs to be augmented with good usage properties. Specifically it is limited as follows:

Q. Wang, D. Pfahl, and D.M. Raffo (Eds.): ICSP 2008, LNCS 5007, pp. 10–11, 2008.
© Springer-Verlag Berlin Heidelberg 2008

Despite a common acceptance of a modular vision of methods, every method engineering approach has developed its own notion of a method component and its own proprietary repository. Method repository availability is therefore, restricted.

There is no standard component interface and this inhibits component retrieval.

Locating the needed component may require searching several repositories rather than having them in one centrally available place.

As a consequence, ME approaches remain locally used by their providers without been largely adopted by other organizations even if a standardization effort has been made in [2]. Furthermore, it is nowadays acknowledged that contingency factors change continuously during the project life cycle imposing a"continuous change management". This last feature raises the problem of dynamic adaptation of methods which has not been considered by current ME approaches.

In order to overcome these problems, the talk will develop the position of Method as a Service (MaaS).

We propose to adopt a service-based paradigm and by analogy to SaaS (Software as a Service) to consider a method as a service (MaaS). By adopting the SOA for ME, we aim to develop a method engineering approach driven by the needs of method clients whereas implementation details of method services will remain under the control of method providers.

Our belief if that the adoption of service technologies for ME will increase the accessibility of method services and will facilitate their dynamic composition. Last (but not least), it will provide a platform permitting an easy execution of method services compositions that is missing today.

The talk will demonstrate the feasibility of the MaaS concept and will outline its further development.

References

1. Aaen, et al.: A tale of two countries: CASE experience and expectations. The Impact of Computer Supported Technology on Information Systems Development, pp. 61–93. North Holland Pub., Amsterdam (1992)
2. International Standards Organization / International Electrotechnical Commission: Meta-model for Development Methodologies. Software Engineering, ISO/IEC 24744 (2007)
3. Karlsson, F., Agerfalk, P.J.: Method-user centred method configuration. In: Ralyte, J., Agerfalk, P.J., Kraiem, N. (eds.) Proceedings of SPRE 2005, Paris, France (2005)
4. Russo, et al.: The use and adaptation of system development methodologies. In: Proceedings of the International Resources Management. Association Conference, Atlanta (1995)
5. Welke, R.J., Kumar, K.: Method Engineering: a proposal for situation-specific methodology construction. In: Cotterman, Senn (eds.) Systems Analysis and Design: A Research Agenda, pp. 257–268. Wiley, Chichester (1992)
6. Wijers, G.M., van Dort, H.E.: Experiences with the use of CASE tools in the Netherlands. Advanced Information Systems Engineering, 5–20 (1990)
7. Yourdon, E.: The decline and fall of the American programmer. Prentice Hall, Englewood Cliffs (1992)

Macro-processes Informing Micro-processes: The Case of Software Project Performance

Paul L. Bannerman

NICTA, Australian Technology Park, Sydney, NSW, Australia
Paul.Bannerman@nicta.com.au

Abstract. This paper explores the operational context of software processes and how it can inform the micro-process level environment. It examines the case of software project performance, describing a novel explanation. Drawing on the management literature, project performance is modeled as the contested outcome of learning as a driver of success and certain barrier conditions as drivers of failure, through their effects on organizational capabilities. A case study illustrates application of the theory. Implications of this macro-process case for micro level software process improvement are discussed.

Keywords: software process, macro-process, capabilities, project performance.

1 Introduction

There is growing interest and recognition in the software community of the need to understand the broader context of software processes [23, 33]. For example, the most appropriate software processes are often dependent upon the organizational context. Furthermore, since most software development is done in projects, factors that affect project performance can influence the perceived success of the software artifact produced. The interaction between the macro and micro environment is bi-directional since organizations are dependent on the use of good software processes to produce high quality software. Therefore, they are co-dependent.

As defined in [33], the macro-process environment is concerned with high level behaviors while the micro-process environment deals with the internal workings of processes. Osterweil proposes that software process research has a role in informing macro-process behaviors [33]. This paper takes the complementary view that the macro-process environment may also inform the micro-process environment of software processes. It does this by examining the case of a novel explanation of the tendency of software projects to perform poorly. It illustrates the explanation with a practical example. Implications are drawn from the case for finer-grained processes.

A distinctive feature of the case is that it draws from the management literature to view processes in the higher level construct of organizational capabilities, which are a composite of tangible and intangible organizational knowledge, processes, skills and other assets that are developed through 'learning by doing'.

Projects are an important vehicle in developing software and delivering change to organizations. As such, they are critical enablers or inhibitors of business growth and

Q. Wang, D. Pfahl, and D.M. Raffo (Eds.): ICSP 2008, LNCS 5007, pp. 12–23, 2008.
© Springer-Verlag Berlin Heidelberg 2008

development, depending on the success of the project. A key sticking point, however, is that software projects have a highly variable performance record.

According to Charette [8], software projects have "a long, dismal history" of going awry. In a "Software Hall of Shame", he lists examples of over 30 major failures or losses that occurred in little more than a decade. He argues that billions of dollars are lost each year on failed or under-performing software projects. According to Charette, such failures can jeopardize organizations, imperil national security, and stunt economic growth and quality of life. Indeed, some reports suggest that software projects are more likely to perform poorly or fail than succeed [24], while others indicate that this problem has existed for decades [7, 51].

Extant explanations of the problem focus on factor- and process-based research to identify the drivers of project success. Implicitly, the research assumes that more of a desirable factor or process, or less of an undesirable 'risk' factor or process, improves the likelihood of success. Drawing on management theory (specifically, the resource-based view of the firm and organizational learning theory), this paper extends these views with an alternative theoretical explanation of the problem. It presents a capabilities-based view of software project performance that explains the data in a way the extant approaches have not. This broader conceptualization of processes has implications for the development of thinking at the software process level.

The paper is structured as follows. The following sections review the dominant current explanations of project performance and outline an alternative framing of the problem. Contributing theory to the proposed explanation from the management literature is then introduced, before the extended model is described. Application of the theoretical model is then illustrated with a case study of an Australian DMV. Finally, implications of the case for the micro level software process environment are drawn and conclusions reached on the contribution.

2 Current Explanations

Extant explanations of IT project performance are dominated by factor and process prescriptions in conjunction with assumptions about accumulating improvements through learning.

Factor research focuses on identifying antecedent variables (factors) for which a relationship can be hypothesized with a performance outcome. Well-known examples include a lack of top management commitment and/or user involvement, poorly defined requirements, gold plating and an absence of project management experience. The underlying logic of factor research is that a desirable factor is associated with a positive performance outcome while an undesirable factor is associated with a negative outcome. The limitations of this approach are that it is difficult to establish a definitive set of factors as they tend to vary with project type, stage of the project life cycle, organizational context, and cultural context [36, 45]. Also, by focusing on inputs and outputs, it ignores intervening processes.

Process research in information systems examines interactions between stakeholders and events to find more complex causal relationships between factors and project outcomes (e.g., [43]). However, it reports limited convergence and empirical support [44]. In software engineering, process research is concerned with improving product quality through software processes [16]. Despite many benefits, Jeffery has argued that the performance improvement effect of software process improvement in practice is often smaller than expected, in isolation of other enabling drivers of change [22]. Furthermore, these approaches are only weakly supported by theory.

The strategy underlying the two research streams is simple and compelling: identify factors and processes associated with success (or failure) in practice, and then develop prescriptions to emulate (or avoid) them [44]. It is assumed that, if these factors and processes are properly accounted for, quality will be high, failure will be avoided and the project will be a success. The basic argument is that, if you do 'the right things in the right ways', the outcome will be success. This has led to a proliferation of methodologies on what to do 'right'.

Underpinning the factor and process research streams are several assumptions about learning: learning is a prerequisite for project success [25]; organizations learn from experience [49]; and learning accumulates within and between projects [11]. These assumptions reinforce the view that experience accumulates during and across successive projects, refines the application of desirable factors and processes, resulting in continuous improvement over time and increasing project performance.

3   Reframing the Problem

Taken together, current research seeks to explain why software projects fail by focusing on the *drivers of success*. The logic is that if a project fails, then the project did something wrong. The project failed to take sufficient account of all the factors and processes that research and prior experience have shown are necessary for success. This approach has strong logical and practical appeal.

The problem with this framing, however, is that it does not fit the empirical data that shows there has been limited improvement in software project performance over the years [8, 24]. By reframing the problem, new insights can emerge. If we accept the industry data and adopt the view that high variability in outcomes and low success rates should be expected from such high risk ventures, then what is needed is a causal model that includes *drivers of success* and *drivers of failure*.

A capabilities-based explanation provides such a model, supported by two bodies of management literature: the resource-based view of the firm and related capability-based perspective, and; organizational learning theory. According to this literature, superior performance is associated with developing and maintaining stocks of firm-specific resources and capabilities (including processes) that are developed primarily through learning from experience. Extant research tends to understate the importance of having 'the right resources'. This literature also argues, however, that learning and capability development may be inhibited, blocked or made redundant, creating a capability deficit and propensity to under-perform or fail. These components provide the basis of a capabilities-based explanation of project performance.

4   Contributing Theory

In this section, we profile the management theory underlying the proposed model.

4.1 Resource-Based View and Organizational Capabilities

According to the *resource-based view of the firm* (RBV), organizational performance is a function of internal resources, which are heterogeneously distributed across firms. Firm-specific idiosyncrasies in accumulating and using differentiated resources drive superior firm performance and sustainable competitive advantage [4]. Resources with high performance potential are characterized as valuable, rare, non-tradable, non-imitable, non-substitutable, causally ambiguous and/or socially complex [5, 12].

The capability-based perspective extends this view by emphasizing building and accumulating resources better and faster than competitors [38]. Capabilities, a subset of firm resources, typically comprise an amalgam of intangible assets, knowledge, skills, processes, routines, technologies and values. A firm is modeled as a learning organization that builds and deploys advantageous, firm-specific capabilities and applies them to achieve superior levels of performance [18]. A firm's comparative effectiveness in developing and deploying capabilities determines its marketplace success. Furthermore, its ability to adapt and innovate in identifying, building and leveraging new competencies is a capability in itself, called 'dynamic capability' [48].

The IT literature reports empirical support for a positive relationship between capability and firm performance [41].

4.2 Organizational Learning

In the management literature, organizational learning is the primary generative mechanism of organizational capabilities. Capabilities are developed through learning from experience, or 'learning by doing' [27]. Organizational capabilities are developed and institutionalized in the operating routines, practices and values of organizations in a way that outlives the presence of specific individual members [32]. Routines that lead to favorable outcomes become institutionalized in organizations as capabilities, which are adapted over time in response to further experiential learning. Organizations can also build capabilities through management practices [19, 39].

This view of learning is different to that of the experience factory in software engineering [6]. The latter deals with declarative or explicit knowledge that can be codified in a data repository. In contrast, learning by doing builds tacit knowledge and skill-based capabilities that cannot be encapsulated in a database (other than through links to sources, as in network knowledge management systems).

Learning improves the 'intelligence' of the organization and, thus, its performance. In this sense, the ability to learn from experience is a critical competency, requiring a deliberate investment [11]. Learning takes two forms [1]. One is *continuous*, incrementally improving organizational capabilities (called 'single-loop learning'). The other is *discontinuous* (called 'double-loop learning), resulting in fundamentally different organizational rules, values, norms, structures and routines.

4.3 Learning and Capability Development Barriers

However, the literature also reports that learning and capability development are neither certain nor cumulative. Barrier conditions may arise in the organizational and technological contexts of projects that can inhibit or block learning and capability development and/or make accumulated capabilities redundant or obsolete in the face of new opportunities and challenges [2].

Conditions that can *inhibit* organizational learning and capability development include learning disincentives; organizational designs that create artificial barriers; time compression diseconomies (learning is slow, it cannot be rushed); low aspiration levels; absorptive capacity (the ability to absorb new learning); asset mass inefficiencies (learning requires some prior knowledge); and transformative capacity (the ability to share or transfer learning) [10, 12, 17, 28, 50].

Conditions that can *block* organizational learning and capability development include causal ambiguity (lack of clarity of causal drivers); complexity; tacitness; embeddedness and interconnectedness (capabilities are deeply entrenched in their context so they may be difficult to explicate or share); learning myopia, competency traps and core rigidities (existing learning is favored); the need to unlearn old ways before new learning can occur; organizational inertia; focus diversion (distractions from relevant learning); unjustified theories-in-use (defensive routines); and certain characteristics of projects (e.g., projects are usually too short and focused on other objectives for effective learning to occur within the project) [1, 26, 27, 29, 37, 42, 47].

Finally, conditions that can *negate the value of existing organizational capabilities or make them obsolete* include newness; technological discontinuities; radical business process reengineering (redesigning from a zero-base); staff loss through turnover, downsizing or outsourcing; organizational forgetting; and asset erosion (capabilities can be lost over time) [9, 12, 15, 20, 21, 28, 40, 46].

Individually and in combination, these organizational learning and capability development barriers can significantly diminish the ability of an organization – or project – to perform according to expectation and in a manner assumed by the best practices that are applied. They can offset positive learning effects and devalue or destroy the accumulated capabilities necessary for project success.

5 Alternative Explanation

Based on this literature, poor project performance is not an exception or simply the result of managers not taking account of all relevant factors and process prescriptions. Also, learning from poor results and improving is not enough to ensure success next time. Rather, project performance can be explained by the generative and regressive mechanisms underlying organizational capabilities. Specifically, project performance is a function of the capabilities applied to the project. Learning drives capability development and project success. Barriers to learning and capability development diminish or negate existing capabilities, driving poor performance and project failure. Project performance, then, is the contested outcome of the two opposing effects on capabilities. These relationships are shown in the causal model in Figure 1.

In this model, *learning* is the process of developing capabilities through experience. *Barriers* are conditions that retard, deplete or make organizational capabilities redundant, creating a propensity to fail. *Capabilities* are the differentiated resources that generate operational and strategic value for an organization. *Performance* is the extent to which the outcome of an IT project meets stakeholder expectations.

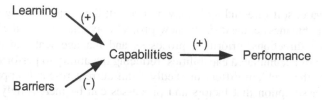

Fig. 1. Model of project performance

The individual relationships between organizational learning and capabilities, and organizational capabilities and performance, are accepted, *a priori*, as hypothesized in the literature and discussed above. The central model-based contributions of this paper are in the negative relationship and the total dynamic of the model.

One general barrier effect, a negative association with capabilities, is shown in the model. In fact, two effects were identified earlier. First, barrier conditions reduce or block the *learning improvement* effect on capabilities; second, and more fundamentally, they can make existing *capabilities redundant or obsolete* for the needs of new or changed conditions. These effects are of different types. The first effect is continuous, interrupting or slowing the incremental accumulation of capabilities. In contrast, the second effect is discontinuous, making existing capabilities obsolete for requirements under the new condition.

Based on these relationships, two central propositions arise.

First, project performance is the contested outcome of the positive effects of learning and the negative effects of learning and capability development barrier conditions on the organizational capabilities available to the project.

Second, in software projects, especially those involving large-scale developments, the initial capability stocks plus the learning that occurs on the project can be less than the effect of the barrier conditions experienced during the project. This results in a net competence liability that limits performance. The barrier effects offset the learning effects so that capabilities for the project are sub-optimal, resulting in a poor performance outcome. When these effects persist, both within and between projects, limited learning accumulates. The organization is in no better position to take on a new project than it was at the start of the previous one.

Software projects are particularly susceptible to the disruptive effects of technology and organization changes, which occur both within and between projects. Hardware, software, processes, tools and methods are constantly changing or becoming obsolete. This occurs on cycle times that vary from a few months for leading-edge technologies, to longer for other technologies. These discontinuities significantly impact people, processes and technologies currently in use, destroying the value of existing capabilities, and requiring resources to be diverted to manage them, as well as affecting the resources needed for future projects. So, if the project cycle time is several years, which is typical for a major system development project, technology will have cycled a number of times, making some capabilities obsolete, refreshing the organization's competence liability and propensity to fail.

On this basis, even when capabilities are developed in the current technologies during a project, it is likely that they are obsolete by the time the next project starts.

Different hardware, software and tools may be needed; the project manager and team changes; and the business context of the new project may change. Similarly, changes in organizational directions, priorities, processes and management can set back or negate the value of accumulated capabilities, reducing the ability to perform well.

This view of the problem differs markedly from current research approaches. In contrast to the assumption that factors and processes can be increasingly applied to deliver a successful outcome, it argues that the shift in factors that would be necessary for success is unlikely to occur, or does not have the desired result, because of the progressive offsetting effects of barriers to learning and capability development. The unpredictable nature of these conditions, in both frequency and magnitude of effect, can produce substantial variation in outcomes from one project to the next within the same organization.

According to this view, it is not sufficient to 'do the right things in the right ways'. It is also critical to 'have the right resources (capabilities)'. While an organization has followed the appropriate guidelines of factor and process prescriptions, the normal ongoing conditions that arise during a software project can damage or destroy the capabilities needed to ensure its success, increasing the likelihood that it might fail. Furthermore, even if the organization is successful, it cannot assume that it can replicate that success in the next project.

This model provides an explanation for the persistent variance in empirical data (e.g., [24]). It also explains why an organization can have an outstanding success with one project and a total failure with the next. This was the experience, for example, of Bank of America with its ERMA and MasterNet projects [30], and of American Airlines with its SABRE and CONFIRM reservation systems projects [34].

6 Illustration

Application of the theory is illustrated by a longitudinal case study of a major system development in an Australian State Government department of motor vehicles (DMV). The case is detailed in [2] and summarized here.

A project was initiated to replace the department's inefficient batch processing mainframe system with a new server-based online system for administration of the State's drivers and motor vehicles. The study examines the initial development and subsequent upgrades from 1989 to 2001.

The initial development was an interesting case of a 'successful failure'. That is, even though the new system was very late, well over budget and significantly descoped in functionality, it ultimately achieved the Department's major business objectives, including savings of $20m a year. Consequently, the success was acknowledged with an industry award for excellence for the system.

Due to this anomalous outcome, the case presented an opportunity to examine the substance of the agency's excellence and performance in system development. One implication of the award is that the initial development 'failure' was a 'glitch', so capabilities would have accumulated and exemplary performance would dominate subsequent development. However, this was not evident. To understand why, the case was examined for evidence of learning accumulation and barrier effects.

The study period featured many organizational and technology changes that occurred concurrently with or as a direct result of ongoing development of the system. The major changes are shown in Figure 2. These occurred in conjunction with a stream of ongoing software version upgrades, escalating design complexity and architecture fragmentation, and other people movements not shown in the figure. To resource the project, the DMV relied heavily on contract developers. While they were highly skilled and experienced professionals, there was no incentive for them to transfer knowledge and skills to staff.

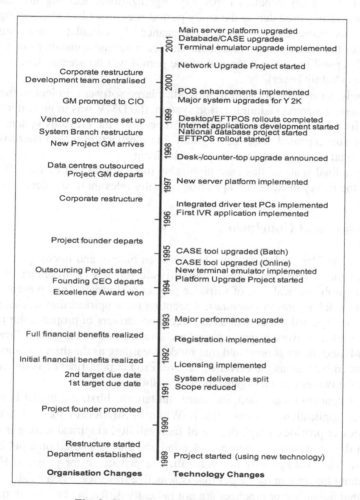

Fig. 2. Chronology of change at the DMV

Changes in the status of eight IT core capabilities adapted from [13] were analyzed in four phases across the study period [2]. The capabilities were: leadership, business systems thinking, building business relationships, infrastructure management, making technology work, building vendor relationships, managing projects, and managing change. Capability strength was measured as low, medium or high for each capability in each phase of the study. Barrier conditions associated with each capability were also identified in each phase. Measurement was aided by empirical indicators developed for each capability and barrier condition, described in [2].

The analysis found that very little cumulative learning occurred in the capabilities during the study period. Furthermore, barrier conditions were found to be high and significantly associated with each capability across the study. In particular, newness discontinuities were found to negatively impact over 80% of the capabilities over the study period. The study concluded that any organizational learning and capability development that occurred during the study period was offset by the effects of recurrent barrier conditions, resulting in the maintenance of a cumulative net competence liability rather than accumulated organizational learning and capability development. The level of capability stocks at the end of the period was no greater than at the start (rather, it was slightly lower).

Accordingly, in moving forward to any other large software project in the future, such as the next generation administration system, the DMV was in no better position to improve its likelihood of success than it had been for the previous system project. The earlier result appeared not to be a 'glitch' but a reflection of an underinvestment in organizational learning and capability development.

The longitudinal scale of this case highlights the learning and barrier effects, but the logic of the theory makes the propositions equally relevant to smaller projects.

7 Discussion and Conclusion

Motivated to consider the interrelationship between macro- and micro- processes and gain insights that might contribute to the software process environment, this paper examines the problematical case of software project performance and presents a novel approach to modeling project outcomes. Accepting the empirical data as indicative of what might be expected rather than as an exception, drivers of project failure are recognized as well as drivers of project success. Drawing on management literature, a capabilities-based theory is proposed that models learning as the driver of success and learning-related barriers as the driver of failure. Project performance is the contested outcome of the two effects on organizational capabilities.

As an independent proposition, there are limitations. First, the model is validated only through application to a case study. While illustration of its explanatory and predictive power provides a high degree of face validity, empirical testing is required to establish the bounds of its relevance. Second, the study is based on a public sector organization. The findings may not generalize to private sector projects. However, there is nothing inherent in the model that is sensitive to sector. There is also evidence to suggest that public sector practices are not radically different [14]. Third, the model is not applied to any specific organizational capabilities (apart from in the illustration). Other research, however, reports progress in identifying capabilities relevant to software engineering [3]. Finally, future research could extend the model by considering, for example, how capabilities are built, their inter-relationships and complementarities, or how they aggregate.

The case has several implications for micro level software process research.

The most immediate implication is that extant factor- and process-based research approaches to macro level problems may not be sufficient on their own to adequately explain the phenomenon. They may benefit, for example, from considering drivers of failure as well as drivers of success, and the organizational resources needed to make them effective. Specifically, the effectiveness of software process best practices may be a reflection of the competencies that underlie and enable their impacts.

Second, software process can be an organizational capability. Software process can be an undifferentiated resource for an organization or a distinctive capability. The choice is the organization's, based on its strategic goals and positioning.

Third, learning does not necessarily accumulate continuously. Software processes, as capabilities, are subject to the same contested dynamic that was described in the case. Strategies for continuous process improvement are likely to be disrupted by discontinuities in learning and capability development.

In support of [33], another implication is the importance of the interaction between macro-processes and micro-processes to the effectiveness of each other. The ultimate 'quality' of software is its fitness for purpose, determined at the macro level, but that quality cannot be achieved or sustained without improving the processes employed to build it. As Jeffery has argued [22], effective software processes occur within a framework of multiple organizational interactions. Also, software project success factors, processes and capabilities may only be some of the critical elements that, in aggregate, reinforce each other to drive project outcomes. Further research is needed to unlock these dimensions and interactions.

Furthermore, because of the delivery context of software (that is, through projects in organizations), the perception of the effectiveness of software processes as reflected in the developed software artifact may be influenced by many other external factors that have nothing to do with software quality. This reinforces the need to understand the macro context and minimize impacts on software process performance from other contingent domains.

A final implication arises for experience-based process improvement and process modeling. The case illustrates that intangibles contribute to performance outcomes as well as explicit process capabilities. Mechanisms are needed to capture and represent capabilities in the software process domain. This is partially recognized by [52].

This paper has highlighted the importance of contextual awareness. Benefiting from the implications will require ongoing interaction between the micro- and macro-process domains and continued recognition that neither environment is an island.

Acknowledgments. The paper benefits from comments provided by Liming Zhu. NICTA is funded by the Australian Government through the ICT Research Centre of Excellence program.

References

1. Argyris, C., Schön, D.A.: Organizational Learning: A Theory of Action Perspective. Addison-Wesley, Reading (1978)
2. Bannerman, P.L.: The Liability of Newness. PhD Dissertation, UNSW, AGSM (2004)

3. Bannerman, P.L., Staples, M.: A Software Enterprise Capabilities Architecture. NICTA Working Paper (2007)
4. Barney, J.B.: Firm Resources and Sustained Competitive Advantage. J Manage 17(1), 99–120 (1991)
5. Barney, J.B.: Gaining and Sustaining Competitive Advantage, 2nd edn. Prentice Hall, Upper Saddle River (2002)
6. Basili, V.R.: The Experience Factory and its Relationship to Other Quality Approaches. Advances in Computers 41, 65–82 (1995)
7. Brooks Jr., F.P.: The Mythical Man Month: Essays on Software Engineering. Addison-Wesley, Reading (1975)
8. Charette, R.N.: Why Software Fails. IEEE Spectrum 42(9), 42–49 (2005)
9. Christensen, C.M.: The Innovator's Dilemma. HarperBusiness, New York (2000)
10. Cohen, W.M., Levinthal, D.A.: Absorptive Capacity: A New Perspective on Learning and Innovation. Admin. Sci. Quart. 35(1), 128–152 (1990)
11. Cooper, K.G., Lyneis, J., Bryant, B.J.: Learning to Learn, from Past to Future. Int. J. Project Manage 20(3), 213–219 (2002)
12. Dierickx, I., Cool, K.: Asset Stock Accumulation and Sustainability of Competitive Advantage. Manage Sci. 35(12), 1504–1511 (1989)
13. Feeny, D.F., Willcocks, L.P.: Core IS Capabilities for Exploiting Technology. Sloan Manage Rev 39(3), 9–21 (1998)
14. Ferlie, E.: Quasi Strategy: Strategic Management in the Contemporary Public Sector. In: Pettigrew, A., Thomas, H., Whittington, R. (eds.) Handbook of Strategy and Management, pp. 279–298. Sage Publications, London (2002)
15. Fisher, S.R., White, M.A.: Downsizing in a Learning Organization. Acad. Manage Rev. 25(1), 244–251 (2000)
16. Fuggetta, A.: Software Process: A Roadmap. In: Proceedings of the Conference on The Future of Software Engineering, pp. 25–34. ACM, New York (2000)
17. Garud, R., Nayyar, P.R.: Transformative Capacity: Continual Structuring by Intertemporal Technology Transfer. Strategic Manage J. 15(5), 365–385 (1994)
18. Hamel, G., Heene, A. (eds.): Competence-Based Competition. John Wiley & Sons, Chichester (1994)
19. Hamel, G.: The Concept of Core Competence. In: Hamel, G., Heene, A. (eds.) Competence-Based Competition, pp. 11–33. John Wiley & Sons, Chichester (1994)
20. Hammer, M.: Reengineering Work: Don't Automate, Obliterate. Harvard Bus. Rev. 68(4), 104–112 (1990)
21. Hannan, M.T., Freeman, J.: Structural Inertia and Organizational Change. Am Sociol Rev 49(2), 149–164 (1984)
22. Jeffery, D.R.: Achieving Software Development Performance Improvement through Process Change. In: Li, M., Boehm, B., Osterweil, L.J. (eds.) SPW 2005. LNCS, vol. 3840, pp. 43–53. Springer, Heidelberg (2006)
23. Jeffery, D.R.: Exploring the Business Process-Software Process Relationship. In: Wang, Q., Pfahl, D., Raffo, D.M., Wernick, P. (eds.) SPW 2006 and ProSim 2006. LNCS, vol. 3966, pp. 11–14. Springer, Heidelberg (2006)
24. Johnson, J.: My Life is Failure. Standish Group International (2006)
25. Kotnour, T.: A Learning Framework for Project Management. Project Manage J. 30(2), 32–38 (1999)
26. Leonard-Barton, D.: Core Capabilities and Core Rigidities: A Paradox in Managing New Product Development. Strategic Manage J. 13, 111–125 (1992)
27. Levitt, B., March, J.G.: Organisational Learning. Annu. Rev. Sociol. 14, 319–340 (1988)

28. Lyytinen, K., Robey, D.: Learning Failure in Information Systems Development. Informa Syst. J. 9(2), 85–101 (1999)
29. March, J.G.: Exploration and Exploitation in Organizational Learning. Organ Sci. 2(1), 71–87 (1991)
30. McKenney, J.L., Mason, R.O., Copeland, D.G.: Bank of America: The Crest and Trough of Technological Leadership. MIS Quart. 21(3), 321–353 (1997)
31. McWilliams, A., Siegel, D.: Event Studies in Management Research: Theoretical and Empirical Issues. Acad Manage J 40(3), 626–657 (1997)
32. Nelson, R.R., Winter, S.G.: An Evolutionary Theory of Economic Change. Harvard University Press, Cambridge (1982)
33. Osterweil, L.J.: Unifying Microprocess and Macroprocess Research. In: Li, M., Boehm, B., Osterweil, L.J. (eds.) SPW 2005. LNCS, vol. 3840, pp. 68–74. Springer, Heidelberg (2006)
34. Oz, E.: When Professional Standards are Lax: The CONFIRM Failure and its Lessons. Commun ACM 37(10), 29–36 (1994)
35. Pettigrew, A.M.: Longitudinal Field Research on Change: Theory and Practice. Organ Sci. 1(3), 267–292 (1990)
36. Pinto, J.K., Slevin, D.P.: Critical success factors across the project life cycle. Project Manage J. 19(3), 67–74 (1988)
37. Polanyi, M.: The Tacit Dimension. Peter Smith, Gloucester (1966)
38. Prahalad, C.K., Hamel, G.: The Core Competence of the Corporation. Harvard Bus. Rev. 68(3), 79–91 (1990)
39. Purcell, K.J., Gregory, M.J.: The Development and Application of a Process to Analyze the Strategic Management of Organizational Competences. In: Sanchez, R., Heene, A. (eds.) Implementing Competence-Based Strategies, pp. 161–197. JAI Press, Stamford (2000)
40. Quinn, J.B., Hilmer, F.G.: Strategic Outsourcing. Sloan Manage Rev. 35(4), 43–55 (1994)
41. Ravichandran, T., Lertwongsatien, C.: Effect of Information Systems Resources and Capabilities on Firm Performance. J. Manage Inform Syst. 21(4), 237–276 (2005)
42. Reed, R., DeFillippi, R.J.: Causal Ambiguity, Barriers to Imitation and Sustainable Competitive Advantage. Acad. Manage Rev. 15(1), 88–102 (1990)
43. Sambamurthy, V., Kirsch, L.J.: An Integrative Framework of the Information Systems Development Process. Decision Sci. 31(2), 391–411 (2000)
44. Sauer, C.: Deciding the Future for IS Failures. In: Currie, W., Galliers, R. (eds.) Rethinking Management Information Systems, pp. 279–309. Oxford University Press, Oxford (1999)
45. Schmidt, R., Lyytinen, K., Keil, M., Cule, P.: Identifying Software Project Risks: An International Delphi Study. J Manage Inform Syst 17(4), 5–36 (2001)
46. Stinchcombe, A.L.: Social Structure and Organizations. In: March, J.G. (ed.) Handbook of Organizations, pp. 142–193. Rand McNally College Publishing Company (1965)
47. Szulanski, G.: Exploring Internal Stickiness: Impediments to the Transfer of Best Practice within the Firm. Strategic Manage J. 17(S2), 27-43 (1996)
48. Teece, D.J., Pisano, G., Shuen, A.: Dynamic Capabilities and Strategic Management. Strategic Manage J. 18(7), 509–533 (1997)
49. Turner, J.R., Keegan, A., Crawford, L.: Learning by Experience in the Project-Based Organization. In: P PMI Research Conf., pp. 445–456. PMI, Sylva (2000)
50. Winter, S.G.: The Satisficing Principle in Capability Learning. Strategic Manag J 21(10-11), 981–996 (2000)
51. Yourdon, E.: Death March. Prentice Hall PTR, Upper Saddle River (1997)
52. Zhu, L., Osterweil, L.J., Staples, M., Kannengiesser, U., Simidschieva, B.I.: Desiderata for Languages to be Used in the Definition of Reference Business Processes. J. Softw. Informatics 1(1), 37–65 (2007)

Improving Software Risk Management Practices in a Medical Device Company

John Burton[1], Fergal McCaffery[2], and Ita Richardson[1]

[1] Lero – the Irish Software Engineering Research Centre, University of Limerick, Ireland
[2] Dundalk Institute of Technology, Dundalk, Ireland
John.Burton@ul.ie, Fergal.McCaffery@dkit.ie,
Ita.Richardson@ul.ie

Abstract. Software is becoming an increasingly important aspect of medical devices (MDs) and MD regulation. MDs can only be marketed if compliance and approval is achieved from the appropriate regulatory bodies. MD companies must produce a design history file detailing the processes undertaken in the design and development of their MD software. The safety of all MD software produced is of primary importance and it is crucial that an effective and efficient risk management (RM) process is in place. The authors have developed a software process improvement RM model that integrates regulatory MD RM requirements with the goals and practices of the Capability Maturity Model Integration (CMMI). This model is known as the RM Capability Model (RMCM). This paper evaluates how introducing the RMCM into a MD company improved their RM process.

Keywords: Risk Management, Process Assessment, Software Process Improvement, Medical Device Standards, Compliance, CMMI, FDA, BSI, Action Research, Evaluation, Verification.

1 Introduction

The MD industry is currently one of the fastest growing industries in the world. According to the World Health Organisation, in 2000, it was estimated that there were over one and a half million different MDs (incorporating MDs containing software) available on the market, representing a total value of over €114 billion [1] and were expected to grow to in excess of approximately €205 billion in 2006.

Software RM within MD companies is a critical area. MD manufacturers that do not devote sufficient attention to the areas of hazard analysis and RM are penalised as failure to comply can result in surrendering their legal right to sell their device in a specific market. However, with so many different standards, regulatory guidance papers and industry guides on RM, the task of collating this information into a usable model is a daunting one. In an attempt to resolve this issue, the RMCM [2] was developed through extracting concepts from a number of industry accepted standards and guides. The RMCM is an extension of the RM process area within the CMMI but is specifically tailored to fulfil the RM regulations of the MD software industry.

Q. Wang, D. Pfahl, and D.M. Raffo (Eds.): ICSP 2008, LNCS 5007, pp. 24–35, 2008.
© Springer-Verlag Berlin Heidelberg 2008

1.1 Medical Device Regulation

Regulatory bodies worldwide are tasked with the job of ensuring that only safe MDs that cannot cause serious harm or injury to a patient or end-user are marketed. Clearance of MDs varies between countries. In the European Union, MD companies receive a European Community (EC) certificate and a CE mark (a European conformity mark). In the United States, the device manufacturer receives a Marketing Clearance (510K) or an Approval Letter for Pre Market Approval (PMA) from the Food and Drug Administration (FDA).

Typically, before a MD company is certified to sell their product in a country, they must follow the registration or licensing procedure of that country. This in turn establishes a contract between the device manufacturer and that country, whereby the device manufacturer is obligated to perform both pre-market and post-market duties as defined in the quality system requirements. The quality system is defined as the organisational structure, responsibilities, procedures, processes and resources required to implement quality management. Applicable requirements are typically directly related to the regulatory classification of the device. This in turn defines the potential of that device to cause harm. However, hazard analysis and RM are key components that are applicable to all classes of device. The regulatory or approved body audits the conformance to the quality system requirements periodically.

1.2 Risk Management in Software

In the US, all MDs containing software are subject to the United States Quality Systems Regulation (QSR), 21 CFR 820 [3]. The regulations stipulate the requirement for risk analysis as part of the design validation process. In Europe, many companies also use relevant US guidance documents [4], therefore the research presented in this paper integrates guidance by US regulatory agencies.

Lack of RM within software projects can lead to failures and loss at several levels. Boehm [5] defined the degree to which a software project may be exposed to failure i.e. risk exposure, as the probability of an unsatisfactory outcome and the loss to the parties affected if the outcome is unsatisfactory. MD industry regulators view "unsatisfactory outcome" and "loss" in terms of loss of life, injury or damage to users, bystanders or the environment, as distinct from schedule and budget over-runs. Their job is to protect the public from MD faulty software and thus reduce the risk of potential injury [6]. An issue facing MD companies producing software is that it is not practical, even in the simplest software programs, to fully test all possible execution paths. Therefore, the quality of software cannot be determined by software testing alone and requires solid software engineering practices [7] with RM implemented as a core practice.

2 Overview of RMCM

The RMCM was developed to assist companies to meet the MD regulations for RM through adopting disciplined software engineering practices. The RMCM design allows relevant elements of the model to be adopted to provide the most significant benefit to the business. The model is based on the CMMI [8] and the regulations used to extend the CMMI framework are those of the FDA [9,10,11,12], ISO 14971 [13], ANSI/AAMI/IEC 62304:2006 standard (IEC 62304) (MD software – Software life cycle processes) [14] and   EN 60601-1-4 [15]. Reference was made to IEC 60812 [16], GAMP 4 [17], TIR 32 [18] and guidance from the AAMI (Association for the Advancement of Medical Instrumentation) on RM [19]. The RMCM contains an assessment method for the software engineering capability of the RM process area in relation to MD software (both application and embedded software). Use of the RMCM is expected to improve the effectiveness and efficiency of RM through mapping MD regulatory guidelines against the CMMI RM process area (Figure 1).

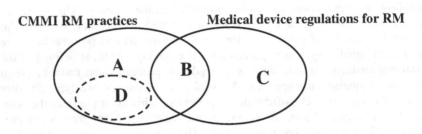

Fig. 1. Composition of the RMCM

The mappings between the MD regulatory guidelines and the CMMI specific practices for the RM process result in RMCM goals and practices which may be either generic (relating to the entire organisation) or specific (relating directly to the RM process). The RMCM determines what parts of the CMMI RM process area (part A of Figure 1) are required to satisfy MD regulations (part B of Figure 1). The RMCM also investigates the possibility of extending the CMMI process areas with additional practices that are outside the remit of CMMI, but are required in order to satisfy MD regulatory guidelines (part C of Figure 1). Additionally, the RMCM provides MD companies with the opportunity to incorporate practices from the CMMI that are not required in order to achieve regulatory compliance but that would greatly enhance their RM process if they were included (part D of Figure 1). The RMCM will help companies to measure their organisational RM capability and to track their progression against the following software process capability levels (see Table 1):

- **RMCM Level Med** – Demonstrate they satisfy the goals and perform practices required to meet the requirements of the various MD regulatory guidelines and standards associated with RM. Involves performing some practices that the CMMI views as generic, although not to the extent of fulfilling any generic goals.
- **RMCM Level 0** – Insufficient practices have been performed to satisfy the requirements of Level Med.
- **RMCM Level 1** – Demonstrate that they satisfy RMCM level Med and the CMMI capability level 1 goal of performing the CMMI RM base practices.
- **RMCM Level 2** – Demonstrate that they satisfy RMCM level 1. Additionally perform CMMI RM Advanced Practices and CMMI capability level 2 generic goal of institutionalising a Managed Process.

- **RMCM Level 3** – Demonstrate that they satisfy RMCM level 2. Additionally perform CMMI Generic Goal to Institutionalise a Defined Process (CMMI Generic Goal 3) for the RM process area.
- **RMCM Level 4** – Demonstrate that they satisfy RMCM level 3. Additionally perform CMMI Generic Goal to Institutionalise a Quantitatively Managed Process (CMMI Generic Goal 4) for the RM process area.
- **RMCM Level 5** – Demonstrate that a process area satisfies RMCM level 4. Additionally perform the CMMI Generic Goal to Institutionalise an Optimising Process (CMMI Generic Goal 5) for the RM process area.

Table 1. Summary of the RMCM

Goal: GG1: Perform the Specific Practices				
GP 1.1 Perform Base Practices				
Specific Goal	CMMI® based Sub-Practices (A)	CMMI® sub-practices to meet MD regulations (B)	Additional Sub-practices to meet MD regulations (C)	Level 1 sub-practices
SG 1: Prepare for RM	6	6	10	0
SG 2: Identify and Analyse Risks	9	4	4	5
SG 3: Mitigate Risks	8	5	6	3
Specific Goal Totals	23	15	20	8
Goal: GG2: Institutionalise a Managed Process				Level 2
	10	6	0	4
Goal: GG3: Institutionalise a Defined Process				Level 3
	2	0	0	2
Goal: GG4: Institutionalise a Quantitatively Managed Process				Level 4
	2	0	0	2
Goal: GG5: Institutionalise an Optimising Process				Level 5
	2	0	0	2
Totals	39	21	20	
RMCM Level Med Sub-practices *(Total of B + Total of C)*				41
RMCM Sub-practices *(Total of A + Total of C)*				59

Table 1 summarises the RMCM, illustrating that the RMCM is composed of 5 Generic Goals (GGs). The first of these GGs requests that three specific goals (SG): (SG1: Prepare for RM, SG2: Identify and Analyse Risks & SG3: Mitigate Risks) are satisfied. Each specific goal is composed of a number of practices and sub-practices, with each practice consisting of a number of sub-practices. This table specifies the RMCM capability levels for sub-practices belonging to a particular practice. For each of the goals to be achieved to a particular capability level, it is necessary for the associated practices and sub-practices (with an assigned capability level less than or equal to the desired capability level) to be performed (detailed in [2]). The generic goals GG2-GG5 are not broken down to the sub-practice level. Therefore, the capability level is assigned at the practice level within these goals.

The RMCM contains 59 sub-practices, with level Med containing 41 of these sub-practices. Only 21 of the 39 CMMI RM sub-practices are included in the RMCM level Med. Therefore, following the MD regulations will only partially meet the goals of this CMMI process area, with only specific goal 1 being fully satisfied. The RMCM also shows that 35 specific sub-practices have to be performed in order to satisfy MD regulations and that only an additional 8 sub-practices are required to satisfy all the CMMI level 1 (or RMCM level 1) requirements. Meeting the goals of the RM process area by performing the CMMI specific practices would not meet the requirements of the MD software regulations as an additional 20 MD specific sub-practices had to be added to meet the objectives of RMCM.

3   Research Methodology

3.1   Action Research

To evaluate the effectiveness of the RMCM in assisting MD companies to improve their software RM procedures and practices, the methodology employed is action research using a five phase multi-cyclical approach [20, 21]. This involves diagnosing, action planning, action taking, evaluating and specifying learning. Action research encompasses aspects of analysis and change, lending itself well to this research where changes to the company's RM procedures and practices are required.

The research presented here involves one organisation (client). It discusses cycle 1 and modifications that have been made to the RMCM which will be included in cycle 2. The client is a privately owned MD company which is bound legally by the regulatory bodies British Standards Institution (BSI) and the FDA, and is regularly audited. The client manufacturers Spirometry devices that are used in the diagnosis and monitoring of lung function. Primary markets include clinical trails, primary care, occupational health, sports medicine, asthma management, emergency services and hospitals.

With the client, we, the researchers, agreed that the research environment would be their R&D department, focusing specifically on software RM. The collaborative effort between ourselves and the client was central to the gathering of system knowledge and other information necessary to understand the anomalies being studied and was also central in enabling the planned intervention. We also had access to the company's appropriate project files, logs and resources.

Diagnosing commenced with discussions with the client on existing process and procedure issues within the software development environment. Given its regulatory requirements, they have a base of documented process and procedures encapsulated in development handbooks, standard operating procedures (SOPs) and templates. The client believed that their RM procedures and templates could be improved significantly to cater for more effective and efficient hazard analysis and RM for their MD software.

In the Action Planning phase, we, with the client, identified the desired future state along with planning the actions required to implement improvements to achieve that state. The desired future state for the organisation was to have in place a BSI / FDA compliant, more comprehensive and reusable software hazard analysis and RM procedure with associated templates (documented framework), which could be used in the production of MD software. This should lead to safer and more efficient software design and device development.

In the Action Taking phase, the RMCM was used to establish the capability level of the MD company's existing software RM and to identify gaps or missing practices. Consequently, a new software RM procedure and template was developed through a controlled and formal process. This was as required by the client's quality management system. The new framework would be used in all future software projects.

In the Evaluation Stage, using the RMCM, the new software RM procedure was assessed. A gap analysis was performed between what was required to satisfy regulatory requirements, as defined by the RMCM's sub-practices, and what existed within the new procedure. Evaluation is discussed in detail in section 4.

Specifying Learning is the final stage of the Action Research cycle. The knowledge gained during this research thus far has been integrated back into the client organisation. This has been explicit knowledge in the form of modified software RM SOPs and templates for use with new software development projects.

3.2 Data Collection and Analysis

Prior to the implementation of the RMCM, we analysed the SOPs and associated design templates (DTs). This allowed us to determine the state of the client's original software RM procedures. Documentation required by regulatory requirements was made available to us by the client, in conjunction with training logs and bug tracking reports. These documents were reviewed following the implementation of the RMCM.

Also, at the end of the implementation period, in-depth interviews were used to collect data, using open-ended questions to provide "good interviews" [21]. Participants were chosen to cover a broad range of software related roles including software development (desktop and embedded applications), software quality and project management. Six pre-arranged interviews were conducted over periods ranging from thirty minutes to seventy-five minutes with Management, Software QA and Software Development. Participants ranged from new to experienced employees with over five years' experience. Interviews were recorded and transcribed verbatim, and to ensure the validity of the transcriptions, were sent to the interviewees for review prior to analysis.

Content analysis [22] was used to analyse the qualitative interview data. Open coding where initial categories were applied to the transcripts was undertaken. This was then re-evaluated using axial coding [22], defining the relationships between the open-coding categories and refining them into suitable sub-categories. The data and categories obtained during the content analysis were then used with the documentation described above in a process of triangulation to strengthen findings or eliminate false or unsubstantiated claims.

At the end of the implementation period, the company's RM procedures were reassessed. Capability was measured and defined in terms of meeting the RMCM's goals and associated practices. The evaluation involved examining each goal and associated practices within the RMCM, identifying what was required to meet the goals of the RMCM and then determining if that goal had been satisfied.

4   Evaluation of the RMCM

In the Action Taking phase, the RMCM was implemented by the client with researcher support for two years on two embedded and three desktop software projects. Prior to the introduction of the RMCM, 9 out of the 35 required base practices (i.e. level Med practices with SG1 to SG3) were adequately addressed by the company's SOPs and DTs. Twenty-six were found to be missing and one was insufficient in that it only partially met the requirement laid out by the RMCM for the practice. The findings are summarised in table 2 below.

Table 2. RMCM Findings prior to the introduction of the RMCM

Goal	Practices to satisfy MD regulations	Practices satisfied by Company
SG 1: Prepare for RM	16	3
SG 2: Identify and Analyse Risks	8	3
SG 3: Mitigate Risks	11	3
GG2: Institutionalise a Managed Process	6	6
GG3: Institutionalise a Defined Process	0	0
GG4: Institutionalise a Quantitatively Managed Process	0	0
GG5: Institutionalise an Optimising Process	0	0
Total	41	15

The initial analysis confirmed that all 6 practices required to satisfy level Med for Generic Goal 2 of the RMCM had been met. However, establishing the policy, planning the process, providing resources, assigning responsibility, training people and identifying stakeholders were ineffective. This was because the base practices (i.e. SG1 –SG3) themselves are insufficient in terms of the practices they address. During evaluation, after 2 years, we found that all required RMCM level Med practices were addressed by the latest revision of the company's software RM procedure. This was as expected, given that the RMCM was used to identify missing or inadequate practices.

The RMCM has had a positive effect on the MD client company. It provided them with a single reference point for determining their RM practice capability, enabling them to quickly identify what practices were missing or inadequate. They also have a source to refer to when addressing missing practices deemed essential by the MD regulators in achieving safe and efficient software.

The following sections further evaluate the impact the RMCM based software RM procedure has upon the MD company since its formal release. The findings have been grouped into logical categories arising from the data collection and analysis process.

4.1 Safety Pre-production

Following implementation of the RMCM, employees recognise that software hazard analysis and RM procedure is one method of ensuring safety pre-production. All team members demonstrated an awareness of the new procedure. However, the project manager also discussed user trials, not mentioned in the RMCM, as a method for ensuring safer software pre-production. Sub-practice 16 of the RMCM mentions the analysis of post-production queries and issues to safeguard against a risk scenario arising post-production that were not originally considered during development. User trials could be used for similar analysis but before the software actually goes into production and therefore shall be considered for the next up-issue of the RMCM.

4.2 Safety Post-production

In ensuring software safety post-production the team members discussed dealing with non-conformance requests (NCRs) through the completion of corrective actions/preventative actions (CAPAs). They also discussed fixing and testing any software related bugs/issues through unit testing and system testing. This is in keeping with the company's procedures, which states "all post-production RM activities are covered by (the company's) CAPA system." Only one team member, a software QA engineer, alluded to updating the software RM report when dealing with post production queries and issues. Sub-practice 16 of the RMCM references how three of the major MD related standards point to this as a very important practice. Therefore it is of concern that only one team member discussed this in relation to safety post-production. The evaluation indicates that both the way in which this practice has been integrated into the client's procedures and the training that individuals have received is not sufficient. On inspection of the company's procedure, in the life-cycle phases section, it states that changes must be analysed "to determine if any changes have taken place that adversely affect the risk analysis and mitigation". This does not appear under the post-production information section. Therefore, this practice must be revisited for cycle two of the company's implementation of the RMCM.

4.3 Requirements Changes

Adequate change control and proper impact analysis of requirements changes are an important element of RM [23]. The RMCM addresses change control in sub-practices 1 and 2 for determining risk sources and risk categories. It also states that as per FDA requirements "it is important to define risk-related functions when analysing requirements" and to "monitor this ongoing source of risk" as requirements change".

During RMCM evaluation it is evident that the team recognises the need to perform software risk analysis following requirements changes - "for every change to the software/module, we should determine if there is any new risk as a result of the change". However, further investigation revealed that it was QA who updated the software RM document 'after the fact' because "the software hazard analysis document was not kept in line with the changes to the software requirements". Additional testing was implemented by QA to ensure there were no adverse side effects. There was no traceability provision from the changes through to verification. The evaluation has highlighted inadequate software risk analysis being performed in the company with respect to change control.

A number of shortcomings were identified in the company's procedures. For example, the software changes specification contained only a header called "hazard analysis", and the procedure did not state what should be done. This led to inconsistencies and insufficiencies in terms of software hazard and risk analysis. The evaluation has resulted in this being addressed for the second action research cycle.

4.4 Training

Analysis of the training records alone suggested that those individuals doing the analysis, mitigations and verification were trained appropriately. However, analysis of interview transcripts pointed to a deviant case for this finding.

Following self-training, where individuals read the internal software RM procedure individuals were not proficient in performing a risk analysis of the software. Frustrations in implementing the new RMCM based procedure were attributed to this. In fact when asked about the positive and negative things about the process it was specific mentions include: "I would introduce better training". Given these findings, cycle 2 shall commence with a detailed training session using practical examples and sample projects. Individuals will be coached interactively in the process. Reviews of the output shall be performed at the various stage gates of the design process.

4.5 Lifecycle Phases for Software RM

There is awareness amongst the team of the safety benefits for performing the software risk analysis at every lifecycle phase as per the RMCM. However the team acknowledged that they did not always follow the procedure.

There was a general consensus that the software risk analysis document was drafted at the requirements stage and then re-visited at the very end of the lifecycle (prior to product launch) but that "sometimes is not properly looked at in between". This was not sufficient because "if we find out at the end that something is missing such as a unit test or code review (mitigations), it can be too late because the development is already done". One interviewee, discussing what happens in reality stated "we might do a draft of the hazard analysis when the specification is being done and then it's closed out and not looked at again until software testing happens". Project files confirmed this was indeed the case.

The primary reasons that the RM was left until the very end of the lifecycle was due to "time constraints" and a cumbersome implementation of the RMCM practices for analysing and categorising risks. The procedure and associated template (based on the RMCM) were recognised as being sufficient in terms of the practices but were seen as adding more work to the process. One interviewee put this down to the company moving from "having no documentation" to "having vast sums of documentation" and in relation to the RMCM software risk based procedure that "this is a relatively new document which we have only had for the past couple of years". Other reasons given for not performing analysis at all stages included training, which was discussed earlier.

This evaluation highlights the need to revisit how the RMCM has been implemented procedurally, to simplify the process without removing compliance in terms of implementing the RMCM practices and to train all team members on the new process. There is also a need for management within the company to ensure adequate time is allocated to the software RM activities for all software projects. The term "requirements" is used within the company to encompass both user requirements and the software/technical requirements. Software risk analysis should commence as early as possible during the user requirements stage. This may highlight specific requirements that require corresponding software requirements or design items to mitigate potential risks, and these should be addressed (in the SRS).

5 Discussion

The evaluation of the RMCM has demonstrated a significant improvement in the company's software RM procedure and required practices in terms of meeting regulatory compliance. Prior to RMCM implementation, the software risk process satisfied 15 of the 41 required regulatory practices. Following its implementation the RM procedure satisfies all required practices. However, we have identified two distinct but inter-related set of changes required for the second action research cycle - (a) changes to the RMCM and (b) changes to the company's procedures.

5.1 Changes to the RMCM

The quality of the User Requirements Specification (URS) and Software Requirements Specification (SRS) has a direct impact on the quality of the RM report. Missing requirements in the URS or SRS may lead to missing analysis on associated risks. Documentation reviews should be implemented as core to this process. The RMCM has been amended to include a sub-practice "Formally Review all Software Lifecycle Design Documentation", within specific goal 3 (Mitigate Risks).

Presently, the term "Requirements" is used within the company to encompass both user requirements and the software/technical requirements. The software RM procedure states that risk analysis must be performed at the requirements stage. However, more specifically, software risk analysis should commence early in the user requirements stage, when the URS is being drafted. The URS may highlight specific requirements that require corresponding software requirements or design items to mitigate potential risks, and these "should be addressed in the SRS"

User trials, not originally considered, shall be added to the RMCM as a method for detecting user related queries, issues and associated risk scenarios pre-production.

The description for sub-practice 23 (defining traceability) of the RMCM shall be amended to include provision of traceability between the user requirements, the technical specification, the associated hazard analysis and the software verification.

5.2 Changes to the Company's Procedures

While employees were aware of RM procedures, training provided to date has been inadequate. Performing the base practices of the RMCM alone is not sufficient - consideration must also be given to performing the level Med practices in GG2 (Institutionalise a Managed Process). Without this, the base practices of GG1 may not be performed sufficiently or by the correct person, and could have a significant negative impact on software risk-analysis and control. Training (GP 2.5) is a practice of GG2 and adequate training must be provided to relevant personnel.

The post-production section of the software RM procedure will be updated to specify that changes requested post-production must be analysed for risks due to the changes. Procedures will be updated to ensure traceability between the software changes specification and the original requirements in the software requirements specification, thus allowing QA to determine correct regression tests.

The software changes specification procedure will be updated to state that software hazard and risk analyses must be performed for all changes listed and added to the software RM file. Thus, traceability will be provided from the changes specification to the corresponding analysis in the software RM file. This will ensure a consistent method of performing risk analysis for software changes.

6 Conclusion

If the company's procedure for implementing the RMCM activities is too cumbersome or hard to follow, it runs the risk of being ineffective or not being implemented in the software projects. The company's procedure for software RM shall be reviewed with respect to making the process simpler without removing any of the level Med required practices. It will be suggested to management within the company that they must ensure adequate time is allocated to the software RM activities for all software projects or else they risk the possibility of negating the impact of the process itself.

This paper has illustrated that the RMCM can be successfully implemented within one MD company, the next stage of this research project will be to transfer the research to other MD companies and to demonstrate whether that the RMCM may be generalised. We also intend extending this research to establish if the RMCM will result in a decrease in medical device accidents related to software.

Acknowledgements

This research has been funded by Science Foundation Ireland through the Cluster project GSD for SMEs (Grant no 03/IN3/1408C) within the University of Limerick, Ireland. This research is supported by the Science Foundation Ireland funded project, Global Software Development in Small to Medium Sized Enterprises (GSD for SMEs) within Lero - the Irish Software Engineering Research Centre (http://www.lero.ie).

References

1. World Health Organisation: Medical device regulations: global overview and guiding principles (2003), ISBN 92 4 154618 2
2. Burton, J., McCaffery, F., Richardson, I.: A Risk Management Capability Model for use in Medical Device Companies. In: 4th Workshop on Software Quality, ICSE 2006, Shanghai, China, May 21, 2006, pp. 3–8 (2006)

3. FDA: Quality Systems for Medical Device & Equipment/Software Manufacturers (QSR). Code of Federal Regulations (April 2005)
4. Donawa, M.: Useful US Guidance on Device Software. Medical Device Technology (December 2005), http://www.medicaldevicesonline.com
5. Boehm, B.W.: Software Risk Management: Principles and Practices. IEEE Software 8(1), 32–41 (1991)
6. FDA Mission Statement, http://www.fda.gov/opacom/morechoices/mission.html
7. Eagles, S., Murray, J.: Medical Device Software Standards: Vision and Status (2001), http://www.devicelink.com/medicaldevicedi/archive/01/05/002.html
8. CMMI Product Team: Capability Maturity Model® Integration for Development, Version 1.2, Technical Report CMU/SEI-2006-TR-008 (2006), http://www.sei.cmu.edu/publications/documents/06.reports/06tr008.html
9. FDA/CDRH: Guidance for the Content of Premarket Submissions for Software Contained in Medical Devices (May 2005), http://www.fda.gov/cdrh/ode/guidance/337.pdf
10. FDA/CDRH: Guidance for Off-the-Shelf Software Use in Medical Devices (September 1999), http://www.fda.gov/cdrh/ode/guidance/585.pdf
11. FDA/CDRH Guidance Document. General Principles of Software Validation, Final Guidance for Industry and FDA Staff (January 2002)
12. FDA Regulations: Code of Federal Regulations 21 CFR Part 820 (April 2006), http://www.accessdata.fda.gov/scripts/cdrh/cfdocs/cfcfr/CFRSearch.cfm?CFRPart=820&showFR=1
13. ANSI/AAMI/ISO 14971: Medical devices – Application of risk management to medical devices (2007)
14. ANSI/AAMI/IEC 62304:2006: Medical device software - Software life cycle processes Association for the Advancement of Medical Instrumentation (July 2006), http://www.techstreet.com/cgi-bin/detail?product_id=1277045 ISBN 1-57020-258-3
15. BS EN 60601-1-4: Medical Electrical Equipment, Part 1 - General requirements for safety (2000)
16. IEC 60812: Analysis technique for system reliability- procedure for failure modes and effects analysis (FMEA) (1985)
17. ISPE: GAMP Guide for Validation of Automated Systems. GAMP 4 (December 2001), http://www2.ispe.org/eseries/scriptcontent/orders/ProductDetail.cfm?pc=4BOUNDFUS
18. AAMI TIR32: Medical device software risk management (2005)
19. AAMI: New Guidance Offered on Software Risk Management 40(2) (2005)
20. Baskerville, R.L.: Investigating Information Systems with Action Research. Communications of the Association of Information Systems 2, article 19 (1999)
21. Susman, G., Evered, R.: An Assessment of The Scientific Merits of Action Research. Administrative Science Quarterly 4(23), 582–603 (1978)
22. Liamputtong, P., Ezzy, D.: Qualitative Research Methods, 2nd edn (2006), ISBN 9 78019551 7446
23. FDA/CDRH: Software related recalls for fiscal years 1983-91. US Department of Health and Human Services (1992)

Framework to Evaluate Software Process Improvement in Small Organizations

Pedro E. Colla[1] and Jorge Marcelo Montagna[2]

[1] EDS ASFO – Av. Voz del Interior 7050 -- EDS Argentina
pedro.colla@eds.com
Facultad Regional Santa Fé – Universidad Tecnológica Nacional
pcolla@frsf.utn.edu.ar
[2] INGAR - Avellaneda 3657 -- CIDISI – FRSF – UTN
mmontagna@santafe-conicet.gov.ar

Abstract. Organizations of all sizes understand the benefits to consider Software Process Improvements (SPI) investments, still many of them and in particular the smaller ones are reluctant to embrace this kind of initiatives. A systemic model is presented in this article as a tool aiming aiming to provide an initial understanding over the behavior of the different organizational variables involved and their complex interactions within a SPI effort, their contribution to the improvement effort, the resulting value sensitivity to model parameters, the systemic relations at large and the limits derived from the holistic interaction of all in order to be used as a scenario analysis tool to identify the SPI strategies which best suit a given organization business context thru the maximization of the value obtained from the investment.

Keywords: Software Process Improvement, SPI, CMMI, Simulation, Dynamic Models. Small Organizations, Software Engineering Economics. Net Present Value.

1 Introduction

For software development organizations, specially small and medium sized, the management dilemma is how to justify the investments required to improve the software processes (Software Process Improvement, SPI) [07] on a business context where bigger competitors, quite of a global scale, undertake similar actions leveraging much larger structures and therefore able to absorb better the costs impacts produced by the SPI initiative [40] . At the same time the consideration of competitors of similar scale which not introducing significant improvements on their core processes enjoy a short term competitive advantage and less margin erosion is needed.

Organizations of all sizes understand the benefits to consider SPI initiatives, still many of them and in particular the smaller ones are reluctant to embrace this approach. Scenarios and results captured by the bibliography [08,28,39] reflects the experiences of large scale organizations leaving smaller ones wondering whether an SPI approach is realistic for them. A perception of larger companies being able to tap

Q. Wang, D. Pfahl, and D.M. Raffo (Eds.): ICSP 2008, LNCS 5007, pp. 36 – 50, 2008.
© Springer-Verlag Berlin Heidelberg 2008

on deeper pockets or leverage corporate financial muscles to fund SPI investments leads to the *a-priori* estimation on smaller companies that formal endeavors to perform structural changes in their software development process through an structured SPI effort are simply outside their realm of possibilities.

This aspect turns out to become of particular relevance since on the national or regional context of emerging economies small and medium software companies offering off-shore services to a globalized landscape are far smaller than the organizational sizes typically referred to at the bibliography.

Even though SPI efforts attempted at small and medium companies has been documented previously [10,13,25,31,32,49] the focus is often placed at qualitative or methodological factors rather than quantitative ones; it seems the implicit assumption is for SPI efforts to be unconditionally a good initiative no matter what the business context where the company operates really is.

This notion has been challenged by several authors [16,23] where the actual affordability and suitability of formal CMMI oriented SPI initiatives for *Small and Medium Enterprises* (SME) is questioned from different perspectives.

The paper proposes a contribution in three areas at the evaluation of SPI initiatives. First a systemic framework aimed to model the main parameters driving an SPI effort and their interrelations in a single model for the overall value gained by the organization on doing the SPI investment is proposed. Although many of the relations can be found dispersed in the referred sources, the consolidation into a single model and the validation of their systemic consistency is a contribution of the research activity performed by the authors.

Second the *Net Present Value* (NPV) is proposed as a suitable instrument to measure that value as part of a decision process as a difference with the economic indicators most often used by the bibliography.

Finally, the third contribution is to run the model under a combination of ranges found in the literature and assumptions made by the authors in order to preliminary explore the usefulness of such instrument for a small or medium sized organization to validate decisions and explore trade-offs using a rational base.

Since actual data aren't fluidly available the analysis is performed through a dynamic stochastic simulation model where the behavior of different factors, their contribution to the improvement effort, the sensitivity of the final result to the model parameters and the practical limits can be explored.

The model is built by identifying the main factors involved at the organization level, the external context and the intrinsic components of the SPI effort as reflected in the available bibliography (see *Investment Modeling*), because of space constraints identified relationships between factors and transfer functions considered in the model has been consolidated in the appendix of the paper (see *Appendix II*).

In order to handle the dispersion of the parameters as reported by the bibliography a Monte Carlo simulation technique is used where the system variables, the uncertainty of the results, the Sensitivity to different investment strategies and the limits for a reasonable return can be explored (see Model *Execution*).

Finally some limits of the approach and conclusions are explored (see *Conclusions*).

1.1 Process Improvement Framework

The SEI CMMI v1.2 reference model guides the deployment of SPI efforts through the formulation of a framework to help develop a comprehensive process that unveils the organization's technologic potential at delivering software products; positive correlation between the maturity level and better performance is backed up by many industry and academic references [03,12,19,28,34,35,47]. The SEI-CMMI model specifies what goals must be achieved at *Process Areas* through the satisfaction of both generic and specific *goals* on each one through the usage of generic and specific *practices* [12,43], actual details of the implemented process is left to each organization to decide.

Although other reference models can equally be eligible for this purpose, the SEI-CMMI receives significant industry acceptance at a global scale, a long standing record of application and some metrics for the results obtained by different organizations as referred by different authors [02,07,19,34,35,38]. The framework is not going without significant criticism. Conradi [16] among others had presented evidences against formal CMMI based SPI approaches to obtain sustainable improvement at many organizations, but at the same time seems to conclude that organizations faces substantial competitive pressure to achieve market required levels of maturity under a globally recognized framework as an essential requirement from international customers trying to reduce the *"buyer risk"* of undertaking off-shore projects.

It's certainly not a surprise that the SEI records shows [43] a significantly higher number of organizations undertaking formal SEI-CMMI evaluations at off-shore markets than typical target markets for off-shore activities like the US and Europe.

2 Investment Modeling

In order to address a SEI-CMMI based SPI initiative the organization will require undertaking a significant effort into developing and implementing policies, plans, processes, instruments and metrics associated with the satisfaction of each one of the *Process Areas* of each *Maturity Level*. The transfer functions has been established starting with the variables and systemic relations relevant to a software process as identified originally by the work on dynamic models formulated by Abdel-Hamid [01] and later proposed by Carrillo [09] and Ruiz [41] as to be used in the analysis of software process improvements efforts; the internal factors of the process improvement modeling has been used as identified by Hayes [27] .

This paper integrates also functional relations dispersed in the bibliography into a consolidated model enabling the study of their systemic behavior as one of the contributions. The model relations are going to be discussed in detail at the next section.

2.1 Implementation Costs

Different authors [19,21,28,42,50] supports the need to invest a significant fraction of the organizational resources through the implementation of a mature process as a *Software Process Improvement Effort* (E_{spi}) which would require a proportion of the *Total Organization Staff* (N) to be allocated to the SPI activities (K_{spi}), the Software Process Improvement Effort is then given by [[Ec 2].

The implementation has to be followed by an institutionalization effort aiming to ensure the implemented processes are effectively understood and used by the organization at large through a sustained *Training Effort* (E_t). Walden [50] among others provide some data on the magnitude of this effort.

The training effort is composed by the *Training Preparation Effort* assumed to be related to the number of *Process Areas* (N_{PA}) to be evaluated on the target maturity level and the effort to deliver the training which is made by the *Training Effort per Person and Process Area* (E_{PA}), the total Training Effort will then be as in [[Ec3]:

The Training Effort would be distributed, assumed evenly in this model, through the entire SPI implementation.

At the same time the formal assessment of the maturity level means to transit a number of informal evaluations as defined by the *Standard CMMI Appraisal Method for Process Improvement* (SCAMPI) Class "C" and "B" or equivalent, followed by a maturity level assessment given by a formal Class "A" appraisal (SCAMPI-A); the SEI and other authors [28,43,48,50] provides a framework to estimate the *Appraisal Preparation Effort* (E_{ap}) and the *Appraisal Delivery Effort* (E_{ad}) the organization has to incur to get ready and perform the appraisal. Also the organization will need to fund during the appraisal the *Appraisal Costs* (C_a) for consultancy fees and other event related expenses; this cost is normalized into effort units for model consistency through the *Cost per Engineer* (C_{PE}) the organization has as in [[Ec 4]. The total *Appraisal Effort* (E_a) is considered to be incurred mostly toward the end of the implementation period and it is given by [[Ec5]

2.2 On-going Returns

Assuming the organization achieves the aimed maturity level after the assessment a fraction of the resources would still be required to maintain, adapt and evolve the implemented process framework deployed in order to ensure a consistent usage as well as an on-going alignment with the organizational goals, the effort to perform this activity is the *Software Engineering Groups Effort* (E_{sepg}) which will be a proportion (K_{sepg}) of the Total Organization Staff (N) as shown by [[Ec 6]

Although it would be reasonable to expect organizations to realize benefits as they move through the implementation of the different practices a conservative approach taken in this model is to assume all benefits will realize only after the organization is formally evaluated on the target maturity level.

At the same time, it is likely that even if the organization fails to achieve a given target maturity level all major software process areas would be in a better performance than at the beginning of the project. This model assumes that no benefit will be collected out of the investment performed unless the maturity level is formally obtained. The benefits of a given maturity level would came in the form of an improved quality as measured by a reduction in the *Cost of Poor Quality* (CoPQ) [17,18,30] , an enhanced capability to meet schedule commitments as well as significant improvements in cycle time and in overall productivity among others [04,07,19,35].

Clark [11], provides the perspective that all benefits could be summarized as a reduction of the non-value added effort expended by the organization to achieve a result in a way that less effort can be required to achieve the same result or more results achieved with the same effort. This can also be seen as an improvement of the overall productivity. The modeling approach used the *Productivity Income* (I_{prod}) as the return of the SPI effort to represent the savings achieved compared with operating in a lower level of maturity; this is considered the source of return of the SPI effort and the main financial reason to justify it. The magnitude of this factor is assumed to be an equivalent fraction (K_{prod}) of the *Total Organization Size* (N) as reflected by [[Ec 7]:

The net *flow of benefit* (V_i) the organization are going to receive as shown by [[Ec8] will occur since the appraisal is completed at *Implementation Time* (t_i) and as long as the *Investment Horizon* (t_p) allowed by the organization to collect resources last. This timeframe is often called the *Recovery Time* (t_r).

Although the nature of the SEI-CMMI improvement process, with several non-rating instances of appraisal, allows for a comprehensive evaluation of the organization progress at implementing the different Process Areas the factual data [44] still suggest the final appraisal success is not guaranteed.

A surprisingly high number of appraisal failures for organizations trying to achieve maturity level 2 and a reduced number for higher maturity levels suggest the need to factor this element in the model.

The *Appraisal Success Rate* (ξ), even with a risk of being too optimistic, corresponding to each maturity level (see *Appendix I*) are considered and reduces the expected flows as seen in [[Ec8] by this rate as shown in [[Ec9].

2.3 Investment Analysis

The *Return on Investment* (ROI) has been extensively used in the bibliography [05,07,19,23,46] as the main indicator to evaluate investments in SPI; it measures the investment as the relation between *expenditures* required and *incomes* obtained within a given timeframe selected by the organization as the *Investment Horizon* (t_p).

Ideally all investments verifying the condition ROI ≥ 1 are desirable to be made. Given different simultaneous investment opportunities the one with the higher ROI should capture in preference the organization resources as it would create the higher wealth in return. This approach has been criticized [35,48] as not providing uniformity among different initiatives making difficult to compare results between different organizations.

At the same time, the ROI has very limited capability [06] to factor a proper compensation for the time and risk value of money. Given the fact that SPI efforts require quite significant investment horizons and are performed by organizations operating at moderate to high risk levels it is relevant to introduce both factors in the decision analysis.

Investment analysis based in the *Net Present Value* (NPV) captures both the time and risk through the discount of the flows over time at a rate called the *cost of the capital* or the *opportunity cost* (r) and therefore it is often referred to as having a better performance at evaluating an investment than other pure economical based methodologies [04,06,22,29]; for this reason it is adopted in this paper as the way to compute the value created.

The NPV discounts the cash flows using the best return the organization could get out of an investment of equivalent risk. Cash flows are typically a sequence of discrete individual flows $\{F_1,..,F_n\}$ whose NPV is given by [Ec 10]. In some cases the flows are better modeled by a continuous function rather than discrete events and therefore it is also possible to represent them as a *continuous flow* F(t) where the expression turns into [Ec11] where the instantaneous *opportunity cost* (δ) is a continuous equivalent capitalization cost. By combining the values of [Ec 2] through [Ec9] normalized to their present value the Net Present Value can be expressed by [

Replacing terms in the [Ec1] a final expression for the NPV used in the model is obtained [Ec1B]

[Ec1B]

$$[Ec1] \quad NPV_i = PV(V_i) - PV(E_a) - PV(E_{spi}) - PV(E_t)$$

Replacing terms in the [Ec1] a final expression for the NPV used in the model is obtained [Ec1B]

$$[Ec1B] \quad NPV_i = \xi \int_{t_i}^{t_p} V_i \times e^{-\delta t} dt - \left[\frac{E_a}{(1+r)^{t_i}} + \int_0^{t_i} (E_{SPI} + E_t) \times e^{-\delta t} dt \right]$$

Although the NPV is intended to reflect cash flows this model uses a normalized cost based on the effort in order to concentrate in the relations between factors rather than the absolute magnitude in any given currency. In this scenario the organization decides at which *Total Organization Size* (N) the operation is desired, which *Maturity Level* (CMMI) as defined by the SEI CMMI v1.2 model wishes their processes to be executed and what is the competitive *Investment Horizon* (t_p) allowed to obtain tangible results from the investment which is required to yield a reasonable return for the time and risk as measured by the opportunity cost (r).

The nature of the improvement effort defines which is the likely *Implementation Time* (t_i) a given maturity level requires and that defines the remaining time to obtain the benefits which make the investment viable.

At the same time each maturity level will drive which percentage of the organization has to be allocated to the SPI Effort (K_spi) as well as the maintenance effort proportion (K_sepg) afterwards and the effort improvement (K_prod) which is realistic to expect as a result. The selected maturity level selected (CMMI) would define the number of *Process Areas* (N_pa) which are going to be implemented as well as the likely training effort (E_pa) associated to each one.

The model assumes the organization progress from one maturity level to the next available level in a discrete and monotonic increasing way.

2.4 Other Investment Critical Factors

Some authors [20,33,38,44] highlights other intangible factors obtained from the SPI investment such as improvements in organizational image, staff motivation, customer satisfaction as well as organizational cultural climate as strong motivations for the effort to be performed. Small and medium sized organizations in particular will depend critically for their survival on several other factors [16,23,25,45] such as the quality of the human resources, the establishment of agile organizational relations, the business model flexibility, the legal context, the organizational model adopted and the decision speed as well as interrelation fabric between areas, the debt taking capability, the critical adaptability speed and the very low capacity to survive on a restricted cash flows environment among others.

Although very important the previously enumerated factors are difficult to incorporate in a model like the one presented by this paper; however all of them can conceptually be considered increasing or decreasing the strengths of the organization and therefore changing the certainty of their results.

As the certainty of the results ultimately drives the risk under which the organization operates these factors should largely be represented by the risk premium component of the opportunity cost the organization uses to evaluate their investment decisions. Then by incorporating the opportunity cost on the model some of the critical factors, even partially, can be captured.

This represents a clear improvement in the analysis of an SPI investment as compared with the more classic usage of ROI and other economic formulations where neither the time nor the risk cost of the money is factored in the investment decision.

2.5 Opportunity Cost

As the organization progressively improves the maturity level as measured by the SEI-CMMI model the bibliography reflects a consistent improvement in the cost and schedule performance. Therefore a reduction in the business risk should drive a reduction of the opportunity cost as well.

In order to compute the variation because of this factor the average variation and the standard deviation of the Net Present Value in a maturity level (μ_i, σ_i) is compared with the same factors when a maturity increase has been made (μ_o, σ_o); the *risk variation factor* (λ)[26] is then defined by [Ec12].

The return provided by a secure financial asset provided by the market, often the yield of the 30 yr US Treasury bonds is used with this purpose, is considered the time compensation for the money ant it is called the *risk free discount rate* (r_f) the *modified cost of opportunity* (r') reflecting the reduction in uncertainty would given by [[Ec13] and all other factors being equal a reduction in the opportunity cost would improve the NPV which can be considered a legitimate additional value created by the increased level of maturity achieved through the SPI effort. Previous effort by the authors provided some insights in the possible range of values this factor could take [14,15].

3 Model Execution

In order to compute the model it is implemented using a GoldSim® platform [29] where the variables, relations and typical value distributions are defined as per the Equations shown in *Appendix II*.

When computed in this way the typical NPV evolution of a simulation instance can be seen at Figure 1; the expenditures in the deployment of the SPI actions drives the NPV to become more and more negative; towards the end of the implementation time (t_i) the rate of change accelerates as the expenditures reaches a maximum when appraisal related costs are incurred.

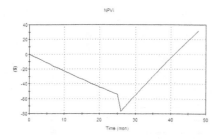

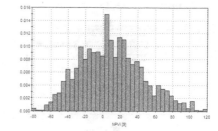

Fig. 1. NPV evolution with time on a typical SPI simulation run

Fig. 2. NPV Probability distribution for a typical SPI simulation run

Once the new maturity level is obtained at time t_i after a successful appraisal the organization starts to collect productivity gains net of the process maintenance costs which drives an improvement of the NPV until it eventually, if allowed enough time, become positive, the moment in time the NPV becomes positive is where the investment has been fully paid back in financial terms.

The fact most variables can not be assigned with unique values but for ranges or probabilistic distributions of possible values makes the model to be far from being deterministic; the bibliography reports ranges of values for each parameters and in some cases suggest some possible distributions; this information is used to run the model with an stochastic methodology in order to evaluate the range of possible results; a sample outcome for a given run would be, as seen in Figure 2, where a typical probability distribution of the NPV is shown summarizing the results of the stochastic evaluation of the model.

By computing the area below the curve for values where a positive NPV is obtained the probability of a project success can be assessed; each organization could then match their own risk acceptance profile with the investment parameters that yield an acceptable outcome.

The results of a run with variations in all major parameters is shown in Figure 3; the model highlights increases in the NPV as to be sensible to Organizational Size (N), the CMMI level at which the organization is willing to achieve and the Investment Horizon (t_p); increases in these factors also increases the NPV outcome.

As either the Appraisal Cost (C_a) and the Opportunity Cost (r) increase the NPV is reduced. The Cost per Engineer (C_{PE}) improves the NPV as it gets higher likely because the fixed SPI costs gets diluted by the higher returns provided by the improved productivity from the operation in a higher maturity level by a more expensive group.

Several scenarios are explored by means of varying the external parameters of the model. Just to perform a quick overview of the main trends it's assumed a typical organization are assumed to have a staff of 100 persons, trying to achieve a maturity level given by CMMI Level 3, they will allow a total investment horizon of 48 months, will operate in the offshore environment with a typical cost per engineer of

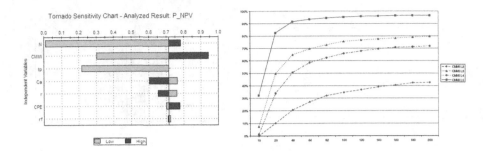

Fig. 3. NPV Sensitivity to Organizational Factors

Fig. 4. Dependency of Organization Size

USD 30K per year and will financially take as the opportunity cost an effective annual rate of 15%. All scenarios are ran varying one of the parameters through the range of interest while keeping the rest set at the previous values in order to be able to evaluate the variation dynamics.

3.1 Organization Size Sensitivity

Running the model for different maturity levels and organizational sizes the probability to obtain a viable project increases with the size of the organization as seen in Figure 4; this can be interpreted as the effect of the critical mass required for the productivity gains to offset the investment required. In this implementation of the model the apparent difficulty of organizations to achieve CMMI Level 2 is derived from the relatively high failure rate this level has as reported by the SEI-CMMI and other sources [43], although this result strikes as odd at first glance it results reasonable on deeper analysis, specially counting on the fact that the number of failed attempts at maturity level increases are likely to be much higher but not captured by any formal framework.

On a higher level of analysis there are no significant differences in the ranges of parameters observed during the SPI effort with the organization size other than the obvious capability to sustain a larger investment horizon, to perceive the investment as less risky for the entire operation and having fewer dependencies on cash flow issues associated with the appraisal effort. While the options larger organizations might have at their disposal in terms of the key strategies to adopt for their SPI might be larger than in smaller organizations the behavior of their outcomes and parameters does not necessarily are different.

3.2 Investment Horizon Sensitivity

As the Investment Horizon increases the likelihood of a successful project increases as well. Considering the time to implement and the time to recover the model suggest 48 months to realistically be the horizon required to obtain returns at reasonable risk as shown in Figure 5.

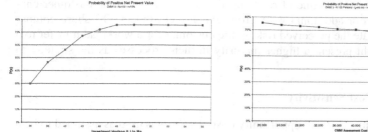
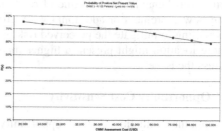

Fig. 5. Dependency from Investment Horizon   **Fig. 6.** Dependency from Maturity Appraisal Costs

3.3 Appraisal Cost Sensitivity

Many small organizations might perceive a formal CMMI appraisal is too upscale for them. Then the model is used to validate that perception by a simulation. The result shows in Figure 6 the probability of achieving a positive NPV is influenced very little by the Appraisal Costs suggesting this shouldn't be a strong consideration when undergoing an SPI investment.

3.4 Cost per Engineer Sensitivity

Through the model formulation a typical off-shore cost per engineer (C_{PE}) has been considered, especially to seize the relative impact of the fixed appraisal costs in the overall cost of the project. The impact of varying this parameter can be seen in Figure. 7. As expected the higher the Cost per Engineer is the better the results of the SPI effort are projected to be.

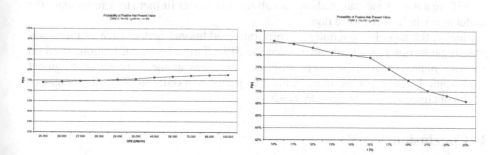

Fig. 7. Dependency from Cost per Engineer   **Fig. 8.** Dependency from Opportunity Cost

It is remarkable that although this should suggest a bigger drive to undertake SPI efforts in business contexts where the C_{PE} is higher (typically target for off-shore offerings) evidence shows [43] exactly the contrary which requires as a conclusion that other factors needs to be considered. Among the factors to make candidate to capture this behavior is the value of reducing the *"buyer risk"* for the customer enabling new customers or additional work from existing customers. Off-shore companies willing to mitigate the perceived risk on the customer for a workload transfer to a remote location might present a higher maturity in their processes as the strategy to address the issue.

3.5 Opportunity Cost Sensitivity

Through the evaluation a typical opportunity cost of 15% was used as assumed to be a reasonable value for technology companies. It is natural to evaluate the impact for organizations discounting their investment projects at different levels representative of the operational risks at different industries and business contexts.

The results shown in Figure. 8 shows that NPV results deteriorates as the organization operates in more volatile segments of the market where the risk is higher and therefore the opportunity cost should reflect that.

This back ups the findings by Conradi [16] who suggested that many small organizations could not afford to step into an investment with a large horizon because of the demanding nature and volatility of the markets they choose to operate.

3.6 Limitations and Further Work

Many simplifications has been adopted in the formulation of the model, therefore the results has opportunity for improvement and should be taken as preliminary; the ranges used for the parameters requires further research and confirmation.

The model is evolving from a research and theoretical construct and further validation with practical observations needs to be done.

Additional factors are needed to identify additional benefits explaining organizations with lower Cost per Engineer to embrace SPI efforts often than these with higher costs as it should make sense based on the current set of benefits.

Data ranges for typical parameters has been integrated from different sources and even if the author's validation shows no obvious conflicts further steps to validate the model as a whole needs to be done.

Finally, the model also requires incorporating additional factors such as the intangible organization impacts obtained from the SPI effort; a better calibration based on maturity improvement experiences from organizations at the National or Regional level would be an important improvement to perform in order to verify the ranges of results obtained in the bibliography holds.

4   Conclusions

The model formulation and validation process can be regarded as complex but the actual execution to evaluate a given organizational environment and decision options can be quite straightforward; the end results is given in standard financial analysis terms and therefore should be easily integrated into a conventional investment analysis case.

The work suggest the usefulness to enable small organizations facing a SPI investment decision with the ability to use the model as a tool during the decision process; the match between the outcome of the model and results reflected by the bibliography are encouraging.

For this organizational target to have the possibility to evaluate the trade-offs between different investment scenarios is one of the benefits of the approach, even considering further work is required to refine the parameters used and the need to capture some additional elements to better explain the empirical evidence.

The usage of the NPV as the main evaluation of the investment seems to add flexibility and to better capture the realities of the financial pressure small organizations have when facing this type of investment.

The preliminary execution of the model suggest that maturity improvements to up to CMMI L3, which is typically considered the gate to participate in larger international projects, can be achieved by relatively small organizations with reasonable risk and organizational sacrifice.

The results to achieve higher maturity levels are aligned also with what the authors estimate is the reasonable growth of a successful organization in the technology markets in the implementation time of the higher maturity levels and still are within the realm of relatively small companies.

A realistic investment horizon seems to be 48 months, the probability of a successful investment with smaller horizon although not zero is considerably smaller.

Organization, especially SMEs, will require help to hedge the difference between the payback required by their financial resources and the investment horizon required by SPI initiatives. Therefore the model might also bring some aid to formulate industry or government policy to create financial and economic instruments to sponsor SPI initiatives.

The sensitivity of the final result is very much depending on the implementation schedule as this factor is having a two fold impact on the NPV because if the time gets larger the implementation costs would typically be greater and the returns will be farther into the future therefore reducing their financial attractiveness.

The need of placing emphasis in methodologies, best practices and tools to reduce this time as a gate factor for smaller companies to become enabled to operate as high maturity organizations is strongly suggested by the results.

The appraisal cost has a lower impact in the overall investment performance than often assumed; although in need of being optimized the results suggest this is not necessarily a priority direction to be taken by the industry.

The organizations operating in highly volatile market segments, and therefore discounting their capital investment at higher opportunity costs would have objective issues on implementing formal projects unless there is income or underlying assets outside the software development projects that gets impacted in their valuation because of the higher certainty yield by the operation at higher maturity levels.

References

[1] Abdel-Hamid, T.K., Madnick, S.E.: Software Project Dynamics: An Integrated Approach. Prentice-Hall, Englewood Cliffs (1991)
[2] Agrawal, M., Chari, K.: Software Effort, Quality and Cycle Time. IEEE Transactions on Software Engineering 33(3) (March 2007)
[3] Bamberger, J.: Essence of the Capability Maturity Model. Computer (June 1997)

[4] Barbieri, S.: Framework the Mejora de Procesos de Software. MSE Thesis. UNLP, Argentina

[5] Boria, J.: A Framework for understanding SPI ROI, Innovation in Technology Management. In: PICMET 1997: Portland International Conference on Management and Technology, July 1997, pp. 847–851 (1997)

[6] Brealey, R.A., Myers, S.C.: Fundamentos de Financiación Empresarial, 4ta ed. McGraw-Hill

[7] Brodman, J., Johnson, D.: ROI from Software Process Improvement as Measured in the US Industry. Software Process Improvement and Practice 1(1), 35–47

[8] Capell, P.: Benefits of Improvement Efforts, Special Report CMU/SEI-2004-SR-010 (September 2004)

[9] Carrillo, J.E., Gaimon, C.: The implications of firm size on process improvement strategy. In: PICMET apos 1997: Portland International Conference on Management and Technology, July 27-31, 1997, pp. 807–810 (1997)

[10] Cater-Steel, A.P.: Process improvement in four small software companies. In: Software Engineering Conference, 2001. Proceedings, Australian, August 27-28, 2001, pp. 262–272 (2001)

[11] Clark, B.K.: Quantifying the effects of process improvement on effort. Software, IEEE 17(6), 65–70 (2000)

[12] Clouse, A., Turner, R.: CMMI Distilled. In: Ahern, D.M., Mellon, C. (eds.) Conference, COMPSAC 2002. SEI Series in Software Engineering (2002)

[13] Coleman Dangle, K.C., Larsen, P., Shaw, M., Zelkowitz, M.V.: Software process improvement in small organizations: a case study. Software, IEEE 22(16), 68–75 (2005)

[14] Colla, P.: Marco extendido para la evaluación de iniciativas de mejora en procesos en Ing de Software. In: JIISIC 2006, Puebla, México (2006)

[15] Colla, P.: Montagna M. Modelado de Mejora de Procesos de Software en Pequeñas Organizaciones. In: JIISIC 2008, Accepted Paper, Guayaquil, Ecuador (2006)

[16] Conradi, H., Fuggetta, A.: Improving Software Process Improvement. IEEE Software 19(I4), 92–99 (2002)

[17] Demirors, O., Yildiz, O., Selcuk Guceglioglu, A.: Using cost of software quality for a process improvement initiative. In: Proceedings of the 26th uromicro Conference, 2000, September 5-7, 2000, vol. 2, pp. 286–291 (2000)

[18] Devnani, S.: Bayesian Análisis of Software Cost and Quality Models. PhD Thesis, USC-USA (1999)

[19] Diaz, M., King, J.: How CMM Impacts Quality, Productivity, Rework, and the Bottom Line. CrossTalk 15(I3), 9–14 (2002)

[20] Dyba, T.: An empirical investigation of the key factors for success in software process improvement. IEEE Transactions on Software Engineering 31(I5), 410–424 (2005)

[21] El Emam, K., Briand, L.: Cost and Benefits of SPI. Int'l SE Research Network Technical Report ISERN-97-12 (1997)

[22] Focardi, S.: A primer on probability theory in financial modeling The intertek group, Tutorial 2001-01

[23] Galin, D., Avrahami, M.: Are CMM Program Investment Beneficial? Analysis of Past Studies – IEEE Software, 81–87 (November/December 2006)

[24] GoldSim – Simulation Software (Academic License), http://www.goldsim.com

[25] Guerrero, F.: Adopting the SW-CMMI in Small IT Organizations. IEEE Software, 29–35 (January/February 2004)

[26] Harrison, W., et al.: Making a business case for software process improvement. Software Quality Journal 8(2), November

[27] Hayes, W., Zubrow, D.: Moving On Data and Experience Doing CMM Based Process Improvement, CMU/SEI-95-TR-008 (1995)

[28] Herbsleb, J.D., Goldenson, D.R.: A systematic survey of CMM experience and results Software Engineering. In: Proceedings of the 18th International Conference, March 25-30, 1996, pp. 323–330 (1996)

[29] Hertz, D.: Risk Analysis in Capital Investment. Harvard Business Review Nr 79504 (September 1979)

[30] Houston, D., Keats, B.: Cost of Software Quality: Justifying Software Process Improvement to Managers. Software Quality Professional 1(2), 8–16 (1999)

[31] Illyas, F., Malik, R.: Adhering to CMM L2 in medium sized software organizations in Pakistan. In: IEEE INMIC 2003, pp. 434–439 (2003)

[32] Kelly, D.P., Culleton, B.: Process improvement for small organizations. Computer 32(10), 41–47 (1999)

[33] Koc, T.: Organizational determinants of innovation capacity in software companies. Computers & Industrial Engineering – Elsevier Science Direct 53, 373–385 (2007)

[34] Krishnan, M.S., Kellner, M.I.: Measuring process consistency: implications for reducing software defects. IEEE Transactions on Software Engineering 25(I6), 800–815 (1999)

[35] Lawlis, P.K., Flowe, R.M., Thordahl, J.B.: A Correlational Study of the CMM and Software Development Performance. Crosstalk, 21–25 (September 1995)

[36] McGarry, F., Decker, B.: Attaining Level 5 in CMM Process Maturity. IEEE Software, 87–96 (November/December 2002)

[37] McGibbons: Proceedings of the 7th Software Process Engineering Group Conference (SEPG), Boston (1995)

[38] McLain: Impact of CMM based Software Process Improvement MSIS Thesis, Univ of Hawaii (2001)

[39] Niazi, M., Wilson, et al.: Framework for assisting the design of effective SPI implementation strategies. Elsevier JSS (accepted, 2004)

[40] Raffo, D., Harrison, W., Settle, J., et al.: Understanding the Role of Defect Potential in Assessing the Economic Value of SPI. In: International Conference on SE, June 2000, Limerick, Ireland (2000)

[41] Ruiz, M., Toro, M., Ramos, I.: Modelo Dinámico Reducido – Informe Técnico LSI-2001-01, Departamento de Lenguajes y Sistemas Informáticos Universidad de Sevilla (2001)

[42] Rico, D., Pressman, R.: ROI of Software Process Improvement: Metrics for Project Managers and Software Engineers. J. Ross Publishing, Inc.,(February 2004) ISBN-13:978-1932159240

[43] SEI-CMU CMMI site, http://www.sei.cmu.edu

[44] Siakas, K.V.: What has culture to do with CMMI? In: IEEE Proceedings of the 28th Euromicro Conference (2002)

[45] Stalhane, T., Wedde, K.: SPI, Why isn't it more used? In: Euro SPI 1999 (1999)

[46] Statz, J., Solon, B.: Benchmarking the ROI for SPI, Gartner-Teraquest Report 2002 (2002)

[47] Tvedt, J.: A modular model for predicting the Impacts of SPI on Development Cycle Time. PhD Thesis dissertation

[48] Van Solingen, R.: Measuring the ROI of Software Process Improvement. IEEE Software, 32–38 (May/June 2004)

[49] Varkoi, T., Lepasaar, M., Jaakkola, H.: Priorities of process improvement outcomes based on process capability levels. In: Proceedings Conference on Quality Software, 2001. Second Asia-Pacific, December 10-11, pp. 349–353 (2001)

[50] Walden, D.: Overview of a Business Case: CMMI Process Improvement. In: NDIA/SEI CMMI Presentation, Proceedings 2nd Annual CMMI Technology Conference and User Group (2002)

[51] Wilson, D., Hyde, K.: Intangible benefits of CMM-based software process improvement. Software Process: Improvement and Practice 9(4), 217–228 (2004)

Appendix I-Model Parameters

Parm	Name	UM	Min	Med	Max	Reference
Ksepg	% Organization to SEPG	%Org	0,8%	0,8%	0,8%	[15,20,30,35]
Kprod	Productivity Gain after SPI	%Org	8,0%	22,0%	48,0%	[07]
Kspi	% Organization to SPI	%Org	0,8%	0,8%	2,3%	[15,20,35]
Ca	Assessment Costs	Person/Md	8,0	12,0	16,0	Based on $20K-$30K-$40K range
Eae	Appraisal Execution Effort	Person/Md	2,7	2,7	6,5	[09,20],10Persx2Wks+3Persx2W
Eap	Appraisal Preparation Effort	Person/Md	0,6	0,9	1,3	[09,10,20]
ti	Time to Implement	Months	18,0	20,0	32,0	[10,15,18,20,35,37]
Etp	Training Preparation Effort	Person/Hr	12,0	18,0	24,0	[Authors estimation]
Epa	Training Effort per PA-Person	Person/Hr	4,0	6,0	8,0	[20,41]
CMMI Level			λ(**)	Npa	ξ (*)	
Level 3			0,633	21	94%	

(*) McGibbon [44] and SEI Assessment Data Base [50] / (**) Colla & Montagna [11,12,13]

Appendix II-Modeled Relations and Equations

[Ec 2] $E_{spi} = K_{spi} \times N$	[Ec3] $E_t = \left[(E_{PA} \times N) + E_{tp}\right] \times N_{PA}$	[Ec 4] $E_{ca} = \left(C_a \middle/ C_{PE}\right)$
[Ec5] $E_a = E_{ap} + E_{ad} + E_{ca}$	[Ec 6] $E_{sepg} = K_{sepg} \times N$	[Ec 7] $I_{prod} = K_{prod} \times N$
[Ec8] $V_i = \left(K_{prod} - K_{sepg}\right) \times N$	[Ec9] $V_i = \xi \times \left(K_{prod} - K_{sepg}\right) \times N$	[Ec 10] $NPV = \sum_{t=0}^{n} \frac{F_t}{(1+r)^t}$
[Ec11] $NPV = \int_0^\infty F(t) \times e^{-\delta t} dt$ $\delta = Ln(1+r)$	[Ec 12] $\lambda = \frac{\mu_i \, \sigma_o}{\sigma_i \, \mu_o}$	[Ec13] $r' = r_f + \lambda \times (r - r_f)$

On Deriving Actions for Improving Cost Overrun by Applying Association Rule Mining to Industrial Project Repository

Junya Debari[1], Osamu Mizuno[1], Tohru Kikuno[1],
Nahomi Kikuchi[2], and Masayuki Hirayama[2]

[1] Graduate School of Information Science and Technology, Osaka University
1-5 Yamadaoka, Suita, Osaka 565-0871, Japan
{j-debari,o-mizuno,kikuno}@ist.osaka-u.ac.jp
[2] Software Engineering Center, Information-technology Promotion Agency
2-28-8, Honkomagome, Bunkyo-ku, Tokyo 113-6591, Japan
{n-kiku,m-hiraya}@ipa.go.jp

Abstract. For software project management, it is very important to identify risk factors which make project into runaway. In this study, we propose a method to extract improvement action items for a software project by applying association rule mining to the software project repository for a metric of "cost overrun". We first mine a number of association rules affecting cost overrun. We then group compatible rules, which include several common metrics having different values, from the mined rules and extract improvement action items of project improvement. In order to evaluate the applicability of our method, we applied our method to the project data repository collected from plural companies in Japan. The result of experiment showed that project improvement actions for cost overrun were semi-automatically extracted from the mined association rules. We can confirm feasibility of our method by comparing these actions with the results in the previous research.

Keywords: association rule mining, project improvement actions, cost overrun.

1 Introduction

In recent software development, avoiding runaway projects has become a pressing need to be resolved. However, the sources of the project success and failure are derived from a wide range of the factors in the software development. Therefore, identifying or avoiding the sources of the runaway projects is usually realized based on the experience of the software developers. Utilizing empirical analysis of various project data to control the software project is required.

In the most of development field in Japan, project data including various software metrics are collected. However, usually, such data are not utilized for project control. In many cases, reasons are following two-folds: (1) Since the data include much noises and omissions, the analysis of the data is difficult, and (2) There are less time to tackle with such problems for industries. Therefore, ease to use procedure for the project control using a data-driven or experience-based methodology is required.

Q. Wang, D. Pfahl, and D.M. Raffo (Eds.): ICSP 2008, LNCS 5007, pp. 51–62, 2008.
© Springer-Verlag Berlin Heidelberg 2008

We have conducted studies to predict the final status of software projects based on the data collected in the development field [1]. The results of the studies show only possibility of project runaway. So it is difficult to know the cause of the result. Furthermore, since these studies aimed to offer global guide for development organization, it is not sufficient to deal with individual problems in a software project.

Therefore, a method to extract factors that lead projects runaway and to feedback knowledge from extracted factors to individual development project is required. To do so, we introduced association rules mining for extracting such factors [2]. However, association rule mining have several limitations. For example, according to the parameters used for mining, too many or too few rules are found. Furthermore, although many similar rules (intuitively, similar rules are rules whose antecedents include almost the same metrics) are usually extracted by the association rule mining, we have to investigate essential rules to feed back to development field.

This paper focuses on the analysis to extract the project attributes that affects cost overrun by association rule mining. The experiment is conducted for the year 2006 version of the IPA/SEC repository consisting of 1,419 samples of enterprise software development projects in Japanese companies. The IPA/SEC repository has been developed and maintained by Software Engineering Center (SEC), Information-technology Promotion Agency (IPA), Japan [3].

Briefly speaking, we can feed back the result of analysis to the existing development process as follows: At first, just after the requirements analysis, a metrics set for pre-evaluation M_0 is collected. Based on the M_0 and the pre-constructed model, we predict whether the project is going to excess the estimated cost or not. When the predicted result indicates a fear of cost excess, we construct a plan to avoid the excess of the cost, and then conduct the development.

In this analysis, we used association rule mining to determine the metrics set M_0 and the model to predict the cost excess. We also used association rule mining to extract the actions (that is a set of association rules) for each project to avoid the fear of cost excess.

The rest of this paper is organized as follows: Section 2 addresses the objective of this study. The data repository used in this research is described in Section 3. The analysis using association rule mining for the cross-company data in Japan is described in Section 4. A case study of this approach is shown in Section 5. Related works of this study is described in Section 6. Finally, Section 7 concludes this paper.

2   The Proposed Approach

The objective of this study is to construct an approach to extract improvement plans for the cost excess in the software development. This approach is an extension of existing software development process. Figure 1 shows an outline of this approach.

The main procedure of the proposed approach is as follows:

Phase 1. Before the project begins, we extract improvement actions from industrial project repository. We describe this approach in Section4.

Phase 2. Just after the requirements analysis of a certain software project, we collect a metrics set for pre-evaluation M_0 from the software project.

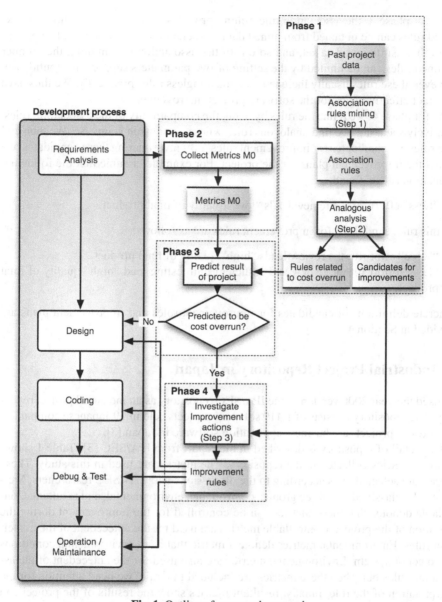

Fig. 1. Outline of proposed approach

Phase 3. Based on the M_0 and the pre-constructed model, we predict whether the project is going to excess the estimated cost or not. We use association rule mining to determine the metrics set M_0 and the model to predict the cost excess.

Phase 4. When the predicted result indicates a fear of cost excess, we construct a plan to avoid the excess of the cost, and then conduct the development. We also use association rule mining to extract the actions (that is a set of association rules) for each project to avoid the fear of cost excess.

As for phase 3, the association rule mining provides some merits as follows: unexpected rules can be obtained from mined data, association rules mining can be applicable to the insufficient data set, and so on. In the association rule mining, the number of mined rules can be limited by the setting of two parameters support and confidence. However, these rules usually include much meaningless rules practically. We thus have to extract effective rules for the software project improvement.

As for phase 4, we refine the rules by using the compatibility of the association rules. Intuitively speaking, we find analogous rules whose conclusion is inverse. We then call such rules as "candidates for improvement rules". By investigating these candidates, we extract the improvement plans for the project. For example, assume that the following association rule is found:

– "Less" effort for the review leads "low" quality of final product.

For this rule, candidates for improvement rules are as follows:

– "More" effort for the review leads "high" quality of final product.
– "Less" effort for the review and sufficient unit testing lead "high" quality of final product.

Concrete definitions of candidates for improvement rules and improvement plans are provided in Section 4.

3   Industrial Project Repository in Japan

We used the year 2006 version of the IPA/SEC repository as an industrial project repository. The repository consists of 1,419 software projects held in 19 Japanese companies. The most of projects are business application software in Japan [3].

The detail of repository is described in the report from IPA/SEC [3]. Table 1 shows a part of metrics collected in the repository. The metrics are used in this study. These metrics are selected ones according to the discussions with IPA/SEC researchers. Metrics can be classified into three groups: controllable, environmental, and resultant. Controllable denotes that these metrics can be controlled for the improvement during the execution of the project. Controllable metrics are used for the antecedent of the association rules. Environmental metrics denote a metric that is an environmental conditions of project or system. Environmental metrics are also used for the antecedent of the association rules but when these metrics are included in a rule, we need attention for the interpretation of the rule. Finally, resultant metrics show the results of the project and they are considered as a conclusion of the association rules. We can find 38 metrics as controllable, 47 metrics as environmental, and 6 metrics as resultant.

4   Analysis by Association Rule Mining (Phase 1)

4.1   Association Rule Mining

Association rule mining is a data mining method, which extracts a data set called an association rule. This represents relations of factors. An association rule $X \Rightarrow Y$ means

Table 1. Metrics used in this study

Controllable metrics		
New customer	Category of business	New cooperate company
New technology	Role and responsibility	Manifestation of priority of goal
Room for development site	Use of operation tools	Evaluation of plan (cost)
Evaluation of plan (quality)	Evaluation of plan (duration)	Test organization
Use of project management tools	Use of configuration management tools	Use of design support tools
Use of document management tools	Use of debug/test tools	Use of CASE tools
Use of code generator	Use of development methodology	Use of development framework
Environment and noise of development site	Degree of manifestation of requirements specification	Involvement of user for requirements specification
Experience for the system of user	Experience for the business of user	Acknowledgement of user for design
Acknowledgement of user for requirements specification	Degree of understanding of user for the design	Role and responsibility clarification between users and developers
Involvement of user in the acceptance testing	Skill of project managers	Skill and experience of developers in business area
Skill and experience of developers in languages and tools	Skill and experience of developers in development platform	Skill and experience of developers for analysis and design
Ratio of FP per package	Quantitative criteria of quality assessment	
Environmental metrics		
Domain of business	Domain of business (category)	Detail of business
Purpose of system	Type of development projects	Place of development
Configuration of development projects	Type of use	Number of users of system
Number of sites of system	Maximum number of simultaneous users	Use of Web technology
Process of on-line transaction	Use of DBMS	Type of system
Use of COTS	Type of operation	Architecture
Target of development: Linux	Target of development: Windows	Development life cycle model
Reference to similar projects	Number of stakeholders for requirements	Requirements for reliability
Requirements for availability	Requirements for performance	Requirements for maintainability
Requirements for portability	Requirements for running cost	Requirements for security
Legal regulation	Actual FP (uncalibrated)	Duration in months (planned)
Duration in months (actual)	Planned effort of development project	Quality assurance organization
Maximum number of developers	Average number of developers	Actual effort (5 phases)
Actual SLOC	FP per month	SLOC per effort
Actual duration of overall development	Does duration match COCOMO model?	Effort per actual duration
Actual FP per effort	Actual FP per duration	
Resultant metrics		
Customer satisfaction (subj. evaluation)	Success of the project (self evaluation)	Cost overrun
Quality evaluation	Duration overrun	Number of failures

that if an event X happens, an event Y happens at the same time. An event X is called antecedent, and Y is called conclusion. In this study, events X and Y are described as a form of "metrics name = value", for example, "Cost overrun = good".

"Support" and "confidence" are the parameters evaluating the importance of association rules. Support means the frequency of an association rule. Support of an association rule $X \Rightarrow Y$ is the probability that the event X and the event Y happen simultaneously in the data set. Confidence of the association rule is the conditional probability of the event X given the event Y. Confidence means the relationship between X and Y.

We set the minimum value of support and confidence for mining because combinatorial explosion occurs without the threshold value of support and confidence.

4.2 Outline of Analysis

The outline of analysis performed for this study is as follows:

Step 0. First, we collect and prepare the data for analysis.
Step 1. We apply association rule mining to the data. The conclusion of association rules are "Cost overrun = good" or "Cost overrun = bad".

Step 2. We extract Improvement Rules from the rules mined in the previous step.
Step 3. We inspect software project improvement actions from improvement rules.

In the following subsections, we describe the detail of each step.

4.3 Analysis for Cost Overrun

First, we explain steps 0 and 1 in which the analysis to obtain the association rules related to the cost overrun is performed.

Step 0: Collecting Software Project Data. At first, we collect data from software development and determine necessary metrics. The data from software development projects have various metrics, and thus we need to choose metrics. In this step, we prepare these data.

Step 0.1. We define goals to improve, and pick metrics indicating goals up.
Step 0.2. We choose metrics as parameters, and examine collected data carefully.
Step 0.3. We classify metrics into controllable, environmental, resultant. Metrics of controllable and environmental are used as antecedent of association rules, and metrics of resultant are used as conclusions of association rules.
Step 0.4. We decide data sets cut from collected data.

Step 1: Association Rule Mining. In this study, we perform association rule mining with the following steps:

Step 1.1. We decide the conclusion of association rules. In this study, we chose "Cost overrun".
Step 1.2. We decide the minimum of support and the minimum of confidence.
Step 1.3. We apply association rule mining to the data, and store mined rules.

Thus, a lot of association rules are stored. In the next step, we extract important rules from these rules.

4.4 Analysis for Project Improvement

Before explaining steps 2 and 3, we introduce the notion of analogous rules and project improvement actions, which are key idea of this study. Then we explain the steps to obtain the project improvement actions.

Idea of Project Improvement Actions. Here, we explain software improvement actions. First, we define "analogous rules" as follows:

When we find an association rule r_1, we define $M_{r_1}^A$ as the group of metrics in antecedent of the rule r_1, and define $M_{r_1}^C$ as the group of metrics in conclusion of the rule r_1.

In a similar way, we define $M_{r_2}^A$ and $M_{r_2}^C$. $M_{r_2}^A$ is the group of metrics in antecedent of the rule r_2, and $M_{r_2}^A$ is the group of metrics in conclusion of the rule r_2.

If $M_{r_2}^A \supseteq M_{r_1}^A$ and $M_{r_2}^C = M_{r_1}^C$, the rule r_1 and the rule r_2 are "analogous rules" about the group of metrics.

Example 1. Assume that the following rule r_1 exists.
  – Effort of review = low $\Rightarrow$ Cost overrun = bad
The "analogous rules" of the rule r_1 is as follows.
  – Effort of review = high $\Rightarrow$ Cost overrun = good
  – Effort of review = high $\wedge$ Effort of test = high $\Rightarrow$ Cost overrun = good
  – Effort of review = high $\wedge$ Effort of test = low $\Rightarrow$ Cost overrun = bad
  However, the next rule is not a analogous rule because the antecedent of the rule is different.
  – Effort of test = high $\Rightarrow$ Cost overrun = good

Here, we try to derive software project improvement actions in following method. We focus on the rule r_1 and the analogous rules. The conclusion of the rule r_1 is "Cost overrun = bad". The contrast value of this is "Cost overrun = good". If the conclusion of the rule r_2 is "Cost overrun = good", we call this rule "improvement rule". We define R_r^I as the group of "improvement rules".

Example 2. Again, assume that the rule r_1 exists, which is the same as example 1.
  – Effort of review = low $\Rightarrow$ Cost overrun = bad
  Since the improvement rules are the rules whose conclusion is "Cost overrun = good", the improvement rules are extracted as follows:
  – Effort of review = high $\Rightarrow$ Cost overrun = good
  – Effort of review = low $\wedge$ Effort of test $\Rightarrow$ Cost overrun = good

In this way, we get R_r^I. Then, we define M_r^I as the group of metrics indicating the actions of project improvement. The derivation of M_r^I is following. First, we derive M_t^A from each rule t in R_r^I. Next, we make M_r^I. The next expression represents M_r^I.

$$M_r^I = \bigcup_{t \in R_r^I} M_t^A$$

Then, we derive the project improvement actions from M_r^I. This process is not automatic. The project improvement actions are derived by experienced manager, developer, and researcher.

Hence, we explain about the actions of software project improvement. The existence of analogous rules means that the situations of software development are similar. If situations are similar and conclusions are different, it is probable that these conclusions are turned by changes of antecedent of the rules. Because he group M_r^I includes these cases, collecting M_r^I means collecting factors changing project situations. Therefore, we think of M_r^I as the project improvement actions in this study.

Step 2: Extracting Improvement Rules. The procedure of this step is as follows:

Step 2.1. We focus the rule r whose conclusion is "Cost overrun = bad". First, we search r', whose metrics in antecedent is comprised in the antecedent of r. The conclusion of r' is "Cost overrun". Because there are a lot of rules such as r', we define these rules as R_r'.

Step 2.2. If the conclusion of $r' \in R_r'$ is "Cost overrun = good", r' is defined as r^I (improvement rule). We define the group of r^I as R_r^I.

Step 2.3. We make M_r^I from the metrics in the antecedent of R_r^I, and make candidates of project improvement actions from M_r^I.

Step 3: Inspecting Project Improvement Actions. In this step, we validate project improvement actions from M_r^I.

Step 3.1. As we mentioned before, controllable metrics are considered as risk items with corrective actions which mitigate the risks during the project. Accordingly, we accept controllable metrics as project improvement actions by priority.

Step 3.2. Environmental metrics have a high probability of difference in the constrained condition of the software projects. Therefore, we don't consider these metrics as improvement actions.

5 Case Study: Application to Actual Development

5.1 Result of Analysis (Step 0 – Step 3)

In this case study, we prepared the data set as mentioned in Section3, and applied the method to the data set. We extracted 421 projects which have the target metrics "Cost overrun".

First, we set the minimum support and the minimum confidence of association rule mining. The minimum support is 0.01 and the minimum confidence is 0.9. The conclusions of association rules are "Cost overrun". The number of the rules whose conclusions are "Cost overrun = good" is 545,836 and the number of rules whose conclusions are "Cost overrun = bad" is 180. Next, we extract improvement rules from these association rules. As a result, we find 35 rules have improvement rules and R_r^I. In addition, the number of improvement rules is 4,116. The total amount of time of mining association rules and extracting improvement rule is 320 minutes.

Example 3. We extracted an association rule r_1. The support of this rule was 0.01, and the confidence was 1.00.

r_1:   Evaluation of plan (cost) = partially clear and feasible
    $\wedge$ Involvement of user for requirements specification = relatively
    $\wedge$ Requirement for performance = medium
    $\Rightarrow$ Cost overrun = bad

The rule r_1 indicates that the cost overrun becomes bad if evaluation of plan for cost is indecisive or the execution feasibility is not examined in planning phase, the user basically involves for requirements specification, and requirement for performance is not so strict.

For the rule r_1, an improvement rule r_1^I was found as follows. The support of the rule r_1^I was 0.26, and the confidence was 0.92.

r_1^I: Evaluation of plan (cost) = very clear and feasible
    $\wedge$ Involvement of user for requirements specification = relatively
    $\wedge$ Requirement for performance = high
    $\Rightarrow$ Cost overrun = good

The rule r_1^I indicates that the cost overrun becomes good if evaluation of plan for cost is precise and the execution feasibility is examined in planning phase, the user basically involves for requirements specification, and requirement for performance is high.

From r_1 and r_1^I, we obtained a project improvement action as follows: when the user basically involves for requirements specification,

1. Evaluate cost plan precisely.
2. Examine the feasibility of plan.
3. Make requirement for performance high.

However, because requirement for performance is an environmental metrics, the item 3 cannot be an improvement action item. Thus, a project improvement action is follows:

Action 1. If the user involvement for requirements specification and requirement for performance is high, evaluate cost plan precisely and examine the plan's feasibility.

In general, evaluation of plan must be done with clear criteria and its feasibility of execution must be assured. If plan is not constructed precisely, a fear to overrun the planned cost becomes large.

Example 4. Let us show the other example. We extracted the following rule r_2. The support of the rule was 0.01, and the confidence was 1.00.

r_2:   Category of business = legacy
 ∧ New technology = used
 ∧ Evaluation of plan (cost) = very clear and feasible
 ∧ Actual FP per effort = low
 ⇒ Cost overrun = bad

The rule r_2 indicates that cost overrun becomes bad if the category of business is not new, the project uses new technology, evaluation of plan for cost is precise and the execution feasibility is examined, and actual FP per effort is low.

We then found r_2^I as an improvement rule for r_2 as follows. The support of r_2^I was 0.02 and the confidence was 0.92.

r_2^I: Category of business = legacy
 ∧ New technology = not used
 ∧ Evaluation of plan (cost) = very clear and feasible
 ∧ Actual FP per effort = high
 ⇒ Cost overrun = good

The rule r_2^I indicates that cost overrun becomes good if the category of business is not new, the project doesn't use new technology, evaluation of plan for cost is precise and the execution feasibility is examined, and actual FP per effort is high. Thus, the following improvement action can be derived from r_2^I: when the category of business is legacy and the evaluation of cost plan is very clear and feasible,

1. Do not use new technology.
2. Execute project under condition of high Actual FP with less man-hours.

However, since FP per effort is an environmental metric, the item 2 cannot be an improvement action. Thus, the improvement action is as follows:

Action 2. If the category of business is legacy, the evaluation of cost plan is very clear and feasible, and actual FP per effort is high, then do not use new technology if possible.

Obviously, new technology requires much effort to learn or skilled engineers. This usually results unexpected increase of costs.

Discussion. In this case, these two examples derive somewhat obvious rules from the project repository. Although one characteristic of association rule mining is to derive unexpected rules from huge repository, the result of analysis in this study could not derive such unexpected rules. However, from the other point of view, we can consider that these rules are formulated knowledge or experience of the skilled engineers. Thus, our approach can be applicable to the purpose of formalization of experiences.

Furthermore, our approach can contribute to simplify the factors related to the cost overrun. Since various metrics and rules related to the cost overrun are mined, our approach can simplify them as improvement actions.

5.2 A Case Study from Result of Analysis (Phase 1 – Phase 4)

Here, we show a case study of applying our approach to actual development data.

According to the result of analysis, we can prepare the following metrics set M_0: New technology, Involvement of user for requirements specification, Requirements for performance, Evaluation of plan (cost), Evaluation of plan (quality), Degree of manifestation of requirements specification. Furthermore, we have already obtained improvement rules, R_r^I.

In our analysis, developers of each project fill out the metrics set M_0 at the end of requirement analysis. Assume that a project answers that "New technology = used" and "Evaluation of plan (cost) = vague". From the mined rules, we can see that these answers tend to result excess of cost in projects. Thus, in this case, the following rules are extracted from R_r^I as actions for improvement:

(1)   Category of business = legacy
   $\land$ New technology = not used
   $\land$ Evaluation of plan (quality) = very clear and feasible
   $\land$ Actual FP per effort = high
   $\Rightarrow$ Cost overrun = good

(2)   Evaluation of plan (cost) = very clear and feasible
   $\land$ Involvement of user for requirements specification = enough
   $\land$ Degree of understanding of user for design = relatively
   $\Rightarrow$ Cost overrun = good

(3)   Evaluation of plan (cost) = very clear and feasible
   $\land$ Involvement of user for requirements specification = relatively
   $\land$ Requirements for performance = high
   $\Rightarrow$ Cost overrun = good

According to these rules, developers can find that use of new technology and vague evaluation of planned cost have a certain risk for cost excess. Furthermore, looking into rules in more detail, developers also find other factors to be improved. For example, enough involvement of user for requirements specification lead less cost overrun. From these information obtained from improvement rules, actual improvement plan is constructed.

6   Related Works

Estimation of cost overrun is an important problem from a viewpoint of economics of the software development. Methods and guidelines to prevent cost overrun have been proposed so far [4,5].

Association rule mining is applied to various field of research in order to extract useful information from huge databases [6]. In the software engineering, for example, Michail et al. mined pattern of reuse of libraries in an application by the association rules mining [7]. Mined information is used for reconstruction of class library. Besides, Zimmermann et al. tried to apply association rule mining to change history of revision management system in order to extract combinations of files and modules which are usually modified simultaneously [8]. Garcia et al. tried to extract interesting rules from project management data [9]. They proposed an algorithm for refining association rules based on incremental knowledge discovery and provided managers with strong rules for decision making without need of domain knowledge. Their approach, however, is only validated on the project simulator. Chawla et al. applied association rules network(ARN) approach to the data of open source software(OSS) projects [10]. Using ARNs we discover important relationships between the attributes of successful OSS projects. In general, conditions of successful projects differ between OSS and industrial projects. Our approach mainly aims to find improvement actions from a viewpoint of industrial software development.

Analysis of the IPA/SEC repository is now performed from various aspects [11, 12, 13]. Although their objective is to estimate cost or to specify dominant factors on the success of projects, our objective is to extract improvement actions to improve cost overrun.

7   Conclusion

In this study, we proposed an approach to extract improvement action items for a software project by applying association rule mining to the software project repository for a metric of "Cost overrun". By using the association rule mining and notion of analogous rules, our procedure can extract rules for project improvement actions. In order to evaluate the applicability of our approach, we conducted a case study with the project data repository collected from plural companies in Japan. The case study showed that project improvement actions for cost overrun were semi-automatically extracted from the mined association rules.

As future work, we have to compare our method with methods by using other cost estimation models in order to confirm the usefulness of our method.

References

1. Takagi, Y., Mizuno, O., Kikuno, T.: An empirical approach to characterizing risky software projects based on logistic regression analysis. Empirical Software Engineering 10(4), 495–515 (2005)
2. Amasaki, S., Hamano, Y., Mizuno, O., Kikuno, T.: Characterization of runaway software projects using association rule mining. In: Münch, J., Vierimaa, M. (eds.) PROFES 2006. LNCS, vol. 4034, pp. 402–407. Springer, Heidelberg (2006)

3. Software Engineering Center, Information-technology Promotion Agency (ed.): The 2006 White Paper on Software Development Projects (in Japanese). Nikkei Business Publications (2006)
4. Masticola, S.P.: A simple estimate of the cost of software project failures and the breakeven effectiveness of project risk management. In: Proceedings of the First International Workshop on The Economics of Software and Computation (ESC 2007), p. 6 (2007)
5. Lederer, A.L., Prasad, J.: Nine management guidelines for better cost estimating. Commun. ACM 35(2), 51–59 (1992)
6. Han, J., Kamber, M.: Data Mining: Concepts and Techniques. Morgan Kaufmann Publishers, San Francisco (2001)
7. Michail, A.: Data mining library reuse patterns using generalized association rules. In: Proceedings of the 22nd international conference on Software engineering, pp. 167–176 (2000)
8. Zimmermann, T., Weißgerber, P., Diehl, S., Zeller, A.: Mining version histories to guide software change. IEEE Trans. on Software Engineering 31(6), 429–445 (2005)
9. García, M.N.M., Román, I.R., Penalvo, F.J.G., Bonilla, M.T.: An association rule mining method for estimating the impact of project management policies on software quality, development time and effort. Expert Syst. Appl. 34(1), 522–529 (2008)
10. Chawla, S., Arunasalam, B., Davis, J.: Mining open source software (oss) data using association rules network. In: Whang, K.-Y., Jeon, J., Shim, K., Srivastava, J. (eds.) PAKDD 2003. LNCS (LNAI), vol. 2637, pp. 461–466. Springer, Heidelberg (2003)
11. Mitani, Y., Kikuchi, N., Matsumura, T., Ohsugi, N., Monden, A., Higo, Y., Inoue, K., Barker, M., Matsumoto, K.: A proposal for analysis and prediction for software projects using collaborative filtering, in-process measurements and a benchmarks database. In: Proc. of International Conference on Software Process and Product Measurement, pp. 98–107 (2006)
12. Ohsugi, N., Monden, A., Kikuchi, N., Barker, M.D., Tsunoda, M., Kakimoto, T., Matsumoto, K.: Is this cost estimate reliable? – the relationship between homogeneity of analogues and estimation reliability. In: Proc. of First International Symposium on Empirical Software Engineering and Measurement, pp. 384–392 (2007)
13. Furuyama, T., Kikuchi, N., Yasuda, M., Tsuruho, M.: Analysis of the factors that affect the performance of software projects (in Japanese). Trans. of Information Processing Society of Japan 48(8), 2608–2619 (2007)

Software Multi-project Resource Scheduling: A Comparative Analysis

Fei Dong[1,2], Mingshu Li[1], Yuzhu Zhao[1,2], Juan Li[1], and Ye Yang[1]

[1] Institute of Software, Chinese Academy of Sciences
[2] Graduate University of Chinese Academy of Sciences
{dongsquare, zhaoyuzhu, lijuan, ye}@itechs.iscas.ac.cn,
mingshu@iscas.ac.cn

Abstract. Software organizations are always multi-project-oriented, in which situation the traditional project management for individual project is not enough. Related scientific research on multi-project is yet scarce. This paper reports result from a literature review aiming to organize, analyze and make sense out of the dispersed field of multi-project resource scheduling methods. A comparative analysis was conducted according to 6 aspects of application situations: value orientation, centralization, homogeneity, complexity, uncertainty and executive ability. The findings show that, traditional scheduling methods from general project management community have high degree of centralization and limited capability to deal with uncertainty, and do not well catered for software projects. In regard to these aspects agile methods are better, but most of them lack scalability to high complexity. Some methods have balanced competence and special attention should be paid to them. In brief, methods should be chosen according to different situations in practice.

Keywords: software multi-project management, agile methods, resource allocation and scheduling, survey.

1 Introduction

Most project life cycles share a common characteristic: cost and staffing levels are low at the start, peak during the intermediate phases, and drop rapidly as the project draws to a conclusion [37]. As for individual participant, energy input does not remain unchanged along the whole life cycle. Sharing human resources across projects can decrease idle time and increase utilization of resources, and also facilitate sharing common technologies and components so as to reduce development cost. It can serve as ways of knowledge transferring and cross-training too.

Traditional Project Management (PM) focus on individual project, however, up to 90%, by value, of all projects are carried out in the multi-project environments [46], and multi-PM is a new trend in PM community [15]. Software organizations commonly work in multi-project environments [25], but little systematic study concentrates on managing multiple software projects, and little research about multi-project comes from software development community. Just take IEEE database as an example, we searched ((multiple projects) <or> (project portfolio) <or> (program management)) on Nov 27

Q. Wang, D. Pfahl, and D.M. Raffo (Eds.): ICSP 2008, LNCS 5007, pp. 63–75, 2008.
© Springer-Verlag Berlin Heidelberg 2008

2007 and obtained 219 papers (unrelated articles included), among which only 45 come from software (or computer science, information system) community. In a representative PM journal, International Journal of Project Management (IJPM), we searched ("multiple projects" OR "multi-project" OR "project portfolio" OR "program") in latest papers after year 2000, and got 78 results. Only three of them have an author from Information System area.

Table 1. Representative paper statistic

Source	Total	With author(s) from software community	%
IEEE	219	45	20.5
IJPM	78	3	3.8

Resource management is one of chief problems in multi-PM [34]. Existing mass research in PM community should be learned, however, software development is a knowledge intensive activity with high creativity and uncertainty, and experiences in other industries can not be borrowed mechanically. Human resource usually represents the major cost of software projects, and its allocation and scheduling are really important as well as difficulty. There are so many methods extracted in section 2, but more research should be done in finding which of them are more useful and suitable to different application environments and constraints. This paper takes an initial attempt to compare and evaluate the resource scheduling methods from different disciplines, especially on software multi-PM.

The rest of the paper is composed as follows. Section 2 presents a short overview of existing multi-project resource scheduling methods. Section 3 summarizes 6 aspects of application situations for subsequent analysis. Section 4 analyzes the referred methods from the 6 aspects. Section 5 presents a simple discussion, limitation of this paper and future work.

2   An Overview of Multi-projects Resource Scheduling Methods

Multi-project: Several related terms are frequently used such as *Project Portfolio* and *Program*. Since some confusion exists regarding these terms [17], we borrow the framework defined by PMI standards to differentiate them. A *portfolio* is a collection of projects and/or programs and other work grouped together to facilitate effective management of that work to meet *strategic* objectives [38]. A *program* is a group of *related* projects managed in a *coordinated* way to obtain benefits and control not available from managing them individually [39]. PM, Program Management and Project Portfolio Management have incremental strategic levels [38]. The focus level in this paper is the same with program management. But "program" is often used interchangeably with portfolio, and has an intuitive meaning in software community, i.e. software code. So we choose the term "multi-project" to avoid ambiguity.

As well, resource management has different abstract levels accordingly. We focus on relatively tactical resource scheduling. **Resource scheduling** is to determine schedule dates on which activities can be performed with required resources. The term "resource" in this paper usually refers to human resources, unless the context indicates otherwise. *Aspect* in this paper means a way in which something can be viewed. And we refer to *Method* as a kind of procedure or technique.

For the confusing terms mentioned above, we conducted a survey in many complemented ways as follows:

1. Key words search. An Internet search via Google Scholar was conducted. To obtain practices in software area, IEEE and ACM were searched particularly.
2. Classical or authoritative materials, e.g. PMI standards[38][39]
3. Web forum. There is little research paper about agile multi-PM, while indeed there are some explorations in industry. We browsed famous forums where agile practitioners gather [52] and also asked active posters.

The extracted methods are listed in Table 2.(The abbreviation is for later references.) Some of them are self-explained or able to find reference in related literature, while some need explanations (no details due to space limitation).

Table 2. Multi-project resource scheduling methods

Methods	References	Abbreviation
One project at a time/ manage as individual project/ non-multi-project	[12]	*Individual*
Networking optimization algorithm/ heuristics methods (with uncertainty mechanism)	[13][19][21] [26][43] [48]	*Network*
Critical Chain methodology	[3][25][33][45]	*Critical Chain*
Resource modeling and simulation	[1][5][25] [32][40][41]	*Resource Modeling*
Multi-agent planning and scheduling	[16] [27]	*Multi-agent*
Scrum of Scrums/ Shared Resources Team/ Virtual team member/ Dual responsibility system (Differentiated Matrix)	[9][12][51] [52]	*Virtual team*
Fixed core team with flexible resource transfer	[22] [31] [52]	*Core team*
Pair Programming across multiple projects	[24] [52]	*Pair programming*
Exchange by turns	[52]	*Exchange*
Multi-product team	[12][30] [52]	*Multi-product*
Classify resources and schedule with different mechanism	[20]	*Classification*

Resource constrained project scheduling problem (RCPSP) has been treated by multiple approaches [19]. The problem for multi-project is treated as a generalization of RCPSP by adding artificial activity nodes as the start and end of each project as well as of multi-project. Thus multi-project is similar to a large project with projects as sub-projects, and methods in individual PM context can be borrowed, e.g. exact methods, heuristics methods, and meta-heuristics methods. Since they are based on a large multi-project network, with activity on node, we classify them into one kind called *Networking optimization algorithm*. PM environment is always with high uncertainty. *Algorithms dealing with uncertainty* in individual PM context [21] can serve as reference: reactive scheduling, stochastic project scheduling, fuzzy project scheduling, robust (proactive) scheduling, and sensitivity analysis. *Critical chain methodology* is a kind of proactive scheduling, but its contribution to multi-project scheduling mainly rests on the use of Theory of Constraint and scheduling basing on capacity constraining resource [45].

Software development depends on individuals' knowledge and skills. Different tasks ask for different skills. Researches in process enactment/instantiation are engaged in this direction. We classify rigid resource definition [40], policy-based resource allocation [41], continuous simulation of resource states by Systems Dynamics [1], agent-based resource modeling [53] and so on into one category called *Resource modeling and simulation*. The optimization algorithms used on project networking above can also be applied here. We treat *Multi-agent planning and scheduling* methods as a special category for it is a distributed algorithm.

The uniqueness of software development, distinct from mass manufacturing, is creativity, uncertainty and dependence on people, leading to agile movement [4] and agile PM. Agile methods attach vital importance to adaptation to real situations when running project with continuous iterations. Besides, they advocate to plan by features rather than activities in traditional methods, to plan and self-organize by the whole team rather than plan and assign tasks to developers by managers, and to monitor the team collectively rather than individually [10].Agile practices can be enlarged by *Scrum of Scrums* [44] for large project or multi-project. *Shared Resources Team*, a sort of Scrum of Scrums in XBreed[51], composed of team leaders or technique leaders, is responsible for extract reusable component from teams or projects. These organizations are similar with those of *Virtual team member* [9], *Dual responsibility system* and *Differentiated Matrix* [12], and we conclude them into one category. In Feature-Driven Development [31] methodology, a feature team consists of stable members and transferable ones, and developers can choose relevant feature teams flexibly. In multi-PM, such thought, named *Fixed core team with flexible resource transfer*, is also appropriate. *Pair Programming* [6] (or pair design et al) is also means of transferring staff *across projects* [24]. Agile methods do not advocate staffing projects of different importance according to people's competence, e.g., unattractive maintenance project should be done *by turns* rather than by fixed team or staff.

Some managers simply expand the size of a single project to accommodate multiple distinct products, i.e., *Multi-product team*. The expanded team contains too many people to operate effectively. But it may be a good practice in mini organization, e.g. a small IT department with a manager, 3 or 4 programmers, a network manager, a database manager and a business analyst in charge of tens of mini projects. It is appropriate to organize all features of projects into one backlog [30] [52].

Resources could be divided into multiple categories to decrease complexity of their scheduling. Project members are divided into 3 categories in [20]: all-around project members, experts and service employees. Different scheduling pattern could be used for different kind of resources. PMI [39] proposed several common tools, i.e. expert judgment, meetings, policies and procedures. They are so common that have been diffused in the above methods, and we won't discuss them separately.

3   A Comparison Framework

Different multi-projects require different management approaches and organizational structures. We summarize 6 aspects of application situations (see Table 3.) to evaluate the various methods systematically and comparably (see next section).

Value orientation. The preferential goal of multi-PM, and how the resources are regarded, ultimately lead to different resource scheduling methods. More emphasis on product innovation and quality, or resource utilization and cost? Can the resources be scheduled like machines or should they be respected and encouraged? These orientations depend on the requirement of (multi-)project strategy, innovation and knowledge management in the organization and so on. (Multi-)Project at different stage, e.g. development or testing, may have different requirements.

Table 3. Aspects of application situations for evaluation of various methods

Aspect	Description	Key references
Value orientation	Goal of resource scheduling or management. Attitude to the labors involved in the projects.	[8][12]
Centralization	The degree of centralization or federation of multi-project	[2][18][34] [49]
Homogeneity	The degree of similarity or diversity of multiple projects	[15][17][18][29] [34][35][36][49]
Complexity	The complexity of multi-project, counting up complexity of all individual projects and their interdependency.	[3] [8] [28][29] [34][49]
Uncertainty	Clarity of objective, degree of change, and risk of the multi-project and all its projects.	[8] [28]
Executive ability	Personality, knowledge, experience, competence and cooperation of participants. Supporting process or tool and culture to implement multi-PM.	[8][11] [12] [18] [29][34][42][47]

Centralization. Are resources scheduled at a central point, or mainly scheduled by every autonomous project and adjusted when necessary? This means different multi-project organization structure and also communication cost across projects or departments. Sometimes the degree of centralization or federation can be changed for efficient management; sometimes be hindered by existing mechanism or authority.

Homogeneity. Managing heterogeneous projects as a multi-project would be much complex [34]. Projects within a multi-project are usually closely related in some way, in addition to using common resources [3]. Have most projects in a multi-project used, or do they suit for one kind of methodology? What is the similarity of projects? The homogeneities facilitate adoption of a common PM approach, and resource or component reuse. Similarities among projects may be as such: common goal, similar size/duration, sharing resources, interlaced scope, potential reusable component, common technology, same business sector, common customer/contractor, under surveillance of same regulatory agency, comparative criticality/risk/priority, same location, and compatible methodology. Various common attributes among projects possibly need different management methods.

Complexity and **Uncertainty**. The 2 aspects are easy to understand since frequently used as indicators when comparing traditional and agile methods in individual PM condition (e.g. [8][28]). It is likely that some method can only deal with a certain situation with high/low complexity/uncertainty. Besides complexity of every project (e.g. team size, mission criticality, team location, domain knowledge gaps, see [28] for extensive explanation) and project quantity, the influential factors to multi-project complexity include degree of interdependency among projects.

Executive ability. Different methods ask for diverse executing competence and cost. Established supporting processes or tools, ability and cooperation of participants, may be prerequisite for methods implementation. Organization culture, maturity, complexity and institutionalization also affect methods selection and balancing.

4   Comparison Results and Analysis

In this section, the 11 methods stated in section 2 are compared and evaluated from the 6 aspects defined in section 3. A sketch map is shown in Table 4. and detailed comparison and evaluation by every aspect are presented in the following subsections. The scales "●", "◐" and "○" stand respectively for high, medium and low degree for aspects *Centralization*, *Homogeneity*, *Complexity* and *Uncertainty*. Their meanings for *Value orientation* and *Executive ability* are explained in the responding subsections.

Table 4. Summary of evaluation for the methods

Aspects \ Methods	Individual	Network	Critical Chain	Resource Modeling	Multi-agent	Virtual Team	Core Team	Pair Programming	Exchange	Multi-product	Classification
Value orientation	●	○	○	●	◐	●	●	●	●	○	◐
Centralization	○	●	●	●	◐	○	○	○	○	●	◐
Homogeneity	○	●	●	◐	◐	◐	◐	○	○	●	◐
Complexity	◐	◐	◐	◐	◐	●	○	○	◐	○	●
Uncertainty	○	○	●	○	◐	◐	●	●	◐	●	●
Executive ability	◐	○	○	○	○	●	●	●	●	●	◐

4.1   Value Orientation

Companies may save on production costs by sharing resources across projects, but they risk technical compromises [34] and placing too many restrictions on creativity of engineers [12]. And similar to attitudes to multi-tasking in individual project context, many practices suggest people or team focus on one project at a time. Thus *Individual* PM encourages concentration or creativity rather than resource utilization. Companies may pursue project quality or lead-time at cost of dedicated and redundant resources. But resources are always scarce for too many projects in organization, and resource utilization is the starting-point of most multi-project scheduling methods. *Network* can choose various optimization goal or priority rule such as minimum lead time, maximum resource utilization, and minimum project slack, however, treating people as machine may not be applicable in software industry. *Critical Chain* is based on Theory of Constraint to maximize throughout of the whole system rather than load balancing or certain resource utilization. *Resource Modeling* means to assign right people right task so as to increase productivity and product quality, attaching more importance to people knowledge and experience. *Multi-agent* is intended for an adaptive and distributed decision making for dynamic requirements. Agile methods such as *Virtual Team, Core Team* and *Pair Programming* aim to deal with schedule uncertainty and knowledge sharing or component reuse, and they trust people's initiative and communication. *Exchange* is out of the consideration for collective cohesion, and also a way of cross-training, showing highly respects to people. *Multi-product* is to decrease institutionalization in mini organizations. *Classification* recognizes different types of resources need different scheduling methods. Everyone has its own consideration. We use "●" to express more emphasis on people or project individuality, "○" for more emphasis on resource utilization and "◑" between them.

4.2 Centralization

A frequently asked question about multi-project is: is it just a large project? The answer is "No". Regarding multi-project as a large virtual project and mechanically borrowing the methods for single project would lead to [29]: a vicious circle of bureaucratic management, a linear lifecycle without flexibility to respond timely to business change, and many rote technologies. Just think of the origin of PM, coordinating multiple projects does not reduce the need to integrate the functional areas of individual projects but probably makes this coordination even more important as well as more difficult [12]. Both cross-functional integration and cross-project management are necessary for effective multi-PM.

Individual PM possibly allocates resources centrally before projects start but little interference after carrying out. *Network, Critical Chain, Resource Modeling* and *Multi-product*, are basically central methods, allocating resources to "everywhere". They ignore the root why a project forms to overcome the difficulties in traditional functional organization. General speaking, relevance between projects is weaker than that within a project and project teams should be relatively stable, leaving scheduling across projects as tools dealing with uncertainty and cross-training. Some heuristic rules can be added to "decentralize" these methods. For example, *Multi-agent* [16] fixes a set of permanent agents for a group and dynamically allocates marketable agents across groups. Agile methods such as *Virtual Team, Core Team, Pair Programming* and *Exchange* are federal, scheduling autonomously by every project and adjusting at a central point such as a meeting. *Classification* has relatively high centralization (to classify the resources) and depends on concrete methods for every resource type. The federal methods may suffer from lacking a central view of multi-project for senior or top management, out of this paper scope (see [23] [50] for more).

4.3 Homogeneity

Homogeneous projects facilitate adoption of a common PM approach. Advantages are said to be [35]: a consistent reporting mechanism and thus comparable progress reports across these projects; a consistent calculating basis for resource requirements enabling identification of bottle neck and resource sharing. Most methods advocate grouping similar projects together. Of course, heterogeneity is unavoidable in practice. We assume using uniform (or tailored) method, rather than multiple methods, in a multi-project; otherwise projects should be divided into multiple "multi-project"s.

Individual PM needs no similarity between projects. Homogeneity matters little for *Exchange*, determined by the goal of cross-training. *Critical Chain* needs common resource as synchronizer. *Network*, *Resource Modeling* and *Multi-Agent* ask for common supporting tool or exchangeable data format to run (on computer). Multi-project with strongly interrelated projects, e.g. "decomposed" from a common goal, might be scheduled more centrally, like a large project. It is true in particular for *Network*. It is suggested to group projects with similar priority together, otherwise less important projects might never get scarce resources possessed by high priority projects. *Resource Modeling* and *Multi-Agent* can theoretically schedule projects sharing no resources, by assigning projects corresponding resources. Then they are the same with *Individual* PM.

Common attributes among projects, e.g. interlaced scope, common technology, and potential reusable component, also make sense for agile methods such as *Virtual Team*, *Core Team*, and *Pair Programming*. After all, the main purpose of multi-project scheduling is to share resources and their skills. *Pair Programming* is a controversial practice but useful in expert and novice cases. An expert (rare resource) can pair up with a stable project member who can serve as maintenance staff to shorten the queue time of request for expert from other projects. A new coming developer can work together with a stable project member who is familiar with the project to speed up learning curve. It can help resources shift among heterogenic projects. *Multi-product* is not a good practice in PM, but may work in relatively extreme cases, e.g. component-based development, product line, or in a mini organization. *Classification* schedules shared and unshared resources respectively.

4.4 Complexity

Individual PM can solve high complexity with managed interfaces. It is advised to decompose a mega project into several projects to decrease its risk. As well, if a multi-project is extra huge, it's better to divide it into smaller groups. *Network* intends to solve high complexity, but Resource Constrained Multi-Project Scheduling Problem, as a generalization of classical job shop scheduling problem, belongs to NP-hard optimization problems [7], and some optimization algorithms would crash for a large activity network. This makes heuristic procedures the only available means for complex problems in practice. The outcome schedule of *Network* may add price to context switch or communication, unsuitable for work with high initiating threshold. *Critical Chain* can solve high complexity from project size or amount, but may be oversimplified when involving various resources and diverse utilization rate among projects.

Resource Modeling and *Multi-Agent* can model/simulate complex resources or situations but it is even harder to schedule them by automatic algorithms. Opponents of agile methods criticize they are only applicable for small and medium-sized projects and lack scalability for large ones. Considering the relatively high complexity in multi-project environments, agile methods seem to be helpless. Experiences of *Core Team*, *Pair Programming* and *Multi-product* are mainly from small-and-medium companies, and their applicability for high complexity remains to be demonstrated. Maybe they need to be complemented by other methods. Differentiated Matrix organization, a similar form to *Virtual Team* observed in agile context, is successful in large company [12]. *Exchange* as cross-training can apply in any complexity. All of above can be balanced by *Classification*.

4.5 Uncertainty

Individual PM without scheduling resources between projects loses a coping mechanism for uncertainty, and need resource redundancy for safekeeping. *Network* needs whole or accurate information nearly impossibly available in software PM environment with high uncertainty. When projects lag behind their schedules, resources scheduled to other projects are not possible to activate. Although there are some mechanisms to deal with uncertainty in progress, e.g. project or resource buffer in *Critical Chain*, they assume the network of activities/tasks known at the start, which is less common in reality of software development. When changes occur, the networking has to be restructured and optimized again. *Resource Modeling* and *Multi-Agent* tend to model/simulate dynamic availability and capability of resources, but its scheduling is similar to *Network*. Agile methods are born to deal with uncertainty. They advocate iterative planning and scheduling. In addition, *Core Team* for example, project managers, architects and main programmers are fixed members to maintain a stable project, while others can transfer among projects as required to deal with uncertainty. *Pair Programming* can act as an aid in transferring staff across projects. A *Virtual Team* member can apportion his own time among various projects to cope with uncertainty. *Exchange* can run like *Core Team* if need. *Multi-product* can adjust time for different products. *Classification* depends on concrete methods for every category.

4.6 Executive Ability

Individual PM asks for enough even redundant resources and depends on document to communicate with related projects. It is difficulty for *Network*, *Resource Modeling* and *Multi-Agent* to model projects and resources formally, and computer-supported systems are frequently the only practical way to handle the large volume of detailed information involved [3]. They need integrative system and standard process to collect and update data. *Resource Modeling* needs extra detailed formal description and classification of people's skills and tasks requirements as well, requiring unnecessary heavy workload in small companies where a staff must play many roles. It is enough for *Critical Chain* to keep as little as one resource effectively utilized to maximize the throughput of the system[33]. This simplification is why *Critical Chain* is practicable and popular. Division of labor is clear-cut too for *Classification*. Agile methods ask for cooperation and initiative of people--in fact prerequisite of all methods. Take *Network* as an example: if a project manager can not argue for higher priority by ordinary means, he may push the project into crisis to gain priority and resources[14]. In *Virtual Team*, *Core Team*, *Pair Programming* and *Exchange*, resource transfer is usually based on negotiation in meeting and relies on people cooperation. Managers may feel hesitate to help other projects, considering a major risk that resources lent out would not come back when need [14]. And it is better to transfer between 2 iterations, except expert, to keep every iteration stable and avoid unnecessary complexity. To achieve this smoothly, processes of synchronizing the increment control points of related projects are in need [47]. *Multi-product* should also carefully plan its iteration and concentrate on only one product every time, asking for culture embracing agile. We use "●" to express more emphasis on people ability, "○" for more emphasis on process capability and "◐" between them.

5 Discussion and Conclusion

We can conclude from the aspects of *Value orientation* and *Executive ability* that, some methods emphasize on people while others on process – classical balance in software community. The methods can be roughly classified into 3 categories: heavy-weight, light-weight, and medium. Like condition of single project [28], heavy-weight methods suit for situations of high *complexity* and low *uncertainty*, and light-weight for low *complexity* and high *uncertainty*. However, multi-projects, compared to projects, face a higher level of *complexity* and *uncertainty* [36], as a result balanced methods combining advantages of the 2 types are in need. Considering the notable trend of individual software PM that traditional approaches and agile methods are coming from opposite to fusion [8], *Classification*, *Multi-agent*, *Critical Chain* and *Virtual Team* have relatively high overall performance and call for attention.

Generally, some similarity among projects is asked to facilitate efficient multi-PM. Heavy-weight methods have higher degree of *centralization* and *homogeneity* than light-weight. Research indicates autonomic management with cooperation is more efficient than central management and individual PM [2]. Federation thought shown in agile methods should be learned. The balance between stability and flexibility should adjust according to complexity, similarity, and relevancy of projects.

Due to space limitation, we do not discuss some important aspects of methods such as supporting to senior/top management and other processes. Multi-project resource allocation syndrome is not an issue in itself, rather an expression of many other, more profound, organizational problems [14]. We discuss some organization structure of multi-project but have no enough space for whole organization context (see [12] for more information). Change on organization structure is quite radical reformation. They can serve as a kind of methods but are preconditions in most cases.

Much work needs to do in finding which of the various methods fits which situations. A more elaborated matching algorithm with measurable factors that actively contributes to the *aspect* is under consideration. Case study and questionnaire need to conduct to improve and validate the framework brainstormed in this paper. After more analysis, various multi-projects situations may be clustered into several patterns to reduce the problem complexity. We also plan to take in the good points of various methods and conclude a consolidated method with more scalability.

Acknowledgments. This research is supported by the National Natural Science Foundation of China under grant No. 60573082, the National Basic Research Program (973 program) under grant No. 2007CB310802, the Hi-Tech Research and Development Program of China (863 Program) under grant No. 2006AA01Z155.

References

1. Abdel-Hamid, T.K.: The Dynamics of Software Project Staffing: A System Dynamics Based Simulation Approach. IEEE Trans. Software Engineering 15(2), 109–119 (1989)
2. Al-jibouri, S.: Effects of resource management regimes on project schedule. Int. J. Proj. Manag. 20(4), 271–277 (2002)
3. Archibald, R.D.: Managing High-Technology Programs and Projects, 3rd edn. John Wiley, Hoboken (2003)
4. Agile Alliance, http://www.agilealliance.com
5. Ash, R.C.: Activity scheduling in the dynamic, multi-project setting: choosing heuristics through deterministic simulation. In: Proc. Winter Simulation Conference, vol. 2, pp. 937–941 (1999)
6. Beck, K.: Extreme programming explained: embrace change, 2nd edn. Addison-Wesley, Reading (2005)
7. Blazewicz, J., Lenstra, J.K., Kan, A.H.G.R.: Scheduling subject to resource constraints: Classification and complexity. Discrete Applied Mathematics 5, 11–24 (1983)
8. Boehm, B., Turner, R.: Balancing Agility and Discipline: A Guide for the Perplexed. Addison-Wesley, Reading (2004)
9. Briscoe, T.D.: Virtual team members: a case study in management of multiple projects in a limited resource environment. In: PICMET 1997: Portland Int. Conf. on Management and Technology, pp. 378–382 (1997)
10. Cohn, M.: Agile Estimating and Planning. Prentice-Hall, Englewood Cliffs (2006)
11. Cooper, R.G., Edgett, S.J., Kleinschmidt, E.J.: Portfolio management: fundamental for new product success, Working paper (2006), http://www.prod-dev.com/pdf/wp12.pdf
12. Cusumano, M.A., Nobeoka, K.: Thinking beyond lean: how multi-project management is transforming product development at Toyota and other companies. The free press (1998)
13. Dean, B.V., Denzler, D.R., Watkins, J.J.: Multiproject staff scheduling with variable resource constraints. IEEE Trans. Engineering Management 39(1), 59–72 (1992)
14. Engwall, M., Jerbrant, A.: The resource allocation syndrome: the prime challenge of multi-project management. Int. J. Proj. Manag. 21, 403–409 (2003)
15. Evaristo, R., van Fenema, P.C.: A typology of project management: emergence and evolution of new forms. Int. J. Proj. Manag. 17(5), 275–281 (1999)
16. Fatima, S.S.: TRACE-An Adaptive Organizational Policy for MAS. In: 11th Int. Workshop on Database and Expert Systems Applications (DEXA 2000), p. 722 (2000)
17. Ferns, D.C.: Developments in programme management. Int. J. Proj. Manag. 9(3), 148–156 (1991)
18. Gray, R.J.: Alternative approaches to programme management. Int. J. Proj. Manag. 15(1), 5–9 (1998)
19. Goncalves, J.F., Mendes, J.J.M., Resende, M.G.C.: A Genetic Algorithm for the Resource Constrained Multi-Project Scheduling Problem, AT&T Labs Techniccal Report TD-668LM4 (2004)
20. Hendricks, M.H.A., Voeten, B., Kroep, L.H.: Human Resource Allocation in a Multiproject Research and Development Environment. Int. J. Proj. Manag. (1999)
21. Herroelen, W., Leus, R.: Project scheduling under uncertainty: survey and research potentials. European Journal of Operational Research 165, 289–306 (2005)
22. Hodgkins, P., Luke, H.: Agile Program Management: Lessons Learned from the VeriSign Managed Security Services Team. In: AGILE 2007, pp. 194–199 (2007)

23. Karlstrom, D., Runeson, P.: Combining Agile Methods with Stage-Gate Project Management. IEEE Software 22(3), 43–49 (2005)
24. Lacey, M.: Adventures in Promiscuous Pairing: Seeking Beginner's Mind. In: AGILE 2006 (2006)
25. Lee, B., Miller, J.: Multi-project software engineering analysis using systems thinking. Software Process Improvement and Practice 9, 173–214 (2004)
26. Levy, N., Globerson, S.: Improving multiproject management by using a queuing theory approach. Project Management Journal (2000)
27. Li, J., Liu, W.: An agent-based system for multi-project planning and scheduling. In: IEEE Int. Conf. Mechatronics and Automation, vol. 2, pp. 659–664 (2005)
28. Little, T.: Context-adaptive agility: managing complexity and uncertainty. IEEE Software (2005)
29. Lycett, M., Rassau, A., Danson, J.: Programme Management: a critical review. Int. J. Proj. Manag. 22, 289–299 (2004)
30. Nocks, J.: Multiple Simultaneous Projects with One eXtreme Programming Team. In: AGILE 2006, pp. 170–174 (2006)
31. Palmer, S.R., Felsing, J.M.: A Practical Guide to Feature-Driven Development. Pearson Education, London (2002)
32. Patanakul, P., Milosevic, D., Anderson, T.: Criteria for project assignments in multiple-project environments. In: Proceedings of the 37th Annual Hawaii Int. Conf. on System Sciences, p. 10 (2004)
33. Patrick, F.S.: Program Management - Turning Many Projects into Few Priorities with Theory of Constraints. In: Proceedings of the Project Management Institute Annual Seminars and Symposium (1999)
34. Payne, H.: Management of multiple simultaneous projects: a state-of-the-art review. Int. J. Proj. Manag. 13(3), 163–168 (1995)
35. Payne, J.H., Turner, J.R.: Company-wide project management: the planning and control of programmes of projects of different type. Int J Proj Manag 17(1), 55–59 (1998)
36. Pellegrini, S.: Programme Management: organising project based change. Int. J. Proj. Manag. 15(3), 141–149 (1997)
37. PMI: A guide to the project management body of knowledge (PMBOK® Guide), 3rd edn. Project Management Institute (2004)
38. PMI: Organizational project management maturity model (OPM3™) knowledge foundation. Project Management Institute (2003)
39. PMI: The standard for program management. Project Management Institute (2006)
40. Podorozhny, R., et al.: Modeling Resources for Activity Coordination and Scheduling. In: 3rd Int Conf on Coordination Models and Languages (April 1999)
41. Reis, C.A.L., Reis, R.Q., Schlebbe, H., Nunes, D.J.: A policy-based resource instantiation mechanism to automate software process management. In: SEKE (2002)
42. Reyck, B.D., et al.: The impact of project portfolio management on information technology projects. Int. J. Proj. Manag. 23, 524–537 (2005)
43. Scheinberg, M., Stretton, A.: Multiproject planning: tuning portfolio indices. Int. J. Proj. Manag. 12(2), 107–114 (1994)
44. Schwaber, K., Beedle, M.: Agile Software Development with Scrum. Prentice-Hall, Englewood Cliffs (2001)
45. Steyn, H.: Project management applications of the theory of constraints beyond critical chain scheduling. Int. J. Proj. Manag. 20(1), 75–80 (2002)
46. Rodney, T.J.: The Handbook of Project-Based Management. McGraw-Hill, New York (1992)

47. Vähäniitty, J., Rautiainen, K.: Towards an Approach for Managing the Development Port-folio in Small Product-Oriented Software Companies. In: Proceedings of the 38th Hawaii Int. Conf. on System Sciences (2005)
48. Vaziri, K., Nozick, L.K., Turnquist, M.A.: Resource allocation and planning for program management. In: Proceedings of the Winter Simulation Conference, vol. 9 (2005)
49. Vereecke, A., et al.: A classification of development programmes and its consequences for programme management. Int. J. Operations & Prodction Manage 23(10), 1279–1290 (2003)
50. Wallin, C., Ekdahl, F., Larsson, S.: Integrating Business and Software Development Mod-els. IEEE Software (2002)
51. XBreed,
http://www.agilealliance.com/resources/roadmap/xbreed/xbreed_aspect
52. Yahoo! Group of extreme programming, scrum and agile project management,
http://tech.groups.yahoo.com/group/extremeprogramming/~/scrumdevelopment/~/agileprojectmanagement/
53. Zhao, X., Chan, K., Li, M.: Applying agent technology to software process modeling and process-centered software engineering environment. In: SAC, pp. 1529–1533 (2005)

Project Assets Ontology (PAO) to Support Gap Analysis for Organization Process Improvement Based on CMMI v.1.2

Suwanit Rungratri[1] and Sasiporn Usanavasin[2]

[1] Ph.D.in Information Technology Program, Graduate School,
Sripatum University, Bangkok, Thailand
suwanit_r@hotmail.com
[2] Master of Science Program in Software Engineering, Graduate School,
Sripatum University, Bangkok, Thailand
sasiporn.us@spu.ac.th

Abstract. In this paper, we introduce an ontology called *Project Assets Ontology (PAO)* that describe concepts of CMMI Maturity and Capability levels, Generic and Specific Goals, Generic and Specific Practices including concepts of Typical Work Products (an organization's project assets) of 22 Process Areas that may be produced in a software development project based on CMMI v.1.2 model. This ontology can be used to enable a CMMI Maturity/Capability assessment tool for automatic generation of metadata description that describe an organization's project work products. With the support of PAO and the generated metadata descriptions, the tool can automatically perform a preliminary CMMI gap analysis, which can lead to time and cost reductions in assessing the CMMI Maturity/Capability level of the organization.

Keywords: CMMI, Ontology, Process Improvement, Gap Analysis, Maturity Level Assessment.

1 Introduction

Due to the high competition in software industry in both global and local markets, many organizations try to gain competitive advantage over their competitors by focusing on product quality improvement, cost reduction and schedule acceleration. To achieve the objectives, those organizations have recently given their interests and efforts toward improving their organizational process. CMMI v.1.2 model [1] has become one of the most effective and internationally recognized as a guideline for software process improvement [2]. Having a CMMI certified is now becoming an essential requirement that clients are looking for when they want to outsource their work or assign a software development project to a software house. However, for any software house to be certified by CMMI is not easy and it is costly because it involves a number of changes in many processes in the organization. Moreover, several documents and procedures have to be reorganized and generated to provide evidence that the organization has actually

Q. Wang, D. Pfahl, and D.M. Raffo (Eds.): ICSP 2008, LNCS 5007, pp. 76–87, 2008.
© Springer-Verlag Berlin Heidelberg 2008

performed a number of practices and achieved goals that comply with CMMI model during appraisal process.

Gap analysis is an important initial step for an organization process improvement. The gap analysis helps the organization to recognize its current maturity/capability level by finding the differences between its current practices and the guidance given in CMMI model. In other words, the gap analysis tells how well the organization's current practices aligned with the specific practices recommended by CMMI for each of 22 process areas (PAs). This is usually when a CMMI consultant team comes in to help locating the gaps and to assist the organization to create the process improvement action plan once the gaps are found. Performing gap analysis process is time-consuming as it requires a consultant to manually reviews a number of the project assets (work products such as policies, plans and other documents that were produced in software development projects), conduct several meetings as well as interview the project members in order to recognize what practices already aligned with the CMMI recommendations and what practices are missing.

In this paper, we introduce an ontology called *Project Assets Ontology* (PAO) and a *CMMI v.1.2 based Gap Analysis Assistant Framework* (CMMI-GAAF) that can be used to support an organization and a CMMI consultant for conducting a gap analysis process more effectively. PAO describes concepts of assets or work products of a software development project that conform to typical work products that can be referred as evidences for all CMMI practices and goals. In the CMMI-GAAF, the organization's project assets will be analyzed and a metadata description for each project asset will be generated using PAO. The generated metadata descriptions will be processed further in order to identify gaps between the organization's current practices and CMMI specific practices. The findings will be shown in a representation of a *Practice Implementation Indicator Description* (PIID) sheet [3], which can be used as a preliminary assessment tool for the organization's Maturity/Capability assessment/appraisal.

This paper is organized as follows. Section 2 explains the structure of CMMI v.1.2 model and Section 3 discusses some of the related works. Our proposed PAO and its usage for CMMI gap analysis are introduced in section 4 and 5, respectively. Section 6 discusses concluding remarks and future works.

2   CMMI v.1.2 Model

Capability Maturity Model Integration for Development version 1.2 [4] was developed by Software Engineering Institute (SEI) at Carnegie-Mellon University. It consists of best practices that address development and maintenance activities applied to products and services in many industries including aerospace, banking, computer hardware, software, defense, automobile manufacturing, and telecommunications [10]. Although, in this paper, we focus on the software industry but the proposed idea and framework can also be applied for other industries that exploit CMMI for products and services development.

Table 1. Five Maturity Levels defined in CMMI v.1.2

Level	Process Areas	Acronym
5 Optimizing	Organizational Innovation and Deployment	OID
	Causal Analysis and Resolution	CAR
4 Quantitatively Managed	Organizational Process Performance	OPP
	Quantitative Project Management	QPM
3 Defined	Requirements Development	RD
	Technical Solution	TS
	Product Integration	PI
	Verification	VER
	Validation	VAL
	Organizational Process Focus	OPF
	Organizational Process Definition	OPD
	Organizational Training	OT
	Integrated Project Management for IPPD	IPM+IPPD
	Risk Management	RSKM
	Decision Analysis and Resolution	DAR
2 Managed	Requirement Management	REQM
	Project Planning	PP
	Project Monitoring and Control	PMC
	Supplier Agreement Management	SAM
	Measurement and Analysis	MA
	Process and Product Quality Assurance	PPQA
	Configuration Management	CM
1 Initial		

CMMI v.1.2 recommends best practices for 22 process areas (PAs) and provides two representations in terms of capability and maturity levels: *continuous representation* and *staged representation*. The *continuous representation* offers maximum flexibility when using a CMMI model for process improvement and it uses the term "capability levels" that enables organizations to incrementally improve processes corresponding to an individual process area selected by organization [4]. In this representation, the organization may choose to improve the performance of a single process area, or it can work on several process areas that are closely aligned to the organization's business objectives. The *staged representation* offers a systematic, structured way to approach model-based process improvement one stage at a time. [6]. In this representation, the 22 PAs are organized into five "maturity levels" as shown in **Table 1**. The staged representation prescribes an order for implementing process areas according to Maturity levels, which define the improvement path for an organization from the initial level to the optimizing level. Achieving each Maturity level ensures that an adequate improvement foundation has been laid for the next Maturity level and allows for lasting, incremental improvement.

In CMMI v.1.2, each PA is comprised of three components, which are *required components* (represented in rounded rectangle), *expected components* (represented in diamond) and *informative components* (represented in oval) as shown in **Fig.1**.

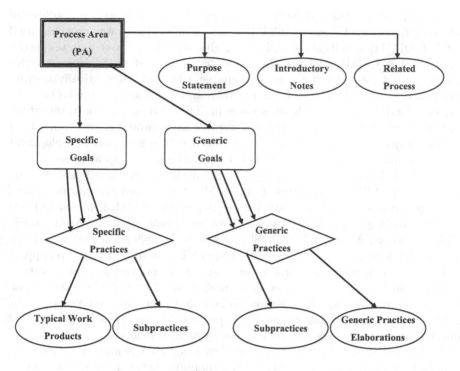

Fig. 1. CMMI v.1.2 Model Components [10]

The *required components* describe what an organization *must achieve* to satisfy a process area. This achievement must be visibly implemented in an organization's processes. The required components in CMMI are the specific and generic goals. Goal satisfaction is used in appraisals as the basis for deciding whether a process area has been achieved and satisfied. The *expected components* describe what an organization *may implement* to achieve a required component. These components refer to the specific and generic practices. These practices are the essential guidance for any organizations who wish to implement process improvement or preform CMMI appraisals. Finally, the *informative components* provide details that help organizations to get started in thinking about how to achieve the required and expected components. Subpractices, typical work products, amplifications, generic practice elaborations, goal and practice titles, goal and practice notes, and references are examples of informative model components.

To support a gap analysis process, our PAO cover concepts of the CMMI required components (generic and specific goals), the expected components (generic and specific practices), and the informative components (typical work products).

3   Related Works

Some of the previous studies had introduced ontologies and tools for supporting an organizational maturity level assessment/appraisal based on CMMI models.

One of them is Soydan and Kokar's work [6]. They developed an ontology of the capability maturity model, CMMI v.1.1. This ontology was created based on OWL-DL [11] specification and it contains 309 classes and four properties that represent CMMI v.1.1 recommended practices and goals. However, this ontology is not sufficient if we want to enable a tool to automatically identify what practices that already conform to CMMI and which are missing for the sake of an organization's maturity level assessment. Therefore, in our study, we extend their ontology by including concepts of typical work products and concepts of possible project assets, which may be produced within a software development project, in order to enable a tool to perform an automatic gap analysis.

Lee, Wang, Chen and Hsu [7] proposed an ontology-based intelligent decision support agent (OIDSA) for supporting CMMI *Project Monitoring and Control (PCM)* process area. In their study, they only focused on CMMI Maturity Level 2 so their ontology only covers seven process areas referenced in CMMI model.

The Appraisal Assistant Beta 3 [8] is a software application that was developed by the Software Quality Institute, Griffith University, in order to support the CMMI assessment and appraisal processes. This tool can generate a variety of reports such as appraisal/assessment findings and strength/weakness summaries of an organization. For the tool to be able to generate those reports, the appraisers have to manually review many project documents and input a lot of information regarding those assets into the system, which is time-consuming.

The CMMiPal 1.0 is a tool that was developed by Chemututi Consultants [9] It provides a function to facilitate the mapping between an organization's processes and CMMI elements that are referenced in Maturity Level 1 to Level 3. Similarly to the work in [8], the appraisers have to manually fulfill the necessary information regarding the organization's goals, practices and work products into the system in order for the system to generate the reports for gap analysis.

In this paper, we introduce an ontology called *Project Assets Ontology (PAO)* that describe concepts of CMMI Maturity and Capability levels, generic and specific goals, generic and specific practices of the 22 process areas including concepts of typical work products and project assets that may be produced in a software development project based on the CMMI v.1.2. This ontology can be used to support a tool for an automatic generation of project assets' metadata descriptions and enabling the tool to automatically perform a preliminary gap analysis for an organization based on CMMI Maturity/Capability assessment process, which can lead to time and cost reductions.

4   Project Assets Ontology(PAO)

An ontology is a representation of a set of concepts within a domain and the relationships between those concepts. It is used to reason about the properties of that domain, and may be used to define the domain.[5] PAO is an ontology that represents a set of possible assets or work products that may be produced within a software development project. The concepts of assets in PAO were created based on the concepts of typical work products for all practices and goals in 22

PAs that are referenced in CMMI v.1.2 model. The main intended use of PAO is to support the analysis process of a software project's asset as well as to support the synthesis process of a metadata description that describes the asset. This metadata document will be further processed by our tool called CMMI-GAAF in order to identify which of the organization's practices already aligned with CMMI practices and goals based on the visible implementation (evidence) of the project's asset. With the use of PAO and the supporting framework, a CMMI consultant can use the tool to perform a preliminary gap analysis automatically. Moreover, the organization can also use the tool to conduct self-evaluation of its Maturity or Capability level as a starting point for the organization process improvement.

PAO is built as an extension to the CMMI Ontology [6] based on OWL specification [11]. It consists of 601 classes (173 classes of specific practices and 428 classes of typical work products), five objects properties representing different relationships (i.e., *attains*, *satisfies*, *achieves* , *referTo*, *producedBy*) between those classes, and a number of data properties that defined a set of possible assets or evidences of information that can refer to each typical work product referenced in CMMI v.1.2. **Fig.2** shows a portion of the logical abstraction of our PAO.

In **Fig.2**, a set of possible project assets such as a *Project_Plan*, *Schedule* and *Task_Dependency* can be considered as parts of *Task_Description*, which can also be referred to as one of the *Typical_Work_Products* that is produced

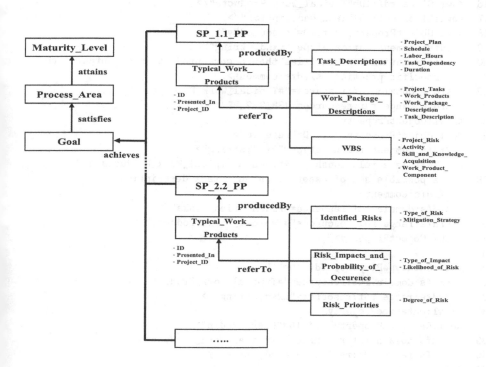

Fig. 2. A Portion of Project Assets Ontology (PAO)

by performing a specific practice *SP_1.1* in *Project Planning* (*PP*). Similarly, a document that contains information about type of risks and strategy for handling the risks can be considered as *Identified_Risks*, which can also be considered as evidence of the *Typical_Work_Products* that is produced by the specific practice *SP_2.2_PP*. The following OWL description shows a partial description of PAO based on Fig.2.

```
1  <?xml version="1.0"?>
2      All required Name Space declaration go here.
3  <owl:Class rdf:ID="SP_1.1_PP">
4   <rdfs:comment rdf:datatype="http://www.w3.org/2001/XMLSchema#string">
5      Specific Practice 1.1 for CMMI Project Planning </rdfs:comment>
6  <owl:equivalentClass
7    rdf:resource="&CMMI_Ont/#SP_1.1_Estimate_the_Scope_of_the_Project"/>
8  </owl:Class>
9  ...
10  <owl:Class rdf:ID="SP_2.2_PP">
11  <rdfs:comment rdf:datatype="http://www.w3.org/2001/XMLSchema#string">
12      Specific Practice 2.2 CMMI Project Planning </rdfs:comment>
13   <owl:equivalentClass
14     rdf:resource="&CMMI_Ont/#SP_2.2_Identify_Project_Risks"/>
15  </owl:Class>
16  <owl:Class rdf:ID="Typical_Work_Products"/>
17  <owl:Class rdf:ID="Task_Description"/>
18  <owl:ObjectProperty rdf:ID="producedBy">
19   <rdfs:comment rdf:datatype="&xsd;string">
20   This relationship specifies that a work product is an output from a
21      specific practice. </rdfs:comment>
22    <rdfs:domain rdf:resource="#Typical_Work_Products "/>
23    <rdfs:range rdf:resource="#SP_2.2_PP"/>
24  </owl:ObjectProperty>
25  <owl:ObjectProperty rdf:ID="referTo">
26    <rdfs:comment rdf:datatype="&xsd;string">
27     This is a relationship between a Typical_Work_Products and
28     a possible set of assets such as a task description.
29    </rdfs:comment>
30    <rdfs:domain rdf:resource="#Identified_Risks"/>
31    <rdfs:range rdf:resource="#Typical_Work_Products"/>
32  </owl:ObjectProperty>
33  ...
34  <owl:DatatypeProperty rdf:ID="ID">
35    <rdfs:domain rdf:resource="#Typical_Work_Products"/>
36    <rdfs:range rdf:resource="&xsd;string"/>
37  </owl:DatatypeProperty>
38  <owl:DatatypeProperty rdf:ID="PresentedIn">
39    <rdfs:domain rdf:resource="#Typical_Work_Products"/>
40    <rdfs:range rdf:resource="&xsd;string"/>
41  </owl:DatatypeProperty>
42  <owl:DatatypeProperty rdf:ID="Project_ID">
```

```
43    <rdfs:domain rdf:resource="#Typical_Work_Products"/>
44    <rdfs:range rdf:resource="&xsd;string"/>
45  </owl:DatatypeProperty>
46  <owl:DatatypeProperty rdf:ID="Type_of_Risk">
47    <rdfs:domain rdf:resource="#Identified_Risks"/>
48    <rdfs:range rdf:resource="&xsd;string"/>
49  </owl:DatatypeProperty>
50  <owl:DatatypeProperty rdf:ID="Mitigation_Strategy">
51    <rdfs:domain rdf:resource="#Identified_Risks"/>
52    <rdfs:range rdf:resource="&xsd;string"/>
53  </owl:DatatypeProperty>
54  ...
```

5 PAO for CMMI Gap Analysis

Most of the organizations that wish to acquire CMMI certifications have to go through a gap analysis process as an initial requirement for their maturity level assessment before they can decide on what strategy and plan are needed to achieve their process improvement objectives. In this section, we will illustrate how PAO can be used to enable a tool to perform an automatic gap analysis that will reduce time and cost for the organization.

Fig.3 shows our ongoing work called *CMMI v.1.2 based Gap Analysis Assistant Framework (CMMI-GAAF)* that we have been implementing and with the

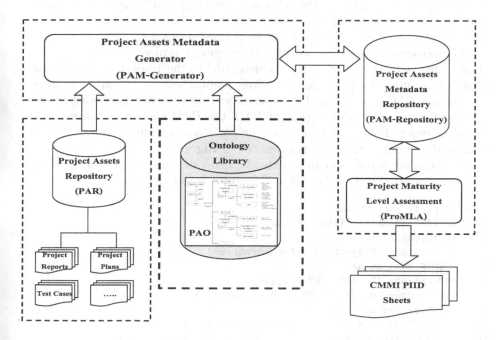

Fig. 3. CMMI v.1.2 based Gap Analysis Assistant Framework (CMMI-GAAF)

Initial Project Risk Assessment

Risk	Risk Level L/M/H	Likelihood of Event	Mitigation Strategy
Project Size			
Person Hours	H: Over 20,000	Certainty	Assigned Project Manager, engaged consultant, comprehensive project management approach and communications plan
Estimated Project Schedule	H: Over 12 months	Certainty	Created comprehensive project timeline with frequent baseline reviews
Team Size at Peak	H: Over 15 members	Certainty	Comprehensive communications plan, frequent meetings, tight project management oversight
Number of Interfaces to Existing Systems Affected	H: Over 3	Certainty	Develop interface control document immediately
Project Definition			
Narrow Knowledge Level of Users	M: Knowledgeable of user area only	Likely	Assigned Project Manager(s) to assess global implications
Available documentation clouds establishment of baseline	M: More than 75% complete/current	Likely	Balance of information to be gathered by consultant

Fig. 4. A Portion of a Project Planning document (a Sample Project Asset)

support of PAO, we will introduce this work as an automatic tool for gap analysis process. The framework consists of five components, which are *1) Project Assets Repository (PAR), 2) Project Assets Ontology (PAO), 3) Project Assets Metadata Generator (PAM-Generator), 4) Project Assets Metadata Repository (PAM-Repository), and 5) Project Maturity Level Assessment (ProMLA).*

This framework allows the software development project members to store all documents (assets) that were produced within the project or used in the project (e.g., project reports, project plans, requirement documents, test cases, etc.) in the *PAR*. These stored documents will be read and processed by the *PAM-Generator*. With the support of *PAO*, the *PAM-Generator* can generate metadata descriptions of those assets. The portion of a sample asset, a Project Planing document in this case, is presented in **Fig.4**

The following description illustrates the generated metadata description of the sample asset (Fig.4) by the PAM-Generator based on PAO.

```
1  <WP:Typical_Work_Product >
2     <WP:ID> Identify_Risks </WP:ID>
3     <WP:PresentedIn>
4          Initial Project Risk Assessment.doc
5     </WP:PresentedIn>
6     <WP:Project_ID> ABC </WP:Project_ID>
7     <WP:producedBy> SP_2.2_PP </WP:producedBy>
8     <WP:Risk_Assessment>
9        <WP:Type_of_Risk>Person_Hours</WP:Type_of_Risk>
10       <WP:Degree_of_Risk>Over 20,000</ WP:Degree_of_Risk>
11       <WP:Likelihood_of_Risk>Certainty</ WP:Likelihood_of_Risk>
```

```
12       <WP:Mitigation_Strategy> Assigned Project Manager,
13             engaged 6 consultant, comprehensive project management
14       </WP:Mitigation_Strategy>
15    </WP:Risk_Assessment >
16    <WP:Risk_Assessment>
17       <WP:Type_of_Risk> Estimated Project Schedule </WP:Type_of_Risk>
18       <WP:Degree_of_Risk> Over 12 months </ WP:Degree_of_Risk>
19       <WP:Likelihood_of_Risk> Certainty </WP:Likelihood_of_Risk>
20       <WP:Mitigation_Strategy> Created comprehensive project
21             timeline with frequent baseline reviews
22       </WP:Mitigation_Strategy>
23    </WP:Risk_Assessment>
24    ...
25 </WP:Typical_Work_Products>
```

Maturity Level	PA	SG1							SG2							SG3				
		SP1.1	SP1.2	SP1.3	SP1.4	SP1.5	SP1.6	SP1.7	SP2.1	SP2.2	SP2.3	SP2.4	SP2.5	SP2.6	SP2.7	SP3.1	SP3.2	SP3.3	SP3.4	SP3.5
5	OID	NA	NA	NA	NA				NA	NA	NA									
	CAR	NA	NA						NA	NA	NA									
4	OPP	NA	NA	NA	NA	NA														
	QPM	NA	NA	NA	NA				NA	NA	NA	NA								
3	RD	S	S						S	S	NA					S	S	NA	NA	NA
	TS	S	S						S	S	S	S				S	S			
	PI	S	S	S					S	S						S	NA	NA	NA	
	VER	S	S	S					S	NA	NA					S	S			
	VAL	S	S	S					NA	NA										
	OPF	NA	S	S					S	S						S	S	NA	NA	
	OPD+IPPD	NA	S	S	S	S	S		S	NA	NA									
	OT	S	S	NA	S				S	S	NA									
	IPM+IPPD	S	S	S	S	S	S		S	NA	NA					S	NA	NA	NA	NA
	RSKM	S	S	S					S	NA						NA	NA	NA		
	DAR	S	NA	NA	S	S	S													
2	REQM	S	S	S	S	S														
	PP	S	S	S	S				NA	S	NA	S	S	NA	S	S	S	NA		
	PMC	S	S	S	NA	NA	NA	NA	S	S	NA									
	SAM	S	S	S					S	S	S	NA	NA							
	MA	S	S	NA	NA				NA	S	S	S								
	PPQA	S	NA						S	S										
	CM	S	S	NA					S	S						NA	NA			

PA: Process Area, SG: Specific Goal, SP: Specific Practice, S: Satisfied, NA: Not Available

Fig. 5. Example of a resulting PIID Sheet

All of the generated metadata documents will be stored in *PAM-Repository* and will later be processed by the *ProMLA* for identifying the list of CMMI practices and goals that the organization may already performed and achieved. In addition, a list of absent practices and a list of documents that must be made will also be specified. The *ProMLA* will generate the findings in a form of a *Practice Implementation Indicator Description* (PIID sheet) [3] that provides a summary of the organization's current Maturity level, as shown in **Fig.5**.

Without PAO, the organization and the consultants may have to spend a great deal of time to manually dig into hundreds of documents for reviews in order to discover the gaps between the organization's current practices and the CMMI recommendations.

With the use of PAO and the generated metadata descriptions, we can reduce some of manual work by exploiting the automated tool to analyze the available project documents and to identify and generate the preliminary gap reports, which we expect that it would result in time and cost reductions.

6   Concluding Remarks and Future Work

In this paper, we introduce our ontology called *Project Assets Ontology* (*PAO*) that describe the concepts of CMMI Maturity levels, generic and specific goals, generic and specific practices of 22 process areas including the concepts of typical work products and a set of possible assets that may be produced in a software development project based on the CMMI v.1.2 model. We also introduce our ongoing work called *CMMI v.1.2 based Gap Analysis Assistant Framework* (*CMMI-GAAF*) with an intention to illustrate how PAO can be applied in order to support an organization to conduct a gap analysis process more effectively to assess its Maturity level.

Without PAO and the supporting tool, an organization has to put a lot of effort in term of time and money for examining and reviewing a number of documents in order to discover the gaps between the organization's current practices and the CMMI recommendations. With the use of PAO and the metadata descriptions of the project assets, the tool can automatically indicate some of the existing gaps, which can help the organization to reduce time and cost consumptions of its gap analysis process.

For our future work, we attempt to complete the implementation of our framework, *CMMI-GAAF*. In addition, we intend to perform a number of experiments based on real projects' work products and also evaluate our framework based on the accuracy of the gap analysis findings.

References

1. Kulpa, K., Johnson, A.: Interpreting the CMMI: A Process Improvement Approach. Taylor & Francis, Abington (2003)
2. Loon, H.: Process Assessment and ISO/IEC 15504: A Reference Book. Springer, Heidelberg (2004)
3. Berauer, R.: The Use of Tailored Practice Implementation indicators for Process Definition and Assessment Preparation. In: National Defense Industrial Association 3rd Annual CMMI Technology Conference and User Group Denver, Colorado (2003)
4. CMMI Product Team: CMMI for Development Version 1.2: Improvement Processes for Better Products. Carnegie Mellon. Software Engineering Institute, USA (2006)
5. Ontology, http://en.wikipedia.org/wiki/Ontology
6. Soydan, G., Kokar, M.: An OWL Ontology for Representing the CMMI-SW Model. In: International Workshop on Semantic Web Enabled Software Engineering (SWESE 2006), USA (2006)
7. Lee, C., Wang, M., Cheng, J., Hsu, C.: Ontology-based Intelligent Decision Support Agent for CMMI Project Monitoring and Control. In: Fuzzy Information Processing Society (NAFIPS 2006), IEEE Press, Canada (2006)

8. Software Quality Institute, Griffith University: The Appraisal Assistant Beta 3, http://www.sqi.gu.edu.au/AppraisalAssistant/about.html
9. Chemuturi Consultants: CMMiPal 1.0: CMMiPal Description, http://www.softpedia.com/get/Others/Finances-Business/CMMiPal.shtml
10. Chrissis, M., Konrad, M., Shrum, S.: CMMI:Guidelines for Process Integration and Product Improvement. Addison-Wesley, New York (2007)
11. The World Wide Web Consortium (W3C): Web Ontology Language (OWL), http://www.w3.org/2004/OWL

Towards Individualized Requirements Specification Evolution for Networked Software Based on Aspect

Zaiwen Feng, Keqing He, Yutao Ma, Jian Wang, and Ping Gong

State Key Lab of Software Engineering,
Wuhan University
430072 Wuhan City, Hubei Province, China
fengzaiwen@sina.com

Abstract. Networked software is a kind of Internet-based online complex software system produced through interaction and cooperation between networks and users who act as both consumer and producer of the system composed of web services. To meet a mass of individualized requirements, specifications for common requirements of the domain need to modify and evolve. Aiming at the concern, we propose a 3-step process of requirements evolution modeling of networked software. Focusing on the first step, the paper analyzes inducements for individualized requirements evolution, proposes a meta-model to describe the evolutionary requirements specification of networked software based on aspects, and presents a case study to demonstrate the usage of our approach. Finally a process for implementing the individualized requirements evolution is proposed. So it is helpful to guide the modeling for evolutionary requirements specifications and implement individualized requirements from common specifications.

Keywords: requirements specification, evolution, OWL-S, aspect.

1 Introduction

Before developing a software production, we should make sure what users want to do. The purpose of software requirements engineering is to define problems which the software will solve [4]. The final artifact of requirements engineering is software requirements specification that explicitly defines users' requirements. The general process of software requirements engineering is composed of requirements eliciting, analyzing, modeling, checking and evolution. Requirements evolution concerns how to reflect user's evolutionary requirements into primitive requirements specification.

Software paradigm has changed with the born of Service-Oriented Architecture after 2000. For the new paradigm, software artifacts can be aggregated by software resources on Internet. Based on the background, we propose *Networked Software* (NS below) that is a complex system of which topology structure and activity can be evolutionary dynamically [1] [13]. To solve the problem of modeling for requirements of the NS, some researchers have been done on meta-model for requirements, language for acquiring requirements, requirements analysis of complex system, dynamic composition of requirements and methodology for modeling requirements evolution [4]. To describe the individualized and diversiform requirements for user of the NS, the

Q. Wang, D. Pfahl, and D.M. Raffo (Eds.): ICSP 2008, LNCS 5007, pp. 88–99, 2008.
© Springer-Verlag Berlin Heidelberg 2008

meta-models of domain requirements modeling framework which support context-awareness named *RGPS* is proposed [5]. In addition, to capture the individualized and diversiform requirements in the mode of intercommunication between users and network which is specific for the NS, a service-oriented requirements language named *SORL* is proposed [12]. In the requirements engineering of NS, *common domain requirements specifications* are stored in domain knowledge repository. Under the support of RGPS, SORL and domain requirements specification, the individualized requirements of the user of the NS can be elicited dynamically, and matched by domain requirements specification which is represented in the form of *domain process model* described by OWL-S in domain knowledge repository finally.

But sometimes the domain requirements specification stored in domain knowledge repository probably cannot fulfill the individualized requirements for the user of the NS completely. For example, the common domain requirements specification for *arrange trip for traveler* only provides the user three traffic patterns: by train, by air or by car. If someone plans to travel by ship, his requirements cannot be fulfilled by common domain requirements specification. In the scenario similar to the example, we should design a method to make the common domain requirements specification evolved to fulfill the user's individualized requirements. To address this problem, we import *aspect* to support modeling for the evolutionary requirements, and design the corresponding process that implements the evolution of common domain requirements specifications.

One of our contributions is proposing OWL-S^A and its meta-model that can describes the evolutionary requirements, the other is designing the process supports individualized requirements evolution. The outline of the paper is arranged as follows: In Section 2, we introduce RGPS and the requirements evolution stages based on it. The catalogue of inducements for individualized requirements evolution is analyzed in Section 3. In Section 4 we propose the meta-model and corresponding definitions of OWL-S^A. In Section 5 the process for implementing the individualized requirements evolution is proposed. In Section 6, related work is reported. Finally, in section7, we conclude the paper and outline our future work.

2 Requirements Evolution Modeling of NS

2.1 RGPS: Meta-models of Domain Modeling Framework for NS

In traditional software engineering, requirements specification is the normal document which is used to describe the requirements for the user of the software. Several requirements modeling methodology have been proposed in traditional software requirements engineering, such as: Role-oriented requirements modeling methodology, as well as Goal-oriented, Process-oriented and Service-oriented requirements modeling methodology [14-16]. The requirements modeling methodologies and the corresponding established requirements specifications are different from one another. It is necessary to propose universal requirements modeling language and methodology to instruct somebody to edit requirements specification. After studying various requirements modeling methodology, meta-models which describe the requirements specification models from each viewpoints have been proposed. That is RGPS: meta-models of domain modeling framework for NS [4][5]. RGPS is composed of four meta-models:

- Role Meta-Model: describes the roles of the users of NS, actors and the contexts which actors are in, intercourse between different roles, and the business rules which intercourse must abide by.
- Goal Meta-Model: describes the requirements goals of the user, including functional and non-functional goal, which can be decomposed to operational goal further. An operational goal can be realized by business process. The decomposition of goal is not completed until the lowest goals are all operational goals.
- Process Meta-Model: describes the business process, including functional description such as IOPE (input, output, precondition and effect), and non-functional description such as Qos expectation and individualized business context expectation. A process can realize functional goal and promote the realization of non-functional goal.
- Service Meta-Model: describes the solution based on service resource, including functional and non-functional attributes. A service solution realizes the business process.

The domain expert defines a number of domain requirements specifications stored in domain knowledge repository in each lay of RGPS, which correspond to the requirements of different users group of the NS. In fact, it is the application of *mass-customization*. In Process layer, a great deal of domain requirements specifications represented as domain process model are defined. Requirements of the user are elicited, analyzed, which is finally matched to common domain requirements specifications described by process model.

2.2 Requirements Evolution Modeling Based on RGPS

As described above, the domain requirements specification represented as domain process model is custom-made for a user group. But actually the user requirements is always individualized, which is not fulfilled by common solution. In traditional software engineering, the software capability may grow as the user of software claims more requirements. As a new software paradigm, NS can make the user feel that he is producing a software system himself through intercommunication between user and network. In fact, the important feather of NS is self-evolution capability. That is to say, NS can continually absorb new common user's requirements from the network, extend or integrate the old domain requirements specifications to the greater ones, and form the universal domain requirements specification which can fulfill almost all the users of the domain finally. Generally speaking, the requirements evolution modeling based on RGPS is divided to the following three stages [4]: (1) Weaving the individualized requirements specification into the domain requirements specification, the requirements specification fulfilling the individualized requirements case is set up. (2) Aggregation. The requirements specification from different roles and different goals are aggregated to several classes. The specifications in each class are integrated. The universal domain requirements specification is set up. (3) Optimization. The universal domain requirements specification is optimized according to complex network environment and the current context.

The corresponding content in stage one of requirements evolution modeling is proposed in the paper below.

3 Inducement for Individualized Requirements Evolution

The inducement leading to the evolution of domain process model includes three points: (1) Additional functional requirements: Common domain process model cannot fulfill the individualized user's functional requirements. For example, the domain process model: *constructing* does not comprise atomic process: *supervising*. If the user claims that the whole constructing process can be supervised by the third party, the process model should be evolved. (2)Additional business context requirements: one or some processes in process model are put different business context expectation. For example, there is a process model named *plan the travel abroad* which comprises an atomic process: *arrange the travelling routine*. Now the traveler hopes specially that the arranged travelling routine consumes no more than 7 days. Thus the process model needs evolving. (3) Additional non-functional requirements. For example, there is another atomic process named *pay for the travel* in the process model *plan the travel abroad*. The traveler hopes higher security in the process of paying for the travel. Thus the process model needs to be evolved.

4 Description Model for Evolutionary Requirements Specification

If the common domain requirements specification is not enough to fulfill the user's individualized requirements, the requirements specification is driven to evolve. The requirements specification is represented by process model in the process layer of RGPS framework, and process model is represented by the extension of OWL-S. But process meta-model has not enough capability to model the individualized evolutionary requirements specification because the OWL-S does not support modeling *where the evolution happens, when the evolution happens* and *how the evolution happens.* After studying some features of AOP, we defined OWL-S^A based on OWL-S that has capability to describe the attributes of the evolutionary requirements specification.

4.1 Brief Introduction of OWL-S and Aspect-Oriented Programming

OWL-S [2] is proposed by W3C which describes services. OWL-S makes the computer understand the semantics of services. It describes the service through a normal ontology based on OWL. Described by semantic markup language, services can be automatic discovered, invoked and composited.

OWL-S release 1.1 defines three ontologies to describe services: *service profile*, *service model* and *service grounding*. Service profile gives the basic capability of service such as IOPE. Service model describes the constitution of service from the viewpoint of process flow. And service grounding describes how a concrete instance of service can be accessed.

In traditional software development, scattered and tangled code always exists in many modules of the software. The scattered and tangled sections lead verbose software code and make it difficult to debug, modify and maintain the program. The goal of Aspect-Oriented Programming (AOP) is to solve this issue [7]. AOP insists on aggregating the scattered and tangled code to a whole modularity, named as *aspect*. An aspect comprises *pointcut, join point*, and *advice*. Join point is a well-defined point in a program's execution, Pointcut predicates on join points. It is a collection of selected join points. And advice is a piece of code that is executed whenever a join point in the set indentified by a pointcut is reached [8]. There are some AOP languages now such as: AspectJ, AspectC++, and AspectWerkz.

4.2 OWL-S^A: Describing the Evolutionary Requirements

In process layer of RGPS, the OWL-S is used to describe the domain process model. It is the proposal of the new individualized user's requirements that drives the domain process model to evolve. Only the domain process model is tailored can the requirements evolution be realized. Aspect is a good solution to realize the customization of the process model. Several evolution points within one process or several evolution points within several processes can be described easily by aspect, as well as the evolutionary content that happens near evolution point. So it is convenient to add, modify or remove evolutionary elements from several evolution points of one or several process model with aspect and the evolution of process model is realized. Furthermore, the modularity of evolutionary element at the requirements stage will be brought to the design and implementation stages smoothly. Thus the runtime evolution of NS can be realized.

Since aspect is introduced to realize the requirements evolution, first we need to describe how the evolution happens. Besides, we also need to describe the point where the evolution happens and what something of evolution is. In fact, it is necessary to set up a unified modeling language to describe the requirements evolution.

OWL-S^A is proposed to describe the evolutionary requirements. OWL-S^A is based on OWL-S, 'A' of OWL-S^A refers to aspect, and *pointcut-advice model* in AspectJ is exerted in it. In OWL-S^A, an *aspect* describes an evolutionary requirements specification, which comprises one or several *pointcut-advice pair*s. One *pointcut* and one or several *advice*s constitute a pointcut-advice pairs.

In a requirements specification described by OWL-S^A, *pointcut* describes the position where the evolution takes place. *Advice* describes the content of requirements evolution. Advice also has an attribute: *evolutionOrder*, which illuminates the order between the evolutionary requirements specification and evolutionary position. The meta-model of OWL-S^A is presented in Fig.1.

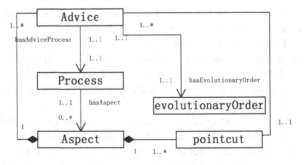

Fig. 1. Meta-Model for OWL-S^A

(1) Describing the position of evolution

When we describe the evolutionary requirements specification, the position of evolution should be described firstly. *Xpath* [11] is always used to address a certain node in an XML document tree. Since domain process model is mainly described in OWL-S, which adopts XML syntax, it is appropriate to use Xpath to locate some certain position of OWL-S^A.

There are two types of pointcut in OWL-S^A. One is the performance to the certain process in the process model. The inserting, substituting, or removing action takes place on or near the certain process when we perform the certain process in the process model, so the process model evolves. This type of pointcut is demonstrated as following:

`//process:CompositeProcess[@rdf:ID="CP1"]//process:perform[@rdf:ID="Step1"]`

When we insert or substitute new process to the process model, the input or output parameter of the process model would be added or modified. So the other type of pointcut is the declaration of input or output parameter of the process model. The type of pointcut is demonstrated as following:

`//process:CompositeProcess[@rdf:ID="CP1"]//process:hasInput[@rdf:ID="I1"]`

(2) Description of evolutionary content

Advice describes the content of requirements evolution. The evolutionary content is either the performance of new process that is inserted or substituted near pointcut, or the added input (or output) parameter to the process model. The inserted or substituted new process may be either atomic process or composite process described by OWL-S. The inserted or substituted evolutionary process is usually invoked by a control construct *Perform*, in which there are some data binding relationships. Data binding of performance is composed of two sections. One is the input data binding represented by *InputBinding*, the other is the output data binding represented by *ProducedBinding*. InputBinding describes the data source of evolutionary process. ProducedBinding describes the destination of output data of evolutionary process.

It is not always that the evolutionary process has data bindings with conjoint processes in the process model, which is due to the order type of the process model. There exist two types of order in process model: *business logic order* and *data flow order*. The business logic order is defined by business flow. There is not always data binding In this case. For example, the business flow prescribes that the process "*send mobile phone message to somebody*" takes place before "*send Email to somebody*". There could be no data binding between the two processes. Another data flow order is defined by the order of data binding in process model, and there exist data bindings between the two nearby processes. For example, the process "*select cargo*" must precede the process "*pay for the cargo*" in the process model "*e-business shopping*", since the output of "*select cargo*", such as "cargo list", is one of inputs of the process "pay for the cargo".

In summary, three patterns of the data binding exist between evolutionary process and other processes when the evolutionary process is imported into the process model. (1) Complete data binding. The new process receives all the outputs of preceding process as the inputs of its, and pushes all the outputs of its to the inputs of the succeeding process. (2)Complete non data binding. It is the business logic order between the new process and other processes, no data binding exists. Thus the process model adds some inputs and outputs corresponding to the new process. The new process sets up data binding to the added inputs and outputs of process model. (3) Partial data binding. The new process receives output of preceding process as its partial input, and pushes its partial output to the succeeding process. At the same time, the process model adds some inputs and outputs corresponding to the rest of inputs and outputs of the new process. And the rest of inputs and outputs of the new process sets up data binding to the added inputs and outputs of process model.

There is an issue arising if the evolutionary process has data binding to point process. A pointcut is probably composed of several join points which are represented corresponding performed processes. Thus the inserted new process probably has several data bindings to different join points of the pointcut. Here a variable is defined to solve the issue: *ThePointcutPerformed*, The variable is introduced as the extension to OWL-S, which represents the collection of processes that represent join points.

```
<swrl:Variable rdf:ID="ThePointcutPerform">
  <rdfs:comment>
    A special-purpose variable, used to refer, at runtime, to the execution instances of the point-
    cut process definition.
  </rdfs:comment>
</swrl:Variable>
```

In a specification describing evolutionary requirements in OWL-S, the *pointcut* describes the position where evolution takes place, and *advice* describes evolutionary content in the pointcut. The sequence between evolutionary content and evolutionary position is represented by evolutionaryOrder. As an attribute of advice, evolutionary-Order is composed of four values: *before, after, around* and *parallelTo*. Before, after or parallelTo represents that the imported new process is performed before, after or parallel to the process designated by pointcut. Around represents the imported new process substitute the process designated by pointcut.

4.3 A Case Study

We present an example to illustrate the evolutionary requirements specification described in OWL-S^A. There is a domain process model *construction*, which involves 6 sub-processes: project planning, blueprint designing, builder team recruitment, material purchasing, building and project checking. They are sequent in the process model. The user argues the individualized requirements to domain requirements specification.

Req1:
He hopes the recruited builder team has no bad record before.

Req2:
He hopes the third party supervises material purchasing, building and project checking.

It means the domain process model needs to be tailored to fulfill the individualized user's requirements. After requirements analysis based on RGPS framework, we get that the evolutionary requirements are composed of: (1) Substitution of the old process *builder team recruitment* for the new process with no bad record. (2) Introduction of process *supervising* after *material purchasing, building* and *project checking*. Scenario is the following.

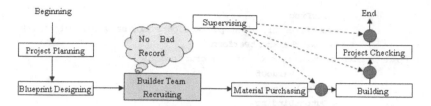

Fig. 2. Construction process model evolution scenario

The evolutionary requirements specification about **Req2** is demonstrated in the following code list. We add *ThePointcutPerform* to support data binding between pointcut and imported new process in OWL-S[A].

```
<Aspect name = "Supervising">
  <pointcut name = "xxx">
    //CompositeProcess[@rdf:ID=construction]//
    Perform[@rdf:ID="Mateiral Purchasing"]
    //CompositeProcess[@rdf:ID=construction]// Perform[@rdf:ID="Building"]
    //CompositeProcess[@rdf:ID=construction]//
    Perform[@rdf:ID="Project Checking"]
  </pointcut>
  <advice evolutionOrder= "after">
      < Perform rdf:ID = "SupervisingPerformed">
        <process rdf:resource="&aux;#Supervising">
        <hasDataFrom>
            <InputBinding>
                <theParam rdf:resource="&aux, #I11"/>
  /*I11 is the input of Supervising*/
                <valueSource>
                  < ValueOf>
                    < theVar rdf:resource="#OP"/>
  /*OP refers to output of the performed pointcut.*/
                    < fromProcess
                    rdf:resource="#http://www.daml.org/services/owl-
                    s/1.1/Process.owl#ThePointcutPerformed"/>
  /*Setup data binding to the variable of pointcut process.*/
                  <ValueOf>
                </valueSource>
              </InputBinding>
          </hasDataFrom>
          <Produce>
            <ProducedBinding>
              <OutputBinding>
                <theParam rdf:resource="#O11"/>
  /*O11 is the output of Supervising*/
                <valueSource>
                  <ValueOf>
                    <theVar rdf:resource="#O1"/>
```

```
                    <fromProc-
                    essrdf:resource="#http://www.daml.org/services/owls/1.1/Proce
                    ss.owl#TheParentPerform"/>
    /*set up data binding to output O1 of Construction*/
                            <ValueOf>
                             </valueSource>
                          </OutputBinding>
                     </ProducedBinding>
            </Produce>
         </Perform>
    </advice>
</Aspect>
```

5 Process of Requirements Evolution Modeling

Requirements evolution process is driven by the user's individual requirement. In section3, inducements of requirements evolution are analyzed including functional requirements, some non-functional Quality expectation and business context expectation. After acquiring the user's individualized requirements, which is then through requirements analyzing and modeling based on RGPS framework, we get the evolutionary position and expected process that supports evolution. Meta-model of OWL-S^A describing the evolutionary specification is proposed in section 4. In this section we will illustrate the process of requirements evolution modeling.

In general, the process of individualized evolution modeling is composed of two basic stages: discovery of process specification in domain knowledge and the modification to the domain process model.

It is necessary of stage1 because the evolution of domain process model needs some evolutionary elements represented as atomic process or composite process. If no suitable process provides inserting or substituting operation, the evolution of domain process model maybe pauses. Discovery of process requirements specification comprises *semantic matching* and *Quality/Contextual matching*. The semantic matching finds the process that fulfill the user's requirements by the semantics of input or output based on domain ontology in domain knowledge repository. Based on semantic matching, the Quality/contextual matching finds the process that fulfills the user's Quality requirement or individualized business context requirement in the domain knowledge repository. It is necessary to refer that the process meta-model, as the extension of meta-model of OWL-S, has the capability to describe user's quality or contextual requirement.

If user argues additional functional requirements, semantic matching will help to find evolutionary element. If user argues additional contextual or quality requirements, the semantic matching and Quality/Contextual matching are both needed.

Stage2 is the modification to the domain process model. If user argues more functional requirements, usually some new processes are imported to domain process model. If user argues additional contextual or quality requirements, new process with more suitable Quality or contextual expectation substitutes corresponding one in the domain process model.

6 Related Works

Aspect technology had been applied in the domain of requirement engineering. Awais Rashid et.al propose a general model for aspect oriented requirements engineering(AORE), which supports separation of crosscutting functional and non-functional properties at requirement level [17]. In [18] Awais Rashid et.al further proposes an approach to modularize and compose aspectual requirements and concrete realization with viewpoints and XML. Ivar Jacobson et.al proposes a method which utilizes *use case* to modeling for crosscutting in software requirements stage in [19], and *use case slice* is designed based on use case in software design stage in order to constitute the model for the whole system. [20] shows aspects can be discovered during goal-oriented requirement model. [17-20] demonstrates how to apply aspect to several software requirements models in order to modularize the concern in software requirement stage and improve the software quality. The paper combines aspect to requirements specification represented as process model to describe evolutionary requirements.

Anis Charfi et.al proposes the application of AOP at the level of the workflow process definition language [8]. They argued that AO4BPEL could be used to modularize the concerns in process-oriented BPEL workflows. AO4BPEL enhances the modularity and flexibility of BPEL, and supports dynamic adaption of composition at runtime. OWL-S^A encapsulates the evolutionary requirements specification from a process model in OWL-S. The difference between OWL-S^A and AO4BPEL is: (1) OWL-S^A is used to describe the evolutionary requirements specification, however, AO4BPEL is used to addresses dynamic adaption at the time of running of service composition as well as BPEL. (2)There are some difference in definition between OWL-S^A and AO4BPEL, because the structures of OWL and BPEL are different.

Yanbo Han classifies various types of workflow adaption, and discusses potential mechanisms for achieving adaptive workflow management in [3]. Boris Bachmendo proposed the method for workflow adaption using aspect in [9], and Qinyi Wu focused on code for defines the permissible sequences of execution for activities in BPEL and encapsulate code in synchronization-aspect [10]. He also presented tool *DSCWeaver* to enable extension to BPEL. Bart Verheecke et.al proposed WSML [18] between client and Web Service. Web service composition can evolve by the support of WSML through the selection of services. But their works do not focus on the adaption of requirements specification represented as process.

7 Conclusions

In the paper, we demonstrate process and method on the first step of requirements evolution modeling of the NS: individualized requirements evolution modeling. Firstly we analyze the inducements of the individualized requirements evolution. Generally, it is due that the domain common requirements specification can not fulfill the user's individualized requirements. Then we define OWL-S^A which can describe the evolutionary requirements specification. And the meta-model of it is proposed at the same time. Finally, the process of requirements evolution modeling is proposed, which involves discovery of specification and tailoring of domain process model. The paper brings a new method to the requirements evolution modeling of NS.

As a representation of requirements specification, OWL-S is not suitable to construct the Web Service composition at runtime. In fact, BPEL [6] is the most popular language to set up and execute web service composition flow. So the transformation from OWL-S to BPEL is necessary. At the same time, as the representation of evolutionary specification, OWL-S^A needs to be mapped to aspect in BPEL, such as AO4BPEL. Thus, with the help of dynamic weaving tool, such as AO4BPEL engine [8], weaving aspect to the executable web service composition flow will be implemented finally. Therefore, we will study on the mapping relation between OWL-S^A and aspect in BPEL in the future, and corresponding tool will be developed.

Acknowledgements

This research project was supported by the National Basic Research Program of China (973) under Grant No.2006CB708302 and 2007CB310801, the National High Technology Research and Development Program of China (863) under Grant No.2006AA04Z156, the National Natural Science Foundation of China under Grant No.90604005, 60703018 and 60703009, and the Provincial Natural Science Foundation of Hubei Province under Grant No.2005ABA123, 2005ABA240 and 2006ABA228.

Reference

1. He, K., Liang, P., Peng, R.: Requirement emergence computation of networked software. J. Frontier of Computer Science in China 1(3), 322–328 (2007)
2. David, M., Mark, B., et al.: OWL-S: Semantic Makeup for Web Services (November 2004), http://www.w3.org/Submission/OWL-S/
3. Yanbo, H., Amit, S.: A Taxonomy of Adaptive Workflow Management, http://pbfb5www.uni-paderborn.de/www/WI/WI2/wi2_lit.nsf/0/a7 fac9b815f26c87c1256c8e00669076/$FILE/CSCW98Workshop%20han-sheth-bussler.pdf
4. Jin, Z., He, K., Wang, Q.: Software Requirements Engineering: Part of Progress of Studying. J.Communications of CCF (in Chinese) (November 2007)
5. Jian, W., Keqing, H., Bing, L., Wei, L., Rong, P.: Meta-models of Domain Modeling Framework for Networked Software. In: Proceedings of The Sixth International Conference on Grid and Cooperative Computing (GCC 2007), pp. 878–885 (2007)
6. Tony, A., Francisco, C., et al.: BPEL4WS V1.1 specification (May 2003), http://download.boulder.ibm.com/ibmdl/pub/software/dw/specs/ ws-bpel/ws-bpel.pdf
7. Gregor, K., John, L., Anurag, M., Chris, M., Cristina, L., Jean-Marc, L., John, I.: Aspect-Oriented Programming. In: Aksit, M., Matsuoka, S. (eds.) ECOOP 1997. LNCS, vol. 1241, Springer, Heidelberg (1997)
8. Anis, C., Mira, M.: AO4BPEL: An Aspect-oriented Extension to BPEL. J.World Wide Web, 309–344 (October 2007)
9. Boris, B., Rainer, U.: Aspect-Based Workflow Evolution, http://www.comp. lancs.ac.uk/~marash/aopws2001/papers/bachmendo.pdf

10. Qinyi, W., Calton, P., Akhil, S., Roger, B., Gueyoung, J.: DSCWeaver: Synchronization-Constraint Aspect Extension to Procedural Process Specification Languages. In: IEEE International Conference on Web Services (ICWS 2006), Chicago, US, pp. 320–330 (2006)
11. W3C: XML Path Language, Version 1.0 (November 1999), http://www.w3.org/TR/xpath
12. Liu, W., He, K.Q., Wang, J., et al.: Heavyweight Semantic Inducement for Requirement Elicitation and Analysis. In: IEEE Proceedings of 3rd International Conference on Semantics, Knowledge and Grid (SKG 2007), Xi'an, China, October 29–31, 2007, pp. 206–211 (2007)
13. He, K.Q., Peng, R., Liu, J., et al.: Design Methodology of Networked Software Evolution Growth Based on Software Patterns. J. Journal of Systems Science and Complexity 19(3), 157–181 (2006)
14. Lamsweerde, A.: Goal-oriented requirements engineering: a guided tour. In: Proceedings of the 5th IEEE International Symposium on Requirements Engineering, August 2001, pp. 249–263. IEEE Press, Toronto, Canada (2001)
15. Hans-Erik, E., Magnus, P.: Business Modeling with UML: Business Patterns at Work. John Wiley & Sons, Inc., New York (2000)
16. Yu, E.: Modeling strategic relationships for process reengineering. Ph.D thesis, Department of computer science, University of Toronto (1994)
17. Awais, R., Peter, S., Ana, M., Joao, A.: Early Aspect: a Model for Aspect-Oriented Requirements Engineering. In: IEEE Joint International Conference on Requirement Engineering, Essen, Germany, September 2002, pp. 199–202 (2002)
18. Awais, R., Ana, M., Joao, A.: Modularisation and Composition of Aspectual Requirements. In: Proceedings of the 2nd International Conference on Aspect-oriented Software Development (AOSD), Boston, USA, pp. 11–20 (2003)
19. Ivar, J., Pan-Wei, N.: Aspect-Oriented Software Development with Use Cases (Chinese Version). Publishing House of Electronics Industry, Beijing (2005)
20. Yu, Y., Leite, J.C.S.d.P., Mylopoulos, J.: From Goals to Aspects: Discovering Aspects from Requirements Goal Models. In: Proceedings of 12th IEEE International Conference on Requirements Engineering, Kyoto, Japan, September 2004, pp. 38–47 (2004)

Requirement-Centric Traceability for Change Impact Analysis: A Case Study

Yin Li[1,2], Juan Li[1], Ye Yang[1], and Mingshu Li[1]

[1] Institute of Software, Chinese Academy of Sciences
[2] Graduate University of Chinese Academy of Sciences
{liyin, lijuan, ye, mingshu}@itechs.iscas.ac.cn

Abstract. Requirement change occurs during the entire software lifecycle, which is not only inevitable but also necessary. However, uncontrolled requirement change will lead to a huge waste of time and effort. Most studies about the change impact analysis assume changes take place in code, which results in the analysis only at the source code level and ignoring the requirement change is the fundamental cause. This paper introduces a Requirement Centric Traceability (RCT) approach to analyze the change impact at the requirement level. The RCT combines with the requirement interdependency graph and dynamic requirement traceability to identify the potential impact of requirement change on the entire system in late phase. This approach has been successfully applied to a real-life project, and the benefits and lessons learned will also be discussed.

Keywords: Change Impact Analysis, Requirement Interdependency, Dynamic Requirement Traceability, Information Retrieval.

1 Introduction

It's common knowledge that software requirements are volatile, because of the change of business strategy and the rapid evolution of the technology. Lacking of effective way to manage the evolution of the requirement will lead to project disaster. Change Impact Analysis (CIA) is "the activity of identifying the potential consequences, including side effects and ripple effects, of a change, or estimating what needs to be modified to accomplish a change before it has been made" [1].

Traditionally, most studies on CIA aim to analyze the change impact from the perspective of maintenance. For example, the program slicing [2] is code analysis technique which receives great attention in supporting the program modification. It produces the decomposition slice graph from the program items (e.g. variable), and based on this graph the change impact can be gained through the propagation path [3]. Essentially, these code based CIA techniques are helpful to the programmer to catch the influencing details, but it is hard for high level decision maker to understand the impact and make a wise decision. Moreover, they assume the change occurs in code and ignore the fact that in many cases requirement changes are the source.

The reasons stated above motivate us to treat the change from the decision maker's view. In this paper, we report our experience in applying RCT based on requirement

Q. Wang, D. Pfahl, and D.M. Raffo (Eds.): ICSP 2008, LNCS 5007, pp. 100–111, 2008.
© Springer-Verlag Berlin Heidelberg 2008

specification to assessing the change impact of a practical project through requirement interdependency graph and traceability matrix in late phase. The requirement interdependency is identified at the beginning of the project and maintained along with the development. The traces from the requirements to the artifacts are automatically generated by the information retrieval. When comes a requirement change proposal, the quantitative impact can be calculated through the interdependency graph and traceability matrix. At last, the project was completed successfully within budget on time.

The rest of the paper is organized as follows. Section 2 describes the process of RCT. Section 3 reports the data analysis and lessons learned in our practice. We compare our method with the related work in Section 4. The paper is concluded in Section 5 with a summary and directions for future work.

2 The Model and Application of RCT

The model and application of RCT falls into four major phrases: *Interdependency Modeling*, *Trace Detection*, *Impact Analysis* and *Decision Making*. Requirement interdependency and dynamic requirement traceability are the basis of our approach, and correspond to the *Interdependency Modeling* and *Trace Detection* respectively. The process is depicted in Fig 1.

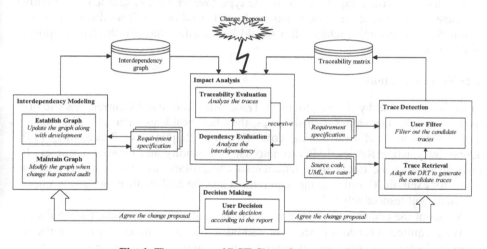

Fig. 1. The process of RCT Chang Impact Analysis

These relations among the requirements are established in the phase *Interdependency Modeling*. The *Trace Detection* phase is to establish the traces from the requirement to other artifacts. The more artifacts the requirement traces to, the more change cost it will be. When comes a change proposal, it's analyzed in *Impact Analysis* according to dependency graph and traceability matrix. Eventually, the quantitative change impact is computed to help the decision maker. If the change is accepted, the requirement dependency graph and traceability matrix will be updated.

2.1 Interdependency Modeling

The purpose of this phase is to construct the relations among requirements using requirement interdependency. It's a bridge to enumerate all the indirect traces of the affected requirement.

Requirements relate to each other and these relationships are called interdependency. Researches on it have different classification of interdependency [9-11]. Dahlstedt et al compiled these different classifications into an integrated view and developed "an overall, neutral model of requirement interdependencies" [12].

Table 1. Åsa G's Interdependency Types [12]

Category	Description	Type
STRUCTURAL	The structure of the requirement set	*Requires, Explains, Similar_to, Conflict_with, Influences*
COST/VALUE	The cost and value of realizing requirement	*Increase/Decrease_cost_of, Increase/Decrease_value_of*

The purpose of our approach is to estimate the impact of requirement change, which includes addition, modification and deletion. The added requirement may conflict with other existed requirements, so the type *Confict_with* is selected. To modify or delete a requirement, the requirements which depend on it will need some modification. So this dependent relationship should be identified through the type *Requires* and *Explains*.

2.2 Trace Detection

Trace is established by the Requirement Traceability activity. As current traceability methods usually manually establish traces, they face problems such as hard to maintain, error-prone and overrunning cost. Dynamic Requirement Traceability [14] adopts Information Retrieval (IR) to automate traceability and improve accuracy. It takes generating the traces from requirements to artifacts as searching the internet using, for example, Google. So the requirement and the artifact are expressed as query and document respectively [8].

We adopt the common used Vector Space IR Model [7] to compute the similarity between requirements and artifacts. The candidate traces are ranked by the similarity score in descending order, and threshold value is introduced to filter out the fault traces. It indicates that the higher score the artifact gets, the more it correlates with the query. More detail about IR can be seen in [7].

Compared to Cleland-Huang's [14] and Hayes's [13] work on dynamic requirement traceability, we had to establish traces between the Chinese requirement specifications and the English source code. Therefore, we used the Google Translate [15] to translate the Chinese requirement to English requirement, and then the synonyms between requirement and code were matched through the WordNet [16]. For the limited length of the paper, we ignore the detail of this process.

The result of traces generating by IR can be evaluated by the metrics of recall and precision [7], where

Precision = No. of relevant documents retrieved / No. of documents retrieved
Recall = No. of relevant documents retrieved / No. of relevant documents

Maximum precision is thinking of how to retrieve more highly considered relevant documents, and maximum recall can be gained by reducing the threshold value. Hayes introduced a harmonic mean of precision and recall called **F-measure** [13]. This measurement balances the precision and recall, and the max of value indicates the "best achievable combination of precision and recall". It is computed as $f = \dfrac{1+b^2}{\dfrac{b^2}{recall} + \dfrac{1}{precision}}$. Here, b represents the relative importance between recall and precision. $b<1$, $b=1$ and $b>1$ mean precision more important, equal important, recall more important respectively. So, the IR system is trying to balance precision and recall simultaneously according to different consideration.

2.3 Impact Analysis

When comes a requirement change proposal, it is analyzed in the *impact analysis* phase and the impact is represented as the number of affected artifacts. Briefly speaking, the algorithm, which is described below, mainly contains two parts: to find out all the affected requirements through interdependency graph; to get all the change and affected requirements' traces through the traceability matrix.

```
(1) Judge the change type, if type = 'addition', goto 2;
    else if type = 'modification', goto 3;
    else if type = 'deletion', goto 4;
(2) If newReq conflicts with existed req: ExistedReqList
    for each req in ExistedReqList
        if req needs to do some modification, goto 3;
        else if req needs to be deleted, goto 4;
(3) For each dependent dreq of modifyReq
        get dreq's traces to artifacts into IA;
        revise IA to IA';//eliminate repeated change impact
        calculate number(IA')* Wchange * df(i) into cost; //i
        is set to 1 initially
        add cost into cc;
        set modifyReq = dependOnReq, i=i+1 and goto 3;
(4) For each dependent dreq of deleteReq
        get dreq's traces to artifacts into IA;
        revise IA to IA';//eliminate repeated change impact
        calculate number(IA')* Wdelete * df(i) into cost; //i
        is set to 1 initially
        add cost into cc;
        set deleteReq = dependOnReq, i=i+1 and goto 4;
```

In step (1), we judge the change type. If the type is 'addition', the conflict requirements should be identified through analyzing the whole requirement set (2). To modify or delete the conflict requirements, the algorithm will move to corresponding modification (3) or deletion (4) module.

The total change impact is the sum of the impact of every affected requirement. The impact of affected requirement is the product of three parts: the number of current traces, the change type weight and depression factor.

The number of requirement traces should be revised, for the affected requirements trace to the same artifact in some cases, which leads to the repeatedly calculated impact. Therefore, we take the maximal impact as their whole impact to the artifact, and the impact set of every requirement will be revised.

The modification type and deletion type should have different trace weights, which comes from general knowledge that the influence in deletion is larger than in modification. In algorithm, w_{change} and w_{delete}, which are set to 0.2 and 1 respectively based on our experience, represent the weight of modification and deletion.

The third part is the depression of impact through the dependent relationship, which is called *df* short for depression factor. Obviously, this factor is the function of *i*, i.e. the distance from the change source to the affected requirement. In our practice, we set this factor to $\frac{1}{2^{i-1}}$. The formula tells us that the farther the affected requirement is from the original change requirement, the less it will be influenced.

2.4 Decision Making

In this last phase, we use the ratio of the number of affected artifacts to the number of total artifacts compared with *high risk ratio* and *low risk ratio* predefined by experts to help determine the risk of current requirement change and take actions accordingly. Basically, if the ratio exceeds high risk ratio, this change will be refused automatically; if the ratio is lower than low risk ratio, it will be accepted automatically; when the ratio stays at the middle area, the impact detail will be analyzed to determine change or not. And finally, if the change is approved, the interdependency graph and traceability matrix will be updated correspondingly. The process is showed in Fig 2.

According to different project type, team and schedule, the high and low risk ratios are different, which are determined by the experts through discussion.

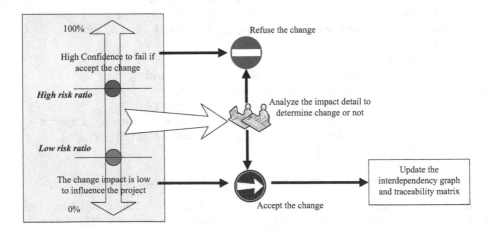

Fig. 2. Change impact during development

3 Quantitative Change Impact Analysis

The proposed method was validated using data from a software project which was developing a *Requirement Management* System (RM). RM aims to provide seamless connection between requirement and development, which incorporates with another in-house software project management product. Table 2 lists the project context.

At the beginning of each iteration, we model the dependencies among requirements. The traceability between the requirement and the artifact is established automatically with the development at any time. During the development, 10 requirement change proposals were evaluated through our method, and the high and low risk ratios were originally set to 20% and 5% respectively based on a group of experts' discussion. The project manager (PM) made convincible decision to manage requirements change, which plays an important role in the success of project.

Table 2. Project context

Project Characteristics	Description
Project type	Web based application
Development process	iterative
Development tool	Java/applet/struts/jsp/ajax, mysql, tomcat4
Team size	5
Developer skill	experience
Project duration	30 weeks
Project scale	43 requirements, 70 KLOC, 468 classes
Logical module number	7
Deployment package	pmreq.jar, pmapplet.jar, pmwss.jar
Change proposal time	10
Project status	Successfully completed on time

3.1 Construct Requirement Interdependency

The whole system can be divided into 7 modules, and the dependencies among these modules can be seen in Fig 3. P1, P2 and P3 represent the java package pmreq.jar, pmreqapplet.jar and pmwss.jar which encapsulate the server side's logic, the rich UI

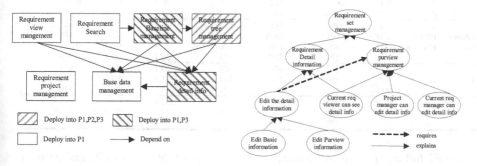

Fig. 3. Modules dependency graph   **Fig. 4.** An example of interdependency graph

implementation by java applet and the interface provided to other modules respectively. The symbol of P1, P2 and P3 will also be used in section 3.2.

The high level relationships among the modules help us define the relationships among requirements in fine-grained. Due to the limitation of the paper length, only a part of the detailed graph is shown in Fig 4.

3.2 Establish the Requirement Traceability Automatically

The source code is the main artifact, so we use the traces between the requirement and code to demonstrate the analysis of impact. The traces from requirement to the code were generated in three parts, for the implementation was deployed into P1, P2 and P3. The result of full data set is shown in Table 3. We use the F-measure to evaluate the synthetical accuracy of precision and recall, and the parameter b in F-measure was set to 3, which means recall is more important than precision. The F-measure of three packages reaches its maximum in *chosen set*, and the data collected in other sets is organized by decreasing and increasing the threshold value.

For different java package, the precision and recall are not the same. In P1, when the threshold value was set to 0.2, the maximum f-measure value was gained, and the precision and recall reach at 26.7% and 73.9%. In P2 and P3, the recall reaches at 92% and 90.4%, which are almost 20 percentage points higher than P1. The precision in P2 and P3 is also higher than P1. For the reason that P1, deployed on server side, encapsulates the business logic and provides the uniform access to the database, and then all the modules depend on it. For example, the class *BaseDBOperation* encapsulates the atomic access to the database, but doesn't refer to any requirements. However, it contains the word '*base*' also contained in requirement *base data management* and *baseline management*, so the similarity computed by IR among them is higher than threshold value and that leads to the fault trace.

Table 3. Dynamic retrieval result on all data set

Set No.	Java Package	Threshold value	All correct No.	Retrieved No.	Correct retrieved No.	Precision (%)	Recall (%)	F-measure b=3.0
	P1	0.15	295	1143	218	20.7	80.3	0.624
1	P2	0.14	600	2423	563	23.2	93.8	0.72
	P3	0.1	198	735	187	25.4	94.4	0.743
	P1	0.18	295	946	226	23.9	76.6	0.628
2	P2	0.16	600	2123	556	26.2	92.7	0.739
	P3	0.12	198	651	182	27.9	91.9	0.748
	P1	**0.2**	**295**	**815**	**218**	**26.7**	**73.9**	**0.629**
Chosen	**P2-full**	**0.18**	**600**	**1889**	**552**	**29.3**	**92**	**0.757**
Set	**P2-part**	**0.15**	**600**	**1363**	**556**	**40.8**	**92.7**	**0.821**
	P3	**0.14**	**198**	**578**	**179**	**30.1**	**90.4**	**0.758**
	P1	0.23	295	677	204	30.1	69.1	0.614
4	P2	0.2	600	1681	534	31.8	89	0.754
	P3	0.16	198	500	171	34.2	86.3	0.749
	P1	0.25	295	595	197	33.1	66.8	0.606
5	P2	0.22	600	1517	518	34.1	86.3	0.749
	P3	0.18	198	439	159	36.2	80.3	0.715

The P2-full and P2-part in P2 means the full requirement traces to P2 and parts of requirement traces to P2. The precision in P2-full is 10 percentage points lower than in P2-part. As stated above, P2, embedded in the Jsp pages, is Java Applet and only used for the modules of *requirement tree management* and *requirement detail info*. So, the requirements in other modules shouldn't trace to P2, and then we eliminate requirements of other modules and the result was showed in P2-part.

The P3 uses Webservice to encapsulate P1's function, and provides the interfaces to the P2 and other in-house tools. The F-measure of P3 is 0.758, it's because the higher level encapsulation of the function can better align to the requirement than lower level realization in P1 and P2. Another reason is the habit of programmers. P3 is the interface to other tools and modules, so the naming of the code item follows the words in requirement.

It's worthwhile to mention that the 43 requirements and 468 classes would produce 20124 potential traces! The analyst needs to do the inspection to find out the real traces, which is a huge waste of time and error-prone. When applying the RCT, the analyst only needs to inspect the 745 potential traces (the number is computed by the data in column *Retrieved No.* of *Chosen Set*) on average.

3.3 Change Impact Analysis

There were 10 change proposals during the development, and they are briefly illustrated in Fig 5. The symbol A., D. and M. represent the change type Addition, Deletion and Modification. For example, the change proposal #2 was to add some functions in implementation phase, and predicated and actual impact was zero and one respectively.

These change proposals were introduced in implementation phase and the impact were calculated through the requirement interdependency graph and the traceability matrix following our algorithm. All of these change proposals are accepted except #10, which will be discussed in section 3.4.

Compared between predicted and actual impact of different change type, we found that most of the predicated impact is almost equal to the actual impact, but #2 and #3 have some exceptions. The #2 and #3 belong to the addition type, and they don't conflict with any existed requirements. However, the actual impact (one) isn't equal to the predicated impact (zero). The reason is that the new functions were inserted into existed class.

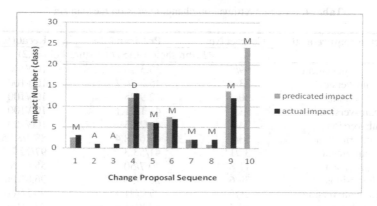

Fig. 5. Change impact during development

3.4 Details in Change #10: Modify *Version Management*

Initially, in order to provide fine-grained management of the evolution of the requirement set, we used the main version and subordinate version (sub version) to
record the history of requirement. The main version is used for recording the requirement content evolution, and the sub version keeps track of the evolutive tree structure
under the requirement. However, this function was argued by its practicability, and
the customer proposed to delete the sub version. The change proposal was analyzed
by our approach and the result indicated that it would cost a lot of resources to modify
this function. So the PM decided to delay this modification to next version of RM.

The interdependency graph is shown in Fig 6. Obviously, the modification of *version management* would lead to some modification of, for instance, *add main-version*.
The impact analysis algorithm estimated the impact through the change type and
distance between change requirement and affected requirements.

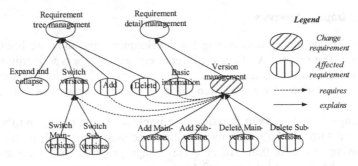

Fig. 6. The impact of modifying *Version Management*

The dynamic retrieval result on these change and affected requirements is shown in
Table 4. These requirements have no implementation in P3, so the data is collected
from P1 and P2. For example, the precision of *switch versions* is 29.4% (in P2 with
threshold 0.15) and 30% (in P1 with threshold 0.2).

Table 4. Dynamic retrieval on changing version mechanism

Affected requirement	Correct No.	Precision(%)	Recall(%)
		P2 (threshold=**0.15**) / P1 (threshold=**0.2**)	
version management	39/5	35.5/16.1	100/100
add main-version	33/4	45.2/26.7	100/100
add sub-version	30/4	42.9/25	100/100
del main-version	23/4	41.1/21.1	100/100
del sub-version	24/4	40/23.5	100/100
basic information	53/2	61.6/18.4	88.3/87.5
add requirement	32/11	41/53.3	97/72.7
del requirement	11/8	40.7/50	55/62.5
switch versions	30/6	29.4/30	96.8/100
switch main-versions	26/5	37.7/21.7	96.3/100
switch sub-versions	32/4	43.8/21	94.1/100

The recall of candidate traces from *version* related requirements to code reaches at 100% for the meaning of '*version*' is unique in all the modules. On the contrary, the word '*base*' residing in several modules (for instance, *base data management*, *basic requirement information*, *requirement baseline management*) has different meaning, which leads to the lowest precision and recall of P1.

We compared the precision and recall between the chosen and individual threshold in Fig 7. The chosen threshold is the uniform value (0.2 in Fig 7) to filter all the requirements' candidate traces, and the individual threshold is one requirement's value to filter its candidate traces when the F-measure reaches maximum. Basically, the recall of the two thresholds has little difference, but the precision in chosen threshold set is less than in individual set. Especially in *version management*, the precision in individual set is two times as in chosen set.

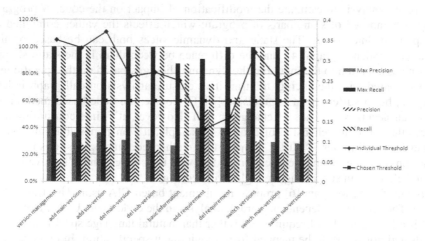

Fig 7. Comparison of precision and recall between chosen and individual threshold

The calculated impact of this change is 24 (classes), and the ratio of the impact number to the total class number (468 classes) is 5.1%, lower than high risk value but higher than low risk value. The affected classes were analyzed in detail, and we found that these classes are too complex to be modified. So PM decided to delay the modification to the next version.

3.5 Discussion

We got at least three benefits from applying the RCT:

1. Our approach addresses the change on the requirement specification rather than code, which can help the non-technical people who don't know the detail of the code to predict the change cost quantitatively.
2. The impact to both requirements and artifacts was unified into the number of artifacts, which is easy to use and understand.

3. It's time-saving to apply the IR to automatically establish the traces among the requirements and artifacts, and is highly probable to adopt in practice. Without the dynamic generating approach, the analyst has to analyze every possible relation among requirements and artifacts, and the candidate traces number is $Num_{req} \times Num_{artifact}$.

Also, we found the weakness of this approach. The precision and recall of the traces are not good enough to totally automatically calculate the change impact, and the user inspection is also needed to filter the traces.

4 Related Work

There are mainly three kinds of techniques: static and dynamic program slicing, call graph based analysis to estimate the modification of impact on the code. A program slicing is composed of some parts of program which affects the values computed at some point of interest [2]. The static and dynamic slices both can be based on the program dependency graph [4], and the difference between them is the static slicing makes no assumption to the input but the dynamic slicing is based on the specific test case. Compared with the slicing, the transitive closure analysis on call graph is less expensive, but it suffers from imprecision [3]. Of course, the code based method results in an accuracy analysis of change impact. However, it's time-consuming and requires the full comprehension of code; for example, it's an impossible mission to catch every detail in our 70 KLOC project. Our method pointing against this problem focuses on the requirement specification to deal with the change, and it's proved practical and effective in supporting the high level decision.

Hassine [5] and Maryam [6] propose requirement based CIA using Use Case Map (UCM). They move the dependency graph analysis in the code to the UCM. However, UCM is a formal model of requirement rather than natural language specification and it needs additional cost to be mapped from requirement specification. In practice, this mapping is too complex for us to adopt in our project. On the contrary, we take an easier and more practical way which is to construct the interdependency graph among requirements. The impact analysis is through not only interdependency graph, but also traceability matrix among requirements and artifacts.

5 Conclusion and Future Work

In this paper, we introduced a practical approach, called Requirement-Centric Traceability, to do the CIA from the requirement perspective rather than code. It incorporates with requirement interdependency analysis and dynamic requirement traceability to calculate the change impact completely. Firstly, according to the three change types, we choose several interdependency types to model the requirement relationship. Then, the candidate traces from requirements to artifacts are generated automatically by IR method, and the actual traces can be gained by user inspection. Therefore, the cost of this activity is reduced to the least based on the IR. When comes a change proposal, the decision maker can show the quantitative impact result to change or not instead of experiential judgment. The interdependency graph and the traceability matrix may be updated when the change is accepted.

We have applied the approach to our 5-people and 30-week project. The result demonstrated that it is feasible to estimate the change impact. The PM can evaluate the change cost from high level perspective rather than details in the code.

Our future work will concentrate on how to improve the accuracy of the traces and also keep the automation level.

Acknowledgments. This research is supported by the National Natural Science Foundation of China under grant No. 60573082, the National Basic Research Program (973 program) under grant No. 2007CB310802, the Hi-Tech Research and Development Program of China (863 Program) under grant No. 2006AA01Z155.

References

1. Bohner, S.A., Arnold, R.S.: Software change impact analysis. IEEE Computer Society Press, Los Alamitos (1996)
2. Weiser, M.: Program slices: formal, psychological, and practical investigations of an automatic program abstraction method. PhD thesis, University of Michigan (1979)
3. Law, J., Rothermel, G.: Whole Program Path-Based Dynamic Impact Analysis. In: ICSE 2003, Portland, Oregon (2003)
4. Tip, F.: A Survey of Program Slicing Techniques. J. Programming Languages 3(3), 121–189 (1995)
5. Hassine, J., Rilling, J., Hewitt, J., Dssouli, R.: Change Impact Analysis for Requirement Evolution using Use Case Maps. In: Proc. of the 8th Int. Workshop on Principles of Software Evolution, pp. 81–90 (2005)
6. Maryam, S., Jameleddine, H., Juergen, R.: Modification Analysis Support at the Requirements Level. In: IWPSE 2007 (2007)
7. Baeza-Yates, R., Ribeiro-Neto, B.: Modern Information Retrieval. Pearson Education, London (1999)
8. Antoniol, G., Canfora, G., Casazza, G., De Lucia, A., Merlo, E.: Recovering Traceability Links between Code and Documentation. IEEE Transaction on Software Engineering, 970–983 (2002)
9. Pohl, K.: Process-Centered Requirements Engineering. John Wiley & Sons, Chichester (1996)
10. Ramesh, B., Jarke, M.: Toward Reference Models for Requirements Traceability. IEEE Transactions on Software Engineering 27(1), 58–93 (2001)
11. Robinson, W.N., Pawlowski, S.D., Volkov, V.: Requirements Interaction Management, GSU CIS Working Paper 99-7, Department of Computer Information Systems, Georgia State of University, Atlanta (1999)
12. Dahlstedt, A.G., Persson, A.: Requirements Interdependencies - Moulding the State of Research into a Research Agenda. In: Ninth International Workshop on Requirements Engineering: Foundation for Software Quality in conjunction with CAiSE 2003 (2003)
13. Hayes, J.H., Dekhtyar, A., Sundaram, S.K.: Advancing Candidate Link Generation for Requirements Tracing: The Study of Methods. IEEE Transaction on Software Engineering, 4–19 (2006)
14. Cleland-Huang, J., Settimi, R., Duan, C., Zou, X.: Utilizing Supporting Evidence to Improve Dynamic Requirements Traceability. In: Proceedings of the 13th IEEE International Requirements Engineering Conference (RE 2005), pp. 135–144 (2005)
15. Google Translate, http://www.google.com/translate_t
16. WordNet, http://wordnet.princeton.edu/

Scaling Up Software Architecture Evaluation Processes

Liming Zhu, Mark Staples, and Ross Jeffery

NICTA, Australian Technology Park, Eveleigh, NSW, Australia
School of Computer Science and Engineering, University of New South Wales, Australia
{Liming.Zhu, Mark.Staples, Ross.Jeffery}@nicta.com.au

Abstract. As software systems become larger and more decentralized, increasingly cross organizational boundaries and continue to change, traditional structural and prescriptive software architectures are becoming more rule-centric for better accommodating changes and regulating distributed design and development processes. This is particularly true for Ultra-Large-Scale (ULS) systems and industry-wide reference architectures. However, existing architecture design and evaluation processes have mainly been designed for structural architecture and do not scale up to large and complex system of systems. In this paper, we propose a new software architecture evaluation process – Evaluation Process for Rule-centric Architecture (EPRA). EPRA reuses and tailors existing proven architecture analysis process components and scales up to complex software-intensive system of systems. We exemplify EPRA's use in an architecture evaluation exercise for a rule-centric industry reference architecture.

1 Introduction

A software architecture is defined as "the structure or structures of the system, which comprise software elements, the externally visible properties of those elements, and the relationships among them" [1]. Most current architecture research reflects this definition by focusing on designing and evaluating structural components and connections. However, such views of architecture are not suitable for all situations. As systems become larger, more decentralized and continue to change, it is difficult for a prescriptive structural architecture to allow flexibility and evolvability . In such situations, an architecture should focus on providing quality-centric architectural rules rather than structural prescription [2, 3]. An architecture rule is defined as principles that need to be followed by structures within a system [4]. An architectural rule may be satisfied by several potential structural architectures. They are usually flexible, evolvable and survivable architectures for a whole industry or an Ultra-Large-Scale system. Just as in urban design planning, the rules have an economics rationale and a quality focus, with little formal control. Rule-centric architectures are for software "cities", rather than software buildings.

A number of architecture evaluation processes, such as Architecture Trade-off Analysis Method (ATAM) [5], Software Architecture Analysis Method (SAAM) [6] and Architecture-Level Maintainability Analysis (ALMA) [7], have been developed to evaluate quality-related issues for software architectures. Recently, a number of process components common to many of these processes have been extracted [8].

Q. Wang, D. Pfahl, and D.M. Raffo (Eds.): ICSP 2008, LNCS 5007, pp. 112–122, 2008.
© Springer-Verlag Berlin Heidelberg 2008

These process components are relatively atomic and generic and have been proven useful for evaluating structural architectures. However, all these evaluation processes do not scale up to system of systems due to their focus on structural architectures and strict step-based processes.

In this paper, rather than extending an existing architecture evaluation process for rule-centric architecture, we instead use the extracted common process components directly. We propose a new process – Evaluation Process for Rule-centric Architecture (EPRA) by selecting, reusing, and tailoring existing process components [8]. The focus of EPRA is not on prescribing methodical steps but rather on adapting existing analysis process components in the context of rule-centric architecture. The adapted process components are loosely organized into several traditional evaluation phases.

We have used EPRA in evaluating a rule-centric reference software architecture for Australia's mortgage lending industry. This systematic process identified a number of trade-offs among these rules and improved them by explicitly providing contexts and condition guidelines for applying the rules. The process also tremendously increased our confidence in releasing the reference architecture.

The paper is organized as follows. Section 2 will explain the motivation of the work. We will explain the process component adaptation and composition in EPRA in section 3. An industry case study is used to illustrate EPRA in section 4. We discuss our experience in using EPRA in section 5. We conclude and propose some future work in section 6.

2 Motivation and Background

This work is entirely motivated by immediate industry needs recognised through our industry engagements. Vertical industries have been developing e-business standards to improve their business-to-business interoperability, and to foster efficient and organically-grown industry-wide systems. NICTA has been working with a leading Australian e-Business industry standardization body – Lending Industry XML Initiative (LIXI) [9] – that serves the lending industry in Australia. The LIXI e-business standards are essentially a set of governing rules for systems supporting the current and future lending industries in Australia.

Until recently, LIXI standards have been composed of XML-based business data models (associated with message exchange patterns) and Business Process Modelling Notation (BPMN)-based business process models. Business data and process models alone have limited power to regulate the healthy evolution of the whole system. We were consequently asked by LIXI to help devise a reference architecture and associated development processes to supplement their e-Business standards.

Both the LIXI standardization body and NICTA realized that the role of a reference architecture in this case is significantly different from traditional technical reference architectures, which only exemplify a possible arrangement of structural components and connectors. This is because the LIXI context has a number of complicating characteristics:

1. Decentralization: Data, development processes, evolution and operational control are all decentralized. LIXI is a non-profit organization with no standard enforcement power. Its membership is voluntary.
2. Inherently conflicting requirements: Most parties want complexity to reside in others' parts of the overall system, want information to be shared, but do not want to share their own information. Technical solution companies provide and favor intermediary gateways and custom-built applications, while smaller players typically want commoditized applications and to remove intermediaries.
3. Continuous evolution with heterogeneous elements: The whole ecosystem can't be stopped and re-engineered. Day-to-day lending activities have to go on, and horizontal interactions with the larger financial and government systems also exert constant influence.
4. No clear people/system boundary: The scale of the companies involved varies widely. Some companies have sophisticated systems that can automate most tasks while others still rely on fax and manual processing. Messages and activities in the e-Business standards can map to systems or people depending on the specific parties and the characteristics of individual transactions.

The LIXI eco-system resembles the characteristics of an Ultra-Large-Scale (ULS) system. In order to address both the business perspective and ULS system challenges, the reference architecture needs to balance consistency and variety, address competing needs from different parties and consider trade-offs between prescriptive guidance and an ability to evolve.The reference architecture for LIXI should provide governing quality-centric rules rather than structural prescriptions. These rules also act as guidance to the distributed design and development process.

To analyze such a rule-centric architecture we need a new architecture evaluation process. We therefore developed EPRA from the basis provided by the proven process components of traditional architecture evaluation processes.

3   Evaluation Process for Rule-Centric Architecture (EPRA)

3.1   Adapt Architecture Analysis Process Components for Rule-Centric Architecture

We analysed the ten common process components in architecture analysis and evaluation for their suitability, and adapted them for rule-centric architectures in the context of ULS systems.

Inevitably, our approach is not yet fully mature, as rule centric architecture is still relatively new compared to structural architecture approaches. Also, the EPRA process were developed to support the immediate needs of a commercial project. Nevertheless, the process has proven useful in the project, and has a theoretical grounding in the process components of Kazman et al [8]. We discuss the ten process components below.

1. *Explicit elicitation of business goals.* As for all types of architecture, the ultimate purpose is to satisfy business goals. Our method requires a presentation of business goals. Depending on the level of abstraction, we observe that certain business goals

can be presented as business rules. Such business rules are especially useful in evaluating architecture rules since there is a smoother mapping between the two. Competing goals are another major concern for ULS systems. More flexible rules are essentially designed for addressing this problem. We adapt the process component by introducing a new process artefact - perspective-based goals and tailoring the corresponding activities, so a rule can be evaluated under different perspectives. The essence of this new process component is about *perspective-based business goals and rules elicitation*.

2. *Active stakeholder participation and communication.* As mentioned above, in ULS systems rule-centric architectures can be used across entire industries to provide flexibility and evolvability. These architecture rules need to be applied to different competing and collaborative companies in different contexts, resulting in different concrete structural decisions. A single common understanding among stakeholders is not expected. The essence of adapting this process component is similar to the last one – to recognise the different perspective of different stakeholders. Two levels of understanding are considered. One is a rule-level understanding, i.e. the understanding of the industry reference architecture. The other is instance-level understanding, i.e. the understanding of applying the rules to a specific system from a particular stakeholder's perspective.

3. *Explicit elicitation of architecture documentation and rationale.* The documentation of architecture rules is different from the documentation of structural architectures. Some architecture description languages can express architectural constraints which are enforced on the implementation at run-time. However, there is an extremely limited ability to express meta-level rules to allow structural change at design-time and run-time. Textual descriptions can be used. An architecture description language in the form of UML profiles for describing design decisions including design rules has been proposed [10], but is not yet mature. We also found that it is useful to document exemplary structural architectures derived by following the rules. These exemplars can be for a specific technology binding or from the perspective of a particular system. They act as a way of documenting possible contexts and results for applying the rules. The essence of this process component is to elicit rule-centric architecture documentation explicitly and provide illustrative exemplary structural architectures whenever necessary.

4. *Use of quality attribute scenarios.* Business goals and rules need to be related to quality scenarios for design and evaluation purposes. Considering the genericity of rule-centric architecture, the scenarios they can be evaluated against tend to be general scenarios or a range of concrete scenarios. These concrete scenarios can be perspective-based or technology- and context-based. This allows flexibility in the final structural architectures derived from these rules. The essence of this technique is to use *general* scenarios with associated perspective or context-based concrete scenarios in evaluation. In our adapted process component, we also suggest categorizing quality attributes scenarios into business goal categories [11] in addition to the quality attribute categories. This enables explicit trade-off and coverage analysis between rules and business goals.

5. *Mapping of quality attribute scenario onto the architecture representation.* The architecture representation in rule-centric systems are rules. When rules are being applied in specific technology and organizational contexts, structural representations will emerge. In our adapted technique we suggest several mappings. The first mapping is from general quality attribute scenarios to rules. Further mappings can be provided from example concrete scenarios to example structures derived for a specific technology bindings or other context-oriented interpretation of rules. The essence of the process component is to understand different types of mappings.

6. *Representation of design primitives, called tactics.* We consider this an essential technique in the evaluation of rule-centric architectures. Firstly, we observe rules are often the application of one or more tactics. This is similar to extracting tactics from structural architectures and design patterns [12] for evaluation purposes. Secondly, architectural tactics are now being directly used in quality attribute reasoning models by manipulating model parameters [13]. Having corresponding tactics for each rule and further using them in quality reasoning models improve the efficiency of the evaluation process for rule-centric architecture. The essence of this process component is to extract architectural tactics from architectural rules.

7. *Use of templates to capture information.* Our process component reuses the 6-part template [1] for capturing quality scenarios. For design rules and rationale, a set of templates based on an informal UML profile for design decisions [10] can be used. An enumeration of all the tags and stereotypes in this UML profile can produce an initial template.

8. *Explicit elicitation of costs and benefits.* For evaluating rules and making architecture improvement over rules, it is necessary to elicit information on costs. Since rules were developed at a certain level of genericity, the contextual implications of applying rules (e.g. on organization capabilities and existing infrastructure) are very important in cost-benefit analysis for rule-centric architecture. The goal of this process component is to have context-based cost analysis, rather than analysis from a single perspective such as the standardization body. Our initial failure to realize this in our industry engagement made much of our first attempts at analysis invalid.

9. *Use of quality attribute models for architecture analysis.* As suggested in [8], certain quality attribute models (e.g. for performance and reliability) are well established while others (e.g. for interoperability, variability and security) are not. The process component essentially evaluates how a rule improves or impedes quality attributes and associated business goals by investigating how it manipulates parameters in the quality attribute reasoning models. Due to the lack of reasoning models for the quality attributes that are important for ULS systems, we had to invent our own informal reasoning models. Rigorous parameters can be replaced by informal factors. This has proven very useful in guiding qualitative analyses.

10. *Use of quality attribute design principles derived from the quality attribute model.* This process component concerns the same problem illustrated in the last item. When a collection of design principles (tactics) for a quality attribute exist, an evaluation analysis is usually about whether the rules follow these principles properly in its specific context. When such collections of principles do not exist, the evaluation analysis has to rely on parameter manipulation in their reasoning models, or even on informal reasoning.

3.2 EPRA

As mentioned previously, EPRA is not intended to give a prescriptive step-wise process, but instead to adapt existing process components for rule-centric systems and loosely organize them into phases. This is intended to improve the process scalability and usefulness to distributed design and development.

An evaluation method for rule-centric architecture does not change the normal phases of an evaluation. Depending on how exemplary structure architectures would be evaluated along with a rule-centric architecture, interactions between EPRA and other evaluation processes may occur. This is represented in Figure 1 which illustrates EPRA's conceptual flow and corresponding process components.

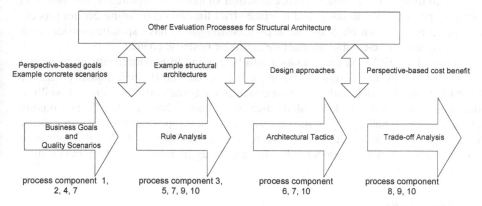

Fig. 1. Rule centric analysis process components in EPRA

- **Phase I: Business Goals and Quality Scenarios**
  - Process component: Perspective-based business goals/rules elicitation
  - Process component: Multiple-level based participation and understanding
  - Process component: Use of general scenarios and example concrete scenarios
  - Process component: Use of templates for general scenarios
  - Interaction with business goals and concrete scenarios for example structural architecture evaluation
- **Phase II: Rule Analysis**
  - Process component: Documentation of rules and example structural architecture
  - Process component: Mappings from quality scenario onto rules on different levels
  - Process component: Use of templates or ADL for capturing architecture rules
  - Process component: Use of quality attribute models for perspective-based analysis
  - Process component: Compare rules with design tactics derived from the quality attribute model
  - Interaction with architecture analysis for example structural architecture evaluation
- **Phase III: Architectural Tactics**
  - Process component: Extracting architectural tactics from rules
  - Process component: Use of templates for tactics extraction and documentation

- Process component: Compare rules with design tactics derived from the quality attribute model
- Interaction with design approaches for example structural architecture evaluation
- **Phase IV: Tradeoff Analysis**
  - Process component: Perspective and contextual based cost benefit analysis
  - Process component: Use of quality attribute models for perspective-based analysis
  - Process component: Compare rules with design tactics derived from the quality attribute model
  - Interaction with perspective-based cost benefit analysis

As shown, some of the process components are used in different phases. This is similar to many other evaluation processes, and supports an explorative, dynamic and iterative process. We do not intend to place strict limitations on using certain process components in certain phases – the important thing is to have specific consideration for the issues of rule-centric architecture and their business context.

Inputs of an EPRA-based evaluation will be elicited from participants or recovered from existing informal design and business documentation. However, quality attribute based reasoning models and architecture tactics for certain attributes are not well understood and are often lacking. Methodically evaluating how a rule affects a quality attribute can be challenging. In our case study, we developed our own interoperability issue matrix as a substitute for a more formal reasoning model. We also extracted architectural tactics for interoperability from existing literature so as to compare rules with these tactics.

4 Case Study

4.1 LIXI Reference Architecture Evaluation Using EPRA

The case study background was introduced in section 2. We performed a full evaluation for this reference architecture by following EPRA. The following shows some results of our evaluation:

Phases I: Business Goals and Quality Scenarios

We categorize these goals using the categories proposed in [11]. The followings are just a few examples:

Category: Reduce Development Cost – Manage Flexibility

Cost reduction for the lending industry is a major driver behind the standard. The overall goal is to achieve cost reduction in the area of cross-organization transactions, which will consequently benefit individual organizations.

Quality attribute general scenario 1: When an organization wants to conduct e-business transactions with a new partner, the cost of re-development should be very low if both parties are in compliance with LIXI standard. Ideally, little reconfiguration should be required, and re-development should be minimized.

Category: Reduce Development Cost – Distributed Development

The business goal is to enable parallel and distributed development with no central control or collaborative overhead except the LIXI standards.

Quality attribute general scenario 1: When systems are developed in total isolation by following the LIXI standards and reference architecture, they should be able to interoperate with minimal re-development effort.

For example, depending on the rules and design of a particular system, the re-development effort could shift between two parties. Within the lending industry, banks have the ability to accommodate relatively large development effort. On the other hand, small brokers and valuers usually do not invest substantially in IT development. An intermediary can be introduced to decouple the involving parties, centralize all possible changes and conduct transaction matching. However, from the perspective of the intermediary, a reasonable transaction volume based premium should be paid to cover the re-development cost. Smaller players can be supportive of an intermediary because of their incapability to deal with changes effectively. However, from the perspective of large players, the goal is to leverage their central influence by absorbing such intermediaries.

All these different perspective are captured for later phases of EPRA.

Phase II: Rules Analysis

The following are two sample sets of rules (development process guidelines) from a list of 40 rules in the LIXI context, with commercial sensitive information removed:

1) Semantic Alignment Rules

Semantic alignment provides architectural mechanisms for minimizing the effort needed to integrate components built independently. LIXI standards provide an ontology vocabulary and associated XML Schema for defined LIXI messages. The purpose of architectural support for semantic alignment is to enable linking of technical elements with business semantics to provide: 1) enough flexibility to technical elements, and 2) interoperability between technical elements by consulting the business meaning at both design-time and run-time. The reference architecture provides two set of rules for achieving semantic alignment in the context of service oriented architecture. Both also act as suggestive enforcement mechanisms for auditing business standards compliance:

Semantic annotation (lightweight) This allows the service architecture to be developed without initially considering business standards. Developers can then annotate technology elements by referring to the common vocabulary through XML reference or semantic web service mechanisms. This is a bottom-up approach and relatively lightweight. When two systems communicate, they can know what each other means business-wise even though labels might differ.

Model Driven (heavyweight) Another approach is a top-down one. High-level BPMN models can be translated into a technical BPEL (Business Process Execution Languages) models. A similar approach can be used to translate business messages into web service messages. The transformation rules (manual or automated) then can be exposed for interoperability purposes.

2) Minimum Service Interface Rules

The business world is essentially a service oriented world. The technology world has recently been catching up by introducing the "service" concept, either as SOAP-based Web services, REST-ful services and other forms. The governing rules and development processes for service interface designs should follow this principle. The set of rules we propose in the reference architecture for LIXI use a loose message-centric interface approach. Messaging behaviors are specified by content structure and exchange protocols. Service interfaces should not expose abstractions as remote procedures. Essentially, we advocate the use of a single operation on a service – ProcessLIXIMessage – but allow more complicated interfaces to exist. This rule encourages maximum flexibility in the face of constant evolution. Shared contexts are carried within messages. Message processing can either be hidden behind the service or exposed as metadata.

Phases III: Architectural Tactics

By analyzing the above rules, we extract a number of architectural tactics for interoperability. Currently, there are no large collections of interoperability tactics. However, a number of papers and technical reports [14-20] have documented current approaches for achieving interoperability. A critical analysis activity in this phase is to use a reasoning model for quality attributes to determine if a proposed rule or tactic improves or hinders important quality attributes. Formal reasoning models for architectural interoperability (the main quality attribute we are investigating) do not yet exist, and so we have had to invent an informal model with informal issues (rather than well-defined parameters) for our evaluation. Using this simple matrix approach, we were able to analyze each rule and tactic systematically.

Phases IV: Trade-off Analysis

The trade-off analyses conducted for the LIXI reference architecture fall into two categories:

- Trade-off analysis between different quality attributes
- Trade-off analysis based on different perspectives

The two types of trade-off analysis also interact with each other. Some trade-off analyses will result in an explicit trade-off decision being made and the rationale captured. Other trade-off analyses will result in perspective-based trade-off decisions being captured as guidelines for different perspectives.

For example, an explicit trade-off decision is made between interoperability and flexibility by not prescribing operational interfaces. We sacrifice immediate interoperability for flexibility and evolvability.

5 Discussion

The full evaluation of EPRA in the LIXI context has not yet finished. However, since we are using proven common architecture analysis process components in EPRA, we are reasonably confident about the feasibility and effectiveness of the process. We have learned a number of lessons in this exercise:

1. Reusing process components is very effective in constructing a new method. Our method leverages existing expertise among stakeholders and evaluators. Actually, these process components are more familiar and user-friendly to participants than well-known evaluation methods such as ATAM .
2. Devising a reference architecture is a very explorative activity. A non-stepped process like EPRA has proved to be very appropriate compared to other more formal processes. We initially tried to directly use ATAM but found a lot of input information was hard to produce and tempted us to jump between phases very frequently.
3. We feel there is a need for a more systematic trade-off analysis process for EPRA. The number of trade-off points has increased tremendously due to perspective-based analysis and rule-structure level-based analysis. CBAM [21] and AHP [22] have demonstrated to be useful, but we need to further investigate their scalability.

6 Conclusion

The needs we have observed in our industry engagement have prompted our research into a new evaluation process. We believe as more systems are connected in a decentralized manner, the software world will evolve towards the ULS system vision. In this paper we have proposed EPRA, an architecture evaluation process for systems with rule-centric architectures. This systematic process helps identify trade-offs among these rules and improved them by explicitly providing contexts and condition guidelines for applying the rules. EPRA is constructed by loosely connecting and adapting existing process components to improve its scalability and usefulness to distributed design and development processes.

We have used EPRA in an architecture evaluation for the rule-centric reference architecture of the LIXI lending industry organization in Australia. The process has helped us to improve the reference architecture significantly and has increased our confidence in releasing it into the industry. Nonetheless, as a new process, EPRA is not yet either mature or widely tested, and we are currently working to validate it in different contexts.

Acknowledgements

NICTA is funded by the Australian Government's Department of Communications, Information Technology, and the Arts and the Australian Research Council through Backing Australia's Ability and the ICT Research Centre of Excellence programs.

References

1. Bass, L., Clements, P., Kazman, R.: Software Architecture in Practice. Addison-Wesley, Reading (2003)
2. Northrop, L., Kazman, R., Klein, M., Schmidt, D., Wallnau, K., Sullivan, K.: Ultra-Large Scale Systems: The Software Challenge of the Future. SEI, Pittsburgh (2006)

3. Zhu, L., Staples, M., Jeffery, R.: Reference Architecture for Lending Industry in ULS Systems. In: Kazman, R. (ed.) 1st ICSE Workshop on Software Technologies for Ultra-Large-Scale (ULS) Systems (2007)
4. Bosch, J.: Software architecture: the next step. In: Oquendo, F., Warboys, B.C., Morrison, R. (eds.) EWSA 2004. LNCS, vol. 3047, Springer, Heidelberg (2004)
5. Kazman, R., Barbacci, M., Klein, M., Carriere, S.J.: Experience with Performing Architecture Tradoff Analysis. In: 21th International Conference on Software Engineering, pp. 54–63. ACM Press, New York (1999)
6. Kazman, R., Bass, L., Abowd, G., Webb, M.: SAAM: A Method for Analyzing the Properties of Software Architectures. In: Proceedings of the 16th International Conference on Software Engineering, pp. 81–90 (1994)
7. Bengtsson, P., Lassing, N., Bosch, J., Vliet, H.v.: Architecture-level modifiability analysis (ALMA). Journal of Systems and Software 69(1-2), 129–147 (2004)
8. Kazman, R., Bass, L., Klein, M.: The essential components of software architecture design and analysis. Journal of Systems and Software 79, 1207–1216 (2006)
9. Architectural-level risk analysis using UML. IEEE Transaction on Software Engineering (2003)
10. Zhu, L., Gorton, I.: UML Profiles for Design Decisons and Non-Functional Requirements. In: 2nd International Workshop on SHAring and Reusing architectural Knowledge - Architecture, Rationale, and Design Intent (SHARK/ADI 2007), colocated with ICSE 2007 (2007)
11. Kazman, R., Bass, L.: Categorizing Business Goals for Software Architectures. SEI (2005)
12. Zhu, L., Ali Babar, M., Jeffery, R.: Mining Patterns to Support Software Architecture Evaluation. In: 4th Working IEEE/IFIP Conference on Software Architecture, pp. 25–36. IEEE, Los Alamitos (2004)
13. Bachmann, F., Bass, L., Klein, M.: Deriving Architectural Tactics: A Step Toward Methodical Architectural Design (2004)
14. Metcalf, C., Lewis, G.A.: Model Problems in Technologies for Interoperability: OWL Web Ontology Language for Services (OWL-S). Software Engineering Institute (2006)
15. Lewis, G.A., Wrage, L.: Model Problems in Technologies for Interoperability: Web Services. Software Engineering Institute (2006)
16. Hohpe, G., Woolf, B.: Enterprise integration patterns: designing, building, and deploying messaging solutions. Addison-Wesley, Boston (2004)
17. Carney, D., Smith, J., Place, P.: Topics in Interoperability: Infrastructure Replacement in a System of Systems. SEI (2005)
18. Carney, D., Fisher, D., Place, P.: Topics in Interoperability: System-of-Systems Evolution. SEI (2005)
19. Carney, D., Fisher, D., Morris, E., Place, P.: Some Current Approaches to Interoperability. SEI (2005)
20. Carney, D., Anderson, W., Place, P.: Topics in Interoperability: Concepts of Ownership and Their Significance in Systems of Systems. SEI (2005)
21. Kazman, R., Asundi, J., Klein, M.: Quantifying the costs and Benefits of Architectural Decision. In: 23rd International Conference on Software Engineering (ICSE), pp. 297–306 (2001)
22. Zhu, L., Aurum, A., Gorton, I., Jeffery, R.: Tradeoff and Sensitivity Analysis in Software Architecture Evaluation Using Analytic Hierarchy Process. Software Quality Journal 13, 357–375 (2005)

Software Project Similarity Measurement Based on Fuzzy C-Means

Mohammad Azzeh, Daniel Neagu, and Peter Cowling

Department of Computing, University of Bradford,
Bradford, BD7 1DP, U.K.
{M.Y.A.Azzeh, D.Neagu, P.I.Cowling}@brad.ac.uk

Abstract. A reliable and accurate similarity measurement between two software projects has always been a challenge for analogy-based software cost estimation. Since the effort for a new project is retrieved from similar historical projects, it is essentially to use the appropriate similarity measure that finds those close projects which in turn increases the estimation accuracy. In software engineering literature, there is a relatively little research addressed the issue of how to find out similarity between two software projects when they are described by numerical and categorical features. Despite simplicity of exiting similarity techniques such as: Euclidean distance, weighted Euclidean distance and maximum distance, it is hard to deal with categorical features. In this paper we present two approaches to measure similarity between two software projects based on fuzzy C-means clustering and fuzzy logic. The new approaches are suitable for both numerical and categorical features.

Keywords: Software Project Similarity, Fuzzy Logic, Fuzzy C-means.

1 Introduction

Software projects similarity measurement is the key accuracy of software cost estimation by analogy. It plays significant role in identifying closest projects to a project being estimated which in turn affects estimation accuracy [12].

The use of similarity measures between two software projects has been evaluated and confirmed in previous researches of software cost estimation. The most widely used approaches are based on nearest neighborhood techniques such as Euclidean distance [1], Manhattan [3], Weighted Euclidean distance [12] and Maximum measures [11]. In these algorithms the closest analogue to a project p_i is the project with maximum similarity. Stamelos et. al. [19], and Mendes et. al. [11,12] compared between different types of distance metrics in analogy software estimation and revealed that using different distance metrics yield dissimilar results which indicate the importance of distance between software projects on effort estimation. According to Idri et al [7], software projects environment has significant impact on the similarity between two software projects, in that software projects within single company give different similarity than projects gathered from cross companies [8].

In general, nearest neighborhood based techniques suffer from several disadvantages [16, 17]. First, they depend mainly on numerical features and binary data. Thus,

Q. Wang, D. Pfahl, and D.M. Raffo (Eds.): ICSP 2008, LNCS 5007, pp. 123–134, 2008.
© Springer-Verlag Berlin Heidelberg 2008

it is difficult to handle categorical variables. Second, they are sensitive to the irrelevant features and missing values as discussed in [17]. Moreover, the attributes employed should first be normalized in order to have same degree of influence to further processing.

In order to overcome the limitations in the current similarity measures between software projects we proposed alternative approaches based on fuzzy C-means clustering and fuzzy logic [10, 22] which has several advantages over nearest neighborhood techniques. First, it groups the most similar projects together in the same cluster and represent their features values in the same fuzzy set. This eventually will enhance prediction accuracy. Second, it handles uncertainty and imprecision, where each attribute is described by several fuzzy sets instead of using single values.

The prime objective of this paper is to measure similarity between two software projects in terms of similarity between two fuzzy sets that they most belong to. For example, let A be the fuzzy set that has maximum membership value for project p_x and let B be the fuzzy set that has maximum membership value for project p_y. The similarity between two projects in terms of feature j is denoted as $SM_j(F_j(p_x), F_j(p_y))$ which is intuitively identical to $SM_j(A,B)$ in this work. However, in order to find which cluster does software project p most belong to, we use max operator as depicted in equation 1. The overall similarity is aggregated by calculating the average of all similarities between fuzzy sets in each feature as discussed in section 4.1.

$$\mu_{C_i}(p) = \max\{\mu_{C_1}(p), \mu_{C_2}(p), ..., \mu_{C_c}(p)\} \tag{1}$$

The reminder of the paper is organized as follows: Section 2 discusses related work. Section 3 introduces the Fuzzy c-means clustering algorithm. Section 4 presents our proposed method of similarity distance measurement between two software projects. Section 5 presents dataset. Section 6 compares the efficiency of our method with the most often used distance metrics in literature. Finally, section 7 summarizes our work and outlines the future studies.

2   Related Works

To our knowledge, there is relatively little research in literature concerned with similarity between two software projects based on the fuzzy logic. Idri et al [7] proposed a new approach based on fuzzy logic to measure the similarity between software projects that are represented by categorical variables. They stated that the equality between two software projects is not null when they have membership different from zero to at least one same fuzzy set of F_j. They built rule base engine for each attribute to find distance between two software projects using max, min and i-or operators. It is interesting to observe from their work that Kleenes-Dienes aggregation is not valid for software project similarity, using i-or operator gave better and stable results than max and min operators. However, they claimed that each organization must initially determine appropriate linguistic quantifier that complies with their situation in order to obtain better results.

3 Fuzzy C-Means Clustering

Like clustering algorithms which assign a data point to distinct cluster, Fuzzy c-Means (FCM) algorithm assigns membership values to each observation in all derived clusters. FCM aims at minimizing objective function $J_m(A)$ to local minima which depends on the initial chosen of membership values. Different initial membership will lead to different local minima [1, 6, 13].

Indeed, there is no standard way to pre-assign number of clusters unless another algorithm is being used [9]. In addition, it is recommended to use weighting parameter $m=2$ in fuzzy clustering [13, 20]. After clustering data using FCM the next step is construct fuzzy model based on clustered data. In literature [6, 21] there are two main ways to construct fuzzy model from data, the first is the expert knowledge which is formed in if-then-rules where parameters and memberships are tuned using input and output data. The second is no prior knowledge about the system, so the model is built based on particular algorithms. However, the fuzzy model was constructed based on the second approach where membership functions obtained by FCM and projection as explained in [21].

4 Software Project Similarity Approach

4.1 The First Approach

To explain our first approach in more details, let p_x, p_y be two software projects described by M features F_j $(j=1...M)$, for each feature (linguistic variable) there are several fuzzy sets A_k^j obtained by FCM and fuzzy identification as mentioned in section three where k represents the number of clusters. Particularly, we impose our approach to use fuzzy sets as *normal* fuzzy sets [15]. Our algorithm is described by the following steps:

1. for each linguistic variable, find fuzzy set A_x^j that represents maximum membership value of $F_j(p_x)$ and fuzzy set A_y^j that contains maximum membership value of $F_j(p_y)$ by using maximum operators as depicted in equation 1.
2. for each linguistic variable, find SM_j (A_x^j, A_y^j) using *approaching degree* (see next paragraph). In terms of one feature, $SM_j(F_j(p_x), F_j(p_y))$ is intuitively identical to SM_j (A_x^j, A_y^j).
3. find overall similarity between two M features software projects:

$$SM(p_{x,}p_y) = \underset{j=1}{\overset{M}{avg}} \left(SM_j(F_j(p_x), F_j(p_y)) \right)$$

(2)

Consequentially, the closes analogue to a particular project is the project with maximum similarity.

The approaching degree mentioned in step 2 is a method used to assess the similarity between two given fuzzy sets in a particular universe of discourse X [15]. Let assume $S(X)$ be a power set of normal fuzzy sets with $A_k^j \neq 0$ and $A_k^j \neq X$. Let A, B be two normal fuzzy sets where $A, B \in S(X)$. The similarity degree between two fuzzy sets A and B is assessed as shown in equation 3:

$$SM(A,B) = min\left((A \bullet B), \overline{(A \oplus B)}\right) \tag{3}$$

where $(A \bullet B)$ the inner product is defined by equation 4 and $(A \oplus B)$ is the outer product defined by equation 5:

$$(A \bullet B) = max(min[\mu_A(x), \mu_B(x)]) \ , x \in X \tag{4}$$

$$(A \oplus B) = min(max[\mu_A(x), \mu_B(x)]) \ , x \in X \tag{5}$$

Particularly, when the value of $SM(A,B)$ approaches a value 1, this represents that the two fuzzy sets A and B are "more closely similar". When $SM(A,B)$ approaches a value 0, the two fuzzy sets are "more dissimilar".

In software cost estimation, it is interesting to define a suitable fuzzy set membership function that copes with the problem domain. We have chosen Gaussian membership function for this research. The final form of similarity measure for one feature is given in equation 6 [14]:

$$SM(A,B) = min\left(e^{\left[\frac{-(a-b)^2}{(\sigma_A + \sigma_B)^2} \right]}, 1 \right) \tag{6}$$

where a, b are the mean values; and σ_A, σ_B are the standard deviation of Fuzzy membership functions A and B respectively. In fact, the inner product of two fuzzy sets represents the membership value of intersection point between them.

Definition 1. Let p_x and p_y be two software projects described by M features. Let $F_j(p_x)$ mostly belong to fuzzy set A_x^j and $F_j(p_y)$ mostly belong to fuzzy set A_y^j. The similarity between two software projects in terms of features j is given as:

$$SM_j(F_j(p_x), F_j(p_y)) = min\left(e^{\frac{-(x-y)^2}{(\sigma_x + \sigma_y)^2}}, 1 \right) \tag{7}$$

where x, y are the mean values and σ_x, σ_y are the standard deviation for A_x^j and A_y^j respectively.

Definition 2. The Overall similarity between two software projects p_x and p_y is given by equation 8:

$$SM_1(p_x, p_y) = \underset{j=1}{\overset{M}{avg}}\left(SM_j(F_j(p_x), F_j(p_y))\right) \tag{8}$$

4.1.1 Example

Let assume there are three projects (p_1, p_2, p_3) described by feature j as shown in figure 1; we want to asses which project is closer to p_1. Let p_1 mostly belong to fuzzy set B with parameters $(b=30, \sigma_B=9)$, and p_2 mostly belong to fuzzy set D with parameter $(d=50, \sigma_D=12)$, while p_3 mostly belongs to fuzzy set E with parameters $(e=70, \sigma_E=14)$. According to definition 1:

$$SM_j(F_j(p_1), F_j(p_2))=min(\,e^{\frac{-(b-d)^2}{(\sigma_B+\sigma_D)^2}},1) = min(\,e^{\frac{-(30-50)^2}{(9+12)^2}},1)=min(0.404,1)=0.404.$$

$$SM_j(F_j(p_1), F_j(p_3))=min(\,e^{\frac{-(b-e)^2}{(\sigma_B+\sigma_E)^2}},1) = min(\,e^{\frac{-(30-70)^2}{(9+14)^2}},1)=min(0.049,1)=0.049.$$

Thus, we conclude that project p_2 is closer to project p_1 than project p_3.

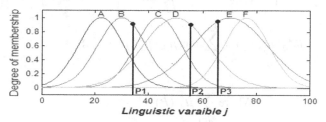

Fig. 1. Fuzzy sets for linguistic variable j

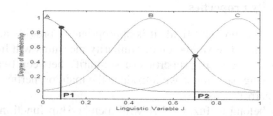

Fig. 2. Fuzzy linguistic variable with three fuzzy sets where p2 belongs to two clusters with same maximum membership value

It is also worth to point out that using this approach could cause problems when a particular project belongs to two fuzzy sets at the same time with same maximum membership as shown in figure 2. For example, to compute similarity between p_1 and p_2 $(SIM_j(p_1, p_2))$ there are two ways; first, if we assume that p_2 belongs to fuzzy set B then the two projects p_1, p_2 are similar with degree over zero. Second, if we assume that p_2 belongs to fuzzy set C then p_1, p_2 are more dissimilar and approaches 0 which is not realistic in this case. To avoid this problem we restrict our model to use the fuzzy set that presents larger similarity.

4.2 The Second Approach

Our second similarity approach is mainly concerned with partition matrix that is obtained by FCM. The final partition matrix contains membership of a project in each particular cluster as shown in table 1.The similarity between two software projects is computed based on similarity between their fuzzy values as shown in equation 9 [15]. In this case, we have to decide how to assign membership for a new project. The simplest way is to use distance formula that is applied in FCM algorithm which tends to assign any new project to different clusters with a particular membership value.

Table 1. Fuzzy partition matrix for software projects

Project	Cluster A_1	Cluster A_2	...	Cluster A_k
P_1	$\mu_{A_1}(p_1)$	$\mu_{A_2}(p_1)$	...	$\mu_{Ak}(p_1)$
P_2	$\mu_{A_1}(p_2)$	$\mu_{A_2}(p_2)$	...	$\mu_{Ak}(p_2)$
...	...	...	...	...
P_n	$\mu_{A_1}(p_n)$	$\mu_{A_2}(p_n)$	...	$\mu_{Ak}(p_n)$

$$SM_2(p_x, p_y) = \sum_{i=1}^{k} \min(\mu_{A_i}(p_x), \mu_{A_i}(p_y)) \tag{9}$$

$$\text{Where } \sum_{i=1}^{k} \mu_{A_i}(P) = 1 \tag{10}$$

4.3 Project Similarity Properties

As in other software measurement fields it is appropriate to provide an evaluation for our similarity approaches. The validation of similarity measures will help us to ensure that our model respects the main properties of similarity between two software projects [7]. In the following paragraphs we introduce the main properties that are used to assess our model in narrow sense [5].

Let $F_j(p_x)$ mostly belong to fuzzy set A with membership function parameters (a, σ_A) and $F_j(p_y)$ mostly belong to fuzzy set B with membership function parameters (b, σ_B).

Property 1. Similarity between a software project p_x to itself is equal to one.
For feature j. According to equation 7:

$$SM_j(F_j(p_x), F_j(p_x)) = \min(e^{\frac{-(a-a)^2}{(\sigma_A + \sigma_A)^2}}, 1) => \min(e^0, 1) => \min(1,1)$$ which produces 1.

Then the overall similarity will be calculated using equation 8.

$$SM_1(p_x, p_x) = \underset{j=1}{\overset{m}{avg}}(SM_j(p_x, p_x)) = avg(1,1....,1) = 1.$$

A significant issue arises when we deal with one linguistic variable. It can be seen that when two projects have different crisp values falling in the same fuzzy set they have unity similarity degree same as similarity between project to itself. This seems not true and contradicts to the crisp set approach, where similarity between two close projects is not necessary to be unity unless they have the same feature value. For the second approach, this definition is true according to equations 9 and 10, let $p_x = \{\mu_{A_1}(p_x), \mu_{A_2}(p_x), ..., \mu_{A_k}(p_x)\}$ then:

$SM_2(p_x, p_x) = min(\mu_{A_1}(p_x), \mu_{A_1}(p_x)) + ... + min(\mu_{A_k}(p_x), \mu_{A_k}(p_x)) = 1.$

Property 2. The similarity between two different projects p_x and p_y must be less than similarity of project p_x to itself $SM(p_x, p_y) < SM(p_x, p_x)).$

The $SM_j(F_j(p_x), F_j(p_x))$ produces 1 as discussed in property 1. However, Since $a \neq b$

and $\sigma_A \neq \sigma_B$, the inner product $(A \bullet B) = e^{\frac{-(a-b)^2}{(\sigma_A + \sigma_B)^2}}$ will be less than 1 because it represents the membership value of intersection point between two different fuzzy sets which is always less than 1, and consequentially:

$SM_j(F_j(p_x), F_j(p_y)) = min(e^{\frac{-(a-b)^2}{(\sigma_A + \sigma_B)^2}} < 1, 1) = e^{\frac{-(a-b)^2}{(\sigma_A + \sigma_B)^2}}$ which it is less than 1.

Therefore the overall similarity $SM_1(p_x, p_y)$ will be definitely less than 1 because when any similarity degree is less than 1 then the average will be also less than 1.

On the other hand, when two different projects described by one feature fall in the same cluster then the similarity will be always 1: $SM_1(p_x, p_y) = SM_1(p_x, p_x)$. This contradicts with Property 2 that say the similarity between two different projects should be less than similarity between a project to itself.

For the second approach, we have seen earlier that $SM_2(p_x, p_x)$ is always equal to one therefore $SM_2(p_x, p_y)$ will not exceed this value according to equations 9 and 10 because similarity will sum only the minimum membership of both fuzzy sets.

Property 3. $SM(p_x, p_y) = SM(p_y, p_x)$
Since $(a-b)^2 = (b-a)^2$ and $(\sigma_A + \sigma_B)^2 = (\sigma_B + \sigma_A)^2$ then:

$SM_j(F_j(p_x), F_j(p_y)) = min(e^{\frac{-(a-b)^2}{(\sigma_A + \sigma_B)^2}}, 1) \equiv SM_j(F_j(p_y), F_j(p_x)) = min(e^{\frac{-(b-a)^2}{(\sigma_B + \sigma_A)^2}},$

1) which yields:

$SM_1(p_x, p_y) = \overset{m}{\underset{j=1}{avg}}(SM_j(F_j(p_x), F_j(p_y))) \equiv SM_1(p_y, p_x) = \overset{m}{\underset{j=1}{avg}}(SM_j(F_j(p_y), F_j(p_x)))$

For the second approach:
$min(\mu_{A_1}(p_1), \mu_{A_1}(p_2)) \equiv min(\mu_{A_1}(p_2), \mu_{A_1}(p_1))$ according to reflexive property of fuzzy operations.

Property 4. Let p_x, p_y, p_z be three projects where p_x mostly belong to fuzzy set A, and p_y mostly belong to fuzzy set B, p_z mostly belong to fuzzy set C, and $F_j(p_x) < F_j(p_y) < F_j(p_z)$ for all features then $SM(p_x, p_z) < min(SM(p_x, p_y), SM(p_y, p_z)).$

Let a, b, c are the mean values and $\sigma_A, \sigma_B, \sigma_C$ are the standard deviation of fuzzy sets A, B, C respectively. Let assume $a < b < c$, and $\sigma_C \leq \sigma_A \leq \sigma_B$.
Since $|a-c| > |a-b|$ and $|a-c| > |b-c|$ then consequentially

$$e^{\frac{-(a-c)^2}{(\sigma_A+\sigma_C)^2}} < e^{\frac{-(a-b)^2}{(\sigma_A+\sigma_B)^2}}, \text{ and } e^{\frac{-(a-c)^2}{(\sigma_A+\sigma_C)^2}} < e^{\frac{-(b-c)^2}{(\sigma_B+\sigma_C)^2}} \text{ which satisfy that:}$$

$$SM_j(F_j(p_x), F_j(p_z)) < min(SM_j(F_j(p_x), F_j(p_y)), SM_j(F_j(p_y), F_j(p_z)))$$

This property is not true in case of $\sigma_B < \sigma_A << \sigma_C$ because $(\sigma_A + \sigma_C) > (\sigma_A + \sigma_B)$ and $(\sigma_A + \sigma_C) > (\sigma_C + \sigma_B)$, therefore :

$$SM_j(F_j(p_x), F_j(p_z)) > min(SM_j(F_j(p_x), F_j(p_y)), SM_j(F_j(p_y), F_j(p_z)))$$

5   The Dataset

The analysis presented in this paper was based on ISBSG Repository (release 10, January 2007) which currently contains more than 4000 software projects gathered from different software development companies [6]. Seven effort drivers were selected including 3 numerical attributes (Adjusted Function points, Maximum Team size, and productivity) and 4 categorical attributes (development types, Business type, Application types, and organization types) in addition to the effort. We omitted the projects with missing values which results in 480 projects. Categorical variable must be handled because each of them has many categories. Rather grouping projects according to their nature, we intend to merge each categorical variable into two homogeneous categories and replaced by ordinal values (1=Low Effort, 2=High Effort). For example, in case of organization type, one would say that "*wholesale & retail trade*" and "*financial*" types would naturally be grouped in the same category but they are not. The merging was conducted using mean effort value of each category based on work of [18] in which the categories that has same impact on the mean effort have been placed together in the same group. We do consider this categorization is an ad hoc approach which follows a data driven context. Only Development type was categorized into three categories (1 = Enhancement, 2 = New Development, 3 = Redevelopment) according to the type of software development followed.

6   Results and Discussion

The results shown in Tables 2 and 3 were obtained using leave-one-out cross-validation. The results obtained in Table 2 represent a sample of the similarity between software projects using our first approach. However, it can be seen that the maximum similarity between two software projects is always equal to one and obtained when two projects are similar (i.e. $SM(P_x, P_x)$). It is also observed that there is violation in property 3 because the FCM algorithm generates different initial membership values every time we run the leave-one-out cross validation. The way to solve this problem is to use the same initial membership function every time. It is worth to point out that the similarity between two different projects does not exceed similarity between a project to itself which consequentially respects Property 2.

The results obtained for the second approach as shown in Table 3 indicate that there is no violation in the similarity properties. Similarity between any project to itself is always equal one. In addition, the similarity between two different projects

Table 2. Similarity value between software projects using first approach

	P1	P2	P3	P4	P5
P1	1	0.97	0.86	0.93	0.656
P2	0.97	1	0.684	0.959	0.635
P3	0.87	0.684	1	0.841	0.568
P4	0.93	0.956	0.845	1	0.58
P5	0.65	0.626	0.569	0.59	1

Table 3. Similarity value between software projects using second approach

	P1	P2	P3	P4	P5
P1	1	0.406	0.148	0.263	0.405
P2	0.406	1	0.318	0.11	0.186
P3	0.148	0.318	1	0.469	0.604
P4	0.263	0.11	0.469	1	0.92
P5	0.405	0.186	0.604	0.92	1

did not exceed one and still over or equal zero. The first approach has an advantage over the second approach in terms of the feature impact. The first approach takes into account the similarity between two projects in each feature while the second approach takes the distribution of membership values across clusters.

In order to assess the performance of each similarity approach on software effort estimation, we compared our two approaches against Euclidean and weighted Euclidean distance in analogy estimation as shown in Table 4. This validation is analogous to Case-based reasoning techniques but it did no take in account its parameters (features subset selection, adaptation rules and case adaptation). For all similarity measures we first compared the actual effort with closest analogy, and then with the mean of K nearest neighbors where K=3. The results shown in table 4 represent the comparison between four similarity measures based on Mean Magnitude of relative errors (MMRE) and Performance indicator (Pred(e)). Pred(e) calculates how many MRE values fall below 25%. MMRE is the mean of estimating error for all individual estimates. MMRE has been criticised that is unbalanced in many validation circumstances and leads to overestimation more than underestimation [16]. Another approach called balanced mean magnitude relative error measure (BMMRE) [16] was proposed to overcome the limitation of MMRE. The new approach has been criticised to be more effective in measuring estimation accuracy.

$$MMRE = \frac{1}{n}\sum_{i=1}^{n} \frac{\mid actual_i - estimated_i \mid}{actual_i} \tag{11}$$

$$BMMRE = \frac{1}{n}\sum_{i=1}^{n} \frac{\mid actual_i - estimated_i \mid}{\min(actual_i, estimated_i)} \tag{12}$$

According to Table 4 , Effort estimation based on our two approaches contribute to better estimation accuracy than those based on Euclidean distance and weighted

Euclidean distance in terms of MMRE, BMMRE and Pred(0.25). The results of the MMRE evaluation criterion for both proposed approach are significant. Using mean of three analogies in the first approach gives slightly better accuracy. Whilst for the second approach, the good results achieved when two and three analogies have been used. In case of Pred(0.25) evaluation criteria, the best result obtained when using mean of three analogies in the first proposed approach, even though the other results in both proposed approaches are still significant. So we can figure out that using two approaches gives better results than using conventional geometrical distance measures.

In Comparison with Idri et al [7] approach who used fuzzy logic to measure similarity between software projects. Their approach was mainly dedicated to ordinal categorical data, especially for COCOMO model. Moreover, there is a lack of evidence of how their approach could be useful for other datasets described by Nominal categorical data. Our approaches show how nominal categorical data can be also used in software projects similarity measurement. Their model was fuzzified based on experience where productivity ratio was used to find boundary of each fuzzy set. In our model we used automatic fuzzification process based on fuzzy c-means algorithm which seems more reliable than relying on experience. The aggregation operators (min and max) always give the extreme values and do not seem contributing in identification of the closest projects. While in our model we tried to take the influence of similarity between two software projects in each feature.

Table 4. Comparison between proposed similarity measures against Euclidian distance and Weighted Euclidean distance on Effort estimation

Evaluation Criteria	First proposed approach		
	One Analogy	*Mean of two analogies*	*Mean of three analogies*
MMRE	18.23%	16.06%	13.55%
BMMRE	22.4%	17.7%	17.0%
PRED(25%)	72%	78%	84%
	Second proposed approach		
	One Analogy	*Mean of two analogies*	*Mean of three analogies*
MMRE	20.3%	16.6%	16.8%
BMMRE	26.6%	23.4%	22%
PRED(25%)	72%	74%	74%
	Euclidean Distance		
	One Analogy	*Mean of two analogies*	*Mean of three analogies*
MMRE	59.4%	62.8%	65.6%
BMMRE	62.2%	60.1%	64.7%
PRED(25%)	44.4%	44.6%	45.4%
	Weighted Euclidean Distance		
	One Analogy	*Mean of two analogies*	*Mean of three analogies*
MMRE	59.4%	55.2%	56.7%
BMMRE	62.2%	59%	59.3%
PRED(25%)	44.4%	47.9%	50.2%

7 Conclusions

In this paper we introduced new approaches to measure similarity between two software projects based on fuzzy C-means and fuzzy logic. The approaches have been validated to their appropriateness for software projects. Both approaches do respect the main properties for similarity measures between two software projects. The first approach showed better MMRE results in terms of one analogy (closest project) than second approach. In general the results obtained showed that there is no significant difference between two proposed approaches and they contribute to better effort estimation accuracy than using conventional distance measures.

As discussed in the introduction, most geometrical distance based techniques applied to software cost estimation suffer from irrelevant features and dealing with categorical variables. The methods hereby proposed overcome these disadvantages by:

1. handling categorical in the same way numerical attributes are handled where they are represented by fuzzy sets.
2. using Fuzzy C-means has the advantage to group close projects together in the same cluster and then represent them in the same fuzzy set.
3. using Fuzzy logic has also advantage in dealing with uncertainty rather than single values.

However, the limitations of solution proposed this paper are: first, when two different projects feature values fall in the fuzzy set and is given unity similarity degree as similarity between a project to itself, therefore the similarity should be based on composition of values of project intersects each fuzzy set. Second, our approach is restricted to Gaussian membership function. Third, the project must be defined by more than one feature. Lastly, the fuzzy set must satisfy normal conditions.

There are sometimes factors affecting similarity measure such as using irrelevant features which has significant impact on similarity measurement, thus, decreasing estimation accuracy. The solution is to use either weight setting for each feature or remove irrelevant features. Weigh setting is difficult to determine and it is hard to be defined by expertise. The validation of using weight setting in our approaches will be for future improvement.

We are therefore continuing to extend our approach by addressing the limitation and restrictions mentioned earlier.

Acknowledgments. We would like to thank ISBSG Repository for granting us permission to utilize their datasets in this research.

References

1. Bezdek, J.C.: Pattern Recognition with Fuzzy Objective Function Algorithms. Kluwer Academic Publishers, Norwell (1981)
2. Dvir, G., Langholz, G., Schneider, M.: Matching attributes in a fuzzy case based reasoning. In: 18th International Conference of the North American on Fuzzy Information Processing Society, NAFIPS, New York, pp. 33–36 (1999)
3. Emam, K.E., Benlarbi, S., Goel, N., Rai, S.: Comparing case-based reasoning classifiers for predicting high risk software components. J. Systems and software 55, 301–320 (2001)

4. Esteva, F., Garcia-Calves, P., Godo, L.: Fuzzy Similarity-based models in Case-based Reasoning. In: Proceedings of the 2002 IEEE International Conference on Fuzzy systems, Honolulu, USA, pp. 1348–1353 (2002)
5. Fenton, N., Pfleeger, S.L.: Software metrics: A rigorous and practical approach, International Computer. Thomson Press (1997)
6. Huang, S.J., Chiu, N.H.: Optimization of analogy weights by genetic algorithm for software effort estimation. J. Information and software technology 48, 1034–1045 (2006)
7. Idri, A., Abran, A.: A fuzzy logic based set of measures for software project similarity: validation and possible improvements. In: Seventh International Software Metrics Symposium, London, pp. 85–96 (2001)
8. Jeffery, R., Ruhe, M., Wieczorek, I.: A comparative study of two software development cost modeling techniques using multi-organizational and company-specific data. J. Information and software technology 42, 1009–1016 (2000)
9. Krishnapuram, R., Frogui, H., Nasraoui, O.: Fuzzy and Possibilistic Shell Clustering Algorithms and Their Application to Boundary Detection and Surface Approximation – Part 1&2. J. IEEE Trans. Fuzzy Systems 3, 29–61 (1995)
10. Martin, C.L., Pasquier, J.L., Yanez, C.M., Gutierrez, A.T.: Software Development Effort Estimation Using Fuzzy Logic: A Case Study. In: Sixth Mexican International Conference on Computer Science, Mexico, pp. 113–120 (2005)
11. Mendes, E., Mosley, N., Counsell, S.: A replicated assessment of the use of adaptation rules to improve Web cost estimation. In: International Symposium on Empirical Software Engineering, pp. 100–109 (2003)
12. Mendes, E., Mosley, N., Counsell, S.: Do adaptation rules improve web cost estimation? In: Fourteenth ACM conference on Hypertext and hypermedia, Nottingham, pp. 173–183 (2003)
13. Michalewics, Z., Fogel, D.B.: How to solve it: Modern Heuristics. Springer, New York (2002)
14. Musflek, P., Pedrycz, W., Succi, G., Reformat, M.: Software Cost Estimation with Fuzzy Models. J. ACM SIGAPP Applied Computing Review 8, 24–29 (2000)
15. Ross, T.J.: Fuzzy Logic with engineering applications. John Wiley & Sons, Chichester (2004)
16. Shepperd, M., Schofield, C.: Estimating software project effort using analogy. J. IEEE Trans. On software engineering 23, 736–743 (1997)
17. Shepperd, M., Schofield, C., Kitchenham, B.: Effort estimation using analogy. In: 18th International Conference on Software Engineering, Berlin, pp. 170–178 (1996)
18. Sentas, P., Angelis, L.: Categorical missing data imputation for software cost estimation by multinomial logistic regression. J. Systems and Software 79, 4040–4414 (2006)
19. Stamelos, I., Angelis, L., Morisio, M.: Estimating the development cost of custom software. J. Information and management 40, 729–741 (2003)
20. Xie, X.L., Beni, G.: A Validity Measure for Fuzzy Clustering. J. IEEE Transaction on pattern analysis and machine intelligence 13, 841–847 (1991)
21. Xu, Z., Khoshgoftaar, T.: Identification of fuzzy models of software cost estimation. J. Fuzzy Sets and Systems 145, 141–163 (2004)
22. Zadeh, L.: Toward a theory of fuzzy information granulation and its centrality in human reasoning and fuzzy logic. J. Fuzzy sets and Systems 90, 111–127 (1997)

An Empirically–Based Process to Improve the Practice of Requirement Review

Juan Li[1], Lishan Hou[1], Zhongsen Qin[1,2], Qing Wang[1], and Guisheng Chen[3]

[1] Institute of Software, Chinese Academy of Sciences
[2] Graduate University of Chinese Academy of Sciences
[3] China Institute of Electronic System Engineering
{lijuan,houlishan,qinzhongsen,wq}@itechs.iscas.ac.cn,
cgs@tsinghua.edu.cn

Abstract. Requirement quality serves as the basis of the whole software development. How to improve and assure the quality of requirements is one of the most difficult issues. Aiming to improve requirement review in a software company, we propose a role-based requirement review process based on the idea that requirement quality should meet needs of all roles involved to the largest extent, and not only determined by the number of defects found in requirements. This process helps reviewers focus on their own concerns and find more defects related to their tasks, and provides a quantitative method to analyze and evaluate the quality of the requirement document. We also provide a case study to illustrate the new process and report some preliminary results.

Keywords: requirement review, role-based, quantitative, requirement quality characteristic.

1 Introduction

Requirements are important inputs of many key activities in software projects, such as project planning, designing and testing. Many studies have shown that requirements deficiencies are one of prime causes for project failures, and over 40% of problems in the software development cycle result from the poor quality requirements [1]. Requirement review is one important way to control requirement quality. Current researches mainly assess the requirement quality from the number of deficiencies found in requirements and propose several effective methods to check out deficiencies as many as possible. Basili et al. adopt a multi-perspectives method and enable the stakeholders to review the requirements specification from different views [2]. This method has been proven to check out more defects than other methods, such as ad-hoc reading and checklist-based reading [2],[3]. Gantner et al. emphasize that sufficient time for individual preparation of the reviewers is a crucial success factor for reviews [4]. In addition, many researches focus on the automatic assessment of requirement document with natural language checking technology [5].

In a Chinese company A which was rated CMMI Level 4, how to control requirement quality at the early phase has always been a serious problem for a long time.

Q. Wang, D. Pfahl, and D.M. Raffo (Eds.): ICSP 2008, LNCS 5007, pp. 135–146, 2008.
© Springer-Verlag Berlin Heidelberg 2008

Poor requirement quality results in much testing and developing effort. In order to resolve this problem, we propose a role-based requirement review process, which addresses that requirement quality should satisfy all the reviewers to the largest extent. This process not only helps inspectors concentrate on their own perspectives to improve review efficiency, but also provides quantitative analysis method based on defects and the satisfaction of inspectors. In the case study of this paper, requirement documents were reviewed according to the new process and some preliminary results were provided.

The remainder of this paper is organized as follows. Section 2 introduces the problems in the requirement review process in company A. Section 3 proposes the role-based quality evaluation process with a case study. Section 4 illustrates the case study and summarizes some lessons learned. Section 5 contains the conclusion and future work.

2 Problem Description

Our research was conducted in company A, a Chinese software company with 170 employees. It passed CMMI4 assessment in 2005. From 2002, Company A has successfully developed a software product line, called L in this paper. The product line has a core architecture and each new release adds features addressing key customers' needs. The New features are generally requested by a Marketing Unit (MU), expressing both market needs and strategic corporate concerns.

In May 2007, one important version of L (V3.0) was released. 2468 bugs were found during test. Among these bugs, there were 481 requirement-related bugs and the effort of modifying them takes 80% of total reworking effort. The cause classification of these 481 bugs is shown in Fig. 1.

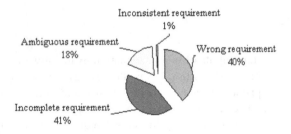

Fig. 1. Cause classification

Software Requirement Specification (SRS) review was an important way for this company to control requirement quality. The review process is shown in Fig. 2. The most important step is Review Meeting. Project Manager (PM), MU, Software Quality Assurance engineer (SQA), testers, and designers joined this meeting and checked SRS based on their own skills and experiences. If there were severe defects, SRS had to be modified and reviewed again. Otherwise, SRS could be put forward into the next phase.

Through interviewing with those reviewers, we found there were three main problems in the current process: (1) Reviewers were often distracted by the problems they did not really care about. For example, the structure of SRS was not important to testers and designers. But they often found this kind of defects because they did not know who should care about. (2) The efficiency of requirement review meeting was low. In the review meeting, some reviewers often fell into argument, and the others had to wait. (3) Reviewers lacked a quantitative method to judge whether the quality of SRS was satisfying. The quality was only judged according to the number of severe defects.

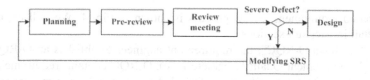

Fig. 2. Current review process

We checked records of 13 requirement reviews of two projects in 2007 (L2.9 and L3.0). There were 397 defects and the number of defects found by different roles is shown in Fig. 3. Table 1 shows concerns of different roles, and we can see that different roles have different viewpoints on the requirement quality. For instance, SQA mainly cares about requirement description format, while testers mainly focus on requirement verifiability. Also there are intersections among perspectives of these roles.

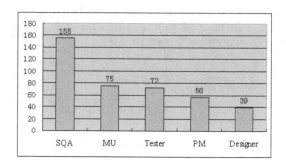

Fig. 3. Requirement defect distribution

Table 1. Concerns of different roles

	Correctness, Completeness, Unambiguity	Realizability	Verifiability	Description format
SQA	28%	0	0	72%
MU	82%	0	0	18%
Tester	10%	0	79%	11%
PM	39%	48%	5%	8%
Designer	16%	74%	0	10%

Based on the above analysis, we conclude that the current requirement review process should be improved. The new process should meet three main objectives. Objective 1: Help reviewers focus on their own concerns and check out more role-related defects; Objective 2: Improve the defect discovering efficiency (Number of Defect/Effort); Objective 3: Provide a quantitative method to evaluate the quality of SRS. We propose a role-based requirement review process, which will be described in section 3.

3   The Role-Based Requirement Review Process

The role-based requirement review process is shown in Fig. 4. We will explain the steps in detail in later sub-sections.

In step "Establish O-RQC", the requirement engineer establishes an O-RQC (Organizational Requirement Quality Characteristic). O-RQC contains requirement quality attributes for different specific roles. Detailed check items for every attributes are provided. In step "Specify Multi-role RQC", the requirement engineer tailors O-RQC into Multi-role RQC, which contains the multi-role checklist for a project. In step "Review", people review SRS separately according to the multi-role checklist. In step "Calculate and Analyze Review Result", the review result shows whether the requirement quality satisfies all the inspectors. PM can make decision on whether SRS should be modified or delivered into the next phase. If two people have different opinions on the same quality attributes, they and the requirement engineer will resolve the problem in step "Meeting".

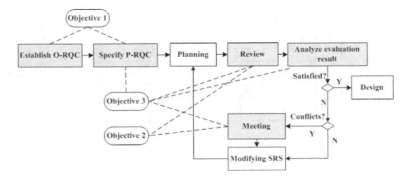

Fig. 4. Role-based requirement review process

3.1   Establish O-RQC

O-RQC provides a series of quality characteristics which describe different perspectives of requirement quality in company A. In O-RQC, the requirement quality is classified into three levels: requirement content quality, requirement description quality, and requirement sufficiency quality.

Requirement content quality: Requirement content means what function or performance of the system should be provided to customers. It emphasizes writing the "right" requirements.

Requirement description quality: Requirement description means the way requirements are described and organized, including the requirement description language and document format. It emphasizes writing requirements "right".

Requirement sufficiency quality: Requirements are important inputs of many tasks. Different tasks have different needs on requirement quality. Requirement sufficiency emphasizes getting an "enough" requirements specification for different tasks. For example, if testers cannot specify test cases based on requirements, the requirement quality is not good enough for them.

At every level, there is a group of Quality Characteristics (QCs), as shown in Fig. 5. Each QC is divided into several sub-QCs, and each sub-QC can be described by a list of check items. According to these check items, reviewers can check SRS step by step.

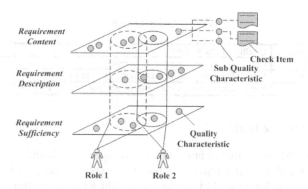

Fig. 5. O-RQC

To specify QC, we try to follow as much as possible a standard terminology, in particular the one defined by IEEE 830[6]. It provides 8 characteristics of a good SRS including "correct", "unambiguous", "complete", "consistent", "ranked for importance and/or stability", "verifiable", "modifiable" and "traceable". We distribute these QCs onto the 3 above levels separately. Also one change is made in order to develop consistent QCs to evaluate requirements: "ranked for importance and/or stability" is divided into "important" and "stable", and "ranked" becomes the sub QC of these two QCs. In the end, we introduce some QCs not included in IEEE830, especially those on sufficiency level. The characteristics at different levels are listed in Table 2. The QCs and sub-QCs represented in bold are not presented in IEEE 830.

As shown in Table 2, some QCs of IEEE 830 distribute both on Content and Description level. That is because in IEEE 830, the definition of these QCs includes both content and description. Also, on sufficiency level, we add new QCs to describe different roles' needs. A brief description of each QC added is presented as follows:

Usable: Expresses the value to customers and end users. If the function or performances meet their needs, then the requirements are usable.

Realizable: Indicates if the requirement can be realized under the constraints of current technologies, the schedule and the personnel capability.

Important: Shows how essential the requirement is for the market. Some requirements are desirable and some are necessary.

Stable: Evaluates the probability of the requirement will change in the development.

Profitable: Expresses the ability of the requirement to yield advantageous returns or results for the company.

The QCs are divided into sub-QCs. The sub-QCs provided by IEEE 830 are maintained and new sub-QCs for some QCs in IEEE 830 are added. For instance, on description level, we add several sub-QCs for the use case model, which is used to describe requirements in company A. There are 14 QCs, 31 sub-QCs and 64 check items in Q-RQC totally.

Table 2. QC in O-RQC

Quality Level	Quality Characteristic
Content	Correct, Complete, Consistent, **Usable**
Description	Modifiable, Complete, Unambiguous, Consistent
Sufficiency	**Realizable**, verifiable, traceable, **Important, Stable, Profitable**

3.2 Specify Multi-role RQC

The O-RQC lists the main quality attributes the company A should care, but for different projects, not all the QCs must be cared. For a specific project, PM and the requirement engineer tailor O-RQC into the multi-role RQC according to the project context and the responsibility of every role. The multi-role RQC provides checklists for different roles.

According to the characteristics of project: For those time-to-market projects, the product needs to be delivered to the market as soon as possible. In order to get customers' feedback, the "important" and "usable" requirement should be realized first. Not all the requirements should be realized, so "unambiguous" is not the first met QC. But for those projects without the schedule pressure, or using waterfall development model, the "unambiguous" is the very first QC that should be satisfied.

According to different roles: Different roles have different concerns on the requirement quality. For example, testers care more about "Verifiable" and designers care more about "Realizable". PM and the requirement engineer choose those QCs important for different roles.

Furthermore, one QC may be related with many roles, and we use the Weight of Role to deal with different importance of multi-role on the same characteristic. The higher the weight, the more important the role is. We use the expert experience method to specify weights of roles.

3.3 Review

Based on the Multi-role RQC, inspectors review requirements according to their own checklist alone. They need to record defects and feed back their satisfaction for every QC.

There are three types of defects: severe defect, slight defect and advice. Severe defects means, if they are not corrected, the function or performances will be wrong or not be realized. Slight defect means the defect that does not affect the whole system realization. Advice means the recommendation on SRS.

In addition, the quality of QC is measured through the reviewers' satisfaction. A three-category rating scale is used which includes "2-Satisfying", "1-Acceptable", "0-Dissatisfying".

3.4 Calculate and Analyze Review Result

After reviews, the requirement engineer calculates the review result represented by the satisfaction degree. Here we provide two kinds of satisfaction degree: Satisfaction degree of every QC (SDqc), Satisfaction degree of the SRS quality (SD$_{SRS}$). The range of these two satisfaction degree value is from 0 to 2. 0~1 means the quality is dissatisfying; 1 means acceptable; 1~2 means satisfying.

SDqc: Expresses the satisfaction degree of every QC based on all the related roles' viewpoints and severe defect ratio. For example, if satisfaction degree of "Correct" is 1, that means the "Correct" of SRS is acceptable for all the stakeholders.

SD$_{SRS}$: Means the quality satisfaction degree of SRS based on the Multi-role RQC. If the SD$_{SRS}$ is 1, that means the SRS' quality is acceptable.

We introduce the following symbols to illustrate our calculating method. Suppose there are m quality characteristics and n roles in the requirement inspections.

QC={qc$_1$,..,qc$_m$} is the set of all QCs, in which qc$_i$(i=1,..,m) is one QC. Role={R$_1$,..,R$_n$} is the set of all roles, in which R$_j$(j=1,..,n) is one role. Each role may be acted by several people. R={P$_1$,...,P$_k$} Role is the set of people acting the same role. W$_{qc}$(R) means the weight of the role R for the characteristic qc; SD$_{qc}$(Pk) means the score of the characteristic qc marked by the person P$_k$; SD$_{qc}$(R) means the score of the characteristic qc marked by the role R; Num$_{dft}$(R) means the number of the defects found by the role R. Num$_{sdft}$(R) means the number of the severe defects found by the role R.

$$SD_{qc}(R) = \frac{1}{k}\sum_{i=1}^{k} SD_{qc}(P_k) \tag{1}$$

$$SD_{qc} = \sum_{j=1}^{n} SD_{qc}(R_j) * W_{qc}(R_j) * (1 - \frac{Num_{sdft}(R_j)}{Num_{dft}(R_j)}) \tag{2}$$

$$SD_{SRS} = \frac{1}{m}\sum_{i=1}^{m} SD_{qc} \tag{3}$$

4 Case Study

In this section, we illustrate the process through a case study. We want to prove the three objectives are achieved by the new process. To address this need, the study uses six reviewers to re-evaluate the requirement documents of previous projects according to the new process proposed in this paper. The findings from this study are then compared with the earlier findings of reviews in previous projects to gain useful insights about the applicability of the new process. Also, we invited the requirement engineer of previous projects to take part in the whole process to learn more experiences.

4.1 Study Design

SRS. The SRSes inspected during this study were requirements documents of a previous project L3.0. The product had three large functions modules and every module had individual SRS. These three SRSes were numbered SRS_1, SRS_2, SRS_3.

Reviewer. There were six reviewers drawn from project teams. These participants had about at least 2 years of experience in the field and did not attend previous requirement review of L3.0. They had different experiences and skills: one PM, one designer, one tester, one marketing unit engineer and one SQA.

Review Process. People reviewed these three SRSes according to the process proposed in section 3. Firstly, the participants received training on the new process and the context of the previous project. Secondly, the requirement engineer of project L3.0 specified Multi-role RQC and determined the weight of role. Thirdly, participants performed their own inspection of SRSes according to the multi-role checklist

Table 3. Multi-role RQC used in the Case

Quality Characteristic	Role				
	PM	Designer	Tester	SQA	MU
Content					
Correct	√				√
Complete		√	√		
Consistent					
Usable	√				√
Description					
Complete		√	√	√	
Unambiguous					
Modifiable				√	
Consistent				√	
Sufficiency					
Realizable	√	√			
Verifiable			√		
Traceable					
Important	√				
Stable					
Profitable					√

Table 4. Weight of role

	Correct	Usable	Content Complete	Description Complete	Realizable
PM	0.5	0.4			0.6
MU	0.5	0.6			
Designer			0.5	0.5	0.4
Tester			0.5	0.4	
SQA				0.1	

alone to identify and record defects as many as possible. Also, they recorded their subjective remark about QC. At last, the defect lists, efforts and remarks of six people were collected and processed. In processing, the requirement engineer caculated the review result for every SRS and analyzed their quality.

Multi-role RQC and weight of role. We interviewed the PM of L3.0 to learn about the project context. L3.0 was a time-to-market project and the product needed to be delivered to market as soon as possible. So QCs like "Important" and "Usable" were important, but "Unambiguous" was not the first met QC. Table 3 lists the QCs in Multi-role RQC of this case. For the space is limited, the sub-QCs chosen are not shown in detail.

Also, the requirement engineer defined the weights of the roles because she was the expert and knew well about the sample project. The weights of roles are shown in Table 4. For example, PM and MU both care about "Correct". The weight of PM is 0.5 and equal to the weight of MU. The sum of weights equals 1.

4.2 Data Collection and Analysis

Table 5 lists the data collected in the three reviews. In Table 5, for every QC, there are three rows to describe the information of satisfaction and the defect amount. The first row shows the review data of SRS_1, the second shows data of SRS_2, and the third shows data of SRS_3. The last column lists the review result we calculated according to formula (1)~(2). According to formula (3), we got the value of every document: $SD_{SRS1}=0.684$, $SD_{SRS2}=1.415$, $SD_{SRS3}=0.468$. From these values, we can see the quality of SRS_2 is satisfying, and the other two are dissatisfying. Although there were some differences, the requirement engineer of L3.0 considered that the result reflected the true quality of the three SRSes by and large.

Now we take SRS3 as an example to illustrate the analysis process. Fig. 6 shows SDqc and satisfaction degrees of reviewers for every QC. We can see most QCs' quality is unsatisfying except "Important", "Realizable" and "Profitable". We take "Verifiable" and "Content Complete" for instances. In project L3.0, the SRS_3 was reviewed once and delivered into design. But during the test phase, many bugs were found due to the poor quality of SRS_3. Most of them were caused by incomplete and unverifiable requirements. In our study, the satisfaction degree of "Verifiable" and "Content Complete" were dissatisfying, because the multi-role checklist helped reviewers find more defects. But several results are not consistent with the real situation. For example, the quality of "Correct" was dissatisfying in this study, but the MU

Table 5. Review data of three documents

	P1		P2		P3		P4		P5		P6		SD_{qc}
	S	D	S	D	S	D	S	D	S	D	S	D	
Correct	1	5:2							1	2:1			0.55
	1	3:0							2	4:0			1.5
	1	4:2							0	2:2			0.25
Usable	2	2:0							1	5:0			1.4
	2	2:0							2	4:0			2
	1	3:1							0	3:2			0.93
Important	0	4:2											0
	1	3:0											1
	1	5:0											1
Content Complete			1	2:0	1	0:0	1	1:0					1
			2	2:0	1	2:0	2	2:0					1.75
			1	7:4	0	5:4	1	2:1					0.5
Description Complete			2	2:0	1	3:0	1	0:0			0	2:2	1.4
			1	2:0	2	1:0	1	2:1			1	2:0	1
			1	9:1	0	4:4	1	1:1			1	3:1	0.51
Consistent											1	4:2	0.5
											1	2:1	0.5
											0	2:2	0
Modifiable											1	1:1	1
											2	2:1	1
											0	3:2	0
Verifiable					1	4:2	1	3:3					0.29
					2	6:0	2	0:0					2
					0	6:6	0	10:7					0
Realizable	0	3:3	1	4:1									0.3
	1	5:0	2	2:0									1.4
	2	0:0	1	7:2									1.49
Profitable									1	5:3			0.4
									2	0:0			2
									0	0:0			0

Note: *P1- Person 1 (PM), P2- Person 2 (Designer), P3-Person 3(Tester), P4-Person 4 (Tester), P5-Person 5 (Marketing Unit Engineer), P6-Person 6 (SQA); S-Satisfaction degree, D-Number of defect: Number of severe defect*

in project L3.0 thought the functions were correct because they had got good feedbacks from customers. This is because their understandings about the function were different. So O-RQC provides detailed and operable checking items for designers, testers and SQA, but for MU and PM, this method can only provide guidance and the result highly depends on the experiences of reviewers. We also found that on "Description Complete", two testers had different opinions. Then we had a meeting with P3 and P4. P3 was dissatisfied with the QC because he found 4 severe defects in half

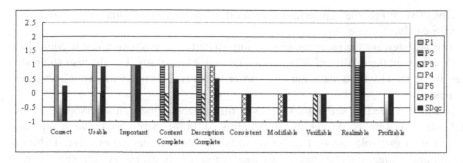

Fig. 6. SD_{qc} and satisfaction degree of reviewers for SRS$_3$

an hour and P4 considered the QC was satisfying because he found only 1 severe defect in an hour. Therefore satisfaction degree was determined by both the number of severe defects and the speed of defect discovering. So their marks were reasonable and need not to be changed.

4.3 Discussion

In order to learn about the effects of the process, we interviewed the six people attended SRS reviews and the requirement engineer. Based on their opinions and data collected in the case, we want to prove the new process has achieved the three objectives proposed in section 2.

Objective 1: Help reviewers focus on their own concerns to find more defects related with their tasks;

All the reviewers mentioned the multi-role checklist helps them concentrate on their own perspectives. The defects are all related with concerns of reviewers. Reviewers need not to consider those unrelated perspectives.

Objective 2: Improve defect discovering efficiency;

We compared the defect discovering efficiency of the case with that of project L3.0, as shown in Table 6. For every SRS, the row in grey lists the data of this case and another lists data from project L3.0. We found the efficiency was improved. Although in this case study, the data set was not large, it also could prove the effects of new process to some extent.

Table 6. Comparison between review data of the case and project L3.0

	Size (Page)	Number of reviewer	Number of Defect	Effort (Human Hour)	Defect Discovering Efficiency
SRS1	20	6	52	6	8.67
		6	24	12	2
SRS2	11	6	46	6.8	6.76
		12	38	24	1.58
SRS3	16	6	75	8	9.34
		11	12	22	0.55

Objective 3: Provide a quantitative method to analyze and evaluate the total quality of SRS easily.

The requirement engineer mentioned the quantitative evaluation result could help her learn about the quality of SRS and analyze problem easily, but she also suggested that there should be a data analysis process because some data were subjective ratings.

In addition, we find some weaknesses in this process. Firstly, if a person plays several roles, the weights of roles should be adjusted. In this paper, we only consider one person with one role. Secondly, the weights of roles are very subjective. Different person and project context may affect their values. It is necessary to apply the new process in more projects to assure its effectiveness.

5 Conclusion

The process proposed in this paper is motivated by the factual problem in a Chinese company. We propose a role-based requirement review process to help reviewers analyze and assess requirement quality. We apply the new process in a case study and discuss its advantages and drawbacks. In the future, we will apply this process into more projects and improve the process continuously.

Acknowledgments. This research is supported by the National Natural Science Foundation of China under grant No. 60573082, the National Basic Research Program (973 program) under grant No. 2007CB310802, the Hi-Tech Research and Development Program of China (863 Program) under grant No. 2006AA01Z155.

References

1. The Standish Report (2004), http://www.standishgroup.com/chronicles/index.php
2. Basili, V.R., Green, S., Laitenberger, O., Lanubile, F., Shull, F., Sørumgård, S., Zelkowitz, M.V.: The Empirical Investigation of Perspective Based Reading. Empirical Software Engineering: An International Journal 1(2), 133–164 (1996)
3. He, L., Carver, J.: PBR vs. Checklist: A Replication in The N-fold Inspection Context. In: 2006 International Symposium on Empirical Software Engineering, pp. 95–104. ACM Press, New York (2006)
4. Gantner, T., Barth, T.: Experiences on Defining and Evaluating An Adapted Review Process. In: The 25th International Conference on Software Engineering, pp. 506–511. IEEE Press, New York (2003)
5. Ormandjieva, O., Hussain, I., Kosseim, L.: Toward A Text Classification System for the Quality Assessment of Software Requirements Written in Natural Language. In: Fourth International Workshop on Software Quality Assurance, pp. 39–45. ACM Press, New York (2007)
6. IEEE Standard Association, IEEE recommended practice for software requirements specifications, IEEE Std-830 (1998), http://standards.ieee.org/reading/ieee/std_public/des-cription/se/830-1998_desc.html

Capability Assessment of Individual Software Development Processes Using Software Repositories and DEA

Shen Zhang[1,2], Yongji Wang[1,3], Ye Yang[1], and Junchao Xiao[1]

[1] Laboratory for Internet Software Technologies, Institute of Software,
The Chinese Academy of Sciences, Beijing 100080, China
[2] Graduate University of Chinese Academy of Sciences, Bejing 100039, China
[3] State Key Laboratory of Computer Science, Institute of Software,
The Chinese Academy of Sciences, Beijing 100080, China
{zhangshen, ywang, ye, xiaojunchao}@itechs.iscas.ac.cn

Abstract. Effective capability assessment of individual software processes is a key issue involved in validating the past and adjusting future development processes. While most of the current assessment approaches have been successfully demonstrated in academic communities, new challenges in metric data extraction and further analysis still arise when considering actual industrial applications. In this paper, we propose a novel integrated method for capability assessment of individual software development processes. Firstly, our method facilitates the capability metrics extraction task by making use of software repositories as the data source, enabling recording of data effortless and more accurate. Then, we decompose these metrics at the individual-level of granularity by exploring different human identities from various sources. Finally, the data envelopment analysis (DEA) is also adopted to assist our method to carry out an objective and quantitative assessment for individual software processes under MIMO constraints. Empirical illustrations from a practical case study illustrate the effectiveness of the proposed method.

Keywords: individual software development process (IDP), software repository, data envelopment analysis (DEA), multi-input-multi-output (MIMO).

1 Introduction

People are well regarded as the largest source of variation in project performance, those organizations that have been able to sustain people performance improvement programs have demonstrated impressive gains in productivity and quality [1]. Among the published studies, the P-CMM [2] and PSP [3], which are both developed by SEI, have been widely recognized as two of the most notable and influential workforce practices. The P-CMM organizes a series of increasingly sophisticated practices into a course of action for evaluating and improving workforce capability, while PSP is also a performance and process improvement technique aimed at individual software engineers and small software organizations. For both P-CMM and PSP, their principal objective is to assess the current personal practices and then galvanize the organization

Q. Wang, D. Pfahl, and D.M. Raffo (Eds.): ICSP 2008, LNCS 5007, pp. 147–159, 2008.
© Springer-Verlag Berlin Heidelberg 2008

and individual to take action on needed improvements immediately following the assessment [2,3]. However, some challenges still arise, especially regarding the industrial applications [4,5].

Firstly, an undue burden is placed on developers and empowered teams due to the extensive overhead of collecting measures manually, and a rather lengthy training time of 150 to 200 hours for PSP users and 2-3 months for a P-CMM assessment team creates extra workload too [2,5].

Secondly, implementing P-CMM and PSP in an industrial setting also involves privacy and integrity issues, the temptation for developers to alter their practice measures can lead to measurement dysfunction [6].

Thirdly, they are both more prone to subjective bias, but inadequate for objective-quantitative assessment. In P-CMM, the assessing phase tasks are conducted by the assessment team through interviews, workforce discussion and questionnaires [2], so the lack of delicate objective quantitative analysis makes it inadequate for accurate capability estimations and improvement suggestions. While in PSP, the estimated data required in the measurement program inevitably leads to biased results.

Fortunately, the software repositories and data envelopment analysis (DEA)[7] offer alternatives to overcome these challenges. In this paper, a novel integrated method is proposed for the assessment of individual development processes, and it can be expected to be ultimately incorporated into P-CMM and PSP to assist in raising the efficiency and effectiveness of their capability assessment processes. In our method, firstly, we facilitate the process metrics extraction task by making use of software repositories as the data source, enabling recording of data effortless and more accurate. Secondly, we decompose the process metrics at the individual-level of granularity by exploring different human identities from various sources. Finally, based on these metrics, a DEA model is presented for the quantitative capability assessment of individual development processes (**throughout this paper, we use the terms "IDP" interchangeably with "individual development process"**).

This paper is outlined as follows. Section 2 discusses the state of the art. In section 3, we first present our work done in the direction of the capability measures extraction from the software repositories, then focus on the DEA-based assessment of individual process capability. The experimental results are reported in section 4. Section 5 closes with a conclusion.

2   Related Work

2.1   Software Repositories

Software repositories such as version control systems, defect tracking systems and mailing lists contain a wealth of valuable information. Such information is not only useful for managing the progress of software projects, but also as a detailed log of the evolution of human activities during development.

Software practitioners and researchers are beginning to recognize the potential benefit of collecting the vast amount of information contained in software repositories. [13] presents a method to track the progress of students developing a term project, using the historical information stored in their version control repository.

However, due to the lack of statistical information on defects, the impact of quality factors hasn't been taken into consideration in their work. Keir et al. [14] outline their experiences of mining and analyzing a set of assignment repositories, the focus of their work is on the extraction of quantitative measures of students' performance. They recognize static error as an important performance indicator but ignore to integrate field defect information from defect reports.

2.2 Data Envelopment Analysis

As we observed in our previous work[9,10], the software development process, which commonly takes the cost, effort, etc. as input and the program size, defects, etc. as output, is doubtless a multi-input-multi-output (MIMO) process. Besides, [8] also points that, in software engineering, it seems more sensible to compare the performance with the best practice rather than with some theoretical optimal (and probably not attainable) value. DEA offer us an opportunity to evaluate the relative performance under MIMO constraints.

Data Envelopment Analysis (DEA) developed by A. Charnes and W. W. Cooper [7] in 1978 is a non-parametric programming-based performance assessment model. It can be used to analyze the relative performance of a number of units, which can be viewed as a multi-input-multi-output system consuming inputs to produce outputs. DEA is superior to ordinary statistical regression in situations where multiple inputs and outputs exist with no objective way to aggregate scores into a meaningful index of production. At present, DEA has been extensively accepted in performance analysis research and then applied to benchmarking of projects and processed. For example, [8] illustrates how to evaluate the performance of ERP projects by using DEA, and a DEA-based empirical study on benchmarking software tasks as well as an evaluation approach for project quality is also presented in our previous work[10,11]..

3 Approach Overview

Fig. 1 illustrates the flow chart of the proposed assessment method.

Our work extends the state of the art in the following ways:

It enables the extraction of data from the following information sources to return four groups of predictors:

• Program features mined from source code
• Software changes recorded in version control system
• Pre-release defects exposed by static analysis tool
• Field defects (customer reported software problems requiring developer intervention to resolve) found in defect tracking system

It adopts a decomposition strategy to decompose the organizational-level metrics at the individual-level of granularity by identifying the different identities of the involved people from various sources.

It proposes the DEA model to deal with the multi-input-multi-output capability assessment of individual development process, the IDP-related metric sets are classified into input and output metrics to be used in this model.

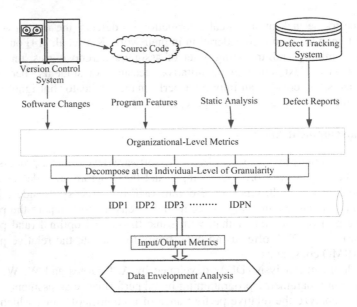

Fig. 1. The Capability Assessment Method

3.1 Metric Extraction

Identifying and collecting predictors (metrics available before release) are prerequisites activities for our assessment method. Since our study only focuses on the most commonly software repositories such as VCS and defect tracking systems, the predictors we extracted can be mainly divided into four classes.

Table 1. Predictors collected in our study

Predictors	Description
Predictors-1	The first group of predictors comes from parsing the source code directly, such as the metrics related the flow of program control, number of distinct operations and statements, degree of modularity of a program, and number of instances of certain formatting habits.
Predictors-2	For the second group of predictors, we used static analysis technique [15] to examine all source files outputted from IDP. Static analysis technique can detect many types of higher-level features of code, particularly style violations or bad practices, such as buffer overflows, null pointer dereferences, the use of uninitialized variables, etc. Most of these static programming errors are important quality predictors and good candidates for pre-release defects.
Predictors-3	The third group of predictors is extracted from VCS repositories, these predictors largely represent individual behavior and work habits. They include things like the number of VCS operations per day, number of update transactions per module, average number of lines of code added or deleted per day, how often to make modifications or add new features to existing code, and more.
Predictors-4	The final group comes from defect tracking systems. Our aim is to assess the quality of individual software process from the end user's perspective. They include things like the number of defect records with high severity level, number of defect records that are fixed before current release, and more.

All the four groups of predictors can be transformed into standard *product metrics* and *development metrics* for software process measurement.

The first two groups of predictors, which are mined from source code directly or indirectly, can be categorized as *product metrics*. The *product metrics* measure the attributes of any intermediate or final product of the software development process. Similarly, the last two groups of predictors, which are extracted from the VCS and the defect tracking system, can be categorized as *development metrics*. The development metrics measure the attributes of the development process.

3.1.1 Metrics Extraction at the Individual-Level of Granularity

In view of the definition of *product* and *development* metrics, all of them are commonly applicable to the process assessment at the organizational level, but not available for immediate use of process assessment at the individual level. In general, the team development process for a massive software project, which may involve dozens of people, can be regarded as an aggregation of many small individual processes. Therefore, the data of the *product* and *process* metrics, such as the total numbers of LOC added and field defect, can also be attributed to all of the people involved in the development work. To this end, we also adopt some strategy to "*decompose*" these organizational-level metrics at the individual-level of granularity.

Since each person can appear with many identities in various repositories real life names (such as in copyright notices), user account with associated e-mail addresses, etc. The goal of our strategy is to mine the user identities from the metric data and then match each piece of metric data to certain IDP by referring to these user identities. To illustrate this strategy, we give the following examples. In our examples, we use a specific VCS tool CVS and Java programming language as a demonstration.

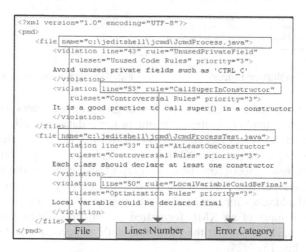

Fig. 2. Example of PMD Outputs

In the first example, we adopt static analysis technique to extract the second group predictors from source code. Tool support is necessary for this work, so we call API of PMD [17] to examine a snapshot of Java code. PMD uses its pre-defined ruleset files and source code as inputs, then returns the errors' locations and their descriptions as outputs. **Fig. 2** shows an example of PMD outputs.

To match these metric data to certain individual software processes, we must acquire the corresponding developer identity. Since only VCS and defect tracking systems are required to have at least a mandatory identity in order to participate, source code does not hold mandatory identities. Therefore, it is necessary to combine the PMD outputs and the VCS log outputs in order to determine the developer identity. In this example, the VCS log is retrieved from a CVS repository by issuing *CVS annotate* command. **Fig. 3** illustrates the combination process above. The top part of **Fig. 3** depicts a sample static error taken from the **Fig. 2**, so we can locate the error in line 43 of the source file *JcmdProcess.java*. On the other hand, the bottom part of **Fig. 3** represents the *CVS annotate* outputs on the modification for line 43 of source file *JcmdProcess.java*, so we can identify that the developer with a CVS account *ezust* is just the person who made this error in version 1.1 on the date of 15-Jun-06.

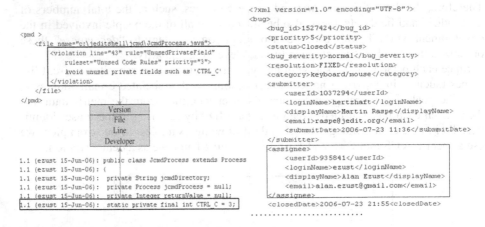

Fig. 3. Combination Process   **Fig. 4.** Snippet from SourceForge.net

For the second example, we extract the fourth group of predictors from defect reports held in a defect tracking system. To obtain these data, we call API of HTML tidy [19] to convert the defect reports to XHTML format via HTTP, then extract the necessary defect properties from the XML documents based on a pre-defined schema. Besides some intrinsic defect properties, each report also contains the identity information of the developer who brought the defect. The identity is a user account with associated e-mail addresses for the developer to login into the defect tracking system. **Fig. 4** depicts a snippet of an XML formatted defect report from Sourceforge.net. From **Fig. 4**, we can confirm that the developer with an account *ezust* should be responsible for the bug 1527424.

In the above two examples, a CVS account *ezust* is identified in the second group of predictors, while a defect tracking system account *ezust* is identified in the fourth group of predictors. However, we still need to determine whether these two accounts can be attributed to the same real person and his individual software process. Moreover, since each person can appear with one or more identities in a repository, some other CVS account names such as *p_ezust, ezust1* and *ezust_alan* may refer to the same person *ezust* as well. For our goal is to mine the user identities from the metric data and then match each piece of metric data to corresponding developer and his individual software process, it is vital to clarify the relationship of different identities and match them for the completeness and accuracy of our assessment study.

A heuristic-based method [12] has been proposed to identify the developers' identities by matching the different identifiers from software repositories, but even the authors themselves also admit "some matches will be false, and some will be missing, which can cause problems." Therefore, we use a more simple approach to ensure the accuracy of the data in our study. We first establish a people identity set by consulting the developers under study for their user accounts in various repositories, then we adopt a string-matching technique to match these identity information based on the people identity set, so a much lower probability for matching failure can be achieved.

Due to the software repository and language-specified constraints, several predictors in this section may vary slightly. However, as long as the software organizations adopt VCS and defect tracking system to maintain the evolution of software development processes, all four groups of predictors extraction and their decomposition processes can proceed automatically without human intervention.

3.2 Capability Assessment Model

The acquisition of individual-level metrics is an essential prerequisite of our assessment method, while choosing statistical methods for further analysis of the metrics data is also identified as a vital step.

In this section, we will present a short introduction to the DEA model, and place emphasis on the actual meaning for individual capability assessment.

Since the IDP is a multi-input-multi-output (MIMO) process, which commonly takes the cost, effort, etc. as input and the program size, defect density, etc. as output, the four groups of predictors stated in section 3.1 are taken as the input/output metrics in our IDP capability assessment model,

Let us assume that there are n IDPs to be evaluated. Each IDP consumes varying amounts of m different inputs to produce s different outputs. Specifically, the input and output metrics of IDP_j can be written as:

$$input\ metrics: \ x_j = \left(x_{1j}, x_{2j}, \cdots, x_{mj} \right)^T > 0, \quad j = 1, \cdots, n$$

$$output\ metrics: y_j = \left(y_{1j}, y_{2j}, \cdots, y_{sj} \right)^T > 0, \quad j = 1, \cdots, n$$

The DEA BCC model is written as:

$$\left(D_{BC^2} \right) = \begin{cases} \min(\theta) \\ \sum_{j=1}^{n} x_j \lambda_j \leq \theta x_{j0} \\ \sum_{j=1}^{n} y_j \lambda_j \geq y_{j0} \\ \sum_{j=1}^{n} \lambda_j = 1 \quad \lambda_j \geq 0, j = 1, \ldots, n \end{cases} \tag{1}$$

Where the scalar variable θ in (1) represents the capability score, and it ranges from 0 to 1. If IDP_{j0} receives the maximal value $\theta = 1$, then it is of relative high capability, but if $\theta < 1$, it is of relative low capability, Furthermore, since the value of θ means that the IDP_{j0} can still achieve a minimal decrease of θ times in its inputs without decreasing the production for any outputs, its capability is relatively lower when the θ is relatively smaller.

The λ in model (1) is the peer weight. Each IDP can be presented by a linear combination of the whole IDP set, such as: $IDP_{j0} = \lambda_1 IDP_1 + \cdots + \lambda_j IDP_j + \cdots + \lambda_n IDP_n$. In fact, only a relative high-capability IDP_j may have a peer weight $\lambda_j > 0$, so we can define a reference set RS_{j0} for each IDP_{j0} as: $RS_{j0} = \{IDP_j : \lambda_j \neq 0, j = 1, \ldots, n\}$. Here, each high-capability IDP_j in the reference set is called as a peer of the IDP_{j0}, The corresponding peer weight λ_j indicates the important degree of the peer IDP_j to the given IDP_{j0}. In our study, via the peers $\{IDP_j\}$ and their weights $\{\lambda_j\}$, researchers can further determine which peer (the IDP of relative high capability) is of the biggest improvement value to the low-capability IDP_{j0} and thus need to be learned more from.

4   Experimental Results and Analysis

In this section, we demonstrate the IDP capability assessment approach on a development team in ISCAS. The organization (ISCAS) which we collect data from is one of the leading research and development organizations in China and has high software process capability maturity level (CMMI level 4). The work of the developers in IS-CAS is entirely performed under strict quantitative CMMI-based processes management and maintained in organizational software repositories, such as CVS, firefly, bugrat and so on. Besides, the organization imposes strict defect reporting/tracing/fixing procedures on their development processes. Thus, the data quality and relative completeness of the defect reports can be sufficiently guaranteed. Since the ISCAS is responsible for a China "863" project *SoftPM* [16], which is being developed in pure Java with hundreds of person-years of development behind it, 30 developers within the project team are selected for our experimental study.

We collect the following predictor data from *SoftPM*'s software repositories. In the CVS repository, we successfully evaluate 4,904 Java source files stored in 657 directories. Upon inspecting these files, 2,871 CVS commits with the corresponding

Table 2. Input and output assessment metrics of IDPs

Metric	Type	Meaning	Unit
Total Schedule (TS)	Input	The sum of actual time devoted to individual software process i	Person hour
Cost	Input	Total money invested in individual software process i during the development period	Chinese yuan
Scale	Output	Total source lines of code produced by individual software process i	LOC
Pre-Defect	Output	Total static errors found across all files in individual software process i	Pre-defects
Field Defect	Output	Total defect records found in individual software process i during the development period in all releases	field defects

15,301 revisions, which can be linked to 96 developers, are also obtained up to date. Then, we perform a static analysis on the source code to identify 89,722 static errors as well as the relationships between them and individual engineers. Furthermore, we extract a total number of 3,532 defect reports from the defect tracking systems, after filtering out 228 duplicate reports and 472 invalid reports, a final number of 2,832 defect reports are recorded, and most of them can be tracked to their assigners.

To simplify the experimental verification in this paper, we only derive five most direct metrics (**Table 2**) for assessing individual software development processes.. The time and money consumed by development processes should be taken as the input metrics, while other metrics defined in **Table 2** are regarded as the output metrics in our DEA model. Moreover, we also provide an explanation here:

The *total schedule (TS)* is actually computed from the accumulation time intervals between check-out time and check-in time of the version changes brought about by IDP i. Since some time intervals may overlap each other, we eliminate the overlapping time intervals during the sum process.

We choose money as one of the sample metrics, the reason is that the time and money are always taken as the most representative factors in empirical software engineering models such as COCOMO. Since no cost-related information can be found in software repositories, we have to consult managers about this.

The two metrics which require for transformation in **Table 2** are: *pre-defect* and *field defect*. Because an increase in an input should contribute to increased output and increasing the *pre-defect* and *field defect* are undesirable outputs, we adopt the [TRβ] transformation to transform these metrics which are undesirable outputs in DEA terminology. For a detailed discussion of the [TRβ] transformation, readers may refer to our previous work [11].

Based on sample metrics defined in **Table 2**, the collected metric data of each IDP are shown in **Table 3**.

The capability score θ for the 30 IDPs is calculated using DEA model in 3.2 and presented in **Fig.5**. We observe that there are 9 IDPs of relative high capability, while the other 21 IDPs are all of relative low capability, since their capability score are smaller than 1.

Table 3. Statistics for the 20 IDPs' input/output metrics

IDP	TS	Cost	Scale	Pre-Defect	Field Defect	IDP	TS	Cost	Scale	Pre-Defect	Field Defect
1	9130	291561	79248	1156	18	16	1548	43670	6118	6746	163
2	595	17503	5061	2460	87	17	585	23433	6352	6600	67
3	12054	454094	83144	2230	42	18	748	28891	10891	2863	95
4	1737	47061	24020	6517	82	19	662	18457	4418	7414	176
5	6137	166813	72578	3053	54	20	395	12209	4749	7487	164
6	3855	112353	34593	5943	131	21	2333	80532	25938	5495	86
7	575	19617	7177	4532	131	22	635	23904	7632	7512	132
8	1903	56987	12964	8311	188	23	1902	55517	10696	6555	187
9	861	34423	9451	7541	133	24	352	10252	5228	6548	114
10	310	11179	4059	6257	153	25	428	17498	4476	5555	179
11	908	28278	6318	7041	168.	26	2005	68137	15677	6560	153
12	250	10219	3972	7162	178.	27	406	14479	6285	7556	157
13	683	27526	5379	6470	119	28	675	20640	6445	7561	143.
14	6245	250275	33206	6428	143	29	1167	46381	8708	7548	148.
15	495	19451	5338	7336	96	30	535	21229	5203	8545	158

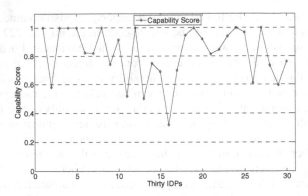

Fig.5. Capability Score θ

Table 4. Peer sets and peer weights

IDP	P1	Peer 1 Weight	P2	Peer 2 Weight	P3	Peer 3 Weight	IDP	P1	Peer 1 Weight	P2	Peer 2 Weight	P3	Peer 3 Weight
1	1	1.0000	×	×	×	×	16	4	0.1019	12	0.8166	24	0.0815
2	12	0.1330	24	0.8670	×	×	17	4	0.0038	27	0.9962	×	×
3	3	1.0000	×	×	×	×	18	4	0.2597	27	0.7403	×	×
4	4	1.0000	×	×	×	×	19	8	0.1605	12	0.6679	27	0.1716
5	5	1.0000	×	×	×	×	20	4	0.0277	12	0.7951	24	0.1773
6	5	0.3989	12	0.2033	27	0.0487	21	4	0.8751	5	0.0645	12	0.0605
7	4	0.0503	27	0.9497	×	×	22	4	0.0645	8	0.0305	27	0.9051
8	8	1.0000	×	×	×	×	23	8	0.8950	12	0.1050	×	×
9	4	0.1785	27	0.8215	×	×	24	24	1.0000	×	×	×	×
10	12	0.9307	24	0.0693	×	×	25	8	0.0950	12	0.9050	×	×
11	4	0.0964	5	0.0060	12	0.8976	26	5	0.1769	12	0.6548	27	0.1683
12	12	1.0000	×	×	×	×	27	4	0.0645	8	0.0305	27	0.9051
13	12	0.3917	27	0.6083	×	×	28	4	0.0043	8	0.0125	27	0.9831
14	3	0.2856	5	0.0033	8	0.7111	29	4	0.0926	8	0.1169	27	0.7905
15	12	0.4094	27	0.5906	×	×	30	8	0.0058	12	0.0390	27	0.9551

As depicted in **Fig.5**, these individual development processes have been clearly classified into relatively high-capability and low-capability ones. According to the reference relationships (the peer sets and the peer weights, see Section 3.2) among the 30 IDPs shown in **Table 4**, the developers with high-capability processes can learn how to make better improvements by comparing against a peer process or a combination of peer processes. For example, managers can find that IDP11 derives a peer set {IDP4, IDP5, IDP12}. By further investigating the peer weight of each peer in this peer set, IDP11 can determine IDP12 as the most suitable one to borrow best practices from, because IDP12 has the biggest peer weight (0.8976) in the peer set. The peer set and the most valuable development process to emulate for the other IDPs in **Table 4** can be derived in a similar way.

Table 5. Reference number and total reference weight

IDP	Reference Number	Reference Weights	IDP	Reference Number	Reference Weights	IDP	Reference Number	Reference Weights
1	1	1.0000	5	6	1.6496	24	5	2.1951
3	2	1.2856	8	10	3.0578	27	15	10.6341
4	13	2.8193	12	15	8.0096	×	×	×

To sum up, by investigating the reference relationships, managers can establish different reference sets for each relatively low-capability IDP. Moreover, with the aid of peer weights of the peers, developers can further find which process is of the biggest improvement reference value to his own IDP.

Moreover, the reference number and total weight, which indicate the relative importance and reference value among the high performance IDPs, are also computed, as shown in **Table 5**. The IDP27, which has been referred 15 times and has a total reference weight more than 10, is doubtless the most useful when the comparison with the best individual software processes is sought.

Besides, we can also draw a sound conclusion from the above results: Our statistical model can measure IDPs with similar scale and ensure that relatively large-scale development processes are compared with other relatively large-scale ones and relatively small-scale development process with relatively small ones. To make it clear, we can refer to **Table 4** for the peer set. From **Table 4**, we find that each relative low-capability IDP_i chooses a peer IDP, which has the largest peer weight and the most similar input and output scale, as the most suitable one to borrow best practices from. For example, IDP7 (input: 575 hours, 19617 yuan) choose IDP27 (input: 406 hours, 14479 yuan) to emulate, while IDP10 (input: 310 hours, 11179 yuan) choose IDP12 (input: 250 hours, 10219 yuan) to learn the best practices from. The results surely show that our model has the ability to establish different capability benchmarks for IDPs of different scales.

ISCAS proposes an individual performance-related pay (IPRP) scheme [18], which links salary to the result of an individual appraisal of job performance, in a variety of organizational contexts. At present, the developers' performance scores are drawn upon the findings from project managers' interpretation and daily reports of work. A performance score with a greater value means a piece of high-performance work and leads to an increase in the bonus rate applied to the base salary, and vice versa.

From the above analysis results, it is found that the our assessment model seems to be more reasonable for scoring personal capability and enabling organization to establish different process performance benchmarks for IDPs of diffident scale than the current IPRP scheme. Indeed, we have planned to put our assessment method into use to improve the IPRP scheme of ISCAS in the near future.

5 Conclusions

In this paper, we present a novel combined method for capability assessment of individual software processes and practices. Our method facilitates the process metrics extraction task by making use of software repositories as the data source, enabling recording of data effortless and more accurate. Then, the process metrics are decomposed at the individual-level of granularity by exploring different human identities from various sources. Since software repositories provide the necessary foundation for the assessment process execution, the proposed method is generally applicable to any software organizations that adopt software repositories to maintain the evolution of software development processes.

Besides the feasible mechanisms for metrics extraction and decomposition from software repositories, the DEA model has also been adopted to measure the capability of individual software development processes under MIMO constraints

Empirical illustrations from a practical case study illustrate the effectiveness of the proposed methodology. The results show that our method is quite helpful in scoring individual capability to facilitate the IPRP scheme adopted in most software companies. Furthermore, this appraisal approach can be expected to be ultimately incorporated into P-CMM and PSP to assist in raising the efficiency of their capability assessment programs.

Acknowledgements

This research is supported by the National Natural Science Foundation of China (60473060, 60573082, 60673022), and the National Hi-Tech Research and Development Plan of China (2006AA01Z185, 2006AA01Z182)

References

1. Biberoglu, E., Haddad, H.: A survey of industrial experiences with CMM and the teaching of CMM practices. Journal of Computing Sciences in Colleges 18(2), 143–152 (2002)
2. Curtis, B., Hefley, W.E., Miller, S.A.: People Capability Maturity Model (P-CMM) Version 2.0. Addison-Wesley Professional, Reading (2001)
3. Humphrey, W.S.: Introduction to the Personal Software Process. Addison-Wesley, Reading (1997)
4. Johnson, P.M., Disney, A.M.: A critical Analysis of PSP Data Quality: Results from a Case Study. Journal of Empirical Software Engineering 4(4), 317–349 (1999)
5. Morisio, M.: Applying the PSP in Industry. IEEE Software 17(6), 90–95 (2000)
6. Nasir, M.M., Yusof, A.M.: Automating a modified personal software process. Malaysian Journal of Computer Science 18(2), 11–27 (2005)
7. Charnes, A., Cooper, W.W., Rhodes, E.: Measuring the Efficiency of Decision Making Units. European Journal of Operational Research 2(6), 429–444 (1978)
8. Stensrud, E., Myrtveit, I.: Identifying High Performance ERP Projects. IEEE Transaction on Software Engineering 29(5), 387–416 (2003)
9. Liping, D., Qiusong, Y., Liang, S., Jie, T., Yongji, W.: Evaluation of the Capability of Personal Software Process Based on Data Envelopment Analysis. In: Li, M., Boehm, B., Osterweil, L.J. (eds.) SPW 2005. LNCS, vol. 3840, pp. 235–248. Springer, Heidelberg (2006)
10. Shen, Z., Yongji, W., Jie, T., Jinhui, Z., Li, R.: Evaluation of Project Quality: A DEA-based Approach. In: Wang, Q., Pfahl, D., Raffo, D.M., Wernick, P. (eds.) SPW 2006 and ProSim 2006. LNCS, vol. 3966, pp. 88–96. Springer, Heidelberg (2006)
11. Li, R., Yongji, W., Qing, W., Mingshu, L., Shen, Z.: Empirical Study on Benchmarking Software Development Tasks. In: Wang, Q., Pfahl, D., Raffo, D.M. (eds.) ICSP 2007. LNCS, vol. 4470, pp. 221–232. Springer, Heidelberg (2007)

12. Robles, G., Jesus, M., Gonzalez-Barahon: Developer identification methods for integrated data from various sources. In: Proceedings of the 2005 international workshop on Mining software repositories, St. Louis, pp. 1–5 (2005)
13. Liu, Y., Stoulia, E., German, D.: Using CVS Historical Information to Understand How Students Develop Software. In: 1st International Workshop on Mining Software Repositories, Edinburgh, pp. 32–36 (2004)
14. Mierle, K., Laven, K., Roweis, S., Wilson, G.: Mining student CVS repositories for performance indicators. In: Proceedings of the 2005 international workshop on Mining software repositories, St. Louis, pp. 1–5 (2005)
15. Vanek, L.I., Culp, M.N.: Static analysis of program source code using EDSA. In: Proceedings of the International Conference on Software Maintenance, Miami, pp. 192–199 (1989)
16. Qing, W., Mingshu, L.: Measuring and Improving Software Process in China. In: Proceedings of the 4th International Symposium on Empirical Software Engineering, Australia, pp. 17–18 (2005)
17. PMD, http://pmd.sourceforge.net/
18. Harris, L.: Rewarding employee performance: line managers' values, beliefs and perspectives. Int. J. Hum. Resource. Manag. 12(7), 1182–1192 (2001)
19. HTML TIDY, http://www.w3.org/People/Raggett/tidy/

Scoping Software Process Models - Initial Concepts and Experience from Defining Space Standards

Ove Armbrust[1], Masafumi Katahira[2], Yuko Miyamoto[2], Jürgen Münch[1],
Haruka Nakao[3], and Alexis Ocampo[1]

[1] Fraunhofer IESE, Fraunhofer-Platz 1, 67663 Kaiserslautern, Germany
[2] Japanese Aerospace Exploration Agency, 2-1-1, Sengen, Tsukuba, Ibaraki, 305-8505, Japan
[3] Japan Manned Space Systems Corporation, 1-1-26, Kawaguchi, Tsuchiura, Ibaraki, 300-0033, Japan

```
{armbrust, ocampo, muench}@iese.fraunhofer.de,
katahira@computer.org,
miyamoto.yuko@jaxa.jp,
haruka@jamss.co.jp
```

Abstract. Defining process standards by integrating, harmonizing, and standardizing heterogeneous and often implicit processes is an important task, especially for large development organizations. However, many challenges exist, such as limiting the scope of process standards, coping with different levels of process model abstraction, and identifying relevant process variabilities to be included in the standard. On the one hand, eliminating process variability by building more abstract models with higher degrees of interpretation has many disadvantages, such as less control over the process. Integrating all kinds of variability, on the other hand, leads to high process deployment costs. This article describes requirements and concepts for determining the scope of process standards based on a characterization of the potential productzs to be produced in the future, the projects expected for the future, and the respective process capabilities needed. In addition, the article sketches experience from determining the scope of space process standards for satellite software development. Finally, related work with respect to process model scoping, conclusions, and an outlook on future work are presented.

1 Introduction

Many facets of process technology and standards are available in industry and academia, but in practice, significant problems with processes and process management remain. Rombach [1] reports a variety of reasons for this: Some approaches are too generic, some are too specific and address only a small part of daily life. Many approaches are hard to tailor to an organization's needs. In addition, some approaches impose rather strict rules upon an organization – but since not everything can be foreseen, there must be room for flexibility. Yet it remains unclear what must be regulated, and what should be left open. In general, support for process problems is plentiful, but very scattered, without a systematic concept addressing problems in a comprehensive way. One result of this unsatisfactory support is an unnecessarily high number of process variants within an organization. For example, each department of a company may have its own process

Q. Wang, D. Pfahl, and D.M. Raffo (Eds.): ICSP 2008, LNCS 5007, pp. 160–172, 2008.
© Springer-Verlag Berlin Heidelberg 2008

variant, all of them varying only in details, but existing nevertheless and needing to be maintained in parallel.

A traditional countermeasure taken to overcome this phenomenon is to define fixed process reference standards like the German V-Modell® XT [2], which fulfill the requirements of maturity models such as CMMI or ISO/IEC 15504 [3]. While this potentially reduces the number of variants, it often also leads to very generic processes that are no great help in dealing with daily problems, and that do not provide the necessary variability for coping with changing contexts. Thus, processes and their variations must be modeled in order to be understood, but at the same time, the modeling extent must be limited, in order to maintain high quality of the modeled processes and achieve high user acceptance.

Together, these circumstances have gradually turned software process management into a complex problem – and this process is nowhere near finished. As a consequence, software process management challenges comprise, but are not limited to, the following key issues:

– How can processes be characterized? Such a characterization is necessary in order to decide which process parts should become mandatory, variable, or be left out completely.
– How can stable and anticipated variable process parts be identified?
– In order to account for unanticipated changes, process models must be variable to some extent – but what is the right degree of variability?
– How can variable processes be adequately described in a process model?
– How can process models be tailored efficiently, based on the particular demand?
– On which level(s) of granularity should process engineers work?

We propose a systematic approach of Software Process Scoping to address these questions. We define Software Process Scoping as the *systematic characterization of products, projects, and processes and the subsequent selection of processes and process elements, so that product development and project execution are supported efficiently and process management effort is minimized.*

This paper is structured as follows. Section 2 names a number of requirements that a Software Process Scoping approach addressing the issues listed above should satisfy. Section 3 explains our initial solution, followed by the description of its application at JAXA in Section 4. We give an overview of what process scoping means in the aerospace domain and describe our experiences. Related work and its relationship to Software Process Scoping are analyzed in Section 5. Finally, we draw some conclusions and give an outlook in Section 6.

2 Requirements for Software Process Scoping

Based on the problems observed with software process management, we have phrased a number of requirements for an approach to scoping software processes.

(1) First of all, the approach should **support software product development** by providing an appropriate selection of necessary processes. This means that for a collection of existing, planned, and potential products developed in specific projects, the

approach should determine the extent and provide a selection of software development processes that supports the creation of these products by providing, for each product and project, the processes needed.

(2) Second, in order to support the selection process, the approach should provide ways to **characterize software products, projects, and processes** accordingly. Since the approach is supposed to provide tailored processes for an organization, it must also provide ways to select these processes, based on process characteristics and the specific needs of projects and (future) products to be developed.

(3) Third, in order to minimize process management effort, the approach should provide ways to **distinguish stable process parts from variable ones.** Many products and projects often share large parts of the processes, with none or only minimal variations. Managing all these variants independently significantly increases process management effort. Therefore, the approach should identify stable and variable process parts, and provide a systematic method for classifying process parts accordingly, so that process management effort can be effectively decreased.

(4) Fourth, in order to cope with the unforeseen, the approach should provide ways to **incorporate unanticipated variability in a controlled manner,** such as process changes during project runtime. This requirement comes from the fact that usually, not all events can be foreseen, and thus need to be taken care of as they occur. In some cases, this requires process changes. The approach should support these changes in such a way that it sensibly constrains and guides process changes after the start of a project.

As necessary preconditions for Software Process Scoping, the following two requirements must also be fulfilled by the process modeling mechanisms used:

(1) The process modeling approach should provide ways to **store stable and variable parts within one process model,** in order to facilitate model management. Obviously, the information about whether a process part is stable or variable, and the variability's further circumstances must be stored somehow. We suggest storage within one combined model in order to facilitate further support, e.g., through tools.

(2) The process modeling approach should provide ways to **cost-efficiently instantiate such a combined model into a project-specific process model** without variability. This means that the combined model is transformed, and during this transformation, all variabilities are solved, resulting in a single process model without any remaining variability.

These requirements are by no means complete. They may need to be amended, refined or changed – however, they seem to be a good starting point to venture further. In the following section, we will present an initial solution that at least partially satisfies these requirements.

3   Initial Solution

One possible solution addressing the requirements mentioned is the concept of a *software process line* (see Fig. 1): *Scoping* determines the members of such a process line, *process domain engineering* constructs a process repository containing all stable and variable process parts as well as a decision model governing when to use which variant. *Process line instantiation* extracts from the process repository one specific process instance without variability for each project, which can then be further adapted during *customization*. These activities are supported by a number of approaches, such as *software process commonality analysis [4], process model difference analysis [5], [6]* and *rationale support for process evolution [7], [8]*. In this software process line environment, scoping and process domain engineering proactively cope with stable and anticipated variable processes, while customization (often also just called "process tailoring") re-actively integrates unanticipated variability into a descriptive process model.

Software Process Line Engineering Core

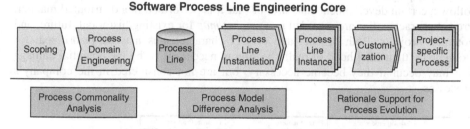

Software Process Line Engineering Support

Fig. 1. Software process line overview

The fundamental difference between this software process line concept and well-known concepts of software process tailoring is that within a software process line, an organization's processes are actively prepared for a number of anticipated needs beforehand and then possibly tailored further to incorporate unanticipated changes, whereas classic process tailoring typically modifies a process individually for a specific project, e.g., for the creation of product P1 in cooperation with suppliers S1 and S2, to be delivered to customer C1. Within a process line, scoping would evaluate how many products of the product P1 type are anticipated to be produced in the future, how often cooperation with suppliers S1 and S2 would presumably occur, and how many projects with customer C1 are likely to happen. Taking this into account, scoping then defines mandatory and optional process parts as determined by the results of the evaluation, and process domain engineering provides the appropriate process model which reflects the scoping results.

The software *process* line concept is in fact quite similar to software *product* lines: In a product line, a software product is systematically prepared to suit future anticipated needs by determining a common core and various variants satisfying different specific needs. The software process line concept transfers this idea to software processes in such a way that it prepares an organization's processes to suit future anticipated (process) needs by determining a common process core and variable process parts that satisfy specific needs. Since product creation and processes have a very close relationship, a combination of both approaches seems only too reasonable, and was, in fact, already envisioned by Rombach in [1].

In this article, we focus on the concept of scoping. Scoping determines what to include in the process line and what not, based on characteristic features described in product, project, and process maps.

Product characteristics determine which process capabilities are needed to develop the respective product(s). These characteristics may include, for example, that a product is safety-critical, or that its requirements are only vaguely known at the beginning of development. Product characteristics are determined in a *product map* for current, future, and potential products.

Project characteristics also influence which process capabilities are needed in development projects. Such characteristics may be, for example, that a project must follow a certain development standard, or that it is performed in a distributed manner. Project characteristics are recorded in a *project map* for existing/historical, future, and potential projects. Both product and project characteristics may be prioritized, for example by their likelihood of really becoming necessary, or by the potential damage that may occur if they become necessary, but are not considered in the company's processes.

Product Characteristics

	Existing Products			Future Products				Potential Products		
	P1	P2	P3	P4	P5	P6	...	P7	P8	P9
Safety critical										
Reqs vague										
...										

Project Characteristics

	Existing Projects			Future Projects				Potential Projects		
	P1	P2	P3	P4	P5	P6	...	P7	P8	P9
SPICE compliance										
distributed										
...										

Process Characteristics

	Existing Processes			Future Processes			Potential Processes		
	P1	P2	P3	P4	P5	P6	P7	P8	P9
ISO 12207 compliant									
Risk-based									
...									

Fig. 2. Product, project, and process map sketches

Once the product and project characterizations are complete, they form a set of demands for the company's processes. For example, product characterization may lead to the insight that for every product, its certification according to a certain standard is mandatory. Project characterization may reveal that in all upcoming projects, SPICE compliance is a must, while support for distributed development is only needed for some projects. Together, these results demand processes that are SPICE-compliant and allow for the necessary product certification by default, while explicit support for distributed development is less important.

Available processes are characterized using the same attributes, describing the capabilities of a process in a *process map* for existing, future, and potential processes and thus providing the counterpart to the demands of products and projects. By matching the prioritized product and project characteristics to the process characteristics, the scope of the future company processes is determined, with "must have"-process features being part of the standard process and optional features representing capabilities needed only in some cases. In our simple example, SPICE-compliant processes that also support the desired certification would be included as a core for every development project, while explicit support for distributed development would be an optional feature that can be invoked on demand. Capabilities needed only very seldom or never are left out; in case they become necessary, the project-specific process tailoring will supply them.

Fig. 2 shows sketches of the three tables explained above. The topmost table displays product characteristics for existing, future, and potential products, with future products being concretely planned and potential products being a possibility, but not yet devised in any way. The middle and bottom tables contain project and process characteristics, featuring the same three-way distinction, where existing processes are processes in daily use, future processes are processes that have been prepared for application, but have not been institutionalized yet, and potential processes are processes that might become used, but have not been adapted or prepared for use within the organization yet.

4 Case Study

In this section, we are reporting on our experiences from an ongoing effort within the Japanese Space Exploration Agency (JAXA) to provide a process line for their space software development. Our focus hereby lies on scoping for satellite software development (see Fig. 3). In the next section, we will describe the project context and results. Following up on that, we will share our experiences.

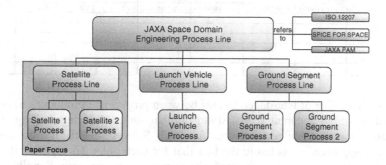

Fig. 3. JAXA process line overview

4.1 Process Scoping in the Aerospace Domain

The ultimate goal of the ongoing project we are reporting on is to provide a software process line for JAXA's space software development. This includes satellite software, launch vehicle software, and ground segment software (see Fig. 3). So far, the first version of a satellite software process line has been finished, the scoping portion of which provided characterizations of two products (satellites) developed in two projects. In this domain, there is a very strong correlation between product and projects, since each product is unique. Nevertheless, a meaningful project and product characterization is not trivial. In our case, it became apparent very soon that while attributes for project characterization often had only two possible values (e.g., "National" and

"International" for the "Collaboration type" attribute), this was not the case for product characterization. For example, complexity, criticality, and size were determined on a 3-piece scale by experts.

Tables 1 and 2 show an extract of the characterizations of the projects and products, respectively. So far, only satellite products and projects have been characterized: however, similar work for the launch vehicle and ground segment is currently going on. Due to confidentiality reasons, subsystems and suppliers are represented by numbers. In Table 2, higher numbers mean higher rating of the respective attribute.

Table 1. Excerpt from project characterization

		Satellites		Launch Vehicle		Ground Segment	
		Sat1	Sat2	LV1	LV2	GS1	GS2
Project Characteristics	Collaboration type	National	International				
	Mission type	Engineering	Science				
	Subsystem	1, 2, 3	3				
	Supplier	1, 2	1				
	...						

Table 2. Excerpt from product characterization

		Satellites				Launch Vehicle		Ground Segment	
		Sat1			Sat2				
		Subsystem1	Subsystem2	Subsystem3	Subsystem3	LV1	LV2	GS1	GS2
Product Characteristics	Complexity	3	2	1	1				
	Criticality	2	3	1	1				
	Size	3	3	2	2				
	Stable Requirements	yes	yes	yes	no				
	...								

There are a number of interdependencies between project and product characterization data that are not apparent at first sight, but that surfaced during scoping efforts. For example, the unstable requirements for Sat2, Subsystem3 require an iterative development approach – this led to the fact that for each potential supplier, it had to be checked whether such a process could be supported. In our case, Supplier 1 was chosen and had to adapt (for Sat2) their processes to the international collaboration type. Other interdependencies led to conflicts, e.g., the collaboration type "international" demanded that documentation had to be made available in English upon request, suggesting one set of potential suppliers, but the mission type suggested a different set – this was solved by prioritizing characteristics.

4.2 Experiences

Translating the project and product characterizations into requirements for the process proved not to be an easy task. Most "soft" product characteristics such as complexity, size, or criticality could not be used to directly derive new or changed processes. In fact, these factors mostly did not lead to qualitative process changes (i.e., new or changed activities or work products), but influenced project planning in such a way that the number of reviews was increased, or that the amount of independent V&V was increased. This was not modeled in detail in the software process line: instead, only high-level directives and quality requirements were given, which have to be implemented individually by the suppliers.

Project characterization, on the other hand, led to a number of variation points within the process itself. While some findings did not change the process itself (e.g., the requirement that for international projects, documentation was to be produced in English upon request), others did. For example, for international cooperation projects with ESA, a new activity was introduced for analyzing hardware/software interaction, producing the new work product FMECA (Failure Mode, Effects, and Criticality Analysis). Especially for exploratory science projects, the usual process standard was perceived as being too heavy. As a consequence, the number of quality assurance activities was reduced, and the requirements and design rationales were waived. Also, source code quality assurance measures were decreased for this type of project.

The variations were modeled using the graphical software process modeling tool [9] SPEARMINT™. Process parts that were optional in some cases were marked accordingly, with a detailed description of when to consider the respective part. Fig. 4 displays the result: The characterization information was used to derive the satellite-specific process line from the generic JAXA Space Domain Engineering Process Line. It contained a number of variable parts, the work products FMECA and Rationale for Design being shown. The rules describing these optional parts are as follows:

(Opt1.1) *if (collaboration type == international) then (produce FMECA)*
(Opt1.2) *resolve (Opt7)*
(Opt2.1) *if (mission type == engineering) then (produce Rationale for Design)*

For Opt1, two rules were defined: one that governs the creation of the FMECA, and one requiring resolution of variation point Opt7, which is concerned with the activities creating the FMECA work product (not shown). For Opt2, one rule was sufficient. Using these rules, the satellite process line could then be instantiated into two specific satellite processes. From one of these, the formerly optional parts were erased, whereas in the other one, these parts were now mandatory: The resulting Satellite 1 Process supports a national science-type project, the Satellite 2 Process an international engineering-type project.

The resulting process model contains 76 modeled activities, 54 artifacts, 18 graphical views depicting product flow, and another 18 graphical views depicting control flow. Transferring the new process model into daily practice, however, has proved to be no simple task. The modification of standards in the aerospace domain cannot be done on-the-fly because many stakeholders are involved and the consequences of software failures (possibly stemming from a faulty standard) are potentially grave. So far, the software process line we have developed has been published as an appendix to the official JAXA software standard. It has therefore not yet replaced the current standard, but JAXA engineers and their suppliers are encouraged to examine the process line and to provide comments and feedback.

Our experiences with the scoping approach taken were positive. From interviews with JAXA process engineers, we have feedback that our scoping approach helped them to focus on the relevant processes and saved a significant amount of effort in

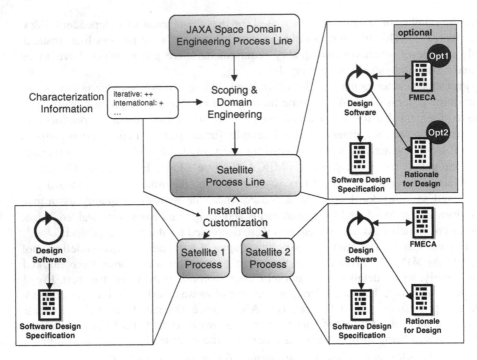

Fig. 4. JAXA satellite process line architecture (excerpt)

later modeling and standardization phases. The classic approach would have developed two independent processes for satellite development, so with the process line, the expected maintenance complexity has been decreased as well due to the fact that only the variable parts have to be considered separately, while for most of the process line, there is only one process to be maintained instead of two.

Regarding the requirements formulated before, we can state that the first three requirements concerning Software Process Scoping are already well addressed by the approach. The fourth requirement (incorporate unanticipated variability in a controlled manner) has not been addressed yet so far, which we accredit to the short lifetime of the process line: There just were no unanticipated process changes necessary yet. Considering the first process modeling mechanism requirement (storage of stable and variable parts within one process model), the JAXA project has shown that it is not feasible for larger process models to manage variable parts manually. Therefore, the tool used has been enhanced, so that it supports the definition and display of variable process elements. The second requirement (cost-efficiently instantiate a combined common/variable model into a project-specific process model), however, has not been addressed at all. JAXA did not want to provide a number of process model variants to its engineers, but instead opted for one combined model highlighting all variable parts, and describing within the model when to follow which variant. This was feasible for the relatively low number of variants; however, we expect that for larger process models with more complex variants, instantiations will become necessary.

5 Related Work

In this section, we connect some related work to the issue of Software Process Scoping. As a basis for all scoping activities, descriptive process modeling [10] is necessary for identifying essential process entities. Becker describes an 8-step approach to descriptive process modeling. During the first step, the objectives and scope of the modeling effort are determined. This narrows the extent of the model, but the approach considers only solitary process instances on the project level, not a set of processes with variabilities. Nevertheless, descriptive process modeling can be used to determine isolated, real processes that can be used as input for a variant analysis.

Bella et al. [11] describe their approach to defining software processes for a new domain. Based on a reference process model, they used descriptive process modeling to document the as-is processes and utilized this model as a basis for deriving suitable processes for engineering wireless Internet services. Through a number of iterations, they collected qualitative and quantitative experience and adapted the processes where necessary. Their focus thus was the past; they evaluated only past events and processes. Software Process Scoping also considers the future in terms of expected products and projects.

The idea of systematically combining software product lines with matching processes was described by Rombach [1]. We consider Software Process Scoping as one potential building block of such a combined approach.

Characterization and customization approaches exist for a number of software engineering concepts, for example, for inspections [12], [13]. However, they are constrained to characterizing a limited number of methods of a class of methods (in the above case, the class of inspection methods). This comprises only a fraction of a Software Process Scoping approach, namely, that when scoping determines the need for certain characteristic features in an inspection approach, the above characterization can be used to determine which inspection approach should be used.

Denger [14] broadens the scope to quality assurance activities in general and provides a framework for customizing generic approaches to the specific needs of a company. The goal of the framework, however, is to optimize only a single factor (software quality), whereas Software Process Scoping as proposed in this article aims at optimizing multiple factors, which can be chosen freely through the product and project characterization vectors.

Avison and Wood-Harper [15] describe an approach to supply an organization with a number of methods from which a suitable one can be selected for different purposes. The authors admit that the necessary method competence for a multitude of methods is hard to achieve in reality, and therefore suggest that alternatives should be included within a single method already. Based on our experience, we support this assumption and consider this for Software Process Scoping by representing variability on different levels of abstraction.

Fitzgerald et al. [16] describe an approach taken at Motorola, which involves tailoring up-front to encompass expected deviations from the organization standard, and dynamic tailoring during project runtime, to encompass unanticipated circumstances. This corresponds to our requirements 1 and 4.

In the software product line domain, scoping has been considered in a number of publications. Clements and Northrop [17] describe three essential activities for software product line development, with scoping being a part of one of them. The authors give a detailed description of what scoping is for and what it should accomplish, but do not provide practical guidance on how to actually do it in a project. This has been done by Schmid [18]. He developed a product- and benefit-based product line scoping approach called PuLSE-Eco 2.0, which defines the scope of a software product line depending on the economical benefit of the products to be produced. The latest version of the approach is described in [19], integrating 21 customization factors that can be used to adapt the generic approach to a company's specific needs. These works were used as a basis for the Software Process Scoping approach and terminology; however, product line scoping focuses on products only and does not consider process or other context factors. Bayer et al. developed a product line based on scoping a number of business processes [20]. Their product line reflects business processes, and by determining the scope of the business processes to be implemented in software, they determined the scope of the product line. However, no more information on how scoping was done is disclosed.

Under the name of Quality Function Deployment [21], Cohen published a method for clearly specifying and ranking customer needs and then evaluating each proposed product or service capability systematically in terms of its impact on meeting those needs. This corresponds to the Software Process Scoping concepts of product/project mapping and process mapping, respectively, but is also strictly limited to products and services.

There is currently only little research going on that tries to provide a similarly systematic approach for software processes. So far, adapting processes (also known as "process tailoring") is done either generally for an organization, resulting in a single process standard, or individually for every project, resulting in a large number of process variants. Most available tailoring instructions are very generic, e.g., in international standards such as ISO/IEC 12207:1995 [3] or the German V-Modell XT [2]. However, due to their general applicability, they rarely provide more than phrases like "pick the activities and work products necessary for the purpose", and thus provide only little help in actually tailoring a process.

6 Conclusions and Outlook

In this paper, we presented an idea for systematically selecting and adapting software processes, depending on the project and product structure of an organization. We formulated four requirements for the approach and two requirements for supporting process modeling mechanisms, presented an initial solution addressing these requirements, and presented an application of our idea in the space software engineering domain.

Our experiences encourage us to continue on this path, and to expand the process line from satellite software development both horizontally to other branches (launch vehicle, ground segment) and vertically (JAXA-wide). The experience we collected so far supports the requirements we have set up. However, since process scoping research is yet in its infancy, a number of open questions remain. Until now, it is unclear which decision models can help to determine which process elements should be part of the process line, and which should not. A meaningful limitation of characterization attribute values (e.g., for attributes such as "complexity" or "criticality") and their objective assessment is another open issue. Furthermore, thorough investigation is needed on the subjects of how to handle different levels of abstraction in processes and characterizations (especially when talking about variability on these levels of abstraction, introduced, for example, by a vertically growing process line), how to describe interdependencies among variable parts and characterization attributes, and how to sensibly limit the number of characteristics and variation points.

Following up on what we have learned so far, our next steps will be the horizontal expansion and the inclusion of more satellite projects and products in the base of our process line, and the concurrent refinement of our approach.

Acknowledgements

We would like to thank Ms. Sonnhild Namingha from Fraunhofer IESE for reviewing the first version of this article. We also thank the anonymous reviewers for their valuable comments on the first version of this article.

References

[1] Rombach, H.D.: Integrated Software Process and Product Lines. In: Li, M., Boehm, B., Osterweil, L.J. (eds.) LNCS, Springer, Heidelberg (2006)
[2] V-Modell XT, http://www.vmodellxt.de/
[3] International Organization for Standardization: ISO/IEC 12207:1995, Geneva, Switzerland (1995)
[4] Ocampo, A., Bella, F., Münch, J.: Software Process Commonality Analysis. Software Process - Improvement and Practice 10(3), 273–285 (2005)
[5] Soto, M., Münch, J.: Focused Identification of Process Model Changes. In: Wang, Q., Pfahl, D., Raffo, D.M. (eds.) ICSP 2007. LNCS, vol. 4470, Springer, Heidelberg (2007)
[6] Soto, M.: Delta-P: Model Comparison Using Semantic Web Standards. In: Proceedings of the Workshop Vergleich und Versionierung von UML-Modellen (VVUM 2007), co-located with the GI-Fachtagung Software Engineering 2007, March 27, 2007, Hamburg (2007)
[7] Ocampo, A., Soto, M.: Connecting the Rationale for Changes to the Evolution of a Process. In: Münch, J., Abrahamsson, P. (eds.) PROFES 2007. LNCS, vol. 4589, pp. 160–174. Springer, Heidelberg (2007)
[8] Ocampo, A., Münch, J.: The REMIS Approach for Rationale-Driven Process Model Evolution. In: Wang, Q., Pfahl, D., Raffo, D.M. (eds.) ICSP 2007. LNCS, vol. 4470, pp. 12–24. Springer, Heidelberg (2007)
[9] Spearmint/EPG,
      http://www.iese.fhg.de/fhg/iese/research/quality/pam/index.jsp
[10] Becker, U., Hamann, D., Verlage, M.: Descriptive Modeling of Software Processes, Kaiserslautern, Germany (ISERN Report 97-10)

[11] Bella, F., Münch, J., Ocampo, A.: Observation-based Development of Software Process Baselines: An Experience Report. In: Proceedings of the Conference on Quality Engineering in Software Technology (CONQUEST), Nuremberg, Germany, September 22-24 (2004)

[12] Biffl, S., Halling, M.: Managing Software Inspection Knowledge for Decision Support of Inspection Planning. In: Aurum, A., Jeffery, R., Wohlin, C., Handzic, M. (eds.). Springer, Berlin (2003)

[13] Schweikhard, T.: Identification of inspection-variation-factors for a decision-support-tool. Diploma Thesis, Fachbereich Informatik, Technische Universität Kaiserslautern (2006)

[14] Denger, C., Elberzhager, F.: A Comprehensive Framework for Customizing Quality Assurance Techniques, Kaiserslautern (2006)

[15] Avison, D.E., Wood-Harper, A.T.: Information Systems Development Research: An Exploration of Ideas in Practice. The Computer Journal 34(2), 98–112 (1991)

[16] Fitzgerald, B., Russo, N.L., O'Kane, T.: Software Development Method Tailoring at Motorola. Communications of the ACM 46(4), 65–70 (2003)

[17] Clements, P., Northrop, L.: Software Product Lines: Practices and Patterns. Addison-Wesley, Reading (2002)

[18] Schmid, K.: Planning Software Reuse - A Disciplined Scoping Approach for Software Product Lines. PhD Thesis. Fachbereich Informatik, Universität Kaiserslautern (2003)

[19] John, I., Knodel, J., Lehner, T., Muthig, D.: A Practical Guide to Product Line Scoping. In: Proceedings of the 10th International Software Product Line Conference (SPLC 2006), Baltimore, Maryland, USA, August 21-24 (2006)

[20] Bayer, J., Kose, M., Ocampo, A.: Improving the Development of e-Business Systems by Introducing Process-Based Software Product Lines. In: Münch, J., Vierimaa, M. (eds.) PROFES 2006. LNCS, vol. 4034, pp. 348–361. Springer, Heidelberg (2006)

[21] Cohen, L.: Quality Function Deployment: How to Make QFD Work for You. Addison-Wesley Longman, Amsterdam (1995)

Detection of Consistent Patterns from Process Enactment Data

Ming Huo, He Zhang, and Ross Jeffery

National ICT Australia
University of New South Wales, Sydney, Australia
{ming.huo, he.zhang, Ross.Jeffery}@nicta.com.au

Abstract. Software process improvement has been a focus of industry for many years. To assist with the implementation of process improvement, we provide an approach to recover process enactment data. The goal of our method is to uncover the actual process used and thereby provide evidence for improving the quality of a planned software process that is followed by an organization in the future. The recovered process model (or patterns) is presented at the same level of abstraction as the planned process model. This allows an easy and clear method to identify the distance between a planned process model and the actual project enactment. We investigate the enactment of a defined software process model from the view of understanding the opportunity for process model improvement from the viewpoint of the project managers in the context of a small software development organization. We collected data from one of our collaboration organizations and then applied our method to a case study. The consistencies between a planned process model and the project enactment were measured. The outcomes of our method provide precise information including qualitative and quantitative data to assist project managers with process improvement in future practice. The main contribution of our work is to provide a novel approach to assist software process improvement by recovering a model from process enactment data.

Keywords: agile method, process recovery, software process modeling, software process improvement.

1 Introduction

One basic implicit assumption in software process research is that improving the software process will improve the software product quality, and increase project success rates. There are three main reasons to improve software process quality. The first reason is to improve the quality of software products [7]. The second reason is that improving process quality can increase the probability of software project success [7]. Lastly, software process improvement also contributes to an increase in the development team's productivity by reducing rework effort [3]. Hence software process improvement has been a long term industry pursuit. Practitioners from research areas and industry continue to explore techniques to improve software processes. They are curious as to what is really happening in the implemented stage, such as if the process

Q. Wang, D. Pfahl, and D.M. Raffo (Eds.): ICSP 2008, LNCS 5007, pp. 173–185, 2008.
© Springer-Verlag Berlin Heidelberg 2008

model is applicable for a project and how appropriate it is, and if there is a distance between a planned process and the project enactment and so on.

Under these demands, we produced a systematic approach that aims to reveal what took place during process implementation. The goal of our approach is to uncover the actual process used at a fine-grained granularity and provide strong evidence to assist project managers in improving their defined software process model. Our work focuses on analyzing the low-level process enactment data. Instead of studying a software process as a completed instance, we investigate each development team member's behaviors and project tasks that compose a software process during a project development. Software process has long been considered as a complex procedure due to human involvement [6, 7]. Our work concentrates on the time sequence of the process stages that are carried out by development team while producing a software product.

We collected data from one of our collaborating software development companies. These data concern the development team's behavior and project tasks, the design of which is based on a defined software process model. By applying our approach to these data, process patterns are discovered. They are presented at the same level of abstraction as the pre-defined process model. We have applied our approach to three case studies. One case study showed how to detect conflicts between the project enactment and the predefined process detected by using our approach which is presented [8]. In this paper, we report the other one that mainly focuses on presenting how we discover the consistent elements of the processes.

Section 2 introduces the background of our method. Section 3 explains our method in detail. Following this, in section 4, examples are exhibited by using our case study data. Section 5 discusses the major difference between our work and previous research, and then is followed by highlighting our contributions. Finally, Section 6 draws the conclusion and outlines our future work.

2   Related Work and Background

2.1   Related Work

Process mining techniques have been used to extract non-trivial and useful information from event logs. Although the idea of process mining is not new, it has been developed mainly in the business process area, especially in workflow management systems [15]. Due to the wide use of information system, such as ERP, WFM and CRM, the process mining technique has also been adopted in these fields.

Process mining seeks to recover a process model from records of people's daily activities. The recovered process model is a type of abstract presentation of these activities. The goal of process mining is to unveil what people are doing in the real world. It analyzes this data and then seeks to identify rules or patterns in people's daily work, such as efficient working rules or bad habits that may cause problems. Process mining can be used in the software process area as well. Software process improvement needs the support of precise information on any deviation between the planned process model and the project process instantiation.

In the software process domain, Cook and Wolf performed a similar investigation [5]. They developed a data analysis technique and called it process discovery. The data of process events are captured from an on-going process. Following this, a formal process model is generated from these data. The goals of their approach include 1) reducing the cost of developing a process model, 2) demoting the error proneness in developing a process model, and 3) lowering the barrier of adopting a process model by introducing automated assistance in creating formal models.

However, there are two major limitations when utilizing Cook and Wolf's method in software process analysis. The first issue is that hundreds of process data instances have to be collected [2, 12, 14]. It is very difficult to collect sufficient data on many projects that consistently follow one process model. In this context, the data might never be enough to recover a single consistent process model. The second problem is that the recovered model is a low-level process model defined generally in the terms of daily activities. Most pre-defined software process models, such as the waterfall model and spiral model are moderately high-level process models. There is a distinct gap between these and the enactment activities. In this paper, we present a methodology that copes with the two limitations noted in [5]. We start by collecting low-level project data, which is then mined to recover process patterns.

2.2 Preliminaries

In this section, we explain the primary definitions and notations used in our method before we detail our approach. There are six primary definitions, which are: 1) Petri-net, 2) path in a process model, 3) conflict, 4) consistent pattern, 5) frequency, and 6) pattern amount.

In Definition 1, we propose the basic assumptions and notations of a Petri-net as we used. We employ Petri-nets in our approach for two main reasons. One is to provide a unified format for representing different software process models across organizations. The other reason is for easy comparison of the final outcomes with the pre-defined process model. Definition 2 shows how a path is defined among the process elements.

Definition 1: A Petri-net N can be defined as
   1. O is a finite set of elements.
   2. V is a subset of the set O: $V = \{v_i \mid v_i \in O\}$
   3. P is the place[1] and it indicates the paths.
   4. R is a set of relations on the set V and P, in the other words, the transitions among the process elements and places.
   At this stage, a process model is represented in its Petri-net format, $N = (O, P, R)$.

Definition 2: Path. In a Petri-net $N = (O, P, R)$, for any two elements v_i, v_j, there is a path from v_i to v_j iff
   $\exists\, p \in P$ s.t. $(v_i, p) \in R$ & $(p, v_j) \in R$, or
   $\exists\, v_k$ s.t. there exists a path from v_i to v_k and a path from v_k to v_j.
   If there is a path from v_i to v_j we say that v_i happens before v_j, and all tasks that are categorized to v_i should complete before any task that belongs to v_j starts. Definition 3

---

[1] A place, presented as P, indicates the paths between two process elements.

defines how a conflict part is detected between a project enactment and the pre-defined process model. Definition 4 presents how a consistency part is mined out. Meanwhile, we need to count the occurrence time of each consistency and conflict. It is called frequency. Definition 5 defines how a frequency of a conflict (inconsistency part) and a consistency pattern is counted.

Definition 3: Conflict. A conflict is an inconsistent part between a pre-defined process model and its project enactment. Given a task t_1 and E_1, E_1 is the process element that t_1 belongs to, i.e., $E_1 = V_t(t_1)$. Similarly for task t_2 and E_2, $E_2 = V_t(t_2)$. t_1 and t_2 are called conflict iff: There exists a path from E_1 to E_2 and start(t_2) < end(t_1).
For example, when classify tasks to process elements, we use $T(v_i)$ to present the set of tasks that belong to a process element. $T(v_i) = \{t_i \mid t_i \text{ is a task and } t_i \text{ belongs to } v_i\}$

Definition 4: Process Pattern Content: A process element sequence Ptn = $\{E_i \mid 1 \leq i \leq k, E_i$ is a process element $\}$ is a process pattern with length k iff $\exists$ k tasks $t_1,\ldots,t_k$ s.t.
1. $\forall\ 1 \leq i < j \leq k$, there exists a path from E_i to E_j in the process model;
2. $\forall\ 1 \leq i \leq k$, $Vt(t_i) = E_i$, which means E_i is the process element that t_i belongs to;
3. $\forall\ 1 \leq i \leq k-1$, End($t_i$)< Start($t_{i+1}$), which means t_i and t_{i+1} are sequential.
This set of tasks is named as a supporting task-set for this process pattern Ptn.

Definition 5: Process Pattern Frequency. The support of a process pattern Ptn is defined as the number of the unique supporting task-sets for this process pattern Ptn.

Definition 6: Process Pattern Amount in one process element: the total number of the frequencies of all the pattern types.
One step in our method, data pre-processing (Section 3.2), involves experts' subjective opinions. We use Kappa method to verify the data pre-processing result. Cohen's Kappa is a chance-corrected measure of agreement among raters. It has long been used to quantify the level of agreement among raters in classifying any types of subjects [4]. The Kappa value is computed as (1).

$$K = \frac{P_o - P_e}{1 - P_e}$$

(1)

P_o is observed agreement and P_e is expected agreement. They are computed as (2).

$$P_o = \sum_{i=1}^{k} P_{ii}, \quad P_e = \sum_{i=1}^{k} p_i^1 p_i^2$$

(2)

$K=0$ means that agreement is not different from chance and $K=1$ means perfect agreement. The conclusion can be drawn when K value is above 0.8 [11]. In our method, we accept the results only when the Kappa value is above 0.8.

3 Process Recovery Approach

This section presents our process discovery approach in general. The full explanation of our approach is published in [8]. Here we give a brief overview of our approach.

There is normally a pre-defined process model to guide the process enactment in an organization. There are four major phases in our method: 1) representation of a pre-defined process model being followed by an organization, 2) data pre-processing, 3) process mining, and 4) analysis of a recovered process model or patterns from two aspects, consistency and inconsistency with a pre-defined process model. Each of these phases also includes several steps.

Phase 1. This phase is to use Petri-nets to represent an organization's pre-defined process model. The definition of Petri-net is explained in Definition 1.

Phase 2. The gathered data need to be pre-processed. This phase includes three steps. The first step is to formalize the data set collected from industry by using formal notations. The next step is to categorize the data to each pre-defined process element. The process elements are the steps designed inside a model. For example, in a process model, which is designed from eXtreme Programming, there are some process elements such as 'unit test', 'code', 'acceptance test', etc. We call this procedure as task classification. The third step is to verify the results of task classification by using the Kappa statistic.

Phase 3. Process mining is applied in this phase. The qualified results of task classification are as the inputs for this phase. There are two types of outcomes, i.e., consistent and inconsistent patterns. The recovered consistent process patterns are part of the pre-defined process model. On the contrary, the inconsistent patterns are the conflicts between the pre-defined process model and the project enactment.

Phase 4. The final phase of the method is to analyze these outcomes. Meanwhile, problems and findings are discovered.

3.1 Phase 1: Process Representation

We transform a pre-defined process model into Petri-net format. Petri-net has been extensively used as a process modeling language due to its formal definition and graphical characteristic [13]. Below we describe the basic assumptions and notations of a pre-defined process model:

1.   After a process model has been established in an organization or a development team, the development team will follow it during their projects.
2.   A process is composed of a set of sequenced steps or tasks which we call process elements in our approach.
3.   There are relationships and constraints among the process elements, e.g. to start software implementation, the team needs to accomplish the software design first.
4.   There should be a set of well-defined steps in a process model, such as the instruction or explanations of each process element.

A process model with the above basic characteristics can be formally represented in a Petri-net format. Definition 1 defines a Petri-net. Definition 2 defines a path. We allow 'one-to-many' paths among process elements.

3.2 Phase 2: Data Pre-processing

The collected data needs pre-processing before process mining stage. There are three steps in this phase. To ensure the classification quality and to evaluate the agreement degree, the Kappa statistic is used [10].

Data formalization: Given a task t, start(t) represents the start date or time of task t and End(t) represents the end date or time of the task. The precision of the start and end time of a task in our case study is accurate to the date. Obviously, we have End(t)>Start(t). We use $V_t(t_i)$ to represent the process elements that task t_i belongs to: $V_t(t_i)$ = {v_j| $t_i \in T(v_j)$ }, where $T(v_j)$ is the set of tasks that belongs to v_j. For example, two tasks with ID 1 and 2, t_1 and t_2, are designed for writing the code. Then, we categorize t_1 and t_2 to 'Code' process element. The presentations are, $V_t(t_1)$ = { 'Code' }, $V_t(t_2)$ = { 'Code' }, and T(Code)={t_1,t_2}.

Data classification: This step is to categorize each task to a process element in O. In Definition 1, O is a finite set of process elements. The raters need to possess comprehensive knowledge of the pre-defined process model. They also need to understand the project content. In addition, a list of the task descriptions is provided to the raters. They do the classification individually.

Verification of task classification: This step aims to verify the results of task classification. In our approaches, we do not accept the classification until the K value is above 0.8.

3.3 Phase 3: Process Mining Approach

We investigated many process mining algorithms. A most suitable algorithm, the alpha algorithm was chosen and revised to fit our needs. The main content of the alpha algorithm is to detect the temporal relationship among tasks and then build the connection and transitions among these tasks [14].

After task classification (data pre-processing), each task is categorized to a project element v_i in O. The next step is to mine the data in order to recover the process patterns from the data set. We focus on the temporal relations between two tasks to investigate if there is a temporal dependency between them. For example, if one task is always followed by another task, it is likely that there is a temporal dependency between them. Furthermore, if such dependency exists, it implies that a connecting transition exists between these two tasks, and there has to be a *place* connecting the transitions in the Petri-net [14]. The temporal relationship is searched in the whole data set. While accumulating the temporal relationship and the connecting places, the process patterns are generated and gathered piece by piece.

Example: Given any two tasks t_i, t_j we say that t_i and t_j have temporal relationship $t_i \rightarrow t_j$ iff End(t_i) < Start(t_j), and then we add a directed line from t_i to t_j. We already know that each task has its own process element character. For example, Task 1, t_1 is described as 'writing C code'. In the task classification phase, t_1 is categorized as 'Code' (one of the pre-defined process elements). Task 2 is recorded as 'testing the bar function' (t_2). It is classified as 'Test'. We found that there is a temporal relationship between t_1 and t_2 because t_2 ends before t_1 starts, End(t_2) < Start(t_1). We say that there is a temporal relationship between t_2 and t_1, i.e. $t_2 \rightarrow t_1$. Because $V_t(t_1) = \{\text{'Code'}\}$ and $V_t(t_2) = \{\text{'Test'}\}$, we say there is a temporal relationship from 'Test' to 'Code'. The temporal relationship in the task level also reflects the corresponding relationship at the process element level in the pre-defined process model.

However, we cannot simply claim that the development team is doing testing before coding only by one occurrence of this temporal relationship. It needs to be validated by counting its frequency in the next phase explained in Section 3.4.

3.4 Phase 4: Measurement of Outcomes

Compared with the pre-defined process model, two types of patterns are mined out. They are the consistency patterns, which are consistent with the pre-defined process model, and the conflicts, which are the inconsistent patterns.

The frequency of each pattern is determined by its unique supporting task-sets. For example, a pattern, $Ptn=\{E_{17}, E_{18}, E_{20}\}$ (E_i is a process element). Its supporting tasks are t_{10}, t_{17} and t_{71}. $V_t(t_{10})=\{E_{17}\}$, $V_t(t_{17})=\{E_{18}\}$ and $V_t(t_{71})=\{E_{20}\}$, we call these three tasks as Task-set 1. If there are other three tasks, such as Task-set 2, which also support the pattern and the tasks in Task-set 1 and 2 are not all the same, the frequency of this pattern can go up to 2. Hence, the frequency is the number of the unique supporting task-sets. Counting the frequency assists us in identifying the heavily adopted parts of a pre-defined process model. The frequency provides quantitative information on the usage of a pattern.

4 Case Study

We have cooperated with an Australian software firm for many years. The company decided to customize ISO 12207 as their fundamental process model. Attending to repeatedly follow their pre-defined process, the company provides guidance to the development team members by virtue of an Electronic Process Guideline[2].

4.1 Case Study Background

This section describes a case study done by using our method and the results from analysis. Instead of enumerating all the details of each step, we present the patterns

Table 1. Project Information

Project Information		
Team size	10 persons	
Total Effort	2212.25 man-hours	
Duration	717 days	
Closed year	2002	
Total task number	138	
Task Classification	EPG Tasks	106 (82%)
	None-EPG Tasks	23 (18%)
Kappa Agreement	0.810	

[2] The detailed information on EPG is published in paper [9].

we discovered and the potential problems found from comparing the mined process pattern with the pre-defined process model. Table 1 shows the project information.

4.2 Results of Consistency

In this case study, the recovered patterns range from length 3 to 11. Fig.1 lays out their distributions. The detected patterns are grouped by their lengths. Each column presents the amount of patterns in different length. The frequencies of each pattern are also counted. The patterns are divided into two groups. One group holds the patterns with high frequency and the other group contains the low frequency patterns. The frequency is one of the key indicators to measure the importance of a pattern because the patterns with high frequencies reveal two main issues. First, the patterns with high frequency must have been adopted heavily during the project development or more development effort was spent on them. They might be the **essential** parts of the pre-defined process model. Second, the high frequency patterns are **important** to future projects as well inside the organization because of the high probability of reuse. It is subjective to determine if the frequency of a pattern is classified as high.

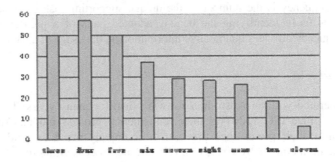

Fig. 1. Distributions of Patterns from Length 3 to 11

Table 2. Content of patterns with length 3

Length 3 Pattern's Content and Frequency	
Content	Frequency
Ptn1={ E_{18}, E_{17}, E_{18}}	27.8%
Ptn2={E_{17}, E_{18}, E_{24}}	23.3%
Ptn3={ E_{17}, E_{18},E_{25}}	10.7%
Ptn4={ E_{17}, E_{18},E_{22}}	8.8%
Ptn5={ E_{17}, E_{18},E_{19}}	6.2%
EPG Element ID	E_{17}= 'Detailed Design' E_{18}= 'Code' E_{19}= 'Test' E_{22}='Write User Documentation' E_{24}='Setup Hardware for Installation' E_{25}= 'Installation and Test'

We convert the frequency of each pattern from absolute numbers to percentage within the patterns of the same length. In this case study, the patterns with frequency above 1% from length 3 to 11 are considered for further analysis. We show the content of the top 5 high frequency patterns in length 3 as examples. Table 2 lists their content and frequencies.

The highest frequency pattern among length 3 patterns is Ptn1=$\{E_{18}, E_{17}, E_{18}\}$. There is a loop in it. In EPG model, a cycle between 'Detailed Design' and 'Code' exists. Ptn1 is consistent with EPG. Based on its frequency, it is apparent that Ptn1 is followed heavily during the development, which means the system design might not be completed in one time. Meanwhile, some other patterns, such as Ptn2, Ptn3 and Ptn5 indicate that the team starts from design and then coding. It discloses that the team leans towards a short iteration that mainly focuses on design and coding, i.e. the team was doing a bit of design and then coding it. We use Ptn2 as an example and show its Petri-net format in Fig. 2.

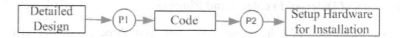

Fig. 2. Pattern 2 in Petri-net Format

Similar investigations were performed in patterns with length from 4 to 11. We found the cycle of 'Detailed Design' and 'Code' also appeared in the pattern across different lengths. The patterns from length 4 to 11 but all with a frequency above 1% are compared. From the comparisons, the longest pattern that happened mostly during project development is identified. We summarize the patterns in Petri-net format in Fig.3. In this pattern, there is a path directly from 'Test' to 'Setup Hardware for Installation', which means 'Write User Documentation' might be skipped during project development. Similar to the path from 'Code' to 'Setup Hardware for Installation', it shows that in some circumstance, the development team skipped the tasks of 'Test' and 'Write User Documentation'.

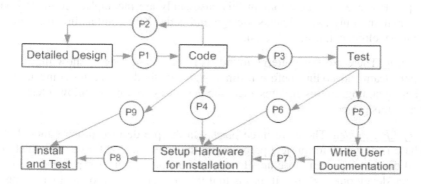

Fig. 3. Case Study Patterns

We conclude some findings from the analysis of the consistency patterns. The development team did not follow the project preparation procedures designed in their pre-defined process model, because there is no consistency detected in project design stage of the pre-defined model. However, no pattern found in this phase reveals that the development team may have their procedures for preparing the project. This phase might be not as useful as it was planned to this project.

The iteration of 'Detailed Design' (E_{17}) and 'Code' (E_{18}) is repeated heavily and up to four times. A pattern with length 11 is found to have this iteration four times and its frequency is up to 28.6% among all the length 11 patterns, Ptn={E_{18}, E_{17}, E_{18}, E_{17}, E_{18}, E_{17}, E_{18}, E_{17}, E_{18}, E_{22}, E_{24}} (E_{22}='Write User Documentation', E_{24}='Setup Hardware for Installation'). Regarding this fact, we can claim that the team was doing a bit of design, and coding it, then again back to design. The occurrence of the path from 'Code' to 'Test' is not high, which implies that the team might follow a test-driven process unconsciously.

4.3 Summary of Detected Problems and Findings

The analysis of a case study should be carried out from three aspects, 1) analysis of the conflicts, 2) investigations of the patterns, and 3) review of non-EPG tasks. In this case study, we only present the analysis of consistency patterns due to the page limit. Generally, the detected problem and findings emphasize three aspects; 1) iterations composed by project design and code, 2) test driven, and 3) scope of EPG model.

Iteration Composed by Project Design and Code: The analysis of consistency patterns shows that this project follows a short iteration in which the development team design a bit and then code a little. In the data set, the first design happened on 21st, Feb, 2001 and the first coding on the next day. The development team designed for one day and then coded for another day. They were apparently trying to finish a small function each time in a short iteration. The design and coding were coupled tightly. The interval between the design task and code task ranged from one day to thirty days. However, most design-code iterations happened closely to each other, which is similar to eXtreme Programming (XP) method. In XP, each iteration lasts 1 to 3 weeks [1]. However, the iterations in this case study are incomplete compared with XP's, containing only two elements: design and code. XP iterations involve iteration planning, development, test, and so on.

Test Driven: There are few patterns found which are expecting to show that the development team did coding before testing. Agile methods suggest writing unit test cases before coding. In this circumstance, the team was tending to follow a test driven practice in this project.

Scope of EPG model: There are three phases in the pre-defined process model. The first phase is designed for project preparation, the next phase is for development, and the third one is for project close up. However, most of the detected patterns are gathered in the development phase. It means that the project preparation and wrapping up stages have not been extensively adopted or recorded by the development team. The project manager may need to consider re-designing these two phases, if necessary.

From the analysis of the process patterns, several agile practices were identified at the project enactment level. This seems reasonable because the project's characteristics were likely suitable for adopting agile methods.

5 Discussions and Comparison with Previous Work

Scalability: We have applied our approach on three different sized projects including the case study presented in this paper. In the other two case studies, one is a team with 6 persons, and its total effort is 1652.25 man-hours. The other one is composed of 14 persons and 3524.5 man-hours. We won't enumerate them to save space. Each case study is a typical representative of different sized software development projects. These case studies proved that our approach is applicable to different sized projects, including small to middle sized projects and even to project modules.

Data type: The alpha algorithm tries to recover a whole process model and the data set must be complete [2]. A complete data set means that all process elements are adopted. Our algorithm is able to process an incomplete data set. The incomplete data set is produced when the development team skips some process elements while following the pre-defined process model during development. In our approach, we try to find the process patterns first. If the recovered process patterns contain all the pre-defined process elements, it can be treated as a full process model.

Data size: Data type and required amount: Previous work used a similar approach in the software process context. Their approach involved statistical methods where the amount of data required is large, normally more than hundreds of cases. It is difficult to gather enactment data from hundreds of projects which follow the same process model within the similar project environment. The required data size of our approach could be as small as one single project (as shown in case study).

Mining method: Our approach does not include any statistical method. On the other hand, most of the process mining approaches do include it. We try to find the temporal relations from the data set and then to detect the connecting places (see definition 1) from the relations. These places make up the recovered process patterns.

Output: The output of previous work presents the relationships among the daily activities, such as "code check-in", "code inspection" and so on. The recovered process model or patterns through our method are in the same context as the pre-defined process model. The major advantage is that a high-level process pattern or model can be captured. This is the most distinctive difference with previous work.

6 Conclusion and Future Work

This paper presents our approach to recover process patterns based on project enactment. In our approach, process patterns are discovered in the same format as a pre-defined process model, which can be designed from any general process methods or models, e.g. waterfall model. In the previous research, the recovered process remains at the same level as the raw data. The breakthrough from our work is that we can discover higher-level process patterns or models at the same level as the pre-defined process. Furthermore, our work makes project enactment become comparable with the planned process model. The deviations between a pre-defined process model and the discovered process patterns can be taken as the input for software process improvement, evolution or tailoring. The value of our method can be summarized as: 1) providing evidence of how a process executes during development, 2) identifying the coverage of the process model, 3) extracting the process patterns from live data, 4) discovering the conflicts and consistence between the defined process model and its enactment model.

From our case studies, we find some issues needs to be improved in our future work. Our current work has not provided a method to deal with noise data. The noise data are the tasks that do not belong to the predefined process model. Currently our approach does not take these data into account. Another limitation is that while the project is a moderate-large sized project, it needs to be divided into its modules or components. Our approach has no clear instructions on which type of projects should be divided into modules. In addition, our work only deals with the sequential temporal relation at current stage. We need to investigate the relationships among process elements, such as concurrency or choices, which remain as future work. Also after mining process patterns, how to accurately compare them with the defined process model and to present the deviation quantitatively will be investigated. Last but not least, a comprehensive process amendment mechanism for using these results will be proposed in the future.

Acknowledgement. NICTA is funded by the Australian Government as represented by the Department of Broadband, Communications and the Digital Economy and the Australian Research Council through the ICT Centre of Excellence program.

References

1. Extreme Programming: A gentle introduction,
   http://www.extremeprogramming.org
2. Alves de Medeiros, A.K., Weijters, A.J.M.M., van der Aalst, W.M.P.: Using Genetic Algorithms to Mine Process Models: Representation, Operators and Results. BETA Working Paper Series, WP 124, Eindhoven University of Technology, Eindhoven (2004)
3. Boehm, B.: A view of 20th and 21st century software engineering. In: 28th International Conference on Software Engineering, pp. 12–29. ACM, Shanghai, China (2006)
4. Cohen, J.: A coefficient of agreement for nominal scales. Educational and Psychological Measurement 20, 37–46 (1960)
5. Cook, J.E., Wolf, L.A.: Discovering models of software processes from event-based data. ACM Trans. Softw. Eng. Methodol. 7, 215–249 (1998)
6. Curtis, B.: Modeling the software process: three problems overcome with behavioral models of the software development process (panel session). In: 11th International Conference on Software Engineering, pp. 398–399. ACM, New York (1989)
7. Fuggetta, A.: Software process: a roadmap. In: Proceedings of the Conference on The Future of Software Engineering, pp. 25–34. ACM Press, Limerick, Ireland (2000)

8. Huo, M., He, Z., Jeffery, R.: A Systematic Approach to Process Enactment Analysis as Input to Software Process Improvement or Tailoring. In: APSEC 2006, XIII Asia Pacific Software Engineering Conference, pp. 401–410. IEEE Computer Society Press, Los Alamitos (2006)

9. Jeffery, R., Kurniawati, F.: The Use and Effects of an Electronic Process Guide and Experience Repository: A Longitudinal Study Information and Software Technology. Information and Software Technology 48, 57–566 (2005)

10. Henningsson, K., Wohlin, C.: Assuring fault classification agreement - an empirical evaluation. In: ISESE 2004, International Symposium on Empirical Software Engineering, pp. 95–104 (2004)

11. Krippendorff, K.: Content Analysis: An Introduction to Its Methodology. Sage Publications, Newbury Park, CA (1980)

12. Wen, J.W.L., van der Aalst, W.M.P., Wang, Z., Sun, J.: A Novel Approach for Process Mining Based on Event Types. BETA Working Paper Series, WP 118, Eindhoven University of Technology, Eindhoven (2004)

13. Murata, T.: Petri nets: Properties, Analysis and Applications. Proceedings of the IEEE 77(4), 541–580 (1989)

14. van der Aalst, W., Weijters, T., Maruster, L.: Workflow Mining: Discovering Process Models from Event Logs. IEEE Transactions on Knowledge and Data Engineering 16(9), 1128–1142 (2004)

15. van der Aalst, W.M.P.: Verification of Workflow Nets. In: Azéma, P., Balbo, G. (eds.) ICATPN 1997. LNCS, vol. 1248, pp. 407–426. Springer, Heidelberg (1997)

A Deviation Management System for Handling Software Process Enactment Evolution

Mohammed Kabbaj, Redouane Lbath, and Bernard Coulette

Université de Toulouse II – IRIT
5, allées Antonio Machado, F-31058 Toulouse Cedex 9, France
Tel.: +33 (0) 561 50 39 85, Fax: +33 (0) 561 50 25 40
{kabbaj, lbath, bernard.coulette}@univ-tlse2.fr

Abstract. An important problem encountered in Process-centered Software Engineering Environments (PSEE) is that software development processes are subject to permanent evolution during enactment. Without managing evolution, PSEEs are condemned to fail in being adopted in software industry. This article presents an original approach to process enactment evolution, based on formal management of process deviations. Deviations are defined as operations that violate process constraints. Once a deviation is detected, a deviation-tolerance model attached to the preset process is used to decide whether to accept or to reject the deviation.

Keywords: Software Process Modeling, Process Enactment, Process Deviation, Process Enactment Evolution, Dynamic Adaptation of Software Processes.

1 Introduction

After the apparition of Process-centered Software Engineering Environments (PSEEs), researchers and practitioners have realized that process models must be flexible enough to allow process changes to face unexpected situations [4]. Processes need to continuously undergo changes and refinements to increase their ability to deal with customer's requirements and expectations of the market. Consequently, PSEEs must accept a permanent evolution of process models, and tolerate and manage inconsistencies and deviations. This requirement reflects the nature of a creative activity such as software development, where consistency is the exception, not the rule [1][3]. The objectives of the work presented in this paper are to support process enactment evolution, by managing the deviations that occur during the enactment time. Addressed processes are those of organizations where the software process corresponds to « The Defined Level » of maturity according to the Capability Maturity Model [5].

The problem of process evolution is well known in software process community but only a few works [2] [7] [8] have addressed it. As discussed in section 2.4, existing approaches do not respond real-world situations that require context-dependant handling of process evolution. To contribute to solve this problem, we propose an innovative approach, which stems from the following postulate: "*absence of deviation is the exception, not the rule.*" In other words, we consider that process models are

Q. Wang, D. Pfahl, and D.M. Raffo (Eds.): ICSP 2008, LNCS 5007, pp. 186–197, 2008.
© Springer-Verlag Berlin Heidelberg 2008

needed to guide humans, not to be enforced prescriptively. Humans must always be allowed to decide whether to follow process models whenever they need to face unexpected situations or to improve process models. Our approach [10] is based on detection and management of process deviations, by making two process models coexist: a preset process model that guides development, and an observed process model that is dynamically constructed by observing visible actions of human actors. Deviations are defined as operations executed by human actors that violate process constraints. A first-order logic representation of the preset process' constraints, the observed process model, and operations, is used in order to rigorously characterize deviations as *operations that cannot be deduced from that logical representation*. Once a deviation is detected, context-dependant deviation-tolerance rules attached to the preset process are used to decide whether to accept or to reject the deviation.

This paper is organized as follows. Section 2 deals with problems and concepts of process deviation and process enactment evolution. Section 3 outlines the approach we propose, and illustrates it through a simplistic example. Section 4 deals with implementation aspects. Section 5 concludes the paper and gives some perspectives.

2 Software Process Deviation Problem

2.1 Consistency of Supported Software Processes

First of all, let us define some of the terms used in the remainder of this paper (see [6] for more detailed definitions). A *process model* is a static description of the expected software process expressed in a Process Description language. It is typically composed of activities (tasks), which represent work items to be executed by a human or automated resource. An *actual process* is the actual software process as it is performed in the real world. During process model enactment, a PSEE has a partial view of the actual process. This partial view of the actual process owned by the PSEE is called the *observed process*. At each instant, it may be described by a history of the activities that users perform under the PSEE .

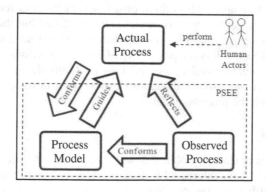

Fig. 1. Software process consistency relationships in ideal situation

2.2 Concepts of Deviation and Inconsistency

People behave differently in different situations and, therefore, it is hard to capture in advance in a formal process model all the possible behavior of a complex and dynamic system like software process development. Unforeseen situations may always occur. Typically, the effect of an unmanaged failure or exception is an action that breaks the consistency relationships shown in Figure 1. This often leads to the impossibility of continuing executing the process under the PSEE's control. To better clarify possible effects of undesired events not adequately managed by the PSEE, we use the following terminology [6]. A *deviation* is an action performed that is not described in the predefined process or that violates constraints expressed in the process. An *inconsistency* is a state of software process resulting from a process deviation. An *actual process deviation* is an action that breaks the consistency relationship between the actual process and the process model. Usually, actual process deviations are the result of an exception. An *observed process deviation* is an action performed within the PSEE that is not reflected in the process model. These deviations break the consistency relationship between the observed process and the process model. An *environment deviation* is an action that breaks the consistency relationship between the actual process and the observed process. It typically occurs when human actors perform a relevant action out of the PSEE control. The PSEE has then an incorrect view, so it cannot correctly support the actual process anymore. A PSEE is said to be *coherent* [9] if it is capable of tracking all developers' actions.

2.3 Dealing with Process Deviation

To face an unexpected situation, three different responses are possible [8]: (1) *Nothing* is done: the process model is not modified and actions needed to cope with the unexpected situation are performed out of the PSEE control. Consequently, the PSEE cannot analyze the deviation, nor can it support developers in reconciling the actual process with the process model. (2) *Model-changing*: the PSEE provides mechanisms to change the process model on-the-fly. Actions needed to cope with the unexpected situation are added to the model and the PSEE is given the new process model to enact. The result of this approach is that consistency of process relationships is restored. (3) *Model-relaxing*: the process model is not modified but the PSEE provides mechanisms to explicitly deviate from the model without the need of modifying the process model. The PSEE offers the possibility of executing actions necessary to cope with the unexpected situation under its control, by explicitly deviating from the process model. The PSEE can analyze deviations and support developers in reconciling the actual process with the process model.

2.4 Related Works

Although the process deviation problem is well known in software process community, only a few works have addressed it. In a previous research work, we developed RHODES [7], a PSEE that manages dynamic inconsistencies through an exception handling mechanism. However, process deviations are not supported. Other significant works dealing with process enactment evolution are those of SPADE [2], and SENTINEL [8]. SPADE assumes that humans do not change the way they work unless they change the process model. The process deviation problem is tackled by providing features for changing process models "on-the-fly". This approach may be effective to cope with major deviations from process models that are expected to occur again in the future, but the approach is unsuitable for situations that require minor or temporary deviations. SENTINEL tolerates deviations while critical requirements of processes are not violated. But it makes no difference between deviations according to their origin, and has no consistency handling policies. However, practical situations of real-world software development require context-dependent tolerance of deviations.

Besides these works that aim to allow process performers to deviate from the process model, there are many other works dealing with process evolution and/or process inconsistencies, but with a different focus such as process improvement, process elicitation, etc. For example, [12] proposes an algebraic approach based on the π-calculus to detect inconsistencies between a process model and its performance, and help process designers locate and resolve the inconsistencies; [13] provides a viewpoints-based approach to manage inconsistency for process analysis and improvement; [14] presents a pattern-matching technique for process elicitation.

3 Proposed Approach

Figure 2 gives an overview of our approach. The Enacting Process Model represents the process model that actually guides development. The Observed Process Model represents a description of the actual process reflecting visible human actors' actions. The Deviation-Tolerance Model consists of deviation-tolerance rules that describe tolerance to process deviations.

The Deviation Detection System is a module in charge of detecting process deviations. Role of the Deviation Management System is to decide whether to accept or to reject deviations according to DTM. Details are given in the following sections.

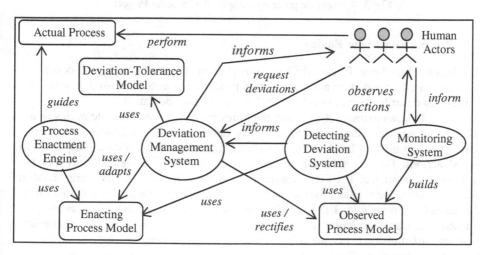

Fig. 2. General overview of our approach

3.1 Modeling Process Models

The Enacting Process Model (EPM) mentioned in figure 2 represents a process model that actually guides the development process. Initially, it is obtained by instantiating a generic process model, which represents the "ideal" process that describes the know-how and policies of a software development organization. The generic process model conforms with a UML process meta-model described in [11], which is an extension of SPEM. It allows specification of activities with associated pre-conditions, post-conditions, invariants, roles played by actors, tools to be used, artifacts, and guidance for achieving activities. EPM is created by customizing the generic process model to a particular software project, i.e. by defining specific activities, assigning roles and resources, and setting correct initial states.

An example of EPM, called "Student Project", is shown by figure 3. It is a simplistic process favored by our students in developing small-size software within a few weeks. The process consists of two activities: Design which produces a design model from specifications, and Coding which produces software code that implements the design model. The process involves roles of designer, and developer.

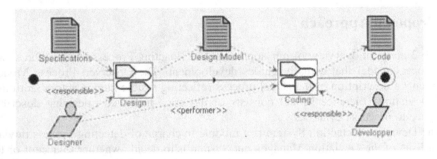

Fig. 3. A simplistic process example: the "Student Project"

3.2 Process Enactment Engine

The Process Enactment Engine (PEE) is a module in charge of enacting process models. It is based on structure and behavior of process elements expressed as state machines that describe their nominal life cycles, i.e. without deviations.

Figure 4 shows extracts of the state machines expressing nominal life cycles of activities and artifacts. States are connected by either *automatic* transitions that correspond to conditions to be checked, or *manual* transitions that constitute responses to users' actions. For example, for an activity, the state *Enactable* indicates that the activity is instantiated. The State *Activatable* indicates that the activity's precondition and precedence are verified, thus it can be launched. The transition from *Enactable* to *Activatable* is *automatic*. The state *Enacting* indicates that the activity is being performed. The transition *launch* corresponds to a user action (launch the activity) and it is a *manual* transition. For an artifact, the state *Initial* indicates that the artifact is ready for elaboration. The state *Drafta* indicates that the artifact is ready for evaluation and revision, and the state *Draftβ* means that it is ready for validation.

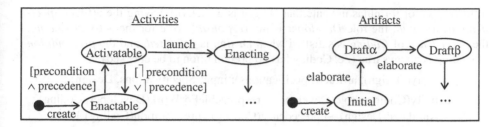

Fig. 4. Extracts of nominal behavior for enactment of process elements

3.3 Monitoring System

The Observed Process Model (OPM) represents a description of the actual process that reflects visible actions that human actors perform while carrying out the process. The Monitoring System collects events relating to the performed process in order to build OPM. Without deviations, OPM indicates at each instant parts of process model that have been performed and parts that have to be performed in the next instant. So, in this case, OPM would represent trace of following the process without deviation.

The Monitoring System receives events from observers of process elements and observers of operations that human actors may execute (e.g. launch an activity, validate an artifact). The observers of process elements are event listeners to changes of significant process elements' properties (e.g. state of an activity). The observers of operations generate an event whenever an operation is executed.

3.4 Detecting Deviation System

Deviations correspond to operations that do not conform to the process elements' nominal behavior, or break process elements' relationships (e.g. "launching an activity whose precondition is not satisfied", "pursuing an activity whose invariant has been violated"). The Detection Deviation System (DDS) receives events relating to operations executed by human actors from the Monitoring System. Role of DDS is to analyze events in order to determine whether executed operations conform with process' structure and behavior or constitute deviations.

Logical Formalization of Process Models. A UML description of the process model does not allow direct exploitation of the model to detect violations of constraints. A logical formalization is more appropriate for checking constraints and, thus, for detecting process deviations. The idea is to consider the union of the structure and the nominal behavior of the enacting process model, and the observed process model, as a set of first-order logical formulas from which non-deviating operations are deductible. Consequently, deviations can be characterized as operations that are not deductible from that set of formulas.

The logical description of the enacting process model's structure is obtained from its UML description by translating types and relationships into first-order logic formulas[1]. For example, let us consider the simplistic process shown by figure 3. The

---

[1] The translation is achieved automatically from XMI representation of UML diagrams.

following set of formulas indicate that *Design* is an activity having the artifact *Specifications* as *input*, the role *Developer* is the *responsible role* for the activity *Coding*, the *precedence* of *Coding* is satisfied when *Design* is *validated*, and the *precondition* of Coding is always true (i.e. Coding has no precondition to be checked):

{ activity(Design); artifact(Specifications); input(Specifications, Design) ;

activity(Coding); role(Developer); responsibleForWork(Developer, Coding) ;

validated(Design) → precedence(Coding) ; precondition(Coding) } .

The logical formalization of the observed process model is a set of first-order logic formulas that represent current states of process elements, and operations performed by human actors. For example, let us consider the process shown by figure 3. To indicate that the activity *Design* has been launched by *Designer* and its state has moved to Enacting, the observed process model will contain the following formulas:

{operation(launch, Design, Designer); enacting(Design)} .

As discussed in section 3.2, process elements are associated with state machines that describe nominal behavior for enactment. The logical representation of this behavior is obtained by translating state machines into a set of implicative first-order logic formulas. For example, the extract of the state machine associated with activities, shown by Figure 4, is translated into the following set of formulas, where w stands for an activity and r for a role:

{ $\forall$w (initial(w) → enactable(w)) ;

$\forall$w ((precondition(w) ∧ precedence(w) ∧ enactable(w)) → activatable(w)) ;

$\forall$w $\forall$r ((activatable(w) ∧ responsibleForWork(r, w)) → operation(launch, w, r)) ;

$\forall$w $\forall$r (operation(launch, w, r) → enacting(w)) } .

Detecting Deviations. Operations executed by human actors are represented by logical formulas in the observed process model (e.g., operation(launch, Design, Designer)). If we analyze the implicative formulas describing the process' nominal behavior, we can easily see that: an operation is not a deviation if and only if it can be deduced from the logical representation of the process model and the observed model.

Formally, if M is the union of the set of formulas that describe structure and behavior of an enacting process model, and the set of formulas that describe the observed process model, and O is an operation executed by human actors, then:

$$O \text{ is not a deviation } \Leftrightarrow M \vdash O .$$

For example, let us consider the process StudentProject shown by figure 3, and let us suppose that: *Design* is in state *enacting* (i.e. not validated yet), the activity *Coding* is in state *Enactable* (i.e. not activatable yet), and *Coding* is launched by the role *Developer*. According to the nominal behavior of activities listed above, *Coding* can be legally launched only when it is in state *Activatable*, which cannot be reached if Coding's precedence is not satisfied, i.e. if *Design* is *not validated*. Thus, in this context, the operation constitutes a deviation. Formally, the situation can be characterized as follows[2]:

---

[2] The set M is restricted here to only those formulas that are relevant to the example's context.

ο = operation(launch, Coding, Developer) .

M = { ∀w∀r ((activatable(w) ∧ responsibleForWork(r, w)) → operation(launch, w, r)) ;

validated(Design) → precedence(Coding) ;

enacting(Design) ; enactable(Coding) ; responsibleForWork(Developer, Coding) } .

M ⊢/— ο . Thus, ο constitutes a deviation.

3.5 Deviation-Tolerance Model

The deviation-tolerance model describes tolerance to process deviations. It helps process designers authorize deviations in order to meet specific needs, and thus improve process models' flexibility. It consists of deviation-tolerance rules that indicate tolerability of deviations in terms of numeric value ranging from 0 to 1, called deviation-tolerance index (DTI). Two threshold values are defined: tolerance threshold (TT) and non-tolerance threshold (NT) as shown by figure 5. So, the interval [0,1] is partitioned into three intervals: zero-tolerance interval, from 0 to NT; uncertainty interval, from NT to TT; and tolerance interval, from TT to 1. Deviations marked with values belonging to the zero-tolerance interval are automatically rejected. Deviations marked with values belonging to the tolerance interval are automatically tolerated. Deviations marked with values within the uncertainty interval are context-sensitive, i.e. the decision of whether rejecting or tolerating them remains in the hands of human actors. Moreover, the two threshold values may be dynamically adjusted in order to authorize more flexibility and context-sensitive response to deviations.

reject deviations	*reject / accept deviations*	*accept deviations*
Zero-tolerance Interval	Uncertainty Interval (context-sensitive decision)	Tolerance Interval
0 NT	TT	1

Fig. 5. Intervals of deviation-tolerance values

Description : "In case of violation of precedence of an activity w, then if any input of w is in the state Draftβ with at least a 90% degree of achievement, the deviation is to be qualified as minor and is to be tolerated (with DTI=0.9)".	
Deviation : ∃ r (operation(launch, w, r) ∧ ¬ precedence(w))	
Context : ∀ P (input(P,W) → (Draftβ(P) ∧ GreaterThan(achievement(P), 90%)))	
Qualification : minor	Deviation Tolerance Index : 0.9

Fig. 6. An example of deviation-tolerance rule attached to activities

Deviation-tolerance rules are associated to process elements (activities, artifacts, etc.). Figure 6 gives an example. A rule relates to a single deviation and consists of different parts: a natural-language description, a qualification (minor or major), a logical formula that characterizes the deviation, a logical formula that describes the context of tolerating or rejecting the deviation, and a deviation-tolerance index.

Deviations qualified as minor are considered to be without significant impact on process models, thus they do not imply the modification of process models. In contrast, deviations qualified as major are considered to be with significant impact on process models, meaning that the enacting process model has to be adapted accordingly.

With respect to generic process elements' structure and nominal behavior, we have identified about thirty context-independent deviations (e.g., launching an activity whose precondition is not satisfied, not performing a planned activity, etc.). A logical characterization of deviation is a first-order logic formula that describes a context-independent deviation. It indicates an illegal operation and violated constraints of the process model. For example, if we analyze the description of the rule shown by figure 6, we see that it clearly relates to context-independent deviation "violation of precedence", which can be characterized as shown by deviation part in the figure.

The context part of a rule aims to take into account specific and context-dependent aspects of actual processes. Such aspects are expressed through a first-order logic formula, in terms of observed process elements' states. For example, the context part of rule shown by figure 6 states that "all input are in state Draftβ with at least 90% degree of achievement" and can be described by the formula shown by the context part in the figure.

The set of the context-independent deviations has not to be considered as a fixed set for all situations. It is defined through the deviation-tolerance rules, and may change as these rules change, dynamically, according to unexpected situations.

Specifying deviations through deviation-tolerance rules is equivalent to adding alternative enactment paths to the process model. The benefit of the rules formalism described above mainly resides in the first-order logic's power of expressiveness.

3.6   Deviation Management System

Detected deviations and human actors' requests for deviations are submitted to the Deviation Management System whose role is to decide whether to accept or to reject deviations, according to the deviation-tolerance model. It uses both model changing and model relaxing approaches (discussed in section 2.3). If an accepted deviation is assumed to be of a deep impact on the process, the enacting process model is adapted according to the deviation (model changing). Otherwise, the enacting process model remains unchanged and thus the deviation is tolerated (model relaxing).

The deviation to be considered is analyzed in order to determine the relating process element. Then, deviation-tolerance rules attached to the process element are considered. Rules that match with the deviation and whose context part matches with the current context of the development are selected. Finally, the rule of the weakest deviation-tolerance index is used to set a tolerance value to the deviation. Actions envisaged for a deviation depend on two different criteria: (1) the interval that the deviation's tolerance value belongs to (zero-tolerance interval, tolerance interval, or uncertainty interval); and (2) the qualification of the deviation, minor or major.

Regarding the tolerance value assigned to a deviation, three cases are possible:

(1) The value belongs to the tolerance interval, i.e. the deviation is acceptable. Then, the deviation is automatically tolerated.

(2) The value belongs to the zero-tolerance interval, i.e. the deviation is incompatible or unacceptable with the development. Then the deviation is automatically rejected and, the observed process model is reset to its state previous, eventually (for detected deviations, not for requested deviations).

(3) The value belongs to the uncertainty interval. Then, a human decision is requested to whether accept or reject the deviation. Risks, costs, and reconciliation actions to keep project's coherence should be considered before making decision.

Regarding the qualification of a tolerated deviation, two cases are possible:

(1) The deviation is qualified as a minor deviation. Then the deviation is assumed to be an exceptional and temporary deviation that requires no change of the enacting process model. It continues to be enacted for guiding the development (application of the model relaxing principle discussed in section 2.3).

(2) The deviation is qualified as a major deviation. Then, the deviation is assumed to be of a deep impact on the process, which requires changing the process model. The enacting process model is modified[3] according to the deviation (application of the model changing principle discussed in section 2.3).

4 Implementation

A prototype system of our approach, called DM_PSEE (Deviation Management PSEE) has been developed under ECLIPSE 3.2. Plugins EMF and UML2.0 are used for editing generic process models and their associated deviation-tolerance rules, graphically. Checking of conformity to the process metamodel PMM is implemented in Java. Figure 7 shows the Student Project example, described in section 3.1, and associated tolerance-deviation model edited within DM_PSEE.

To automate building of enacting process models, each generic process' element is mapped into a Java process execution class that includes enacting aspects of the process element (e.g. process element states, degree of achievement, operations, etc.). The process enactment engine implements (in Java) state machines that describe nominal behavior of processes (presented in section 3.2). A user interface allows human actors to see process elements and their current state, and to execute different operations (e.g. login, launch an activity, terminate an activity, invalidate an artifact, validate an artifact, etc.). The process enactment engine also ensures resource management such as role assignation, artifact versioning, etc. The monitoring system is implemented as a set of java listeners that collect events relating to process execution classes. Events indicate either changes of process elements states, or operation executed by human actors. Collected events are used to build the observed process model. The detection deviation system is implemented in the Prolog language, thanks to an Eclipse plug-in

---

[3] Changing the generic process model is not necessary. Only its instance, the enacting process model, has to be adapted to restore consistency relationships discussed in section 2.1.

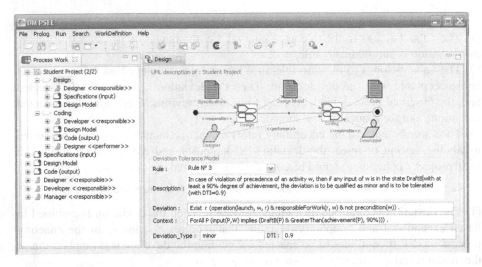

Fig. 7. DM_PSEE prototype: editing process models and associated deviation-tolerance rules

Prolog. The first-order logic representation of process models (presented in section 3.4) is described as a set of Prolog clauses to be used for deducing illegal operations executed by human operators, and thus for detecting deviations. Tolerance-deviation rules and the management deviation system are implemented in Prolog as well.

5   Conclusion and Perspectives

An important problem encountered in PSEE is that software development processes are subject to permanent dynamic evolution. This article presents an original approach to support process enactment evolution. Addressed processes are those corresponding to the "Defined Level" of the Capability Maturity Model.

The approach makes two process models coexist: a preset process model that guides development, and an observed process model. A first-order logic representation of process models is used for detecting process deviations. Tolerance to deviations is expressed as a set of rules that specify tolerance for accepting or refusing deviations. Our approach is founded on a postulate: "absence of deviation is the exception, not the rule". It considers that process models are needed just to guide humans, who must always remain the masters of decision, and be allowed to decide whether to follow process models whenever they need to face unexpected situations. Such a view makes our approach very innovative and radically different from the approaches proposed so far. A prototype system has been developed. The language Prolog has been used for logical representation of process models and rule-based reasoning for detection and management of deviations.

The simplistic example described in sections 3 has been used as a case study for validation. It could show feasibility of the approach but a real-world validation, through industrial processes, remains to be done. In addition to real-world validation, our future work will concern this important issue: in case of process adaptation after a major deviation, how to ensure that changes do not generate new inconsistencies with the process observed until the detection of the deviation?

References

1. Balzer, B.: Tolerating Inconsistencies. In: 13th International Conference on Software Engineering (ICSE 1991), Austin, Texas, pp. 158–165 (1991)
2. Bandinelli, S., et al.: SPADE: An Environment for Software Process Analysis, Design and Enactment. In: Finkelstein, A., et al. (eds.) Software Process Modeling and Technology, pp. 223–244. Wiley, London (1994)
3. Gervais, M.-P., Blanc, X., Bendraou, R.: UML4SPM: a UML2.0-Based Metamodel for Software Process Modeling. In: Briand, L.C., Williams, C. (eds.) MoDELS 2005. LNCS, vol. 3713, pp. 17–38. Springer, Heidelberg (2005)
4. Berande, P.: Understanding and Evaluation of Software Process Deviations. Master Thesis, Blekinge Institute of Technology, Sweden (2002)
5. Capability Maturity Model Integration, http://www.sei.cmu.edu/cmmi
6. Casati, F., Cugola, G.: Error Handling in Process Support Systems. In: Romanovsky, A., Dony, C., Knudsen, J.L., Tripathi, A.R. (eds.) ECOOP-WS 2000. LNCS, vol. 2022, pp. 251–270. Springer, Heidelberg (2001)
7. Coulette, B., et al.: RHODES: a Process Component Centered Software Engineering Environment. J. ICEIS, 253–260 (2000)
8. Cugola, G.: Tolerating Deviations in Process Support Systems via Flexible Enactment of Process Models. J. IEEE Transactions on Soft. Eng. 24(11), 982–1001 (1998)
9. Cugola, G., et al.: A Framework for formalizing Inconsistencies in Human-Centered Systems. J. ACM Trans. On Soft. Eng. and Methodology 5(3), 191–230 (1996)
10. Kabbaj, M., Lbath, R., Coulette, B.: A Deviation-tolerant Approach to Software Process Evolution. In: 9th Int. Workshop on Principles of Software Evolution, in conjunction with the 6th ESEC/FSE Joint Meeting, Dubrovnik, Croatia, pp. 75–78 (2007)
11. Lbath, R., Coulette, B., et al.: A multi-Agent Approach to a SPEM-based Modeling and Enactment of Software Development Processes. In: 7th Int. Conf. on Software Engineering. and Knowledge Engineering (SEKE), Taipei, Taiwan, pp. 241–246 (2005)
12. Qiusong, Y., et al.: An Algebraic Approach for Managing Inconsistencies. In: Wang, Q., Pfahl, D., Raffo, D.M. (eds.) ICSP 2007. LNCS, vol. 4470, pp. 121–133. Springer, Heidelberg (2007)
13. Sommerville, I., et al.: Managing process inconsistency using viewpoints. J. IEEE Transactions on Software Engineering 25(6), 784–799 (1999)
14. Soto, M., et al.: Focused Identification of Process Model Changes. In: Wang, Q., Pfahl, D., Raffo, D.M. (eds.) ICSP 2007. LNCS, vol. 4470, pp. 182–194. Springer, Heidelberg (2007)

Assessing Quality Processes with ODC COQUALMO

Raymond Madachy and Barry Boehm

University of Southern California Center for Systems and Software Engineering
941 W. 37th Place, Los Angeles, CA, USA
{madachy, boehm}@usc.edu

Abstract. Software quality processes can be assessed with the Orthogonal Defect Classification COnstructive QUALity MOdel (ODC COQUALMO) that predicts defects introduced and removed, classified by ODC types. Using parametric cost and defect removal inputs, static and dynamic versions of the model help one determine the impacts of quality strategies on defect profiles, cost and risk. The dynamic version provides insight into time trends and is suitable for continuous usage on a project. The models are calibrated with empirical data on defect distributions, introduction and removal rates; and supplemented with Delphi results for detailed ODC defect detection efficiencies. This work has supported the development of software risk advisory tools for NASA flight projects. We have demonstrated the integration of ODC COQUALMO with automated risk minimization methods to design higher value quality processes, in shorter time and with fewer resources, to meet stringent quality goals on projects.

Keywords: quality processes, defect modeling, orthogonal defect classification, COQUALMO, COCOMO, system dynamics, value-based software engineering.

1 Introduction

The University of Southern California Center for Systems and Software Engineering (USC-CSSE) has been evaluating and updating software cost and quality models for critical NASA flight projects. A major focus of the work is to assess and optimize quality processes to minimize operational flight risks. We have extended the COQUALMO model [1] for software defect types classified with Orthogonal Defect Classification (ODC). COQUALMO uses COCOMO II [2] cost estimation inputs with defect removal parameters to predict the numbers of generated, detected and remaining defects for requirements, design and code. It models the impacts of practices for automated analysis, peer reviews, and execution testing and tools on these defect categories. ODC COQUALMO further decomposes the defect types into more granular ODC categories.

The ODC taxonomy provides well-defined criteria for the defect types and has been successfully applied on NASA projects. The ODC defects are then mapped to operational flight risks, allowing "what-if" experimentation to determine the impact of techniques on specific risks and overall flight risk. The tool has been initially calibrated to ODC defect distribution patterns per JPL studies on unmanned missions. A

Q. Wang, D. Pfahl, and D.M. Raffo (Eds.): ICSP 2008, LNCS 5007, pp. 198–209, 2008.
© Springer-Verlag Berlin Heidelberg 2008

Delphi survey was completed to quantify ODC defect detection efficiencies, gauging the effect of different defect removal techniques against the ODC categories.

The approach is value-based [3] because defect removal techniques have different detection efficiencies for different types of defects, their effectiveness may vary over the lifecycle duration, different defect types have different flight risk impacts, and there are scarce resources to optimize. Additionally the methods may have overlapping capabilities for detecting defects, and it is difficult to know how to best apply them. Thus the tools help determine the best combination of techniques, their optimal order and timing.

ODC COQUALMO can be joined with different risk minimization methods to optimize strategies. These include machine learning techniques, strategic optimization and the use of fault trees to quantify risk reductions from quality strategies.

Empirical data is being used from manned and unmanned flight projects to further tailor and calibrate the models for NASA, and other USC-CSSE industrial affiliates are providing data for other environments. There will be additional calibrations and improvements, and this paper presents the latest developments in the ongoing research.

2 COQUALMO Background

Cost, schedule and quality are highly correlated factors in software development. They essentially form three sides of a triangle, because beyond a certain point it is difficult to increase the quality without increasing either the cost or schedule, or both. Similarly, development schedule cannot be drastically compressed without hampering the quality of the software product and/or increasing the cost of development. Software estimation models can (and should) play an important role in facilitating the balance of cost/schedule and quality.

Recognizing this important association, COQUALMO was created as an extension of the COnstructive COst MOdel (COCOMO) [2], [4] for predicting the number of residual defects in a software product. The model enables 'what-if' analyses that demonstrate the impact of various defect removal techniques. It provides insight into the effects of personnel, project, product and platform characteristics on software quality, and can be used to assess the payoffs of quality investments. It enables better understanding of interactions amongst quality strategies and can help determine probable ship time.

A black box representation of COQUALMO's submodels, inputs and outputs is shown in Fig 1. Its input domain includes the COCOMO cost drivers and three defect removal profile levels. The defect removal profiles and their rating scales are shown in Table 1. More details on the removal methods for these ratings are in [2]. From these inputs, the tool produces an estimate of the number of requirement, design and code defects that are introduced and removed as well as the number of residual defects remaining in each defect type.

The COQUALMO model contains two sub-models: 1) the defect introduction model and 2) the defect removal model. The defect introduction model uses a subset of COCOMO cost drivers and three internal baseline defect rates (requirements, design, code and test baselines) to produce a prediction of defects that will be introduced

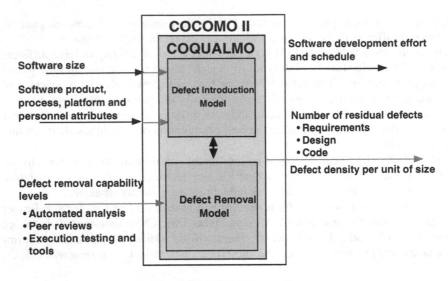

Fig. 1. COQUALMO overview

Table 1. Defect removal practice ratings

	Very Low	Low	Nominal	High	Very High	Extra High
Automated Analysis	Simple compiler syntax checking	Basic compiler capabilities	Compiler extension Basic req. and design consistency	Intermediate-level module Simple req./design	More elaborate req./design Basic dist-processing	Formalized specification, verification. Advanced dist-processing
Peer Reviews	No peer review	Ad-hoc informal walk-through	Well-defined preparation, review, minimal follow-up	Formal review roles and Well-trained people and basic checklist	Root cause analysis, formal follow Using historical data	Extensive review checklist Statistical control
Execution Testing and Tools	No testing	Ad-hoc test and debug	Basic test Test criteria based on checklist	Well-defined test seq. and basic test coverage tool system	More advance test tools, preparation. Dist-monitoring	Highly advanced tools, model-based test

in each defect category during software development. The defect removal model uses the three defect removal profile levels, along with the prediction produced by the defect introduction model, to produce an estimate of the number of defects that will be removed from each category.

2.1 ODC Extension

ODC COQUALMO decomposes defects from the basic COQUALMO model using ODC [5]. The top-level quantities for requirements, design and code defects are decomposed into the ODC categories per defect distributions input to the model. With more granular defect definitions, ODC COQUALMO enables tradeoffs of different detection efficiencies for the removal practices per type of defect. Table 2 lists the ODC defect categories used in the model, and against which data is collected.

Table 2. ODC defect categories

Requirements	Design/Code
• Correctness	• Interface
• Completeness	• Timing
• Consistency	• Class/Object/Function
• Ambiguity/Testability	• Method/Logic/Algorithm
	• Data Values/Initialization
	• Checking

This more detailed approach takes into account the differences between the methods with specific defect pairings. Peer reviews, for instance, are good at finding completeness defects in requirements but not efficient at finding timing errors for a real-time system. Those are best found with automated analysis or execution and testing tools.

The model also provides a distribution of defects in terms of their relative frequencies. The tools described in the next section have defect distribution options that allows a user to input actuals-based or expert judgment distributions, while an option for the Lutz-Mikulski distribution is based on empirical data at JPL [6].

The sources of empirical data used for analysis and calibration of the ODC CO-COQUALMO model were described in [7]. The quality model calculating defects for requirements, design and code retains the same calibration as the initial COQUALMO model[1]. The distribution of ODC defects from [6] was used to populate the initial model with an empirically-based distribution from the unmanned flight domain at JPL. The Lutz-Mikulski distribution uses the two-project average for their ODC categories coincident across the taxonomy used in this research for design and code defects. Their combined category of "Function/Algorithm" is split evenly across our two corresponding categories.

A comprehensive Delphi survey [8], [9] was used to capture more detailed efficiencies of the techniques against the ODC defect categories. The experts had on average more than 20 years of related experience in space applications. The ODC Delphi survey used a modified Wideband Delphi process and went through two rigorous iterations [9]. The results are summarized separately for automated analysis, execution testing and tools, and peer reviews in Fig. 2, Fig. 3 and Fig. 4 respectively.

The values represent the percentages of defects found by a given technique at each rating (sometimes termed "effectiveness"). The different relative efficiencies of the defect removal methods can be visualized, in terms of the general patterns between the methods and against the defect types within each method. For example, more automated analysis from very high to extra high increases the percent of checking defects found from 65% to almost 80%.

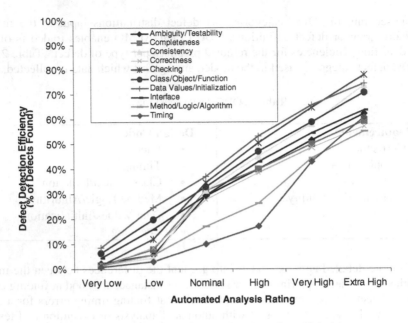

Fig. 2. Automated analysis ODC defect detection efficiencies

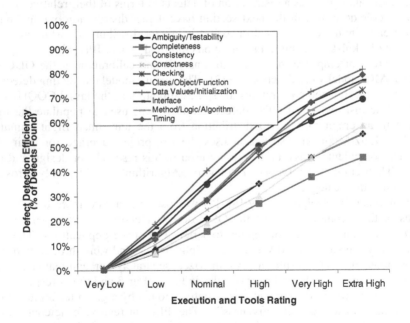

Fig. 3. Execution testing and tools ODC defect detection efficiencies

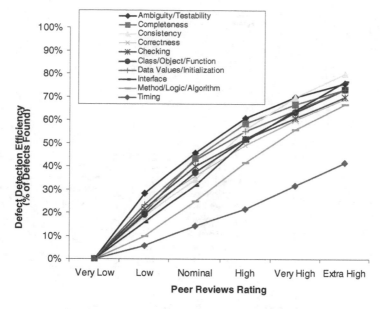

Fig. 4. Peer reviews ODC defect detection efficiencies

2.2   ODC COQUALMO and Risk Minimization

Different methods for risk analysis and reduction have been performed in conjunction with ODC COQUALMO, which can produce optimal results in less time and allow for insights not available by humans alone. In [11] machine learning techniques were applied on the COQUALMO parameter tradespace to simulate development options and measure their effects on defects and costs, in order to best improve project outcomes. Another technique to reduce risks with the model is a strategic method of optimization. It generates optimal risk reduction strategies for defect removal for a given budget, and also computes the best order of activities [12].

An integration of ODC COQUALMO has also been prototyped with the DDP risk management tool [13], [14], which uses fault trees to represent the overall system's dependencies on software functionality. These experiments to optimize quality processes are described in more detail in [15].

3   ODC COQUALMO Tools

There are different implementations of ODC COQUALMO. There are static versions in a spreadsheet and one that runs on the Internet that estimate the final levels of defects for the ODC categories. The Internet-based tool at http://csse.usc.edu/tools/odc_coqualmo.php now supersedes the spreadsheet. It has the latest defect detection efficiency calibrations and is our base tool for future enhancements. The inputs to the static model are shown in Fig. 5, while Fig. 6 shows an example of ODC defect outputs. A dynamic simulation version models the defect generation and detection rates

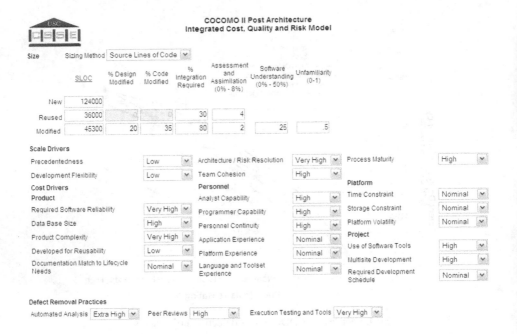

Fig. 5. COQUALMO sample inputs

over time for continuous project usage, and provides continuous outputs as shown in the next section.

3.1 Dynamic Simulation Model

This section summarizes a continuous simulation model version using system dynamics [10] to evaluate the time-dependent effectiveness of different defect detection techniques against ODC defect categories. As a continuous model, it can be used for interactive training to see the effects of changes midstream or be updated with projects actuals for continuous usage on a project [10].

The model uses standard COCOMO factors for defect generation rates and the defect removal techniques for automated analysis, peer reviews and execution testing and tools. The model can be used for process improvement planning, or control and operational management during a project.

COQUALMO is traditionally a static model, which is a form not amenable to continuous updating because the parameters are constant over time. Its outputs are final cumulative quantities, no time trends are available, and there is no provision to handle the overlapping capabilities of defect detection techniques. The defect detection methods and the defect removal techniques are modeled in aggregate, so it is not possible to deduce how many are captured by which technique (except in the degenerate case where two of the three methods are zeroed out).

In this system dynamics extension to ODC COQUALMO, defect and generation rates are explicitly modeled over time with feedback relationships. It can provide

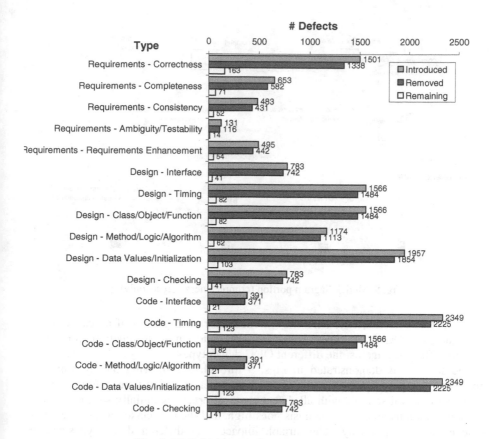

Fig. 6. ODC COQUALMO sample defect outputs

continual updates of risk estimates based on project and code metrics. This model includes the effects of all defect detection efficiencies for the defect reduction techniques against each ODC defect type per Fig.2, Fig 3 and Fig. 4.

The defect removal factors are shown in the control panel portion in Fig. 7. They can be used interactively during a run. A simplified portion of the system diagram (for completeness defects only) is in Fig. 8. The defect dynamics are based on a Rayleigh curve defect model of generation and detection. The buildup parameters for each type of defect are calibrated for the estimated project schedule time, which may vary based on changing conditions during the project.

(1=very low, 2=low, 3=nominal, 4=high, 5=very high, 6=extra high)

Fig. 7. Defect removal sliders on interactive control panel

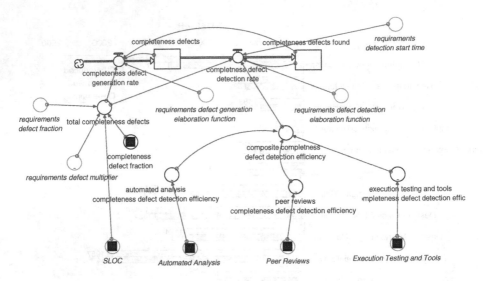

Fig. 8. Model diagram portion (completeness defects only)

The defect detection efficiencies are modeled for each pairing of defect removal technique and ODC defect type. These are represented in graph functions for defect detection efficiency against the different ODC defect types.

The scenario is demonstrated in Figs. 9 through 11, showing the dynamic responses to changing defect removal settings on different defect types. Fig. 9 shows the defect removal settings with all defect removal practices initially set to nominal. At about 6 months automated analysis goes high, and then is relaxed as peer reviews is kicked up simultaneously. The variable impact to the different defect types can be visualized in the curves.

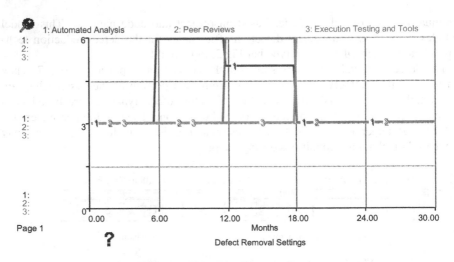

Fig. 9. Defect removal setting changes

The requirements consistency defects are in Fig. 10, showing the perturbation from the defect removal changes. The graph in Fig. 11 from the simulation model shows the dynamics for code timing defects, including the impact of changing the defect removal practices in the midst of the project at 18 months. At that time the setting for execution testing and tools goes high, and the timing defect detection curve responds to find more defects at a faster rate.

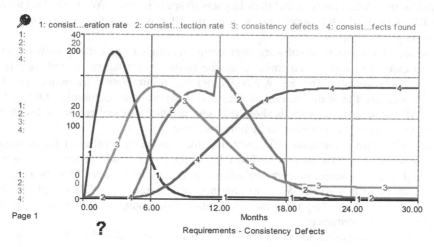

Fig. 10. Requirements consistency defect dynamics (*1: requirements consistency defect generation rate, 2: requirements consistency defect detection rate, 3: requirements consistency defects, 4: requirements consistency defects found*)

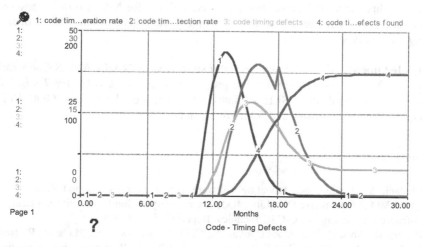

Fig. 11. Code timing defect dynamics (*defect removal practice change at time = 18*) (*1: code timing defect generation rate, 2: code timing defect detection rate, 3: code timing defects, 4: code timing defects found*)

4 Conclusions and Future Work

Software estimation models can and should play an important role in facilitating the right balance of activities to meet quality goals. By predicting software defect introduction and removal rates, ODC COQUALMO is useful for identifying appropriate defect reduction strategies. The extension for ODC defect types provides more granular insight into defect profiles and their impacts to specific risks. We have shown that the ODC COQUALMO model can be used in different ways to reason about and optimize quality processes.

The use of value-neutral software engineering methods often causes software projects to expend significant amounts of scarce resources on activities with negative returns on investment. The use of models and risk minimization techniques can be used to optimize the scarce resources. Results of experiments combining ODC CO-QUALMO with various methods show they can produce optimal results in less time and allow for insights not available by humans alone.

The ODC defect detection efficiency functions are being evaluated for different domains and operational scenarios. The ODC Delphi survey will be revisited for the extra high usage of defect removal techniques, and to address issues identified by the experts so far in this work. We will continue to integrate the ODC COQUALMO model with complementary techniques to support risk management practices, and to compare their performances.

We are also analyzing additional empirical case studies. Model calibration data is being used from manned and unmanned NASA flight projects, as well as other USC-CSSE data sources including industrial affiliates who serve as contractors on space projects. There are also affiliates in commercial domains undertaking ODC defect analysis for which specialized calibrations are being done. With more comprehensive data the quality model will be further improved, tailored for NASA projects and other organizations, and integrated with complementary methods for value-based decision making on quality strategies.

Acknowledgments. This work was partially supported by NASA AMES Cooperative Agreement No. NNA06CB29A for the project *Software Risk Advisory Tools*. The authors wish to thank the CSEE affiliates who contributed data, the ODC Delphi participants, Dr. Mike Lowry and John Powell at NASA.

References

1. Chulani, S., Boehm, B.: Modeling software defect introduction and removal: CO-QUALMO (COnstructive QUALity MOdel), University of Southern California Center for Software Engineering, USC-CSE Technical Report 99-510 (1999)
2. Boehm, B., Abts, C., Brown, A., Chulani, S., Clark, B., Horowitz, E., Madachy, R., Reifer, D., Steece, B.: Software Cost Estimation with COCOMO II. Prentice-Hall, Englewood Cliffs (2000)
3. Biffl, S., Aurum, A., Boehm, B., Erdogmus, H., Grünbacher, P. (eds.): Value-Based Software Engineering. Springer, Heidelberg (2005)
4. Boehm, B.: Software Engineering Economics. Prentice-Hall, Englewood Cliffs (1981)

5. Chillarege, R., Bhandari, I., Chaar, J., Halliday, M., Moebus, D., Ray, B., Wong, M.: Orthogonal Defect Classification - A Concept for In-Process Measurements. IEEE Transactions on Software Engineering 18(11), 943–956 (1992)
6. Lutz, R., Mikulski, I.: Final Report: Adapting ODC for Empirical Analysis of Pre-Launch Anomalies, version 1.2, NASA Jet Propulsion Laboratories, JPL Caltech report (2003)
7. Madachy, R.: Risk Model Calibration Report, USC Center for Systems and Software Engineering, Report to NASA AMES (2006)
8. Madachy, R.: JPL Delphi Survey for V&V Defect Detection Efficiencies, USC Center for Systems and Software Engineering, Report to NASA (2006)
9. Madachy, R.: Calibration of ODC COQUALMO to Predict V&V Effectiveness, USC Center for Systems and Software Engineering, Report to NASA AMES (2007)
10. Madachy, R.: Software Process Dynamics. IEEE-Wiley, Hoboken NJ (2008)
11. Menzies, T., Richardson, J.: XOMO: Understanding Development Options for Autonomy. In: 20th International Forum on COCOMO and Software cost Modeling, USC (2005)
12. Port, D., Kazman, R., Polo, B., Nakao, H., Katahira, M.: Practicing What is Preached: 80-20 Rules for Strategic IV&V Assessment, Center for Strategic Software Engineering, Technical Report, CSSE-TR20051025, University of Hawaii at Manoa (2005)
13. Feather, M., Cornford, S.: Quantitative Risk-based Requirements Reasoning. Requirements Engineering 8(4), 242–265 (2005)
14. Feather, M., Cornford, S., Hicks, K., Johnson, R.: Applications of Tool Support for Risk-informed Requirements Reasoning. Computer Systems Science and Engineering 20(1), 5–17 (2005)
15. Madachy, R., Boehm, B., Richardson, J., Feather, M., Menzies, T.: Value-Based Design of Software V&V Processes for NASA Flight Projects. In: AIAA Space 2007 Conference (2007)

Accurate Estimates without Calibration?

Tim Menzies[1], Oussama Elrawas[1], Barry Boehm[2], Raymond Madachy[2],
Jairus Hihn[3], Daniel Baker[1], and Karen Lum[3,*]

[1] LCSEE, West Virginia University, Morgantown, WV, USA
tim@menzies.us, oelrawas@mix.wvu.edu, danielryanbaker@gmail.com
[2] CS, University of Southern California, Los Angeles, California, USA
boehm@sunset.usc.edu, madachy@usc.edu
[3] JPL, California, USA
jairus.hihn@jpl.nasa.gov, karen.t.lum@jpl.nasa.gov

Abstract. Most process models calibrate their internal settings using historical data. Collecting this data is expensive, tedious, and often an incomplete process.

Is it possible to make accurate software process estimates without historical data? Suppose much of uncertainty in a model comes from a small subset of the model variables. If so, then after (a) ranking variables by their ability to constrain the output; and (b) applying a small number of the top-ranked variables; then it should be possible to (c) make stable predictions in the constrained space.

To test that hypothesis, we combined a simulated annealer (to generate random solutions) with a variable ranker. The results where quite dramatic: in one of the studies in this paper, we found process options that reduced the median and variance of the effort estimates by a factor of 20. In ten case studies, we show that the estimates generated in this manner are usually similar to those produced by standard local calibration.

Our conclusion is that while it is always preferable to tune models to local data, it is possible to learn process control options *without* that data.

1 Introduction

Without precise knowledge from an organization, it is difficult to make precise estimates about software processes at that site. For example, initial development effort estimates may be incorrect by a factor of four [7] or even more [17].

It can be very difficult to find relevant data within a single organization to fully specify all the internal parameters inside a process model. For example, after 26 years of trying, we have only collected less than 200 sample projects for the COCOMO database. There are many reasons for this, not the least being the business sensitivity associated with the data. Therefore, in this paper, we explore what can be decided from process models *without* local data.

For this experiment, we adopt the following framework. We say that a process model P yields estimates from a combination of $Project$ and $Model$ variables:

---

* This research was conducted at WVU, USC, and NASA's Jet Propulsion Laboratory partially under a NASA sub-contract. Reference herein to any specific commercial product, process, or service by trade name, trademark, manufacturer, or otherwise, does not constitute or imply its endorsement by the United States Government.

Q. Wang, D. Pfahl, and D.M. Raffo (Eds.): ICSP 2008, LNCS 5007, pp. 210–221, 2008.
© Springer-Verlag Berlin Heidelberg 2008

$$estimates = P(Project, Model)$$

P describes the space of influences between variables. and may take many forms:

- discrete-event models [19, 16];
- system dynamics models [1];
- state-based models [3, 13, 23];
- rule-based programs [28];
- standard programming constructs such as those used in Little-JIL [11, 33];
- or the linear models used in COCOMO [7, 9], PRICE-S [29] and SEER-SEM [15].

The strength of each influence is controlled by the $Model$ variables. Taken together, the process model P and the $Model$ variables store what we've leaned from the *past*.

$Project$ variables, on the other had, concern a *new* situation that should be analyzed using past knowledge. For example, P could assert "$effort \propto pcap$" (programmer skills is proportional to development effort) while $Model$ could assert the proportionality constant of -0.7 (i.e. "$effort = -0.7pcap$"). Finally, $Project$ could assert that programmer skills are "in the upper range"; e.g. for a COCOMO model "$pcap \in \{4, 5\}$".

We say $Project$ and $Model$ variables can be:

- $fixed$ to one value such as "programmer capability ($pcap$) is nominal";
- $free$ to take on any legal value. In COCOMO, a free $pcap$ can take values

$$\{veryLow = 1, low = 2, nominal = 3, high = 4, veryHigh = 5\}$$

- or $float$ to some subset of the whole range. For example, a manager might declare that "our programmers are in the upper ranges"; i.e. this $pcap$ floats in a particular part of the entire $pcap$ range ($pcap \in \{4, 5\}$).

The range of legal values for variables increases from $fixed$ to $float$ to $free$:

$$(|fixed| = 1) < |float| < |free|$$

This paper reports an experiment that frees *both* the $Model$ and $Project$ variables. At first glance, such an experiment may seem perverse, particularly if the goal is to reduce uncertainty. Free variables range over a larger space than fixed variables: the more free variables, the wider the range of $Estimates$. If we free both $Model$ and $Project$ variables then, surely, this will result in greater $Estimate$ uncertainty?

However, our analysis is not just some passive observer of a large space of options. Instead, it is an active agent that seeks parts of the options space where predictions can be made with greater certainty. We augment a Monte Carlo analysis with two tools. SA is a *simulated annealing algorithm* that minimizes $Estimates$. RANKER is a *variable pruning algorithm*, that seeks the *smallest* number of $Project$ variables that *most* reduce the $Estimates$. The combination of SA+RANKER is called STAR[1].Since it knows the most influential $Project$ ranges, STAR can discover (and then constrain) the factors that most most impact $Estimates$.

---

[1] The name is a geek joke. In regular expressions, the star meta-character "*" matches any characters. That is, just like STAR, it can be used to search a wide range of options.

case study	Monte Carlo SCAT	STAR STAR
flight	712	44
ground	389	18
OSP	629	68
OSP2	84	31

Fig 1a: variance, in months.

case study	Monte Carlo SCAT	STAR STAR
flight	1357	86
ground	737	38
OSP	1951	410
OSP2	297	182

Fig 1b: median, in months.

Fig. 1. Effort estimates seen in 1000 simulations of the *Project* ranges found by STAR. "Variance" (left hand side) shows the difference between the 75th and 50th percentile. "Median" (right hand side) shows the 50th percentile estimate.

When compared to state-of-the-art process models, the effects of a STAR-style analysis are quite dramatic. Figure 1 compares STAR's estimates to those generated by SCAT [22, 21, 20], a COCOMO-based tool used at NASA's Jet Propulsion Laboratory. SCAT fixes *Model* and perform a Monte Carlo simulation of the *Project* ranges. Each row of Figure 1.A is one case study:

- *flight* and *ground* systems software from NASA's Jet Propulsion Laboratory;
- *OSP* is the GNC[2] for NASA's Orbital Space Plane (prototype);
- *OSP2* is a newer version of OSP.

Note that, for all four case studies, STAR reduces the variance and median estimates to a small fraction of SCAT's estimates, sometimes as much as a factor of 20 (in Figure 1a: $\frac{712}{44} \approx 20$; in Figure 1b: $\frac{737}{38} \approx 20$).

The rest of this paper describes STAR. We extend prior work in two ways. Prior reports on STAR [26] were based on limited case studies; here we report ten new case studies showing that our main effect (reduced median and variance) holds in a wide range of cases. Also, prior reports on Figure 1 [25] failed to check the validity of those results. The ten case studies discussed below show that STAR's estimated are shown to be close to those generated via standard local calibration, despite being generated from a large space of *Project* and *Model* options. This validity check greatly increases our confidence in the STAR method.

It is unknown if our results apply to software process models more complex than STAR's COCOMO-style of models. However, our results to date suggest that other process models could make reasonably accurate predictions without local data by:

- finding the fewest number of variables that most effect model output;
- constrain them;
- check for stable conclusions in the constrained space.

2   Related Work

In terms of the framework of this paper, related work may be divided into:

---

[2] GNC= guidance, navigation, and control.

- *Prediction*: fix *Model* and *Project* and generates fixed *estimates*.
- *Calibration*: import an log of fixed *estimates* and *Project* variables, find fixes to *Model* that best explain how *Project* inputs lead to *estimation* outputs.
- *Monte Carlo* studies: fix the *Model* values (perhaps to values learned via calibration), import floating *Project* values, generates a range of possible *estimates*.

In the field of effort estimation:

- *Prediction* is used to create one point estimate for a project; e.g. COCOMO [7, 8],PRICE-S [29] and SEER-SEM [15].
- *Calibration* is useful for learning from historical data; e.g. see Boehm's local calibration procedure [7, p526-529] or the COSEEKMO toolkit [24].
- *Monte Carlo* studies are useful for conducting what-if queries across a range of possible projects [30]. Such Monte Carlo studies are conducted by many tools including COBRA [10], CrystalBall [5], SCAT [21, 20], and 2CEE [6].

To the best of our knowledge, this work is the first to try freeing *both* the *Project* and *Model* variables. Even in the field in *search-based software engineering*, we have not seen anything like this study. It is true that search-based SE often uses non-liner search methods like SA. A recent review of 123 search-based SE papers [31] showed that much of that work relates to testing (e.g. SA to minimize test suites for regression testing) while only a handful of those papers related to the kinds of early project process planning discussed here. For example, Aguilar-Ruiz et.al. [2] and Alvarez et.al. [4] apply search-based methods for effort estimation. One facets that distinguished STAR from other methods is that we are searching over more than just the effort models explored by the Aquilar-Ruiz & Alvarez teams. Also, unlike standard data mining approach, we do not try to learn better *Model* variables from historical data.

3   STAR

STAR's current implementation explores three software process models:

- The COQUALMO software defect predictor [9, p254-268].
- The COCOMO software effort predictor [9, p29-57].
- The THREAT predictor for project effort & schedule overrun [9, 284-291].

COQUALMO models two processes (defect introduction and defect removal) for three phases (requirements, design, coding). COCOMO assumes that effort is exponentially proportional to some *scale factors* and linearly proportional to some *effort multipliers*. COCOMO estimates are development months (225 hours) and includes all coding, debugging, and management activities. The THREAT model contains a large set of two-dimensional tables representing pairs of variable settings are problematic. For example, using the *rely* vs *sced* table, the THREAT model would raise an alert if our tool decides to build a system with high *rely* (required reliability) and low *sced* (schedule available to the development).

STAR samples the space of possibles models inside COCOMO and COQUALMO using the following technique. Internally, COCOMO and COQUALMO models contain

scale factors (exponentially decrease effort)		strategic?	tactical?
	prec: have we done this before?	✓	
	flex: development flexibility		✓
	resl: any risk resolution activities?		✓
	team: team cohesion		✓
	pmat: process maturity	✓	
upper (linearly decrease effort)	acap: analyst capability	✓	
	pcap: programmer capability	✓	
	pcon: programmer continuity	✓	
	aexp: analyst experience	✓	
	pexp: programmer experience	✓	
	ltex: language and tool experience	✓	
	tool: tool use		✓
	site: multiple site development	✓	✓
	sced: length of schedule		✓
lower (linearly increase effort)	rely: required reliability		✓
	data: secondary memory storage requirements		✓
	cplx: program complexity		✓
	ruse: software reuse		✓
	docu: documentation requirements		
	time: runtime pressure		
	stor: main memory requirements		✓
	pvol: platform volatility		
COQUALMO defect removal methods	auto: automated analysis	✓	✓
	execTest: execution-based testing tools	✓	✓
	peer: peer reviews	✓	✓

Fig. 2. The variables of COCOMO, COQUALMO, and the THREAT model

many linear relationships. Nominal values of $x = 3$ change some estimate by a factor of one. These COCOMO lines can hence be modeled as a straight line $y = mx + b$ passing through the point $x, y = 3, 1$. Such a line has a y-intercept of $b = 1 - 3m$. Substituting this value of b into $y = mx + b$ yields $y = m(x - 3) + 1$. COCOMO's effort slopes are either positive or negative, denoted m^+, m^- (respectively):

- The positive slopes m^+ represents the variables that are proportional to effort; e.g. *increasing* required reliability also *increases* the development effort.
- The negative slopes m^- represents the variables that are *inversely* proportional to effort; e.g. *increasing* analyst capability *decreases* the development effort.

Based on decades of experiments with calibrating COCOMO models, we have identified variables with different slopes. These following COCOMO variables have m^+ slopes: cplx, data, docu, pvol, rely, ruse, stor, and time. Also, these variables have m^- slopes acap, apex, ltex, pcap, pcon, plex, sced, and site (for an explanation of those terms, see Figure 2). Further, based on decades of calibration of COCOMO models, we assert that effort estimation, m^+ and m^- have the ranges:

$$-0.178 \leq m^- \leq -0.078$$
$$0.073 \leq m^+ \leq 0.21 \tag{1}$$

Using an analogous procedure, it is possible to derive similar equations for the CO-COMO scale factors, the COQUALMO scale factors/effort multipliers/ defect removal variables (for full details, see [26]).

With the above machinery, it is now possible to define a Monte Carlo procedure to sample the space of possible THREAT/COCOMO/COQUALMO *Models*: just randomly selecting $\{m^-, m^+\}$. As to sampling the space of possible THREAT models, this is achieved by adding random variables to the cells of THREAT's tables.

STAR tries to minimize defects (D), threats (T), and development effort (E). This is a non-linear optimization function: e.g. reducing costs can introduce more defects. For this reason, we use simulated annealing (SA) to explore trade-offs between models. SA is best explained in comparison to the Metropolis algorithm.

A *Metropolis* Monte Carlo algorithm [27] improves on basic Monte Carlo as follows. New solutions are created by small mutations to some *current* solutions. In the case of STAR, an "solution" is some randomly selected part of the space of possible *Projects*. If a new solution is "better" (as assessed via an *energy function*), it becomes the new *current* solution used for future mutations. STAR's energy function is
$$E = \sqrt{\overline{E}^2 + \overline{D}^2 + \overline{T}^2}/\sqrt{3} \text{ where } \overline{x} \text{ is a normalized value } 0 \leq \frac{x - min(x)}{max(x) - min(x)} \leq 1.$$
Energy ranges $0 \leq E \leq 1$ and *lower* energies are *better*. If a new solution does not have lower energy, a Boltzmann acceptance criteria is used to probabilistically decide to assess the new state: the worse the new state, the less likely that it becomes the new current state.

A *simulated annealer* (SA) [18] adds a "temperature" variable to the Boltzmann accept criteria such that, at high temperatures, it is more likely that the algorithm will jump to a new worst current state. This allows the algorithm to jump out of local minima while sampling the space of options. As the temperature cools, such jumps become less likely and the algorithm reverts to a simple hill climber.

Our *RANKER* algorithm instruments the internals of SA. Whenever a solution is assigned some energy, that energy is added to a counter maintained for each variable setting in *Projects*. When SA terminates, RANKER sorts all variable ranges by the sum of the energies seen during their use. The ranges that are lower in the sort order are associated with lower energy solutions; i.e. lower defects, efforts, threats. RANKER then conducts experiments where it fixes the first N ranked ranges and lets the remaining variables float. N is increased till some minimum energy point is reached. A *policy* are the project settings that achieve that minimum energy point.

The last two columns of Figure 2 show the results of Delphi panel session at JPL where the COCOMO variables were separated into those *tactical* variables that can be changed within the space of one project, and those *strategic* variables that required higher-level institutional change (and so may take longer to change). For example, the panel declared that *pmat* (process maturity) is hard to change within the space of a single JPL project. In the sequel, all our RANKER experiments will be divided into those that just use the *strategic* variables and those that just use the *tactical* variables[3].

4   Experiments

Figure 3 shows various *Projects* expressed in term of *float*ing and *fixed* variables. For example, with JPL's flight systems, the *rely* (required reliability) can float anywhere

---

[3] Note that these definitions of *strategic* and *tactical* choices are not hard-wired into STAR. If a user disagrees with our definitions of strategic/tactical, they can change a simple configuration file.

project	float variable	low	high	fixed variable	setting
OSP	prec	1	2	data	3
	flex	2	5	pvol	2
	resl	1	3	rely	5
	team	2	3	pcap	3
	pmat	1	4	plex	3
	stor	3	5	site	3
	ruse	2	4		
	docu	2	4		
	acap	2	3		
	pcon	2	3		
	apex	2	3		
	ltex	2	4		
	tool	2	3		
	sced	1	3		
	cplx	5	6		
	KSLOC	75	125		
OSP2	prec	3	5	flex	3
	pmat	4	5	resl	4
	docu	3	4	team	3
	ltex	2	5	time	3
	sced	2	4	stor	3
	KSLOC	75	125	data	4
				pvol	3
				ruse	4
				rely	5
				acap	4
				pcap	3
				pcon	3
				apex	4
				plex	4
				tool	5
				cplx	4
				site	6

project	float variable	low	high	fixed variable	setting
flight	rely	3	5	tool	2
	data	2	3	sced	3
	cplx	3	6		
	time	3	4		
	stor	3	4		
	acap	3	5		
	apex	2	5		
	pcap	3	5		
	plex	1	4		
	ltex	1	4		
	pmat	2	3		
	KSLOC	7	418		
ground	rely	1	4	tool	2
	data	2	3	sced	3
	cplx	1	4		
	time	3	4		
	stor	3	4		
	acap	3	5		
	apex	2	5		
	pcap	3	5		
	plex	1	4		
	ltex	1	4		
	pmat	2	3		
	KSLOC	11	392		

Fig. 3. Four case studies

X	variable = setting
1	pmat = 4
2	ltex = 4
3	acap = 3
4	apex = 3
5	prec = 2
6	pcon = 3
7	execution testing and tools = 6
8	peer reviews = 6
9	automated analysis = 6

X	variable = setting
1	ruse = 2
2	cplx = 5
3	resl = 3
4	tool = 3
5	sced = 2
6	stor = 3
7	flex = 5
8	automated analysis = 6
9	peer reviews = 6
10	docu = 2
11	execution testing and tools = 6
12	sced = 1

Fig.4.A: controlling only strategic *Project* variables

Fig.4.B: controlling only tactical *Project* variables

Fig. 4. Some RANKER results on OSP. The settings shown under the plots describe the policy that leads to the policy point.

in the upper range; i.e. $rely \in \{3, 4, 5\}$. However, for flight systems, *sced* (schedule pressure) is tightly defined (so *sced* is fixed to the value 3).

Figure 4 and Figure 5 shows the results of STAR. The variable ranges are sorted along the x-axis according the order generated by RANKER. At any x value we see the results of fixing the ranges $1..x$, letting all ranges $x + 1...max$ float, then running 1000

X	feature = range
1	pmat = 3
2	site = 6
3	pcon = 5
4	plex = 4
5	pcap = 5
6	ltex = 4
7	apex = 5
8	prec = 5
9	acap = 5
10	automated analysis = 6
11	execution testing and tools = 6
12	peer reviews = 6
13	acap = 4

X	feature = range
1	resl = 5
2	cplx = 1
3	execution testing and tools = 6
4	flex = 5
5	docu = 1
6	ruse = 2
7	data = 3

Fig.5.A: controlling only strategic *Project* variables   **Fig.5.B:** controlling only tactical *Project* variables.

Fig. 5. Some RANKER results on JPL ground systems. The settings shown under the plots. describe the policy that leads to the policy point.

Monte Carlo simulations. In the results, "median" refers to the 50th percentile band and "spread" refers to the difference between the 75th and 50th percentile in the 1000 generate estimates.

For this paper, we ran SA+RANKER on the four case studies of Figure 3, plus a fifth study called "ALL'" that used the entire COCOMO ranges, unconstrained by a particular project. Each study was repeated twice- one for controlling just the strategic variables and once for controlling just the tactical variables. This resulted in ten experiments.

Some of the results from four of those experiments are shown in Figure 4 and Figure 5 (space restrictions prevent us from showing all the results). In those four experiments (and in the other six, not shown) the same effect was observed. Minimum effort and defects was achieved after fixing a small number of *Project* variables (in Figure 4.A, Figure 4.B, Figure 5.A, and Figure 5.B, that number was at X={9,12,13 7} respectively). At these minimum points, the median and spread estimates were greatly reduced. We call this minimum the *policypoint* and use the term *policy* to refer to the intersection of the case study defined in Figure 3, and the ranges found in the range between {$1 \leq x \leq policypoint$}.

Figure 4 and Figure 5 are the reports we would offer back to the manager. Start at the top of this list, we would advise, and apply as many oft eh top N things that you can. Do not waste time implementing policy changes off this list.

In terms of controlling uncertainty, the reduction in the spread estimates at the policy point is particularly interesting. Note that this reduction in model uncertainty was achieved by only controlling a few of the *Project* variables while letting all other *Project* and *Model* variables float free. That is, in these case studies, projects could be controlled (development effort and defects reduced) without using historical data to constrain the *Model* variables.

For each of our ten experiments, a set of random *Projects* were generated, consistent with the policies; i.e.

- If the policy fixes a value, then the *Project* contains that value;
- Otherwise, if the variable is found Figure 3, it is drawn from those constraints;

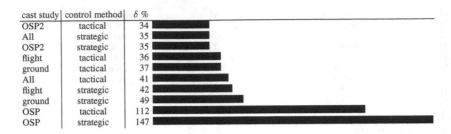

cast study	control method	δ %
OSP2	tactical	34
All	strategic	35
OSP2	strategic	35
flight	tactical	36
ground	tactical	37
All	tactical	41
flight	strategic	42
ground	strategic	49
OSP	tactical	112
OSP	strategic	147

Fig. 6. Median $\delta = (estimate(STAR) - estimate(lc))$ between effort estimates generated by conventional means (LC) and STAR

– Otherwise, the variable's value is selected at random from background knowledge of the legal range of the Figure 2 variables.

For each set, the following procedure was repeated 20 times. Ten examples were removed at random and Boehm's local calibration (LC) procedure [7, p526-529] was used to train a COCOMO model on the remaining $Project$ examples[4]. LC's estimates were then compared to the estimates generated by STAR's simulation at the policy point (i.e. floating over both the policy and the $Model$ ranges). Figure 6 show the median difference in the estimates generated by LC or STAR . Note that, in $\frac{8}{10}$ cases, the difference is under 50%. The reason for the large deltas seen in $\frac{2}{10}$ of the results (from the OSP case study) are currently unknown but are a subject of much current exploration.

The median δ values of Figure 6 are around 0.4; i.e. a STAR estimate of 100 months could really range for 60 to 140 months. Compared to the effort estimate reductions shown in the introduction, δ is quite small. Recall that STAR reduced effort estimates to a small part of the initial values, sometimes a factor of 20; i.e by a factor that is much larger than 0.4. Clearly, even if STAR is wrong by ±40%, then the overall benefits to be gained from applying STAR's policies are still dramatically large.

5   Discussion

Given all the randomized exploration STAR performs over the space of possible $Models$, this discrepancy is very small. and those discrepancies are dwarfed by the much larger effort reductions of Figure 1.

How are we to explain the remarkable effectiveness of STAR in managing uncertainty? Researchers in planning and theorem proving have recently shown that as model complexity grows, other constraining effects may appear such as "master variables"; i.e. a small number of settings that control all other settings [12, 32]. Such master variables can greatly reduce the search space within large models.

We hypothesize that software process models also contain master variables; i.e. much much of uncertainty in a model is due to the influence of a small subset of model

---

[4] LC was chosen since, in extensive experiments, we have found this decades old procedure to be remarkably competitive with current data mining methods [14] including bagging and boosting [6].

variables. If so, then after (a) ranking variables by their ability to constrain the output; and (b) applying a small number of the top-ranked variables; then it should be possible to (c) make stable predictions in the constrained space.

6 Conclusion

In studies with one widely-used suite of effort/ detect/ threat predictors for software systems, we have shown that:

- *Estimation* median values can be greatly reduced (see Figure 1). In comparisons with other effort estimation tools, the reduction can quite dramatic. In the best case our tools found *Project* ranges that yields estimates that were 5% of estimates found by other means.
- *Estimation* variance can be reduced by only floating the *Project* values and leaving the *Model* values free (see Figure 4 and Figure 5).
- Within the space of *Project* options that most reduce *Estimation* median and variance, the predictions made by our process models are remarkably similar to those made by conventional methods (see Figure 6).

The first result suggests that it may be highly advantageous to use STAR. Projects designed around STAR's recommendations will be will be delivered sooner and have fewer bugs or threats.

The second result is of much practical importance since it means we do not require calibration data to tune the *Model* variables. If process models can be deployed without calibration, then they can be used with much greater ease and *without* the requirement for an expensive and time-consuming period of data collection.

The third result is showing that (a) this method can find and remove the major sources of uncertainty in a project; (b) in the reduced space, it is possible that the estimates in the resulting constrained space will be close to estimates found via tuning on historical data. In the above discussion section, we commented that this result has precedent in the AI planning and theorem proving literature.

Finally, we comment on the external validity of these results. Compared to many other process models[5] this combination of effort/threat/defect models is relatively simple. As model complexity grows, then the space of possible *Estimates* can grow exponentially and STAR's controlling effect may disappear. Therefore it is clear that we can not claim that, for *all* process models, that *Estimate* variance can be controlled by just constraining *Project*, not *Model*, variance.

Nevertheless, data collection for the purposes of model calibration remains as a expensive, tedious, and often incomplete process. Our results suggest that such data collection may be, for some process models, an optional activity (caveat: provided that a process model exists that specifics the general relationships between concepts in a domain). Our hope is that the results of this paper encouraging enough that other software process modeling researchers will try the following strategy. *First*, find the fewest number of variables that most effect model output. *Next*, constrain them. *Finally*, check for stable conclusions in the constrained space.

---

[5] See Software Process journal, issue on Software Process Simulation, vol. 7, No. 3-4, 2002.

If these results from STAR generalize to more complex models, then is should be possible to make reasonably accurate predictions without local calibration data.

Note that if such stability is *absent* in more complex models, and those models are being used in domains with data collection problems, then we would argue that that is a reason to abstain from such complexity, and use COCOMO-style models instead.

References

1. Abdel-Hamid, T., Madnick, S.: Software Project Dynamics: An Integrated Approach. Prentice-Hall Software Series, Englewood Cliffs (1991)
2. Aguilar-Ruiz, J.S., Ramos, I., Riquelme, J., Toro, M.: An evolutionary approach to estimating software development projects. Information and Software Technology 43(14), 875–882 (2001)
3. Akhavi, M., Wilson, W.: Dynamic simulation of software process models. In: Proceedings of the 5th Software Engineering Process Group National Meeting, Costa Mesa, California, April 26-29, 1993, Software engineering Institute, Carnegie Mellon University (1993)
4. Alvarez, J.L., Mata, J., Riquelme, J.C., Ramos, I.: A data mining method to support decision making in software development projects. In: ICEIS 2003: Fifth International Conference on Enterprise Information Systems (2003)
5. Bailey, J.: Using monte carlo and cocomo-2 to model a large it system development (2002)
6. Baker, D.: A hybrid approach to expert and model-based effort estimation. Master's thesis, Lane Department of Computer Science and Electrical Engineering, West Virginia University (2007), https://eidr.wvu.edu/etd/documentdata.eTD?documentid=5443
7. Boehm, B.: Software Engineering Economics. Prentice-Hall, Englewood Cliffs (1981)
8. Boehm, B.: Safe and simple software cost analysis. IEEE Software, 14–17 (September/October 2000), http://www.computer.org/certification/beta/Boehm_Safe.pdf
9. Boehm, B., Horowitz, E., Madachy, R., Reifer, D., Clark, B.K., Steece, B., Brown, A.W., Chulani, S., Abts, C.: Software Cost Estimation with Cocomo II. Prentice-Hall, Englewood Cliffs (2000)
10. Briand, L.C., Emam, K.E., Bomarius, F.: Cobra: A hybrid method for software cost estimation, benchmarking, and risk assessment. In: ICSE, pp. 390–399 (1998)
11. Cass, A.G., Staudt Lerner, B., Sutton, S.M., Jr., McCall, E.K., Wise, A., Osterweil, L.J.,: Little-jil/juliette: A process definition language and interpreter. In: Proceedings of the 22nd International Conference on Software Engineering (ICSE 2000), June 2000, pp. 754–757 (2000)
12. Crawford, J., Baker, A.: Experimental results on the application of satisfiability algorithms to scheduling problems. In: AAAI 1994 (1994)
13. Harel, D.: Statemate: A working environment for the development of complex reactive systems. IEEE Transactions on Software Engineering 16(4), 403–414 (1990)
14. Jalali, O.: Evaluation bias in effort estimation. Master's thesis, Lane Department of Computer Science and Electrical Engineering, West Virginia University (2007)
15. Jensen, R.: An improved macrolevel software development resource estimation model. In: 5th ISPA Conference, April 1983, pp. 88–92 (1983)
16. Kelton, D., Sadowski, R., Sadowski, D.: Simulation with Arena, 2nd edn. McGraw-Hill, New York (2002)
17. Kemerer, C.: An empirical validation of software cost estimation models. Communications of the ACM 30(5), 416–429 (1987)

18. Kirkpatrick, S., Gelatt, C.D., Vecchi, M.P.: Optimization by simulated annealing. Science 220(4598), 671–680 (1983)
19. Law, A., Kelton, B.: Simulation Modeling and Analysis. McGraw-Hill, New York (2000)
20. Lum, K.: Software cost analysis tool user document (2005)
21. Lum, K., Bramble, M., Hihn, J., Hackney, J., Khorrami, M., Monson, E.: Handbook for software cost estimation (2003)
22. Lum, K., Powell, J., Hihn, J.: Validation of spacecraft software cost estimation models for flight and ground systems. In: ISPA Conference Proceedings, Software Modeling Track (May 2002)
23. Martin, R., Raffo, D.M.: A model of the software development process using both continuous and discrete models. International Journal of Software Process Improvement and Practice (June/July 2000)
24. Menzies, T., Chen, Z., Hihn, J., Lum, K.: Selecting best practices for effort estimation. IEEE Transactions on Software Engineering (November 2006), Available from: http://menzies.us/pdf/06coseekmo.pdf
25. Menzies, T., Elrawas, O., Baker, D., Hihn, J., Lum, K.: On the value of stochastic abduction (if you fix everything, you lose fixes for everything else). In: International Workshop on Living with Uncertainty (an ASE 2007 co-located event) (2007), Available from: http://menzies.us/pdf/07fix.pdf
26. Menzies, T., Elwaras, O., Hihn, J., Feathear, M., Boehm, B., Madachy, R.: The business case for automated software engineerng. In: IEEE ASE 2007 (2007), Available from: http://menzies.us/pdf/07casease-v0.pdf
27. Metropolis, N., Rosenbluth, A., Rosenbluth, M., Teller, A., Teller, E.: J. Chem. Phys. 21, 1087–1092 (1953)
28. Mi, P., Scacchi, W.: A knowledge-based environment for modeling and simulation software engineering processes. IEEE Transactions on Knowledge and Data Engineering, 283–294 (September 1990)
29. Park, R.: The central equations of the price software cost model. In: 4th COCOMO Users Group Meeting (November 1988)
30. Raffo, D.M., Vandeville, J.V., Martin, R.: Software process simulation to achieve higher cmm levels. Journal of Systems and Software 46(2/3) (April 1999)
31. Rela, L.: Evolutionary computing in search-based software engineering. Master's thesis, Lappeenranta University of Technology (2004)
32. Williams, R., Gomes, C., Selman, B.: Backdoors to typical case complexity. In: Proceedings of IJCAI 2003 (2003), http://www.cs.cornell.edu/gomes/FILES/backdoors.pdf
33. Wise, A., Cass, A., Staudt Lerner, B., McCall, E., Osterweil, L., Sutton, S.M., Jr.: Using little-jil to coordinate agents in software engineering. In: Proceedings of the Automated Software Engineering Conference (ASE 2000) Grenoble, France (September 2000), Available from: ftp://ftp.cs.umass.edu/pub/techrept/techreport/2000/UM-CS-2000-045.ps

Investigating Factors Affecting the Usability of Software Process Descriptions

Mohd Naz'ri Mahrin, David Carrington, and Paul Strooper

School of Information Technology and Electrical Engineering
The University of Queensland, St. Lucia
4072 Queensland, Australia
{mahrin, davec, pstroop}@itee.uq.edu.au

Abstract. This paper presents the findings of our investigation into factors that affect the usability of software process descriptions from three sources of information: the literature on software process descriptions, data we collected from a survey of practitioners at the 5th Australia SEPG conference, and an analysis of core elements of software process metamodels. To understand how the identified factors can be used to evaluate process descriptions, we used several factors as a set of criteria for a qualitative comparison of a number of process descriptions. As a result, we discovered some gaps between the sample process descriptions and those usability factors.

Keywords: Software Process Descriptions, Usability, Metamodels.

1 Introduction

The software process is important to the success of software development projects and needs to be adapted in various project environments. Process performers are responsible for enacting the process by interpreting process descriptions. In this paper, a software process description is defined as a representation of a software process created to facilitate process enactment and evaluation, and to serve as a medium for communicating software process information.

Producing a usable software process description is essential, since usability problems may translate into difficulty during process enactment. The demand for systematic and usable software process descriptions is high [13] but in practice, process descriptions suffer from usability problems, including complexity and inflexibility of their structure, incompleteness of process information, and inconsistent process instructions [16, 21, 23].

A growing number of studies have examined the key success factors that affect software processes (e.g. [19]) but there is little research dealing with the factors that affect the usability of process descriptions. A study by Kellner et al. [14] investigated usefulness and usability issues of software process descriptions and proposed some factors to be considered when designing and developing process descriptions, such as: process descriptions should be "up-to-date", "well-structured", "consistent in presentation style", and "tailorable". We believe there is a need to investigate the application of these factors to existing process descriptions and observe how these factors can affect the usability of process descriptions.

Q. Wang, D. Pfahl, and D.M. Raffo (Eds.): ICSP 2008, LNCS 5007, pp. 222–233, 2008.
© Springer-Verlag Berlin Heidelberg 2008

In this paper, we attempt to answer a basic research question: what key factors make a software process description usable? To answer this question, we conducted a series of investigations from three sources of information: the literature on software process descriptions, data we collected from a survey of practitioners at the 5th Australia SEPG conference, and an analysis of core elements of software process metamodels. To understand how the identified factors can be used to evaluate process descriptions, we used several factors as a set of criteria for a qualitative comparison of a number of process descriptions.

The motivation for this research is based on the premise that process descriptions should be usable because of the important roles they have [4, 14, 23]:

- To help process performers understand, communicate and enact the process.
- To facilitate monitoring and control of the execution process.
- To facilitate process evolution and reuse.
- To support process management, evaluation and improvement.
- To support automated execution of software process (whenever possible).
- To provide a foundation for building a software engineering culture.

The remainder of this paper is structured as follows: Section 2 presents the literature in the field of software process descriptions. Section 3 focuses on the usability factors investigation and results. A comparative review of a number of software process descriptions is presented in Section 4, followed by research implications and conclusions in Section 5.

2 Software Process Descriptions

Bunse et al. [2] emphasise that the description of software development processes is a prerequisite for software process improvement (SPI), to explain the roles, activities and techniques applied by an organisation. Process descriptions support effective communication from project to project and among peers in software project organisations and can help demonstrate an organisation's capabilities to customers. They can also serve as process asset evidence when certifying an organisation according to external process improvement models such as the Capability Maturity Model Integrated (CMMI) [3]. Derniame et al. [5] state that process descriptions can be used to drive software process enactment, which is one of the goals of software process technology.

Before process performers can enact a process description in a specific software project environment, the process description needs to be instantiated. According to Wang et al. [23], instantiating a process description to suit a specific project environment is crucial, since activities, techniques, work products etc. need to be adapted to the specific project environment.

To promote a structured way of describing software processes, a software process metamodel can be used as a reference. The Software Process Engineering Metamodel (SPEM) [17] is a software process metamodel introduced by the Object Management Group (OMG). In general, a software process metamodel provides a common structure for software process engineers to describe process elements including tasks, roles, work products and their interrelationships. According to Henderson-Sellers

[10], process descriptions developed based on a metamodel are expected to be more extensible, configurable and tailorable to individual and project-specific needs.

Process descriptions may be paper-based (known as process handbooks) or electronically-based (known as electronic process guides) documents. Commonly, process descriptions employ a combination of text and graphics [14]. For example, a generic structure of a process description might contain structured narrative text descriptions for the specific processes, methods, techniques, roles, guidance, etc. The graphical representations of process descriptions often contain decision tables or decision trees, graphical aids such as process flow diagrams, activity diagrams and work product dependency diagrams.

Paper-based process descriptions are traditionally used to communicate and disseminate process knowledge, but experience has shown that process handbooks are not widely accepted by process performers. For example, paper-based process descriptions are not very user-friendly which may cause difficulty for process performers wanting to find required information quickly. It is also difficult to distribute up-to-date process knowledge in printed form [1, 14]. Some examples of paper-based process descriptions are: the Personal Software Process (PSP) [12], and the Software Engineering Process Reference Model (SEPRM) [23].

The online EPG appears to be the trend for disseminating process knowledge across projects and process performers [16]. EPGs have advantages in terms of flexibility to manage process information structure, increased maintainability and availability to all users [14]. Some online examples of EPGs are: OpenUP/Basic, XP and SCRUM (available at [7]), UPEDU [22] , and OPF [18].

To some process performers, reading information through a computer screen is not as efficient as reading information on paper. Hornbæk et al. [11] summarised the potential obstacles when reading information through a computer screen, including cumbersome navigation, a lack of overview of the document, lower tangibility of electronic documents compared to paper, uncertainty over of the length of document, lower reading speed caused by poor screen resolution, and possible fatigue if reading for an extended period.

3 Usability Factors Investigation and Results

Our investigations concentrated on identifying factors that enhance the usability of software process descriptions. We considered three sources of input: existing literature on software process descriptions, data from a survey of practitioners at the 5th Australia SEPG conference, and software engineering process metamodels.

3.1 Potential Factors from Literature Reports

Our literature search was performed in the digital libraries of well-known publishers in computer science and software engineering with "software process descriptions" and "process guides" as the search key. We identified four papers that suggested ideas for effective process descriptions. Such ideas are considered in our investigation and the ideas relevant to usability are presented in Table 1. The small number of relevant studies can be viewed as evidence that there is limited research in the software process description field on usability issues.

Table 1. Potential usability factors from literature reports

Potential Factor	Researcher			
	Kellner et al. [14]	Moe et al. [15]	Scott et al. [21]	Henderson-Sellers [10]
▪ Up-to-date	Yes			
▪ Well-structured	Yes			Yes
▪ Consistency of presentation style	Yes		Yes	
▪ Understandable	Yes			
▪ Tailorable	Yes	Yes	Yes	Yes
▪ Checklist	Yes	Yes		
▪ Searching features	Yes		Yes	
▪ Include the basic process elements and their relationships	Yes			
▪ Use diagrams, tables and narrative effectively	Yes			
▪ Description of best practice		Yes		
▪ Enable integration with other CASE tools		Yes	Yes	
▪ Collaborative process description development (between process engineer and process performer)		Yes		
▪ Templates for all documents to be produced		Yes	Yes	
▪ Use graphical overview of the process	Yes		Yes	
▪ Details on how to carry out tasks (e.g. steps etc)			Yes	
▪ Provide forum or experience sharing facility			Yes	
▪ Provide completed work product examples			Yes	
▪ Use software process metamodels				Yes
▪ Link to project databases to access examples			Yes	

Many factors are identified by multiple authors. For example, Kellner et al. [14], Moe et al. [15] and Scott et al. [21] all consider ability to tailor as an important feature for process descriptions. Work product templates and integration capability between process descriptions and CASE tools are other repeated factors.

On the other hand, some factors are identified by only one author. For example, a link between process descriptions and project databases to access example documents and provide a forum or experience sharing infrastructure was highlighted only by Scott et al. [21].

3.2 Potential Factors from Exploratory Survey

We conducted an exploratory survey during the 5th Australia SEPG conference to understand how software practitioners develop and use process descriptions. We distributed approximately 70 self-administered questionnaires and 14 were returned with data appropriate for our analysis.

The questionnaire consisted of seven questions and took approximately five minutes to complete. Five questions were about how software practitioners within their organisation develop and use process descriptions. One question was specifically on the factors that make process descriptions usable and the last question was about the willingness of the respondent to be involved and to contribute to our research. The usability factors listed by respondents are presented in Table 2.

Table 2. Potential usability factors from exploratory survey

Original words/phrases	Potential Factor
▪ Minimal information ▪ Not complex ▪ Simple	Simple
▪ Easy to understand ▪ Clear and unambiguous ▪ Use understandable terminology ▪ Software engineers have same understanding ▪ Content – needs to be clear	Understandable
▪ Customizable – able to suit process to the project. Can be changed by practitioners over time ▪ Tailorable – to any project and to any existing methodology in organisation. ▪ Multiple versions for different project types (e.g. safety critical, small, customer-driven, embedded).	Tailorable
▪ Repeatable ▪ Reusable	Reusable
▪ Easy to implement ▪ Easy to administration	Operable
▪ Consider local situation by taking input from software engineers ▪ Own by the whole organization – not limited to process group only	Collaborative process description development
▪ Perform audit review to process description from time to time	Process audit
▪ Metrics to measure	Metrics
▪ Provide help desk	Provide help desk
▪ Reporting ▪ Provide feedback mechanism	Provide feedback
▪ Explain to team on how to use and their purpose	Provide training
▪ Realization	Realization
▪ Immediately available – accessible in work environment.	Immediately available

We noticed some overlap in the meaning of words or phrases used by respondents to name the factors, for example: "easy to understand", "clear and unambiguous" and "use understandable terminology" are quite similar in meaning. Such words and phrases were reviewed and aggregated as shown in the "potential factor" column of Table 2.

3.3   Potential Factors from Software Engineering Process Metamodels

We also investigated the elements of software process descriptions as defined in software engineering process metamodels including SPEM [17], Open Process Framework (OPF) [18], and Unified Method Architecture (UMA) [6].

The focus is on the foundational elements (roles, work products, activities, and guidance) that underlie process descriptions. These four core elements are the main concern in our investigation. See Figure 1 for the relationships between these core elements and Table 3 for their definitions. We limit our investigation to these core elements because they are an essential part of any process description.

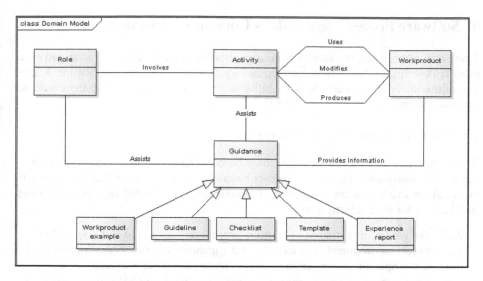

Fig. 1. Software Process Descriptions Core Elements and their Relationships

Table 3. Core Elements of Software Process Descriptions

Factor	Definition
Activity	Activity is a work element that defines basic units of work. It describes work performed by a role, assisted by guidance and associated with work products. An activity may consist of atomic elements called *steps*.
Role	Role is a performer of, or a participant in, an activity. A role defines a set of related skills, competencies, and responsibilities of an individual or individuals (a.k.a. performers or agents). It may be a human or a computerised tool.
Work product	Work product is a general term for activity inputs and outputs, descriptions of content elements that are used to define anything used, produced, or modified by an activity.
Guidance	Guidance is a general term for additional information related to role, activity, and work product. Guidance provides information to assist a performer in creating a work product, how to perform an activity, and so on. Examples of guidance are: checklists, work product examples, guidelines, experience reports, and templates.

Work products and roles are quite tangible and visible, e.g., they can be touched as well as seen. The activity is difficult to touch, but it can be observed from an explicit process description. Guidance is a general term for additional information related to roles, activities, and work products. In particular, guidance provides information to assist a performer on how to create a work product, how to perform an activity, and so on. Guidance can appear in many forms, such as templates, examples, and guidelines.

In the context of software architectural design, Folmer et al. [8] suggest that guidance can have a positive effect on usability and considering usability issues early at the architectural level can improve the usability of that software system. Analogously, we suggest that guidance can affect the usability of process descriptions and detecting usability problems prior to enactment is essential. We have therefore considered guidance elements as one of the potential usability factors.

4 Software Process Descriptions Comparative Review

This section discusses the results from a qualitative comparison of several software process descriptions based on selected usability factors as identified in Section 3. The aim of this study is to observe how usability factors have been applied in these sample process descriptions.

4.1 The Comparative Review Criteria

There are many usability factors that could be considered as our comparison criteria, but for this study we select a small subset based on our assumption that this subset is essential for every process description. In particular, the selected factors and a brief justification for their selection are:

- *Tailoring guide:* Instantiating a software process description to suit a specific software project environment is crucial and the capability of process descriptions to be tailored to a specific project environment prior to enactment is crucial too.
- *Searching feature and help support:* Searching features and help support will support users when using a process description.
- *Enable integration with CASE tools:* The capability of a process description to integrate with CASE tools can support users to perform tasks.
- *Use of a process metamodel:* A software process description based on a process metamodel is expected to be better structured, more consistent in terms of presentation style and easier to tailor.
- *Use of diagrams, tables and narrative:* Combinations of these presentation styles are expected to make a process description more presentable.
- *Consistency of presentation style:* A consistent presentation style to describe process elements can make process information more readable and searchable.
- *Well-structured:* A well-structured process description can also make process information more readable and searchable.
- *Supported by guidance:* Guidance for the three foundational elements of process descriptions (roles, work products and activities) is expected to assist users with enacting the process.

4.2 Selected Software Process Descriptions

Many paper-based and electronically-based process descriptions have been developed internally by software organisations, the open source community or third-party vendors. For the purpose of our comparison, the focus is on one paper-based and two electronically-based process descriptions. The reviewed process descriptions are:

- Open Unified Process (OpenUP) [7]: This electronically-based process description was developed using the Eclipse Process Framework Composer (EPFC). EPFC is an open-source product produced by the Eclipse Process Framework Project [6]. In brief, OpenUP applies iterative and incremental approaches within a structured software development lifecycle. OpenUP embraces a pragmatic, agile philosophy that focuses on the collaborative nature of software development. It is not tied to any specific CASE tools and provides a tailorable process description to address a variety of project types.

- Unified Process for EDUcation (UPEDU) [22]: This is an electronically-based process description developed by Rational Software Corporation and École Polytechnique de Montréal. UPEDU has been customized from the Rational Unified Process (RUP) for the educational environment. It provides a disciplined approach to assigning tasks and responsibilities within a development organisation. Its goal is to ensure the production of high-quality software that meets the needs of end users within a predictable schedule and budget.
- Personal Software Process (PSP) [12]: PSP is a set of paper-based process descriptions developed by Watts S. Humphrey. PSP was designed to facilitate project control, management, and improvement by individual software engineers using a structured framework of forms, guidelines, and scripts. The purpose of PSP is to train a software engineer to be able to manage and assess their ability to plan, track the performance, and measure the quality of developed products. In this paper, we analysed only the simplest PSP process: PSP0.

4.3 Software Process Descriptions Comparison

The result of our comparison is presented in tabular form and is divided into two categories: a comparison based on criteria given in Section 4.1 (in Table 4) and a detailed comparison based on guidance criteria for producing work products (in Table 5). We investigated work product guidance in detail because we believe this is a key aspect of making process descriptions more usable. In the following we discuss the findings and issues to be highlighted from the data in Table 4.

- *Tailoring guide:* Both EPGs provide a tailoring guide only for work products, but not for activities and roles. To us, tailoring guides for activities and roles are also important and the absence of tailoring guides may negatively affect the usability of process descriptions. We found that no specific section of the PSP0 description discussed tailoring.
- *Searching feature and help support:* All the sample descriptions provide ways for users to search process information and help support. For PSP0, the index at the back of the PSP book [12] is considered a tool for searching process information.
- *Enable integration with CASE tools:* None of the sample descriptions explain how to integrate process descriptions with CASE tools.
- *Use of process metamodel:* For OpenUP [7], information about the underpinning process metamodel is provided in the "overview" section. UPEDU discusses process metamodels in one section of the UPEDU textbook [20]. No information was found about process metamodels in the PSP description.
- *Use of diagrams, tables and narrative:* These presentation styles are present in both EPGs and the PSP book.
- *Consistency of presentation style:* Both EPGs provide consistency of presentation style. PSP0 is also consistent in presentation style based on a tabular structure.
- *Well-structured:* All sample process descriptions are considered well-structured, but the EPG examples have more dynamic structure compared to PSP0. For example,

the relationships between process core elements (roles, work products and activities) of EPGs are structured by using hyperlinks and hypertext technology.

- *Supported by guidance:* Not all sample process descriptions are supported by guidance according to the core process elements structure shown in Figure 1. In fact, some core process elements were not supported by any guidance, for example, none of the roles in OpenUP other than the "architect" role.

Table 4. Software process descriptions comparison

Criteria	Software Process Descriptions		
	OpenUP - V1.0 (EPG)	UPEDU (EPG)	PSP0 (Paper-based)
Tailoring guide	Yes (for each work product)	Yes (for each work product)	No
Searching feature and help support	Yes (via web search)	Yes (via web search)	Yes (via textbook index)
Enable integration with CASE tools	No	No	No
Use of process metamodel	Yes (Unified Method Architecture)	Yes (Unified Software Process Metamodel)	No
Use of diagrams, tables and narrative	Yes	Yes	Yes
Consistency of presentation style	Yes	Yes	Yes
Well-structured	Yes	Yes	Yes
Support by guidance	Yes (for each discipline[1])	Yes (for each discipline)	Yes (for each work product)

From Table 5, we can see that different types of guidance are provided as support. "Example" appears to be the preferred form of guidance for UPEDU and PSP0, followed by "template", "guideline" and "checklist". For OpenUP, "Checklist" is the main form of guidance, followed by "template", "guideline" and "example".

The detected gaps in both comparisons give us some insights into issues regarding usability that are worth investigating:

- Insufficient guidance for tailoring process descriptions may translate into difficulty instantiating process descriptions for a specific project context. To what extent is it possible to provide sufficient guidance for tailoring and what sort of project context information is useful to support tailoring?
- According to Henderson-Sellers [10], process descriptions developed based on a metamodel are expected to be more extensible, configurable and tailorable to individual and project-specific needs. To what extent can process metamodels support software process engineer to achieve these expectations and how does it affect process descriptions usability?

---

[1] A discipline is a collection of tasks that are related to a major area of concern of software development, for example, requirements, architecture, and project management [6].

Table 5. Software process descriptions (SPD) comparison – details on work product guidance

SPD	Phase	Work Product	Template	Example	Check-list	Guide-line
OpenUP [7]	Architecture	Architecture notebook	Yes	No	Yes	Yes
	Development	Build	No	No	No	Yes
		Design	Yes	No	Yes	No
		Developer test	Yes	No	No	Yes
		Implementation	No	No	Yes	Yes
	Project Management	Iteration plan	Yes	Yes	Yes	Yes
		Project plan	Yes	Yes	Yes	No
		Risk list	Yes	No	Yes	No
		Work items list	Yes	Yes	Yes	Yes
	Requirements	Glossary	No	No	No	No
		Supporting requirements specification	Yes	No	Yes	Yes
		Use case	Yes	Yes	Yes	No
		Use case model	No	Yes	Yes	Yes
		Vision	Yes	No	Yes	No
	Test	Test case	Yes	No	Yes	No
		Test log	No	No	No	No
		Test scrip	Yes	No	Yes	Yes
UPEDU [22]	Requirements	Glossary	Yes	Yes	Yes	No
		Software req. specifications	Yes	Yes	Yes	Yes
		Supplementary specifications	Yes	Yes	Yes	Yes
		Use case	Yes	Yes	Yes	Yes
		Use case model	No	Yes	Yes	Yes
		Use case package	No	Yes	No	No
		User interface prototype	Yes	Yes	No	Yes
	Analysis & Design	Analysis class	No	Yes	Yes	Yes
		Design class	No	Yes	Yes	Yes
		Design model	No	Yes	Yes	Yes
		Design package	No	Yes	Yes	No
		Software architecture document	Yes	Yes	Yes	Yes
		Use case realization	Yes	Yes	Yes	Yes
	Implementation	Build	No	Yes	No	No
		Component	No	Yes	No	No
		Imp. Model (model)	No	Yes	No	No
		Imp. Model (document)	Yes	Yes	No	No
	Test	Defect	Yes	Yes	No	No
		Test case	Yes	Yes	Yes	Yes
		Test evaluation report	Yes	Yes	No	No
		Test plan	Yes	Yes	Yes	No
		Test results	Yes	Yes	No	No
	Configuration & Chg. Mgmt.	Change request	Yes	Yes	No	No
		Configuration mgmt. plan	Yes	Yes	No	No
	Project Management	Iteration plan	Yes	Yes	No	Yes
		Gantt diagrams	No	Yes	No	No
		Measurement plan	Yes	Yes	No	Yes
		Project measurements	No	Yes	No	Yes
		Review record	Yes	Yes	No	Yes
		Risks list	Yes	Yes	No	Yes
		Software development plan	Yes	Yes	No	Yes
		Work order	Yes	Yes	No	No
PSP0 [12]	Planning	Project plan summary	Yes	Yes	No	Yes
		Time recording log	Yes	Yes	No	Yes
		Problem description	No	Yes	No	No
	Development	Requirements statement	No	Yes	No	No
		Defect type standard	Yes	Yes	No	Yes
		Source program	No	No	No	Yes
		Defect recording log	Yes	Yes	No	Yes
	Postmortem	PSP0 used the same work products and the same guidance types in the postmortem phase as in the planning and development phases.				

- Which work product guidance types (template, example, checklist or guideline) are more effective in supporting the usability of process descriptions, particularly for work product descriptions? Is it necessary to provide all these guidance types to support software engineers?

5 Implications of the Study and Conclusions

This study has identified usability factors that need to be addressed when designing and developing software process descriptions. The findings from this study provide initial results regarding factors that impact process description usability, but we have not yet evaluated the actual impact on usability. The factors can be used as a guide for defining basic requirements for selecting or developing process descriptions.

With respect to the software process research roadmap [9] created by the International Process Research Consortium (IPRC), our research aligns with the research node: "specifying processes using evidence", which is categorized under the "software process engineering" research theme. It is our intention to support software process engineers in preparing usability evidence through a set of measurable factors that affect the usability of process descriptions. Without usability evaluation, software process engineers run the risk of designing software process descriptions that are difficult to understand and enact by process performers.

In this paper, we have used a small set of usability factors as a set of criteria for comparative review of three sample process descriptions. As a result, the analysis has detected a number of potential usability issues. The work in this paper is a part of our broader investigation into various aspects of usability for process descriptions. Some other aspects that still need elaboration are:

- Validation of identified usability factors − we plan to ask a panel of software process experts to review our consolidated list of usability factors.
- We plan to apply the refined list of usability factors to a number of process descriptions to evaluate their effectiveness in indicating usability problems.
- We are also interested to investigate further how the identified usability factors can be incorporated to formulate a usability evaluation framework to support the Process and Product Quality Assurance (PPQA) process area of the CMMI [3]. We expect that having a well-defined usability evaluation framework for process descriptions can provide insight into processes, roles and associated work products for effective software process management.

References

1. Becker-Kornstaedt, U., Verlage, M.: The V-Modell guide: experience with a Web-based approach for process support. In: Proc. of the Software Technology and Engineering Practice, pp. 161–168 (1999)
2. Bunse, C., Verlage, M., Giese, P.: Improved software quality through improved development process descriptions. Automatica 34, 23–32 (1998)
3. CMMI-DEV: Capability Maturity Model® Integration (CMMISM), Version 1.2. Software Engineering Institute (2006)

4. Curtis, B., Kellner, M.I., Over, J.: Process modeling. Commun. ACM 35, 75–90 (1992)
5. Derniame, J.-C., Kaba, B.A., Wastel, D. (eds.): Software process: principles, methodology, and technology. Springer, Heidelberg (1999)
6. Eclipse Process Framework (EPF) (Retrieved: March 10, 2007), Available at: http://www.eclipse.org/epf/
7. EPF Wiki (Retrieved: December 8, 2007), Available at: http://epf.eclipse.org/
8. Folmer, E., Gurp, J.V., Bosch, J.: A framework for capturing the relationship between usability and software architecture. Softw. Process: Improve. and Pract. 8, 67–87 (2003)
9. Forrester, E. (ed.): A Process Research Framework: The International Process Research Consortium (IPRC). Software Engineerng Institute (2006)
10. Henderson-Sellers, B.: Process Metamodelling and Process Construction: Examples Using the OPEN Process Framework (OPF). Annals of Software Engineering 14, 341–362 (2002)
11. Hornbæk, K., Frokjaer, E.: Reading patterns and usability in visualizations of electronic documents. ACM Trans. Comput.-Hum. Interact. 10, 119–149 (2003)
12. Humphrey, W.S.: A discipline for software engineering. Addison-Wesley, Reading (1995)
13. Humphrey, W.S. (ed.): The Software Process: Global Goals. In: Li, M., Boehm, B., Osterweil, L.J. (eds.) SPW 2005. LNCS, vol. 3840, Springer, Heidelberg (2006)
14. Kellner, M.I., Becker-Kornstaedt, U., Riddle, W.E., Tomal, J., Verlage, M.: Process guides: effective guidance for process participants. In: Proc. of the Fifth International Conference on the Software Process: Computer Supported Organizational Work, pp. 11–25 (1998)
15. Moe, N.B., Dingsøyr, T., Nilsen, K.R., Villmones, N.J.: Project Web and Electronic Process Guide as Software Process Improvement. In: Richardson, I., Abrahamsson, P., Messnarz, R. (eds.) EuroSPI 2005. LNCS, vol. 3792, Springer, Heidelberg (2005)
16. Moe, N.B., Dybå, T.: The use of an electronic process guide in a medium-sized software de-velopment company. Softw. Process: Improve. and Pract. 11, 21–34 (2006)
17. OMG: Software Process Engineering Metamodel Specification (SPEM) Version 2, OMG document ptc/07-02-01 (Retrieved: March 1, 2007), Available at: http://www.omg.org
18. OPEN Process Framework (Retrieved: March 10, 2007), Available at: http://www.opfro.org/
19. Rainer, A., Hall, T.: A quantitative and qualitative analysis of factors affecting software processes. Journal of Systems and Software 66, 7–21 (2003)
20. Robillard, P.N., Kruchten, P., D'Astous, P.: Software engineering process with the UPEDU. Addison Wesley, Boston (2003)
21. Scott, L., Carvalho, L., Jeffery, R., D'Ambra, J., Becker-Kornstaedt, U.: Understanding the use of an electronic process guide. Information and Software Technology 44, 601–616 (2002)
22. Unified Process for Education (UPEDU) (Retrieved: March 11, 2007), Available at: http://www.upedu.org/upedu/index.asp
23. Wang, Y., King, G.A.: Software engineering processes: principles and applications. CRC Press, Boca Raton (2000)

Degree of Agility in Pre-Implementation Process Phases

Jaana Nyfjord and Mira Kajko-Mattsson

DSV, Stockholm University/KTH, Forum 100, SE-164 40 Kista, Sweden
{jaana,mira}@dsv.su.se

Abstract. In this paper, we investigate the degree of agility in the pre-implementation software process phases within three Canadian organizations. Our results show that although the organizations studied have adopted an agile process, they still do substantial amount of planning upfront, which is typical for heavyweight processes. They claim that this planning is obligatory for carrying out subsequent development effectively.

Keywords: Lifecycle, software process model, comparison, heavyweight.

1 Introduction

Little is known about what exactly happens in the agile pre-implementation software development phases. Most of the current research mainly reports on the status of the implementation phase instead, i.e. the phase during which the teams choose, prioritize, and implement requirements.

In this paper, we investigate the state of the pre-implementation phase within three Canadian software organizations. We do this by comparing the industrial practice against *Pre-Implementation Process Model*, a model that is synthesized from a set of current agile process models. Because some customary planning activities are missing in the current agile models, we have complemented the synthesized model with the activities taken from a standard heavyweight software process model [6]. Our goal is threefold: (1) to identify the state of industrial pre-implementation practice, (2) to compare it to the existing agile process models, and (3) to find out how the industry has approached both agile and heavyweight activities.

The remainder of this paper is as follows. Section 2 presents our research method. Section 3 describes the synthesized *Pre-Implementation Process Model*. Section 4 presents the status within three Canadian organizations. Finally, Sections 5 and 6 make conclusions and suggestions for future research.

2 Research Method

In this paper, we study the process phases that take place prior to implementation. These are *Product Vision Planning, Product Roadmap and Release Planning,* and the first part of the *Implementation* phase called the *Iteration Planning* phase. The shadowed area in Figure 1a outlines our scope. Regarding the remaining phase in the *Implementation* phase, it has already been studied and published in [9]. Some of its results indicate that substantial planning is conducted even in an agile context. This has, in turn, urged us to study the *Pre-Implementation* process phases.

Q. Wang, D. Pfahl, and D.M. Raffo (Eds.): ICSP 2008, LNCS 5007, pp. 234–245, 2008.
© Springer-Verlag Berlin Heidelberg 2008

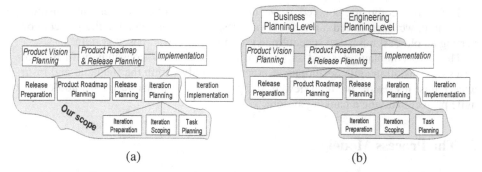

Fig. 1. Pre-implementation phases. **a.** Original model (*left*). **b.** Modified model (*right*).

As a first step, we studied current agile process models. There is a substantial number of published agile process models. However, we decided to base our further work on eXtreme Programming (XP) [3] and Scrum [11]. We selected these because they were the most widely accepted models [5] and because they complement each other [1]. Together, they constitute a comprehensive framework covering both the engineering and management process levels [11].

As a next step, we elicited the activities belonging to their pre-implementation phases, and put them into a synthesized *Pre-Implementation Process Model*. When doing this, however, we observed that some important pre-implementation activities were missing. To ensure the comprehensiveness of our synthesized model and to fulfill our third goal, we complemented it with some heavyweight pre-implementation activities taken from the standard software process model [6]. In this way, we could enquire about their applicability in an agile context. Our synthesized model is presented in Figure 2 and described in Section 3. Each activity is marked with its origin, where *XP* stands for eXtreme Programming, *S* stands for Scrum, and *HW* stands for heavyweight.

After having created the synthesized *Pre-Implementation Process Model*, we created a questionnaire. The questionnaire was open-ended and semi-structured. It covered more than 100 questions. Due to space restrictions, we cannot list them all. However, they mainly concentrated on finding out whether the companies performed the activities as defined in our synthesized model.

Using the questionnaire, we then interviewed the representatives in our companies and established their state of practice. During the course of this work, we realized that they used a set of heavyweight activities. To find out the reasons and to validate the status, we contacted the organizations anew. These reasons are described in Section 5.

Regarding the organizations studied, we interviewed five representatives of the agile development organizations in three Canadian companies. The companies were selected according to their relative ease of access, i.e. by the convenience sampling method [10]. All of them apply a mix of Scrum and XP practices in their projects.

The first company, denoted as *Organization 1*, develops products ranging from ground stations for satellite radar systems to e-commerce applications. Here, we interviewed a process owner, project manager, and chief architect. We studied one small and one middle-sized agile project evolving data transaction systems.

The second company, denoted as *Organization 2*, is an IT management consulting firm. Here, we interviewed a method owner responsible for a small agile project converting an old desktop based scheduling system to a new web-based system.

The third company, denoted as *Organization 3*, is an IT consultancy firm. It focuses on consulting agile development practice, mainly within the financial and insurance industries. Here, we interviewed an agile coach responsible for a middle-sized agile project evolving a banking system.

3 The Process Model

The *Pre-Implementation* process phase covers the following phases: *Product Vision Planning, Product Roadmap and Release Planning,* and *Iteration Planning.* These are described in Sections 3.1-3.3, respectively. They are also listed in Figure 2.

3.1 Product Vision Planning

Organizations generally have an overall picture of their businesses, core values, strategic goals, mission and product portfolios. In the *Product Vision Planning* phase, this overall picture is evolved into a more detailed product vision focusing on product goals, overall business and product structure and return on investment. *Product Vision Planning* guides work in subsequent planning, decision making, and work [11].

As listed in Figure 2, the phase starts with determining the product vision, calculating return on investment (ROI) and creating the business case [11]. In order to understand the client business and to identify business needs, one makes a top-down analysis of the business, its goals, operations, and existing systems. One then creates a business architecture model. This model will provide guidance in identifying functionality in subsequent planning [11]. Similarly, to guide the identification of technical needs, one outlines a system architecture model. One also specifies the overall quality goals and identifies the needs of the development environment [11].

Using the information gathered, one then develops a product vision plan. Here, one identifies the overall system functionality, elicits high-level requirements (product backlog items in Scrum and Stories in XP [3][11]), outlines future releases, and plans resource allocation [4][11]. The requirements are coarsely prioritized and grouped according to the criteria such as ROI or system functionality [11].

Based on the product vision plan, one records an initial high-level requirements specification covering for instance feature descriptions and high-level use cases [4]. Finally, one records the product vision plan [4].

3.2 Product Roadmap and Release Planning

The *Product Roadmap and Release Planning* consists of three sub-phases: *Release Preparation, Product Roadmap Planning* and *Release Planning. Release Preparation* involves preparatory activities for the whole phase. Here, one schedules the planning meetings and gathers all the necessary information, including the product vision plan and high-level requirements specification [4][11].

Fig. 2. Our synthesized process model. S stands for Scrum. XP stands for eXtreme Programming. Bullets (●) and (I) stands for the activities elicited from industry in this study.

In the *Product Roadmap Planning* phase, one outlines a high-level roadmap of future product versions. Here, one studies the product vision plan, identifies new or revises old high-level requirements, creates a requirements list (a backlog in Scrum or a set of Stories in XP [3][11]), and updates the requirements specification [4] [11].

In the next step, one creates a product roadmap outlining future releases. One starts by designating or revising the product releases and their contents using various criteria such as customer priority, business value, criticality, and other [11]. One then determines their schedule and budget [11]. Finally, one records the results [4].

Once the product versions and their release dates are determined, the actual release is planned in the *Release Planning* phase. Here, one creates a high-level plan for the identified releases which one then regularly revisits before each release start [11].

In the *Release Planning* phase, one first studies the product roadmap, requirements list and the current version of the requirements specification [4][11]. To pin down the requirements for the upcoming release, one identifies new or revises old requirements [4]. For each requirement, one assigns business value, identifies risks, estimates development effort, assigns priority value and records the results [3][11]. One then prioritizes and/or re-prioritizes the requirements accordingly [3]. Based on the prioritization results, one then re-organizes the requirements list and groups its items according to the chosen criteria [11]. Its top-priority items should reflect the requirements to be selected for the release [3].

After having defined the preliminary contents of the release, one once again scrutinizes the release scope with respect to the requirements chosen. To determine its final scope, one decides upon the number and length of iterations and assigns requirements to them [3]. One then studies their development feasibility and determines the effort for both the iterations and the release [11]. Finally, one confirms and records the release plan [4].

3.3 Iteration Planning

Iteration Planning is conducted at the start of each iteration. It involves three phases, *Iteration Preparation, Iteration Scoping* and *Task Planning*. Here, the team, product management and other relevant stakeholders meet to plan the implementation work to be conducted in the coming iteration [3][11].

In the *Iteration Preparation* phase, one conducts preparatory activities for starting the iteration, that is, one schedules the iteration planning meeting and collects all the necessary input to plan the iteration effectively [11]. In the next two phases (*Iteration Scoping* and *Task Planning*), one conducts the actual iteration planning. These phases take place during the first day of the iteration [3].

In the *Iteration Scoping* phase, one studies, analyses and prioritizes the requirements planned for the next iteration in order to determine its scope [3]. One first presents a current state of business conditions, and the pending requirements. One may also identify new requirements and include them in the iteration plan. [11]

To facilitate analysis and design, one groups the requirements according to some chosen criteria [4]. One then prioritizes them and revises the extant requirements list [3]. The requirements having the highest priority get selected for the implementation [3]. In cases when the original requirements cannot be squeezed into the iteration or in technically complicated cases, one may suggest alternative requirements that may better fit into this iteration [11].

After having agreed on the requirements to be implemented, one then plans for the iteration and determines its scope. Here, one defines the iteration objective, ensures that each requirement is understood and feasible within the iteration and estimates or re-estimates the development effort [3]. One then agrees upon the iteration plan [4].

In the *Task Planning* phase, one makes an execution plan to implement the prioritized requirements [3]. One first creates or modifies an analysis model for each requirement [7]. One then combines the analysis models, identifies quality problems, and creates traceability among the requirements [4]. Based on these results, one updates or modifies requirements specification accordingly [4].

For each requirement and its analysis model, one identifies/revises design goals, studies architecture, identifies architectonical changes, and creates/modifies a design model, if required [7].

After having agreed upon the analysis and design model, one plans the implementation of each requirement [4][7]. Here, one identifies tasks required for implementing the design model, groups the tasks, estimates or re-estimates resources required for implementing them, estimates combined resources for the entire requirement and signs up for the tasks [3]. For follow-up reasons, one records the task assignments and other relevant data [3].

Based on the outcome from the analysis, design and task planning, one revises the implementation plan [3][4]. One then specifies the acceptance tests constituting the criteria for accepting or rejecting each requirement implementation [3]. Finally, one confirms the iteration plan and updates the iteration plan anew, if required.

4   Status within the Organizations Studied

This section presents the status within the organizations studied based on the interview results.

4.1   Product Vision Planning

On a general level, our results indicate that many of the activities described in the *Product Vision Planning* phase are typically done in the agile projects studied, but to varying degrees, depending on the project type, size, criticality, and resources.

Our results also show that the organizations studied have two levels of planning, the *Business* and *Engineering* planning levels. *Product Vision Planning* takes place upfront on the *Business* level. It is not carried out on the *Engineering* level. However, it is required as input to the *Engineering* planning level.

The product vision plan is always produced on the *Business* level in the studied organizations. Besides a project go/no-go decision, the product vision plan provides a foundation for the subsequent product, release and iteration planning. In *Organization 1* and *Organization 2*, it is called *Operational Concept*. It gives a high-level view of the system needs, its context and its operational characteristics. Regarding *Organization 3*, they do not use the term *Operational Concept*, but refer to a similar outcome. This outcome seems to be less formal than the *Operational Concept*.

Regarding the *Product Vision Planning* activities as listed in our model, all the five interviewees have confirmed that their organizations carry out the majority of them. They create product visions, conduct high-level business and architecture analyses, identify the overall system functionality requirements and quality goals. The activities that do not to take place in any of the organizations studied are the ROI calculation, requirements prioritization, requirements grouping, and mapping the requirements onto the releases. All but the ROI calculation take place in later planning phases.

Regarding the ROI analysis, the coarse-grained granularity character of the functionality requirements does not allow the organizations studied to make any meaningful ROI calculations. The interviewees claim that they simply lack appropriate tools for making certain calculations. Hence, business stakeholders do not even try to quantify ROI. However, our interviewees agreed that with appropriate tools, the activities concerning ROI calculations should take place in this phase.

When studying the *Product Vision Planning* phase in our organizations, we have observed a new activity that has neither been suggested by Scrum nor by eXtreme Programming. It concerns contract writing.

Contracts are always written in all the studied organizations in this phase. However, in *Organization 3*, they may be finalised after the start of a project. A project may start based on an oral agreement. *Organization 3* does so in order to avoid time consuming interaction with legal departments.

4.2 Product Roadmap and Release Planning

The *Roadmap and Release Planning* phase is conducted by all the organizations studied. As shown in Figure 1b, it takes place on the *Engineering* planning level and is generally called the *Release Planning* phase in all of the organizations. It starts after a decision to initiate a project has been made and a product vision plan has been produced.

All the organizations studied have defined a *Product Roadmap Planning* phase. During this phase, they break down the product vision plan (their *Operational Concept*) into an overall high-level product roadmap. This roadmap outlines the evolution of the product and delineates the product releases. The time span of the product roadmap varies from months to years.

All the organizations studied have also defined a *Release Planning* process. However, they conduct it formally only in cases of evolution and maintenance projects or where the product is known for other reasons. They do not conduct it as formally in some specific innovative projects. *Organization 1*, for instance, does not conduct it in small projects where entirely new products are developed. The reason for this is the fact that one does not exactly know in advance what is to be built.

Regarding the projects that undergo the release planning, the practice does not differ much in the organizations studied. In *Organization 1*, this phase is also called *Iteration 0*. Its obligatory input is the *Operational Concept* which provides a basis for (1) identifying key system features and their dependencies, (2) eliciting and analyzing requirements, (3) creating the requirement specification, (4) making estimations, and for (5) creating/updating/revising a backlog. Requirements are primarily described in terms of use cases at this stage.

Identification of the dependencies between the system features helps in organizing and prioritizing the work. This in turn aids in the identification and planning of high-level work packages to be distributed over several releases.

With the knowledge gained in the former steps, high-level estimations are made and compared against the current known capacity to further scope the releases and their iterations.

Finally, a preliminary backlog is created based on the high-level system functionality requirements as identified in the *Operational Concept.* The backlog is complimentary to the planning documentation. It lists new functionality, enhancements, and problems to be addressed in the future. It is only used as a reminder internally by the team and continuously updated where after ideas or concerns are identified.

Overall, the *Release Planning* phase follows the same process in all the organizations studied. We have however noticed some differences. They mainly concern the practice of architecture analysis, requirements elicitation, analysis and specification, and documentation. In *Organization 1,* for instance, these activities are always carried out. Whether agile or not, architecture and requirements analyses are conducted upfront in all projects, i.e. before the implementation starts. They are conducted in a traditional way with all the required documentation according to an organizational process standard.

In *Organization 2* and *Organization 3,* on the other hand, the degree of formality depends on the size and criticality of a project. Generally, however, release planning encompasses the creation of an architectural model and process flow diagrams. Similarly, the documentation practice of the requirements specification varies. *Organization 3,* for instance, strives to use only *Stories* and the *Informative Workspace* as prescribed by XP [3]. They document them only if need arises.

4.3 Iteration Planning

In all the three organizations studied, the minimum inputs required to start planning the iterations are the product roadmap, release plans and the specification of the overall requirements.

Regarding the *Iteration Preparation* phase, all the organizations studied cover the scheduling and preparation activities. We have however observed one practical difference in this phase. The agile methods do not suggest any document to guide the iteration planning. Regarding the organizations studied, they use a planning document dedicated to this activity. In *Organization 1*, it is called *Work Definition.* It is produced by the chief system engineer prior to the iteration planning start. It describes the requirements preliminarily selected for the iteration. Its purpose is to serve as the main input to the detailed iteration planning. It also provides a high-level or conceptual overview of the upcoming iterations.

Concerning the *Iteration Scoping* phase, all the three organizations follow the activities as defined in our model. This phase is conducted by the development team together with the project manager. They meet with the customer, negotiate the priorities, and determine the scope of the iteration. Business and customer values are the main driving factors for prioritization in all the studied organizations. The *Iteration Scoping* phase takes place on the first day of the iteration.

Task Planning, on the other hand, is conducted by engineers only as it focuses on planning the engineering tasks. It usually takes place immediately after the *Iteration Scoping* phase. In some cases, however, it can take two additional days to complete it. Its duration depends on the complexity of the tasks and the skills of the developers.

Most of the differences in the *Iteration Planning* phase are found in the *Task Planning* phase. *Organization 1* covers the majority of the activities that we have listed in our synthesized model, including thorough requirements analysis and design, task break down and estimation, and recording of the iteration plan. In addition, *Organization 1* conducts an activity that we have not covered in our model. This activity is a form of an official contract between the developer and the chief system engineer, where the developer signs off the undertaking of the assigned tasks in her work package. The contracts are signed on an individual developer level, but the organization combines them and refers to them as a *Team Service Level Agreement*. The reason is that the responsibility for delivering the iteration results is shared by the team.

The *Task Planning* phase in *Organization 2* and *3* is almost similar. It only differs with respect to the documentation practice and contract writing. The developers do not sign any contracts on the developers' level in these organizations. In *Organization 3*, the documentation differs in the sense that the iteration plan and the requirements are primarily put on a *Story wall* [3] that is openly displayed for everyone. Traditional documentation is only conducted if required, for instance if the customer demands it.

5   Comparison of Synthesized Model and the Industrial Practice

In this study, we noticed some discrepancies between the industrial practice and our model. This, in turn leads us to modify our synthesized model to better reflect the industrial state of practice. The modifications are presented in Figure 2. They are marked with bullets next to the activity number and with an *(I)* put after the activity name to indicate that the change is implied by the industrial status. Below, we list and describe the observed differences.

• *Organizational Planning Levels*: The agile models studied do not describe organizational levels of planning. Our study shows evidence that the organizations studied conduct planning on two levels. The levels recognized in the industry are the *Business* and *Engineering* levels. *Product Vision Planning*, as described in our model, takes place on the *Business* level, whereas the *Product Roadmap and Release Planning* and *Iteration Planning* take place on the *Engineering* level. We believe that it is a useful division because it clearly communicates the purpose of the different planning phases. Hence, we modify our model and designate two levels of planning, the *Business* and *Engineering* levels (see Figure 1b).

• *Use of ROI:* Agile models studied suggest measurement of productivity in ROI [11]. The organizations studied however do not make any ROI calculations. They claim that they lack appropriate tools for doing it at this level. Despite this, they agree that it should take place in the *Product Vision Planning* phase. For this reason, we keep the activities involving the ROI calculation in this phase (see Activities *A-1.2* and *A-1.9.5* in Figure 2), and do not modify our synthesized model. Instead, we propose that the research community analyses the current ROI tools to find out reasons for why they are insufficient.

• *Requirements Specification:* The agile process models are vague about pointing out the phase during which requirements are identified, analyzed and specified. As mentioned by the companies, the identification of the overall high-level functionality is already carried out in the *Product Vision Planning* phase (see Activity *A-1.9.4*). It is documented in a product vision plan called *Operational Concept*, a document corresponding to a high-level specification of the overall system functionality. This specification is further evolved in subsequent phases, where each phase adds more detail to it. To address this, we have added the Activity *A-2.14: Create requirement specification* in the *Release Planning* phase to our model (see Figure 2).

• *Use of Backlog:* Scrum defines the backlog as a prioritized list of requirements that drives the release planning, iteration planning and implementation [11]. Scrum also suggests that it be maintained by a product owner [11]. In all the organizations studied, the objective of the backlog differs from the one defined in Scrum. It is maintained by the team and serves only as a complementary list of work to be done internally within the team. Other documents are used for planning and organizing the iteration work, such as the *Operational Concept* and *Work Definition*. This observation does not lead us to make any observable changes in our model. We believe that one should be free to decide on the media used for planning and managing the iterations. We however clarify that a backlog can be used as a complimentary driving wheel of iterations [8], by adding the Activity *A-2.21 Create/update backlog, if needed* in the *Release Planning* phase in Figure 2.

• *Contract Management:* Generally agile models value customer collaboration over contracts [2]. Our results show that the organizations studied negotiate contracts before the *Product Roadmap and Release Planning* phase. The reason claimed is that some contract items such as for instance budget constitute an important prerequisite for carrying out product and release planning. Only one of the organizations studied may start some projects based on an oral agreement and good-will. However, a contract is always written. For this reason, we add a new activity for contract writing in the *Product Vision Planning* phase (see *A-1.12* in Figure 2).

• *Iteration Planning Practice:* Scrum suggests that the planning of iterations be prepared by scheduling meetings and by gathering the necessary information [11]. We have found that the iteration preparation activity involves a study of a document called *Work Definition*, produced prior to the iteration planning. It functions as a driving wheel of the iteration planning sessions by providing an overview of the iteration plan. We believe that this is a relevant aspect to consider in addition to the two already existing activities of the *Iteration Preparation* phase (see activities *A-3.2* and *A-3.3* in Figure 2). Creating such a document also results in new input to the *Iteration Scoping* phase. Hence, we add two new activities. These are *A-3.1 Create Work Definition* in the *Iteration Preparation* phase and *A-3.4 Study Work Definition* in the *Iteration Scoping* phase.

• *Duration of Task Planning:* Agile models suggest that the *Task Planning* take place during the first day of the iteration [3]. Time-wise, it was clear however that it took longer than one day in the organizations studied. Within middle-sized projects in *Organization 1* and *3*, planning the tasks could sometimes take up to three days. Hence, we extend the number of days dedicated to *Task Planning* to 1-3 days instead (see Figure 2). We also propose that the models revise their suggestions for the duration length of this activity.

• *Personal/Team Service Level Contracts:* The agile models do not suggest any contract writing on the developers nor on the team level. However, this is a practice that is spreading in one of the organizations studied. It is claimed that it is a necessary quality assurance activity. At the end of the iterations, the deliverables provided by the developers and teams are measured against these contracts [9]. In this respect, we have identified one additional activity relevant for the *Iteration Planning* phase, i.e. an activity where the developer signs under her work assignment. For this reason, we add a new activity to our model, see Activity *A-3.28 Write Personal/Team Service Level Agreement* in the *Iteration Planning* phase in Figure 2.

• *Validation of the Status:* Finally, when analyzing the pre-implementation phases, we observed that the organizations had implemented various activities typical for heavyweight processes. These concern activities such as requirements elicitation, analysis and specification, architectural analysis and design, documentation practice, guidelines regarding scalability, risk management and thorough task planning.

This observation has made us contact the interviewees anew to find out the reasons. Our interviewees claim that the degree of agility of the pre-implementation phases varies among projects. It depends on the phase in the product lifecycle, project type, its size, criticality, innovative character, degree of uncertainty, risk taking, permission from stakeholders' side to take risk, and budget. For instance, the majority of their fixed budget projects follow a more traditional pre-implementation approach whereas other yet unfunded projects follow a more agile approach. Also, in small, innovative, creative and totally new projects, one has difficulties to conduct detailed planning in advance. Hence, one mainly outlines product vision and high level requirements within the pre-implementation phases and allows the rest to be resolved within the later phases.

The claims made by the interviewees are well aligned with those of Scrum, stating that the primary difference between planning a fixed price/fixed date projects and new, unfunded projects is the degree to which the system must be analyzed and specified prior to the project start [11].

Finally, our interviewees claim that good planning upfront in the *Pre-Implementation* phases allows more agility in the *Implementation* phase. The key issue is to set up an instructive plan and then let the teams decide on the implementation process approach. With good and thorough plans, any degree of agility works well as long as long as one keeps control of the product vision, goals and fulfillment of these goals.

6   Final Remarks

The synthesized process model we have built is based on a subset of the existing agile process models. It also reflects the state of practice within the *Pre-Implementation* phases of three software organizations. Our results show that the organizations studied have adopted an agile approach. However, the degree of agility is lower than the degree of agility as observed in the *Implementation* phase [9]. The organizations studied have added some traditional activities in the *Pre-Implementation* phases. The reason for this is mainly the fact that larger, critical, fixed-budget projects involving for instance the evolution and maintenance of existing business critical systems require more traditional planning. The organizations however dare introduce more agility into smaller, more innovative, creative, and risky new projects. This observation makes us conclude that two different agile planning paths are developed: (a) one for projects requiring more upfront planning, such as for instance evolution and maintenance projects, and (b) another one for projects requiring less formal and more agile planning, such as for instance totally new innovative projects.

References

[1] Abrahamsson, P., et al.: Agile Software Development Methods: Review and Analysis. VTT Electronics (2002)

[2] Beck, K., et al.: Manifesto for Agile Development, http://agilemanifesto.org

[3] Beck, K.: Extreme Programming Explained: Embrace Change, 2nd edn. Addison-Wesley, Reading (2004)

[4] Bruegge, B., Allen, H.: Object-Oriented Software Engineering: Using UML, Patterns, and Java. Prentice-Hall, Englewood Cliffs (2004)

[5] Charette, R.: The Decision is in: Agile vs. Heavy Methodologies. Cutter Consortium 2(19) (2001), http://www.cutter.com/content/project/fulltext/updates/2001/epmu0119.html

[6] IEEE Standard 12207.0-1996 - Software Life Cycle Processes. IEEE Inc. (1998)

[7] Jeffries, R., Anderson, A., Hendrickson, C.: eXtreme Programming Installed. Addison-Wesley, Reading (2000)

[8] Merriam-Webster Dictionary, Online: http://www.m-w.com/dictionary/backlog

[9] Nyfjord, J., Kajko-Mattsson, M.: Agile Implementation Phase in Two Canadian Organizations. In: Proceedings of 19th Australian Software Engineering Conference (2008)

[10] Robson, C.: Real World Research. Blackwell Publishing, Malden (2002)

[11] Scrum: Scrum Methodology: Incremental, Iterative Software Development from Agile Processes. Rev. 0.9. Advanced Development Methods Inc. (2003)

Support IT Service Management with Process Modeling and Analysis

Beijun Shen

Dept. of Computer Science and Engineering, Shanghai Jiaotong University,
Shanghai 200240, China
bjshen@sjtu.edu.cn

Abstract. We propose a generic approach for introducing process modeling and analysis technology into IT Service Management (ITSM) to facilitate management of efficient IT services with guaranteed quality. Our approach consists of five steps: identifying core processes in ITSM, establishing the scope of applicability, defining the processes using the Flex language, executing/automating the processes, and analyzing the processes to find improvement opportunity. We illustrate our approach by applying it to a bank's IT incident management process.

Keywords: Process Technology, Process Modeling and Analysis, IT Service Management.

1 Introduction

In the past two decades, there have been considerable advances in software engineering and management. Tremendous efforts have been made to make software development an engineering discipline, and many new process modeling, analysis, simulation, automation and optimization techniques have evolved. Concurrently with these increasing understandings of the possible mechanics of continuous software process improvement, has come the realization that software development is only one of a multitude of diverse domains in which the continuous improvement of processes can lead to important benefits. So it is suggested to apply these process technologies in many other domains to lead to superior products and outcomes [1]. Some practices have indicated they are effective in some specific domains [1][2][3].

In this paper, we attempt to apply process modeling and analysis technology to IT service management (ITSM). ITSM is a discipline that strives to better the alignment of IT efforts to business needs and to manage the efficient supply of IT services with guaranteed quality. Like in the early days of the software engineering discipline, when dissatisfaction of customers with the often unsuccessful outcome of software development projects drove the focus from providing the individual programmer with ever better tools to adaptation of engineering, now there is a fundamental shift happening in the ITSM field. Here it is mostly companies' discontent with a perceived

Q. Wang, D. Pfahl, and D.M. Raffo (Eds.): ICSP 2008, LNCS 5007, pp. 246–256, 2008.
© Springer-Verlag Berlin Heidelberg 2008

lack of transparency in IT provisioning that drives the rising interest in organizational aspects of ITSM. This paper reports our approach to manage IT service from a formal point of process and presents a case study conducted at a bank.

The rest of the paper is organized as follows: Section 2 discusses related work. Section 3 presents our generic approach for introducing process modeling and analysis technology into ITSM, followed by a detailed case study in section 4. Section 5 concludes the paper.

2 Related Work

There have been some attempts at process technology application in other domains such as government [2] and medical care [3]. The notation of process in those domains is far less well developed than they are in software engineering. Thus these other domains have much to gain from the application of software process technologies [1]. Process is also the core of IT service management; however no related works have been reported to apply software process modeling, analysis, and optimization technology to this domain.

Another relevant piece of work is from researches of IT service management. Due to its increasing role in the enterprise, various IT frameworks have been developed to provide guidelines to the IT industry. Among them, IT Infrastructure Library (ITIL) [4] has developed into a de facto standard for the domain. The release of ISO 20000 [6], which is based on the ITIL, will probably bring even wider adoption of ITIL in the industry. However ITIL does not dictate IT service processes but provides a comprehensive, consistent and coherent set of best practices for ITSM. It should be also noted that IT Service CMM was drafted as a capability maturity model for IT services providers [7]. However, IT Service CMM aims to measure the capability of the IT service processes of organizations, and doesn't provide any guideline for process modeling, analysis and automation.

Moreover, there is some existing work describing definition and automation of aspects of service management. S. Jansen provided a process model for customer configuration updating that can evaluate the practices of a software vendor in these processes [8]. A. Keller proposed a general approach for automating ITSM [9].

In spite of its relevance, its wide distribution and a large number of publications, a generic and comprehensive approach to manage IT service from a formal point of process is lacking. Our work employs modeling, analysis and automation techniques that are applicable to reasoning about the software processes, and applies these techniques to ITSM to improve its management efficiency and quality.

3 Our Approach

In this section, we present a generic approach to apply process technology in IT service management, which can also guide the practices in other domains. Our approach

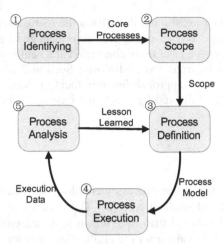

Fig. 1. Generic approach to apply process technology in ITSM

comprises five steps, as shown in figure 1, and each of them will be described detailedly in following subsections.

3.1 Identify Core Processes for the Domain

To identify the best-practice processes for ITSM, we turn to the IT Infrastructure Library (ITIL), which deals with the control and monitoring of IT services based on principles of classical service provision. Within the ITIL there are two areas of ITSM: service support [4] and service delivery [5]. Each of them defines five processes, as depicted in figure 2. Service support also has a chapter for service desk guidance. The service desk is however a business function and not a process.

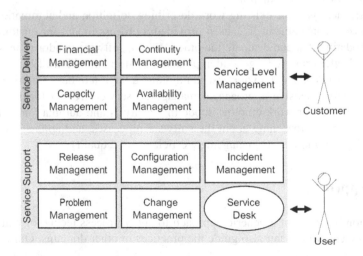

Fig. 2. Core Processes of ITSM

3.2 Establish the Scope of Applicability

We find that not all of these ten ITSM processes are best suited for making them more efficient through the applicability of software process technology. So we adopt the following basic ITSM process characteristics [10] to establish the scope of applicability:

1) Recurrence: degree of the recurrence frequency of process instances.

2) Cycle Time: average duration of a process instance from the event that triggers it to its conclusion.

3) Organizational Complexity: a compound measure, based on the number of distinct parties involved in the process and the complexity of their interactions.

4) Service Level Impact: a measure of how lacking effectiveness in process execution influences the service level compliance.

5) Structure: a measure of how concrete an activity flow structure can be defined for the process.

According to these characteristics, the ITSM processes are evaluated [10] as shown in table 1. Among these ten processes, incident management, problem management and change management are "classic" processes, which involve multiple actors in a clearly structured activity flow. This makes them best suited for process modeling, analysis, and automation. Incidentally, those are also the processes that are determined to have the most immediate impact on service level compliance and shortest cycle times.

Table 1. Characteristics of ITSM processes

ITSM process	Recurrence	Cycle Time	Complexity	SL Impact	Structure
incident management	high	low	high	high	high
problem management	medium	medium	medium	medium	high
configuration management	-	-	low	low	low
change management	medium	medium	high	medium	high
release management	low	high	high	medium	medium
service level management	low	high	medium	low	low
financial management	-	-	low	low	low
capacity management	-	-	low	low	low
IT service continuity management	-	-	low	low	low
availability management	-	-	low	low	low

3.3 Define the Processes

According to ITIL, ITSM processes can be defined through four aspects:

- Resource Management (RM) is designed to manage resources, including human, facilities, and the work environment.
- Management Responsibility (MR) is designed to define functions and their inter-relations within the organization, including responsibilities and authorities.
- Service Realization (SR) is that sequence of processes required to achieve the services.
- Measurement Analysis Improvement (MAI) is designed to define, plan and implement the measurement and monitoring services needed to assure conformity and achieve improvement.

For this research, we use our process language - Flex [11][12][13], to define incident management, problem management and change management. We use its resource model to represent RM, its cooperation model to represent MR, its function model and product model to represent SR, and its KPI (Key Performance Indicator) feature to support MAI. The Flex is a flexible and scalable process modeling language designed for software process originally. It has two representations, one is the formal representation Flex/BM which allows expert to tailor, and the other is the pre-defined high level graphical representation Flex/PL based on Flex/BM. At current preliminary research phase, Flex/PL is selected as the modeling language; and later on Flex/BM will be customized to reflect features of ITSM. These modeling works are supported by our Process-sensitive engineering environments – E-Process [14], which also assists analysis, automation and measurement of process models.

3.4 Automate and Execute the Processes

Automation is regarded as an appropriate means of containing and even reducing the labor costs of ITSM. In ITSM processes, some of their activities will be amenable to automation (such as deploying a change in Change Management) whereas others will not (such as obtaining change approvals from Change Control Boards). Therefore, in this step involves identifying the candidate activities for automation, determining whether the value of automating them outweighs the cost of developing and maintaining the automation, and selecting a final set of process activities to automate.

We implement the Flex-annotated ITSM processes using our E-Process environment, to automatically coordinate the process's activities and the flow of information between them. And also automated and manual activities within the same overall process are integrated harmoniously in E-Process.

3.5 Analyze the Process Model and Identify Improvement Opportunity

During process execution, relevant parameters are constantly monitored and KPI related data are collected, which are the basis of process analysis. Our suggested ITSM process analysis techniques include KPI measurement, value analysis, competitive comparison, benchmarking, risk analysis, and postponement analysis.

The goal of this step is to identify defects and shortcomings in these processes, and propose improvement to the processes. To achieve it, several best practices for ITSM processes are summarized as followings:

1) Task elimination: delete tasks that do not add value from a client's viewpoint.
2) Task automation: introduce technology if automated tasks can be executed faster, with less cost, and with a higher quality.
3) Task simplifying: simplify intermediate steps, and merge similar or sequential tasks into one.
4) Parallelism: introduce concurrency within a process to reduce lead times.
5) Balance: eliminate process inefficiencies, such as bottlenecks and workload imbalances, for more effective resource utilization.
6) Empower: give workers most of the decision-making authority and reduce middle management.

7) Outsourcing: relocate work to a third party that is more efficient in doing the same work, to reduce costs.
8) Contact reduction: combine information exchanges to reduce the number of times that waiting time and errors may show up.
9) Buffering: subscribe to updates instead of complete information exchange.
10) Case-based work: removing constraints that introduce batch handling may significantly speed up the handling of cases.

4 Case Study

To demonstrate the efficiency of our approach, a case study on an incident management was conducted in a real organization.

4.1 Background of the Case Project

The case organization described herein is a commercial bank. Since 1967, this bank has been serving neighborhoods and businesses in the New York Chinatown area with the very best in community banking services. Its business has increased by leaps and bounds over the years. It provides customers with a wide variety of banking products and outstanding personal service. Striving and succeeding in a competitive service industry, the bank pays close attention to optimizing its business processes.

Like many other organizations, the bank has developed IT support services delivered by help desks, which is responsible to achieve good customer relations by restoring the failed services/incident in minimum time. As the bank's business becomes increasingly dependent upon its IT services, the need to react quickly and effectively to any incidents has become vital. An ITSM Process Improvement project was initiated in 2005 within the bank, whose goal is to find an effective and consistent way to address all IT related incidents, aligned with best practices from ITIL model.

4.2 As-is Analysis

Incident management at the bank is concerned with restoring normal service operation as quickly as possible and minimizing its adverse impact on business operations. The original incident management process (as-is process) at the bank consisted of the following four main tasks:

1) Incident reporting: Occurring incidents are detected and recorded.
2) Incident analysis and diagnosis: Recorded incidents are investigated to give initial support to the customer.
3) Incident resolution: Recorded incidents are closely examined in order to restore service.
4) Incident review and closure: The given solution is evaluated and the recorded incident is formally closed.

For the purpose of further analysis, we defined this as-is process in Flex/PL language, as shown in figure 3. Our efforts at process modeling led to a number of important results.

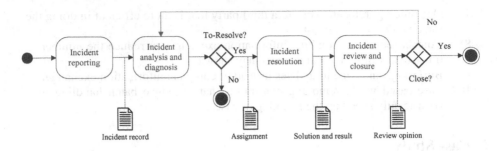

Fig. 3. As-is process of incident management

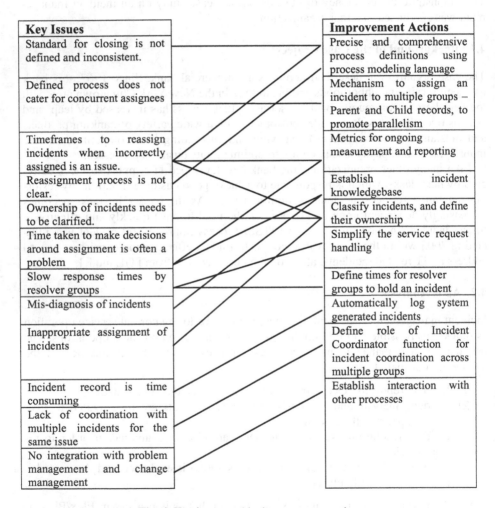

Key Issues	Improvement Actions
Standard for closing is not defined and inconsistent.	Precise and comprehensive process definitions using process modeling language
Defined process does not cater for concurrent assignees	Mechanism to assign an incident to multiple groups – Parent and Child records, to promote parallelism
Timeframes to reassign incidents when incorrectly assigned is an issue.	Metrics for ongoing measurement and reporting
Reassignment process is not clear.	Establish incident knowledgebase
Ownership of incidents needs to be clarified.	Classify incidents, and define their ownership
Time taken to make decisions around assignment is often a problem	Simplify the service request handling
Slow response times by resolver groups	Define times for resolver groups to hold an incident
Mis-diagnosis of incidents	Automatically log system generated incidents
Inappropriate assignment of incidents	Define role of Incident Coordinator function for incident coordination across multiple groups
Incident record is time consuming	Establish interaction with other processes
Lack of coordination with multiple incidents for the same issue	
No integration with problem management and change management	

Fig. 4. Key issues and its improvement actions

First, those involved in executing and managing the process gained a substantial increase in understanding the overall goals of the process, as well as recognition of the effect of regulations and standards on the process. Several different organizational subunits were involved in various stages of the incident management process. The view of most of these subunits was rather parochial, focusing on a specific subtask with little appreciation for overall implications. Such situations frequently led to suboptimization with respect to overall organizational goals.

In addition to providing mechanisms for representing process models, E-Process provides a number of powerful analysis capabilities. A wide variety of static analyses were made to check the model for completeness and consistency, such as, checking for missing sources or targets of information flows, no exception handling, unreachable states, and activities without ownership.

Furthermore, we carried out several deeper analyses on the as-is process, using the dynamic performance data. These included KPI measurement, value analysis, competitive comparison, risk analysis, and postponement analysis. Herein best practices from ITIL were also embraced.

These analyses identified several key issues, and led to a series of recommendations for changes in the as-is process, as shown in figure 4.

4.3 To-be Process

Based on proposed recommendations, we redesigned the incident management process, streamlining the process and improving its timeliness. Figure 5 illustrates the model of to-be incident management process.

Recording ensures that there are no lost incidents or service requests, allows the records to be tracked, and provides information to aid problem management and planning activities. The process includes the use of technology to provide self-service facilities to customers, which reduces the workload and personnel requirements of the service desk.

Service requests, such as a request for change or a batch job request, are also recorded and then handled according to the relevant processes for that type of service request.

Incidents undergo classification to ensure that they are correctly prioritized and routed to the correct resolver groups. Complex incidents can be separated into several parts to be resolved in parallel. Incident management includes initial support processes that allow new incidents to be checked against known errors and problems so that any previously identified workarounds can be quickly located.

Incident management then provides a structure by which incidents can be investigated, diagnosed, resolved, and then closed. The process ensures that the incidents are owned, tracked, and monitored throughout their life cycle.

It should be noted that each activity in the incident management process is subprocess, which is composed of several sub-activities.

This overall incident management process was modeled and analyzed in E-Process environment, while it was automated using another workflow system, which is more flexible than the Enactment tool of E-Process.

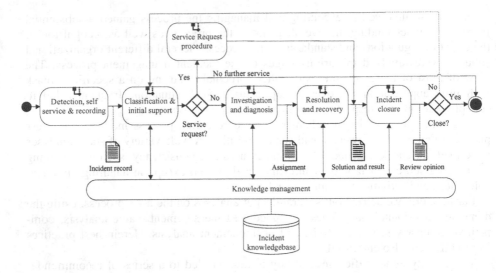

Fig. 5. To-be process of incident management

4.4 Process Execution and Evaluation

After five months of dedicated work, the redesigned process was in place and use of process technologies was starting to pay dividends in increased availability, higher productivity, and faster cycle time for services. Figure 6 and 7 show some of the incident management process improvement results.

The re-designed process provides a seamless incident management workflow aligned with industry-leading incident management best practices. Through avoiding duplication of work and dropped incidences, freeing up IT resources and lowering costs, the productivity and efficiency in incident management is increased. Moreover, IT service quality is improved with faster resolution of disruptive events, resulting in increased IT customer satisfaction.

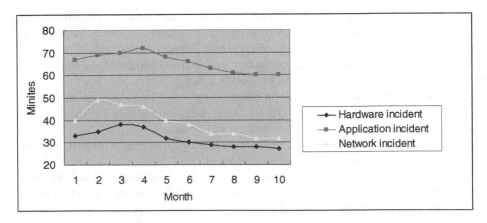

Fig. 6. Average cycle time to resolve incidents

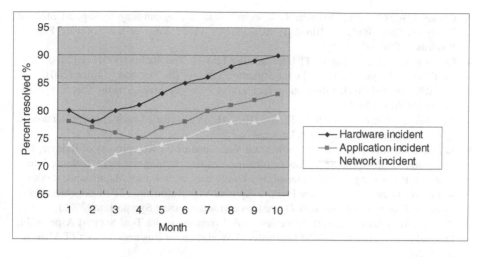

Fig. 7. Ratio of incidents resolved in fixed duration

5 Conclusion and Future Work

This paper describes how process technology can be used to support IT service management. Technologies such as process modeling, analysis, and automation have proven to be an important part of ITSM. These technologies form the basis for service process improvement and their deployment often leads to increased understanding of the process by managers and participants.

Moreover, there are several additional efforts that would be highly beneficial to the application of software process technology. One is to customize Flex/BM language to reflect features of ITSM. Another valuable contribution would be to apply process technology to other modern service domains such as logistics and telecommunication. We look forward to carrying out these future works and playing our part in contributing to the maturation of ubiquitous process engineering as a technique in facilitating growth of the modern service industry.

Acknowledgements. This research is partially supported by the National Natural Science Foundation of China (Grant No. 60373074). Also, I appreciate all project members and the help offered by Prof. W. Bandara and Prof. Hengming Zou.

References

1. Osterweil, L.J.: Ubiquitous Process Engineering: Applying Software Process Technology to Other Domains. In: Proceedings of International Software Process Workshop and International Workshop on Software Process Simulation and Modeling (2006)
2. Raunak, M.S., Chen, B., Elssamadisy, A., Clarke, L.A.: Definition and Analysis of Election Processes. In: Proceedings of International Software Process Workshop and International Workshop on Software Process Simulation and Modeling (2006)

3. Clarke, L.A., Chen, Y., Avrunin, G.S., et al.: Process Programming to Support Medical Safety: A Case Study on Blood Transfusion. In: Proceedings of the Software Process Workshop, China (2005)
4. CCTA (ed.): Service Support, IT Infrastructure Library. The Stationary Office (2000)
5. CCTA (ed.): Service Delivery, IT Infrastructure Library. The Stationary Office (2001)
6. ISO/IEC 20000-1:2005: Information Technology - Service Management- Part 1: Specification, ISO/IEC (2005)
7. Niessink, F., Clerc, V., Tijdink, T., van Vliet, H.: IT Service Maturity Model Version1.0 (2005), http://www.itservicecmm.org
8. Jansen, S., Brinkkemper, S.: Definition and Validation of the Key process of Release, Delivery and Deployment for Product Software Vendors: turning the ugly duckling into a swan. In: Proceeding of IEEE International Conference on Software Maintenance (2006)
9. Keller, A., Brown, A.B.: A Best Practice Approach for Automating IT Management Processes. In: Proceeding of Network Operations and Management Symposium (2006)
10. Brenner, M.: Classifying ITIL Processes — A Taxonomy under Tool Support Aspects. In: Proceedings of First IEEE/IFIP International Workshop on Business–Driven IT Management (2006)
11. Chen, C., Shen, B.: Towards Flexible and High-Level Process Modeling Language. In: Proceedings of International Symposium on Future Software Technology (2001)
12. Chen, C., Shen, B., Gu, Y.: A Flexible and Formalized Process Modeling Language. Journal of Software 13(8) (2002)
13. Shen, B., Chen, C.: The Design of a Flexible Software Process Language. In: Proceedings of Software Process Workshop/Workshop on Software Process Simulation (2006)
14. Shen, B., Gu, C.et al.: A Distributed Architecture for Process-Sensitive Engineering Environment. In: Proceedings of Conference on Software: Theory and Practice (2000)
15. Battell, N., Brooks, T.: Service Management Functions: Incident Management (2005), http://www.microsoft.com/technet/itsolutions/cits/mo/smf/smf incmg.mspx
16. Bandara, W., Cornes, J., Rosemann, M.: Business Process Redesign in Information Technology Incident Management: A Teaching Case. In: Proceedings of the 16th Australasian Conference on Information Systems (2005)

The Secret Life of a Process Description:
A Look into the Evolution of a Large Process Model

Martín Soto, Alexis Ocampo, and Jürgen Münch

Fraunhofer Institute for Experimental Software Engineering
Fraunhofer-Platz 1
67663 Kaiserslautern, Germany
{soto, ocampo, muench}@iese.fraunhofer.de

Abstract. Software process models must change continuously in order to remain consistent over time with the reality they represent, as well as relevant to
the task they are intended for. Performing these changes in a sound and disciplined fashion requires software process model evolution to be understood and
controlled. The current situation can be characterized by a lack of understanding of software process model evolution and, in consequence, by a lack of
systematic support for evolving software process models in organizations. This
paper presents an analysis of the evolution of a large software process standard,
namely, the process standard for the German Federal Government (V-Modell®
XT). The analysis was performed with the Evolyzer tool suite, and is based on
the complete history of 600 versions that have been created during the development and maintenance of the standard. The analysis reveals similarities
and differences between process evolution and empirical findings in the area of
software system evolution. These findings provide hints on how to better manage process model evolution in the future.

Keywords: process modeling, process model change, process model evolution,
model comparison, V-Modell® XT.

1 Introduction

In his seminal paper from 1987 [1], Leon Osterweil pointed out the similarities between software processes and software programs. 20 years later, however, it is clear
to us that his vision of process descriptions similar in its degree of formality and detail
to actual computer programs has been much harder to realize than he actually envisioned. In fact, the majority of contemporary, practical software process descriptions
still contain a large proportion of informal material in the form of natural language
text. This does not mean, however, that process descriptions must be completely
informal. Indeed, they are often highly structured and use standardized, uniform terminology. They also often contain an intricate lattice of internal and external cross-
references that are not only intended to guide the reader in navigating the description
but also ensure the description's internal consistency. The presence of this complex
internal structure, and the consistency requirements associated with it, clearly make
process descriptions look similar to software systems in many respects.

Q. Wang, D. Pfahl, and D.M. Raffo (Eds.): ICSP 2008, LNCS 5007, pp. 257–268, 2008.
© Springer-Verlag Berlin Heidelberg 2008

One aspect of this analogy that has undergone little research until now is the evolution of large process descriptions and its relation to the much better understood field of software evolution. As every process modeling practitioner can attest to, changing a process description over time while preventing its structure from deteriorating or its consistency from being lost is a difficult task. Still, it remains unclear up to what extent maintaining a software process description is similar to maintaining a software system, and how much of the existing software maintenance knowledge can be extrapolated to the process realm. While considering this fundamental question, a number of more concrete questions may arise, for instance:

- if an evolving process description increases its complexity over time unless work is done to reduce it;
- if most changes of process models are performed only on a few parts of a process description;
- if changes performed shortly before a release cause more post-release changes than changes performed earlier before a release;
- if parts of process models that have been changed many times have a higher probability of additional changes.

We expect the answers to such questions to be useful for supporting process management activities better than they can be supported nowadays. Knowing, for example, that changing certain areas of a process description may potentially imply further changes in the near future, could be used to inspect these changes more carefully or to avoid changing certain parts of a process description for minor reasons.

Our current knowledge of process model evolution is not sufficient to answer these questions on an empirical basis. This is caused, in part, by the fact that mechanisms and tools for analyzing process model evolution and visualizing the results are widely missing. Another reason is that only few organizations have a history of the versions of their process models in sufficient detail, that is, including versions in between releases and documented justifications (i.e., rationale) for the changes introduced in each new version.

In this article, we present preliminary results aimed at understanding process model evolution. Our findings are based on detailed evolution data for a large and complex process description: the German V-Modell® XT. This description is interesting not only because of its significance for the German information technology domain, but also because of its large size and complexity. The V-Modell describes about 1500 process entities, and its printed documentation is over 700 pages long.

In order to perform our analysis, we applied novel comparison and annotation techniques to identify the changes made to the model over its versioning history, and to link these changes, whenever possible, with their underlying rationale. By doing this, we obtained a comprehensive, integrated representation of the V-Modell's life along three major public releases and over 600 individual versions. With this information as a basis, we have been able to answer a number of basic questions related to the V-Modell's evolution. These questions, as well as the way we approached them, form the core of this article.

The rest of the paper is structured as follows: Section 2 gives a short overview of the evolution of the V-Modell® XT. Section 3 briefly discusses the techniques used to perform our analysis of the model. Section 4 presents our analysis in more detail, and discusses its results. The paper closes with an overview of related work, a summary, and an outlook on future work.

2   The German V-Modell® XT and the History of Its Evolution

The German process standard V-Modell [2] (not to be confused with Royce's V-Model [3]) has a long history, and an ever increasing significance for the German IT landscape. Its origin dates to the mid-eighties. In 1997, the so-called V-Modell 97 was officially released as a software development standard for the German federal government. The standard remained unchanged until 2004, when a consortium of industrial and research institutions received public funding to perform a thorough update of the model. The result was the new V-Modell® XT, which was established as German federal standard for software development. Since its inception, the model has seen continuous updates, represented by three major and two minor releases. Also, since a few months ago, an English version has also been available, which is kept synchronized with the original German version.

The V-Modell® XT is a high-level process description, covering such aspects of software development as project management, configuration management, software system development, and change management, among others. In printed form, the latest English version at the time of this writing (version 1.2.1) is 765 pages long and describes about 1500 different process entities.

Internally, the V-Modell® XT is structured as a hierarchy of process entities interconnected by a complex graph of relationships. This structure is completely formalized, and suitable for automated processing. The actual text of the model "hangs" from the formalized structure, mainly in the form of entity and relationship descriptions, although a number of documentation items (including a tutorial introduction to the model) are also integrated into the structure in the form of *text module* entities. Actual editing of the model is performed with a software tool set created specially for the purpose. The printed form of the V-Modell® XT is generated automatically by traversing the structure in a predefined order and extracting the text from the entities found along the way.

The V-Modell® XT contents are maintained by a multidisciplinary team of experts, who work, often concurrently, on various parts of the model. In order to provide some measure of support to this collaborative work, the model is stored as a single XML file in a standard code versioning system (CVS). As changes are made by the team members, new versions are created in this system. As usual for a versioning system, versions can, and often do, include a short comment from the author describing the changes. Also, an Internet-based issue tracking system is available so that model users can report problems with the model. This system often includes discussions between team members and users about how certain issues should be resolved. Not all actual changes in the model can be traced to a particular issue in the tracking system, but many of them can.

The change logs show that, since its initial inception, the model has been changed often and for a wide variety of reasons. Changes can be as simple as individual spelling or grammar corrections, or as complex as the introduction of a whole set of processes for hardware development and software/hardware integration. The richness and complexity of this change history makes the V-Modell a very interesting target for evolution analysis.

3 Analyzing the Evolution of a Process Description

The first step in order to analyze the evolution of this process description was to read its versioning history into our Evolyzer model comparison system. Although a description of the internal operation of Evolyzer is beyond the scope of this paper (see [4] for details), a short explanation of its workings is in order. The basis of the system is a model database that can contain an arbitrary number of versions of a model. The formalism used for representing the models is the RDF notation [5] and the whole model database can be queried using a subset of the SPARQL [6] query language for RDF.

The central characteristic that distinguishes Evolyzer from other RDF storage systems is its ability to efficiently compare versions of an RDF model. Given two arbitrary versions, the system is able to compute a so-called *comparison model* that contains all model elements (RDF statements, actually) present in the compared versions, marked with labels indicating whether they are common to both versions, or are only present in one of them, and, in the latter case, in which one of the versions they are present. Given the high level of granularity of this comparison, identifying changes in it by direct inspection is generally a difficult task. For this reason, change identification is performed by looking for special *change patterns* in the comparison model (see [4] for a detailed explanation.) This not only makes it possible to look for changes that are specific, in their form or structure, to a particular model schema, but allows for restricting change identification to particular areas of the model or to specific types of model elements.

For the present study, we attempted to read 604 versions from the original versioning repository into our system. These versions were created in somewhat more than two years time, with three major and one minor public releases happening during that period. Since Evolyzer uses the RDF notation for model representation (this is necessary in order for our comparison technique to work at all), each V-Modell version was mechanically converted from its original XML representation into an RDF model before reading it into the system. This conversion did not add or remove information, nor did it change the level of formalization of the original process description. Process entities described in the original XML through XML elements were translated into RDF resources (the original XML already contained unique identifiers, which were reused for the RDF resources) and the text associated to them was stored as RDF property values. Relations encoded in XML as element references were converted into RDF relations. The conversion process was successful for all but 4 of the 604 analyzed versions. These 4 versions could not be read into our repository because their corresponding XML files contained syntax errors.

After importing the version history, we proceeded to compare the versions pairwise to identify individual changes happening from one version to the next. As changes, we considered the addition or deletion of entities, the addition or deletion of relations between entities, and the alteration of text properties. We identified these changes by defining corresponding change patterns and searching for them in the version comparisons.

Information about each of the identified changes including type, version number and affected process entities was encoded in RDF and stored in the repository together with the model versions. This allowed us to easily go from the change information to the actual model contents and back from the models to the changes as necessary for our analysis (see [7] for the details of how this cross referencing works.)

4 An Exploratory Look into a Process Description's Evolution

The resulting RDF repository containing detailed information about the V-Modell's change history provided the basis for our exploratory analysis of the model's evolution. Our long-term research goal is to formulate explicit verifiable hypotheses about process model evolution, but in order to do that, observation is a first, indispensable step. For this reason, the fundamental objective of the present analysis was to observe and informally characterize the evolution of the model. We attempted to do that by formulating rather open questions and then trying to extract data from the change repository and visualize them in such a way that we could attempt to address the questions by direct observation.

Given the complex structure of the V-Modell® XT, we concentrated our analysis on only one part of it, namely, the so-called *process modules*,[1] a number of large entities that act as containers for a good number (but not all) of the finer-grained entities in the model. We did this for two reasons. First, the process modules contain the "meat" of the description, namely, the process entities used to describe the actual process steps and products: activities, products, roles, and the relationships among them. Second, since process modules are the official means for tailoring the model to specific project types, they correspond to sensible components of the whole description, and are thus more likely to produce meaningful results when observed independently from each other.

Additionally, and for the sake of simplicity, we decided to reduce this analysis to changes affecting the text descriptions contained in the entities, and to exclude the relationships connecting entities. In the following, we present the analysis questions, together with the approach we took to analyze them, the resulting visualization, and the results we derived from it.

4.1 Complexity Over Time

The starting point of the analysis is the question of whether the V-Modell has increased its complexity over time. This question is related to Lehman's law with respect to system evolution, which states that the complexity of a system increases over time unless work is done to reduce it ([8], cited in [9]). To address this question, we chose a simple metric for the model complexity, namely, the total number of entities contained in each process module. By running a special query and performing simple postprocessing of the results, we determined this number for each process module and

---

[1] In German, process modules are called *Vorgehensbausteine,* a term that would rather correspond to *process building blocks.* We decided, however, to stick to the translation used by the official English version of the V-Modell® XT.

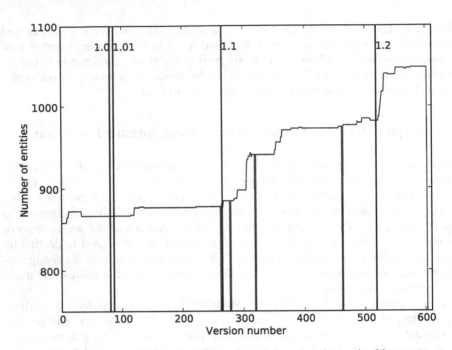

Fig. 1. Number of entities in the process modules along the version history

for each of the 604 analyzed versions, and produced individual plots displaying the process module's size for each version number. Due to space limitations, we are omitting the individual plots (22 in total) but Figure 1 shows the total size accumulated over the 22 process modules for each version number.

The curve in Figure 1 shows a clear growing tendency, going from around 850 to over 1000. Pronounced growth is observed after two of the releases, probably pointing to major changes that were held back until the release. The analysis of the plots covering specific process modules (not included here) shows a similar growing tendency. Significant reductions of the entity count can only be observed in cases where a module was split at some point. As the cumulative graph shows, however, this did not affect the total element count. Some "dents" can be observed at the 4 points were versions could not be read.

Even despite major restructuring, the total number of entities in the V-Modell® XT increased significantly during the observed period. This growth can be attributed, at least in part, to model enhancements such as the introduction of processes for hardware development. Still, these results suggest that monitoring the complexity of process descriptions and possibly taking measures to keep it under control can be a valuable strategy for maintaining complex process models.

4.2 Distribution of Changes Over Time and Over the Model

The next questions are concerned with the way changes affect different parts of the model: How are changes distributed among versions, and how do they relate to releases? How are they distributed over the process modules?

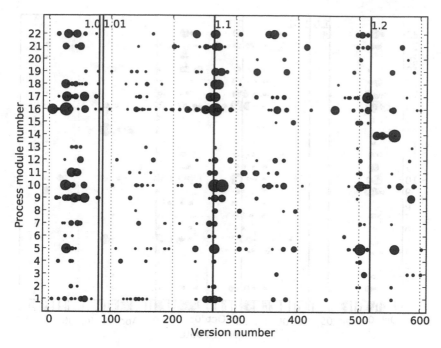

Fig. 2. Changes discriminated by process module along the version history

Our approach to addressing these questions was to display the changes in such a way that the process module affected by the change, as well as the time and size of the changes, become visible. Figures 2 and 3 are two such displays.

The X-axis in Figure 2 shows the version number (from 1 to 604), whereas the Y-axis shows the process modules (numbered arbitrarily). There is a circle wherever a version changed an entity in a particular process module. The size of the circle is proportional to the number of changes affecting entities in the module. Figure 3 is similar to Figure 2, but the X-axis corresponds to actual calendar times. Changes are displayed at the locations where their corresponding versions were checked in. Since versions are not distributed uniformly across time, this figure also contains a "version density" bar at the bottom that has black bars at the points in time where versions actually happened.

Several points are worth mentioning about these figures. First, activity concentrates around releases. Activity before a release probably corresponds to release preparation, whereas activity after a release points to changes held back and introduced after the release. Both of these points were corroborated verbally by members of the V-Modell development team, and can also be confirmed by inspecting the version logs. An interesting observation is that the version-based graph (Figure 2) also looks busy around releases, implying that versions close to a release often collect more changes in a single version than versions far from the release. If this were not the case, the "congestion" around releases would only be observable on the time-based graph. A partial explanation for this phenomenon is that a number of the versions grouping several

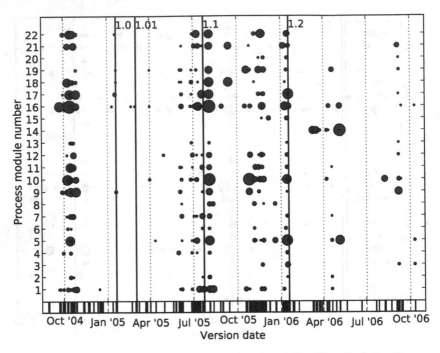

Fig. 3. Changes discriminated by process module, against time

changes are related to reviews or to other bulk corrections that result in many small changes spread over the model. Still, it is possible that some of the "congested" versions are the result of changes being rushed into the model shortly before a release.

One aspect that is evident on the time-based graph is that release 1.0 looks delayed with respect to its preparatory "burst" of activity, with a period of low activity before the actual release date. According to the team members, the bulk of the preparatory work was done for the model's "presentation in society" at a public event in November 2004. Only minor corrections were made until the official release in February 2005. This can also be observed by looking at the version density bar, which shows clear peaks of activity around the releases, except for release 1.0.

Finally, the version-based graph shows us a number of process modules that present more activity than the remaining ones: 10, 16, 5 and, to some extent, 1. Although this is often related to their larger size, change activity seems not to be strictly proportional to size, and also seems to depend on the relative importance of the various modules (we need to investigate both of these points in more detail). The graphs also show that process modules often undergo "bursts" of activity that calm down later on, such as the one observed in process module 10 between releases 1.1 and 1.2. This suggests that, similar to what happens in software development, complex changes have to be performed step-wise and often introduce errors that must be corrected later.

The previous observations point in different ways to the similarities between process model and software evolution. In particular, one should not believe that change management is simpler or less risky for process models than it is for software systems. Practices such as inspections, configuration management, or issue management are most probably advisable for complex modeling projects and may even be necessary in order to achieve high-quality results over time.

4.3 Changes in Detail

Our last question is concerned with the relationship between local and global changes: Does the evolution of individual modules look similar to the evolution of the whole model? To address this question, we decided to analyze the change history of one single process module in more detail.

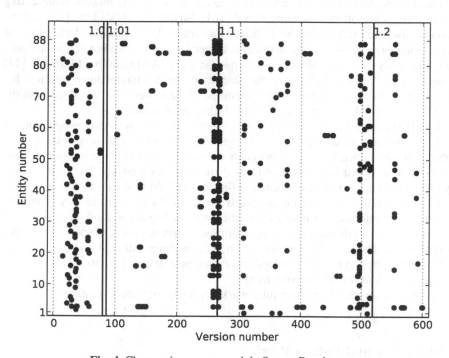

Fig. 4. Changes in process module *System Development*

Figure 4 shows the changes happening to single entities in one particular module, *System Development*, (number 10 in the previous two figures). The X-axis corresponds to the version number, whereas the Y-Axis shows the entity number (entities were numbered arbitrarily). A dot is present where a version changes a particular entity.

The first observation is that this figure presents a pattern similar to the one in Figure 2, with changes concentrating around the releases. Also, shortly before the releases, there are versions affecting many entities at a time. This corroborates a similar observation made in the previous section.

An interesting point is that several instances of changes happening in sequence to a particular entity can be seen on the graph. Although the change logs show that this may happen for a variety of reasons, it would be interesting to analyze whether it has a statistical significance, that is, when an entity was changed, there is a higher probability that it will be changed in the near future. Also, it would be interesting to determine which types of changes are more likely to cause such follow-up changes. Knowing this would make it possible to better handle similar changes in the future.

5 Related Work

Several other research efforts are concerned, in one way or another, with comparing model variants syntactically, and providing an adequate representation for the resulting differences. Most of them, however, concentrate on UML models representing diverse aspects of software systems. Coral [10], SiDiff [11], UMLDiff [12] and the approach discussed in [13] deal with the comparison of UML models. Although their basic comparison algorithms are applicable to our work, they are not concerned with providing analysis or visualization for specific uses. Additionally, FUJABA [14] manages model versions by logging the changes made to a model during editing, but is not able to compare arbitrary model versions. Models must also be edited with the FUJABA tool in order to obtain any useful change information.

Mens [15] presents an extensive survey of approaches for software merging, many of which involve comparison of program versions. The surveyed works mainly concentrate on automatically merging program variants without introducing inconsistencies, but not, as in our case, on identifying differences for analysis. The Delta Ontology [16] provides a set of basic formal definitions related to the comparison of RDF graphs. SemVersion [17] and the approach discussed by [18] are two systems currently under development that allow for efficiently storing a potentially large number of versions of an RDF model by using a compact representation of the raw changes between them. These works concentrate on space-efficient storage and transmission of change sets, but do not go into depth regarding how to use them to support higher-level tasks (such as process improvement).

We are not aware of any previous work on analyzing the evolution of process descriptions.

6 Summary and Future Work

Software process descriptions are intended to be faithful representations of the actual processes used to develop and maintain software systems. This fact implies a twofold challenge for process engineers: On the one hand, descriptions must be continuously improved in order to make them closer to the actual process and to make them more accessible to their users. On the other hand, as processes are improved and expanded to deal with new development challenges, descriptions must be changed accordingly. We have used novel tools and techniques to gain some insight into the evolution of a large, practical process description. We expect to use the results of the initial observations, such as those presented here, for formulating specific hypotheses to guide our future research.

A number of research directions seem promising. Currently, we are in the process of analyzing the results of the connection of the V-Modell's change history with two sources of information related to the rationale of the changes: the human edited version log and the issue tracking system [7]. We expect this to give us more insight into the dynamics of the change process: what causes changes in the first place and how the various motivations for change affect process descriptions at different points in their evolution. In particular, this may help us identify areas of the process that may be continuously causing problems, so that future improvement efforts can concentrate on them.

A final, more general question is related to process adoption. The introduction of good practices to an organization's software process involves complex learning and an increase in the necessary level of discipline. For this reason, finding an appropriate strategy for introducing good practices over time in a non-disruptive, coherent way can be very difficult. We consider that studying process evolution may teach us how to effectively introduce good practices into new organizations or into groups within an organization.

Acknowledgments. We would like to thank Rubby Casallas from Los Andes University, Bogotá, Colombia, for her valuable comments on a draft of this article. We would also like to thank Sonnhild Namingha from Fraunhofer IESE for proofreading this paper. This work was supported in part by the German Federal Ministry of Education and Research (V-Bench Project, No. 01I SE 11 A).

References

1. Osterweil, L.: Software processes are software too. In: Proceedings of the 9th International Conference on Software Engineering, IEEE Computer Society, Los Alamitos (1987)
2. V-Modell® XT (last checked 2007-12-20), Available from http://www.v-modell.iabg.de/
3. Royce, W.W.: Managing the development of large software systems: concepts and techniques. In: Proceedings of the 9th International Conference on Software Engineering, IEEE Computer Society, Los Alamitos (1987)
4. Soto, M., Münch, J.: Focused Identification of Process Model Changes. In: Wang, Q., Pfahl, D., Raffo, D.M. (eds.) ICSP 2007. LNCS, vol. 4470, Springer, Heidelberg (2007)
5. Manola, F., Miller, E. (eds.): RDF Primer. W3C Recommendation (2004) (last checked 2007-12-20), available from http://www.w3.org/TR/rdf-primer/
6. Prud'hommeaux, E., Seaborne, A. (eds.): SPARQL Query Language for RDF. W3C Work-ing Draft (2006) (last checked 2006-10-22), available from http://www.w3.org/TR/rdf-sparql-query/
7. Ocampo, A., Soto, M.: Connecting the Rationale for Changes to the Evolution of a Process. In: Münch, J., Abrahamsson, P. (eds.) PROFES 2007. LNCS, vol. 4589, Springer, Heidelberg (2007)
8. Lehmann, M.M.: On Understanding Laws, Evolution, and Conservation in the Large-Program Life Cycle. The Journal of Systems and Software 1(3), 213–231 (1980)
9. Endres, A., Rombach, D.: A Handbook of Software and Systems Engineering. Pearson, London (2003)
10. Alanen, M., Porres, I.: Difference and Union of Models. In: Stevens, P., Whittle, J., Booch, G. (eds.) UML 2003. LNCS, vol. 2863, pp. 2–17. Springer, Heidelberg (2003)
11. Kelter, U., Wehren, J., Niere, J.: A Generic Difference Algorithm for UML Models. In: German Software Engineering Conference 2005 (SE 2005) (2005)

12. Xing, Z., Stroulia, E.: UMLDiff: an algorithm for object-oriented design differencing. In: Proceedings of the 20th IEEE/ACM International Conference on Automated Software Engineering, Long Beach, CA, USA (2005)
13. Lin, Y., Zhang, J., Gray, J.: Model Comparison: A Key Challenge for Transformation Testing and Version Control in Model Driven Software Development. In: OOPSLA Workshop on Best Practices for Model-Driven Software Development, Vancouver (2004)
14. The Fujaba Manual (last checked 2007-09-06), available from `http://wwwcs.uni-paderborn.de/cs/fujaba/`
15. Mens, T.: A State-of-the-Art Survey on Software Merging. IEEE Transactions on Software Engineering 28(5) (2002)
16. Berners-Lee, T., Connolly, D.: Delta: An Ontology for the Distribution of Differences Between RDF Graphs. MIT Computer Science and Artificial Intelligence Laboratory (CSAIL) (last checked 2006-03-30), Online publication
    `http://www.w3.org/DesignIssues/Diff`
17. Völkel, M., Enguix, C.F., Ryszard-Kruk, S., Zhdanova, A.V., Stevens, R., Sure, Y.: SemVersion - Versioning RDF and Ontologies. Technical Report, University of Karlsruhe (2005)
18. Kiryakov, A., Ognyanov, D.: Tracking Changes in RDF(S) Repositories. In: Proceedings of the Workshop on Knowledge Transformation for the Semantic Web, KTSW 2002, Lyon, France (2002)

Simulating Worst Case Scenarios and Analyzing Their Combined Effect in Operational Release Planning

Ahmed Al-Emran[1], Puneet Kapur[2], Dietmar Pfahl[1,3,4], and Guenther Ruhe[1]

[1] University of Calgary
{aalemran, dpfahl, ruhe}@ucalgary.ca
[2] Chartwell Technology Inc.
pkapur@chartwelltechnology.com
[3] Simula Research Laboratory
dietmarp@simula.no
[4] University of Oslo, Department of Informatics
dietmarp@ifi.uio.no

Abstract. Operational release planning (ORP) is concerned with assigning human resources to development tasks in software projects such that a defined set of product features can be completed under given constraints. In this paper, we present a simulation-based approach to study the impact of uncertainty. Uncertainty parameters considered in this paper are related to the features themselves (functionality, effort) and to developers (availability and productivity). The effect of variation of these four parameters (two static and two dynamic) on make-span is studied in isolation and in combination. This is done for three levels of (stochastic) pessimism ("bad", "worse", and "worst"). In addition to that, a comparison is done with a deterministic worst case scenario. To illustrate the applicability of the method and usefulness of results, we have conducted an explorative case study at Chartwell Technology Inc.

Keywords: Release planning, resource allocation, uncertainty, discrete-event simulation.

1 Introduction and Motivation

Software release planning is performed at both strategic and operational levels. At the strategic level, managers deal with prioritizing and assigning features to successive releases so that both technical and resource constraints are met with maximized customer satisfaction. We consider features to be "a logical unit of behavior that is specified by a set of functional and quality requirements" [1]. Once strategic planning is done (i.e., which features will be implemented in which releases), operational release planning (ORP) takes place, and focuses on the development on one particular release. It deals with the assignment of developers to necessary tasks that needed to be carried out in order to realize each of the selected features for that particular release.

"Uncertainty is inherent and inevitable in software development processes and products" [2] and may arise from inaccurate or incomplete information, from linguistic imprecision and from disagreement between information sources. Uncertainty can

Q. Wang, D. Pfahl, and D.M. Raffo (Eds.): ICSP 2008, LNCS 5007, pp. 269–281, 2008.
© Springer-Verlag Berlin Heidelberg 2008

be assumed in both informal knowledge (uncertainty due to lack of understanding and/or incomplete information) and in formalized knowledge (uncertainty due to imprecise information).

The focus of this paper is to study the impact of uncertainty due to imprecise information related to features and their effort as well as related to developers, their availability and their productivity. More precisely, we study the following factors:

1. The effort required to accomplish different tasks in order to realize a defined set of features in the release. This parameter will be referred as "Effort" in the later sections.
2. Additional features may need to be included in a release in order to accommodate change requests from customers. This parameter will be referred as "Feature" in the later sections.
3. Each developer has different skill levels for different types of tasks. Depending on the skill level of the assigned developer, the duration of a task varies, which impacts the release make-span. This parameter will be referred to as "Productivity" in later sections.
4. Availability of developers may be restricted due to illness or reassignment and may cause a delayed delivery of products to customers. This parameter will be referred to as "Developer" in later sections.

"Effort" and "Productivity" parameters are considered to be static since the variation of these two parameters are done at beginning of each simulation runs but kept unchanged across each time step. On the other hand, "Feature" and "Developer" parameters are dynamic since their occurrence and time of occurrences are stochastic.

The impact of these parameter variations on release make-span are studied both in isolation and in combination and at three levels of pessimism: "bad", "worse", and "worst". Three research questions are formulated and evaluated through an explorative case study conducted at Chartwell Technology Inc. The overall approach is based on a simulation-based risk analysis method which is adapted from the framework ProSim/RA [3] and implemented via the simulation model DynaReP [4].

The structure of the paper is as follows. Section 2 describes related research on operational release planning. Section 3 formalizes the ORP problem and introduces the research questions investigated. Section 4 describes the solution approach and its necessary instantiation for the case study environment. Section 5 describes the conducted case study, its results and relation to the research questions introduced. Section 6 discusses threats to validity. Finally, Section 7 presents conclusions and suggestions for follow-up research.

2 Related Work

In the context of project scheduling, Chang et al. proposed the application of genetic algorithms (GA) for software project management [5]. It is now well known that there are strong differences in the skills and productivity of software developers [6] which was not considered in the proposed method of Chang *et al.* for scheduling minimization. More recently, Duggan *et al.* proposed a GA-based task allocation optimizer [7]. However, the proposed approach fails to work on fine-grained level where each of the work packages (e.g., features) can be further divided in several overlapping smaller work units (e.g., tasks).

In the context of release planning, the method: EVOLVE* can perform strategic release planning [8] whereas OPTIMIZE$_{RASORP}$ provides solution for both strategic and operational release planning simultaneously [9]. However, the impact of uncertainty has not been investigated. Optimized staffing for product releases in deterministic way has been conducted by Kapur et al [10].

From the context of simulation, Kellner et al. proposed several fundamental directions for applying process simulation in software engineering [11]. All of these directions are in some way approaching the inherent uncertainty of software processes and related data. Control and operations management is one of them. Padberg pointed out that software engineering currently offers little help to software project managers on how to develop good schedules for their projects [12]. He proposed a stochastic Markov decision model for software projects in order to compute optimal scheduling strategies for allocating developer teams to software components considering completion time and rework uncertainties. However, the author has mentioned that although he succeeded in computing an exact optimal policy for a given small sample project, it is unlikely that realistic project with dozens of components can be exactly optimized with the proposed approach [13].

3 The Operational Release Planning Problem – Problem Statement and Three Related Research Questions

3.1 Problem Statement

We assume a set F of features f(1), …, f(N) will be developed in the next release. In ORP, the realization of each feature requires a sequence of individual tasks. For our purposes, the vector T consists of S different types of tasks t(1),…,t(S). Task types correspond to the fundamental technical, managerial or support contributions necessary to develop software in general. Typical task types are design, implementation and testing. Note that certain dependency relationships between task types can apply, e.g., testing cannot be started before some or all of the implementation has been finished. The possible dependency relationships are represented by a set called DEP.

The set of all possible feature development tasks is denoted as TASK and its elements are actually executable work packages or simply "tasks" denoted as task(i,j), with i = 1, …,N, and j = 1,…,S. Human resources (e.g., different types of developers, analysts, external collaborators) are intended to perform the different tasks needed to create the features. Our resource allocation process addresses the assignment of the individual human resources to tasks. Each developer is working on just one task at a time. An additional assumption is that for each task only one developer is allowed to work on it. In the case that different developers are allowed to work on the task, the original task would need to be further decomposed.

In order to differentiate among skills of developers, we introduce an average skill level with a normalized productivity factor of 1.0 for each type of task. This allows us to consider more or less skilled developers having a higher or lower productivity factor than 1, respectively. We assume that the project manager can judge the different degrees of productivity of the developers.

We consider a pool D of developers denoted by d(1),..., d(M). Each developer can perform one or more types of development activities with a specific productivity. The productivity factor p(k, j) of a developer d(k) for performing a task of predefined type t(j) indicates if the developer is able to perform the task at all (p(k, j) ≠ 0), and if 'yes', how productive he/she is performing that task (on average). We note that the assignment of a skill level for the different developers in dependence of a whole class of tasks is a simplification of reality as there might be further differentiation even within different areas of e.g. testing. While in principle the granularity of the definition of a task is flexible, we have to keep the model reasonable in size and consequently do not consider this advanced aspect.

Each task can be associated with an effort eff(i,j), where i corresponds to feature f(i) and j corresponds to task type t(j). Effort eff(i,j) then denotes the estimated effort needed to fulfill a task. Note that the duration needed to perform the tasks depends not only on the workload (i.e., effort), but also on the productivity of the developer assigned to this task. ST and ET are sets of starting times and end times of all the tasks, respectively.

Solving the ORP problem means finding an assignment x(i,j,k) of developers d(k) ∈ D to tasks task(i,j) ∈ TASK such that the overall release make-span is minimized. Introducing the space X for all vectors x fulfilling all resource and technological constraints, the problem becomes:

Min {Max {ET(task(i,j)): i = 1,...,N, j = 1,...,S}, x ∈ X}

3.2   Research Questions Studying the Impact of Uncertainty

Our impact analysis is focused on investigation of different kinds of worst case behaviors. For each of the four factors ("Effort", "Feature", "Productivity", and "Developer"), we have defined four levels of pessimism (bad, worse, worst, extreme). We have formulated the following three research questions (RQ) that also will be addressed by our proposed method (Section 4). They will also be investigated in the case study (Section 5):

- RQ1: Considering the impact of each factor in isolation: Is there some variation between factors in the degree of impact?
- RQ2: Considering the impact of the factors in conjunction: What is the tendency of impact for combined occurrence of factors?
- RQ3: Considering the four stages of pessimism for both the factors in isolation and in conjunction: How is the tendency of impact on make-span?

4   The Proposed Approach

4.1   The Simulation Model and Integrated Heuristic

The simulation model used to perform the case study is an enhanced version of DynaReP (Dynamic Re-Planner) originally introduced in last year's ICSP conference [4]. DynaReP is a discrete-event process simulation model developed using EXTEND™

(http://www.imaginethatinc.com). The simulation model is able to perform operational release planning as well as automatic re-planning of operational releases in respond to some unexpected events (e.g., developer dropout, change in effort, etc.). For this research, DynaReP has been enhanced in a way so that it is now has the ability to accommodate the stochastic nature of the process required by the case study conducted. The description of the ten high level block of DynaReP can be found in [4] and more detailed information can be found in [14].

The heuristic used in DynaReP for assigning developers to tasks essentially consists in matching the next available developer with the highest task-specific productivity to the next waiting task that belongs to an incomplete feature with the largest effort. Note that for some special situations, this naive assignment procedure may result in undesired developer allocations. To avoid such a worst case situation, one threshold variable is defined per task type and the heuristic does not allow developers to be assigned to tasks of a type for which their productivity is not greater than the corresponding threshold. The optimal threshold values for different tasks are computed by the simulation model itself. According to the heuristic, a developer d(k) will be assigned to a task task(i,j) if the following conditions are fulfilled:

- There is work still pending for the task task(i,j), i.e., the respective feature f(i) is incomplete.
- The effort of the feature f(i) given by $\Sigma_{j=1,...,S}$ eff(i,j) for all i= 1,...,N is the maximum efforts among all incomplete features.
- The productivity p(k,j) of a candidate developer d(k) related to a specific task type t(j) is greater than the threshold productivity for t(j).
- The candidate developer with sufficient productivity is currently idle.
- For j ≠ 1, at least the percentage of task(i,j-1) (as defined by DEP) needs to finished and task(i,j) can not be finished before task(i,j-1).

4.2 The Method

In order to perform the analysis of the impact of uncertain problem parameters in the ORP, we adapt a risk analysis procedure called ProSim/RA (Process Simulation based Risk Analysis) [3]. The result is a five step procedure that applies modeling, baselining, simulation, and analysis of ORPs. For a given ORP problem <F, T, TASK, D, E, P, DEP, ST, ET> the steps are:

- STEP 1: Determining the baseline solution.
- STEP 2: Identifying uncertain attributes and defining uncertainty ranges.
- STEP 3: Defining observation variables.
- STEP 4: Conducting MCPS analyses.
- STEP 5: Interpreting simulation results.

STEP 1 – Determining the Baseline Solution

The analysis of the impact of uncertainty is always done in relation to a baseline solution. To determine the baseline solution, we apply the process simulation model DynaReP that uses effort and productivity data supplied by Chartwell Technology Inc.

The generated solution will be referred to as the "Baseline" in later sections (not shown due to space limitation). The make-span of the baseline ORP is 15 weeks.

STEP 2 – Identifying Key Uncertainty Parameters and Defining Their Uncertainty Ranges

Uncertainty in the project data can be related to various parameters of the ORP problem. In our study, we focus on the impact of uncertainty in ORP for parameters "Effort" (E), "Productivity" (P), "Feature" (F), and "Developer" (D) by defining probability distributions for these parameters. In order to provide our industrial partner important information on which type of uncertainty, both in isolation and in combination, affects the ORP and to what extent, we considered three levels of pessimism representing three categories of worst case scenarios – bad, worse, and worst. Each of these levels of pessimism comes with their own probability distribution for the OPR parameters E, P, F, and D. In case of E and P variation, the probability distribution sampling simply represents error in the estimation process. Occurrence of this variation is static in nature since the sampling from provided distribution in done only at the beginning of each simulation run. For feature addition (F) and/or developer dropout (D), it reveals the dynamic natures of the system since the occurrence of the events are stochastic.

Table 1 shows three levels of variation conducted on selected "Effort" and "Productivity" parameters in terms of percentage with respect to their original values. In case of "Feature" and "Developer", the values represent the number of additional features/developer dropout in percentage with respect to total number of features/developers considered in the baseline plan (i.e., 35 features and 15 developers). Each of the first 12 cases shown in Table 1 represents different probability distribution sampling patterns for effort and productivity estimates, as well as number of newly added features or number of developer dropout. Each of these parameter values are varied based on the triangle distributions of the type TRIANG (min, peak, max). The "peak" represents the most probable value whereas "min" and "max" represent the minimum and maximum values, respectively. In case of "Effort" and "Productivity" parameters, the sampled value from TRIANG determines how much variation in percentage need to be made in terms of the original effort/productivity values.

In case of "Feature" and "Developer", the distribution range is always from 0% to 30% but the peak is 0%, 15%, and 30% for bad, worse, and worst levels, respectively. This represents the amount of new features/developer dropout compared to the baseline case. The effort values for the tasks of additional features are again sampled from a probability distribution. These probability distributions are determined considering the input task effort data used to generate baseline solution and finding the best fitted distribution curve.

Cases A-D are deterministic worst cases where only one simulation run is conducted and the corresponding parameters are forced to be sampled from the most extreme end rather than sampling from a defined distribution.

STEP 3 – Defining Observation Variables

The observation variables of ORP are the parameters of interest that are supposed to be affected by the input variations due to the defined probability distribution in Step

2. In our case study the observation variable considered is the release make-span that represents the duration of a release in calendar weeks from the beginning of a release construction to the end of its realization. Due to the variation in problem parameters, the duration of a release may change.

STEP 4 – Conducting MCPS Analyses

In this step the simulations defined in the previous steps are conducted. MCPS (Monte Carlo enhanced Process Simulation) means using Monte Carlo based sampling for problem parameters from the distributions defined in STEP 2 and executing Process Simulation using the sampled values to determine process outcomes. In this study 50 simulation runs are conducted per scenarios at a particular level of pessimism.

STEP 5 – Interpreting Simulation Results

The results from simulation runs conducted in the previous step are analyzed. The analysis usually involves summary and descriptive statistics (mean, standard deviation, minimum and maximum values) expressing corresponding impact.

Table 1. ProSim/RA levels of pessimism and corresponding parameter variation

Cases	Levels of Pessimism	Varied Parameter	Input		
			Min	Peak	Max
1	Bad	Effort	-20%	0%	30%
2		Productivity	-30%	0%	20%
3		Feature	0%	0%	30%
4		Developer	0%	0%	30%
5	Worse	Effort	-10%	0%	40%
6		Productivity	-40%	0%	10%
7		Feature	0%	15%	30%
8		Developer	0%	15%	30%
9	Worst	Effort	0%	0%	50%
10		Productivity	-50%	0%	0%
11		Feature	0%	30%	30%
12		Developer	0%	30%	30%
A	Extreme	Effort	-	50%	-
B		Productivity	-	-50%	-
C		Feature	-	30%	-
D		Developer	-	30%	-

Table 2. Impact on make-span due to variation of parameters

Varied	Pessimism Level			
	Bad	Worse	Worst	Extreme
Effort (E)	10%	12%	23%	47%
Productivity (P)	16%	22%	30%	93%
Feature (F)	21%	28%	49%	153%
Developer (D)	10%	16%	22%	47%
E + P	21%	35%	53%	173%
E + F	24%	40%	47%	253%
E + D	16%	31%	49%	100%
P + F	31%	44%	58%	340%
P + D	21%	35%	56%	163%
F + D	24%	43%	53%	273%
E + P + F	30%	61%	84%	507%
E + P + D	24%	47%	78%	293%
E + F + D	32%	54%	80%	381%
P + F + D	38%	58%	98%	547%
E + P + F + D	43%	79%	114%	828%

5   Case Study

In order to demonstrate the applicability of the proposed approach and results of the study, we have conducted a case study based on real-world release planning data for ongoing product development at the Chartwell Technology Inc. which is a leading developer and supplier of Internet gaming software systems to the online and mobile gaming industry.

5.1 Case Study Data

The studied ORP problem involves the following problem parameters:

- A total of 35 features to be developed: $F = \{f(1), ..., f(35)\}$.
- Each feature involves 3 task types: $T = \{t(1), ..., t(3)\}$.
- A pool of 15 available developers: $D = \{d(1), ..., d(15)\}$.
- The estimated work volume for each task, and the estimated productivity of each developer per task type are supplied by Chartwell Technology Inc.
- DEP represents additional dependencies beside start-start & end-end dependencies among the tasks of the same features. That means, a task task(i,j) can start if and only if task task(i,j-1) is started and the task task(i,j) will not be finished before task(i,j-1) is completed. No additional dependencies are considered for this study.

5.2 Case Study Results

5.2.1 Overview

The summary of the results for each of the 15 possible scenarios are shown in Table 2 that contains mean impact values (by running 50 simulations using DynaReP per entry except "extreme" scenarios). An x% impact refers to the fact that the make-span is increased by x% on average compared to the baseline case (i.e., 15 weeks) due to variation of parameters (as shown in Table 1) both in isolation and combination for each of the pessimism level.

5.2.2 Research Question 1

The first four rows of Table 2 provide mean impact information for all four factors in isolation. From the information above we can see that there is no significant difference between the factors "Effort" and "Developer". Even for the extreme case when all task efforts are increased by 50% and 30% of the developers are dropped out, the make-span is not increasing more than 50%. On the other hand, "Feature" is the strongest impacting factor that outperforms all other factors at each of the pessimism levels considered. The effect of the factor "Productivity" always lies in between the effect of "Effort"/"Developer" and "Feature" with a high impact on release make-span.

5.2.3 Research Question 2

Figure 1 shows sorted results based on "extreme" impact. We can see that the more uncertainty factors are combined, the stronger gets the impact. With just three data points per scenario, the formal type of the dependency is hard to judge.

In order to examine the research question in more detail, let us consider the impact of the factor "Productivity" as an example and see the difference when it is considered in isolation and in combination to other factors as shown in Figure 2. When considered in isolation, we can see that the curve representing increase in make-span due to increase in pessimism level is flatter than other curves. The other curves i.e., when an additional factor is combined with "Productivity" or with its one of the superset factors (e.g., "Productivity + Feature") are going much steeper. The observation concludes that with the increase in number of factors in combination (or in isolation) the impact value for all four pessimism level increases in a great deal.

5.2.4 Research Question 3

Figure 1 is providing the impact information per types of parameter variation for both in isolation and in combination. With the increase in pessimism level the make-span

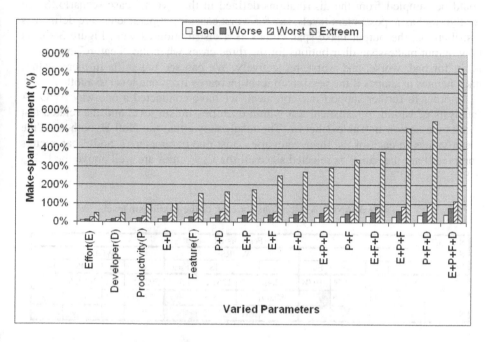

Fig. 1. Make-span increase per variation type

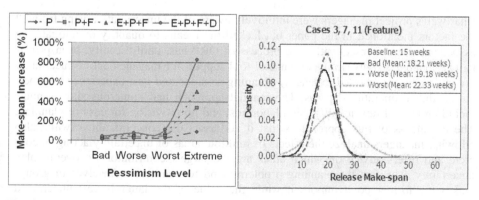

Fig. 2. Make-span trend relative to baseline for different types of combinations

Fig. 3. Distributions fitted[1] to histograms for "Feature" variation in all pessimism levels

---

[1] The fitted curves were generated by Minitab® Statistical Software (www.minitab.com)

is increasing as well. For some factors the increments are not significant (e.g., "Effort") and for some other factor the changes happen drastically (e.g., combination of all factors, and for "Feature" as an individual impacting factor). The reason for having a very sharp increase from "worst" to "extreme" is a switch from stochastic case to deterministic case. The "extreme" case is actually a special deterministic case of "worst" case where all parameter values are set to the highest possible value that could be sampled from the distributions defined in the "worst" case scenario. Since for the stochastic pessimism levels, say for worst case, input parameters are defined as distributions, the output make-span comes as a distribution as well. Figure 3 shows how output make-span distributions for the three cases when the "Feature" parameter is set for bad, worse, and worst, respectively. We can see the shifts in mean values and changes in shapes if the pessimism level increases from one level to another.

In order to further support our argument, we have conducted a one-way ANOVA (analysis of variance) statistical test within each pessimism level and the related test results are shown in Table 3 below. The result shows that the Null Hypothesis: "the mean values in each of the three categories (just one parameter, 2, and 3 parameters combined) are the same" is rejected since all the F_{stat} values are well above the $F_{critical}$ = $F_{2, 11, 0.05}$ = 3.98.

Table 3. ANOVA test results for each of the pessimism level

Sum of Squares (SS)	Pessimism Level											
	BAD				WORSE				WORST			
	SS	df	MS	Fstat	SS	df	MS	Fstat	SS	df	MS	Fstat
SS$_{among}$	561.27	2	280.64	10.04	2522.43	2	1261.21	35.66	5929.52	2	2964.76	40.80
SS$_{within}$	307.58	11	27.96		389.00	11	35.36		799.33	11	72.67	
SS$_{total}$	868.86	13			2911.43	13			6728.86	13		

5.3 Relevance of Results

Chartwell's project managers were intuitively aware of the uncertainty arising from all the factors mentioned in the paper but lacked the means to quantify or mitigate the associated risks. Consequently, the process of ORP has, until recently, been principally a manual activity. In the absence of tool support for management of uncertainty project managers resorted to lengthy planning sessions and past experience to generate candidate operational plans. The manual approach had numerous shortcomings including lack of repeatability, high labor cost and no provision for easy re-planning. The usefulness of this approach is that it addresses the concerns above while also allowing managers analyze the effects of multiple areas of uncertainty acting in concrete and offers advice on which areas are the largest contributors to overall plan uncertainty. The fact the planning problems tend to manifest themselves in groups makes the former point important while the value of the latter is best understood through the following example.

Project Alpha conducted under conditions similar to Case 1 and Case 2 ("Bad Effort" and "Bad Productivity" of Table 1) was under serious risk of schedule slippage. In response, considerable effort was invested in improving the effort estimates with negligible results. Despite the improved effort estimates the project remained behind schedule and exceeded its initial deadline. Traditional software engineering encourages the view that effort uncertainty is the primary influence on make-span and should be paramount in ORP. However Chartwell's experience on Project Alpha, and other projects, shows that increasing the accuracy of effort estimates offers marginal improvements to schedule adherence. Reducing the uncertainty in other areas of the operational plan can provide far greater benefit. This realization is borne out in Chartwell's recent success with Project Beta which was faced with conditions similar to Case 5 and Case 6. This time eschewed improving effort estimates in favor of measures to increase developer productivity (e.g. increased training, co-located teams, etc). Though the level of ORP uncertainty was greater on Project Beta (i.e. Bad vs. Worse) the improvements in developer productivity enabled Project Beta to be delivered on schedule.

Note that in case of both projects Alpha and Beta, the feature set was predetermined by existing commitments to customers and contractual obligations and there was no change in the respective developer pool. Thus, it was not possible to observe the effect of "Feature" and "Developer" uncertainty in these projects. These results have provided valuable insight into the subject matter and it has certainly affected other planning efforts and changed how Chartwell conducts ORP.

6 Threats to Validity

From running a series of coordinated simulation scenarios we have gained additional insight into the nature of worst cases in the context of operational release planning. This question has been confirmed of practical relevance by our case study. In order to better judge the meaningfulness and applicability of the results, we have to carefully check their validity status.

Internal validity is asking for the treatment-outcome construct. There is no restriction here, as for all research questions, we have studied the impact of different types of uncertainty on the overall release duration. The conclusions drawn for all of the 15 different scenarios are based on a set of 50 randomly generated test examples in each case. That means that the treatment-outcome relationship is statistically significant for all the research questions raised.

All the determined solutions for all the worst case scenarios to the ORP problem were obtained from running process simulation with some embedded heuristic for assigning developers to the different tasks. The applied heuristic has been shown to work sufficiently good in general. However, as is the case for heuristics in general, we cannot precisely evaluate the quality of the solution for an individual scenario. This might also impact the comparability between the different scenarios. However, having 50 simulation runs all the time is assumed to be sufficient to overcome the inherent uncertainties with heuristics.

The nature of worst cases was described by triangular distributions for all the stochastic variables. While this is a frequently used assumption, it is not the only one possible. We have applied the equal distribution for one of the fifteen scenarios, and the results have been even more critical than in the case of the triangular function.

Another threat to validity is the underlying model assumptions. Our model is an abstraction from all the details of real-world software release planning where productivity might vary over time and, in addition, might vary also in dependence of not only the task, but also the specific feature. Tasks are typically more differentiated, and the dependencies between tasks are often more dynamic. Despite of all these abstractions, we think that the stated tendencies of the worst-case analysis are remaining the same (if not getting stronger because of the tighter constraints in more detailed models).

Finally, as often the case in simulation, the emphasis of the results should be on the trends, not the detailed numbers. In that sense, we think the presented results based on scenarios derived from a real-world case study are relevant and indicate some fundamental insight not known as such before. However, more comprehensive empirical analysis with real-world data is necessary to improve the level of our understanding and to demonstrate the scalability of results.

While stressing the limitations of the applicability of the results, we also want to emphasize that the overall methodology is applicable more broadly in the context of simulation-based analysis. It is not restricted to discrete event simulation, nor to the operational release planning ORP. The only difference would be the adjustment of the simulation model and the inherent algorithms (heuristics).

7 Summary and Conclusions

Operational software release planning including the assignment of resources to perform tasks necessary to implement the features is of significant practical importance for planning and performing incremental software development. Staffing for product releases is assumed to take about one third of the time of a product or project manager [10]. With all the inherent uncertainties, it is important to pro-actively evaluate the possible impact of worst case scenarios, especially in case of the combined occurrence as suggested by Murphy's Law "Whatever can go wrong will go wrong, and at the worst possible time, in the worst possible way".

We have studied three research questions in this context. From a technical perspective, the importance of our results is based on the following types of analysis of simulation runs: (i) Comparison of the impact of four classes of individual uncertainty factors (both static and dynamic in their influence); (ii) Analysis of the different kinds of combined impact of uncertainties; (iii) Consideration of different levels of negative impact of uncertainty factors; and (iv) comparison between stochastic and deterministic uncertainty.

The results of the simulation-based planning will be the more meaningful the more qualified the data are. Proper design and analysis of measurement data will qualify productivity data (productivity measurement is a research topic of its own) as well as effort estimation. Knowing more about the worst case does not mean being overly pessimistic. Instead, it means to initiate preventive actions already in advance. The expected practical benefit of the simulation method is early risk detection and development of mitigation strategies. These benefits have been confirmed by our industrial case study conducted at Chartwell Technologies.

Future research will be devoted to combine the strengths of the simulation approach(es) with the accuracy and computational power of advanced optimization methods. The method can and will be extended to other criteria than make-span. Based on more comfortable computer and decision support, we foresee more practical applications of the approach allowing to further evaluation of the validity of the stated results.

Acknowledgement

Part of the work presented was financially supported by the Informatics Circle of Research Excellence (iCORE) of Alberta in Canada, and the Natural Sciences and Engineering Research Council (NSERC) of Canada under Discovery Grant no. 327665-06 as well as Discovery Grant no. 250343-07. Chartwell's Jenny Ye and the late Andrew Smith provided valuable contributions for the acquisition of the simulation data and parts of the write-up for section 5. Thanks to Jim McElroy, Kornelia Streb, and Sudipta Sharkar for their efforts and comments on the paper.

References

1. Gurp, J., Bosch, J., Svahnberg, M.: Managing Variability in Software Product Lines. In: Proceedings of LAC 2000, Amsterdam (2000)
2. Ziv, H., Richardson, D.J. Klösch, R.: The Uncertainty Principle in Software Engineering., Technical Report UCI-TR-96-33, University of California, Irvine (1996)
3. Pfahl, D.: ProSim/RA – Software Process Simulation in Support of Risk Assessment. In: Biffl, S., Aurum, A., Boehm, B., Erdogmus, H., Grünbacher, P. (eds.) Value-based Software Engineering, pp. 263–286. Springer, Berlin (2005)
4. Al-Emran, A., Pfahl, D., Ruhe, G.: DynaReP: A Discrete Event Simulation Model for Re-Planning of Software Releases. In: Wang, Q., Pfahl, D., Raffo, D.M. (eds.) ICSP 2007. LNCS, vol. 4470, pp. 246–258. Springer, Heidelberg (2007)
5. Chang, C., Christensen, M., Zhang, T.: Genetic Algorithms for Project Management. Annals of Software Engineering 11, 107–139 (2001)
6. Acuña, S., Juristo, N., Moreno, A.M.: Emphasizing Human Capabilities in Software Development. IEEE Software 23(2), 94–101 (2006)
7. Duggan, J., Byrne, J., Lyons, G.J.: A Task Allocation Optimizer for Software Construction. IEEE Software 21(3), 76–82 (2004)
8. Ruhe, G., Ngo-The, A.: Hybrid Intelligence in Software Release Planning. International Journal of Hybrid Intelligent Systems 1(2), 99–110 (2004)
9. Ngo-The, A., Ruhe, G.: Optimized Resource Allocation for Software Release Planning. IEEE Transactions Software Engineering (accepted, 2008)
10. Kapur, P., Ngo-The, A., Ruhe, G., Smith, A.: Optimized Staffing for Product Releases - Focused Search and its Application at Chartwell Technology. Software Maintenance and Evolution (Special Issue on Search-based Software Engineering) (submitted)
11. Kellner, M.I., Madachy, R.J., Raffo, D.M.: Software Process Simulation Modeling: Why? What? How? Journal of Systems and Software 46, 91–105 (1999)
12. Padberg, F.: Scheduling software projects to minimize the development time and cost with a given staff. In: 8th Asia-Pasific Software Engineering Conference, pp. 187–194 (2001)
13. Padberg, F.: Computing optimal scheduling policies for software projects. In: 11th Asia-Pasific Software Engineering Conference, pp. 300–308 (2004)
14. Al-Emran, A.: Dynamic Re-Planning of Software Releases. Master's Thesis, University of Calgary (2006)

Using Process Simulation to Assess the Test Design Effort Reduction of a Model-Based Testing Approach

Eduardo Aranha and Paulo Borba

Informatics Center of the Federal University of Pernambuco,
PO Box 7851, Recife, PE, Brazil
{ehsa, phmb}@cin.ufpe.br

Abstract. Several researches are being performed to address current software development problems in industry. However, quantifying the benefits of using these solutions in the practice is also a challenge. Usually, pilot studies are run to get evidences about these benefits. Nevertheless, it may be difficult to run these studies due to the required changes in the development process and the lack of available resources. In this work, we address the problem of assessing the test design effort reduction provided by TaRGeT, a tool that supports a Model-Based Testing (MBT) approach. We used process simulation to provide evidence of this effort reduction in a multi-site industry. For that, we modeled, simulated and compared the use of the current and the model-based test design processes. We identified interesting advantages of using process simulation, such as its reduced costs and the possibility to analyze multiple scenarios. We also show some drawbacks of this approach, such as the difficult to create models close to the reality and the lack of processes simulation and comparison support.

Keywords: process simulation, test design effort, model-based testing, process improvement assessment, technology adoption.

1 Introduction

In industry, we usually need empirical evidence of the benefits of a given solution in order to convince people to use it. For instance, Model-Based Testing (MBT) is a testing approach in which test cases are automatically generated from software specifications written in a more formal notation or structure that can be processed by a tool. In this way, MBT can significantly improve test coverage and reduce test design effort [7] [9]. However, although these improvements are expected to occur, they need to be quantified to verify if these benefits justify the effort to change the current process to adopt MBT.

In general, pilot studies are run to evaluate these solutions and to get evidences about their benefits. Nevertheless, pilot studies are usually simples and they are not representative when considering all different environments of a global software development. Also, even pilot studies are difficult to run, since they usually require changes in the development process and the availability of additional resources.

An alternative way to evaluate new solutions and to support their adoption is the use of process simulation [3]. With this technique, we can model processes as currently

Q. Wang, D. Pfahl, and D.M. Raffo (Eds.): ICSP 2008, LNCS 5007, pp. 282–293, 2008.
© Springer-Verlag Berlin Heidelberg 2008

implemented and as planned for future implementation. Then, we run these models to get useful insights, predictions and empirical evidences for questions related to the benefits and drawbacks of each modeled process. Despite of the reduced costs of using process simulation instead of pilot studies, we also can address the uncertainty and the different possible situations existing in a multi-site organization, achieving more representative results through the analysis of these multiple scenarios.

Currently, software testing is being considered so important that organizations can allocate teams exclusively for testing activities [12]. In this context, this work shows the use of process simulation to provide evidences of the effort reduction provided by the use of a new test design process and its supporting tool, called TaRGeT [9].

We run the process simulation considering an industrial setting with multiple developing and testing sites distributed around the world. The simulation model was created using data analysis and expert opinion. Actually, these models can always be refined as data is acquired from new experiments, pilots and case studies. This paper also highlights interesting advantages of using process simulation, such as its reduced costs and the analysis of multiple scenarios. It also presents some drawbacks of this approach, such as the difficulty to create the simulation models.

2 Test Design Processes

In this section, we model two different processes used to design test cases. The first one is the process currently used to create test cases manually in a real company. The second process considers the use of TaRGeT [9], a tool developed to support a Model-Based Testing approach. Both test design processes are presented here using the notation of the process modeling tool used in this work [16].

2.1 Manual Test Design

This process is used to create test cases manually. This probably still the most common process used in industry due to the current lack of appropriate tool support for functional test generation. We modeled this process as shown in Figure 1. There are two types of roles in this process, the test designers and the reviewers.

The first activity of the test designers is the requirements analysis. Basically, the test designers read the requirements and any other source of information that helps to describe the behavior of the application to be tested. The output of this activity is a skeleton of the application behavior, which summarizes how to navigate in the application, what are the alternative flows in case of errors, etc.

With the skeleton of the application behavior, the test designer is able to start the next activity, which goal is to write the test cases. These specifications are commonly written in natural language and they usually describe the test precondition, procedure (list of test steps with inputs and expected outputs) and post-condition [13]. The output of this activity is the set of specified tests (test suite).

Once the test cases are written, they need to be inspected in order to ensure their correctness, the conformity with writing standards and the quality of the text. This activity is detailed in Figure 2. First, two or more reviewers are responsible to read the test specifications and take notes about any identified problem. This activity is called inspection preparation.

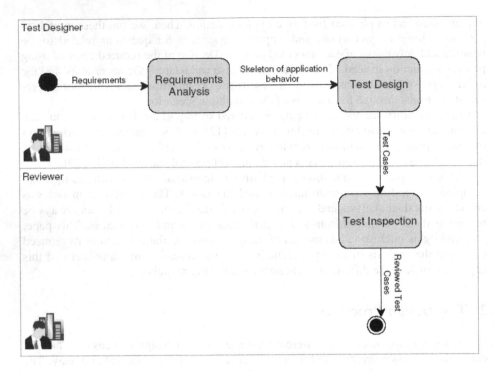

Fig. 1. Test design process for creating test cases manually

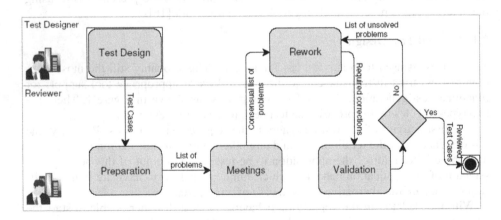

Fig. 2. Details of the test inspection activity

After that, the identified problems are discussed in one or more meetings. The goal of these meetings is to confirm all the identified problems. The test designers are then responsible to rework the test specifications in order to correct all reported problems. Finally, the reworked test cases are validated by one of the reviewers to confirm that the problems were really solved.

2.2 Automated Test Design

Model-Based Testing (MBT) is a technique used to generate test cases from the application requirements. Using this approach, test designers concentrate their efforts in modeling the application behavior using a specific notation instead of in the writing of

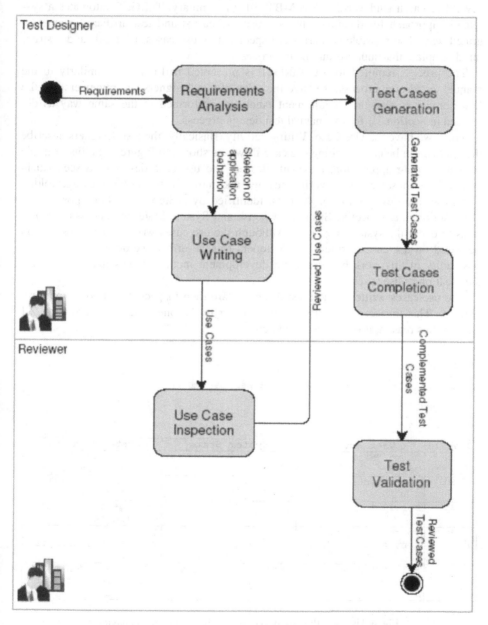

Fig. 3. Test design process for generating test cases automatically

the test specifications. In general, the notation to be used depends on the input required by the MBT supporting tool.

In this work, we consider the use of the Test and Requirements Generation Tool (TaRGeT), which is a MBT supporting tool for automatic test case generation from use case scenarios written in Natural Language (NL) [10]. This tool is a result of several research studies related to MBT [9]. In summary, TaRGeT automates a systematic approach for dealing with use cases scenarios and test artifacts in an integrated way. The possible scenarios are specified as use cases using NL and a structured template that supports automatic processing.

The process required to use TaRGeT is presented in Figure 3. Similarly to the manual test design process, we have the roles of test designers and reviewers and the first activity is also the Requirement Analysis, performed in the same way as described in Section 2.1 for the manual test design process.

Then, we have the Use Case Writing activity. Basically, the test designers describe the application behavior writing use case flows, as shown in Figure 4. In this example of a messaging application, the main flow of the use case describes a scenario in which the user selects his favorite message and moves it to the hot message folder. The flows are described through steps, identified by a Step Id, and composed by a User Action, the respective System Response and System State (the necessary conditions to occur the system response). Although the use cases written by the testers can be based on use cases written by developers to save effort, we do not consider this possibility in this work because some development methodologies may not include the creation of use cases.

The use cases written by the test designers are then inspected by two or more reviewers. This inspection activity is very similar to the one described in Section 2.1 and, for this reason, it is not described here.

Main Flow

Description: The message is moved to Hot Messages folder

From Step: START

To Step: END

Step Id	User Action	System State	System Response
1M	Go to "Message Center"		"Hot Messages" folder is displayed
2M	Go to "Inbox"		All inbox messages are displayed
3M	Scroll to a message		Message is highlighted
4M	Go to "Context Sensitive Menu"		"Move to Hot Messages" option is displayed
5M	Select "Move to Hot Messages" option	Message storage is not full	"Message moved to Hot Messages folder" is displayed

Fig. 4. Use case flow used to describe the application behavior

Based on the reviewed use cases, the test designers use TaRGeT to automatically generate the test cases. Due to some technical limitations, it is not possible to generate all the information required to execute the tests. For this reason, the test designers have to complement the generated test specifications with some additional information, such as some test preconditions or setup information. After that, the information written manually in the test specification must be inspected. We called this last activity by test validation to differentiate from the test inspection activity of the manual test design process.

3   Assessment of Effort Reduction Using Processes Simulation

We want to use process simulation to assess the effort reduction achieved by using the automated test design process instead of using the manual test design process. For that, we created and run simulation models for these test design processes, as described next.

3.1   Simulation Models

For each process, we defined variables that characterize the artifacts used as inputs or outputs of the activities defined in the test design processes. Then, we modeled the effort spent in each activity based on the generated or updated artifacts (activity output). Table 1 lists the artifacts artifact used in the test design processes and describes the variables used to characterize them.

Table 1. Variables used to characterize the artifacts used in the test design processes

Artifact	Variable	Description	Determined by
Requirements	Req	Number of requirements defined in the document.	
Skeleton of application behavior	SkF	Number of control flows identified in the skeleton.	Req
Use cases	UCF	Number of control flows written in the use cases.	SkF
	RwUCF	Number of control flows written in the use cases that required rework after inspection.	UCF
Test cases	MTC	Number of test cases created manually.	SkF
	RwMTC	Number of manually created test cases that required rework after inspection.	MTC
	GTC	Number of test cases generated automatically.	UCF
	CompGTC	Number of generated test cases that required a manual completion.	GTC
	RwGTC	Number of generated test cases that required rework after validation.	CompGTC

In addition, we are considering that all the output artifacts of a process activity can be characterized only by analyzing the input artifacts (see column "Determined by" of Table 1). These relations are modeled as shown by the sample Equations 1 and 2.

$$SkF = \text{round}(\beta_1 * Req) . \tag{1}$$

$$MTC = \text{round}(\beta_2 * SkF) . \tag{2}$$

In Equation 1, the number of requirements (Req) is a variable that has values assigned during the simulation to represent different situations, such as documents with small, medium or large number of requirements. These values are chosen according to a probability distribution, which basically describes the values and probabilities that the random event (e.g., size of the requirements) can take [14]. Then, the number of control flows created in the skeleton of the application behavior (SkF) is determined by Req and β_1, which represents the intrinsic variance and uncertainty of the (linear) relation between SkF and Req. We use the function round to ensure that only integer values are assigned to SkF.

Similarly, we see in Equation 2 that the number of test cases created manually (MTC) is determined by the number of control flows (SkF) and the intrinsic variance and uncertainty (β_2) of this other relation. To easy the reading of this paper, variables having probabilistic distribution (random values assigned during the simulation) appear in italic in the equations and texts.

The probabilistic distributions to use in the simulation model are defined using expert judgment and by the analysis of the available historical data. For instance, we analyzed the relation between the artifacts created in previous projects and then used normal, triangular and other probabilistic distributions that best fitted the data or the expert opinion. Regarding the automated test design approach, the only historical data available were extracted from studies carried out by the TaRGeT development team. This lack of data is a characteristic of new proposed technologies. Since the details of these distributions (types and parameters) are specific for the analyzed industrial setting, we kept the privacy of this information without compromising the contributions of this paper.

As our goal is to assess the effort reduction by using the automated test design process, we need to model the effort required to perform the activities of both manual and automated test design processes. For that, we defined variables and equations related to the effort spent in the activities presented in Section 2.

Basically, we calculate the effort spent in each activity based on their output artifacts. For instance, the effort required to perform the Requirements Analysis activity (RAEffort) is given by multiplying the number of flows in the skeleton of the application behavior (SkF) by the average time required to write each flow ($TSkF$):

$$RAEffort = SkF * TSkF . \tag{3}$$

The variable $TSkF$ and some others used in the next equations represent the time required to generate output artifacts. Probabilistic distributions are assigned to these variables in order to model the uncertainty and variance related to the team productivity for the considered activity of the process.

For calculating the effort spent in the Test Design activity of the manual process (TDEffort), we multiply the number of test cases created manually (MTC) by the average time required to write each test case (*TMTC*) manually:

$$\text{TDEffort} = \text{MTC} * TMTC. \tag{4}$$

The effort spent in the Test Inspection (TIEffort) is the sum of the efforts spent in Preparation (PrepEffort), Meetings (MeetEffort), Rework (RwEffort) and Validation (ValidEffort):

$$\text{TIEffort} = \text{PrepEffort} + \text{MeetEffort} + \text{RwEffort} + \text{ValidEffort}. \tag{5}$$

$$\text{PrepEffort} = \text{MTC} * TPrepTC * Reviewers. \tag{6}$$

$$\text{MeetEffort} = \text{RwMTC} * TMeetTC * Reviewers. \tag{7}$$

$$\text{RwEffort} = \text{RwMTC} * TRwTC. \tag{8}$$

$$\text{ValidEffort} = \text{RwMTC} * TValidTC. \tag{9}$$

Where:
− *TPrepTC* is the average time for reading a test case for the inspection.
− *TMeetTC* is the average time to discuss a test case in a meeting.
− *TRwTC* is the average time to rework a test case.
− *TValidTC* is the average time to verify if the corrections were done.
− *Reviewers* is the number of reviewers attending the inspection.

For the automated test design process, the effort spent in requirement analysis is considered the same as in the manual process. Also, the effort spent in the Use Case Inspection (UCInspEffort) and Test Validation (TVEffort) activities are calculated similarly to the Test Inspection effort for the manual test design process (Equation 5). For modeling the effort of the Test Case Generation activity (*TCGEffort*), we used a probabilistic distribution that represents the effort to use TaRGeT (create a project, import the use cases and generate the tests), which is practically independent of the size of the use cases.

For the Use Case Writing activity, we calculate the spent effort (UCEffort) by multiplying the number of use case flows (UCF) by the average time required to write each one of these flows (*TUCF*):

$$\text{UCEffort} = \text{UCF} * TUCF. \tag{10}$$

For calculating the time spent in the Generated Test Cases Completion (CompGTCEffort), we consider the average time spent to analyze each generated test case (*TAnalyzeGTC*) and the average time spent to complement each test case with missing information (*TCompGTC*).

$$CompGTCEffort = GTC * TAnalyzeGTC + CompGTC * TCompGTC. \qquad (11)$$

Finally, to support the analysis of the effort reduction provided by the automated test design process, we defined equations to calculate the effort spent in each test design process, as well the percentage gain (EffortReduction) of using the automated test design process:

$$ManualProcessEffort = RAEffort + TDEffort + TIEffort. \qquad (12)$$

$$AutomatedProcessEffort = RAEffort + UCEffort + UCInspEffort + TCGEffort \\ + CompGTCEffort + TVEffort. \qquad (13)$$

$$EffortReduction = (ManualProcessEffort - AutomatedProcessEffort) / ManualProcessEffort. \qquad (14)$$

Due to some limitations of the tool used for modeling the process, it did not support the creation of the presented simulation model. Then, we created and run the simulation model in a general purpose simulation tool [15].

3.2 Simulation Results

After running the simulation, we were able to perform several analyses. First, we analyzed the effort reduction by using the automated test design process instead the manual process and the differences of the effort distributions of both processes, as the sample graphs presented in Figure 5, which shows the effort reduction (gain) by using the automated process and the distribution of the effort spent in both process during the simulated situations.

In addition, we analyzed and compare the performance of the test design processes with respect to the effort distribution among their activities. Descriptive statistics and the data generated during the simulation were also a valuable source of information to analyze. Finally, we were able to change the probabilistic distribution of some variables to represent specific situations under investigation, such as during the adoption of the new technology (high productivity with the manual process and low productivity with the automated process).

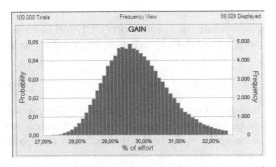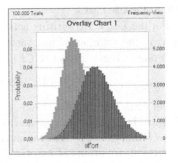

Fig. 5. Sample charts used to analyze the results of the simulation (with illustrative data)

4 Advantages and Drawbacks of This Approach

In this section, we summarize and generalize the advantages and drawbacks of using process simulation to compare two different processes. Regarding the advantages, we verified that:

- The process simulation usually has a low cost than pilot studies.
- Usually, we have historical data about the currently used process and this information can be used to create and validate its simulation model.
- The execution of new empirical studies (pilot projects, case studies, experiments, etc.) can generate data to incrementally calibrate the simulation models. Then, these models can be simulated again at a very low cost to provide more accurate results.
- We can perform the analysis of multiple scenarios, analyzing the application of new processes in specific situations.
- An analysis per process activity can highlight points in the process to improve.

Although all these advantages, some drawbacks of using process simulation to compare processes must be observed:

- Difficulty to create models close to reality. The validity of its results strongly depends on the correct simulation model construction. It may be a challenge to convince managers about the correctness of the model construction.
- New processes have only few data from expert opinion and initial experiments run by the developers of the new process (possibly biased information).
- The relationship between input and output artifacts of the process activities may be non-linear, making more difficult the modeling of these relations.
- The simulation models are valid only for the aspect under investigation, such as effort reduction, and not for others, such as the creation of effective tests.
- Process modeling and simulation tools may be too complex without providing the needed resources.

5 Related Work

In [6], the authors simulated a software development process to analyze different strategies, such as iterative development, pair programming and test automation. They defined parameters to represent the effort to perform the activities in the process (team productivity), the defect introduction rate, the probability of finding bugs, etc. They identified situations were the use of these strategies can provide benefits in terms of effort and bug detection. In our work, we study the automation of the test design process using MBT. The generated tests can then be automated or executed manually.

In [5] and [11], the authors compared different prediction techniques using simulation. Basically, their works simulate data to create datasets with different characteristics. They compared the predictions techniques with these simulated datasets and identified that the best technique can be defined only for particular contexts. In our work, we create a larger number of different situations through simulation to assess the effort spent in two different test design processes.

Mutation testing [8] is a technique to simulate the introduction of software defects in order to evaluate the best set of tests cases able to reveal these defects (kill the mutants). While this paper only considers the effort reduction criteria to assess the test design approaches, Mutant testing can be used to assess these approaches considering the effectiveness of the created tests.

6 Conclusions

In this paper, we presented the use of process simulation to address the problem of assessing the test design effort reduction provided by a Model-Based Testing (MBT) approach. We modeled both manual and automated test design processes. For the automated process, we modeled the process supported by the Test and Requirements Generation Tool (TaRGeT).

We used process simulation to provide evidences of this effort reduction in a multi-site industry. For that, we created a simulation model that characterized the artifacts produced and manipulated during the processes. Then, we modeled the effort spent in each processes activity based on these artifacts. The modeling of each individual process activity make easy the model construction and validation process. All these models were created using expert opinion and data analysis. Actually, these models can be refined as the data is acquired through new experiments, pilots and case studies.

We identified interesting advantages of using process simulation, such as its reduced costs and the achievement of more representative results, since we can simulate several different situations. We also show some drawbacks of this approach, such as the difficult to create models close to the reality and the lack of support of the process simulation tools.

We also believe that similar works can be done to provide evidences about the benefits of solutions for other software development problems. After this study, we believe that process simulation is an interesting alternative to evaluate the impact of using new technologies that require changes in the processes.

Acknowledgments. We would like to thank all anonymous reviewers who have helped us to improve this paper through their valuable comments. Also, the first author is a PhD candidate partially supported by Motorola, grant BCT-0021-1.03/05, through the Motorola Brazil Test Center Research Project. The second author is partially supported by CNPq, grant 306196/2004-2.

References

1. Angelis, L., Stamelos, I.: A Simulation Tool for Efficient Analogy Based Cost Estimation. Empirical Software Engineering 5(1), 35–68 (2000)
2. Ebert, C., De Neve, P.: Surviving Global Software Development. IEEE Software 18(2), 62–69 (2001)
3. Kellner, M.I., Madachy, R.J., Raffo, D.M.: Software process simulation modeling: Why? What? How? Journal of Systems and Software 46(2), 91–105 (1999)

4. Rask, R., Laamanen, P., Lyytinen, K.: Simulation and Comparison of Albrecht's Function Point and Demarco's Function Bang Metrics in a CASE Environment. IEEE Transactions on Software Engineering 19(7), 661–671 (1993)
5. Shepperd, M., Kadoda, G.: Comparing Software Prediction Techniques Using Simulation. IEEE Transactions on Software Engineering 27(11), 1014–1022 (2001)
6. Ur, S., Yom-Tov, E., Wernick, P.: An Open Source Simulation Model of Software Testing, Hardware and Software, Verification and Testing. In: Ur, S., Bin, E., Wolfsthal, Y. (eds.) HVC 2005. LNCS, vol. 3875, pp. 124–137. Springer, Heidelberg (2006)
7. Pretschner, A.: Model-based testing. In: 27th international conference on Software engineering, pp. 722–723. IEEE Press, St. Louis (2005)
8. Fabbri, S.C.P.F., Maldonado, J.C., Masiero, P.C., Delamaro, M.E.: Mutation analysis testing for finite state machines. In: 5th International Symposium on Software Reliability Engineering, pp. 220–229. IEEE Press, Monterey (1994)
9. Nogueira, S., Cartaxo, E., Torres, D., Aranha, E., Marques, R.: Model based test generation: A case study. In: 1st Brazilian Workshop on Systematic and Automated Software Testing, Recife (2007)
10. Schwitter, R.: English as a formal specification language. In: 13th International Workshop on Database and Expert Systems Applications (DEXA 2002), pp. 228–232 (2002)
11. Shepperd, M., Kadoda, G.: Using Simulation to Evaluate Prediction Techniques. In: IEEE METRICS 2001, IEEE Press, Los Alamitos (2001)
12. Broekman, B., Notenboom, E.: Testing Embedded Software. Addison-Wesley, Reading (2002)
13. Jorgensen, P.: Software Testing, A Craftsmans Approach. CRC Press, Boca Raton (2002)
14. Maxwell, K.: Applied Statistics for Software Managers. Prentice Hall, Englewood Cliffs (2002)
15. Crystal Ball, `http://www.crystalball.com`
16. Metastorm Provision, `http://www.metastorm.com`

GENSIM 2.0: A Customizable Process Simulation Model for Software Process Evaluation

Keyvan Khosrovian[1], Dietmar Pfahl[1, 2, 3], and Vahid Garousi[1]

[1] Schulich School of Engineering, University of Calgary, Canada
[2] Simula Research Laboratory, Lysaker, Norway,
[3] Department of Informatics, University of Oslo, Norway
{kkhosrov, dpfahl, vgarousi}@ucalgary.ca

Abstract. Software process analysis and improvement relies heavily on empirical research. Empirical research requires measurement, experimentation, and modeling. Moreover, whatever evidence is gained via empirical research is strongly context dependent. Thus, it is hard to combine results and capitalize upon them in order to improve software development processes in evolving development environments. The process simulation model GENSIM 2.0 addresses these challenges. Compared to existing process simulation models in the literature, the novelty of GENSIM 2.0 is twofold: (1) The model structure is customizable to organization-specific processes. This is achieved by using a limited set of macro-patterns. (2) Model parameters can be easily calibrated to available empirical data and expert knowledge. This is achieved by making the internal model structures explicit and by providing guidance on how to calibrate model parameters. This paper outlines the structure of GENSIM 2.0, shows examples of how to calibrate the simulator to available empirical data, and demonstrates its usefulness through two application scenarios. In those scenarios, GENSIM 2.0 is used to rank feasible combinations of verification and validation (V&V) techniques with regards to their impact on project duration, product quality and resource consumption. Though results confirm the expectation that doing more V&V earlier is generally beneficial to all project performance dimensions, the exact rankings are sensitive to project context.

1 Introduction and Motivation

Empirical research is essential for developing a theory of software development, and, subsequently, for transforming the art of software development into engineering. Engineering disciplines require provision of evidence on the efficiency and effectiveness of tools and techniques in varying application contexts. In the software engineering domain, the number of tools and techniques is constantly growing, and ever more contexts emerge in which a tool or technique might be applied. The application context of a tool or technique is defined, firstly, by organizational aspects such as process organization, resource allocation, staffing profiles, management policies, and, secondly, by the set of all other tools and techniques applied in a development project.

Since most activities in software development are strongly human-based, the actual efficiency and effectiveness of a tool or technique can only be determined through

Q. Wang, D. Pfahl, and D.M. Raffo (Eds.): ICSP 2008, LNCS 5007, pp. 294–306, 2008.
© Springer-Verlag Berlin Heidelberg 2008

real-world experiments. Controlled experiments are a means for assessing local efficiency and effectiveness, e.g., defect detection effectiveness of an inspection or test technique applied to a specific type of artifact, by a typical class of developers. Global efficiency and effectiveness of a tool or technique relates to its impact on the overall development project performance dimensions (duration, quality, effort). Typically, global efficiency and effectiveness are evaluated through case studies.

Controlled experiments and case studies are expensive. Support for making decisions as to which experiments and case studies to perform would be helpful. Currently, these decisions are made relying purely on experience and intuition. This way of decision-making has two major drawbacks. Firstly, numerous mutual influences between entities, involved in a process, make it hard for an expert to estimate to what extent a locally efficient and effective tool or technique positively complements other locally efficient and effective tools or techniques applied in other activities of the chosen development process. Secondly, for the same reasons as mentioned above, it is hard for an expert to estimate how sensitive overall project performance dimensions will react to variations in local efficiency or effectiveness of a single tool or technique. The second point is particularly important if a decision has to be made whether assumed improvements are worthwhile to be empirically investigated within various contexts.

To address the above mentioned challenges, one can provide experts with a software process simulator that generates estimates of the impact of local process changes on overall project performance. For example, if the defect detection effectiveness of a unit test technique A is expected to be 10% better than that of another unit test technique B in a given context, this might yield a simulated overall positive impact of, say, 2% or 20% on end-product quality (plus effects on project duration and effort). If simulations indicate that it has only 2% overall impact or less, it might not be worthwhile to run additional experiments to assess the advantage of technique A over technique B. More complex questions could address the overall effectiveness of varying combinations of different development and V&V techniques. Also, one could ask how much workforce should be allocated to development and V&V activities in order to achieve predefined time, cost and quality goals. One can even go one step further and use process simulators to analyze how better developer skills improve project performance. This, in turn, can be used to assess whether and to what extent investment in training or in hiring better qualified developers would pay off.

Well-known issues of process simulators are related to assessing their validity, and their high development and maintenance costs. This paper offers a solution to the cost-related issue and provides some initial guidance addressing the validity-related issue. A core element of the proposed solution is the simulation framework GENSIM 2.0 (GENeric SIMulator, Version 2.0), which is an enhanced version of an older research prototype (GENSIM [18]).

2 Related Work

The idea of using software process simulators for predicting project performance or evaluating processes is not new. Beginning with pioneers like Abdel-Hamid [1], Bandinelli [4], Gruhn [9], Kellner [10], Scacchi [15], dozens of process simulation models have been developed for various purposes[1]. However, all published models have at least one of the following shortcomings:

- The model is too simplistic to actually capture the full complexity of real-world processes (e.g., GENSIM was used for purely educational purposes [18]).
- The model structure and calibration is not comprehensively reported (e.g., [19]) and thus cannot be independently adapted and used by others.
- The model captures a specific real-world development process with sufficient detail but fails to offer mechanisms to represent complex product and resource models. This has typically been an issue for models using System Dynamics (SD) [7] modeling environments.
- The model structure captures a specific real-world development process (and associated products and resources) in sufficient detail, but is not (easily) adaptable to new application contexts due to lack of design for reusability and lack of guidance for re-calibration (e.g., [17]).

While the third issue can easily be resolved by fully exploiting the modeling constructs offered by commercial process simulation environments such as Extend® [6] and Vensim® [22], the fourth issue has not yet been satisfactorily resolved, neither by researchers proposing proprietary process simulation modeling environments (e.g., Little-Jil [24]) nor by researchers using commercial process simulation environments.

A first attempt to define a set of core structures of process simulation models which could be regarded as a set of basic building blocks of any process simulator was made by Senge in the early 1990s [21]. He identified ten "Systems Archetypes", i.e., generic process structures which embody typical behavior patterns of individuals and organizations. Although these archetypes are certainly a good tool for understanding individual and organizational behavior modes, they are too generic and too qualitative as to be directly applicable for the modeling of software development processes. More recently, following the approach taken by Senge but having software development processes in mind, Madachy suggested a core set of reusable model structures and behavior patterns [14]. This set comprises several very specific micro-patterns (and their implementations) suited for SD process simulation models. Madachy's micro-patterns are well-thought reusable process structures, with very specific purpose and focused scope. They can be interpreted as a bottom-up approach to support reusability of process simulation structure. However, there exist no guidelines that help modelers combine individual micro-patterns to capture more complex, software development specific process structures.

Emerging from suggestions made several years ago [2], the work presented in this paper complements Madachy's micro-patterns by a top-down approach that provides a set of reusable and adaptable macro-patterns of software development processes. The suggested macro-patterns are described in more detail by giving an implementation example of the research prototype GENSIM 2.0. Besides capturing key structural and behavioral aspects of software development processes, GENSIM 2.0 provides a

---

[1] For an overview of software process simulation work done in the past 15 to 20 years, refer to [16]. Currently, a systematic review is being conducted by researchers at National ICT Australia (NICTA) that will offer a more comprehensive overview of work done in the field of software process simulation.

blueprint on how to integrate detailed product and resource models. In GENSIM 2.0, each instance of a process artifact type and resource type, i.e., roles involved in software development, is modeled individually. Since GENSIM 2.0 is the core element of a long-term research program supporting the integration of results from empirical software engineering research conducted worldwide, this paper also presents examples on how to calibrate GENSIM 2.0 to empirical data.

3 The GENSIM 2.0 Model

This section describes the macro-patterns of software development processes, the key parameters associated with these patterns, and their implementation in GENSIM 2.0. Some of the underlying assumptions and heuristics used in the prototype are described. Moreover, examples that illustrate how GENSIM 2.0 can be calibrated to empirical data collected from specific software development processes are presented. All implementation details of GENSIM 2.0 can be found in [11].

3.1 Generic Process Structures (Macro-patterns)

Inspired by the idea of frameworks in software engineering, customizable software process simulation models can be constructed from reusable structures [3, 16, 20] referred to as macro-patterns. An example of a reusable structure representing development (including rework) and verification activities is shown in Fig. 1 on the left-hand side. Associated with activities are input/output products and resources. In addition, each artifact, activity, and resource is characterized by attributes representing states. "Learning" is an example attribute related to resources (e.g., developers), while "maturity" is an example of a state attribute related to artifacts and activities. The right-hand side of Fig. 1 shows state-transitions for development (top) and verification (bottom) maturity. The macro-pattern shown in Fig. 1 is applied to different development phases of a generic development process. Each development/rework/verification sub-process can be complemented by an optional validation (i.e., testing) sub-process.

Fig. 2 shows an example instance of such a generic process (the well-known "V" model) with three levels of refinement, i.e., requirements development and verification (system level), design development and verification (sub-system level), code development and verification (module level), and their validation (test) counterparts. Verification activities could involve, e.g., requirements, design, and code inspections. On each level, one or more artifacts are developed, verified, and validated. In this example process, only development activities are mandatory. Depending on the organizational policies and the type of product under development, verification and validation activities are optional. If defects are detected during verification or validation, rework has to be done (through the development activity in the macro-pattern of Fig. 1). On code level, rework is assumed to be mandatory no matter by which activity defects are found, while rework of design and requirements artifacts due to defects found in other V&V activities than design and requirements verification, respectively, may be optional depending on the organizational or project policies.

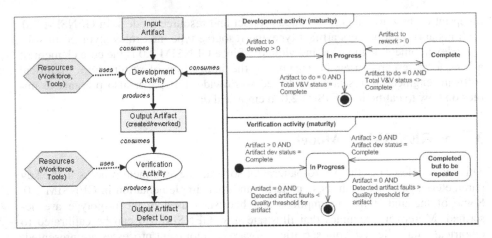

Fig. 1. Macro-pattern for development/verification activity pairs (with state-transition charts)

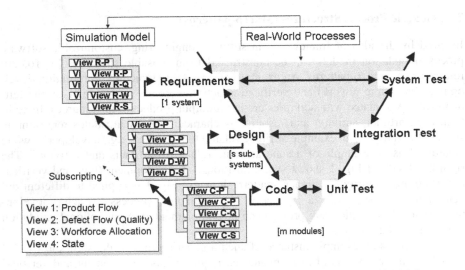

Fig. 2. An example instance of a software development process in GENSIM 2.0

3.2 Model Implementation

GENSIM 2.0 was implemented using the SD simulation modeling tool Vensim, a mature commercial tool widely used by SD modelers. Vensim offers three features in support of reuse and interoperability: views, subscripts, and the capability of working with external DLLs.

In order to capture the main dimensions of project performance (duration, effort and quality) together with different artifact/activity/resource states, the generic process instance shown in Fig. 2 is implemented in four separate views: product-flow (process), defect flow (product quality), workforce allocation (developers, techniques, tools), and project states.

Specific product types are associated with different refinement levels of the development process, i.e., system, subsystem, and module. If a new refinement level is required, e.g., design shall be split into high-level design and low-level design, existing views can easily be reused. The subscripting mechanism provided by Vensim allows for modeling individual work products as product type instances. For example, if one system consists of several sub-systems, and each sub-system of several modules, then each of these products would be identifiable via its subscript value. Vensim's subscripting mechanism is also used to distinguish defect origins and the ISO 9126 quality characteristics that they potentially affect.

Vensim's capability of working with external DLLs was exploited to extract organization-specific heuristics from the SD model and incorporating them into external DLL libraries where they can be changed easily without affecting the model structure. The algorithm that allocates developers to development and V&V activities is an example of such a heuristic. The DLL's main allocation function takes as input headcount and skill levels of the available workforce, workload of all activities, and the minimum skill level required for developers in order to be assigned to different activities. Without going into full detail, the heuristic works as follows. Developers are classified according to the number of different types of activities they are able to conduct. Ability to conduct an activity is given whenever the related skill level of a developer is higher than the minimum required level. First, all developers that are able to work only on one artifact type are assigned to the related activity. Next, those developers that can work on two artifact types are assigned to the related activities proportional to the number of waiting artifacts per type. This procedure is continued until all developers that can be allocated are assigned to activities. The formal definition of the algorithm used by the developer assignment heuristic can be found in [11].

The following list summarizes the most important assumptions underlying the model corresponding to the process instance shown in Fig. 2. These assumptions are explicit and thus can be modified as needed to adapt the model to other organization-specific processes:

- A downstream activity can only begin when working on its input artifact has been completely finished in the upstream activities.
- Working on different modules and subsystems can be done independently.
- The rates at which development/rework and V&V activities are carried out depend on the efficiencies of the chosen techniques, the headcount and average skill level of the assigned development team and the learning status.
- Defect injection rates depend on the headcount and average skill level of the assigned developer team, the development/rework rates and the learning status.
- Defect detection rates depend on the effectiveness of the chosen V&V techniques, the headcount and average skill level of the assigned team and the learning status.
- Learning happens during development/rework and V&V activities.

3.3 Model Parameters

GENSIM 2.0 has a large number of parameters. Parameters can represent model inputs and outputs, or they are used to calibrate the model to expert knowledge and empirical data specific to an organization, process, technique or tool.

Table 1 shows a selected list of 17 (out of 28) parameters related to the macro-pattern code development (including rework) and verification. Corresponding parameters exist for the requirements specification and design related sub-processes.

Input parameters represent project specific information like estimated product sizes and developer skills, as well as project specific policies that define which verification and validation activities should be performed and whether requirements and design documents should be reworked if defects are found in code (by different V&V activities) that actually originate from design or requirements defects.

Calibration parameters represent organization specific information. An example of how model parameters are calibrated is given in Section 3.4.

Output parameters represent values that are calculated by the simulation engine based on the dynamic cause-effect relationships between input and calibration parameters. Which output values are in the focus of interest depends on the simulation goal. Typically, project performance variables such as product quality, project duration, and effort are of interest.

Table 1. A subset of model parameters related to code development and verification

	Parameter Name	Attribute	Type	View
1	Verify code or not	Process	Input	C-P
2	# of modules per subsystem	Product	Input	C-P
3	Code doc quality threshold per size unit	Project	Input	C-Q
4	Required skill level for code dev	Project	Input	C-W
6	Developers' skill level for code dev	People	Input	C-W
8	Maximum code ver. effectiveness	Process	Calibrated	C-P
9	Maximum code ver. rate per person per day	Process	Calibrated	C-P
12	Minimum code fault injection rate per size unit	Product	Calibrated	C-Q
14	Code rework effort for code faults detected in CI	Product	Calibrated	C-Q
16	Code rework effort for code faults detected in IT	Product	Calibrated	C-Q
18	Initial code dev. rate per person per day	People	Calibrated	C-W
19	Initial code ver. rate per person per day	People	Calibrated	C-W
20	Code doc size (actual)	Product	Output	C-P
22	Code development rate (actual)	Process	Output	C-P
24	Code faults undetected	Product	Output	C-Q
26	Code faults corrected	Product	Output	C-Q
28	Code ver. effort (actual)	Process	Output	C-W

#=number, CI=Code Inspection, UT=Unit Test, IT=Integration Test, ST=System Test

3.4 Model Calibration

The possibility to calibrate GENSIM 2.0 is essential for the validity of simulation results. Generally, parameters can be calibrated by using expert judgment or empirical data. Empirical data can either be gathered from organization specific measurement and experimentation or from publications that publish data which is assumed to have been derived from sufficiently similar contexts.

Table 2 shows snapshots of two literature-based calibrations (A and B) of model parameters related to code defect injection, detection, and correction. For the parameters shown, three sources were used: Frost and Campo [8] provide an example of a defect containment matrix from which values for the calibration fault injection rates and verification effectiveness can be derived. Table 2 shows only the code related parameters. Wagner [23] provides much data on typical (average) verification and validation rates, and rework efforts for defects of various document types. According to Wagner, defect rework efforts vary depending on the type of defect detection activity. He observed that defect rework effort increases the later defects are detected. For example, as shown in Table 2 (Calibration A), a code defect detected in system test (ST) requires about 2.4 times as much rework effort than a code defect detected during unit test (UT). Unfortunately, Wagner does not state clearly in which context his numbers are valid. Since there exist other studies (e.g., [5]) which report a much higher distance between rework efforts for code defects found in UT as compared to integration test (IT) and ST, Table 2 shows an alternative calibration. Calibration B applies factors of 2.5 and 13 on correction effort for defects found in UT in order to calculate the rework effort for code defects detected in IT and ST, respectively. Many other calibrations based on data from published sources were made in GENSIM 2.0 but cannot be shown here due to space limitations, but can found in [12].

Table 2. Examples of coding related calibration parameters

Calibration Parameter	Value	
	Calibration A	Calibration B
Minimum code fault injection rate per size unit	14.5 Defect/KLOC [8]	
Maximum code verification effectiveness	0.53 [8]	
Max. code verification rate per person per day	0.6 KLOC/PD [23]	
Code rework effort for code faults detected in CI	0.34 PD/Def. [23]	
Code rework effort for code faults detected in UT	0.43 PD/Def. [23]	
Code rework effort for code faults detected in IT	0.68 PD/Def. [23]	1.08 PD/Def. [5, 23]
Code rework effort for code faults detected in ST	1.05 PD/Def. [23]	5.62 PD/Def. [5, 23]

KLOC = Kilo Lines of Code, PD = Person-Day, Def. = Defect.

4 Model Application

Software process simulation in general – and GENSIM 2.0 in particular – can support software decision-makers in many ways. The following list of possible applications is not exhaustive but gives an idea of the diversity of questions that could be addressed:

- What combinations (and intensity levels) of development, verification, and validation techniques should be applied in a given context to achieve defined time, quality or cost goals?
- What staffing levels should be assigned to achieve time, quality or cost targets?
- Does investment in training pay off for specific development contexts and goals?
- Do investments in improving development, verification, and validation techniques pay off for specific development contexts and goals?
- What are the promising areas of research for improving development, verification, and validation techniques?

To demonstrate the applicability and usefulness to relevant problems software decision-makers are facing, the remainder of this section summarizes results of a model application related to the first question listed above in two different scenarios. Underlying assumptions of the application are: (1) A project has a given set of features (which are assumed to define the size of work products) and a target deadline; (2) The project manager wants to know which verification and validation techniques should be combined to hold the deadline (priority 1) and deliver high quality code (priority 2); (3) The developer team and their skills are given; (4) The requirements, design, and code implementation methods and tools are given.

4.1 Scenario 1

This scenario shows the impact of different combinations of verification and validation (V&V) activities on project duration, product quality, and effort. Verification activities include Requirements Inspections (RI), Design Inspections (DI) and Code Inspections (CI). Validation activities include Unit Test (UT), Integration Test (IT), and System Test (ST). Exactly one technique with given efficiency and effectiveness measures is available per V&V activity. A V&V technique is either applied to all artifacts of the related type (e.g., requirements, design, and code documents) or it is not applied at all.

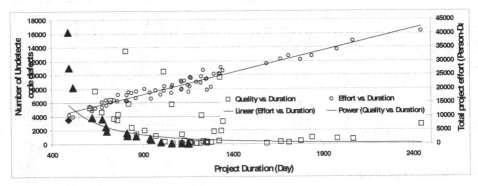

Fig. 3. Quality vs. Duration and Effort vs. Duration (Scenario 1 – Calibration A)

Fig. 3 shows simulation results for model calibration A. Due to space constraints, the results for calibration B are not reported in this paper, but can be found in [13]. Squares represent (Quality, Duration) result value pairs, where quality is measured as the total number of undetected code faults.

Filled triangles represent non-dominated (Quality, Duration) result values, i.e., simulation results to which no other simulation exists with both less undetected defects and less duration. Obviously, for calibration A, there exists a trade-off between Quality and Duration. This is also true for calibration B [13]. By looking at the non-dominated solutions, it can be seen that in order to achieve less undetected defects (higher quality), more time is needed. In fact, if the goal was to explore which combinations of V&V activities should be applied to achieve the target duration, in case there are several eligible V&V combinations, a decision-maker could pick the non-dominated solution with the lowest number of undetected defects.

Circles represent (Effort, Duration) result value pairs, where effort is measured as the total number of person-days spent on all activities (including rework). The only non-dominated solution is represented by the diamond symbol near the lower left end of the (Effort, Duration) regression line. For calibration A, it is the case where only RI is performed.

Differences between simulation results of calibrations A and B are reported in [13]. For instance, on average, simulations with Calibration B take longer and consume more effort. This can be explained by the fact that Calibration B assumes larger per defect rework effort for code defects found in IT and ST than Calibration A.

4.2 Scenario 2

This scenario uses only Calibration B. Scenario 2 shows the impact of different combinations of verification activities and techniques on project duration, product quality, and effort. This scenario assumes that all validation activities UT, IT, and ST are always performed, while verification activities RI, DI, and CI can be performed or not. If a verification activity is performed, one of alternative techniques A or B can be applied. Compared to A-type verification techniques, B-type techniques are 10%

Table 3. Simulation results of Scenario 2

RI	DI	CI	RI-tec	DI-tec	CI-tec	Duration [Day]	Effort [PD]	Quality [UD]
0	1	0		B		1085	28401	96
0	1	0		A		1086	30272	108
1	0	0	B			1102	32830	135
1	0	0	A			1103	34448	145
1	1	0	A	A		1103	26216	89
1	1	0	B	A		1106	25637	86
1	1	0	A	B		1108	25220	82
1	1	0	B	B		1110	24892	81
1	1	1	A	A	A	1135	22032	43
0	1	1		B	A	1138	24297	50
1	1	1	B	A	A	1143	21516	40
1	1	1	B	B	A	1144	20926	36
0	1	1		B	B	1149	23888	45
0	1	1		A	A	1152	25916	61
1	1	1	A	B	A	1156	21253	38
1	1	1	B	B	B	1158	20728	33
0	1	1		A	B	1169	25412	54
1	0	1	B		B	1171	27094	72
1	1	1	A	B	B	1172	21153	35
1	0	1	A		A	1173	29187	90
1	0	1	B		A	1178	27836	82
1	1	1	A	A	B	1179	21865	40
1	1	1	B	A	B	1181	21434	38
1	0	1	A		B	1183	28302	79
0	0	1			B	1355	39446	139
0	0	1			A	1363	40287	149
0	0	0				1394	48683	233

more effective (i.e., find 10% more of all defects contained in the related artifact) and 25% less efficient (i.e., 25% less document size can be verified per person-day).

The simulation of all possible combinations generates $3^3 = 27$ different results (cf. Table 3). The main difference to Scenario 1 is that in addition to the (Quality, Duration) trade-off there exists a simultaneous (Effort, Duration) trade-off. Moreover, as can be seen in Table 3, for the specific values chosen, in cases where only one verification activity is performed, solutions using the B-type technique (i.e., slower but more effective) perform better with regards to project duration, effort consumption, and quality than solutions using the A-type techniques.

When there is a mix of A-type and B-type verification techniques, the picture is more complex. In cases involving only two verification activities, solutions that use B-type techniques more often and/or later seem to slightly extend project duration but consume considerably less effort and leave less defects undetected.

5 Discussion

The scenarios presented in the previous section exemplify how GENSIM 2.0 can be applied for decision support. Many other practical scenarios could have been presented, addressing various aspects of the questions listed at the beginning of Section 4. Two observations can be made with regards to the simulation results in Scenarios 1 and 2. Firstly, the results are consistent with empirical evidence about the effects of performing V&V activities. The more, and – if not all V&V activities are performed – the earlier V&V is done, the better the end product quality. Secondly, the results show that effects of V&V activities on project duration and effort consumption are complex. They depend on the combinations and types of V&V techniques, and the overall project context. The complex behavior partly results from non-linear effects in the model due to learning and the specific workforce allocation heuristic.

To what extent the presented results are reliable depends on the validity of the simulation model. Model validity is mainly affected by three factors: proper implementation of cause-effect structures, proper representation of real-world attributes by model parameters, and proper calibration. As all underlying assumptions (and thus limitations) of GENSIM 2.0 are explicit, it is always possible to judge to what extent the model structure and parameters correspond to an actual organizational process. Moreover, the design of GENSIM 2.0 allows for easy adaptation where and when needed. Finally, calibration to available organization-specific data and expert knowledge is simple as demonstrated by the example shown in Section 3 using external source of information, i.e., data published in scientific papers.

6 Conclusions and Future Work

GENSIM 2.0 is a customizable and publicly available software process simulation model. Different to most SD software process simulation models, GENSIM 2.0 allows for detailed modeling of work products, activities, developers, techniques, tools, defects and other entities by exploiting the subscription mechanisms of Vensim. Moreover, the possibility to use external DLL libraries gives the opportunity to extract potentially time-consuming algorithms from the SD model and thus speed up model execution.

Future work on GENSIM 2.0 will address some of its current limitations. For example, currently it is not possible to represent incremental software development processes easily. Mechanisms will be added to the model that allow for concurrent execution of development cycles following the generic process of which an instance was presented in Fig. 3 (Sub-section 3.1).

GENSIM 2.0 is part of a long-term research program that aims at combining results from empirical studies and company-specific measurement programs with process simulation. While writing this paper, GENSIM 2.0 is calibrated to data from a German research institute and its industrial partners. Once completely calibrated to this data, simulations will be performed to explore which combination of V&V activities (and applied techniques) is most suitable to achieve certain product quality goals, under given resource and time constraints. The quality goals will be defined according to standard ISO 9126.

Acknowledgements

Keyvan Khosrovian and Dietmar Pfahl were supported by Discovery Grant no. 327665-06 of the Canadian Natural Sciences and Engineering Research Council (NSERC). Vahid Garousi was supported by an Alberta Ingenuity New Faculty Award.

References

1. Abdel-Hamid, T.K., Madnick, S.E.: Software Projects Dynamics – an Integrated Approach. Prentice-Hall, Englewood Cliffs (1991)
2. Angkasaputra, N., Pfahl, D.: Making Software Process Simulation Modeling Agile and Pattern-based. In: ProSim 2004, pp. 222–227 (2004)
3. Armbrust, O., et al.: Simulation-Based Software Process Modeling and Evaluation. In: Chang, S.K. (ed.) Handbook of Software Engineering & Knowledge Engineering, Advanced Topics, vol. 3, pp. 333–364. World Scientific, Singapore (2005)
4. Bandinelli, S., Fuggetta, A., Lavazza, L., Loi, M., Picco, G.P.: Modeling and Improving an Industrial Software Process. IEEE Trans. on Soft. Eng. 21(5), 440–453 (1995)
5. Damm, L., Lundberg, L., Wohlin, C.: Faults-slip-through - a concept for measuring the efficiency of the test process. Software Process: Improv. and Practice 11(1), 47–59 (2006)
6. Extend Product Information (March 22, 2007),
   http://www.imaginethatinc.com/
7. Forrester, J.W.: Industrial Dynamics. Productivity Press, Cambridge (1961)
8. Frost, A., Campo, M.: Advancing Defect Containment to Quantitative Defect Management. CrossTalk – The Journal of Defense Software Engineering 12(20), 24–28 (2007)
9. Gruhn, V., Saalmann, A.: Software Process Validation Based on FUNSOFT Nets. In: Proceedings of EWSPT 1992, pp. 223–226 (1992)
10. Kellner, M.I., Hansen, G.A.: Software Process Modeling: A Case Study. In: Proceedings of AHICSS 1989, vol. II - Software Track, pp. 175–188 (1989)
11. Khosrovian, K., Pfahl, D., Garousi, V.: A Customizable System Dynamics Simulation Model of Generic Software Development Processes. Technical Report SERG-2007-07, Schulich School of Engineering, University of Calgary (2007)

12. Khosrovian, K., Pfahl, D., Garousi, V.: Calibrating a Customizable System Dynamics Simulation Model of Generic Software Development Processes. Technical Report SERG-2007-08, Schulich School of Engineering, University of Calgary (2007)
13. Khosrovian, K., Pfahl, D., Garousi, V.: Application Scenarios of a Customizable System Dynamics Simulation Model of Generic Software Development Processes. Technical Report SERG-2007-09, Schulich School of Engineering, University of Calgary (2007)
14. Madachy, R.: Reusable Model Structures and Behaviors for Software Processes. In: Wang, Q., Pfahl, D., Raffo, D.M., Wernick, P. (eds.) SPW 2006 and ProSim 2006. LNCS, vol. 3966, pp. 222–233. Springer, Heidelberg (2006)
15. Mi, P., Scacchi, W.: A knowledge-based environment for modeling and simulating software engineering processes. IEEE Trans. on Know. and Data Eng. 2(3), 283–294 (1990)
16. Müller, M., Pfahl, D.: Simulation Methods. In: Singer, J., Shull, F., Sjøberg, D. (eds.) dvanced Topics in Empirical Software Engineering: A Handbook, pp. 117–153. Springer, London (2007)
17. Pfahl, D., Lebsanft, K.: Knowledge Acquisition and Process Guidance for Building System Dynamics Simulation Models: An Experience Report from Software Industry. Int. J. of Software Eng. and Knowledge Eng. 10(4), 487–510 (2000)
18. Pfahl, D., Klemm, M., Ruhe, G.: A CBT module with integrated simulation component for software project management education and training. Journal of Systems and Software 59(3), 283–298 (2001)
19. Raffo, D.M., Nayak, U., Setamanit, S., Sullivan, P., Wakeland, W.: Using Software Process Simulation to Assess the Impact of IV&V Activities. In: Proceedings of ProSim 2004, Fraunhofer IRB, pp. 197–205 (2004)
20. Raffo, D., Spehar, G., Nayak, U.: Generalized Simulation Models: What, Why and How? In: Proceedings of ProSim 2003, Portland State University, no page (2003)
21. Senge, P.: The Fifth Discipline. Doubleday, New York (1990)
22. Vensim User Manual (March 22, 2007), http://www.vensim.com/
23. Wagner, S.: A Literature Survey of the Quality Economics of Defect-Detection Techniques. In: Proceedings of ISESE 2006, pp. 194–203 (2006)
24. Wise, A.: Little-JIL 1.5 Language Report, UM-CS-2006-51. Department of Computer Science, University of Massachusetts, Amherst, MA 01003 (2006)

RVSim: A Simulation Approach to Predict the Impact of Requirements Volatility on Software Project Plans

Dapeng Liu[1,2], Qing Wang[1], Junchao Xiao[1], Juan Li[1], and Huaizhang Li[1]

[1] Laboratory for Internet Software Technologies, Institute of Software,
Chinese Academy of Sciences, Beijing 100190, China
{liudapeng, wq, xiaojunchao, lijuan, hzli}@itechs.iscas.ac.cn
[2] Graduate University of Chinese Academy of Sciences, Beijing 100039, China

Abstract. Requirements volatility is a common project risk which has severe consequences on software projects. Though its impact on various aspects of software projects has been highlighted extensively, its influence on project plans is not well explored yet. This paper proposes a simulation approach RVSim (Requirements Volatility Simulation) which utilizes requirements traceability and dependency information to predict the impact of requirements volatility on software project plans. RVSim can help analyze the effects of requirements volatility in depth, and provide useful information for users to make better decisions. Moreover, RVSim supports customization for users' own software processes and projects. We also provide a case study to illustrate the applicability and effectiveness of RVSim.

Keywords: Requirements Volatility, Requirements Traceability, Requirements Dependency, Software Process Simulation, Risk Management.

1 Introduction

Software development projects are highly complex and involve various kinds of risks from customers, business environments, resources and so on. Many researchers have reported that requirements volatility is one of the most frequent and severe risks in software projects [1-3]. Requirements volatility often results in cost and schedule overruns, unmet functions and, at times, cancelled projects.

Requirements volatility has great impacts on diverse aspects of software projects. Existing studies have investigated the relationship between requirements volatility and development productivity [4-6], project cost [7, 8], defect density [9], project effort [7], customer satisfaction [6], project duration [7, 8, 10], change effort [11] and software releases [10]. However, the impact of requirements volatility on software project plans is not well explored yet. Project plans, which drive software projects, are highly important for software project management. Researching the impact of requirements volatility on project plans is especially necessary and valuable for improving the project management.

In this paper, we propose a simulation approach named RVSim (Requirements Volatility Simulation) which utilizes requirements traceability and dependency information to predict the impact of requirements volatility on project plans during the

Q. Wang, D. Pfahl, and D.M. Raffo (Eds.): ICSP 2008, LNCS 5007, pp. 307–319, 2008.
© Springer-Verlag Berlin Heidelberg 2008

software development lifecycle. RVSim is able to not only predict the impact of definite requirement changes, but also do impact analysis according to the trajectory of requirements volatility. RVSim can assist software project managers to understand the impact of requirements volatility deeply, make decisions accurately and improve their project plans continuously.

RVSim has three abstraction levels, which support customizing simulation models for users' own software processes and projects. The three levels also improve the reusability of RVSim models, saving users' modeling time greatly. RVSim uses requirements traceability and dependency information to handle requirement changes, which is considered as a main strategy for impact analysis [12].

The remainder of the paper is structured as follows. Section 2 describes RVSim in detail with customization for an iterative software development process for demonstration. Section 3 illustrates the applicability and usefulness of RVSim with the help of a case study. Section 4 discusses the related work. Finally, Section 5 concludes the paper and gives directions of our future work.

2   The RVSim Approach

RVSim is a discrete-event simulation approach. There are four components in the RVSim simulation model, which is shown in Fig. 1.

Requirements Traceability/Dependency Repository (RTDR) stores software requirements traceability and dependency information. Requirements traceability is concerned with tracing information between requirements and other work products such as design documents and codes, while requirements dependency deals with the relationship between requirements. One change on a certain requirement not only influences work products related to the requirement through traceability, but also probably impacts other requirements through dependency. The information in this component is fully utilized by *Requirements Change Event Routines* to accurately analyze the impact of requirements volatility on *Software Project Plan*. We detailedly describe this component in Section 2.1.

Requirements Change Event Generator (RCEG) generates events which

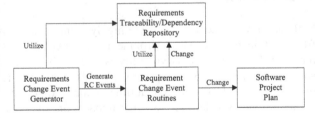

Fig. 1. The RVSim simulation model

represent requirements changes in simulation. There are three types of events in RVSim: Requirements Addition, Requirements Modification and Requirements Deletion [13]. We describe this component in detail in Section 2.2.

Requirements Change Event Routines (RCER) includes three routines responsible for handling the three kinds of events respectively in simulation. We give a detailed description of the three routines in Section 2.3.

Software Project Plan (SPP) is the plan of the software project which is analyzed by RVSim. *Software Project Plan* is changed during simulation, so users can easily see how requirements volatility impacts on the project plan.

When simulating, firstly, *RCEG* generates requirements change events and sends them to *RCER*. Secondly, the corresponding routines are started to deal with these events in order utilizing the information in *RTDR*. Finally, the routines analyze the effects of these events, and then change related part in *SPP* and *RTDR*.

One simulation model hardly covers all kinds of situations because there are so many differences between software projects such as application domains, customers, business environments, organization strategies and so on. Considering this problem, we divide the RVSim model into three abstraction levels, shown in Fig. 2.

The top level is *RVSim-General,* which is the framework of the RVSim model. *RVSim-General* is independent of any software development process, but some contents in it can be customized by users, which are called *"Customizable Points"*. *RVSim-General* provides the general expressions of components and guidelines for user customization.

The middle level is *RVSim-Process*, which is particular for one concrete software development process. *RVSim-Process* simulation model is achieved by customizing the *Customizable Points* defined in *RVSim-General* with rules about the concrete software process. There are some parameters related to real projects defined in a software development process's rules.

The bottom level is *RVSim-Project*, which is particular for one real software development project.

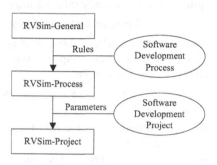

Fig. 2. The three abstraction levels of the RVSim simulation model

RVSim-Project simulation model is achieved by inputting parameters of a real software project defined in the corresponding *RVSim-Process* model, so *RVSim-Process* model is reusable in different software projects using the same software development process.

In order to clearly demonstrate RVSim, we have built a *RVSim-Process* model for an iterative development process. This iterative development process has four phases in every iteration: Requirements, Design, Coding and Test. Because requirements volatility is constructive in Requirements phase and destructive in other three phases [8], the Requirements phase is ignored in the model. It is noted that due to the page limit, some contents of the iterative development process are simplified.

2.1 Requirements Traceability/Dependency Repository

In *RVSim-General, RTDR* is represented as a set:

$$RTDR = \{RTDI_1, RTDI_2, ..., RTDI_N\}$$

Every item $RTDI_i$ (*Requirement Traceability/Dependency Information, $1 \leq i \leq N$, N* is the total number of requirements) contains the traceability and dependency information of one requirement. *RTDI* is defined as a tuple:

$$RTDI = (RequirementID, Volatility, WorkProductSet, DependencySet)$$

where:

- *RequirementID* is the ID of the requirement which traceability and dependency information is contained in this *RTDI*. Assume this requirement is *R*.
- *Volatility* specifies the relative probability the requirement *R* is changed. All values of *Volatility* are held in the *VolatilitySet*, which is a *Customizable Point*.
- *WorkProductSet* is a set of work products related to *R*. It keeps the requirements traceability information of *R*, which is represented as follows:

$$WorkProductSet = \{WorkProduct_1, WorkProduct_2, ..., WorkProduct_M\}$$

Every item *WorkProduct$_j$* ($1 \leq j \leq M$, *M* is the number of work products) contains type, size and size unit of one work product. *WorkProduct* is defined as a tuple:

$$WorkProduct = (Type, Size, SizeUnit)$$

WorkProductSet is a *Customizable Point*.

- *DependencySet* is a set of relationship between requirements. It keeps the requirements dependency information of *R*, which is represented as follows:

$$DependencySet = \{Dependency_1, Dependency_2, ..., Dependency_S\}$$

Every item *Dependency$_k$* ($1 \leq k \leq S$, *S* is the number of requirements depending on *R*) represents a relationship that one other requirement depends on *R*. *Dependency* is defined as a tuple:

$$Dependency = (RequirementID, DependencyStrength)$$

where:

- *RequirementID* is the ID of the requirement depending on *R*. Assume this requirement is R_d.
- *DependencyStrength* specifies the degree to which R_d depends on *R*. All values of *DependencyStrength* are held in the *DependencyStrengthSet*, which is also a *Customizable Point*.

Regarding the *RVSim-Process* model for the iterative development process, we customized all the *Customizable Points* mentioned above. In this iterative process, every requirement is related to three work products: design documents, codes and test cases, which size units are page, line of code (LOC) and test case respectively. Assume the sizes of the three work products are *ds, cs* and *ts,* the *Customizable Points* for the iterative process are expressed as follows:

VolatilitySet = {high, low}, DependencyStrengthSet = {strong, weak}
WorkProductSet = {DesignDocs, Codes, TestCases}
DesignDocs = (DesignDocument, ds, page)
Codes = (Code, cs, LOC)
TestCases = (TestCase, ts, test case)

2.2 Requirements Change Event Generator

In *RVSim-General*, the requirements change event (*RCEvent*) is represented as a tuple:

$$RCEvent = (RCType, RCTime, RTDI, ModificationLevel)$$

where:

- *RCType* is the type of *RCEvent*. There are three types: *RA* (Requirements Addition), *RM* (Requirements Modification) and *RD* (Requirements Deletion).
- *RCTime* is the time when *RCEvent* occurs.
- *RTDI* corresponds to the requirement which is added, modified or deleted.
- *ModificationLevel* specifies the degree to which one requirement is modified if *RCType* is *RM* or *RD*. *ModificationLevel* is null if *RCType* is *RA*. All values of *ModificationLevel* are held in the *ModificationLevelSet*, which is a *Customizable Point. RVSim-General* defines a special value *delete* in the *ModificationLevelSet*, which stands for the *RD* event.

RCEG allows users to specify how requirements change events are generated in one concrete software development process. There are two modes for generating events:

- Definite events inputted by users. This mode is suitable for the situation that one requirement change request has arrived, and the user wants to know the impact of this change on the software project plan.
- Supposed events generated automatically according to user-defined rules, which is a *Customizable Point.* This mode is suitable for the situation that the user wishes to predict the impact according to the trajectory of requirements volatility. The rules can be obtained by analyzing historical project data (like [13, 14]) or by their experience. Users can also do "what-if" analysis by setting up different rules.

As to our *RVSim-Process* model for the iterative development process, we customized *ModificationLevelSet= {delete, major, moderate, minor}. RCEG* adopts the second mode, and the rules are defined as follows:

- Requirement change events occur at a constant interval p $(p>0)$ since the beginning of Design phase in one iteration.
- There are no more requirement change events after a constant period q $(q>0)$ since the beginning of Design phase in one iteration.
- The percents of *RA, RM* and *RD* events are ap, mp and dp respectively ($ap \geq 0$, $mp \geq 0$, $dp \geq 0$, $ap+mp+dp=100\%$).
- For *RA* events, a new *RTDI* corresponding to the new added requirement is generated. In this *RTDI*, the *RequirementID* is generated automatically; the *Volatility* is chosen randomly from the *VolatilitySet*; the *DependencySet* is empty because we believe that no existing requirements depend on a new one; the *Size* of every *Type* is generated randomly between lower and upper limits parameters. For *DesignDocument*, the lower and upper limits are *dll* and *dul*. For *Code*, the lower and upper limits are *cll* and *cul*. For *TestCase*, the lower and upper limits are *tll* and *tul*.
- For *RM* and *RD* events, *RTDI* is chosen from the *RTDR* randomly. A *RTDI* with *Volatility=high* is more likely to be chosen than one with *Volatility=low*.
- For *RM* events, the percents of *major, moderate* and *minor* of *ModificationLevel* is *map, mop* and *mip* ($map \geq 0$, $mop \geq 0$, $mip \geq 0$, $map+mop+mip=100\%$). For *RD* events, *ModificationLevel=delete*.

The time unit in the above rules is *hour*. The time is the working time, not the absolute time. For example, if a project proceeds 24 *hours* and the development team works 8 *hours* per day, it means that 3 days have passed.

2.3 Requirements Change Event Routines

In *RVSim-General*, RCER includes three general routines for the three types of requirement change events in simulation, which are presented in the following.

Requirement Addition Event Routine
Assume the *RA* event is E_A and the new added requirement is R_A. This routine has four steps as follows:

● Put $E_A.RTDI$ into the *RTDR*. The $E_A.RTDI$ corresponds to the requirement R_A.
● Generate dependency relationship that R_A depends on existing requirements in the *RTDR*.
● Create project tasks related to R_A. These tasks produce or use *WorkProducts* in the $E_A.RTDI$.
● Rearrange tasks properly in the *Software Project Plan (SPP)*.

There are three *Customizable Points* in this routine, which are how to generate dependency relationship, how to create project tasks and how to adjust the *SPP*. They all are customized by user-defined rules.

With regard to the *RVSim-Process* model for the iterative development process, the corresponding rules are defined as follows:

● *Rule for dependency information R_A depends on existing requirements:* Assume total number of requirements is N and the number of requirements R_A depends on is N_A, the parameter *dper* (dependency percent) of R_A is defined as follows:

$$dper = \frac{N_A}{N} \times 100\%$$

N_A can be calculated easily by N and *dper*. Choose N_A different requirements from all as ones which R_A depends on. The *DependencyStrength* is chosen randomly from the *DependencyStrengthSet*.
Set up the lower and upper limits of *dper* as *dperll* and *dperul*. *dper* is generated randomly between *dperll* and *dperul*.
● *Rule for new project tasks:* In this iterative development process, one requirement is related to three tasks: design task, coding task and test task, which are in Design, Coding and Test phases respectively. Design task produces design documents; coding task generates software codes; and test task uses test cases.
Set up the productivities of three types of new tasks as *dpro page/hour*, *cpro LOC/hour* and *tpro test case/hour* respectively. The duration of new tasks can be calculated easily by *Size* in the $E_A.RTDI.WorkProductSet$ and the productivities.
● *Rule for adjusting the SPP:* In this iterative development process, overlapping of the phases in one iteration is not allowed. In Design phase, design tasks have precedence relationship the same as the dependency of requirements related to them. For example, if design tasks *T1* and *T2* realize requirements *R1* and *R2* respectively, and *R2* depends on *R1*, then *T2* must be arranged to start after *T1* is

finished. In Coding and Test phases, tasks do not have such precedence relationship, so tasks in the same phase can be parallel. In addition, there is no idle time between tasks.

This rule is also applied to the following *RM* and *RD* events routines for the iterative development process.

Requirement Modification/Deletion Event Routines

The routines for *RM* and *RD* events are very similar, so we present them together here. Assume the event is E_{MD}, and the modified or deleted requirement is R_{MD}. There are four steps in the routines.

- Find the $E_{MD}.RTDI$ from the *RTDR*, and modify or delete it. If $E_{MD}.RCType=RM$, modify the *RTDI* according to the $E_{MD}.ModificationLevel$, but keep the *RequirementID* unchanged. If $E_{MD}.RCType=RD$, remove the *RTDI* from the *RTDR*.
- If $E_{MD}.RCType=RM$, modify the dependency relationship that R_{MD} depends on other requirements in the *RTDR* according to the $E_{MD}.ModificationLevel$.
- Modifying or deleting R_{MD} may influence the requirements depending on R_{MD}. The following pseudocodes express this chain effect:

```
void modifyOrDeleteRequirement
            (RTDI rtdi, ModificationLevel ml)
{
    if (ml==delete)
        delete rtdi from the RTDR;
    else
    {
        modify rtdi according to ml;
        modify dependency relationship of R_MD;
    }
    for(int i=0;i<|rtdi.DependencySet|;i++)
    {
        get a requirement R_d which depends on R_MD;
        get the ModificationLevel ml_d for R_d;
        modifyOrDeleteRequirement(R_d, ml_d);
    }
}
```

- Adjust the *SPP*. Requirements modification or deletion may change duration and precedence relationship of related project tasks, or cause idle time between tasks, so the *SPP* needs to be adjusted.

There are three *Customizable Points* in the routines, which are how to modify the *RTDI* according to the *ModificationLevel*, how to modify dependency relationship of R_{MD}, and how to get *ModificationLevel ml_d for R_d.

With regard to the *RVSim-Process* model for the iterative development process, the corresponding rules are defined as follows:

- *Rule for modifying the RTDI according to the ModificationLevel: major, moderate* and *minor* all represent numeric values between 0 and 1, *major≥moderate≥minor*. For *Size*, set up a parameter *smp* (size modified percent). If the original *Size* of a work product is *S*, the *Size* after modification is *S*(1+smp)*. *smp* is the same for the three types of work products. The range of *smp* is decided by the *ModificationLevel*. For example, assume *major=0.8, moderate=0.5, minor=0.2*. If *ModificationLevel=major*, 50%<|smp|≤80%; if *moderate,* 20%<|*smp*|≤50%; if *minor,* 0<|*smp*|≤20%. *smp* is generated randomly in its range. Keep the *Volatility* and *DependencySet* unchanged.

- *Rule for modifying R_{MD}'s dependency on other requirements:* Set up a parameter *dpermp* to represent the modified percent of *dper*. The range of *dpermp* is also decided by the *ModificationLevel*, that is, 0≤|*dpermp*|≤*ModificationLevel*. *dpermp* is generated randomly in its range.
- *Rule for ModificationLevel of Requirements depending on R_{MD}:* Assume R_d is a requirement depending on R_{MD}, this rule is shown in Table 1, where "*none*" indicates that R_d is not influenced.

Table 1. Rule for *ModificationLevel* of R_d

R_{MD}'s ModificationLevel	DependencyStrength	R_d's ModificationLevel
delete	strong	delete
delete	weak	major
major	strong	major
major	weak	moderate
moderate	strong	moderate
moderate	weak	minor
minor	strong	minor
minor	weak	none

So far we have finished building the *RVSim-Process* model for the iterative development process.

3 Case Study

In this section, we apply the *RVSim-Process* model for the iterative development process to an example software project to illustrate the applicability and usefulness of RVSim.

The objective of the example project is to develop a function module of a large web application in one iteration of the iterative development process. The time limit for the project is three weeks. The development team works 8 hours per day, that is, the project has 120 working hours before the deadline. The human resources are enough for the example project.

The example project gets 4 requirements after Requirements phase. We call them *R1, R2, R3* and *R4* respectively for convenience in the following. Among these requirements, *R1* is the core function of the module; *R2* and *R3*

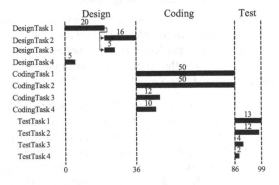

Fig. 3. The original software project plan

are two extension functions based on *R1*; *R4* is an independent function about user interface, which has no dependency relationship with other functions. All requirements are clearly analyzed, but *R3* is a new feature that the development team has never implemented before, which brings some uncertainty. We have made a plan for the example project shown in Fig. 2, where *DesignTaski, CodingTaski* and *TestTaski* are related to the requirement *Ri* ($1 \leq i \leq 4$).

We have developed a tool named *RVSimulator* which implements the *RVSim-Process* model for the iterative development process. *RVSimulator* is developed based on an open source simulation package SimJava[1], and it has a user-friendly graphical interface which can display the adjusted *SPP* after every requirement change event, so users can see how *SPP* evolves due to requirements volatility. For the example project, we plan to use *RVSimulator* to get the probability that the project is finished before the deadline, so the output of *RVSimulator* is the project duration data.

In order to apply *RVSimulator* to the example project, firstly, we build a *RVSim-Project* simulation model for the example project by inputting parameters defined in the *RVSim-Process* model as follows:

Input Parameters in *RCEG*: $p=16$, $q=40$, $ap=25\%$, $dp=25\%$, $mp=50\%$; $dul=8$, $dll=2$; $cul=4000$, $cll=1000$, $tul=30$, $tll=10$; $map=10\%$, $mop=20\%$, $mip=70\%$.
Input Parameters in *RCER*: $major=0.8$, $moderate=0.5$, $minor=0.25$; $dperul=30\%$, $dperll=0$; $dpro=0.4$, $cpro=50$, $tpro=2$.

Secondly, we input the requirements traceability and dependency information, and the software project plan to the *RVSimulator*. The *RTDIi* corresponding to *Ri*($1 \leq i \leq 4$) are expressed as follows:

RTDI1=(1, low, {(DesignDocument, 6, page), (Code, 2000, LOC), (TestCase, 25, test case)}, {(2, strong), (3, strong)})
RTDI2=(2, low, {(DesignDocument, 8, page), (Code, 3000, LOC), (TestCase, 30, test case)}, {})
RTDI3=(3, high,{(DesignDocument, 2, page), (Code, 600, LOC), (TestCase, 6, test case)}, {})
RTDI4=(4, low, {(DesignDocument, 1.5, page), (Code, 500, LOC), (TestCase, 5, test case)}, {})
RTDR = {RTDI1, RTDI2, RTDI3, RTDI4}
In order to illustrate how the *RVSim-Project* model works, we describe one execution of the simulation model in detail in the following.

● The first requirement change is requirement addition, which occurs at time 16. We call the new added requirement *R5*. The event and *RTDI* for *R5* are as follows:
    RCEvent=(RA, 16, RTDI5, null)
    RTDI5=(5, high, (DesignDocument, 6.96, page), (Code, 2032, LOC), (Test-Case, 26, test case), {})
The following is the event routine for this *RA* event.
■   *RTDR = {RTDI1, RTDI2, RTDI3, RTDI4, RTDI5}.*

---

[1] http://www.icsa.inf.ed.ac.uk/research/groups/hase/simjava/

■ *dper=21.04%*, so $N_A= N*dper=21.04\%*4=0.8416\approx1$. It means that *R5* depends on one existing requirement. Choose one requirement randomly, and get *R3*. Generate *DependencyStrength=weak*. After that,

   RTDI3=(3, high, {(DesignDocument, 2, page), (Code, 600, LOC), (TestCase, 6, test case)}, {(5, weak)})

■ Create *DesignTask5, CodingTask5* and *TestTask5* for *R5*. The duration of the three tasks is 6.96/0.4=17.4, 2032/50≈40.6, 26/2=13 hours respectively.

■ Rearrange tasks according to the *Rule for adjusting the SPP*.

RVSimulator displays the *SPP* after adjusted shown in Fig. 4 (a). We see that the project is delayed for 105.4-99=6.4 hours due to this event.

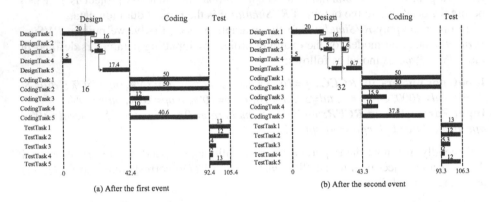

(a) After the first event   (b) After the second event

Fig. 4. The adjusted software project plan

● The second requirement change is requirement modification, which occurs at time 32. The changed requirement is *R3*. The event is

   RCEvent=(RM, 32, RTDI3, moderate).

The event routine for this *RM* event is as follows:

■ Modify the *RTDI3*. *smp=32.72%*. After modification,

   RTDI3=(3, high,{(DesignDocument, 2.65, page), (Code, 796, LOC), (TestCase, 8, test case)}, {(5, weak)})

■ *dpermp=-9%*, so *dper=1/5-9%=11%*, $N_A=11\%*5=0.55\approx1$. Keep unchanged.

■ *R5* depends on *R3*, so *R5* is influenced. For *R5*, *Modification=minor*, *smp=-6.93%, dpermp=5%*. After modification,

   RTDI5=(5, high, (DesignDocument, 6.48, page), (Code, 1891, LOC), (TestCase, 24, test case), {})

■ Adjust the *SPP*. The precedence relationship between tasks does not change. The duration of tasks related to *R3* increases while the duration of tasks related to *R5* decreases.

RVSimulator presents the *SPP* after adjusted shown in Fig. 4 (b). We see that the project is delayed again for 0.9 hours due to this event.

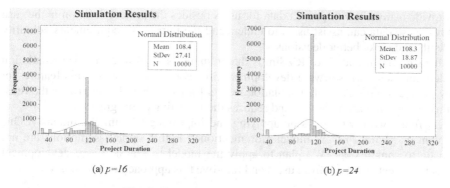

(a) $p=16$ (b) $p=24$

Fig. 5. Simulation results in two situations

So far one simulation execution has been finished because there are no more requirement change events, and Fig. 4 (b) is the final project plan. This plan duration is 7.3 hours longer than the original plan duration (99 hours), but it is still within the time limit for the example project (120 hours).

We simulate 10000 times for the example project, and the simulation results of project duration are shown in Fig. 5 (a), which fit a Normal distribution. From the distribution, we calculate that the probability the project is finished before the deadline is 66.3%. Then we change the parameter $p=24$ to simulate another situation. The simulation results are shown in Fig. 5 (b). The probability the project is finished before the deadline is 73.2% in this situation.

4 Related Work

There are several researches about the impact of requirements volatility on software project schedule [7, 8, 10]. Zowghi et al [8] conducted a survey of 430 software development companies in Australia, and the results showed that over 80% projects were late because of requirements volatility. Stark et al [10] developed a regression analysis model to predict the schedule change percent due to requirements volatility. Pfahl et al [7] built a simulation model for Siemens Corporate Technology to demonstrate the impact of requirements volatility on project duration and effort, and find out the optimal effort invested in requirements engineering.

Discrete-event simulation allows for more detailed statistics on the entities, so RVSim is able to provide more useful information for users to make better decisions. In addition, unlike studies based on specific data or for specific software processes, RVSim supports customization for users to build their own simulation models. We believe it can produce more accurate results for users.

5 Conclusions and Future Work

In this paper, we present a simulation approach RVSim which can predict the impact of requirements volatility on software project plans using requirements traceability and dependency information. RVSim adopts discrete-event simulation which is able to provide many kinds of project data for users besides the project duration in the case study. These data can assist users to understand the impact of requirements volatility in depth, and make better decisions.

One significant feature of RVSim is that it supports users to customize simulation models for their own software development processes and projects. This feature not only produces more accurate simulation results for users, but also improves the reusability of the simulation models and reduces the modeling effort greatly.

Our future work will focus on applying and improving RVSim continuously. One problem of *RVSim-Process* model aforementioned is that some assumptions are not realistic to some extent. We plan to apply the model to real software development projects, collect feedback from users and improve this approach continuously.

Acknowledgments. We would like to thank Prof. Yongji Wang and Ph.D candidate Qiusong Yang for their precious suggestions and advice on this paper. This work is supported by the National Natural Science Foundation of China under grant No. 60573082, 60473060, the National Hi-Tech Research and Development Program (863 Program) of China under grant No. 2006AA01Z155, 2006AA01Z185, 2007AA010303, as well as the National Basic Research Program (973 Program) of China under grant No. 2007CB310802.

References

1. Boehm, B.W.: Software Risk Management: Principles and Practices. IEEE Software 8(1), 32–41 (1991)
2. The Standish Group: The CHAOS Report (1995)
3. Schmidt, R., Lyytinen, K., Keil, M., Cule, P.: Identifying Software Project Risks: An International Delphi Study. Journal of Management Information Systems 17(4), 5–36 (2001)
4. Finnie, G.R., Wittig, G.E., Petkov, D.I.: Prioritizing Software Development Productivity Factors Using the Analytic Hierarchy Process. Journal of Systems and Software 22(2), 129–139 (1993)
5. Lane, M.S.: Enhancing Software Development Productivity in Australian Firms. In: Proceedings of the 9th Australian Conference on Information Systems (ACIS 1998), Sydney, Australia (1998)
6. Zowghi, D., Offen, R.: Nurmuliani: The Impact of Requirements Volatility on the Software Development Lifecycle. In: Proceedings of the International Conference on Software Theory and Practice (IFIP World Computer Congress), Beijing, China (2000)
7. Pfahl, D., Lebsanft, K.: Using Simulation to Analyze the Impact of Software Requirements Volatility on Project Performance. Information and Software Technology 42(14), 1001–1008 (2000)
8. Zowghi, D., Nurmuliani, N.: A Study of the Impact of Requirements Volatility on Software Project Performance. In: Proceedings of the 9th Asia-Pacific Software Engineering Conference, Gold Coast, Australia, pp. 3–11 (2002)
9. Malaiya, Y.K., Denton, J.: Requirements Volatility and Defect Density. In: Proceedings of 10th International Symposium on Software Reliability Engineering, pp. 285–294 (1999)
10. Stark, G., Skillicorn, A., Ameele, R.: An Examination of the Effects of Requirements Changes on Software Releases. CROSSTALK, The Journal of Defense Software Engineering, 11–16 (December 1998)

11. Nurmuliani, N., Zowghi, D., Williams, S.P.: Requirements Volatility and Its Impact on Change Effort: Evidence Based Research in Software Development Projects. In: Proceedings of the 11th Australian Workshop on Requirements Engineering (AWRE 2006), Adelaide, Australia (2006)
12. Jönsson, P., Lindvall, M.: Impact Analysis. In: Engineering and Managing Software Requirements, pp. 117–142. Springer, Heidelberg (2005)
13. Nurmuliani, N., Zowghi, D., Powell, S.: Analysis of Requirements Volatility During Software Development Life Cycle. In: Proceedings of the 2004 Australian Software Engineering Conference (ASWEC 2004), Melbourne, Australia (2004)
14. Nurmuliani, N., Zowghi, D., Williams, S.P.: Characterising Requirements Volatility: An Empirical Analysis. In: Proceedings of the 4th International Symposium on Empirical Software Engineering (ISESE 2005), Noosa, Australia (2005)

Identifying Key Success Factors for Globally Distributed Software Development Project Using Simulation: A Case Study

Siri-on Setamanit[1] and David Raffo[2]

[1] Faculty of Commerce and Accountancy, Chulalongkorn University, Phyathai Rd.,
Pathumwan, Bangkok, Thailand
{siri-on@acc.chula.ac.th}
[2] Portland State University, 631 SW Harrison St., Portland, OR, USA
{raffod@pdx.edu}

Abstract. With the increased pressure to reduce cost, reduce development time, and improve quality, many software companies are moving toward using a Globally Distributed Software Development (GSD) paradigm. Due to the challenges and difficulties with GSD, researchers and practitioners are attempting to identify key success factors for GSD projects. Based on our previous work, we found that the key success factors can be different depending upon specific project characteristics. To ensure a successful outcome, project managers have to focus on the right success factors for their particular project. In this paper, we illustrate how a GSD simulation model can be used to represent a specific project and to identify key success factors for that project. We use a case study from an actual software development firm. We also perform sensitivity analysis to assess the magnitude of the performance impact for the key factors for the specific project. For the case study site, which uses a combination of phase-based and module-based task allocation strategies, we found that team member familiarity, frequency of team meetings, and communication frequency each have a strong impact on total project effort and duration.

Keywords: Globally Distributed Software Development, Success Factors, Process Simulation, Case Study.

1 Introduction

Due to increased competition in software development industry, software companies are under pressure to further reduce costs, decrease development cycle time, and improve software quality. With the advancement of communication media (especially through the use of Internet), many software companies are moving toward developing software in globally distributed setting. Today, there are almost 100 nations participating in globally distributed software development [1].

There are several *potential* benefits from GSD such as reduction in time-to-market, reduction in development costs, better use of scarce resources, business advantages from proximity to customers, and etc. [1-5]. Unfortunately, due to geographical dispersion, time zone differences, coupled with cultural and language differences, communication

Q. Wang, D. Pfahl, and D.M. Raffo (Eds.): ICSP 2008, LNCS 5007, pp. 320–332, 2008.
© Springer-Verlag Berlin Heidelberg 2008

and coordination between development sites can become exceedingly difficult. As a result, it has been reported that some GSD projects have been unsuccessful and have had to be abandoned [2].

Despite these challenges and difficulties, GSD will continue to be a major paradigm in software development industry. Therefore, it is important to identify key success factors for GSD projects and to identify approaches to improve the development process so that full potential GSD benefits can be achieved.

Researchers and practitioners have attempted to identify and understand factors that enable or hinder the success of GSD projects. Several key important factors have been identified such as communication frequency [6-10], time zone differences [2, 11-13], cultural differences [11, 14-19], language differences [2, 11, 13, 20], development site characteristics such as infrastructure, programmer experience and skills [2, 21], etc. Nevertheless, most of this work is based on case studies or experience of the developers on specific projects. Moreover, this work consists of mostly qualitative studies which make it difficult for practitioners to gauge the potential impact these factors may have on their own specific projects.

According to our previous work, we found that the impact (magnitude and direction) of many of the above key factors varied depending on the specific task allocation strategies used on the project [22]. This suggests that GSD practitioners need a methodology to evaluate the impact of key factors as they vary simultaneously on a specific project so that they can focus their effort in improving the factors that will strongly contribute to the success of that specific project.

1.1 Research Objectives

There are two objectives in this paper. First, we strive to illustrate how a Global Software Development simulation model (GSD model) can be used to identify and assess the performance impact of key success factors on a specific project. Second, we show how project managers (PMs) can use a GSD model to select the most important success factors for their particular project and then to identify way to improve them. This enables the PM the ability to focus on the right success factors that have the most impact for their own specific project.

1.2 Organization of the Paper

This paper is divided into 4 sections. Section 1 contains the introduction and motivation for this research. Section 2 briefly discusses the use of a simulation model together with other techniques to identify and assess the impact of GSD success factors for a particular project. Section 3 presents the case study showing the application of the simulation model directed toward project managers who wish to focus their effort on the right factors in order to capture the full benefits of GSD. This application of the GSD model was done in a real world setting. Section 4 presents a conclusion.

2 Methodology

In order to identify and assess the impact of key success factors, a GSD simulation model was used as a platform for experimentation. An overview of this model is presented in Section 2.1. An experimental design is then created to explore the response surface of the key GSD factors contained in the model. Results obtained from the model identify the success factors for the specific GSD project that is being represented. After the key factors have been identified for a specific project, a sensitivity analysis is conducted to further evaluate the impact of the most important success factors for the project. This provides specific guidance to project managers as to where they should focus their efforts.

2.1 A Simulation Model as an Experimentation Platform

In software engineering, it is very costly, time consuming, and nearly impossible to conduct controlled experiments [23]. In addition, it is extremely difficult to separate the impact of any particular factor from other factors especially in large, complex, and dynamic project environments (like GSD projects) [24]. As a result, most GSD studies are primarily exploratory or based on experience on a particular project. Moreover, the studies address only limited aspects of GSD projects. For example, Herbsleb et al. [4] focused on how distance affects cycle time, but not concerned about cultural and language differences or time-zone differences. This makes it a challenge to generalize the findings to other GSD projects that may be conducted under different circumstances or in different development settings.

One of the significant advantages of simulation is that these models can be constructed and calibrated to reflect real world behavior when provided with sufficient empirical data for a specific system (in this case a GSD project). This data is rarely perfect. However, for parameters where there is not sufficient data, ranges, industrial averages or other information can be provided and a consensus as to reasonable values or ranges of values can be determined. It is from this starting point that the simulation model can be used as an experimental platform to investigate and/or evaluate the system under study. Individual parameters or combinations of parameters can then be varied and the magnitude and strength of the impact of these factors on variables of interest can be measured [25]. Thus, a simulation model can enable researchers and/or practitioners to identify and assess the effects of any factor on project performance. As a result, it is far less costly and less risky to perform experimentation using simulation models than to make changes to the GSD project.

The GSD Model. A simulation model was developed to capture important GSD project and process issues. The GSD model used in this paper is classified as a hybrid simulation model combining system dynamics and discrete-event paradigms in order to represent GSD projects. The GSD model includes the factors that were reported to affect GSD project performance. The GSD model has three high-level components: a discrete-event (DES) model, a system dynamics (SD) model and an Interaction Effect (IE) model. The DES model captures how tasks are allocated between development sites. It represents activities performed at each site and the artifact transfer between sites. The SD model captures both overall project environment such as planning and controlling activities and specific characteristic of each development site such as human resource and productivity. The IE model captures the impact when developers work collaboratively with developers from other sites. In addition, the GSD model was designed to be flexible and expandable. Therefore, one can easily modify the GSD model to represent any particular project with different number of development sites, different task allocation strategies, and etc. The detail information about the model and the important GSD factors incorporated in the model can be found in [22, 26-29].

2.2 Experimental Design or Design of Experiment (DOE)

Experimental design or Design of Experiments (DOE) is a statistical technique for organizing and analyzing experiments. DOE can be used to examine the impacts of changes in parameter values on the outcome measures of interest. Important inter-actions in complex systems can be revealed by performing DOE. DOE has been widely used in simulation studies since the 1990s [30]. Law and Kelton [31] pro-vide good overviews of an experimental design and optimization in the simulation context. DOE has also been applied to several simulations of software projects. For example, Houston et al. [32] used DOE to measure the relative contribution of several factors to variations in the response variables in order to behaviorally char-acterize four system dynamics software process models. Wakeland et al. [33] illus-trate the application of DOE combined with Broad Range Sensitivity Analysis (BRSA) on a hybrid model in order to study the impacts of removing inspection steps on duration and latent defects.

A 2^k factorial design, where each of the k factors is allowed to have two values or levels, is a common and useful approach in DOE. It is an economical approach, which is effective in examining the impacts of changes in a model's inputs on its out-puts and also revealing interaction effects [31].

2.3 Sensitivity Analysis

Sensitivity analysis is the process to systematically vary the values of the model's parameters and see how these changes affect its output or behavior. This allows the modeler to examine the impact of uncertainty on a model's input parameters [34, 35]. Sensitivity analysis can be used to compliment a 2^k factorial design. In general, a 2^k factorial design is first conducted in order to identify factors that can have significant impacts on model output measures (i.e. for the purposes of this study, this relates to GSD project performance). After that, sensitivity analysis on these factors can be performed in order to examine the magnitude of the impact to changes in these factors on each performance measure.

3 A Case Study

In this section, we will describe a case study that was conducted at a global software development company in Thailand. We will illustrate how a GSD model was adapted to represent a specific project at the case study site. The model was then used to help project managers identify key project success factors and focus their efforts on the right factors.

3.1 Case Study Overview

This case study was conducted at a global software development company in Thailand. The company is engaged in the development of application software that supports real-time financial applications. This site is one of the seven major development centers located around the world for this company, including the United States, England, Europe, and Asia.

The project under study is named "ABC-1". It is a collaboration project between two development sites: Bangkok, Thailand (BKK) and Chicago, Illinois, USA (USA). The scope of the project ranges from gathering customer requirements to releasing the software. ABC-1 project has 6 major development phases; each phase contains multiple activities. For simplicity and to provide a general understanding, Fig. 1 shows the high-level process flow for ABC-1 project.

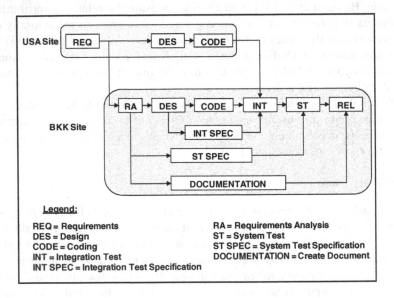

Fig. 1. ABC-1 Top Level Process

One can see that the majority of the work (approximately 70%) is handled by the BKK site. However, the requirements phase which includes requirements gathering, requirements analysis, and requirements specification, all of which require expertise and proximity to the clients, was performed at the USA site. In general, the requirements specification is developed by the USA staff at the beginning of the project. Then, development work is divided into 3 modules. The USA staff designs and codes one module, and the other two modules are sent to BKK.

Once the requirements specification from the USA site is received, the BKK site starts the project by analyzing the specification and creating a detailed design. Most of the communication and feedback between sites occur regularly at this stage until the detailed design is finalized. After that, the communication and coordination activity between the two sites is kept to a minimum. Note that there is no formal integration activity because changes to the code are automatically integrated by the server at the USA site. Nevertheless, there is a formal integration test at the BKK site after the CODE phase.

3.2 Identifying Key Success Factors

First, we tailored the GSD model to represent the ABC-1 project, called "ABC-1" model. This includes configuring the number of development sites, the activities that will be carried out at each site, and the transfer points. We also calibrated the model based on information from survey questionnaires as well as in-depth interviews with the technical director, the ABC-1 project manager, and software developers. We also used secondary data from the project metrics repository.

After performing several tests to verify and validate the model, the model showed stable performance and reasonable results which approximated the actual performance of the ABC-1 project. The next step was to conduct a 2^k factorial design to examine the effects of key factors on ABC-1 project performance measures (total effort and project duration). Based on the literature, expert opinion, and initial experimentation, we identified 7 factors that potentially could have a strong impact on project performance.

A 2^7 factorial design was constructed with 5 replications for each design point (a modest sample size from a statistical viewpoint [31]) for a total of 640 runs. The dependent variables were total effort and project duration. Table 1 shows the factors, their levels, and descriptions.

Table 1. Factor levels in a 2^7 factorial design for ABC-1 project

Factors		Levels	Description
Communication Frequency	2	Low	The level of communication between development sites
		High	
Time-zone (% Overlap of Work Hours)	2	No overlap working hour	Different time-zone means less overlap working hour
		100% overlap working hour	
Culture	2	Same	National culture between two development sites (related to the location of development sites)
		Different	
Language	2	Same	Common language between two development sites
		Different	
Overhead of Distribution (% OH)	2	Low	Additional effort/time required when tasks are distributed across sites including artifact trasnfer and knowledge transfer.
		High	
Member Familiarity	2	Low	The degree that members are familiar with one another (i.e. work together before, kick-off meeting = high)
		High	
Team Meeting	2	Infrequent	The frequency of team meeting during the course of the project
		Frequent	

Key Success Factors for Total Effort. The main effects of all factors on total effort were found to be statistically significant. Fig. 2 shows the main effect plot for the seven key factors on the total effort. To interpret Fig. 2, we look at the direction of the slope of the line on the main effect chart in comparison to the values used in the factorial analysis (x-axis). For example, the first section of Fig. 2 is devoted to the percentage of overlap time. The slope of the line indicates that as the % overlap of work hours varies from 0% to 100%, total effort is reduced since project level productivity of the GSD team is increased by having better coordination through synchronous communication. The other variables can be interpreted similarly.

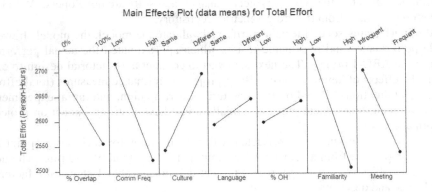

Fig. 2. Main effect plot on total effort

The top three success factors that had the strongest impact on total effort (steep slope) were team member *familiarity*, followed by *communication frequency*, and the frequency of *team meetings*. When developers are familiar with one another, they tend to coordinate better and have higher productivity, thus require lower effort. Frequent communication between developers also leads to higher productivity, resulting in lower project effort. This is particularly true in the Thai culture. Lastly, as mentioned in the literature [2, 12], frequent meetings help improve trust between team members, which further reduces effort.

Key Success Factors for Duration. The main effects of all factors on duration except *team meeting* were statistically significant. Fig. 3 shows the main effect plot for the seven key factors on the total project duration.

The top three success factors with the strongest impact on duration were member *familiarity*, followed by *% overlap of work hours*, and *communication frequency*. Like its effect on total effort, member *familiarity* had a negative relationship with project duration. Increasing *percent overlap of work hours* allowed for increased synchronous communication between developers. Synchronous communication facilitated better coordination between sites and thus improved productivity, which contributed to lower effort required. Since duration was correlated with effort, increased *percent overlap of*

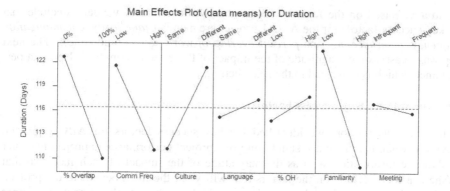

Fig. 3. Main effect plot on duration

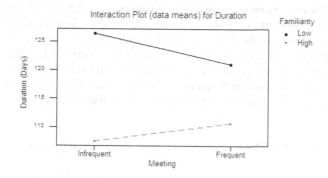

Fig. 4. Interaction plot on duration

work hours contributed to shorter duration. *Frequent communication* between developers also contributed to lower effort, which made the project duration shorter. Note that the interactions between member *familiarity* and *team meeting* are also significant as shown in Fig. 4.

Team meeting helps decrease duration only when team member are not familiar with one another. On the other hand, when developers are familiar with one another, having frequent meeting will increase duration. Using this information together with the result from factorial analysis on total effort in previous section, one can see that when team members have met before or are familiar with one another, frequent meetings did not reduce effort (improve productivity), and actually increased duration. The reason is that the improvement in productivity was not enough to off-set the development time lost when the meeting(s) were held. However, when team members were not familiar with one another, frequent meetings provided significant benefit by reducing effort and duration.

This finding is very important. Almost all research on GSD has mentioned the importance of having frequent meeting during the course of the project. Simply following this suggestion without considering specific project conditions may result in an unfavorable outcome.

Summary. Based on the factorial design that was conducted, we can conclude that the key success factors for the ABC-1 project are member *familiarity, communication frequency, team meeting,* and *percent overlap of work hours* (time-zone). The next step was to assess the magnitude of the impact of these factors on ABC-1 project performance, which is described in the next section.

3.3 Quantifying Key Success Factors

In the previous section, we identified the key success factors for ABC-1 project. However, when making a decision to improve project performance, a project manager needs more information such as the magnitude of the impact of each factor so that he/she can focus efforts on the factors that will yield the most benefit to the project. In this section, we conducted a sensitivity analysis to evaluate the impact of changes in key success factors on project performance.

The Impact of Member Familiarity and Team Meeting. For the ABC-1 project, the degree of member familiarity is at the maximum level since key developers from the BKK site were brought to the USA site for training for 3 months before the project started. Nevertheless, GSD model results showed that member familiarity interacts with team meeting frequency. Hence, we conducted a sensitivity analysis in order to identify the appropriate meeting frequency when team members have high familiarity. Fig. 5 shows the effect of meeting frequency on total effort and project duration.

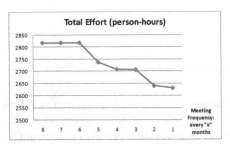 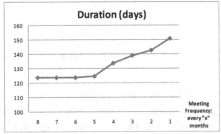

Fig. 5. Effect of team meeting frequency when degree of member familiarity is high

Increasing meeting frequency contributed to lower effort but longer duration (but the effects are not uniform). One can see that the appropriate frequency for team meetings could be every 4 or 5 months which will result in the best combination of total effort and duration (low effort with short duration). However, if the degree of member familiarity is lower or different, the impact of meeting frequency on total effort and project duration can be different. To illustrate the point, we conducted a sensitivity analysis on meeting frequency when team members are not familiar with one another (i.e. never work together before) as shown in Fig. 6.

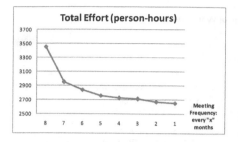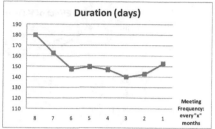

Fig. 6. Effect of team meeting frequency when degree of member familiarity is low

When team members' familiarity is low, it makes much more sense to have more frequent meetings. At the same time, however, having too many meetings can result in longer duration without a significant improvement in productivity to off-set the development time lost when the meeting(s) were held.

The Impact of Communication Frequency. From a factorial analysis, we found that communication frequency has strong impact on total effort and project duration. Therefore, we conducted a sensitivity analysis to evaluate the impact of the changes in communication frequency on total effort and duration. The results are shown in Fig. 7.

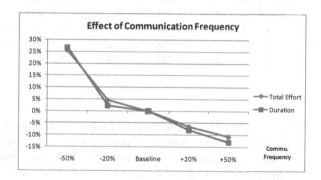

Fig. 7. Sensitivity analysis of communication frequency on total effort and duration

One can see that the impact of the change in communication frequency is relatively low except when communication frequency was reduced by 50%. This implies that it is very important to maintain the level of communication frequency between development sites.

The Impact of Percent Overlap of Work Hours. Based on the discussion with the project manager, it is possible that the developers at the BKK site can adjust their working schedule such that there is an overlap of work hours with the USA site (up to 3 hours or 37.5% overlap). Fig. 8 shows the effect of the increased in percent overlap of work hours on total effort and duration.

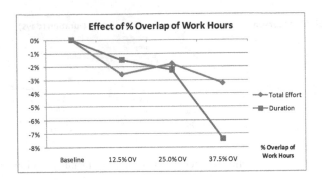

Fig. 8. Sensitivity analysis of percent overlap of work hours on total effort and duration

The impact of percent overlap of work hours is relatively small. It may not be worthwhile to increase overlap of work hours if it will increase the project costs (for example, overtime wages). Nevertheless, it is clear that if we need to reduce project duration, increasing overlap of work hours can help.

3.4 Future Work

The analysis that we performed in this section focused on the impact of the changes of each variable on project performance. This allows project managers to understand and quantify the impact of each key success factor on the project performance. In the future, we can use the ABC-1 model to examine the impact of improvement in several key success factors at the same time in order to find the combined conditions that would make the ABC-1 project realize the full benefits of GSD.

4   Conclusion

In this paper, we illustrate how to use a GSD model to identify and quantify key success factors for specific GSD projects. Key success factors can vary based on specific characteristics such as task allocation strategy, time-zone difference, member familiarity, among others. Simply improving the general set of key success factors without considering the impact each factor may have on the particular project of interest may result in unfavorable outcome. For the case study described in this paper, we found that member familiarity had the strongest impact on project performance. However, there was also an interaction between member familiarity and team meeting frequency. As a result, the project manager would need to be more careful when examining the impact of these factors on project performance and manage any changes that might occur related to these parameters. These factors while generally recognized as important, are rarely mentioned as being critical. However, for this particular project, the GSD model was able to identify them as being most important for this specific real world project. This research emphasizes the importance of using a simulation model to help project managers assess the impact of potential project changes before implementing them and experiencing large, unanticipated negative effects.

References

1. Carmel, E., Tija, P.: Offshoring Information Technology: Sourcing and Outsourcing to a Global Work-force. Cambridge University Press, Cambridge (2005)
2. Carmel, E.: Global Software Teams. Prentice Hall PTR, Upper Saddle River (1999)
3. Gorton, I., Motwani, S.: Issues in co-operative software engineering using globally distributed teams. Information and SoftwareTechnology 38, 647–655 (1996)
4. Herbsleb, J.D., Grinter, R.E., Finholt, T.A.: An empirical study of global software development: distance and speed. In: ICSE 2001, pp. 81–90. IEEE, Toronto, Canada (2001)
5. Norbjerg, J., Havn, E.C., Bansler, J.P.: Global production: the case of offshore programming. In: Krallmann, H. (ed.) Wirtschaftsinformatik 1997, Physica-Verlag, Berlin (1997)
6. Allen, T.J.: Managing the Flow of Technology. MIT press, Cambridge (1977)
7. Kraut, R.E., Egido, C., Galegher, J.: Patterns of contact and communication in scientific research col-laborations. In: Galegher, J., Kraut, R.E., Egido, C. (eds.) Intellectual Teamwork: Social Foundations of Cooperative Work, pp. 149–172. Lawrence Erlbaum Associates, New Jersey (1990)
8. Kraut, R.E., Streeter, L.A.: Coordination in software development. Communications of the ACM 38, 69–81 (1995)
9. Herbsleb, J.D., Grinter, R.E.: Conceptual Simplicity Meets Organizational Complexity: Case Study of a Corporate Metrics Program. In: International Conference on Software Engineering, pp. 271–280. IEEE Press, Kyoto, Japan (1998)
10. Herbsleb, J.D., Grinter, R.E.: Splitting the organization and integrating the code: conway's law revisited. In: International Conference on Software Engineering (ICSE 1999), pp. 85–95. ACM Press, Los Angeles (1999)
11. Carmel, E., Agarwal, R.: Tactical approached for alleviating distance in global software development. IEEE Software 18, 22–29 (2001)
12. Jarvenpaa, S.L., Knoll, K.: Is anybody out there? Antecedents of trust in global virtual teams. Journal of Management Information Systems 14, 29–64 (1998)
13. Keil, L., Eng., P.: Experiences in distributed development: a case study. In: The International Workshop on Global Software Development, Portland, OR USA, pp. 44–47 (2003)
14. Carmel, E.: The explosion of global software teams. Computerworld (1997)
15. Karolak, D.W.: Global Software Development: Managing Virtual Teams and Environments. IEEE Computer Society, Los Alamitos (1998)
16. Battin, R.D., et al.: Leveraging resources in global software development. IEEE Software, 70–77 (2001)
17. Damian, D.E., Zowghi, D.: The Impact of Stakeholders' Geographical Distribution on Managing Requirements in a Multi-site Organization. In: IEEE Joint International Conference on Requirements Engineering, IEEE, Essen, Germany (2002)
18. Ives, B., Jarvenpaa, S.L.: Applications of Global Information Technology: Key Issues for Management. MIS Quarterly, 33–49 (1991)
19. Borchers, G.: The Software Engineering Impacts of Cultural Factors on Multi-cultural Software Devel-opment Teams. In: International Conference on Software Engineering, pp. 540–545. IEEE, Portland, OR, USA (2003)
20. Ishii, H.: Cross-cultural communication and CSCW. In: Harasim, L.M. (ed.) Global Networks: Computers and International Communication, pp. 143–151. MIT Press, Cambridge (1993)
21. Herbsleb, J.D., Moitra, D.: Global software development. IEEE Software 18, 16–20 (2001)
22. Setamanit, S., Wakeland, W., Raffo, D.: Using simulation to evaluate global software development task allocation strategies. Software Process: Improvement and Practice 12, 491–503 (2007)
23. Myers, G.J.: Software Reliability: Principle and Practices. John Wiley & Sons, Inc., New York (1976)

24. Glass, R.L.: Modern Programming Practices: A Report from Industry. Prentice-Hall, Inc, Englewood Cliffs (1982)
25. Rus, I., Biffl, S., Halling, M.: Systematically Combining Process Simulation and Empirical Data in Support of Decision Analysis in Software Development. In: The fourteenth International Conference on Software Engineering and Knowledge Engineering (SEKE 2002), ACM, Ischia, Italy (2002)
26. Raffo, D., Setamanit, S.: A simulation model for global software development project. In: The International Workshop on Software Process Simulation and Modeling, St. Louis, MO (2005)
27. Setamanit, S., Wakeland, W., Raffo, D.: Exploring the Impact of Task Allocation Strategies for Global Software Development Using Simulation. In: Software Process Change, Springer, Heidelberg (2006)
28. Setamanit, S., Wakeland, W., Raffo, D.: Planning and Improving Global Software Development Process Using Simulation. In: The First International Workshop on Global Software Development for the Practitioner, Shanghai, China (2006)
29. Setamanit, S., Wakeland, W., Raffo, D.: Improving Global Software Development Project Performance Using Simulation. In: Portland International Conference on Management of Engineering and Technology Portland, OR, USA (2007)
30. Donohue, J.M.: Experimental Designs for Simulation. In: Tew, J.D., Manivannan, S., Sadowski, D.A., Seila, A.F. (eds.) The 1994 Winter Simulation Conference, pp. 200–206 (1994)
31. Law, A.M., Kelton, W.D.: Simulation Modeling and Analysis. The McGraw-Hill Companies, Inc., New York (2003)
32. Houston, D., et al.: Behavioral characterization: finding and using the influential factors in software process simulation models. Journal of Systems and Software 59, 259–270 (2001)
33. Wakeland, W., Martin, R., Raffo, D.M.: Using Design of Experiments, Sensitivity Analysis, and Hybrid Simulation to Evaluate Changes to a Software Development Process: A Case Study. In: The International Workshop on Software Process Simulation and Modeling, Portland, OR, USA (2003)
34. Sargent, R.G.: Verification and Validation of Simulation Models. In: Cellier, F.E. (ed.) Progress in Modelling and Simulation, pp. 159–169. Academic Press, London (1982)
35. Pegden, C.D., Shannon, R.E., Sadowski, R.P.: Introduction to Simulation using SIMAN. McGraw-Hill, New York (1990)

Hybrid Modeling of Test-and-Fix Processes in Incremental Development

He Zhang, Ross Jeffery, and Liming Zhu

National ICT Australia, Locked Bag 9013, Alexandria NSW 1435, Australia
School of Computer Science and Engineering, University of New South Wales, Australia
{he.zhang, ross.jeffery, liming.zhu}@nicta.com.au

Abstract. Software process simulation modeling has become an increasingly active research area for managing and improving software development processes since its introduction in the last two decades. Hybrid process simulation models have attracted interest as a possibility to avoid the limitations of applying single modeling method, and more realistically capture complex real-world software processes. This paper presents a hybrid process modeling scheme to build an integrated software process model. It focuses on the particular portion of software process by using different techniques on separate but interconnected phases, while still allows for the integrity of modeling development process. We developed a hybrid simulation model of the test-and-fix process of incremental software development. Results conclude that this approach can support the investigation of portions of software process at different granularity levels simultaneously. It also avoids the limitation caused by incomplete process detail of some phases, and may help reduce the effort of building a hybrid simulation model.

Keywords: Software process simulation model, hybrid modeling, test-and-fix, incremental development.

1 Introduction

Software process simulation modeling (SPSM) has become an increasingly active research area for managing and improving software development processes in the last two decades. In [1], Osterweil identified two complementary types of software process research, which can be characterized as macro-process research, focused on phenomenological observations of external behaviors of processes, and micro-process research, focused on the study of the internal details and workings of processes. In SPSM area, the continuous and discrete-event modeling approaches are corresponding to these two types of research.

Our systematic review [2] found that continuous simulation (system dynamics, SD) and discrete-event simulation (DES) are the two most applied paradigms in ProSim[1] community in the last decade. The review also concludes that hybrid process simulation models have attracted interest as a possibility to avoid the limitations of applying

---

[1] International Workshop on Software Process Simulation Modeling.

Q. Wang, D. Pfahl, and D.M. Raffo (Eds.): ICSP 2008, LNCS 5007, pp. 333–344, 2008.
© Springer-Verlag Berlin Heidelberg 2008

single modeling method, and more realistically capture complex real-world software processes. Among the published hybrid SPSM models, SD plus DES has been the most common combination [2].

Many studies published in ProSim series conferences have tried to integrate SD and DES to model software process more realistically. They both have their own advantages and limitations (Section 2). In this paper, we propose a flexible hybrid SPSM solution, and then demonstrate its use for investigating the test-and-fix process of incremental development.

This paper is structured as follows. In Section 2, we review the previous hybrid SPSM approaches, and then propose our hybrid modeling scheme. Section 3 briefly introduces the characteristics of incremental development, describes the conceptual model of software quality applied in this study, and reviews the related models. Section 4 describes the development of an incremental development model by using our proposed hybrid modeling scheme. We include a case example to illustrate the capability and usefulness of the model in Section 5. Finally, we conclude our research and provide future work in Section 6.

2 Hybrid Simulation Modeling

2.1 Previous Hybrid Modeling Approaches

Martin and Raffo's analyzed the manpower utilization using hybrid simulation model [3], which presents how workforce levels vary on the basis of the changes in a set of factors. Their hybrid simulation model was developed to maintain the consistency between the discrete activities and the change of continuous portions. This hybrid model allows investigation of the effects of discrete resource changes on continuously varying productivity, and the influences of discrete tasks on continuously varying defect rates.

Rus *et al.* [4] and Lakey [5] modeled the software process as a set of discrete activities. To achieve continuous modeling and incorporate the feedback loops of system dynamics, they divided the inputs by five, and iterate the activity five times. This solution improves the continuity of calculating the process factors and performances, such as implementation size, defect level, and workforce. It also makes it possible to explicitly analyze the performance of a single discrete process, which is regarded as a difficult task in pure continuous simulation, e.g. system dynamics [3]. However, such approximation of continuous models is coarse, and the time advance might be different between discrete phases.

Table 1. Solutions for hybrid software process modeling

Authors	Martin & Raffo	Rus *et al.* & Lakey	Choi *et al.*	**Zhang *et al.***
Model framework	Continuous	Discrete-event	Discrete-event	**Discrete-event**
Module/phase level	Discrete-event	Continuous	Continuous	**Continuous/ Discrete-event**
Sim tool	Extend	Extend	DEVSim++	**Extend**

Choi *et al.* [6] proposed their hybrid modeling approach by constraining the time advance of discrete-event model to be a small enough constant-time, which enables them to model differential equation system with discrete-event modeling. Therefore, their solution is an enhancement to Rus and Lakey's approach with the refined time advance, which presents the feedback mechanism of system dynamics more effectively in a discrete-event framework.

Table 1 (column 2 to 4) summarizes the characteristics of the above hybrid modeling solutions. These solutions employ continuous and discrete-event modeling at different levels, i.e. modeling portions of continuous model with discrete-event approach, or using finer time advance for modeling discrete activities to observe the continuously varied process performance.

2.2 Flexible Hybrid Modeling Scheme

One limitation of the previous hybrid simulation modeling approaches is that they emphasized continuous and discrete-event modeling at different model levels. For instance, if the model's framework is based on discrete-event, they tried to implement continuous simulation in every single discrete phase. However, the selection of simulation modeling is a function of the characteristics of the system (what we know) and the objectives of our study (what we need) [7]. This principle should not only be applied at model level, but module (or phase) level also.

Our hybrid modeling scheme described in this paper is shown in Table 1 as well (in bold) for comparison with the previous approaches. At model (or framework) level, our approach is discrete-based, which presents the transitions between sequentially connected discrete phases. Whereas, the decision of choosing continuous or discrete-event modeling depends on the answers to the following questions:

- What is the purpose of modeling and simulation of this module/phase?
- Which portion of the investigated process(es) is the focus of our study?
- What are the observed process factors in this phase related to model outputs?
- At what granularity level we possess the information of this phase?

In the real cases, we do not always possess the micro-process level knowledge on all phases of software processes, which limits our capability to carry out fine-grained investigation on portion(s) of processes. The flexible selection of simulation modeling approach on module level, however, can assist our investigation in focusing on the

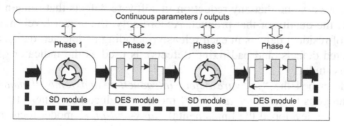

Fig. 1. Flexible hybrid simulation modeling scheme

specific phase or process by using discrete-event approach, while still maintain the overall model integrity by using continuous approach on other portion(s) of the process. By reusing the well-developed the generic continuous modules, it may also help reduce the effort of building a hybrid simulation model. Figure 1 visualizes our flexible hybrid SPSM scheme.

To demonstrate this proposed hybrid modeling approach, one model of incremental development is presented in the following sections as an example.

3   Background

3.1   Incremental Development

Incremental development is a broad term describing a type of software development process, which may cover iterative development, versioned implementation, spiral model, etc [8]. The basic idea is to divide the development into several smaller increments, which are gradually accumulated to become the complete system.

Basically, there are three phases in one increment. They are analysis (design), implementation, and test-and-fix. In this article, we model these phases by focusing on investigation of the test-and-fix process in an intermediate increment. After the current release is implemented, the progress enters a test-and-fix process, where this release is thoroughly tested and the detected defects are cleared. During this period, no new functionality is added into the current release. The purpose of the process is to make sure that each release provides a robust foundation for its succeeding releases.

Compared with waterfall process, the incremental development reflects more typical characteristics of software processes, such as transition, concurrence, and iteration. Each transition is necessary to trigger next phase of process, as well as the releases aggregate to the final product. It is difficult to implement the simulation of an incremental development process, because every single phase in every release (iteration) cannot be omitted from the simulation model. Nevertheless, given the specific research question(s) and the knowledge of different process portions, our hybrid modeling scheme can investigate some portion(s) of the process on a fine-grained level and allow the incomplete process detail in others, while maintain the required model integrity for simulation.

3.2   Software Quality Conceptual Model

In our work, we assume that any reduction in software defects that remain in a product improves the quality of that product. Accordingly, the defect level, measured by the number of residual defects in each release (including undetected defects, detected but uncorrected defects, and bad-fixing defects), is used as the indicator of software quality in this study.

Boehm described the "*software defect introduction and removal model*" in [9], which is analogous to the "*tank and pipe*" model introduced by Jones [10]. Based on their models, we developed the fundamental "*tank-and-pipe*" model focusing on test-and-fix process of incremental development, as shown in Figure 2.

The graphic model shows that defects conceptually flow into a cascade of tanks through various defect source and transferring pipes. To be noticed, we don't include the quality assurance activities, e.g. walk-through and inspection, in our model at current stage. The figure depicts that defects are drained off through the defect detection and defect fixing pipes. The residual defects of current release will be input to next increment. In the following sections of this paper, we use '*error*' as the equivalent term to '*defect*'.

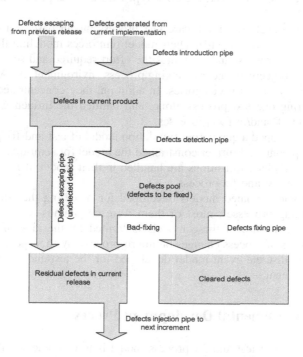

Fig. 2. "*tank-and-pipe*" model of test-and-fix process of incremental development

3.3 Related Models

Some previous researches have investigated the software testing process using quantitative models. A brief description and comments of these models are given separately as below.

Abdel-Hamid and Madnick (AHM) modeled the basic software testing process, which is a sector of their integrated software process model with system dynamics [11]. However, their model is based on the waterfall testing process, rather than the testing process in incremental development. They did not differentiate the newly generated errors and the residual errors from the test-and-fix process of the previous increments, which influence the current testing performance. Plus, as a continuous model, their model neglects the switchover phenomenon (identified in [12]) of error fixing productivity.

Huff *et al.* developed an alternative causal model for the test-and-fix process of incremental development [12]. They quantified the relations by quantitative equations.

Nevertheless, their models did not identify the reproduction of the residual (old) lactive errors in the succeeding increments.

Tvedt developed a comprehensive process model of concurrent incremental development [13]. He considered the impacts on defect creation from engineer's capability, technical risk, and interdependency among the concurrent increments, which is not the case of our process. However, the error types were not explicitly handled across increments.

Cangussu et al. developed a software test process model based on concepts and techniques from control theory [14]. Their model reinforces modeling the continuous feedback during test process, and computes the effort required and schedule slippage to meet the quality objectives under changing process environment. As AHM's model, they did not identify the error categories. In addition, they concentrated on the control-feedback during one test process alone, and omitted the influence between implementation and test (and/or fix) processes.

Zhang et al. developed a qualitative simulation model of test-and-fix process in incremental development, and further constrained the model for semi-quantitative simulation [15]. Though, phase transitions are handled in their model, it is still a continuous-based model of test-and-fix process.

Although the above related models developed for modeling the similar software testing and/or fixing processes, most of them were continuous- or analytical-based models. Therefore, the use of these models is limited by the lack of capability to evaluate the impacts of process changes on micro-process. With respect to our knowledge, there is few discrete-event model developed for the test-and-fix process of incremental development.

4   Modeling Incremental Development Process

The primary purpose of test-and-fix process model is to examine whether the increment can be completed in the desired time period with the required quality, and evaluate the process changes of test-and-fix phase in incremental development.

Overall, the simulation model was developed using Extend^{TM} (by ImagineThat Inc.). Aiming at the model purposes, it consists of two interlinked sub-models: system dynamics model of the design-and-implement process (for defect generation) and discrete-event model of the test-and-fix process (for defect detection and correction).

4.1   Sub-model of Design-and-Implement Phase

One widely used linear model for software implementation is employed as the basic skeleton of this model, i.e. given workforce (wf), release size (s_i), and unit productivity (pd), the elapsed calendar days to complete the release can be calculated by $s_i/(wf * pd)$. However, because we are interested in the processes related to defect generating, detecting and fixing during each increment, more features related to defect generation need to be involved in the sub-model of this phase. In addition, the management and communication overheads and staff capability need to be considered as well when calculating the elapsed time. The high level continuous feedback loops of this model, especially for continuous modules, are shown in Figure 3.

During the implementation phase, there are two basic types of defects generated: active defects and passive defects [11]. An undetected "active defect" may reproduce more active or passive defects in its succeeding increments until it is detected or retired. The undetected "passive defects" remain dormant until they are captured.

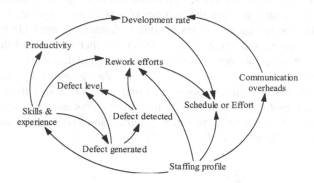

Fig. 3. Continuous feedback loops

We pay more attention on the active and passive defects in implementation process because their combination and reproduction to some extent influence the total amount of available defects introduced to test-and-fix phase. If we suppose the system is developed with an incremental top-down strategy, then in the early releases, most of defects committed are in the core or high level components and become active. If these defects are not detected, they tend to propagate through the succeeding increments that build on one another.

Therefore, the defects generated through each implementation in the model come in two ways. The first is through the development of the incremental size for each release; the second is through the reproduction of the residual (old) active defects.

However, for many undetected active defects, the reproduction will not continue after producing one or two "generations" of defects [11]. In this case, they effectively become undetected passive defects.

Other important assumptions of this sub-model include: no concurrent increment (increment dependency); no change of release size during current increment; and no change of developer's productivity during design-and-implement phase.

4.2 Sub-model of Test-and-Fix Phase

The objective of test-and-fix process is to achieve an "acceptable level of quality", meaning that a certain percentage of defects will remain unidentified at release of the software [16]. During the incremental development, a small percentage of defects may escape from the current test-and-fix process, and remain in the implementation of the next increment (Figure 2).

In the test-and-fix process, a specific test suite is run and analyzed, detected defects are reported, assigned, and eventually fixed. In incremental development, the test cases are usually performed by a standalone team to avoid any potential bias. On the other hand, the work of correcting defects mostly falls to the team who implement the design and coding.

The test suite contains multiple test cases, which are prepared in advance, and ready prior to test-and-fix. We assume that the black-box testing strategy is applied in this process. Different from the implementation, the time spent detecting defects depends on the size of test suite (or the number of test cases in queue) for the current release, instead of the release size (lines of code or function points). On the other side, the time spent on correcting defects relates to the number of detected defects, defect characteristics (e.g. severity), developer's competency, and defect fixing process.

Here we focus on the "new" and "old" defects in the test-and-fix process model, as they are associated with different possibility and effort to detect them [12], which ultimately influences the performance of the testing process. Four types of defect severity are modeled (i.e. "easy", "medium", "hard", and "very hard"), and associated with different fixing efforts as well.

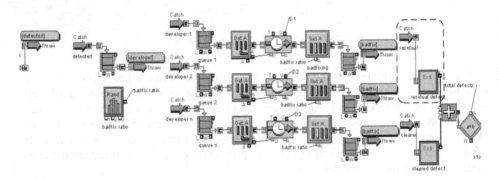

Fig. 4. Portion of test-and-fix process model with three developers

Figure 4 depicts a portion of defect fixing process in test-and-fix phase. At the leftmost, the defects are delivered to developers in terms of different strategies (further discussion in Section 5.2). The time required for fixing a defect is determined by defect severity, its original release, original developer, developer's competency. Besides, the process performance and developer utility are also related to the defect delivery strategies in use. The defect fixing activities may produce a small proportion of bad-fix at the same time, and they are captured by the blocks in dashed-line (Figure 4). Its possibility is handled stochastically in the simulation model.

Other important assumptions of this sub-model include: no change of the predefined test suite in each increment; and the uniform distribution of defects across the test suite (no regression).

4.3 Integration

These two sub-models connect each other iteratively to model the entire incremental development process (as shown in Figure 5). The design-and-implement sub-model is developed using system dynamics, while test-and-fix sub-model by discrete-event approach. At the connection between them, the information flow (output from design-and-implement) is split into information and entity flow. The latter contains two types of entity: defect and developer, which are associated with a set of attributes. The entity flow is accumulated and converted into information flow, then input to next increment. During this course, some important continuous parameters are observed, e.g. effort and defect level. As Extend^{TM} does not offer the capability of controlling the transitions between continuous and discrete-event sub-models in its visual modeling workbench, at current stage, we have to work with ModL language [17] to control the transitions at code level.

The intermediate increment may have multiple exits when performing simulation. This process is not completed until all detected defects are fixed, or a required percentage of test cases are passed within a desired period, and so on.

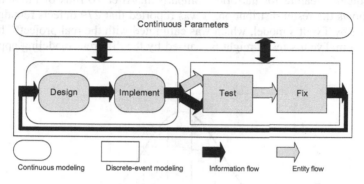

Fig. 5. High level hybrid model structure of incremental development

5   Case Example

5.1   Baseline Project

The baseline project in this section used for comparison is derived from data reported by Tvedt [13]. The characteristics of this project are given in Table 2. The requirements size of the baseline project was 80,000 lines of code written in COBOL. Because the incremental development is applied in this project, it causes 10,667 lines of

Table 2. Characteristics of the baseline project

Attributes	Values
Project size	90,667Loc
Number of increments	3
- Increment 1	26,667Loc
- Increment 2	32,000Loc
- Increment 3	32,000Loc
Project schedule	250days (1 year)
Project team size	15 experienced engineers
Estimated budget	3750 man-days

code as the overheads. Therefore, the total project size became 90,667 lines of code. The project was scheduled to last one calendar year, with a workforce level of 15 full-time engineers from start through finish.

In the baseline project, we assume that the team fixing defects is the same team developing the current release. Further, to maintain the high individual productivity of defect correction, the detected defects should be returned to its original developer for rework.

Tvedt's model was developed using system dynamics. In contrast to our model, his model simulated the concurrent development that allows overlapping between increments. However, at current stage, we do not consider the increment dependency in our model. Thus, it is not necessary to compare the elapsed times. We present the simulated quality feature for the brief comparison. After 20 runs of the simulation, Figure 6 shows the result distribution. It was reported that 279 defects remains in the final product by Tvedt's model, which was calibrated with the real project. The major difference from Tvedt's result might be caused by the different modeling approaches applied.

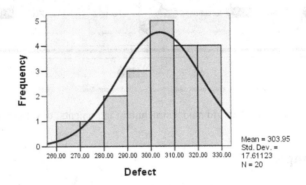

Fig. 6. Defect levels generated through simulations

5.2 Simulated Process Change

Our model focuses on the test-and-fix process of incremental development, which allows us to perform an investigation of possible process changes in this phase. In the baseline project, the detected defects are required to be fixed by its original developer. It may maintain the high productivity of individual developer on every single defect. Nevertheless, in some cases, there might be a long defect queue prior to one developer when another is idle. This situation turns to be more frequent when competency deviations exist among the developers. Experienced developers may produce fewer defects than novices in implementation. On the other hand, they may work more efficiently on defect fixing, while novices are struggling on their long defect list.

For this reason, we try to investigate the impact of corresponding process change. In the new case, an incoming detected defect should be assigned to one developer with the shortest defect queue. When two developers have the shortest queues with the same length, the incoming defect is assigned to the more experienced one.

After 20 runs of simulation, Figure 7 shows the average developer utilities of each release in these two cases. In the baseline case, the average developer utility may vary between 0.1 and 0.9 (Figure 7-a). When we applied the process change, the possible utility falls into the range from 0.6 to 0.9 (Figure 7-b). Moreover, the proposed process change also decreases the deviation of developer utility in the defect fixing process.

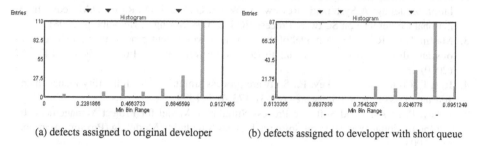

(a) defects assigned to original developer   (b) defects assigned to developer with short queue

Fig. 7. Developer utilities between baseline and proposed process change

6 Conclusion

This paper has proposed a hybrid software process simulation modeling scheme combining continuous and discrete-event methods. Compared with the existing hybrid modeling approaches, its distinct enhancement is that by choosing continuous or discrete-event modeling at phase (module) level, it allows the different zooms applied to each single process phase. It makes the selection of modeling methods more flexible at the low level, which is ultimately determined by our knowledge about the process and the real needs of our simulation. Without loss of model integrity, it may also help reduce the effort of building a hybrid simulation model.

Using this hybrid modeling scheme, we developed a hybrid simulation model of incremental development with focus on the test-and-fix process. We also applied this model for estimating product defect level and investigate the possible process change. The simulation model provides powerful analysis capability, especially for the test-and-fix process, and avoids the limitation of incomplete process detail (on micro-process level) of other phases, normally required by discrete-event modeling.

The future work on this hybrid modeling approach can be carried out in two dimensions: 1) to improve this hybrid modeling scheme and develop hybrid simulation models of other software processes (e.g. agile processes) using this approach; 2) to enhance this hybrid simulation model by considering more interventions that are not included in current model, such as test suite regression, and increment dependency.

Acknowledgement

NICTA is funded by the Australian Government as represented by the Department of Broadband, Communications and the Digital Economy and the Australian Research Council through the ICT Centre of Excellence program.

Reference

1. Osterweil, L.J.: Unifying Microprocess and Macroprocess Research. In: Li, M., Boehm, B., Osterweil, L.J. (eds.) SPW 2005. LNCS, vol. 3840, pp. 68–74. Springer, Heidelberg (2006)
2. Zhang, H., Kitchenham, B., Pfahl, D.: Reflections on 10 Years of Software Process Simulation Modeling: A Systematic Review. In: Wang, Q., Pfahl, D., Raffo, D.M. (eds.) International Conference on Software Process (ICSP) 2008, Springer, Heidelberg (2008)
3. Martin, R.H., Raffo, D.: A model of the software development process using both continuous and discrete models. Software Process: Improvement and Practice 5(2-3), 147–157 (2000)
4. Rus, I., Collofello, J., Lakey, P.: Software process simulation for reliability management. Journal of Systems and Software 46(2-3), 173–182 (1999)
5. Lakey, P.B.: A Hybrid Software Process Simulation Model for Project Management. In: 4th International Workshop on Software Process Simulation Modeling (ProSim), Portland, OR (2003)
6. Choi, K., Bae, D.-H., Kim, T.: An approach to a hybrid software process simulation using the DEVS formalism. Software Process: Improvement and Practice 11(4), 373–383 (2006)
7. Banks, J., Carson, J.S., Nelson, B.L., Nicol, D.M.: Discrete-Event System Simulation. Prentice-Hall, Englewood Cliffs (2005)
8. Karlsson, E.-A.: Incremental Development - Terminology and Guidelines. In: Chang, S.-K. (ed.) Handbook of Software Engineering & Knowledge Engineering, vol. 1, pp. 381–400. World Scientific, Singapore (2001)
9. Boehm, B.: Software Engineering Economics. Prentice-Hall, Englewood Cliffs (1981)
10. Jones, C.: Programming Defect Removal. GUIDE 40 (1975)
11. Abdel-Hamid, T.K., Madnick, S.E.: Software Project Dynamics: An Integrated Approach. Prentice Hall, Englewood Cliffs (1991)
12. Huff, K.E., Sroka, J.V., Struble, D.D.: Quantitative Models for Managing Software Development Processes. Software Engineering Journal 1(1), 17–23 (1986)
13. Tvedt, J.D.: An Extensive Model for Evaluating the Impact of Process Improvements on Software Development Cycle Time. PhD dissertation. Arizona State University (1996)
14. Cangussu, J.W., DeCarlo, R.A., Mathur, A.P.: A Formal Model of the Software Test Process. IEEE Transactions on Software Engineering 28(8), 782–796 (2002)
15. Zhang, H., Keung, J., Kitchenham, B., Jeffery, R.: Semi-Quantitative Modeling for Managing Software Development Processes. In: 19th Australian Software Engineering Conference (ASWEC), IEEE Computer Society, Perth, Australia (2008)
16. Galin, D.: Software Quality Assurance: from Theory to Implementation. Pearson, London (2004)
17. Imagine That Inc.: Extend Developer's Reference Manual, http://www.extendsim.com

Reflections on 10 Years of Software Process Simulation Modeling: A Systematic Review

He Zhang[1,2], Barbara Kitchenham[3], and Dietmar Pfahl[4,5]

[1] National ICT Australia, Locked Bag 9013, Alexandria NSW 1435, Australia
[2] School of Computer Science and Engineering, University of New South Wales, Australia
[3] School of Computer Science and Mathematics, Keele University, UK
[4] Simula Research Laboratory, P.O. Box 134, NO-1325, Lysaker, Norway
[5] Department of Informatics, University of Oslo, Norway
he.zhang@nicta.com.au, barbara@cs.keele.ac.uk,
dietmarp@simula.no, dietmarp@ifi.uio.no

Abstract. Software process simulation modeling (SPSM) has become an increasingly active research area since its introduction in the late 1980s. Particularly during the last ten years the related research community and the number of publications have been growing. The objective of this research is to provide insights about the evolution of SPSM research during the last 10 years. A systematic literature review was proposed with two subsequent stages to achieve this goal. This paper presents the preliminary results of the first stage of the review that is exclusively focusing on a core set of publication sources. More than 200 relevant publications were analyzed in order to find answers to the research questions, including the purposes and scopes of SPSM, application domains, and predominant research issues. From the analysis the following conclusions could be drawn: (1) Categories for classifying software process simulation models as suggested by the authors of a landmark publication in 1999 should be adjusted and refined to better capture the diversity of published models. (2) Research improving the efficiency of SPSM is gaining importance. (3) Hybrid process simulation models have attracted interest as a possibility to more realistically capture complex real-world software processes.

Keywords: ProSim, software process simulation, systematic literature review.

1 Background

Software Process Simulation Modeling (SPSM) was introduced into the software engineering domain by the pioneering work summarized in [1]. In the last two decades, it has been emerging as an effective tool to help evaluate and manage changes made to software projects and organizations. As a major research event, the ProSim workshop[1] series has taken place since 1998, and focuses on the state-of-the-art theories and applications of SPSM research in addressing real-world problems.

In ProSim'98, Kellner, Madachy, and Raffo (KMR) discussed a variety of aspects of software process simulation in their widely-cited paper, "Software process simulation

---

[1] International Workshop on Software Process Simulation Modeling.

Q. Wang, D. Pfahl, and D.M. Raffo (Eds.): ICSP 2008, LNCS 5007, pp. 345–356, 2008.
© Springer-Verlag Berlin Heidelberg 2008

modeling: Why? What? How?" [2], such as the reasons for undertaking simulations of software process models, and simulation approaches/paradigms. However, after almost 10-years (1998 - 2007) progress in software process simulation, it is appropriate to review and update the status of SPSM research, to summarize the 10-years progress, best practice and lessons learned, and propose the possible directions of our future research activities in this domain.

From this viewpoint, this paper reports the preliminary results of a systematic literature review of papers published in the proceedings and journals associated with ProSim since 1998. This paper is part of a larger study and presents only a subset of the research questions and research literature addressed by the larger study. As an anniversary review of the previous work, this paper also partially serves as the latest continuation and enhancement to the topics discussed in the KMR's paper.

2   Systematic Literature Review

In 2004, Kitchenham *et al.* [3] suggested software engineering researchers should adopt "Evidence-Based Software Engineering" (EBSE). EBSE aims to apply an evidence-based approach, which was initially developed in medicine and is being adopted in many domains, to software engineering research and practice. In this context, evidence is defined as a synthesis of best quality scientific studies on a specific topic or research question. The main method of synthesis is a systematic literature review (SLR).

In contrast to an ad hoc literature review, a systematic literature review (also known as systematic review) is a methodologically rigorous review of research results. It is a means of identifying, evaluating and interpreting all available research relevant to a particular research question, or topic area, or phenomenon of interest [4]. A systematic review is a form of *secondary* study, the identified individual studies contributing to a systematic review called *primary studies*.

A systematic literature review involves several discrete activities, which can be grouped into three main phases: planning the review, conducting the review, and reporting the review. A pilot review is recommended for the reviews including multiple research questions or a large set of primary studies.

3   Method

This study follows Kitchenham's methodological guidelines for systematic reviews [4, 5], as adapted for PhD candidates. It was carried out in two stages. This paper reports the review process and the preliminary results from Stage 1. Currently, three researchers are involved in this research, one principal reviewer (a PhD candidate), one secondary reviewer (the candidate's supervisor), plus one researcher acting as the expert panel.

3.1   Research Questions

Each stage of the systematic review is intended to answer the following research questions. This paper only addresses questions 1 to 4.

Q1. What are the purposes or motivations of SPSM in the last decade's practice? Q1 can be split into two sub-questions: Q1.1 How are the purposes identified by KMR supported by SPSM practice in the last ten years? Q1.2 Are any updates required?

Q2. Which simulation paradigms have been applied in the last decade, and how popular are they? Are there any new techniques emerging during this period?

Q3. Which simulation tools are available for SPSM and have been in use in the last decade? And how popular are they?

Q4. On model level, what are problem domains and model scopes focused on by software process simulation models?

Q5. On parameter level, what are the output variables considered when developing software process simulation models of software process?

Q6. Which simulation paradigm is most appropriate for a specific SPSM purpose?

3.2 Search Process

As the review of 10-years' efforts in SPSM, the time frame of sources for our study is constrained to the period from 01 Jan 1998 to 31 Dec 2007. Because the ProSim workshop series (which continued as a special track of ICSP since 2007) are regarded as the most important forum of SPSM, the sources related to ProSim (including ProSim workshop, simulation track of ICSP, and special issues of JSS and SPIP) are the primary data sources for the Stage 1 of this study. The corresponding source and search strategy are summarized in Table 1.

Table 1. Selected sources for Stage 1 of the systematic review

Source	Acronym	Period	Search method
The proceedings of ProSim workshop	ProSim	1998 - 2006	Manual
The proceedings of ICSP conference	ICSP	2007	Manual
Journal of Systems and Software	JSS	1999 - 2001	Manual
Journal of Software Process: Improvement and Practice	SPIP	2000 - 2007	Manual

In Stage 2, we will select the external sources of software process research with high relevance to SPSM for our review. To avoid possible source bias and missing some important work, we will also conduct an online search in some major electronic sources (digital libraries).

We carried out manual search in the ProSim conference proceedings and special issues of the journals published within the proposed time frame during Stage 1. There are over 200 candidate papers. When there are a large number of research questions and a large set of potential primary studies, Kitchenham recommends undertaking a pilot review after the planning phase [4]. The purposes of a pilot systematic review is *"to assess and refine the review protocol, and further to secure the quality of the systematic review"*, We chose the papers published in the special issues (SPIP) of ProSim Workshop 2005/2006 (10 latest journal papers available at the planning phase), which reflect the current state and progress, for our pilot review.

3.3 Inclusion and Exclusion Criteria

There are two major steps in primary study selection: an initial selection and a final selection. The theme for this systematic review, "software process simulation modeling" contains two keywords: "software process" and "simulation modeling". Therefore, as the inclusion criteria, the primary studies identified must employ simulation paradigm(s) for software process research; in the other words, the process model or modeling in the studies can be used for simulation studies.

From the candidate studies retrieved by data sources (Table 1), an initial selection was obtained by reviewing the title, abstract, and keywords of the publications. When an exclusion decision could not be made, the paper's structure, conclusion, and references were also checked. Unless studies could be excluded based on the above criteria, full copies of the papers were obtained and included in the initial selection.

Next, a final selection that satisfied the selection criteria was obtained from the initially selected papers. We excluded:

– Editorials, position papers and keynotes
– Abstracts, posters and slides alone.

We included the most recent and comprehensive versions of duplicated papers or continued studies. For example, some SPSM papers published in the ProSim workshop series were selected for publication in special issues of journals. To avoid duplicate aggregation, we only selected and reviewed the journal articles as they typically enhance the proceedings papers with more details. However, to track any trends over time, the first publication date of the original research paper was recorded during data extraction. The selection process was performed by the principal researcher.

3.4 Study Classification

We initially identified two broad categories of publications by briefly reviewing the most recent papers published in SPW/ProSim 2006 and ICSP 2007 (16 papers on the special tracks of process simulation). One category includes the specific process simulation models or simulators, and their applications; the other discusses the methodology and guidelines for process simulation modeling. Both categories are relevant to most research questions (except Q5).

Based on the results of the pilot review, we refined the study classification into four categories as follows:

– A: Software process simulation models or simulators;
– B: Process simulation modeling paradigms, methodologies, and environments;
– C: Applications, guidelines, and frameworks of adopting process simulation in software engineering practice;
– D: Experience reports of SPSM research and practice.

These four types of studies focus on different aspects of software process simulation research, and may give answers to the research questions on different levels of granularity and from different points of view. We defined the concrete criteria (questions) to facilitate the effective identification of each study category.

The categorization was not a mutually exclusive one, i.e. it is possible that a specific study falls into more than one category. For example, one case could be that the author(s) introduced a novel simulation paradigm to software process research, and then described a simulation model for a specific problem domain by using this paradigm as an example. We allow these studies to be mapped to multiple categories.

3.5 Quality Assessment

The quality of a primary study is assessed with the help of a checklist (Table 2), which specifies the questions to each study category separately. For each question, the study's quality is evaluated as 'yes', 'partial', or 'no', which are scored with the value 1, 0.5, and 0 respectively. The studies were evaluated by the principal researcher, and a selection of approximately 30% was checked by the secondary researcher. Disagreements were resolved by the principal researcher.

Table 2. Study quality assessment checklist

Question	Score
Common questions (for all categories)	
Did the study clearly state the aims/research questions?	y/p/n
Did the study review the related work for the problem?	y/p/n
Did the study discuss related issues, and compare with the alternatives?	y/p/n
Did the study recommend the further continuous research?	y/p/n
Questions for Category A	
Are the model's assumptions explained explicitly?	y/p/n
Is the model construction fully described?	y/p/n
Did the study explain why choosing the applied simulation paradigm(s)?	y/p/n
Are the conditions when the model adoption explained?	y/p/n
Did the study avoid any selection bias exist during experiment design?	y/p/n
Has the model been trialed on an industry scale problem?	y/p/n
Did the study carry out a sensitivity or residual analysis?	y/p/n
Are any model evaluation methods applied on the model?	y/p/n
Does the study interpret the findings?	y/p/n
Questions for Category B and C	
Are the scopes of the method/paradigm/solution clearly defined?	y/p/n
Are the modeling approach/method/environment clearly defined?	y/p/n
Are the problems that the study addresses defined with appropriate SE examples?	y/p/n
Did the study specify the limitations of the argued paradigm/method/solution?	y/p/n
Did the empirical evidence include support the arguments of the study?	y/p/n
Questions for Category D	
Can the experience be used for validating and calibrating simulation model/modeling?	y/p/n
Are the best practices or lessons learnt extracted from experience?	y/p/n

3.6 Data Extraction

The major attributes to be collected for each study through the review are listed in Table 3. They are grouped by the study categories. The 'Q' column indicates which research question(s) is the attribute collected for answering.

Table 3. Attributes collected during data extraction

Q	Attribute	Description
	Common Attributes	
1	Purpose category	The specific purpose for the simulation model or modeling. It can be one of purposes identified by KMR, or any new ones.
2	Modeling paradigm(s)	The paradigm used to build the simulation model. It can be one of identified by KMR, or some other approaches.
	Attributes for Category A	
4	Problem domain	The specific problem domain in SE, e.g. open-source, evolution.
5	Model complexity	Including single-module model or integrate model, the number of modules and levels of the simulation model.
3	Simulation tool	The simulation tools used in executing the process model.
5	Model scope	Including the process phase(s) of life-cycle, and time span.
5	Output variables	The information produced through simulation answers the questions specified with the purpose of the model.
	Attributes for Category B	
4 6	Study's theme	The emphasized and discussed aspects of SPSM in the study.
	Attributes for Category C	
4 6	Focused questions	The specific questions related to SPSM raised in the study
4 6	Proposed solution	The corresponding answers given in the study
6	Application effects	The expected effects caused by the solution.
	Attributes for Category D	
6	Experience source	Where does the experience come from? Industry, government, education/academia, or somewhere else.
6	Outcome of applying SPSM	The result of the application experience, i.e. positive, negative, or mixed.
1 6	Supported arguments	The arguments supported by the experience report.

4 Results

4.1 Primary Studies

In total, 209 papers have been published in the ProSim sources, including the workshop and conference (ICSP) proceedings and the special issues of JSS/SPIP. They form a comprehensive body of knowledge of software process simulation and modeling. Unfortunately, because the electronic proceedings were not available for ProSim'98 - '00, nine papers could not be evaluated in our review. Although we contacted the author(s) for each missing paper individually to request the electronic version, only three of them had responded to us. Hence, there were around 4.3% (9/209) papers missed from the review at the current stage. Nevertheless, we believe that the low proportion will not influence the review results significantly.

By carefully reviewing their titles, abstracts, keywords, conclusions and references, 96 articles were selected from the publications in ProSim sources and identified as the

Table 4. Sources identified for primary studies

	1998	1999	2000	2002	2003	2004	2005	2006	2007	Total
Proceedings	15	13	21	0	32	27	24	8	8	**148**
Missing	*2*	*1*	*6*	*0*	*0*	*0*	*0*	*0*	*0*	*9*
JSS	11	0	12	0	0	0	0	0	0	**23**
SPIP	0	10	0	7	5	7	7	2	0	**38**
Selected	**13**	**9**	**14**	**7**	**16**	**10**	**13**	**6**	**8**	**96**

primary studies. The total number of papers per year and source are summarized in Table 4. The individual primary studies will be available online (systematicreview.org) for public access.

Data extraction was performed by two researchers: the principal and secondary reviewer. The former was responsible for reviewing all primary studies, extracting data, and assessing study quality. The other reviewer selected approximately one third of the papers and performed a secondary review for validation of the extraction and assessment. When the disagreement could not be solved, the final decision was made by the principal researcher.

Table 5 summarizes per year the number of different countries the first authors came from. All contributions to ProSim were mainly from 13 countries. The ProSim workshop became more international since 2000, when the first authors from 7 countries were involved. After that, the number of participating countries varied between 4 and 6.

The results also indicate that USA is the leading country of SPSM research in terms of ProSim publications, where 41 (49%) studies were originated. It is followed by Germany (18%) and UK (17%).

Table 5. Number of countries involved in the ProSim series (workshops and conference)

	1998	1999	2000	2002	2003	2004	2005	2006	2007	Total
Number of Country	3	3	7	5	5	5	6	4	6	**13**

4.2 Classification

Four study categories were identified in the pilot review. By reviewing the full papers, all primary studies were classified into at least one category (A, B, C, and D). Figure 1 shows the distribution of studies per category and year.

Most primary studies were identified as Category A, for both the decade (58%) and each year separately. In total, there have been 61 software process simulation models (simulators) developed and published in ProSim series during the last 10 years. Only 18 primary studies (19%) were identified as Category C, while 29% of primary studies were of Category B and 23% of Category D. 22 studies were classified into two categories, and 3 studies were identified as combinations of three categories.

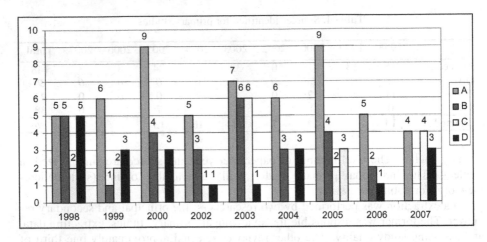

Fig. 1. Summary of study categories distribution

4.3 Quality Assessment

The primary studies were assessed for quality using the checklist in Section 3.7. Although the full score for each study cannot be included in this paper, we present the normalized average quality score per source type (proceedings and journals) and year in Figure 2. The study quality of workshop proceedings was stable from 2000 to 2005. In most cases, the quality of journal articles was equal to or better than the proceedings papers of the same year. Overall, many Category A studies failed to explicitly address the conditions of model/simulator adoption. For Category B and C studies, the limitations associated with the paradigm/method/solution were rarely discussed.

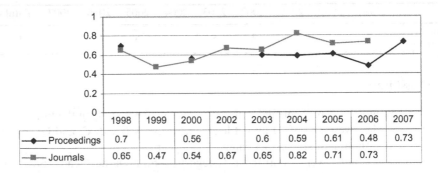

	1998	1999	2000	2002	2003	2004	2005	2006	2007
◆ Proceedings	0.7		0.56		0.6	0.59	0.61	0.48	0.73
■ Journals	0.65	0.47	0.54	0.67	0.65	0.82	0.71	0.73	

Fig. 2. Average study quality per source type and year

5 Discussions

In this section, we discuss the primary answers to our first four research questions (defined in Section 3.1).

5.1 Purposes for SPSM (Q1)

During the process of Stage 1 review, we gradually perceived that it is difficult to handle the purpose identification clearly according to the definitions addressed by KMR. There are two major shortcomings: 1) Ambiguity to some extent exists among their 6 purposes; 2) Since the examples given in KMR's paper were mainly derived from the publications in ProSim'98, the scope of their purposes is limited.

For instance, in terms of their classification, '*planning*' is different from '*strategic management*'. But the latter usually consists of the former at the organizational level or on a long-term scale. As another example, process simulation can help predict size of open source software. However, according to the definition in PMBoK [6], '*planning*' is the process that contains the activities of 'define scope', 'develop management plan', 'identify and schedule activities and resources', which are not the cases in open-source development. Therefore, '*planning*' needs to be refined as '*prediction and planning*' to fit such change.

To clearly represent the purposes for SPSM research identified from the primary studies, they can be grouped at three levels:

Cognitive level
Tactical level
Strategic level

They can be further detailed as 10 purposes. The *cognitive* level contains the purposes of 1) *understanding*, 2) *communication*, 3) *process investigation*, 4) *training and learning*. On the *tactical* and *strategic* levels purposes are similar. They are 5) *prediction and planning*, 6) *control and operational management*, 7) *risk management*, 8) *process improvement*, 9) *technology adoption*, 10) *tradeoff analysis and optimizing*. They differ in scope and impact between the two levels.

5.2 Modeling Paradigms (Q2)

Overall, 10 simulation modeling paradigms were found in the review of Stage 1. Figure 3 shows the paradigms with the applied study number more than one. System dynamics (SD, 49%) and Discrete-event simulation (DES, 31%) were the most widely

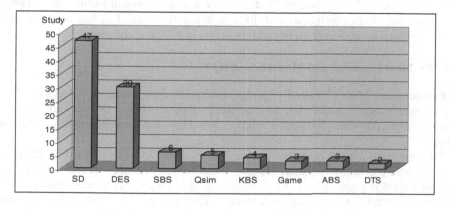

Fig. 3. Study distribution by simulation paradigms

used techniques in SPSM. Other paradigms included state-based simulation (SBS), qualitative(semi-quantitative) simulation (QSIM), knowledge(rule)-based simulation (KBS), role-playing game, agent-based simulation (ABS), and discrete-time simulation (DTS). However, only SD, DES, SBS and KBS were discussed by KMR.

QSIM and ABS are paradigms that are relatively new to software process research. As a special case, DTS was classified as one type of SBS by some studies. In addition, three games (role-playing simulators) were developed with focus on training and learning purposes.

During the last decade, hybrid simulation has been one of the most frequent research themes in the ProSim community. Most of these studies (10 papers) presenting the hybrid simulation focus on the combination of continuous (SD) and discrete-event simulation (DES).

5.3 Simulation Tools (Q3)

With respect to the simulation models/simulators presented in Category A studies, 13 tools were identified. Their application numbers are shown in Table 6. Because some authors did not explicitly mention the simulation tools in their papers, the total application number (38) is less than the number of Category A studies (56).

Table 6. Application of simulation tools

Vensim	Extend	iThink	Qsim	Netlogo	Repast	DSOL	Smalltalk	DEVSim++	DEVSJava	QNAP2	PML	SESAM
12	11	3	2	1	1	1	1	1	1	1	1	1

Due to a large number of SD models developed and published, Vensim[TM] (by Ventana Systems, Inc. www.vensim.com) is the most popular tool for continuous simulation. Since Extend[TM] (by ImagineThat, Inc. www.extendsim.com) offers the capability of building both continuous and discrete simulation model, it has been the first choice by the discrete-event and hybrid modelers in SPSM community.

5.4 Problem Domains and Model Scope (Q4)

Our systematic review extracted 19 problem domains from Category A studies. "Generic development" models the normal development process of software project. Among other domains, software evolution has been the most frequently modeled topic.

To review simulation model scope, we extended the 5 scopes defined by KMR to 7, i.e. single-phase, multi-phase, project, multi-project, product, product evolution, and long-term organization. Table 7 shows the relations between modeled domains and scope extracted from Category A studies. The number in the 'subtotal' row is not

Table 7. Modeling problem domains vs. model scopes

	single phase	multi-phase	project	multi-project	product	evolution	long-term organization	unknown or N/A	Total
generic development			9					1	10
SW evolution			1			7			8
SPI	1	1					1	3	6
requirement	2		1		1			1	5
incremental development	1	2	1					1	5
open-source SD	1			1		2			4
global SD			1			3			4
SW economics	1		1		1				3
SW product-line					1		1		2
agile development			1					1	2
QA		1						1	2
acquisition/outsourcing		1						1	2
SE education			2						2
SW testing	1								1
SW design	1								1
SW services						1			1
productivity analysis			1						1
SD risk mgmt			1						1
SW reliability								1	1
Subtotal	7	5	19	1	2	8	2	9	

always the exact sum of the column. This is because some studies modeled multiple domains, e.g. a combination of global development and evolution.

'Project' was the most frequently modeled study scope, particularly for 'generic development'. 'Product evolution' was the next most studied topic.

5.5 Other Categories

Most studies (17 papers) of Category B discussed methods of building process simulation model more correctly, effectively and efficiently. Some papers introduced novel simulation paradigms (8 studies) and simulation environments (8 studies). 6 studies dealt with the strategic questions, or presented perspectives of SPSM. KMR's paper [2] is the best known example of them.

The low proportion of Category C study (Section 4.2) implies that modelers may need to pay more attention to the methodologies and guidelines needed to support the application and adoption of process simulation modeling in practice.

6 Conclusions and Future Work

The main limitation of our review is that the process recommended for PhD candidates is not as rigorous as that adopted by multiple-researchers. However, it does include a quality assurance check by the secondary researcher and review of the research protocol, and the results by an external researcher.

Our results indicate that: (1) Categories for classifying software process models as suggested by the authors of a landmark publication in 1999 should be adjusted and refined to better capture the diversity of published models. (2) Research improving the efficiency of SPSM is gaining importance. (3) Hybrid process simulation models have attracted interest as a possibility to more realistically capture complex real-world software processes.

Our future work will include a more detailed analysis of the studies of categories B, C and D, and an investigation of the issues raised by our other two research questions (Q5 and Q6). We also intend to extend our systematic review to include studies outside of the ProSim sources (Stage 2).

Acknowledgement

NICTA is funded by the Australian Government as represented by the Department of Broadband, Communications and the Digital Economy and the Australian Research Council through the ICT Centre of Excellence program. Barbara Kitchenham's research is funded by the UK EPSRC project EP/E046983/1.

References

1. Abdel-Hamid, T.K., Madnick, S.E.: Software Project Dynamics: An Integrated Approach. Prentice Hall, Englewood Cliffs (1991)
2. Kellner, M.I., Madachy, R.J., Raffo, D.M.: Software Process Simulation Modeling: Why? What? How? Journal of Systems and Software 46(2-3), 91–105 (1999)
3. Kitchenham, B., Dybå, T., Jørgensen, M.: Evidence-based Software Engineering. In: 26th International Conference on Software Engineering (ICSE), pp. 273–281. IEEE Computer Society, Los Alamitos (2004)
4. Kitchenham, B.: Guidelines for Performing Systematic Literature Reviews in Software Engineering. Software Engineering Group, School of Computer Science and Mathematics, Keele University, and Department of Computer Science, University of Durham (2007)
5. Kitchenham, B.: Procedures for Undertaking Systematic Reviews. Computer Science Department, Keele University and National ICT Australia (2004)
6. PMI: A Guide to the Project Management Body of Knowledge. Project Management Institute (2004)

Integrating Joint Reviews with Automotive SPICE Assessments Results

Fabrizio Fabbrini[1], Mario Fusani[1], Giuseppe Lami[1], and Edoardo Sivera[2]

[1] Istituto di Scienza e Tecnologie dell'Informazione – C.N.R.
56124 Pisa, Italy
{fabrizio.fabbrini, mario.fusani, giuseppe.lami}@isti.cnr.it
[2] Fiat Group Automobiles
Torino, Italy
Edoardo.sivera@fiat.com

Abstract. The continuous changes in customer requirements as well as the ever-increasing market-driven demand for innovation make automotive software projects success strongly dependent on the customer-supplier communication and co-operation throughout the software life cycle. Joint reviews and software process assessments (mostly performed according to the Automotive SPICE model) are popular means used by car manufacturers and their suppliers of software-intensive components to face such a situation. Often these two resource-consuming techniques are performed separately, without mutual support or interaction. This paper presents an approach to integrating joint reviews with software process assessment results. The effectiveness of joint reviews depends on the degree of car manufacturer's knowledge and understanding of the supplier's way of proceeding in software development. We show how assessment results can be used as input to joint reviews to support car manufacturers in conducting joint reviews effectively.

Keywords: Joint Reviews, Software Process Assessment, Automotive SPICE, Software Process Improvement.

1 Introduction

Up to a few years ago, car makers could not completely understand what the software component of Electronic Control Units (ECU) was about, and hardly intervene anywhere in the software development process, that was guarded realm of subsystems suppliers. On the other hand, most suppliers were just emerging from years of experience limited to hardware design, barely coated with low-level software drivers.

Today the competency and experience of car manufacturers in automobile's electronics is much increased, rousing competition that in turn demands for more and more basic and sophisticated functions, ranging from car control to passenger comfort to continuous information exchange between vehicles and their environment. This has led the software to play a key role in the whole car design, now scoring an 80% of the whole project. [1], [2]

Although Software Engineering as a discipline may now be sufficiently mature to guarantee the trustworthiness of software-controlled systems, what is not guaranteed is that ECU manufacturers are actually adopting the most suitable techniques and practices.

Q. Wang, D. Pfahl, and D.M. Raffo (Eds.): ICSP 2008, LNCS 5007, pp. 357–368, 2008.
© Springer-Verlag Berlin Heidelberg 2008

In facts, serious problems interested the earliest cars provided with complex electronic components network, especially those regarding the car body functions. This led manufacturers to reconsider their initially unquestioned acceptance of software as a minor component of car subsystems.

Such a hard situation, that caused huge loss of resources to the automotive industry, was due to several reasons:

-   Cultural transition in designing and producing automobiles from a mechanic (or electro-mechanic) centered approach to an approach where the software plays a crucial role. An important effect of such a cultural gap has been the difficulty of interaction between car makers and their software suppliers. In fact, often car makers' language and competency were different from those of software suppliers, which heavily affected software acquisition capability.
-   Lack of standard approaches and platforms, which caused budget overruns.
-   High complexity of ECU interactions, which determined system integration problems.

In such a context the acquisition of software-intensive systems has become a critical activity for car manufacturers, that need to monitor and control the software development of their suppliers in order to avoid losses in terms of time and quality of product. This paper focuses on the discussion of two widely adopted techniques aimed at enabling the car manufacturer to control and understand the supplier's way to produce software. These are joint reviews and software process assessments.

The paper is structured as follows: Section 2 deals with the most popular techniques used in the practice to controlling, monitoring and evaluating the software suppliers in automotive. In section 3, open problems occurring today in controlling and monitoring supplies in automotive are discussed. In Section 4 an approach is described to integrate joint reviews in software process assessments made according to the Automotive SPICE model [7]. The way such an approach is going to be adopted at FIAT Automobiles Group is also presented. Finally, in Section 5 some conclusions are provided.

2   Controlling Software Suppliers in the Practice

The increasing importance of the electronics in automobiles stimulated a considerable offer of electronic components and systems by many specialised producers. Car makers are thus facing problems of interoperability, integration and distributed intelligence. Acquisition has become a key process because the time-to-market as well the overall functionality of the vehicle depend on the car manufacturers' ability to interact effectively with its own software suppliers.

In the recent past a huge amount of resources have been lost for insufficient management of the technical aspects of the acquisition processes. That caused late releases and after-market problems.

The success of the acquisition process depends on the capability of effectively managing the relationship between customer and suppliers. Customers should improve their ability of assisting and monitoring the software development of their suppliers and suppliers should be more open to customer involvement..

To face this challenge, in practice, many car manufacturers adopt both software process assessments and joint reviews as means to control the capability of their suppliers in producing software. The purposes and the impact of these two approaches are different, in that joint reviews address the ongoing activities of a project and aim at verifying specific requirements of a specific project (in terms of quality and completeness of delivered work products, compliance to plans and process requirements), while software process assessments provide general information of the supplier's software process and are more oriented towards the supplier selection phase.

In the following these two approaches are shortly described and discussed.

2.1 Joint Reviews

Generally speaking, joint reviews are meeting where persons having different roles, responsibilities and perspectives join together to analyse the status of an activity or the content of a product. The purpose of such an analysis is to ensure that agreed objectives and requirements are satisfied. Joint reviews are conducted with a substantial degree of formality and are regulated by precise requirements. [3]

The object, scope and goals of joint reviews can be different depending on the project/product development phase. They can address issues at both project management and technical levels and are held throughout the life of a development project. [4]

On the basis of the authors' experience, two principal types of joint reviews can be identified.

- Internal joint reviews: they involve member of the software development team, and aim at reviewing key work products at specific project's milestones. Typically, they occur when a particular work product (e.g. software requirements, test plans...) is to be released, and such a work product is to be used by different members of the team. In this case, the work product is jointly reviewed in order to achieve a formal agreement on its content.
- External joint reviews: they involve both members of the supplier's software development team and customer representatives. The objective of these joint reviews is either to obtain a formal agreement on the content of specific work products (typically the specifications) or to verify managerial aspects of the supplier's software development project (e.g. respect of planning, compliance with process requirements, control of risks, ...).

In particular, in this paper we consider external joint reviews involving software suppliers (i.e. typically suppliers of Electronic Control Units (ECU) to be integrated into the automobile's network) and car manufacturers (i.e. system integrators).

This kind of joint reviews are an effective mean to control and monitor the advancement of a software development project as well as to verify the quality of the intermediate work products.

2.2 Software Process Assessments

The traditional reliance on Quality Systems Standards such as ISO9001, QS9000 [5] and ISO/TS 16949 [6] has not provided sufficient confidence in the software area.

The car manufacturers, like others in the defense and aerospace industries, have turned to international standards for software process assessment, based on ISO/IEC 15504 (known also as SPICE) [7] and/or the Capability Maturity Model Integration (CMMI) [8], as a mean to identify and control supplier-related risks and to assess supplier's software capability [9], [10], [11]. A common trend in the European automotive industry to face this question consists of principally addressing the improvement of the software acquisition process. While different car makers set up their own improvement program, a commonly adopted policy is the choice of the SPICE model as the principal mean [7] to assess the capability of the suppliers' software process. This choice has been supported by some large-scale awakening effort: In year 2001 an initiative was launched by the Procurement Forum [12] with the principal European car makers, their assessors and representative bodies to address the problems related to software assessments in automotive. In the framework of this initiative, a Special Interest Group (SIG) has been founded with the aim to design a special version of the SPICE model (called Automotive-SPICE) tailored on the needs and peculiarities of the automotive business area [13]. The initiative aimed at creating consensus on commonality of approach in order to avoid that suppliers face multiple assessments from multiple manufacturers using different models and criteria and consume resources that put additional pressure on delivery times. Furthermore, the focus on software capability determination by means of software process assessment has established a common trend among the European Car Makers in using Automotive SPICE as a mean for determining a qualification mechanism. Such a qualification mechanism is based on the definition of a target capability profile that the suppliers shall reach to be admitted in the supply selection.

Benefits derived from the Automotive-SPICE initiative not only can be quantified as an increased degree of satisfaction for the quality of the acquired software product, but include some positive "side effects" as:

- better supplier selection (only supplier having a high capability profile can be selected);
- better project monitoring (customers can identify the principal phases and work products to be controlled during the supplier's software development process);
- better relationship with own suppliers (clearer than before, because based on a deeper knowledge of the suppliers organization and processes and on a common technical language);
- identification of internal improvement areas (both for customer and suppliers) addressing specific processes (e.g. Requirement Management, Testing Management, etc.) and work products.

The strategy adopted by many European Car Makers based on SPICE capability profile as a mean for qualifying their suppliers gives practical benefits and opportunities also for the automotive software suppliers. In particular, it has been provided an important stimulus to accelerate the suppliers' software process improvements. Moreover it can be used as a sort of benchmark where the required capability profile becomes a target to be aligned with the competitors.

3 Capability Determination vs. Project Performance

External Joint Reviews are practices performed by manufacturers to interact with their software suppliers with the aim of monitoring and, if case, driving the performance of the supply-related development project.

In the automotive domain, external Joint Reviews are planned and performed at specific and predefined times conciliating and synchronizing supplier's software development project milestones with car development phases (typically such external joint reviews are performed after requirements elicitation/analysis, at development project planning, once software design has been defined or at software testing planning time). Moreover, Joint Reviews can be iterated when the development project is composed of several incremental cycles.

The principal purpose of these joint reviews is to make the car manufacturer able to understand the status of the supplier's project in order to verify its schedule, the quality of the technical solutions adopted and the compliance to its own needs.

The effectiveness of external joint reviews depends on the amount and quality of information the car manufacturer can have at its disposal. In fact, only having a complete set of information allows the car manufacturer to get full understanding of the status of the supplier's project. For example, the availability of project planning documentation is necessary to understand the suitability of the resources to be allocated to the project.

Unfortunately, often car manufacturers are not able to make the external joint reviews effective because of incomplete evidence provided by the software suppliers. This reduces the benefits that can be expected by the joint reviews.

It is a common practice (principally in the European automotive industry) to require a specific capability profile for potential software suppliers according to the Automotive SPICE model. It is even common practice that car manufacturers sponsor the initial assessment for determining such a capability profile. The return of such an investment is, for the car manufacturer, the possibility to know the capability of a defined set of suppliers' processes taken from the Process Reference Model of Automotive SPICE; such knowledge becomes one of the main criteria used by the car manufacturers for supplier selection.

Moreover, to assess the capability of the software process, assessors use process instances (i.e. processes executed in projects that are representative of the organization's business goals) to collect evidences and consequently rate the Automotive SPICE process attributes.

Nevertheless, car manufacturers cannot be guaranteed that any current supplier's project has the same characteristics of the projects whose process instances were assessed.

In other words, a new project might be designed, planned, managed and conducted with a different level of care, effort and resources, without adopting the same good practices that were in use in assessed process instances.

That should not be surprising. Performing an assessment means to determine, in a disciplined manner, the capability of a set of selected processes.

According to ISO/IEC 15504-1 [7] the process capability is a characterization of the ability of an organization's process to meet current and predicted business goals and it is not involved with the evaluation of the specific techniques and management choices of a project.

In other words, determining the capability of a process means rating the ability of an organization of achieving the outcomes associated with a particular process, no matter how and no matter according what technical or managerial solutions.

So, there is no contradiction if an organization, having a process with high capability level, implements that process in a different (and possibly poorer) way with respect to the standard way it performs. Such a situation does not depend on a defect in the SPICE assessment model, nor on a bad assessment made by the assessors, nor on the fact that the organization under assessment (the software supplier, in our case) was cheating during the assessment. It is simple due to management choices of the supplier, that can decide to devote different care in the project without making invalid the results of the assessment already performed.

4   Integrating Joint Reviews and Software Process Assessments

The integration of software process assessment and external joint reviews is able to provide an added value respect the performance of these two techniques in isolation.

In this section we describe how joint reviews and software process assessment can support each other in the supplier monitoring and control activity.

We present a mechanism where software process assessment results and related evidences can be used to give information to support the car manufacturer in conducting external joint reviews with the supplier.

The mechanism we present is composed of three phases:

Phase 1:   Software Process Assessments: the car manufacturer sponsors software process assessments to a set of important[1] software suppliers. Sponsorship is important because it allows the ownership of the assessment results.
Software Process Assessment reports should be compliant with the requirements contained in the ISO/IEC15504 Part.2 and, in addition, should provide specific information to be used to support the external joint reviews.

Phase 2:   Process mapping: the processes in the assessment scope are mapped on the planned Joint Reviews. Each Joint Review has a purpose, a set of input items and a scope (in terms of activities and work product to be reviewed); they are to be used to guide such a mapping.

Phase 3:   Joint Reviews: the external joint reviews should be prepared and conducted taking into account the additional information from the process assessment the supplier involved in the joint review undertook.

According to what stated in Section 2.1, the objects (i.e. the project aspects to be evaluated) of an external Joint Review can be:

A - Technical solutions adopted in the specific project
B - Management choices adopted in the specific project

---

[1] With the term *important* we intend characterise a supplier that is either a new one or that is supplying a critical component for the vehicle.

C - Quality of Work Product (i.e. documents, artefacts, …) developed

D - Content of the Work Products developed

The kind of evidences collected during an assessment that can be used during a Joint Review depends on the level of capability achieved by a specific process. In fact, the higher the capability levels high the more the amount of useful information available.

In the following we discuss the nature of information that can be obtained from an assessment according to the capability level achieved by the process assessed.

The ISO/IEC 15504 standard, as well as every compliant assessment model including Automotive SPICE, has a five-value scale for measuring the capability of single processes. Processes having the capability level rated as 1 don't provide relevant information to be used in a Joint Review. In fact, capability level 1 means that the process outcomes are obtained but neither the project is managed nor a standard process is in place, then the information collected unlikely can be used to support the joint review of different projects.

For this reason we consider in this paper the evidences derivable from assessments that have reached a capability level 2 or 3. We don't consider capability levels 4 and 5 because, in the practice, the most common assessment profiles required in automotive don't ask for Automotive SPICE capability levels higher than 3. [14]

A process capability level 2 means that the organization is able to manage the process-related activities and artefacts of its own projects. In some sense, evidences collected in a process capability level 2 assessment indicate the potentiality of the organizational unit. Then, the evidences of how the projects used as process instance in the assessment has been managed can be useful in a joint review because it is possible to ask the justification of possible under-management of the reviewed project. Having a process rated at level 3, means that a standard process is adopted, and then the same process (i.e. technical and managerial practices as well as documentation characteristics), should be expected also for the process under joint review. Possible differences shall be justified by the supplier.

In Table 1. a list of possible evidences collectable in a process assessment that can support a joint review is provided. Such evidences are grouped by capability level and cross-mapped with the four types of object a Joint Review can have.

The evidences described in Table 1 are all available after an Automotive SPICE process assessment is made. These evidences and information, if suitably organized and provided, can support Joint Reviews. In the following a couple of examples are provided in order to better explain the use in a joint review of the information described in Table 1.

Example 1: let's suppose to have the Software Requirements Analysis process rated at capability level 2 by an Automotive SPICE assessment. That means that the evidences corresponding to the first line of table 1 are available. In particular, the needs in terms of personal skills (see third bulled in the Management Choices column) and the correspondent responsibility allocation (see second bulled in the Management Choices column), shall be available. Then, if the project used as process instance during the assessment has characteristics similar to those of the project under Joint Review, it should be expected that the human resources allocated to the two projects are almost the same.

Table 1. Evidences collectable in process assessment by capability level

	A Technical solutions	B Management choices	C Quality of Work Products	D Content of Work Products
Capability Level 2	- Criteria for resource allocation exist (tools, facilities, infrastructures ...)	- Definition of project's objectives in terms of quality of artefacts, process cycle, resource usage - Criteria for responsibility allocation in the project exist - Definition of skills profiles needs for the project	- Definition of requirements for work products (structure) - Definition of review and approval criteria for work products - Identification of dependencies among work products	- Definition of requirements for work products (contents) - Review and adjusting of work products
Capability Level 3	- Infrastructures and work environment needed identified - necessary infrastructures and work environment allocated - Data and analysis on the suitability and effectiveness of technical solutions used in project available	- Tailoring guidelines exist - Interaction with other processes are described - Roles and competencies identified - Verification of the project conformance to the standard process - necessary competencies identified - Data available and analysis made on the suitability and effectiveness - necessary resources allocated to the project	- Procedures to support the implementation of the standard process exist	- Verification of the project conformance to the standard process (including work products)

Example 2: let's suppose to have the Software Testing process rated at capability level 3; in this case, the effectiveness and suitability of the technical solutions adopted in the project have been evaluated. The same evidence should be available for the project under review. Then, at joint review time, the supplier can be asked to provide such evidences in order to understand if the project is conducted with appropriate technical support.

4.1 A Pilot Initiative at Fiat Group Automobiles

Fiat Automobiles Group, in cooperation with the System and Software Evaluation Centre of the CNR's Information Science and Technologies Institute (SSEC), is undertaking an activity aimed at improving its capability in managing, controlling and driving the acquisition of software-intensive systems since year 2000 [14], [15], [16]. Such an activity has been mainly based on the performance of SPICE (and, since year 2004, Automotive SPICE) software process assessments with the aim of determining a supplier qualification mechanism based of the achievements of a predefined capability profile. Only suppliers having such a capability profile can be qualified as suppliers. Today FIAT Group Automobiles is able to know the way its own suppliers develop software because it got an understanding of their processes by means these assessments.

In addition, FIAT Group Automobiles is conducting, on a regular basis, external joint reviews (called Design Reviews) with its own suppliers in order to monitor their software projects. These joint reviews aim at verifying the suitability and correctness of key work products and managerial practices; they are primary means to:

- Verify completeness and quality of delivered work products
- Monitor respect of plans and other process requirements
- Monitor and control project risks
- Ensure that safety and security are properly managed
- Manage open issues
- Provide recommendations of alternatives.

The FIAT Group Automobiles design review process requires that four design reviews shall be planned and performed for each project. Specific check-lists have been defined for each design review. In the following these reviews are shortly described:

- Software Requirements Review (SRR): it shall ensure the correctness and completeness of the software requirements to be implemented. In addition the review will focus on project management. The stakeholders of SRR are: project manager, configuration manager, requirements analyst, quality manager. Documents reviewed are: Functional Requirements Specification, Requirements Analysis Report (RAR), and Validation Test Strategy.
- Software Architecture Review (SAR): it shall confirm correctness and completeness of software architecture, agree on the technical approach and on implementation choices. The stakeholders of SAR are: project manager, software engineering manager. Documents reviewed are RAR, Functional Requirements Specification, Software Requirements, Software Architecture, and System Architecture.
- Software Test Readiness Review (STRR): it shall be conducted to confirm successful completion of coding, unit testing and integration testing and to gain confidence for the beginning of the software validation. The stakeholders of STRR are: project manager, software engineering manager, V&V manager. Documents reviewed are: RAR, Functional Requirements Specification, Software Requirements, Software Architecture, Software tests, Software Test Reports, Quality Reports.
- Software Validation Review (SVR): it shall be conducted to confirm successful completion of validation phase, and to gain confidence for the delivery to Fiat Group Automobiles. A successful validation review does not imply acceptance, as the software shall undergo a separate acceptance process after the validation review. Stakeholders of SVR are: project manager, V&V manager, quality manager. Documents reviewed are: Software Requirements, Traceability Matrices, Software Validation Reports, Safety and Security Reports.

Because problems similar to those described in Section 3 occurred, FIAT Group Automobiles, with the support of the SSEC, is going to implement the mechanism described above to integrate Automotive SPICE assessments results with the design reviews. Fiat Group Automobiles is going to sponsor Automotive SPICE software process assessments to a selected group of software suppliers.

The Automotive SPICE assessments FIAT Automobiles Group sponsored until now, had the assessment scope depicted in Figure 1.

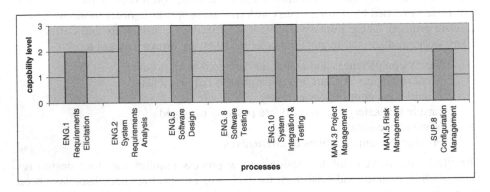

Fig. 1. FIAT Automobiles Group Automotive SPICE assessment scope, until year 2007

To improve the integration between design reviews and Automotive SPICE assessment results, the assessment scope is going to be modified by adding new processes and modifying the target capability levels. The current scope, in fact, doesn't allow an adequate coverage of the four design review phases.

A possible new scope will be composed of the following processes: ENG.1 Requirements Elicitation; ENG.2 System Requirements; ENG.3 System architectural design; ENG.4 Software requirements analysis; ENG.5 Software design; ENG.6

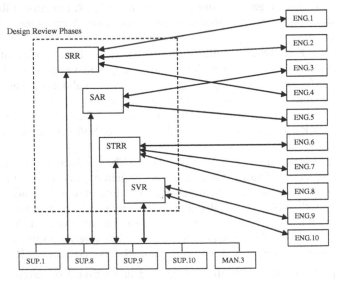

Fig. 2. Mapping between Design Review Phases and Process into the Assessment Scope

Software construction; ENG.7 Software integration test; ENG.8 Software testing; ENG.9 System integration test; ENG.10 System testing; SUP.1 Quality assurance; SUP.8 Configuration management; SUP.9 Problem resolution management; SUP.10 Change request management; MAN.3 Project Management.

In figure 2, the mapping between the design review phases and the processes in the assessment scope is shown. The link between a design review phase and a process indicates that the results of the assessment of such a process should be used in the correspondent review phase.

5 Conclusions and Future Works

In this paper we proposed a mechanism to integrate the Automotive SPICE assessment results into the joint reviews. Such a mechanism allows using the evidences collected during a software process assessment to support the joint reviews between FIAT Group Automobiles and its suppliers of software-intensive devices. To adopt the mechanism we propose, software assessments reporting shall be modified by providing information suitable to be applied in the different design reviews FIAT Group Automobiles performs regularly. The mechanism described in this paper can be considered as a way to conciliate the products based software evaluation and the process-based one.

FIAT Group Automobiles is going to sponsor a number of Automotive SPICE assessments in order to be able to apply such a mechanism on a sample set of important suppliers. The next step will be the definition of techniques to quantitatively evaluate the possible advantages obtained with the application of the mechanism.

References

[1] Leen, G., Hefferman, D., Dunne, A.: Digital Networks in the Automotive Vehicle. IEE Computer and Control Eng. Journal, 257–266 (December 1999)
[2] Kassakian, J.G.: Automotive Electrical Systems: The Power Electronics Market of the Future. In: Proceedings of Applied Power Electronics Conference, APEC 2000, pp. 3–9. IEEE Press, Los Alamitos (2000)
[3] ISO/IEC 12207 Amd 1:2002, Software Engineering – Software life cycle processes
[4] Staples, M., Mahmood, N.: Experiences Using Systematic Joint Review Guidelines. Journal of Systems and Software 80(90), 1425–1437 (2007)
[5] Quality System Requirements (QS-9000 Third Edition) Vers. 03.00. DaimlerChrysler, Ford Motor Company and General Motors Quality Publications (1998)
[6] ISO/TS 16949- Quality Management Systems - Automotive Suppliers - Particular Requirements for the Application of ISO 9001:2000 for Automotive Production and Relevant Service Part Organizations (2002)
[7] ISO/IEC 15504 International Standard. Information Technology – Software Process Assessment: Part 1–Part 5 (2006)
[8] Chrissis, M.B., Konrad, M., Shrum, S.: CMMI Guidelines for Process Integration and Product Improvement. Addison-Wesley, Reading (2004)
[9] Paulk, M.: Top-Level Standards Map: ISO 12207, ISO 15504 (January 1998 TR) Software CMM v1.1 and v2, Draft C. Software Engineering Institute, Carnegie Mellon University, Pittsburgh, PA, 1998 (date of access January 31, 2007), available at
http://www.sei.cmu.edu/pub/cmm/Misc/standards-map.pdf

[10] Hailey, V.: A comparison of ISO 9001 and the SPICE framework. In: SPICE: The Theory and Practice of Software Process Improvement and Capability Determination, IEEE CS Press, Los Alamitos (1998)

[11] Jung, H.W., Hunter, R.: The relationship between ISO/IEC 15504 process capability levels. ISO 9001 certification and organization size: an empirical study Journal of Systems and Software 59, 43–55 (2001)

[12] http://www.procurementforum.org

[13] http://www.automotivespice.com

[14] Fabbrini, F., Fusani, M., Lami, G., Sivera, E.: A SPICE-based Supplier Qualification Mechanism in Automotive Industry. Software Process Improvement and Practice Journal 12(6), 523–528 (2007)

[15] Fabbrini, F., Fusani, M., Lami, G., Sivera, E.: Performing Process Assessment to Improve the Supplier Selection Process - An Experience. In: Proceedings of the Automotive European Software Process Improvement Conference EuroSPI 2002, pp. 267–274 (2002)

[16] Fabbrini, F., Fusani, M., Lami, G., Sivera, E.: Software Process Assessment as a Mean to Improve the Acquisition Process of an Automotive Manufacturer. Software Process Improvment CMM & SPICE in Practice. Verlag UNI-DRUCK, Munchen, 142–154 (2002)

Quantitatively Managing Defects for Iterative Projects: An Industrial Experience Report in China

Lang Gou[1,2], Qing Wang[1], Jun Yuan[3], Ye Yang[1], Mingshu Li[1], and Nan Jiang[1,2]

[1] Institute of Software, Chinese Academy of Sciences
{goulang, wq, ye, mingshu, jiangnan}@itechs.iscas.ac.cn
[2] Graduate University of Chinese Academy of Sciences
[3] Beijing ZZNode Technologies Development Co., Ltd.
jun.yuan@zznode.com

Abstract. Iterative development methodology has been widely adopted in recent years since it is flexible and capable of dealing with requirement volatility. However, how to quantitatively manage iterative projects, and in particular, how to quantitatively manage defects across multiple iterations, remains a challenging issue. There is lack of quantitative defect management support for iterative projects due to the difficulty in selecting appropriate control points and measures to collect and analyze data, and determining the "sweet spot" amount of effort for performing testing and defect fixing activities. In this paper, we first propose the BiDefect (process-performance *B*aselines based *i*teration *Defect* management) method to support quantitative defect management in iterative development. Then we report an industrial experience that a Chinese telecommunications company, ZZNode, successfully applied the BiDefect method in initial estimating, analyzing, re-estimating, and controlling defects for iterative development projects.

Keywords: Measurement, Quantitative process management, Defect Management, Software process improvement.

1 Introduction

Iterative development concepts have been a recommended practice by prominent software engineering thought leaders over the past 30 years [1], esp. during the recent popularity of agile methods. A common theme of iterative development is to avoid a single-pass sequential, gated-step approach. Due to the process agility introduced by iterative concepts, there is a consensus that it is more difficult to implement quantitative management for iterative projects.

Quantitative management is among the advanced features of highly mature processes as defined in CMMI [2], which provides insights on the degree of goal fulfillment and root causes of significant process/product deviation. Quantitative defect management is the key to ensure the production of high quality software, which has been an important part of quantitative quality management. Unfortunately, how to quantitatively manage defects across multiple iterations, remains a challenging issue. Existing defect management methods [3] very few focus on quantitative management support for iterative development.

Q. Wang, D. Pfahl, and D.M. Raffo (Eds.): ICSP 2008, LNCS 5007, pp. 369–380, 2008.
© Springer-Verlag Berlin Heidelberg 2008

Nowadays, iterative development is applied widely in China. The concept of software process improvement and quantitative process management has also been adopted in many organizations. There are more than 200 software organizations deploy CMM or CMMI by 2007, some of them have applied quantitative management, but not all of them get benefit from it in reality [5]. Although two process areas (OPP - Organizational Process Performance and QPM - Quantitative Project Management) and some statistical techniques (e.g. SPC – Statistical Process Control) are described in CMMI [2] for implementing quantitative management, most software organizations still do not know clearly how to apply quantitative management. Therefore, some detail guidance on quantitative management, especially some experience results, is very helpful for software organizations who want apply or are being applied quantitative management.

This paper presents the BiDefect (process-performance *B*aselines based *i*teration *Defect* management) method, developed to address the quantitative defect (including defects from all defect detection activities, e.g., review, inspection and testing) management problems for iterative projects, along with an industrial experience of ZZNode. ZZNode is a leading Chinese telecommunications company, which successfully applied the BiDefect in quantitative defect control for its iterative projects based on the deployment of SoftPM [5]. SoftPM is a toolkit developed by Institute of Software, Chinese Academy of Sciences (ISCAS), which is used to manage software process and has been applied in over 200 organizations. The paper includes both research and experience results based on the collaboration between ISCAS and ZZNode throughout ZZNode's process improvement movement from CMMI ML3 to CMMI ML4.

This paper is organized as follows. The next section describes the challenges of defect management in iterative development. Related work is discussed in Section 3. Section 4 introduces the BiDefect method. Section 5 presents the application of the BiDefect method in quantitative defect management for iterative development in ZZNode. Section 6 concludes the paper and points out future directions of our work.

2   Challenges of Defect Management in Iterative Development

Iterative development has been adopted widely in China in recent years. ZZNode is a high-tech Chinese telecommunications company which has recently adopted iterative development. ZZNode was funded in Oct. 1999 and has about 360 employees today. In Jan. 2005, ZZNode was appraised and rated at CMMI ML 3. After that, ZZNode initiated quantitative process management program towards CMMI ML4. In the last two years, about 40% product lines adopted iterative development. The expectation was to control the quality of iterative development projects through controlling the quality of each iteration release and the final product.

ZZNode applied an adapted iterative development as shown in Fig. 1. The whole iterative development lifecycle includes several iterations and a system testing phase. Through each iteration, different functions are implemented separately and concurrently. When all functions are implemented and passed unit testing, testing for all functions will be performed. After all iterations are finished, product integration and system testing for products developed by all iterations are performed. Normally, the system testing phase includes several testing rounds. Compared to normal iterative development, the adapted iterative development lifecycle can control the quality of product more effec-

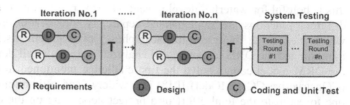

Fig. 1. The adapted iterative development lifecycle

tively because of the system testing stage involved. Through the application of iterative development, three challenges of quantitative defect management appear:

(1) The first challenge is identifying appropriate "control points" in each iteration. Many activities are related to defect, such as defect injection activity, defect detection activity and defect removal activity. For iterative development projects, the same kind of defect related activity is performed many times in the same and different iteration, which makes the defect management more complicated. For example, we can collect and analyze defect data after defect detection activity of each function, which supports precise control. However, it may incur too much effort on analyzing defect data. In addition, the defect data of each defect detection activity vary widely, which may not be appropriate to be placed under quantitative control.

(2) The second challenge is selecting appropriate measures and effective measurement methods. There are many existing defect related measures and measurement methods. How to select an appropriate set of measures and corresponding measurement methods for iterative projects, which support defect management for each iteration as well as the final product and do not incur too much effort of defect analysis, is a challenge issue.

(3) The third challenge is determining the "sweet spot" amount of effort for performing testing and defect fixing activities. If developers spend too much effort in testing, the schedule may very likely be delayed and additional cost may be incurred, however, if they spend too little testing effort, the quality of the software cannot be assured. In addition, the more defects, the more effort is needed to fix and verify them. Unfortunately, how to estimate the defect fixing effort accurately based on the actual defects is difficult.

The above challenges frequently place iterative developers in situations of making quality-schedule-function trade-offs from time to time. Unfortunately, the developers are left with very little help in making such kind of decisions. The goal of the BiDefect method is to solve these challenges.

3 Related Work

There is much research on management of defect related activities [5][6][7][13]. The DRM (phase-based Defect Removal Model) summarizes the relationships among three metrics: defect injection, defect removal, and effectiveness [3]. As a basic concept in DRM, the DRE (Defect Removal Effectiveness) of each phase is analyzed;

this is helpful for waterfall development. However, in iterative development projects, different functions are implemented separately and concurrently in each iteration, which means that there are not clear phases of requirements, design, coding in an iteration and the DRE cannot be and analyzed as in waterfall development. Therefore, the DRM model cannot solve the first challenge mentioned in Section 2. COCOMO (COnstructive COst MOdel) II [8] is a widely-used estimation model, which allows one to estimate the total effort of a project depending on the estimated size. It provides two sets of empirical results on effort distribution for both waterfall and RUP lifecycle phases, which can be used to estimate effort of each phase including testing activities proportionally. COCOMO II cannot predict the effort of defect detecting and fixing accurately. COQUALMO (COnstructive QUALity MOdel) [8] is a quality model extension to COCOMO II. It is used to estimate defects injected in different activities, and defects removed by defect removal activities. COQUALMO does not associate the defects with the effort of defect fixing. Therefore, COCOMO and COQUALMO cannot solve the third challenge mentioned in Section 2.

4 BiDefect Method

This section presents the BiDefect (process-performance *B*aselines based *i*teration *Defect* management) method as shown in Fig. 2. In the acronym, the 'B' stands for 'baselines' established based on organization historical data analysis, and the 'iDefect' means the iteration defects or

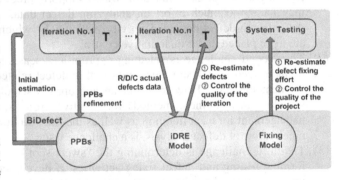

Fig. 2. The BiDefect method

defects during iterative development. The BiDefect method is an integration of three method components: PPBs (Process-Performance Baselines), iDRE (iteration Defect Removal Effectiveness) model, and Fixing model. The PPBs specify the measures and measurement methods for iterative development, which are used to solve the second challenge of defect management in iterative development (see Section 2). The iDRE model identified appropriated control points in each iteration, which is used to solve the first challenge. And the Fixing model are helpful in determining the "sweet spot" amount of effort for performing defect management activities in the system testing process, which can solve the third challenge. The BiDefect method can support initial estimating, analyzing, re-estimating, and controlling defects for iterative development projects.

4.1 PPBs

PPBs are measurement of performance for the organization's set of standard process at various levels of detail, as appropriate [2]. Before establishing PPBs, some defect related measures for iterative development are selected as shown in Table 1. The principles of selecting these measures are: (1) the measures can be collected easily, e.g. there is tool support for data collection; and (2) the measures are closely related to the organization's defect management objectives. In Table 1, the measures No. 1 to 4 focus on all kinds of defects, including defects detected in review, inspection, unit testing, integration testing, system testing, etc; and the measures No.6, 9 and 10 just focus on defects detected in integration testing and system testing activities.

Table 1. Measures for iterative development projects

No.	Measures
1	Defect Injection Rate (DIR) of requirements, design, coding and testing activities = defects injected at the activity / all defects of the project
2	Defect Removal Effectiveness (DRE) of requirements, design, coding and testing activities = defects removed at the activity / (defects existing on activity entry + defects injected during development of the activity)
3	Pre-release defect density = defects removed before product release / product size
4	Post-release defect density = defects detected within one year after product release / product size
5	Productivity = product size / total effort of project
6	Defect Injection Distribution (DID) = defects injected in requirements (or design, coding and testing) / all defects removed in system testing * 100%
7	Percentage of Detecting Effort (PDE) = effort of defect detecting activity in system testing stage / total effort of project * 100%
8	Percentage of Fixing Effort (PFE) = effort of defect fixing activity in system testing stage / total effort of project * 100%
9	Test efficiency = number of defects / defect detecting effort
10	Rework efficiency = number of defects / defect fixing effort

PPBs contain two important indicators: process performance and process capability. The process performance is a measure of actual results achieved by following a process, specified by central line (CL). The process capability is the range of expected results that can be achieved by following a process, specified by upper control limit (UCL) and lower control limit (LCL). In the paper, we used BSR method [9] and XmR (individuals and moving range) control chart [10] to establish PPBs. Due to space limit, we do not describe the process of calculating CL, UCL, LCL in detail.

4.2 iDRE Model

In ZZNode, each iteration release is submitted to customer as an intermediate result, which requires each iteration finish on schedule with high quality. However, as mentioned in Section 2, it is a challenge issue to identify appropriate control points in each iteration for defect management. The iDRE model is established to solve this challenge. As a variant DRE model, the iDRE model is derived from the concept of DRE [3] aiming at controlling the quality of each iteration, as shown in Fig. 3. Since the normal method of analyzing DRE of each phase is not applicable for iterative development (mentioned in Section 3), the iDRE model improves the implementing method to analyze DRE of each kind of activity in iteration instead of

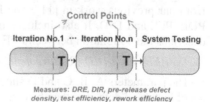

Measures: *DRE, DIR, pre-release defect density, test efficiency, rework efficiency*

Fig. 3. iDRE model

DRE of each lifecycle phase. In addition, the iDRE model collects defect data through each defect related activity, but analyzes them until all functions have been implemented (which means before the testing activity of an iteration). The selected control points in iDRE model are before the testing activity of each iteration. Compared to traditional DRE, the iDRE model is coarse-grained but requires less effort of measurement and analysis. Besides, in many organizations, an iteration often takes not a long period, such as one to two months. Therefore, a coarse-grained quantitative method is more than sufficient. In the iDRE model, the PPBs for DIR, DRE, pre-release defect density, test efficiency and rework efficiency are adopted. The steps for applying iDRE model are:

(1) At the beginning of projects, the defects that could be removed in different kinds of activity of each iteration are estimated based on the PPBs of DRE and DIR. The control limits of the defects number are also defined. Normally, the iteration *(n+1)* is developed based on the iteration *(n)*, but the functions developed in iteration *(n)* will not be tested in iteration *(n+1)*. Therefore, defects that should be removed in each iteration could be estimated separately and no feed-forward of defect results from one iteration to another is needed.

(2) Before the integration testing activities of each iteration, actual defects removed before testing are collected and analyzed. The number of defects that could be removed in integration testing is re-estimated based on the actual defects removed before testing and the quality objectives of the iteration. If the actual defects removed before testing are out of control limits, causal analysis should be performed and corrective actions should be implemented if necessary.

(3) Before the system testing phase, where all iterations are finished, the number of defects removed in all iterations are collected and analyzed. Based on the quality objectives of the project, the number of defects that could be removed in system testing phase is re-estimated. If the re-estimated defects that could be removed in system testing are out of the control limits, causal analysis should be performed and corrective actions should be implemented if necessary. In addition, the defect detecting effort and the defect fixing effort of the system testing activity are re-estimated based on the PPBs of test efficiency and rework efficiency.

4.3 Fixing Model

The Fixing model is established to solve the third challenge of defect management in iterative challenge, which is determining the "sweet spot" amount of effort for performing testing and defect fixing activities. The Fixing model supports quantitatively manage system testing process in iterative development projects, which was derived from our previous work in [11]. The Fixing model includes PPBs of three measures: PDE, PFE and DID. It also includes one regression equation as shown below, which describes the correlation between PFE and DID.

$$PFE = A * DID\_Requirements + B * DID\_Design + C * DID\_Coding + D$$

The parameters A, B, C and D should be specified using multiple regression analysis of historical data, and then be evaluated by statistical method, e.g. F test [12].

By using the PPBs of PDE, PFE and DID, the Fixing model can estimate the amount of effort for performing testing and defect fixing activities, and the number of defects injected in each activity. By using the regression equation, the Fixing model can re-estimated the effort of defect fixing based on the actual defects.. More information about the Fixing model is described in [11].

5 Experience Result of BiDefect

This section presents the experience result of applying the BiDefect method in ZZNode. First, ZZNode established PPBs for iterative development projects based on its historical project data, as shown in Table 2. In ZZNode, all defects (including defects discovered in review, inspection and testing) were submitted by engineers and were collected in SoftPM. These defects were classified into four severities: A, B, C and D, where A is the most serious. After revising the defect reports (e.g., removing duplicated defects, dividing defect reports that recorded multiple defects into several defect reports), ZZNode describe the total defects without distinguishing them by different severity.

Then, ZZNode analyzed the historical data and derived the regression equation for the Fixing model as follows:

$$PFE = 0.1065*DID\_Requirement - 0.0043*DID\_Design - 0.3925*DID\_Coding + 0.3597$$

The regression equation was evaluated using F test [12]. At the confidence level $\alpha=0.05$, the regression equation was linearly prominent.

In ZZNode, several iterative projects applied the BiDefect method, including a few large-scaled projects. Due to space limit, we only take one project as an example to demonstrate the process of using BiDefect. Table 3 summarizes the information about the project.

Table 2. PPBs for iterative projects

PPBs		UCL	LCL	CL
DIR (%)	Requirements	64.1%	8.6%	36.4%
	Design	20.2%	8.0%	14.1%
	Coding	76.0%	13.6%	44.8%
	Testing	9.2%	0.2%	4.7%
DRE (%)	Requirements	85.9%	25.6%	55.8%
	Design	93.9%	2.4%	48.1%
	Coding	52.0%	0.0%	25.5%
	Testing	90.9%	28.0%	59.5%
Pre-release defect density (defects / KLOC)		4.07	3.40	3.70
Post-releases defect density (defects / KLOC)		1.02	0.99	1.01
Software productivity (LOC / Labor Day)		69.20	25.20	47.20
DID (%)	Requirements	9.7%	5.2%	7.4%
	Design	12.2%	5.6%	8.9%
	Coding	80.4%	61.0%	70.7%
	Testing	15.9%	10.1%	13.0%
PDE (%)		2.4%	0.8%	1.6%
PFE (%)		1.6%	0.4%	1.0%
Test efficiency (defects / labor day)		5.59	0.00	2.29
Rework efficiency (defects / labor day)		5.60	0.00	2.61

Table 3. Brief information about the project

Category	Information
# of staff	34 (each staff just involves some activities and divides his/her time on several projects)
Plan Schedule	11 months
Pan Size	224.6 KLOC
Lifecycle	Iterative development (total four iterations in overlap time, and three testing rounds in system testing activity)
Techniques	J2EE
Quality Objectives	Whole project: Post-release defect density <= 0.65 defects/KLOC and no class A defects Each iteration: Post-release defect density <= 0.8 defects/KLOC
Description	To develop the inventory management and service assurance function of the next generation network for PCCW, the biggest telecom operator in Hong Kong, P.R. China.

5.1 Initial Estimation from PPBs

At the beginning of the project, the project manager and experienced engineers planned the project. The estimation for each iteration was specified through the following steps: (1) estimate the size, schedule, and total effort; (2) estimate the defects that should be removed in each iteration based on the PPB of pre-release defect density; (3) estimate defects that should be removed in requirements, design, coding and testing activities based on the PPBs of DIR and DRE; and (4) calculate the escaped defect density of each iteration, and judge whether it satisfy the quality objectives of each iteration. If not, some corrective actions would be performed and the initial estimation should be refined until escaped defect density satisfies the quality objectives. For the selected project, the initial estimation for four iterations all satisfied the quality objectives of each iteration, as shown in Table 4.

Table 4. Estimation and actual performance for each iteration of the project

Measures	Iteration #1		Iteration #2		Iteration #3		Iteration #4	
	Estimation	Actual	Estimation	Actual	Estimation	Actual	Estimation	Actual
Size (KLOC)	117.3	113.8	39.1	42.6	47.5	46.7	20.7	22.5
Schedule (Month)	5.9	6	2.95	3	2.5	2.6	2.5	1.5
Total effort (Labor Day)	2480	2512	829.25	841	968.75	1013.9	270.75	289.75
Total defects removed	346	410	115	154	140	170	61	41
Defects removed at requirements	88	42	29	12	36	15	16	17
Defects removed at design	63	90	21	30	26	38	11	12
Defects removed at coding	67	85	22	34	52	44	12	12
Defects removed at testing	128	193	43	78	27	73	23	0

The system testing phase was estimated by the following steps: (1) estimate the total defect detecting (or fixing) effort in the system testing based on the PPB of PDE (or PFE); (2) estimate the defect detecting (or fixing) effort of each testing round based on the effort distribution which was 50%, 30% and 20% in the project; (3) estimate the total defects that could be removed in system testing activity based on defects escaped from the four iterations and the PPB of DIR in testing; (4) estimate the defects could be removed in each testing round based on the defect distribution which was 50%, 40% and 10% in the project; and (5) calculate the escaped defect density of system testing, and judge whether it satisfy the quality objectives of the project. If not, some corrective actions would be performed and the initial estimation should be refined until escaped defect density satisfied the quality objectives of the project. For the selected project, the initial estimation for system testing activity satisfied the quality objectives of the project, so no corrective actions were needed, as shown in Table 5. The control limits of defects related data were also estimated and

Table 5. Initial Estimation for system testing activity of the project

Estimation	Testing round #1	Testing round #2	Testing round #3
Effort of defect detecting (Labor Day)	40.9	24.5	16.4
Effort of defect fixing (Labor Day)	25.6	15.3	10.2
Total defects detected in system testing	61	49	12

specified in the project plan based on the PPBs. Due to space limit, we do not describe the control limits. The project was performed against the project plan.

5.2 Quantitative Defect Management for Each Iteration Using iDRE

The iDRE model was used to quantitatively manage each iteration. Due to space limit, we take the first iteration as an example. In the first iteration, after all functions were implemented, actual defects removed before testing were collected as shown in Table 4. The control limits of defects removed in requirements, design, coding and testing in the first iteration are shown in Table 6. Compared the actual defects to the control limits, the actual defects removed at requirements, design and coding activity of the first iteration are between the UCL and LCL, which means no abnormality. Then, defects that should be removed at testing activity in the first iteration were re-

Table 6. Control limits for defects removed in each activity

Defects Removed	Requirements	Design	Coding	Testing
UCL	132	119	132	191
LCL	39	3	0	59

estimated. Based on the actual defects removed before testing, the number of defects escaped before testing was calculated, which was 184. The number of defects injected in testing activity of the first iteration was 20. In order to satisfy the quality objectives of the first iteration, the number of defects existed after testing activity should be no more than 0.8*113.8=91. Therefore, the number of defects that should be removed at testing should be at least 184+20-91=113. After the testing activity of the first iteration, actual defect data were collected. As shown in Table 4, 193 defects were removed through the testing activity, which is more than the UCL=191. Given this abnormality, some further causal analysis was performed. First, they analyzed the quality of the product through the interview and data analysis, and found the quality of the product was similar to historical projects. Then, they applied cause-and-effect diagram as shown in Fig. 4. The project team concluded that detecting more defects in the first iteration was a good phenomenon and no corrective action was needed.

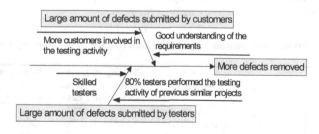

Fig. 4. Cause-and-effect diagram

Similarly, through the development of the later iterations, iDRE model was applied. Before the product integration and system testing phase, where all iterations were finished, the actual number of defects removed in all iterations was collected as shown in Table 4. Fig. 5 shows the defects escaped after testing activity and the defects allowed by the quality objec-

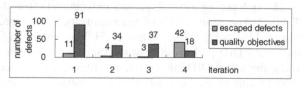

Fig. 5. Satisfaction of quality objectives in each iteration

tives of the four iterations. The first three iterations all satisfied the quality objectives since the defects escaped was less than the defects allowed by the quality objectives. Due to the testing activity in the fourth iteration was moved and integrated with the system testing activity, the fourth iteration did not satisfied the quality objectives.

Based on the actual defects removed in the four iterations, the number of defects that should be removed in the system testing activity was re-estimated, which was 73, based on the quality objectives of the project. Compare to the control limits, the re-estimated defects were between the UCL and LCL. Therefore, no corrective actions were needed. In addition, since the estimated defects that should be removed in the system testing activity were changed, the effort of defect detecting and fixing in the system testing activity was re-estimated based on the PPBs of test efficiency and rework efficiency. The plan for the system testing process was adjusted correspondingly.

5.3   Quantitative Defect and Fixing Management for System Testing Using Fixing

The Fixing model was used to quantitatively manage the system testing process. As mentioned before, the system testing process contained three testing rounds. Based on historical data, defects removed in each testing round were not equal. For the project, the percentages of defects removed in the three testing rounds were 50%, 40%, and 10% respectively. Therefore, based on the total defects that should be removed in the system testing activity (which was 73); defects should be removed in the three testing rounds were 36, 30, and 7 respectively. In addition, based on the PPBs of DID, defects injected in each activity of the three testing rounds were re-estimated correspondingly as shown in Table 7. Based on the re-estimated data for the system testing activity, the project manager refined the plan for each system testing round and performed testing activity against the plan.

Table 7. Re-estimated and actual performance of each testing round in system testing process

Process-performance	Testing round #1		Testing round #2		Testing round #3	
	Re-estimation	Actual data	Re-estimation	Actual data	Re-estimation	Actual data
Effort of defect detecting (Labor Day)	41.2	22.75	28.8	11.75	12.4	7.25
Effort of defect fixing (Labor Day)	26.53	28	26.98	21	13.09	10
Total defects detected in system testing	36	37	30	26	7	6
Defects injected in requirements	3	3	2	1	0	0
Defects injected in design	3	3	3	2	1	1
Defects injected in coding	25	26	21	17	5	4
Defects injected in testing	5	5	4	6	1	1

Through testing round #1, actual defects and effort data were collected as shown in Table 7. The actual DIDs of the requirements, design, coding and testing activities were 8.11%, 8.11%, 70.27% and 13.51% respectively. Compared to the PPBs of DID, the actual DID performance was normal and no corrective actions were needed. By using the actual DID and correlation regression between DID and PFE, the effort of defect fixing in testing round #1 was re-estimated, which was 26.53 labor days. When testing round #1 was finished, the actual effort of defect detecting and fixing were collected in Table 7.

Similarly, the latter two testing rounds were quantitatively controlled by using the Fixing model. Fig. 6 shows the initially estimated (Table 5), re-estimated (Table 7) and actual defects (Table 7) removed in each testing round, as well as the relative variance between initial estimation and actual data (RV1 = ABS (actual data–initial estimation) / initial estimation * 100%) and relative variance between re-estimation and actual data (RV2=ABS(actual data – re-estimation)/re-estimation* 100%). Fig. 6 indicates that the re-estimated defects were more precise than the initial estimation since it is closer to the ac-tual defects.

Supported by the BiDe-fect method, the project finished in time and the quality of the project satis-fied its quality objectives. PCCW, the customer of the project, was satisfied with the project and had con-tracted new projects to ZZNode afterwards.

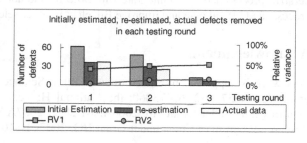

Fig. 6. Initially estimated, re-estimated and actual defects removed in each testing round

5.4 Discussion

In Aug 15, 2007, ZZNode was appraised and rated at CMMI ML4. ZZNode high-lighted some benefits of using BiDefect as follows: (1) better management of defect data repository. The PPBs were established according to organization's defect man-agement objectives. Compared to the previous PPBs, current PPBs are more appropri-ate; (2) quantitatively controlling projects efficiently. The BiDefect method was co-herent to ZZNode's business objectives, and covered the entire lifecycle; (3) promotion of customer satisfaction. From 2006 Q1 to 2007 Q1, the percentage of "Very Satisfied or Satisfied" was increased from 46% to 82%, especially, the percent-age was 100% in 2006 Q4; and (4) improvement of product quality. From 2005 to 2007, the average post-release defect density was decreased year by year and the range of post-release defect density was converged.

Through the implementation of BiDefect, we found that the result of applying BiDefect is most dependent on the availability and quality of historical data in the organization. Therefore, if the historical data is missing or not sufficient, we recom-mend collecting more data from stable process before using the BiDefect method.

6 Conclusions

This paper described a process-performance *B*aselines based *i*teration *Defect* man-agement method named BiDefect, which was developed to solve the three challenges of defect management in iterative development. Its three components: PPBs, iDRE model, and Fixing model, provide support in establishing process-performance base-lines, managing defects in each development iteration, and managing the quality of overall integrated products respectively. The BiDefect method was evolved from the collaboration between ZZNode and ISCAS, which combined research results and ZZNode's best practice. Based on the application of quantitative process management supported by the BiDefect method, ZZNode was appraised and rated at CMMI ML4 in Aug. 2007. Through the implementation of BiDefect, the customer satisfaction of ZZNode had been promoted together with the improvement of product quality.

The future work in our study includes: (1) extend BiDefect to suit more generalized iterative process needs; (2) integrate with SoftPM and automate the defect management process; and (3) validate and improve BiDefect in other selected organizations.

Acknowledgments

This work is supported by the National Natural Science Foundation of China under grant Nos. 60573082, 60473060; the National Hi-Tech Research and Development Plan of China under Grant No. 2006AA01Z182, 2007AA010303; the National Basic Research Program of China under Grant NO. 2007CB310802.

References

1. Larman, C., Basili, V.R.: Iterative and Incremental Development: A Brief History. Computer 36(6), 47–56 (2003)
2. Chrissis, M.B., Konrad, M., Shrum, S.: CMMI(R): Guidelines for Process Integration and Product Improvement. Addison-Wesley Publishing Company, Boston (2006)
3. Kan, S.H.: Metrics and Models in Software Quality Engineering. Addison-Wesley Professional, Reading (2002)
4. Wang, Q., Li, M.S.: Measuring and Improving Software Process in China. In: 4th International Symposium on Empirical Software Engineering, Australia, pp. 183–192 (2005)
5. Fenton, N.E., Neil, M.: A Critique of Software Defect Prediction Models. IEEE Transactions on Software Engineering 25(5), 675–689 (1999)
6. Mizuno, O., Shigematsu, E., Takagi, Y., Kikuno, T.: On Estimating Testing Effort Needed to Assure Field Quality in Software Development. In: 13th International Symposium on Software Reliability Engineering, Annapolis, MD, pp. 139–146 (2002)
7. Jones, C.: Software Assessments, Benchmarks, and Best Practices. Addison-Wesley Professional, Boston (2000)
8. Boehm, B.W., Horowitz, E., Madachy, R., et al.: Software Cost Estimation with COCOMO II. Prentice Hall PTR, Upper Saddle River (2000)
9. Wang, Q., Jiang, N., Gou, L., et al.: BSR: A Statistic-based Approach for Establishing and Refining Software Process Performance Baseline. In: 28th International Conference on Software Engineering, Shanghai, China, pp. 585–594 (2006)
10. Florac, W.A., Carleton, A.D.: Measuring Software Process-Statistical Process Control for Software Process Improvement. Addison-Wesley Publishing Company, Reading (1999)
11. Wang, Q., Gou, L., Jiang, N., et al.: An Empirical Study on Establishing Quantitative Management Model for Testing Process. In: International Conference on Software Process, pp. 233–245. Springer, Minneapolis (2007)
12. Wooldridge, J.: Introductory Econometrics: A Modern Approach. South-Western College Pub., Boston (2002)

An Investigation of Software Development Productivity in China[*]

Mei He[1,2], Mingshu Li[1,3], Qing Wang[1], Ye Yang[1], and Kai Ye[1,2]

[1] Laboratory for Internet Software Technologies, Institute of Software, Chinese Academy of Sciences, Beijing 100080, China
{hemei,mingshu,wq,ye,yekai}@itechs.iscas.ac.cn
[2] Graduate University of Chinese Academy of Sciences, Beijing 100039 China
[3] State Key Laboratory of Computer Science, Institute of Software, Chinese Academy of Sciences, Beijing 100080, China

Abstract. Software productivity conveys fundamental information for many decision making processes, such as in-house development benchmarking and outsourcing strategic planning. However, there is a lack of statistical results on this matter with respect to Chinese software industry. In this paper, through the analysis of 999 industry projects in China, we seek to develop in-depth and comprehensive understanding about software productivity status in China, by identifying significant influential factors and examining their true effects based on our dataset. As a result, Organization is identified as the most significant factor, followed by Development type, Business area, Region, Language, Project size and Team size. Further assessment and findings are also presented with relevant recommendations to increase productivity and improve software processes.

Keywords: Software productivity, empirical analysis, Chinese software industry, globalization of software development, software process improvement.

1 Introduction

New types of software processes such as IT outsourcing and globally distributed development have become widely adopted practices. A successful outsourcing approach requires a systematical consideration and management of many critical factors such as people factors, process factors, product factors, etc. Among these, it is believed that software productivity study provides the most insights to help organizations seeking for a beneficial outsourcing option.

On the other hand, software industry in China has been experiencing great-leap-forward development resulting from this global outsourcing paradigm. As a result, software export value has increased from 3.3 billion RMB in 2000 to 46.8 billion RMB in 2006. An 8-year longitude analysis of the industry size is shown in Fig. 1

---

[*] This work is supported by the National Natural Science Foundation of China under Grant No. 60573082; the National Hi-Tech R&D Plan of China under Grant Nos. 2006AA01Z182 and 2007AA010303; the National Basic Research Program (973 program) under Grant No. 2007CB310802.

Q. Wang, D. Pfahl, and D.M. Raffo (Eds.): ICSP 2008, LNCS 5007, pp. 381–394, 2008.
© Springer-Verlag Berlin Heidelberg 2008

[1-3]. Meanwhile, Chinese software industry is also facing a great deal of challenges, such as scalability difficulty, lack of core technology advance, lack of top-level personnel, and management policy mismatch [3].

During the development course of its software industry, China also grows into one of the major outsourcing service bases. However, there is lack of comprehensive studies on Chinese software industry to provide information on the latest status of software development productivities and its associated issues. Having seen the big numbers in Fig. 1, one may immediately ask what the actual productivity level is like compared to

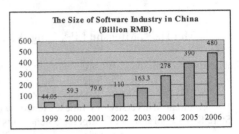

Fig. 1. The size of software industry in China from Year 1999 to 2006 [1-3]

other countries and what are the important factors are on influencing the productivity in China? Such information offers great insights and value to business planner and decision makers, as well as local software organization to make organization/process benchmark and/or fine-tuning prediction models [4].

In this paper, we provide results of an investigation on software productivity in Chinese software industry. To that end, 999 software project data points from the China Software Benchmarking Standard Group (CSBSG) database are used and analyzed in our investigation. The data is from 140 companies which are across 15 regions of China. The investigation is designed in a way to better develop understanding of Chinese software productivity comparable to knowledge published in existing productivity studies. Through this paper, some answers to above questions are concluded, and the characteristics and potential problems of software development in China are elaborated.

The remainder of the paper is organized as follows. Section 2 briefly introduces the motivation and goals of our research. Next, analysis results are addressed in Section 3. Finally, a discussion of the significance of the results and some comments on the future data collection and analysis are summarized to conclude.

2   Motivation and Goals of the Investigation

2.1   Related Work on Software Productivity

Software productivity is generally defined as the ratio of software output to input. Previous research on software productivity has produced different terms such as lines-of-code productivity [5], function point productivity [6, 7], process productivity [8], according to the specific measurement used for software output. As an essential measurement in software development, software productivity is a good indicator for the condition of software process, product, and personnel. There is a consensus that productivity is highly variable across the software industry [5], and results from productivity studies are frequently used as a basis for building organization/process benchmark and/or fine-tuning prediction models.

For the purpose of our study, we are more interested in comparing and analyzing the significant factors affecting productivity defined by different groups of researchers. Table 1 summarizes a comparison of such factors in 5 previous studies.

Table 1. Critical factors influencing productivity in previous studies. N represents the number of projects involved in each database.

Data source	Year	N	Factors discussed
European Space Agency data (from 8 countries) [5]	1996	99	Company, Language, Category, Environment, Team size, Duration, KLOC & a set of COCOMO drivers
Software Technology Transfer Finland (old) [9]	2000	206	Company, Business sector, Operating system, DBMS tools, Hardware platform etc.
STTF (new) [6], [7]	2004 2005	622	Company, Process model, Business sector, Year, Hardware
ISBSG [10]	2003	1238	organization type, business area, development type, primary programming language etc.
ISBSG [11], [12]	2007	>3000	Team size, Language, Dev Type, Platform, Dev techniques, Dev methodology, CASE tool

Though some common factors (e.g. business area, language) appear in different studies, it is interesting for these different studies to conclude different results. An example is that new development projects are found to have a higher productivity in ISBSG data, while other analysis of development type attribute has been inconclusive, showing either no difference [7] or in some situations higher productivity for enhancement projects [12]. Some of these inconsistencies will need to be resolved on the basis of the Chinese real projects.

2.2 Overview of CSBSG Database

To develop further understanding to software productivity status in China, this study uses a dataset of 999 industry projects from the first version of the CSBSG database, as of August 2007. The CSBSG was established in Jan. 2006, and its mission is to advocate and establish domestic benchmarking standards for system and software process improvement in Chinese software industry. The CSBSG projects were collected from 140 organizations and 15 regions across China with the support of government and industry association. Each data point follows the similar format of ISBSG definitions [9]. Table 2 summarizes the general information of our database.

Table 2. Summary of the CSBSG project data

Variable	N	Mean	Median	Min	Max
Project size (LOCs)	999	666341	36109	771	2339728
Effort (person hours)	999	6207	3152	132	134840
Team size	998	9	6	1	110
Development Region	From 9 primary regions including Beijing, Shanghai, Jiangsu, Tianjin, Shandong, Liaoning, Zhejiang, Anhui, Chongqing (#Obs.> 10)				
Business Area	Across 7 primary business areas including Public admin, Energy, Manufacturing, General, Retail & Inventory, Finance, Telecom (#Obs.> 20)				
Language type	Consisting of 7 primary language types: C#, Java, C++, ASP, VB, C, Cobol (#Obs.> 10)				
Development Type	New development, Enhancement, Re-development				

2.3 Research Questions

In addition to identify the significant factors influencing productivity in the CSBSG database, we also attempt to validate different conclusions and findings for previous studies using this dataset. To that end, some research questions are proposed with respect to the CSBSG database.

RQ1: Do organizations differ a lot from each other in productivity?

Every organization carries its own set of characteristics that influence on software productivity. This has been identified as the most significant factor in many literatures such as [5], [7], [13].

RQ2: Does new development always cost more effort than enhancement?

Software projects can be new development, re-development, or enhancement. Some researchers consider new development costs more effort than enhancement [12], and claim that while new development starts everything from scratch, software enhancement simply adds, changes, or deletes software functionality of legacy systems to adapt to changing business requirements [14]. On the other hand, some find them no difference [7], but in one version of ISBSG data, new development projects also show higher productivity [9].

RQ3: What business area corresponds to a higher productivity rate? What corresponds to a lower one?

Business area has been identified as one of the most significant factors influencing productivity for times [5], [6], [7], [10]. However, the most productive area is not consistent from the results of different researchers.

RQ4: Is there a relationship between software productivity and the region/city where the organization is from?

Development region has very rarely been discussed in previous studies, except that some studies give information about productivity by country [15]. However, it is reported that region is one of the most differentiating factors in Chinese software industry [1-3].

RQ5: Does programming language matter in terms of affecting productivity?

Language is also a frequently studied factor in terms of software development and its productivity [5], [9], [11], [12]. In previous research, some have removed the language effect either by considering only programs written in the same language or by converting all data into one language using conversion factors, but a number of researchers have found that productivity varies with the level of the language [5].

RQ6: Will larger team size reduce the productivity?

Team size is included as a variable influencing productivity in several researches [5], [11], [12], [16], and many of them agree that increasing team size will reduce productivity. Then, how about its influencing trend in China?

RQ7: Will larger project size reduce the productivity?

Projects size is a major estimator in almost all effort estimation models, such as COCOMO [17], COBRA [18]. As productivity is identified as a ratio of size and effort, and size is such an important estimator for effort, then the relation between productivity and size is also an interesting issue for many researchers.

3 Analysis Results

General Linear Models (GLM) procedure [19] is a commonly used procedure to analyze the variance of unbalanced data in previous studies [5], [19]. In our study, a GLM procedure was followed to produce a list of factors that significantly influence the productivity based on the whole 999 project data points as listed in Table 3.

Table 3. Variance of productivity explained by each variable

Variables	Type	Variance explained
Organization	Class	91.32%
Development type	Class	25.66%
Business area	Class	21.36%
Region	Class	21.07%
Language	Class	16.33%
Project size	Nonclass	14.84%
Team size	Nonclass	2.63%

The results show that, the single variable which explains the greatest amount of variance of productivity in the dataset is Organization. This is followed by Region, Business area, Development type, Language and Project size. The Team size which is the peak size of development teams explains only 2.63% of the variance in productivity. In the remainder of this section, analysis results based on each variable are discussed and formulated into findings in answering the proposed RQs.

3.1 Productivity by Organization (RQ1)

For the whole dataset, Organization is identified as the most significant factor (91.32%), and this result is similar to the research identifying Company as the most significant one as in [5], [7]. Indeed, organizations adopt different technologies, face to diverse market competition environments, and vary in the way of managing software process, the composition and capability of the personnel and the culture of corporate etc. All of these make individual organizations quite different from each others.

This might be one essential reason why all kinds of estimation model and quality management toolkit, which help organizations better track and control software development, recommend the users to customize and calibrate the models and tools according to the dataset and requirements of their own.

Finding 1 : Organizations in the CSBSG database display great difference in productivity. Due to the significant variance, it is always recommended that one organization be cautious while using cross-organization data as benchmark, estimation or control reference. It is better to build their own database to identify the most relevant aspects and critical factors for enhancement in their own organizational settings.

3.2 Productivity by Development Type (RQ2)

In the CSBSG database, new development projects display obviously higher productivity than enhancement. (Due to the small sample size of Re-development, we focus

our attention mainly on the comparison of New development and Enhancement. 13
project data missing "development type" records are removed from this analysis.)

Table 4. Productivity and the number of projects for each development type

Development type	N	Median productivity
Re-development	39	7.08
New development	683	13.65
Enhancement	264	5.27

Furthermore, productivity of the three development types is compared again in combination with other group breakdown criteria. As shown in Fig. 2, all results concur that the new development projects were developed faster than enhancement development.

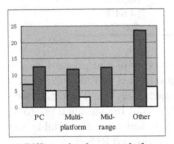

a) Different development platforms

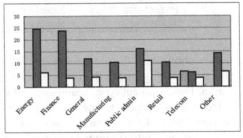

b) Different business areas

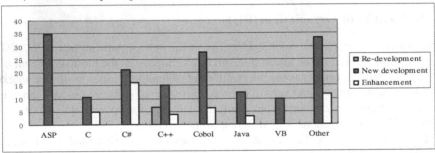

C) Different languages

Fig. 2. Further breakdown comparison results with additional breakdown criteria as: a) development platform; b) business area; c) language

There is no consensus as to which type would cost more effort in existing literatures. Our results correspond to those in [12], where new development type of projects turns out to have higher productivity. However, other researchers suggested the two categories have little difference [7], while some suggested enhancement projects have higher productivity.

Some lessons learned from possible reasons for low productivity in enhancement are: it is better to continue to use the development team or key design personnel to reduce the effort in renewed study. At the same time, in new development, not only the efficiency of producing lines of code, but also the disciplined documentation is important to lay a good foundation for future maintenance or enhancement.

Finding 2 : Productivity in new development is found to be higher than in enhancement in the CSBSG database.

3.3 Productivity by Business Area (RQ3)

We selected the top 7 most frequent business areas (energy, public admin, manufacturing, general, retail, finance, and telecom) in the dataset, grouped the data into 7 subsets accordingly, and compared the median productivity of the 7 subsets. Fig. 3 shows the results, where business areas are arranged in an ascending order in terms of productivity.

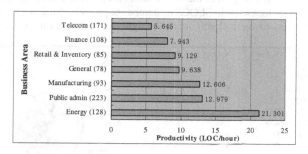

Fig. 3. Productivity by business areas (Number of projects is shown in the parentheses)

For Telecom software, constant evolution is dominant, shaping both software design and software process, and it is now evolving more rapidly than usual on the influence of the Internet [20]. Many telecom software products have to deal with complex and evolving new platforms, unstable requirements, real-time performance, multi-site settings, and high availability and reliability, which justify the low productivity as reported in many other studies [21]. Additionally, the telecom industry in China lacks of fair competition. Immature customer and bureaucracy could be other possible reasons for low productivity in the Telecom area.

For the Finance area, some analysis also revealed its low productivity [10]. Since financial software requires real-time, excessive data exchange, vast data processing, high level security and other complex technologies, the productivity is easier to decrease than other business sectors. Meanwhile, as some information is highly confidential, some banks or investment companies insist finishing internal software development even if the productivity is low.

Nevertheless, productivities in Public Admin, Energy and Manufacturing are relative higher in the CSBSG data. One possible reason may be most of the projects in this subset belonging to administrative management systems. They have comparatively less complexity and more stable requirements. Also, some Chinese government-agencies come to deploy more formal public bidding processes to ensure the quality and efficiency of the entrusted software development team as reported in [22],

[23]. ([23] is a Chinese website proclaiming a government project biding result). At this point, we are in short of detailed information about the application type to carry out further investigation in this matter, due to missing data items in the current CSBSG database. The analysis will be continued in the future when data is available.

Finding 3 *: In the CSBSG database, Telecom and Finance are found to be the lower productivity area, while Public Admin, Manufacturing and Energy are found to be relative more productive.*

3.4 Productivity by Region (RQ4)

In the CSBSG database, Region explains more than 21% of the variation of productivity, and the detailed results about each region is presented in Table 5.

Table 5. Productivity across Region in the whole dataset. Prod, N.Proj, N.Org and N.Bus represent median productivity measured in SLOC/Hr, number of projects, number of organizations and number of business areas covered. The figure on the right shows the region distribution pie chart.

Region	Prod.	N.Proj	N.Org	N.Bus
Zhejiang	28.79	76	6	1
Tianjin	27.68	56	5	2
Shanghai	15.46	17	5	4
Shandong	15.02	21	3	5
Liaoning	9.72	237	23	6
Beijing	8.49	428	73	8
Jiangsu	8.10	90	13	7
Anhui	6.89	29	3	3
Chongqing	6.83	28	2	1
Other	6.90	17	7	6
Total	10.36	999	141	8

Projects Distribution in Main Regions

Table 5 shows that the regions of Zhejiang and Tianjin are the top two highest productivity regions, with median productivity of 28.79Sloc/Hr and 27.68Sloc/Hr respectively, while Beijing is ranked No. 6 with a productivity of 8.49Sloc/Hr. However, the proportion of projects they contribute in the whole dataset varies highly. As mentioned earlier, region is reported as one of the most differentiating factors in Chinese software industry [1-3], thus, in this section, further study is especially developed.

According to three quartiles for the whole dataset, 5.88, 10.23, 20.63 Sloc/Hr, all data is divided into 4 groups in terms of the level of their productivity: low, normal, high, and very high. We define the productivity smaller than 5.88 as "low" level, greater than 20.63 as "very high" level, and so forth. In each level, the number of projects involved in each region is shown in Table 6.

Table 6. Breakdown of projects by Region and productivity levels

Region	Zhejiang	Tianjin	Shanghai	Shandong	Liaoning	Beijing	Jiangsu	Anhui	Chongqing	Other	Total
low	n/a	n/a	1	1	76	126	25	8	6	8	251
normal	n/a	n/a	n/a	1	51	129	25	20	21	3	250
high	26	6	16	13	61	100	26	n/a	n/a	1	249
very high	50	50	n/a	6	49	73	14	1	1	5	249

As shown in Table 6, Beijing has more projects than other regions in all 4 groups. Furthermore, we took the "very high" subset and compared the median productivity of each region using only this subset. In this subset, Beijing is found to be the only region involving all business areas as shown in Table 7.

Table 7. Median productivity and the number of involved organizations and business areas for each region in the "very high" level part

Region	N.Proj	Productivity	N.Org	Business areas ("Other" is omitted)
Liaoning	57	44.90	10	General, Public admin, Telecom
Beijing	70	38.16	20	Energy, Finance, General, Manufacturing, Public, Retail, Telecom
Shandong	6	34.38	1	Energy, General, Manufacturing
Zhejiang	49	34.00	5	Energy
Chongqing	1	31.09	1	Public admin
Jiangsu	14	28.59	3	Energy, Telecom
Tianjin	50	28.36	5	Finance
Anhui	1	21.87	1	Other
Shanghai	0	n/a	0	n/a
Other	5	27.81	3	Public admin, Retail

According to above results, Beijing contributes more proportion in the high-productivity projects and organizations; moreover, it is the only region owning high-productivity projects cross all business areas. Hence, we believe it is a fair conclusion that Beijing is the only high productivity and the most equally developed region across all business domains. In fact, Beijing is also the No. 1 region for software process improvement, since its CMM/CMMI 4/5 organizations account for the largest percentage of all CMM/CMMI 4/5 organizations in the country, i.e. 27.1% [3].

This is consistent with the report result shown in Table 8. That is, no matter in terms of the total number of software organizations in 2006 [24], industry revenue scale, or total number of employees [3], Beijing has absolute advantage over other regions.

Table 8. Software industry sizes in different regions

	Total No. of enterprises	Industry size (Billion RMB)	Employed personnel (Thousand persons)
Beijing	4064	97.2	165
Shanghai	1779	61.7	141
Jiangsu	959	51.2	170
Zhejiang	725	30.6	50
Liaoning	604	27.8	48
Shandong	291	22.4	53
Tianjin	296	12.4	26
Anhui	265	Not available	Not available
Chongqing	249	Not available	Not available

However, there are also limitations to this result, mainly due to the small number of organizations included in some regions. For example, Shanghai only has 5 organizations included in CSBSG database, while its total number of organizations is ranked the 2nd in China as shown in Table 8.

Additionally, due to factors such as fierce personnel competition, preferential policies, and large numbers of excellent enterprises, some developed regions such as Beijing, demonstrates more advantages, and they keep on top in various business areas. On the other hand, despite some regions are less developed and have less resource, they still perform quite well in certain business areas. For instance, some organizations in Tianjin have really high productivity in the finance business area, which indicates that in regions owning less resource, to focus on one type of business area software might be a feasible way to strengthen local software industry.

Finding 4 : In relatively developed regions whose industry size is larger, there are more high-productivity organizations than others and the high-productivity organizations can appear in each business area.

3.5 Productivity by Language (RQ5)

A subset of 7 languages applied by at least 10 projects is listed in Table 9. As a number of researchers have found that productivity varies with the level of the language [6], we also take this issue into account. According to the conversion factors (shown in the last column in Table 9) given by SPR [25], high level languages show relatively higher productivity, and this result is consistent with the finding in [6].

Table 9. Productivity by Language. Since the conversion ratio varies significantly for different versions of VB, the value for VB (without version information) cannot be confirmed.

Language	N	Median productivity	Average LOCs per FP
ASP	14	34.68	14
C#	205	18.68	25
VB	48	9.94	n/a
Java	362	9.58	53
C++	217	7.52	53
C	95	6.41	128
Cobol	24	6.27	107

Also, variance by Language is corresponding to the variance by other factors. Take an example, ASP is shown to be the most productive language, while all the ASP projects are from the energy business area (the highest productivity area). On the other side, in relatively low productivity C projects, 54% are from the telecom domain.

Meanwhile, it is also noticed that the most productive language ASP is not so popular in recent years (after 2005). One possible reason is that while technologies like .NET and J2EE enhance the development efficiency, security, components supported and scalability in Web development, script languages on the server side like ASP appear less frequently in large-scale projects. Correspondingly, in the CSBSG database, the size of projects using ASP just varies from 16 to 23 KLOC. Therefore, while selecting programming languages, not only the productivity but also the performance advantage and limitation of each language should be taken into account.

Except ASP, the languages like C# and Java appearing most frequently in the data-set are also more productive than many other languages, and it also confirms their popular application in real world.

Finding 5 : As to programming language, high level ones are found to be more pro-ductive, and it is coherent to the finding in a European database [6]. Moreover, it is also necessary to consider the software performance required, such as scalability, security etc. while selecting languages

3.6 Productivity by Team Size (RQ6)

Software development teams grow and contract at different phases of the project, and the average team size and peak team size have both been used [13], [17]. As over the

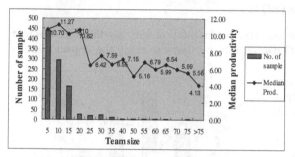

Fig. 4. Productivity by Team size

whole project it is easier to measure than average team size, Team size used in this analysis is measured as the maximal team size.

As shown in Fig. 4, for the 998 data points with "Team size" records, increasing Team size leads to decreasing productivity, which is consistent with the conclusion in [6], [26], and the coordination and com-munications problems that occur while adding more people may cause this trend.

However, 90% of the CSBSG projects are developed by small teams with less than 15 persons. This makes the descending line in Fig. 4 suffer from small sample size. Therefore, we performed a further study on the subset of projects whose team size is no greater than 15. The productivity of those teams is presented in Fig. 5.

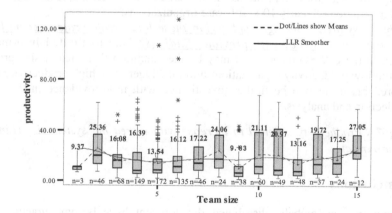

Fig. 5. Productivity by team size (for teams smaller than 15-person). The numbers after 'n=' listed below each box indicate how many projects are involved in this team size, and the num-bers listed above each box are the means of productivity for each team size.

In Fig. 5, the boxplot for each team size indicates the level of project productivity, the horizontal bars within the box show the median value, and the '*'s and '+'s denote extremes and outliers. The tendency for projects decreasing in productivity is not obvious as indicated by the smoother (shown as a dark continuous line in Fig. 5) or the dotted line showing mean productivities. As a result, it is illustrated that teams smaller than 15 persons can be almost controlled in a relatively high-productivity level; however, while the personnel increases largely, due to the lack of disciplined process management and enhanced coordination mechanism, productivity decreases rapidly.

Finding 6 : Increasing team size is found to have a negative influence on productivity. While the teams smaller than 15 persons can be almost controlled in a relatively high-productivity level, productivity for larger teams decreases rapidly.

3.7 Productivity by Project Size (RQ7)

Similar to the way that the continuous size representation was handled into discrete levels in [18], we split the CSBSG dataset into 6 groups to study the impact of software size on productivity. In Fig. 6, the numbers over each column are the sample sizes, and the line connects the median productivity of each group.

Interestingly, the productivity is found to increase while software size increases on the CSBSG database, which demonstrates an economy of scale effect. This result is the opposite of some researchers, who

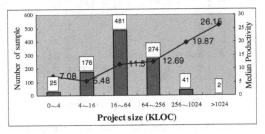

Fig. 6. Productivity with increasing project size

have found that productivity decreases with increasing system size [9], [27], but in agreement with [6], [17]. For a similar result, Agrawal et al. [17] explained that is due to the high maturity for organizations in their study. However, this is not the case in terms of a variation of nearly 1000 software organizations.

What business area, language, and region those large scale projects come from? How to force consistency with previous findings? Due to limited information contained in the CSBSG database, it may be the condition that smaller size projects come from low productivity organizations and the bigger from high productivity ones. Therefore, this result will be further investigated with more evidence in the future data collection and analysis.

Finding 7 : Productivity is found to increase with increasing system size (Lines of code) for our data.

4 Conclusions

IT outsourcing and globally distributed development have become practices with worldwide adoption. Software productivity, as a good indicator for the condition of software process, product, and personnel, conveys the critical information for outsourcing strategic planning and decision making. On the other hand, software organizations frequently rely on productivity as a basic measurement to build organization/process benchmark and/or fine tune prediction models.

There is a consensus that productivity varies highly across the software industry. Results from productivity studies are examined, and their differences in both data sources and conclusions necessities an independent investigation on Chinese software industry before any immediately useful conclusions could be adopted as a solid groundwork for both outsourcing partners and local Chinese software organizations to make their decision on.

To that end, this paper provides an in-depth investigation and draws a more comprehensive picture of software productivity status in Chinese software industry. The most significant factors mostly impacting software productivity are: Organization, Region, Business area, Development type, and Language. Meanwhile, team size and project size also influence productivity significantly in the CSBSG database. In addition to the productivity results for answering the research questions set in this paper, further analysis and assessment are also given by examining characteristics of each factor with respect to current circumstance in Chinese software industry. 7 findings are summarized with recommendations to increase productivity and improve software process.

Finally, we are aware that analysis results involved in this paper have only revealed the surface of this large and complex dataset. For example, some interpretations for the variance of productivity in different business areas are related to the cross influence from other factors; however, further suggestion in handling such interrelation is not offered in this study. For our future work, it is planed to model the interrelationship among these factors in order to minimize the effects of notable cross influence and provide more thorough benchmarking and management guidelincs. At the same time, as the CSBSG database, by now, is the only available and relative comprehensive database to explore the characteristics of software development projects in China, we believe that this study and the continued study based on this database do help researchers and industry better understand software development in China.

Acknowledgements

The authors would like to thank the China Software Industry Association and CSBSG in particular for their tremendous effort in the data collection process and the generosity in sharing the data with us. Also, we appreciate all the help offered by the members in ISCAS-iTechs Lab (especially to Fengdi Shu, Da Yang, Lang Gou, Jing Du, Qi Li and Shujian Wu).

Reference

1. China Software Industry Association: 2002-2003 Annual Report of China Software Industry. Beijing (2003)
2. Ministry of Information Industry of the People's Republic of China and China Software Industry Association: 2006 Annual Report of China Software Industry. Beijing (2006)
3. Ministry of Information Industry of the People's Republic of China and China Software Industry Association: 2007 Annual Report of China Software Industry. Beijing (2007)
4. Olsen, K.B.: Productivity impacts of offshoring and outsourcing: a review (2006), http://www.oecd.org/dataoecd/16/29/36231337.pdf

5. Maxwell, K.D., Wassenhove, L.V., Dutta, S.: Software Development Productivity of European Space, Military, and Industrial Applications. IEEE Transactions on Software Engineering 22(10), 706–718 (1996)
6. Premraj, R., Twala, B., Mair, C., Forselius, P.: Productivity of Software Projects by Business Sector: An Empirical Analysis of Trends. In: 10th IEEE International Software Metrics Symposium (Late Break-in Papers) (September 2004)
7. Premraj, R., Shepperd, M., Kitchenham, B.A., Forselius, P.: An Empirical Analysis of Software Productivity over Time. In: IEEE METRICS 2005, vol. 37 (2005)
8. Putnam, L.H., Myers, W.: Measures for Excellence: Reliable Software on Time, within Budget. Prentice-Hall, Englewood Cliffs (1992)
9. Maxwell, K.D., Forselius, P.: Benchmarking Software Development Productivity. IEEE Software, 80–88 (January/February 2000)
10. ISBSG Benchmark Release 8, http://www.isbsg.org
11. Jiang, Z., Naudé, P., Comstock, C.: An investigation on the variation of software development productivity. International Journal of Computer, Information, and Systems Sciences, and Engineering 1(2), 72–81 (2007)
12. Jiang, Z., Naudé, P.: An examination of the factors influencing software development effort. International Journal of Computer, Information, and Systems Sciences, and Engineering 1(3), 182–191 (2007)
13. Lawrence, M.J.: Programming methodology, organizational environment, and programming productivity. Journal of Systems and Software 2, 257–269 (1981)
14. Kemerer, C.F., Slaughter, S.: Determinants of software maintenance profiles: an empirical investigation. Journal of Software Maintenance 9, 235–251 (1997)
15. Cusumano, M., MacCormack, A., Kemerer, C.F., Crandall, B.: Software development worldwide: the state of the practice. IEEE Software, 28–34 (2003)
16. Agrawal, M., Chari, K.: Software Effort, Quality and Cycle Time: A Study of CMM Level 5 Projects. IEEE Transactions on Software Engineering 33(3), 145–156 (2007)
17. Boehm, B.W.: Software Engineering Economics. Prentice-Hall, Englewood Cliffs (1981)
18. Briand, L.C., Emam, K., Bomarius, F.: COBRA: A hybrid method for software cost estimation, benchmarking and risk assessment. In: Proc. of the 20th Int'l Conf. on Software Engineering, pp. 390–399. IEEE CS Press, Los Alamitos (1998)
19. SAS/STAT User's Guide, version 8, http://www2.stat.unibo.it/ManualiSas/stat/pdfidx.htm
20. Zave, P.: Requirements for Evolving Systems: A Telecommunications Perspective. In: Fifth IEEE International Symposium on Requirements Engineering (RE 2001), August 2001, pp. 2–9 (2001)
21. Tomaszewski, P.: Software development productivity issues in large telecommunication applications. Blekinge Institute of Technology (2005)
22. He, M., Yang, Y., Wang, Q., Li, M.: Cost Estimation and Analysis for Government Contract Pricing in China. In: Wang, Q., Pfahl, D., Raffo, D.M. (eds.) ICSP 2007. LNCS, vol. 4470, pp. 134–146. Springer, Heidelberg (2007)
23. http://www.gd-emb.org/detail/id-27114.html
24. China "Double-soft" Cognizance Website (sponsored by Department of Electronics and Information Product Administration of Ministry of Information Industry of the People's Republic of China), http://www.chinasoftware.com.cn/
25. SPR programming languages table (2003), http://www.spr.com/
26. Brooks, F.P.: The Mythical Man-Month: Essays on Software Engineering. Addison-Wesley, Reading (1975)
27. Behrens, C.A.: Measuring the Productivity of Computer Systems Development Activities with Function Points. IEEE Trans. Software Eng. 9(6), 648–652 (1983)

Optimized Software Process for Fault Handling in Global Software Development

Dirk Macke[1] and Tihana Galinac[2]

[1] Ericsson Deutschland GmbH, Ericsson Allee 1, D-52134 Herzogenrath
Dirk.Macke@ericsson.com
[2] Faculty of Engineering, University of Rijeka, Vukovarska 58, HR-51000 Rijeka, Croatia
Tihana.Galinac@riteh.hr

Abstract. Software development organizations are turning to global software development (GSD) to reach a competitive lead on the global market. This paper presents experiences and results of an Six Sigma based improvement project in a GSD organization. The improvements address better process definition, increase of awareness for different levels of expectations in globally distributed teams, and introduction of regular scanning mechanisms. Success indicators are defined to connect process capability to business value, and are used to measure improvement success by applying SPC techniques.

1 Introduction

Global software development (GSD) as a promising approach for getting competitive advantages on the global market is becoming common practice in the software industry. Coordination, communication and control are the main challenges of GSD as reported by academic and corporate researches, [1]-[5]. The proposed solutions to overcome these challenges are implementation of clear processes as communicating instrument between GSD teams, process support within collaboration information systems, clear responsibilities and roles, and awareness of cultural diversity build on positivism and trust.

The Interest in software process improvement (SPI) has been growing in the software industry for the last decade. There are many SPI models and initiatives – most of them evolved initially from the manufacturing and production industry [6]-[9]. One of such approaches is Six Sigma [10]. There are other published research studies dealing with the application of Six Sigma in software development [11], [12]. The main objection of its usage in the software industry, especially design, is its statistical focus [13]. This is often thought to be inappropriate, since many designers consider themselves more an artist than an engineer. Nevertheless, the growing application of measurements [14], and statistics [15]-[17] is evident in the software industry.

This paper presents a case study performed for an industrial telecom software project within a GSD organization, which aims to achieve operational excellence through continuous improvement programs. The project has applied the Six Sigma Define-Measure-Analyze-Improve-Control (DMAIC) methodology [10].

Q. Wang, D. Pfahl, and D.M. Raffo (Eds.): ICSP 2008, LNCS 5007, pp. 395–406, 2008.
© Springer-Verlag Berlin Heidelberg 2008

The focus of this paper is the improvement of the Fault Handling (FH) process. The FH process constitutes the main interface between the development, and integration and verification (I&V) part of the GSD organization. Faults identified during the I&V phase are reported to the development unit. It is important to stress, that a significant part of the costs within I&V is spent on equipment usage, i.e. lab usage, and IT equipment. Every lost hour for I&V tests means a significant loss of money. Setting the right level of formal and informal communication is of crucial importance to ensure the efficient handling of faults.

The main contribution of the paper is the proposed FH process decomposition, identification of process users, control indicators, and finally the improved FH process itself. Both the presented way of driving improvements in GSD environments and the improved FH process are applicable in any GSD environment. Emphasis is put on describing the use of the Six Sigma methodology, which will be shown as a unique tool for both identifying, and driving the improvements.

2   Research Framework

The case study described in this paper has been performed within an industrial project of the GSD organization at Ericsson A.B.

The GSD organization is developing software for mobile telephony exchanges, and offering complete network solutions as product. The development is done in GSD organization, and face strong quality and reliability requirements, both from national, and international standards bodies and legislation. A short time to market due to a rapidly changing business environment is required. As a consequence, a large amount of global software engineering efforts is needed in order to achieve the required level of competitiveness.

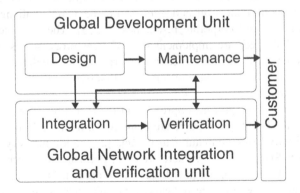

Fig. 1. Global Software Development Organization

The global development (GD) unit is a part of the GSD organization as presented in figure 1. It is distributed within four geographically different design units (Germany, Croatia, Italy, and Greece), which deliver software packages to the global network integration and verification (GNIV) unit. GNIV is distributed over different geographical organizations (Germany, Canada, Croatia, Spain, China and Australia), too. Because the development model is an in-house developed variant of an incremental development model with waterfall increments, the process of handing over smaller packages ('shipments') from GD to GNIV is repeated for each increment during a project.

The research was performed on the fault handling (FH) process, which forms the interface between the GD and GNIV units. The high level process map for the FH process is depicted in figure 2. Four main steps characterize the FH process:

- Fault Detection
- Trouble Report (TR) Handling
- TR Analysis
- Release of Solution/Correction deployment

During the Fault Detection step in GNIV, the product is integrated into different network and hardware configurations, and verified in a real mobile telephony environment (so called end-to-end testing). The product is put under different test conditions such as negative test (NT, probing the code for memory leaks etc.), provocative test (PT, network-level disturbances, such as broken cables, hot-swapping of processor boards etc.), regression test (RT, testing that legacy functionality is still working), etc. These test conditions will be referred to as test types, and will be used later on for analysis purposes. All events experienced while executing the different tests are reported, and stored into a database. The event database is available to all involved GSD units. The main purpose of this database is to avoid work on a particular issue in more than one site in parallel. Otherwise there would be the risk, that geographically separated sites of the GSD organization (potentially also in different time zones), would spend effort on troubleshooting the same issue in parallel, not knowing of similar activities ongoing at another site. By this approach, GNIV can even draw additional testing potential of the global organization, by e.g. continuing troubleshooting in Canada, while engineers in Germany start to finish up for the day.

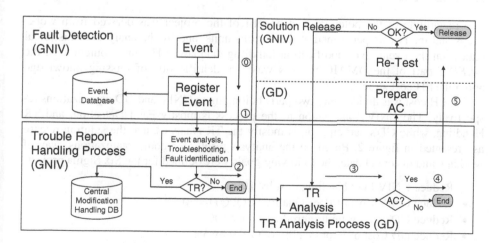

Fig. 2. Fault Handling Process

Once an event is reported, the event analysis, troubleshooting, and/or fault identification is started. When a fault is identified, located, and a temporary solution is proposed, the Trouble Report (TR) is issued in Ericsson's official, company wide modification handling tool. A TR should contain all relevant information, which makes it possible for the GD organization to analyze the fault.

Activities such as troubleshooting, information retrieval, documentation, communication, tools and testing configuration set up issues, belong to the FH process. All these activities are subject to analysis.

The outcome of the TR handling process is a written TR, which is sent to the GD organization, and triggers execution of the next step in the FH process. A TR handler is assigned within the GD maintenance unit, investigates the problem, and develops a proposed solution. An expert, who decides on how to proceed, evaluates the proposed solution. This can either result in no action, an approved correction (AC), or even a product change. After this decision the last step begins with the development of the solution (unless no action is decided), and an answer is sent back to the TR issuer. If the decision was to issue an AC, the designer prepares a correction of the fault. When this correction has been tested and approved (by the GNIV organization), the AC is sent to be released, and included in the product. The main activities within TR analysis and the solution release process are TR analysis, screening, desk check, AC preparation and TR closure. All these activities will be subject to analysis.

3 Approach to Improvements

The original motivation for triggering the improvement project described in this case study was to reduce TR lead time. But the Six Sigma method 'Voice of the Customer' [7] revealed, that the real motivation for the improvement was cost reduction, ideally in conjunction with a productivity increase within the FH process.

3.1 Goal Definition

The magnitude of the potential cost benefit of the project was derived from workshops and interviews performed at the various units, and by the analysis of historical data from the event, and modification handling databases. The main outcome of the *DEFINE* part of the DMAIC process was the identification of missing knowledge about the FH cost structure.

The FH cost was divided into two parts belonging to GNIV and GD organizations respectively. The GNIV contribution to the process is mostly Fault Detection, and TR Handling, while GD's participation is mostly the TR Analysis, and the solution release as presented in figure 2. Based on the analysis results for both organizations, way of working, and historical data, the following goals were defined for the Six Sigma project:

- Reduce GNIV fault handling cost by 10%
- Reduce GNIV Cost of Poor Quality (COPQ) by 30%
- Reduce GD cost for fault reproduction by 10%
- Reduce GD Cost of Poor Quality (COPQ) by 5%
- Improve productivity of GNIV and GD by 10%

(The definition of COPQ is given in the next section.)

3.2 Definitions

The data flow within the FH process presented in figure 2 is graphically represented in figure 3. Circled numbers in figure 3 represent branches, and correspond to the circled numbers in figure 2. Vertical dotted lines represent boundaries between the process steps of the FH process.

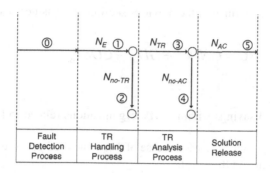

Fig. 3. Fault Handling Data Flow

In order to define the business case and control indicators, we will use the following notational conventions: The number of incoming events detected within the FH process is denoted by N_E. During the TR handling process the total number of N_E faults are divided into two branches, depending if a fault will be registered as TR in the corporate TR database (N_{TR}), or if a fault is handled internally in GNIV, and will therefore not lead to a TR in the corporate TR database (N_{no-TR}). Note that all of these events are considered to be faults within this case study, while not all of them will be handled as TRs – the main difference being, that only TRs will also be handled by the GD organization. The relation of these two classes of faults is obviously

$$N_E = N_{TR} + N_{no-TR} \tag{1}$$

Three reasons leading to N_{no-TR} could be identified: Duplication of an issue (e.g. two testers detecting a fault at different sites in parallel independently of each other, or faults belonging to the same root cause), denoted by N_{no-TR_D}, cancellation of an issue, because there was no fault at all (e.g. diverging opinions between testers in GNIV and designers in GD in what way a certain feature or functionality should work, or simply a misunderstanding of the code), denoted by N_{no-TR_C}, and finally issues, which represent internal faults N_{no-TR_I}, like problems with the test environment etc. All these faults will not lead to an improvement of product quality, albeit requiring the same effort as any other fault, and are therefore considered to be COPQ. These cases sum up to N_{no-TR}:

$$N_{no-TR} = N_{no-TR\_D} + N_{no-TR\_C} + N_{no-TR\_I} \tag{2}$$

Not all registered TRs in the TR database end up with an AC. The amount of registered TRs, N_{TR}, that need to be analyzed by the GD organizations, is split into two categories: TRs going to be fixed with an AC (N_{AC}), and TRs which are not going to be fixed in the current release of the product (N_{no-AC}), e.g. because the fault can only be fixed within a new release (no patch possible), or the fault is too minor to risk late code changes. The sum of all TRs is then

$$N_{TR} = N_{AC} + N_{no-AC} \tag{3}$$

Based on the goals defined in the previous section, the business case (BC) can now be denoted as:

$$BC = GNIV_{as} + GD_{as} - COST_{6\sigma} \tag{4}$$

with

- $GNIV_{as}$ Annual savings within GNIV organizations related to fault handling, including
  - increased efficiency: 10% increase of N_{TR} generated per week,
  - reduced fault handling cost,
  - reduced COPQ: Reduced N_{no-TR} and N_{no-AC},
- GD_{as} Annual savings within GD organization related to FH, including
  - increased efficiency: Increased amount of N_{TR},
  - savings due to less COPQ: Reduced N_{no-TR},
  - decreased effort for fault analysis
- $COST_{6\sigma}$ Cost spent for the Six Sigma improvement project itself, e.g. travel, tools, working hours spent for meetings in the different organizations etc.

To validate the improvement result and goal achievement, the following success indicators were defined:

- Fault Handling Efficiency (*FHE*) defined as

$$FHE = \frac{N_E}{N_{TR}} \tag{5}$$

The smaller the value for *FHE*, the higher the amount of TRs within the total number of events, in other words: Less time and money is spent on issues not leading to an TR, and by this not improving product quality.

- Fault Finding Efficiency (*FFE*) defined as

$$FFE = \frac{N_{no-TR\_1}}{N_{TR}} \tag{6}$$

The smaller the value for *FFE*, the less time and money is spent on troubleshooting internal faults in GNIV, which do not lead to a product quality improvement. This is a direct measure for COPQ in GNIV, with respect to the test environment.

- Fault Handling Effectiveness (*FHEff*) defined as

$$FHEff = N_{no-TR\_C} + N_{no-TR\_D}$$

(7)

The smaller the value of *FHEff*, the less money and time is spent on troubleshooting on 'assumed' faults ($N_{no-TR\_C} + N_{no-TR\_D}$). This is a direct measurement of COPQ in GNIV, with focus on internal processes and testing competence.

- Fault Finding Effectiveness (*FFEff*) defined as

$$FFEff = N_{no-AC}$$

(8)

Here we use N_{no-AC} directly as indicator for the effectivness of fault finding in GNIV. The rationale behind this definition is, that the ultimate goal of I&V is to improve product quality – this can only be done, if a found fault leads to an AC, and by this to improved code (or hardware) in the final product.

These indicators were measured weekly, and the resulting control charts were used for the *CONTROL* part of the Six Sigma project (see section 'Results of the optimized Fault Handling' for details).

4 Data Collection and Analysis

Lack of knowledge on the FH cost structure, effort spent on the individual process steps, and effort distribution over the various involved organizations was identified as the vital data to be analyzed in order to improve the FH process.

Since such data was not readily available, and existing definitions for effort and lead time were widely varying within process steps and organizations, dedicated templates and work instructions were developed, and extensively communicated across the whole GSD organization. The measurements were performed manually by process participants (design and test engineers, and their associated managers). The sample which was taken included 350 measurements in the GNIV unit, and 100 measurements in the GD unit. Central points of contact were established in the GNIV and GD organizations, to support testers, maintenance engineers, and their managers throughout the data collection process. The effort measurements were combined with records from databases used in the FH process such as event data, and TR and AC data from the corporate modification handling database.

The data was analyzed using standard statistical methods:

- for analyzing fault distributions per category we used Pareto charts and/or pie charts to identify the most significantly contributing categories/factors
- for identifying differences between data distributions we used hypothesis tests (t-test)
- if data was not normally distributed we used a Box-Cox transformation to normalize the data

The main results of the analysis is summarized in table 1. In the first column of the table the questions we wanted to answer during the analysis are given. In the second column the conclusions we draw from the analysis are stated. For analysis purposes we differentiate between 'quick' and 'normal' faults 'Quick' faults are defined as faults needing less than one day in the FH handling process. All other faults are considered as 'normal' faults, and typically require a lead-time of 1-2 weeks. The existence of two categories of faults was not anticipated, but a result of the data analysis. Since these two fault categories lead to the identification of different measures in order to improve the FH process, it can be recommended to be very wary of average data from such processes, as long as the arbitrary data distribution has not been analyzed before. Examples of Pareto charts used to obtain the conclusions in table 1 are presented in fig. 4.

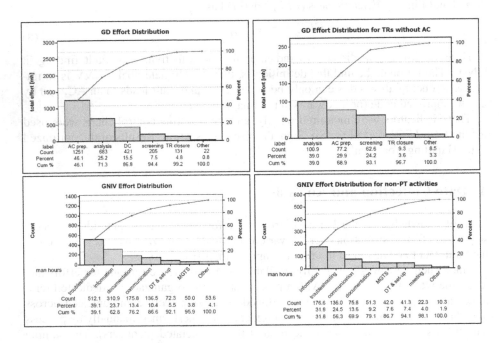

Fig. 4. Effort distributions for GNIV and GD

5   Optimized Fault Handling

Improvements to the FH process presented in fig. 2 were implemented based on the conclusions from the analysis listed in table 1. Actions taken in the IMPROVE part of the Six Sigma project can be summarized as follows:

TR Skeleton. Due to the identified lack of communication and understanding between experts from the GNIV and GD organizations, additional rules and database fields for the corporate TR handling tool were implemented. This was done by means of a template (TR skeleton), which is to be filled out by the TR issuer.

FH Process. Two new work instructions were incorporated into the process, describing handling of the event database, and unifying the way of working between the different GNIV organizations.

PT Process. During analysis of effort spent in software testing, a significant inefficiency was identified while analyzing data from PT test activities. This kind of testing is run over night on a network under full load (mobile telephony traffic), and in the morning all events observed are analyzed. Due to competence limitations often groups of faults having the same root cause were treated individually, causing additional costs both in GNIV and GD organizations. The improved way of working now puts in a mandatory screening step by a senior software engineer.

Screening Control. A main reason of inefficient interaction between GNIV and GD experts is caused by a lack of timely communication. Additional information related to TRs is better obtainable while the test network is still configured. While this sounds straight forward, it is nothing easily achievable in a very dynamic environment with TR turn-around times (time from TR to AC) in the order of magnitude of the lead-time of a test activity. Since the test equipment is very expensive, planning of testing activities with different configurations is a process which sets strict constraints of the flexibility of repeating a particular test, with obvious limitations to the possibilities for fault reproduction. The improvement implemented was to add an additional screening process step in the GD organizations, where the incoming TRs are not only analyzed by priority of the fault itself, but also on re-testability within the GNIV organizations.

6 Results of the Optimized Process Implementation

The results of the improvements proposed in this paper were controlled, verified and validated during the CONTROL phase of the Six Sigma project. The success/control indicators introduced in the 'Definitions' section were used for that purpose. Usage of

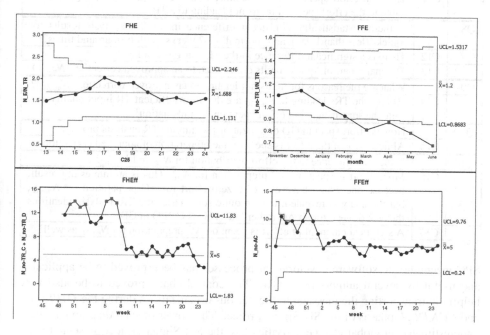

Fig. 5. Moving average charts for the success indicators (SPC)

Table 1. Questions and conclusions from the measurement and analysis phases

Q	C	Information
Q1		How is effort and cost distributed between the different FH activities?
	C1	Almost 40% of the total effort is spent on troubleshooting.
	C2	Significant contribution from information retrieval (24%)
	C3	More effort is spent on documenting faults, than on communication!
Q2		What is the fault distribution between different test activities?
	C4	PT contributes the vast majority to fault finding (~55-60%).
Q3		How is the effort distributed for faults leading to TRs (N_{TR}), and those not leading to TRs ($N_{no\text{-}TR}$)?
	C5	More than 40% of the faults ultimately do not leadt to TRs, i.e. the effort spent does not improve product quality.
Q4		How is effort and cost distributed for PT activities?
	C6	Troubleshooting makes up for 40% of the effort/
	C7	Documenting the TRs takes up 20% of the effort.
Q5		How is effort and cost distributed for non-PT activities?
	C8	Information gathering is the biggest contributor with 30% of the effort. This is significantly more than what is spent/needed in the PT activities.
Q6		Is the effort spent in PT and non-PT activities different?
	C9	There is no statistical significant evidence, that the total effort spent is different.
	C10	There is a significant difference on how the effort is spent.
Q7		Is the effort spent different for faults leading to to TRs (N_{TR}), and those not leading to a TR ($N_{no\text{-}TR}$)?
	C11	The total effort spent on faults leading to a TR is significantly bigger compared to the effort spent on faults not leading to a TR.
Q8		Is there a statistically significant difference in the TR analysis results for 'quick' (less than 1 day), and 'normal' (1-2 weeks) fault turn-around times?
	C12	There is a significant difference in the TR analysis results.
	C13	The major part of 'quick' faults do not lead to an approved correction ($N_{no\text{-}AC}$)
Q9		What are the reasons for faults not leading to an approved correction ($N_{no\text{-}AC}$)?
	C14	50% of the TRs leading to $N_{no\text{-}AC}$ are due to insufficient TR input quality, despite the surprisingly big effort spent on documentation!.
Q10		How is effort spent in GD organizations within the TR analysis process?
	C15	Almost 50% of the effort is spent on the preparation of approved corrections.
Q11		Is there a difference in the effort distribution for N_{AC} and $N_{no\text{-}AC}$?
	C16	More effort is spent on AC preparation for N_{AC}. This is an interesting result, because one would have expected zero effort for AC preparation for $N_{no\text{-}AC}$, but the analysis revealed, that in quite some cases the TR analysis identifies the lack of need for an AC rather late. This is COPQ in GD.
	C17	A significant amount of effort is spent on AC preparation for $N_{no\text{-}AC}$ as well!

SPC techniques to software development processes has been proved to be applicable and useful by several authors [8] – [10]. The control charts proved to be also very helpful in transporting the message to the various organizations during the *IMPROVE* and *CONTROL* phases of the Six Sigma project. The power of such diagrams is often underestimated in global change activities like the Six Sigma project presented here, because often the change management aspect is underestimated in favor of the more technical/statistical work.

The control variables were followed up weekly using moving average charts, and time-weighted control charts. The advantage of using time-weighted control charts is the ability to detect small shifts from the target value. In the figures the horizontal line always represents the target, which needs to be reached in order to fulfill the goals in the 'Goal Definition' section. Measurements below the target value indicate an improvement exceeding the goals. It can be seen from figure 5, that the efficiency of fault finding, and the effectiveness of fault handling could be improved beyond expectations. In the same time, the effectiveness indicator for fault finding, and the fault handling efficiency were stabilizing around the target line. Break-even for the BC (4) ($GNIV_{as} + GD_{as} = COST_{6\sigma}$) was reached approximately six months after implementing the improvements. Since then the improved process generates yearly savings.

7 Conclusion

To reach higher competitiveness, the software development organizations increasingly enter the GSD world. This opens new questions and challenges to the software engineering community. As already reported by many authors, communication, coordination and control are the main challenges. This paper presents experiences and results of an improvement project executed within a GSD organization. The improvement project was based on the Six Sigma DMAIC methodology. The main focus was to increase process effectiveness and efficiency for FH in a GSD organization.

The DMAIC method proved to be a useful tool to gather, analyze, stratify and present non-existing data, and to combine it with existing corporate resources to generate a new view on exiting processes. The approach to use data sampling to create a fact base for argumentation with impacted organizations and practitioners proved to be a powerful tool to change and improve processes, which run largely unattended and without much supervision for many years. All project goals could be achieved, resulting in a significant cost reduction for FH in the GSD.

References

1. Aranda, G.N., Vizcaino, A., Cechich, A., Piattini, M.: Technology selection to improve global collaboration. In: 1st International Conference on Global Software Engineering, pp. 223–232. IEEE Computer Society, Washington (2006)
2. Barbagallo, D.: The challenges of managing a global software engineering capability: Theory to practice. In: 16th Australian Software Engineering Conference, p. 4. IEEE Computer Society, Washington (2005)
3. Herbsleb, J.D.: Global software engineering: The future of socio-technical coordination. In: Future of Software Engineering 2007, pp. 188–198. IEEE Computer Society, Washington (2007)
4. Jonsson, N., Novosel, D., Lillieskold, J., Eriksson, M.: Successful management of complex, multinational R&D projects. In: 34th Annual Hawaii International Conference on System Sciences, p. 8044. IEEE Computer Society, Washington (2007)

5. Ribeiro, M.B., Czekster, R.M., Webber, T.: Improving productivity of local software development teams in a global software development environment. In: 1st International Conference on Global Software Engineering, pp. 253–254. IEEE Computer Society, Washington (2006)
6. Binder, V.R.: Can a Manufacturing Quality Model Work for Software? IEEE Software, 101–105 (1997)
7. Crosby, P.B.: Quality is Still Free: Making Quality Certain in Uncertain Times. McGrow—Hill, New York (1996)
8. Ishikawa, K.: Guide to Quality Control. White Plains, New York (1989)
9. Juran, J.: Juran's Quality Control Handbook. McGrow—Hill, New York (1999)
10. Breyfogle, F.: Implementing Six Sigma. John Wiley & Sons, Hoboken (2003)
11. Galinac, T., Car, Ž.: Software Verification Process Improvement Using Six Sigma. In: Münch, J., Abrahamsson, P. (eds.) PROFES 2007. LNCS, vol. 4589, pp. 51–64. Springer, Heidelberg (2007)
12. Arul, K., Kohli, H.: Six Sigma for Software Application of Hypothesis Tests to Software Data. Sw. Quality J. 12, 29–42 (2004)
13. Binder, V.R.: Six Sigma for Software. IEEE Software 20, 68–70 (2004)
14. Briand, L.C., Emam, K.E., Morasca, S.: On the Application of Measurement Theory in Software Engineering. Empirical Sw. Eng. 1, 61–88 (1996)
15. Eickelmann, N., Anant, A.: Statistical process control: What you don't measure can hurt you! IEEE Softw. 20, 49–51 (2003)
16. Komuro, M.: Experiences of applying SPC techniques to software development processes. In: 28th International Conference on Software Engineering, pp. 577–584. ACM Press, New York (2006)
17. Cangussu, J.W., DeCarlo, R.A., Mathur, A.P.: Monitoring the software test process using statistical process control: a logarithmic approach. In: 4th joint meeting of the European Software Engineering Conference and ACM SIGSOFT Symposium on the Foundations of Software Engineering, pp. 158–167. ACM Press, New York (2003)

Measuring and Comparing the Adoption of Software Process Practices in the Software Product Industry

Mikko Rönkkö[1,2], Antero Järvi[2], and Markus M. Mäkelä[2]

[1] University of Turku, Department of Information Technology, Joukahaisentie 3-5,
20014 Turun yliopisto, Finland
[2] Helsinki University of Technology, Software Business Laboratory, Otaniementie 17,
02015 TKK, Finland
{Mikko.Ronkko, Antero.Jarvi, Markus.Makela}@utu.fi

Abstract. Compatibility of agile methods and CMMI have been of interest for the software engineering community, but empirical evidence beyond case studies is scarce, which be attributed to the lack of validated measurement scales for survey studies. In this study, we construct and validate a set of Rasch scales for measuring process maturity and use of agile methods. Using survey data from 86 small and medium-sized software product firms, we find that the use of agile methods and the maturity level of the firm are complementary in this sample. In addition to providing initial survey evidence of the compatibility of agile methods and process maturity, our study provides a set of validated scales that can be further refined and used in later survey studies.

Keywords: CMMI, agile methods, XP, Scrum, software process improvement, survey research, Rasch model, scale development.

1 Introduction

Compatibility of agile methods and CMMI has been of interest for the software engineering community: The contemporary software process research often discusses combining of agile methods and process maturity as an act of balancing [1]. However, while evidence exists that these approaches can be made to coexists with proper researcher intervention [2-4], there is currently insufficient evidence on the inherent compatibility or conflict of agile approaches and disciplined methods, as is evident considering the number of opinions for [1, 5, 6] and against [7-9] their compatibility. Larger scale evidence beyond case studies is required as validating evidence, as is commonly used in more mature disciplines However, the lack of validated measurement scales has limited the number of software engineering surveys [10].

In this paper, we construct and validate a scale that is relatively compact when compared to other existing scales [e.g. 11], and due to adhering to the stringent documentation requirements [10, 12, 13], can be refined and re-used in other survey studies. Moreover, applying these scales in the Finnish software product industry provides - although on an initial level - much needed large scale empirical evidence on the issue of compatibility and conflict of agile methods and process maturity.

The paper is structured as follows: We will start by reviewing the existing research on process maturity and agile methods. Thereafter, the empirical study section

Q. Wang, D. Pfahl, and D.M. Raffo (Eds.): ICSP 2008, LNCS 5007, pp. 407–419, 2008.
© Springer-Verlag Berlin Heidelberg 2008

explains our scale development and analysis approach, followed by data collection, and the results of statistical analyses. We conclude with a discussion of our results.

1.1 Agile Software Development and Process Maturity

Agile and plan-driven software development methods have distinct origins; agile development has its roots in the software developer camp while plan-driven methods are focused on controlling the complexity of large projects. They were initially - albeit perhaps somewhat falsely as will be discussed below - seen as alternative, contradicting ways to develop software that are based on profoundly different values and principles. This dichotomy can be considered to be well-founded when agile methods are contrasted against full-fledged plan-driven software development methods.

During the recent more than a decade CMMI has established itself as the leading software process improvement framework, and has consequently been often compared with agile development approach [14]. When used in conjunction with plan driven methods CMMI can add more administrative overhead to the process. Agile methods were initially presented as an alternative to the increased overhead, and hence it is widely but somewhat falsely believed that agile software development and CMMI based processes are opposite ends of the same continuum. However it has been argued that agile methods and CMMI are more compatible and can coexist: Agile methods have proved very efficient and effective as team level software development processes [4], while CMMI is a tool for organizational improvement, managing complexity and gaining consistency through the disciplined application of proven practices and processes. Thus the scope of agile methods is primarily the development team, whereas CMMI approaches are used at the organizational level. In our view, the key to successful co-existence of the two is complying with these scopes. In practice, CMMI can provide a framework for scaling up agile methods into the product development level and implementing agile methods in a consistent manner, and provides the framework for putting the required supportive processes in place. On the other hand, agile methods can be used as a very efficient implementation of CMMI process areas in engineering and project management groups, yielding efficiency and adaptability especially in smaller firms where coordination between development teams is not an issue.

The topic of the compatibility of agile and more disciplined development methods has been approached from several perspectives. Valuable insights have been gained through case reports of companies that have adopted agile methods into traditional development organization [2], and of companies using agile development processes that have implemented CMMI, even up to maturity level 5 [15]. In general, the papers report challenges in the process, but eventually a clearly positive outcome indicating that the processes can be made to work. Similarly, agile process frameworks have been modified to fit the requirements of CMMI [16]. Numerous practitioner-oriented papers outline guidelines for bringing agile approaches into traditional organizations. The key contribution of this work is the identification of common pitfalls and conflicts while introducing an agile process, and suggestions for effective approaches for the transition are presented from the perspective of various roles in the organization [17] as well as from the viewpoints of development process, business process and people issues [3]. Some approaches use the situation at hand for tailoring the method for a particular project. Examples include selecting the development method based on situation characteristics [18] and risk-based method [1] for adapting the process framework for a project according to its agile or plan-driven requirements. In addition, some authors have looked closely at the constituents of agile methods and CMMI, trying to identify compatible and incompatible areas using purely conceptual research methods. Rationalizing on these areas using general software engineering experience and expertise, they devise detailed guidance for the combing agile development with CMMI framework [14].While there is a large number of non-empirical research and case studies, survey studies seem sparse limiting the statistical generalizability of the results. For example, in a recent review paper by Bowers, Sangwan and Neill [19] identified only three survey studies investigating the use of XP practices in the industry. In contrast to the lack of large scale empirical evidence for the success of agile methods, strong evidence seems to exist for the positive performance effect of software process maturity [20-22]. However, a majority of the major studies focus on the use of the CMM family of models using appraisal data [cf., 23, 24]. This approach has one key weakness: CMM adoption and appraisals are primarily used by larger firms, due to the cost and effort required [25]. Hence the generalizability of these results outside the population of large project-centric firms can be called into question due to lack of data triangulation [26]. Finally, we are not aware of any studies comparing use of agile methods and the process maturity using survey data and statistical analysis, regardless of the requirement for alternative designs and larger datasets to establish validity of the results [13, 26].

2 Empirical Study

This section explains our empirical scale development and subsequent application of the scales to test an implicit hypothesis about the compatibility of agile methods with process maturity. We structure our reporting of the research in a manner that is used for survey studies [e.g. 20] and complies with the guidelines for survey research in software engineering [10, 13]. We start by explain our scale development procedure and analysis approach, after which we present our data. The empirical section concludes by presenting results in the form of descriptive and analytical statistics.

2.1 Scale Development and Statistical Analysis Approach

In this study we use the CMMI model as a benchmark for maturity and Scrum and XP process areas as surrogate constructs for agile methods. These frameworks were chosen due to the large amount of attention they have received compared to other alternatives.

In survey studies such as this, the use of these different models is often measured with scales. Scale is a set of question or other measures that as an aggregate describe one particular trait or property of the subject that is being analyzed, and scaling refers to the process for calculating a one score describing the degree of the trait being measured [12]. Most commonly these scales consist of a set of Likert-type questions, which are analyzed as a summated scale: Each question consists of a statement and the informants' task is to rate their degree of agreement with the statement. These ratings are converted to numbers (e.g. completely disagree =1, completely agree=7), and the score for the measured trait is established by calculating the sum of the numeric values of the responses. While being simple and widely used, this approach has some weaknesses, of which most important is while summing treats all items in the scale as equal, in reality they might not be that [12, 27]. Consider a scale consisting of the CMMI key practice areas: Measuring process maturity construct with this scale should not only take into account how many practices are implemented, but that implementing level 4 and level 5 items indicate significantly more mature process than implementing the same amount of level 2 and 3 practices. Due to this weakness of the summated scales approach, we decided to use Rasch scaling [27, 28], which has been designed to overcome the problem mentioned above. This method, which has been used in measuring software process in the information system research [29, 30], comes with the disadvantage of increased mathematical complexity and additional requirements for the structure of the data, as explained below.

Rasch scaling takes in answers to a set of questions from numerous respondents, and establishes a difficulty measure for each and ability measure for each respondent based on which items each respondent has answered correctly. In this study the scaling is used to establish scores indicating the adoption of several models (ability measures), and to establish in which order (difficulty measures) particular practices are adopted within the model. The method requires discrete data but does not pose any requirements for the distribution of the data. The only assumption is that the items are progressively more difficult indicators of one underlying measured dimension, thus having a probabilistic Guttman structure [27]. This scaling approach fits measuring software process maturity particularly well, since CMMI provides a recommended order of adoption for the different practices, and consequently, more advanced practices should indicate higher process maturity.

The conformance of the data to the requirements of the scaling algorithm is commonly established by examining the scale and item reliability statistics as well as scale unidimensionality measures [27]. Ability and difficulty are measured on a logit scale, where the zero means the average difficulty or ability and moving one unit to positive direction means doubling of ability or difficulty. If ability and difficulty are equal, the respondent has a 50% chance of answering the item correctly. In other cases the odds of answering an item correctly can be calculated based on the difference of the item difficulty and organizational ability. For example, a respondent with ability of 2 has a 75% chance of answering an item with difficulty of 1 correctly, since the doubling of ability means that the likelihood of failure is decreased by one half. The scaling algorithm establishes the likelihoods of correct answer for each item respondent pair and proceeds to minimize the sum of squares of the differences between the likelihoods predicted by the model and actual performance of the respondents. Readers interested in the mathematical and conceptual details of the scaling algorithm are encouraged to read the original paper by Rasch [28], the derivative work by Andrich [31], or a recent book by Fox and Bond [27]. Practical examples of the use of this analysis method in the context of software process are available in the work by Dekleva and Drehmer [29, 30].

In this study we generated and evaluated five Rasch scales. Three atomic scales were developed for the items indicating different CMMI key practice areas, XP practices, and Scrum practices. Two aggregate scales were developed – "agile" by combining the items from the XP and Scrum scales and "combined" by combining the items from CMMI scale with the items from XP and Scrum scales. Finally, we examine the correlations between these five scores for organizations measured using the developed five scales. In all, this analysis approach gives three sets of results: First, we can estimate the relative difficulty of each practice in the frameworks, or to assess in which order different practices are implemented. Second, using tests for scale unidimensionality, we can assess whether the items in the frameworks have an order of adaptation – as they should with CMMI and probably should not with agile methods. And third, the study enables us to evaluate the possible mutual dependencies between the evaluated frameworks.

All scales were developed specifically for this study., warranting a detailed description of the development of the survey instrument [12, 13] While several survey instruments exist measuring adoption of CMMI key process areas [e.g. 11] and other software process models [e.g. 29], these were considered inappropriate to be used in this study. A key weakness in many of the preexisting scales is that they measure the degree of adoption of the software processes using binary items (not used – used) to measure the use of different processes. However, this dichotomous approach has a poor fit with the reality where different process areas are often first experimented with, then taken into use and finally institutionalized as processes. To remedy this problem, we decided to use seven point Likert scales to allow the respondents to rate to which degree statements applied to their organization. Due to the limitation of the original Rasch model to dichotomous items, we used the rating scale model, or the Rasch-Andrich model [31], departing from the other similar studies [29, 30].

Measuring general process maturity is often implemented through measuring the degree of fit between the development process and a particular framework – most commonly CMM. This approach has a key weakness: It fails to fully appropriate the part of processes maturity that is not directly covered by the framework used in the measurement. To remedy this problem, we use indicative rather than formative measures. That is, our items do not measure elements that constitute a good process, but general elements that reflect that such processes are instituted. In addition, using indicative items has the advantage of reducing the effect of assumptions that the respondents have on the use and goodness of the evaluated frameworks [32]. The weakness of this approach is that one item can act as an indicator for several process areas, but due to the large amount of items per scale, this does not cause problems to the overall validity of the study.

The items for the three atomic scales were based on *CMMI for Development, Version 1.2* [33], XP practices as explained by Beck, [34] and Scrum practices as explained by Schwaber and Beedle [35]. To improve the generalizability of our findings outside product oriented software development, we decided to exclude the integrated product and process development (IPPD) additions to the CMMI. Initially this process resulted in the inclusion of 21 items for CMMI, 12 items for XP and 5 items for Scrum. Although these frameworks have overlap, especially in the more 'common sense good practice' sections, this is not an a problem since all models strive to improve the same underlying dimension of software process capability, and our analysis method – the Rasch model – does not require items to be mutually independent.

The initial descriptions for practices or key practice areas, adopted verbatim from the sources presented above, were considered too long to be included in the survey instrument and often were not clear enough to be understood by a person that is not familiar with the process areas. The items were iteratively reduced in length emphasizing what was important or at the core of the practice. Finally the items were translated to Finnish and tested for clarity with several persons from the industry and reworded for clarity. During this pretesting of the instrument 'Continuous Integration' XP practice was dropped due to insufficient discrimination between 'Product Integration' key practice area of CMMI. The final version of the exact wordings of the scales is reported in the appendix[1].

Scale was analyzed with the *Winsteps 3.63.2* software package using survey data which is described in the next subsection. Recommendations by Bond and Fox [27] were followed for new scale development: Each scaling was performed twice as to first identify and eliminate problematic items and then subsequently repeating the scaling to establish the final measures. This resulted in elimination of four items falling outside the acceptable range of infit values between .7 and 1.4. In addition two items from the CMMI scale were eliminated due to notable conflict with the recommended order of adoption. This final elimination was performed to eliminate the effect of construct operationalization bias, or the effect of badly formulated questions, from the final analyses, as is generally recommended when constructing new scales [27].

2.2 Data

The scales were tested with a sample of firms in the Finnish software product industry. Our data were collected as a follow up survey to the Finnish Software Product Industry Survey. The target population of this parent survey is all Finnish *software product firms*, which includes all firms with the NACE industry code 72.21 (Publishing of software). More details on this population is available in the report of the parent survey [36]. We use the respondents of the parent survey as a population of this study. Since this population is characterized by a large number of very small firms, which are not likely to provide useful data for measuring adoption of software processes, we decided to restrict the sampling frame of this study to include only firms with at least five employees. Moreover, we restricted our sampling frame to include only those firms that reported developing software products, excluding a small number of firms that mainly provided custom development. In all, 123 firms qualified for inclusion in our sampling frame. In the parent survey the CEO had nominated one person as a head of software development, and subsequently this second person was used as an informant for this study.

Data collection was implemented following a modified version of the tailored survey design method [37]. The fact that a firm CEO had already responded was heavily leveraged when contacting the software development managers. We obtained a high response rate via this approach: we received 86 usable responses, a response rate of 70%.

In all, the amount of missing data due to omitting questions was small and since Rasch scaling can effectively accommodate small amounts of holes in the data, missing data analysis did not result in any actions. The possible biasing effect of nonresponse was tested using two different methods. First, we compared the means of control variables age, size, region and industry code, between early and late respondents using

---

[1] The survey was implemented in Finnish and thus the appendix shows the translations of items in English.

t test. No significant differences were found. Second, we compared the sampling frame with the respondents. No differences were found in geographical location, industry code, age or size. Hence we conclude that non-response should not be a problem. However, the small size of the respondent firms in the sample probably limits the generalizability of the results: The mean number of personnel is only 33.0, and only seven firms employ more than 50 people. Descriptive statistics (means and standard deviations) of the 37 Likert responses from 86 development organizations are presented in the appendix.

2.3 Analysis and Results[2]

Rasch scales were analyzed with the *Winsteps 3.63.2* software package. Recommendations by Bond and Fox [27] were followed for new scale development: Each scaling was performed twice as to first identify and eliminate problematic items and then subsequently repeating the scaling to establish the final measures. This resulted in elimination of four items falling outside the acceptable range of infit values between .7 and 1.4. In addition two items from the CMMI scale were eliminated due to notable conflict with the recommended order of adoption. This final elimination was performed to eliminate the effect of construct operationalization bias, or the effect of badly formulated questions, from the final analyses, as is generally recommended when constructing new scales [27].

Table 1 shows the reliability statistics for the five estimated scales. In general, the CMMI and Combined scale show high reliability and the XP and Agile scales are on an acceptable level. The Scrum scale, however, does not reach the acceptable level of Cronbach's alpha [38]. Nevertheless, all scores were used in the correlation analysis.

Unidimensionality of the scales was estimated using principal component analysis of the residuals. This method first removes all variance explained by the Rasch model from the data and groups the remaining items based on the amount of shared residual variance resulting in several contrasts further explaining the covariance of the items. Unidimensionality was assessed by comparing the amount of explained variance and eigenvalue of the model with the corresponding values of the first principal contrast. All scales, excluding the Scrum scale, have a low ratio of principal contrast eigenvalue and model eigenvalue, indicating good level of unidimensionality. To understand the nature of the weak multidimensionality of the scales, item loadings for the first contrast were examined for all scales. If the empirical loadings show a dimension that should be expected based on the existing theory of the relationships between the items, the confidence of the validity of the measures is increased. All loadings had feasible interpretations.

Detailed results of the adoption of different practices compared to other practices are presented in the appendix in the form of item scores. The measures for items in the CMMI scale shows a good and even spread indicating good scale structure and the ability of the scale to accurately measure different levels of process maturity. The results suggest that levels 2 and 3 of the CMMI are adopted in a parallel manner: That is, the need for these process areas seems to arise simultaneously. Level 4, on the

---

[2] More analysis results are available from the first author upon request.

Table 1. Scale Reliability and Unidimensionality Measures

Scale	Cronbach's alpha	Item reliability	Scale Eigenvalue	Scale Variance explained	1st principal contrast Eigenvalue	1st principal contrast Variance explained
CMMI	.91	.98	40.9	56.90 %	3.7	5.10 %
XP	.72	.98	16.5	64.70 %	1.7	6.70 %
Scrum	.65	.90	7.4	59.80 %	1.8	14.10 %
Agile	.77	.96	18.1	56.40 %	2.1	6.60 %
Combined	.93	.97	40.9	56.90 %	3.7	5.10 %

other hand, represents a significant leap from the lower levels, and these practices are not widely adopted. Interestingly, all engineering process areas seem to be adopted relatively early and measurement related process areas later than suggested by CMMI model. Level 5 items appear earlier than expected, which can probably be attributed to error in operationalization. The difference of our empirical observation and the structure of the CMMI model is an interesting finding, since this study – in contrast to many prior studies – does not give the respondents any hints that the questions correspond to the CMMI model, and hence the informants can give more valid data about the adoption of particular practices instead of attempting to perform a self assessment of how far in the CMMI model the organization has proceeded.

On the XP scale, we can see that the items, which can be considered to be general good software development practices, are implemented earlier than practices that are more characteristically agile. Pair programming is rarely used and hence is scaled high. In all, the natural order of the agile methods is present, but not as significantly as with the CMMI model.

Second part of the analysis consisted of calculating the correlations between scores for organizations on the different scales and control variables for the age and size of using *Intercooled Stata 8.2*. Prior to analyzing correlations, Harman's single factor test [32] was performed to assess the possible biasing effect of common method variance. Principal factor analysis of all the items resulted in one dominant factor which accounted for 43% of variance indicating a significant amount of bias. As a remedy, we calculated a summated scale of all the items and calculated partial correlations controlling for this newly formed measure, and compared these values to the non-controlled correlations.

Table 2 shows the correlations and partial correlations for the measures and Figure 1 illustrates the graphical dependency of use of the different models. The strong and significant correlations in the correlation table can be a sign of two issues: there can be a problem with common method variance as discussed earlier or the process areas can be linked. Due large effects sizes, our interpretation of this data is that agile methods and CMMI model share a link in the data: CMMI in general and our scale in particular does not indicate what specific development practices are used, and in this data it seems that several firms are implementing processes through the agile paradigm, which leads to the increased process maturity, which is then indicated by our

Table 2. Correlations and partial correlations between measures

Variable	1	2	3	4	5	6	7
1 CMMI		-.08	-.33 ★★	-.27 ★	.43 ★★	.22 ★	.12
2 XP	.67 ★★		.26 ★	.85 ★★	.68 ★★	-.05	-.23 ★
3 Scrum	.47 ★★	.54 ★★		.69 ★★	.40 ★★	.06	.01
4 Agile	.67 ★★	.91 ★★	.83 ★★		.69 ★★	.01	-.15
5 Combined	.94 ★★	.83 ★★	.66 ★★	.87 ★★		.12	-.08
6 Age	.16	.01	.10	.05	.13		.23 ★
7 Size	.16	-.14	.09	-.05	.09	.23 ★	

Lower diagonal shows correlations, upper diagonal partial correlations.

Two-tailed tests of significance. † = p<.10, ★ = p<.05, ★★= p<.01

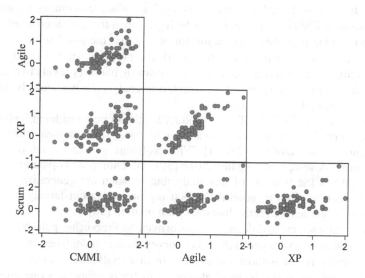

Fig. 1. Scatter plot matrix of scores for organization on the scales

CMMI scale. The presence of high maturity organizations with low agile methods scores, but absence of highly agile but low maturity firms in the upmost scatter plot in Figure 1 supports this interpretation.

3 Discussion and Conclusions

This study has implications for both research and practice. For research, we report the development of scales for measuring process maturity and the use of agile methods.

Particularly the CMMI scale – although clearly suffering from some poorly operationalized items – seems robust and valid to be used in further studies of the software process. While our study used Rasch scaling, this does not limit the further use of these items as a summated scale. For further studies, we recommend either using the scale as a whole, or choosing a set of items with fit values close to one and selecting items having an even spread of difficulty measures across the scale.

For practice, our data show that the practices indicative to CMMI process areas seem to have a natural order of adoption that aligns with the intended order, regardless of whether the model is explicitly used for software process improvement in the organizations, with the exception that process areas belonging to levels two and three seem to be adopted in parallel. However, the construct validity of our measurement approach does not allow us to draw any deeper conclusions about the order of the items. Our research serves primarily as a scale development study, and the results obtained with these scales should be considered currently as initial, and require further validation. Finally, our data show the complementary nature of the CMMI model and agile development methods, which is evident when examining Figure 1: the measured level of CMMI seems to always be higher than the measured level of use of agile methods. One plausible explanation for this is that the good software development practices codified in the agile frameworks, if properly implemented, will take smaller development organizations a long way towards maturity levels two and three. However, due to exploratory nature of correlation analysis, this should be only considered as one possible explanation.

Our study context of small software product firms can be considered both a limitation and a merit. Most previous software engineering surveys have targeted large development organizations [cf., 23, 24]. While software processes certainly differ in large and small development organizations [39], the choice of population limits the generalizability of the findings of this study, but broaden the generalizability of the software process research in general by focusing on a segment largely neglected in previous survey studies thus providing data triangulation [26].

While our sample size and degree of conformance to reporting guidelines [13] can be argued to be at or above par to the other survey studies indentified in the literature review, our study is not without limitations. In this study, we set out to develop a measurement scale to assess the level of process maturity using only one question per key process area to enable construction of more compact survey instrument. Although we attempted to follow good scale development practices, some items in our scale probably have poor construct validity. That is, they measure too narrowly the extent of corresponding process area implementation. On hindsight, to measure something as complex as CMMI structurally, more items per key practice area are clearly needed. However, if one wishes to measure the maturity of the software process in general, adopting the items with the least amounts of error and misfit from our study probably provides a good basis for further scales. On the content side, our study is probably one of the first ones statistically examining the adoption of CMMI and agile methods. We found that process areas on the CMMI levels two and three seem to be adopted in parallel, and seem to be supported by the use of agile methods. This is an interesting finding that should be studied further, not least due to this being a common process combination for a lot of smaller software product firms.

References

1. Boehm, B., Turner, R.: Using risk to balance agile and plan-driven methods. Computer 36, 57–66 (2003)
2. Baker, S.W.: Formalizing agility: an agile organization's journey toward CMMI accreditation. In: Agile Conference, Proceedings, pp. 185–192 (2005)
3. Boehm, B., Turner, R.: Management challenges to implementing agile processes in traditional development organizations. IEEE Software 22, 30–39 (2005)
4. Salo, O., Abrahamsson, P.: Integrating agile software development and software process improvement: a longitudinal case study. In: International Symposium on Empirical Software Engineering, pp. 187–196 (2005)
5. Merisalo-Rantanen, H., Tuunainen, T., Rossi, M.: Is extreme programming just old wine in new bottles: A comparison of two cases. J. Database Manage. 16, 41–61 (2005)
6. Paulk, M.C.: Extreme programming from a CMM perspective. IEEE Software 18, 19–26 (2001)
7. Boehm, B.: Get ready for agile methods, with care. Computer 35, 64–69 (2002)
8. Baskerville, R., Ramesh, B., Levine, L., Pries-Heje, I., Slaughter, S.: Is Internet-speed software development different? IEEE Software 20, 70 (2003)
9. Murru, O., Deias, R., Mugheddu, G.: Assessing XP at European Internet Company. IEEE Software 20, 37–43 (2003)
10. Kitchenham, B.A., Pfleeger, S.L.: Principles of survey research: part 3: constructing a survey instrument. SIGSOFT Softw. Eng. Notes 27, 20–24 (2002)
11. Zubrov, D., Hayes, W., Siegel, J., Goldenson, D.: Maturity Questionnaire. Software Engineering Institute, Pittsburgh (1994)
12. DeVellis, R.F.: Scale development theory and applications. Sage, Thousand Oaks (2003)
13. Kitchenham, B.A., Pfleeger, S.L., Pickard, L.M., Jones, P.W., Hoaglin, D.C., El Emam, K., Rosenberg, J.: Preliminary guidelines for empirical research in software engineering. IEEE Transactions on Software Engineering 28, 721–734 (2002)
14. Turner, R., Jain, A.: Agile meets CMMI: Culture clash or common cause? In: Proc. EXtreme Programming and Agile Methods-XP/Agile Universe 2002, pp. 153–165 (2002)
15. Sutherland, J., Jacobson, C.: Scrum and CMMI Level 5: A Magic Potion for Code Warriors! In: Agile 2007, Washington, DC, IEEE, Los Alamitos (2007)
16. Anderson, D.J.: Stretching Agile to fit CMMI Level 3. In: Agile Development Conference (ADC 2005), pp. 193–201 (2005)
17. Cohn, M., Ford, D.: Introducing an agile process to an organization. Computer 36, 74–78 (2003)
18. Cockburn, A.: Selecting a project's methodology. Software, IEEE 17, 64–71 (2000)
19. Bowers, A.N., Sangwan, R.S., Neill, C.J.: Adoption of XP Practices in the Industry–A Survey. Software Process Improvement and Practice 12, 283–294 (2007)
20. Jiang, J.J., Klein, G., Hwang, H.G., Huang, J., Hung, S.Y.: An exploration of the relationship between software development process maturity and project performance. Information & Management 41, 279–288 (2004)
21. Agrawal, M., Chari, K.: Software effort, quality, and cycle time: A study of CMM level 5 projects. IEEE Transactions on Software Engineering 33, 145–156 (2007)

418   M. Rönkkö, A. Järvi, and M.M. Mäkelä

22. Galin, D., Avrahami, M.: Are CMM program investments beneficial? Analyzing past studies. IEEE Software 23, 81–87 (2006)
23. Harter, D.E., Krishnan, M.S., Slaughter, S.A.: Effects of process maturity on quality, cycle time, and effort in software product development. Management Science 46, 451–466 (2000)
24. Herbsleb, J., Zubrow, D., Goldenson, D., Hayes, W., Paulk, M.: Software quality and the Capability Maturity Model. Communications of the Acm 40, 30–40 (1997)
25. Staples, M., Niazi, M., Jeffery, R., Abrahams, A., Byatt, P., Murphy, R.: An exploratory study of why organizations do not adopt CMMI. Journal of Systems and Software 80, 883–895 (2007)
26. Miller, J.: Triangulation as a basis for knowledge discovery in software engineering. Empirical Software Engineering (in press)
27. Bond, T.G., Fox, C.M.: Applying the Rasch model fundamental measurement in the human sciences. Lawrence Erlbaum Associates Publishers, Mahwah (2007)
28. Rasch, G.: Probabilistic Models for Some Intelligence and Attainment Tests. Danmarks Pædagogiske Institut, Copenhagen (1960)
29. Dekleva, S., Drehmer, D.: Measuring software engineering evolution: A rasch calibration. Information Systems Research 8, 95–104 (1997)
30. Drehmer, D.E., Dekleva, S.M.: A note on the evolution of software engineering practices. Journal of Systems and Software 57, 1–7 (2001)
31. Andrich, D.: Rating formulation for ordered response categories. Psychometrika 43, 561–573 (1978)
32. Lindell, M.K., Whitney, D.J.: Accounting for common method variance in cross-sectional research designs. Journal of Applied Psychology 86, 114–121 (2001)
33. Software Engineering Institute: CMMI® for Development, Version 1.2. Software Engineering Institute, Pittsburgh, PA (2006)
34. Beck, K.: Extreme Programming Explained: Embrace Change. Addison-Wesley Pub. Co., Reading (1999)
35. Schwaber, K., Beedle, M.: Agile Software Development with Scrum. Prentice-Hall, Englewood Cliffs (2001)
36. Rönkkö, M., Eloranta, E., Mustaniemi, H., Mutanen, O.-P., Kontio, J.: Finnish Software Product Business: Results of National Software Industry Survey 2007. Helsinki University of Technology, Espoo, Finland (2007)
37. Dillman, D.A.: Mail and internet surveys the tailored design method. Wiley, Hoboken (2007)
38. Nunnally, J.C., Bernstein, I.H.: Psychometric Theory. McGraw-Hill Book, New York (1994)
39. Strigel, W.: In software processes, organization size matters. IEEE Software 24, 55–57 (2007)

Appendix: Items, descriptive statistics, and results of Rasch scaling

		Descriptives		Rasch results			
	Item	Mean	S.D.	Measure	S.E.	Infit M.S.	Outfit M.S.
CMMI	We deal with programming errors by looking for their fundamental causes from our own ways of working. (CAR)	4.13	1.24	.47	.09	1.19	1.19
CMMI	We use a version management system. (CM)	6.19	1.58	-1.31 [a]	.12	2.75	2.43
CMMI	We make the more important decisions concerning software development by comparing alternatives by using predefined criteria. (DAR)	4.24	1.43	.38	.09	.87	.95
CMMI	We use metrics when monitoring the progress and efficiency of our software development. (MA)	3.33	1.50	.94 [b]	.09	.92	.94
CMMI	We continuously innovate and develop our software development processes to better support our business. (OID)	4.88	1.40	-.19 [b]	.10	.71	.72
CMMI	We maintain a collection of the methods and tools of software development that we have used. (OPD)	4.97	1.70	-.27	.10	1.20	1.18
CMMI	We develop our software process by analyzing strengths, weaknesses, and development opportunities. (OPF)	4.28	1.45	.36	.09	1.01	1.02
CMMI	We monitor our software development process and product quality by metrics. (OPP)	3.14	1.50	1.14	.09	.94	.94
CMMI	We train software developers according to an existing training plan. (OT)	3.31	1.65	.97	.09	1.14	1.10
CMMI	During software development, we continuously focus on the integration of our software components. (PI)	5.38	1.36	-.58	.11	.80	.79
CMMI	We monitor the realization of our software development plans and react to deviations with corrective procedures. (PMC)	4.80	1.31	-.04	.10	.82	.80
CMMI	We design a proper project plan for our larger software development projects. (PP)	5.62	1.42	-.76	.11	1.13	1.15
CMMI	We monitor the quality of our software and software development process. (PPQA)	5.02	1.55	-.22	.10	.95	.95
CMMI	We use numerically-measurable quality and productivity goals in the operative management of software development. (QPM)	2.94	1.64	1.25	.09	1.00	.97
CMMI	We create a requirements document for a product or a component that we develop. (RD)	4.79	1.72	-.03 [a]	.09	1.48	1.52
CMMI	We maintain a real-time account of all requirements for the software we develop. (REQM)	4.69	1.72	.05	.10	1.14	1.10
CMMI	We monitor the risks of software development projects and otherwise carry out risk management operations. (RSKM)	3.76	1.67	.69	.09	1.10	1.14
CMMI	When subcontracting, we actively monitor the progress of the subcontractor. (SAM)	3.13	2.95	-.58	.14	1.34	1.35
CMMI	When developing a software component, we evaluate alternative solutions and pursue reusability. (TS)	5.76	1.19	-.99	.11	.80	.84
CMMI	We evaluate the suitability of a software solution for the task that has been planned for it to perform. (VAL)	6.10	0.95	-1.32	.12	.87	.81
CMMI	We evaluate the correspondence of the functioning and definition of the parts of the software solution being developed. (VER)	5.38	1.20	-.54	.10	.78	.76
XP	We use use cases as the primary tools to define our software. (The Planning game)	4.51	1.49	.08	.09	.89	.83
XP	We do a simple, funcitonal system and later add more features incrementally. (Small Releases)	5.13	1.24	-.41	.10	.74	.75
XP	We strive to ensure that all developers understand the structure and functions of the software (Metaphor)	5.22	1.48	-.44	.10	1.05	1.03
XP	We create unit tests for each new feature that is implemented. (Testing)	4.34	1.64	.18	.09	1.28	1.34
XP	We keep the software we develop as simple as possible. (Simple Design)	5.04	1.35	-.30	.09	.94	.96
XP	We constantly improve - refactor - the existing source code. (Refactoring)	4.80	1.22	-.12	.09	.74	.82
XP	Programming is performed by two developers working as a pair with one computer. (Pair Programming)	2.08	1.37	1.66	.11	1.30	1.19
XP	We do not name responsible persons for each part of the software, but the code is shared and any developer can edit any part of the software. (Collective Ownership)	3.67	2.03	.42 [a]	.08	1.44	1.42
XP	Our developers work overtime for several consequtive weeks. (Reverse coded) (Sustainable pace)	2.73	1.59	-.39 [a]	.09	1.71	1.88
XP	Our developers are in close contact with the users. (Onsite Customer)	4.63	1.57	.00	.09	1.25	1.26
XP	We use common standards and style guides when editing the source code. (Coding Standards)	5.40	1.32	-.64	.10	.91	.90
Scrum	Software development is done in small independent teams.	5.61	1.65	-.56	.11	1.51	1.41
Scrum	Software development is managed usign constantly updated lists of tasks and feature requests.	4.75	1.63	.17	.08	.89	.85
Scrum	Our software development projects are divided into relatively short development periods durign which development team is isolated from the environment.	4.31	1.75	.39	.08	.73	.71
Scrum	We use weekly meetings to which all developers participate.	5.00	1.83	-.02	.08	1.39	1.41
Scrum	Software development is organized into short iterations which include designing, programming and testing activities.	5.01	1.52	.02	.08	.73	.69

[a] Dropped due to large infit mean square.

[b] Dropped due to poor content validity.

All items are anchored as 1=never, 7=always, and 0=does not apply. 'Does not apply' is processed as missing data.

Results of scaling are reported for independent scalings of each framework. Statistics for dropped items are from the initial scaling. All other

Author Index

Lecture Notes in Computer Science

Sublibrary 2: Programming and Software Engineering

For information about Vols. 1– 4336
please contact your bookseller or Springer